HISTORY OF THE LABOR MOVEMENT

IN THE UNITED STATES

VOLUME II

BY PHILIP S. FONER

History of the Labor Movement in the United States, VOLUME I: *From Colonial Times to the Founding of the American Federation of Labor;* VOLUME III: *The Policies and Practices of the American Federation of Labor, 1900-1909;* VOLUME IV: *The Industrial Workers of the World, 1905-1917.*

Business and Slavery
The Life and Writings of Frederick Douglass (4 Vols.)
The Complete Writings of Thomas Paine (2 Vols.)
Jack London: American Rebel
The Fur and Leather Workers Union
The Basic Writings of Thomas Jefferson
The Selected Writings of George Washington
The Selected Writings of Abraham Lincoln
The Selected Writings of Franklin D. Roosevelt
Jews in American History
History of Cuba and Its Relations with the United States (2 Vols.)
The Spanish-Cuban-American War and the Birth of American Imperialism, 1895-1902 (2 Vols.)
The Case of Joe Hill
The Letters of Joe Hill
W.E.B. Du Bois Speaks (2 Vols.)
The Black Panthers Speak
The Bolshevik Revolution: Its Impact on American Radicals, Liberals, and Labor
American Labor and the Indochina War
The Autobiographies of the Haymarket Martyrs
Helen Keller: Her Socialist Years
The Voice of Black America: Major Speeches of Negroes in the United States, 1797-1971
When Karl Marx Died: Comments in 1883
Organized Labor and the Black Worker, 1619-1973

HISTORY OF DISCARDED
THE LABOR MOVEMENT
IN THE UNITED STATES

VOLUME II: From the Founding of the American Federation of Labor to the Emergence of American Imperialism

BY PHILIP S. FONER

INTERNATIONAL PUBLISHERS, *NEW YORK*

To My Daughters
Lidgie and Laura

ABBREVIATIONS USED IN FOOTNOTES AND REFERENCE NOTES

AFL Corr.—American Federation of Labor Correspondence, American Federation of Labor Archives, American Federation of Labor Building, Washington, D. C.

BL.—Bancroft Library, University of California, Berkeley, California.

*GLB.*Samuel Gompers Letter-Books, American Federation of Labor Building, Washington, D. C.

JCL.—Labadie Collection, University of Michigan, Ann Arbor, Michigan.

L of C.—Library of Congress, Washington, D. C.

NYPL.—New York Public Library, New York City.

PHC.—Terence V. Powderly-John W. Hayes Correspondence, Mullen Library of the Catholic University of America, Washington, D. C.

PLB.—Terence V. Powderly Letter-Books, Mullen Library of the Catholic University of America, Washington, D. C.

PP.—Terence V. Powderly Papers, Mullen Library of the Catholic University of America, Washington, D. C.

WSHS.—Wisconsin State Historical Society, Madison, Wisconsin.

ISBN 0-7178-0092-X; 0-7178-0388-0 (paperback)
Library of Congress Catalogue Card Number: 47-19381
PRINTED IN THE UNITED STATES OF AMERICA

CONTENTS

5

PREFACE

In 1947, the first volume of my *History of the Labor Movement in the United States* was published. It covered the period from colonial times to the founding of the American Federation of Labor which dates its inception from 1881, the year the Federation of Organized Trades and Labor Unions was formed.

The present volume carries the story from 1881 to the close of the nineteenth century. While the scope is small in comparison with that covered by the preceding volume, the issues and events discussed are of great importance for an understanding of the emergence of the modern labor movement. The volume covers the two decades which set the mould and the outlook of organized labor for many years to come. These years marked the rise and decline of the Knights of Labor, the early development of the American Federation of Labor, the formation of the Socialist Party, the rise and decline of Populism, the growth of monopoly capitalism and the emergence of American imperialism. During these years the modern labor movement came into being in the United States.

In April, 1897, Professor W. M. Burke of Oberlin College wrote to Samuel Gompers and inquired if the A. F. of L. President could recommend a book that would give a thorough and accurate history of the labor movement during the 1880's and 1890's. Gompers informed his correspondent that the history of the labor movement for the period indicated "is not yet written. . . . Most of it is in the correspondence in the archives of our office and having been so engrossed with the work there have been few to write it, and thus far we have had none who have had the leisure and opportunity to take up this line of work."

The history of the labor movement in the 'eighties and 'nineties has not been ignored since Gompers replied to his correspondent. But none of the books covering these decades, including the monumental work by John R. Commons and his associates at the University of Wisconsin, were based on the source material in the archives of the American Federation of Labor. From its very inception, the files and records of the A. F. of L. remained closed to all but the officials of the organization. Scholars interested in the beginnings of the modern American labor movement were compelled to tell this dramatic and important story without the benefit of the most important source material.

The present writer was fortunate in obtaining access to the vast collection of manuscript sources in the A. F. of L. headquarters. I spent many

months in the basement of the A. F. of L. Building and in the Samuel
Gompers Memorial Room examining thousands of crates, letter boxes and
file drawers containing literally hundreds of thousands of letters and
documents from labor organizations and leaders the world over. I am
indebted to Florence Thorne and others at the American Federation of
Labor for the opportunity to study and make use of this enormous
collection.

Next to the manuscript sources in the A. F. of L. headquarters, the
most important collection examined in the preparation of this volume
was the papers of Terence Vincent Powderly, General Master Workman
of the K. of L., which are in the possession of the Mullen Library of the
Catholic University of America. Consisting of about 75,000 letters, letter-
books, diaries and scrapbooks of press clippings, this collection is an
invaluable source for the understanding of the rise and decline of the
Knights of Labor. I am indebted to Father Henry J. Browne of the
Catholic University of America for the opportunity to study and make
use of this important collection.

In addition to these two major sources, I have had access, in preparing
this volume, to the collections of manuscripts, newspapers, pamphlets
and published and unpublished monographic studies in scores of libraries
and historical societies. I wish to take the opportunity to thank the staffs
of the Wisconsin State Historical Society, the Library of Congress, the
Labadie Collection of the University of Michigan, the Bancroft Library
of the University of California, the Minnesota Historical Society, the John
Crerar Library, Chicago, the British Museum, the Rand School, the
Public Libraries of New York, Boston, Chicago, the libraries of the
following colleges and universities: Wisconsin, Harvard, California,
Southern California, Mount Holyoke, Radcliffe, Cornell, Columbia,
Leland Stanford, Chicago, New York, Minnesota, Howard, Western
Ontario, Princeton, Pennsylvania, Tulane.

PHILIP S. FONER

Croton-on-Hudson, New York
November, 1955

CHAPTER I

The Industrial Scene, 1880-1890

"The times are revolutionary," wrote the fiery labor journalist, John Swinton, in the middle 'eighties. "The energies of mankind in our day are immense. There is an extraordinary activity of the powers of life in our age. The world seems to be whirling more rapidly than ever before. Vast changes have been brought about in our generation; others are in progress; yet others are impending. There is a new spirit abroad, and its manifestations are everywhere. Things are in the saddle. Questions from which there can be no escape are before us." [1]

This contemporary observation is an appropriate introduction to the turbulent years of the 'eighties with their convulsive upheavals and pulsating economic movements. Never before had the nation witnessed labor struggles of such vigor and scope. In cities and towns the armies of labor organized and gave expression to the pent-up bitterness of years of exploitation in a series of strikes which shook the nation to its foundation. "The year 1886," a contemporary report stated, "has witnessed a more profound and far more extended agitation among the members of organized labor than any previous year in the history of our country. . . . The year 1886 will be forever remembered as one of the greatest importance in the battle waged between capital and labor." One historian speaks of 1886 as a "revolutionary year," and in 1887, Frederick Engels, co-founder with Karl Marx of scientific socialism, wrote that during ten months "a revolution has been accomplished in American society such as, in any other country, would have taken at least ten years." [2]

INDUSTRIAL GROWTH

The ending of slavery by the Civil War assured the establishment of industrial capitalism as the dominant economic system throughout the country. At once there took place an almost unprecedented economic expansion. From 1860 to 1894 the United States jumped from fourth to first place in the production of industrial goods, in the latter year accounting for one-third of the world's output, or more than twice as much as Great Britain.

The rise of the United States to a position of industrial preeminence was especially apparent during the 1880's. The number of wage earners in manufacturing increased from nearly 2,750,000 in 1880 to 5,880,000, in 1890, and the percentage of the population engaged in manufacturing for the nation as a whole increased from 5.45 in 1880 to 7.5 in 1890. The railway mileage of the United States expanded from 93,239 to 163,579 in the decade 1880-1890, and by the end of the decade this country had more miles of railroad than all of Europe and about half the mileage of the world. The output of American iron and steel in 1870 was less than that of England and France, but by 1890 the United States had left them far behind and was producing more than one-third of the world's supply. Between 1875 and 1885, the production of steel in Pennsylvania swelled from 143,374 tons to 1,109,034. The total extraction of bituminous coal in 1880 reached 41,800,000 tons; the figure in 1890 was 99,400,000 tons.

Capital investments in manufactures almost tripled in the decade, rising from $2,790,000 in 1880 to $6,525,000 ten years later. Dr. Josiah Strong estimated the wealth of the United States in 1880 at $43,642,000,000 and in 1890 at $61,459,000,000.[3]

RISE OF TRUSTS

The rapid growth of American industry in the 1880's was accompanied by a tremendous concentration of capital and the appearance of giant corporations. The trend towards monopoly operated in almost every branch of industry. Commissioner of Labor Frank A. Fowler of Wisconsin summed up the situation with the statement that "almost every principal necessity is kept up in price by combinations, rings, and pools."[4]

The pool, which appeared after the panic of 1873 and was widely used by railroads, was an organization of business units the members of which controlled prices by apportioning the available market by means of price agreements. In the Interstate Commerce Act of 1887 the pool was declared illegal. This had slight effect on the trend towards monopoly since the pool was already being replaced by the trust. In this form of organization the stockholders deposited with a board of trustees a controlling portion of their stock, receiving stock certificates. The Standard Oil Company used this device as early as 1879, by which time it controlled 95 percent of the oil refining business.

With the remarkable success of the Standard Oil Company, the trust quickly became the most popular form of combination in American industry. In 1884, the American Cotton Oil Trust was formed, followed a year later by the National Linseed Oil Trust. In 1887, there were formed the Distillers' and Cattle Feeders' Company (Whiskey Trust), the Sugar Refining Company (Sugar Trust), the National Lead Trust, the Cordage Trust, and others.[5]

The extent the trust movement had reached by 1890 is well described in the following article in the San Francisco *Argonaut*, reprinted in *Public Opinion* on February 22, 1890:

"The extent to which the organization of trusts has been carried is barely realized by those who have not kept account of the organization of these modern monopolies. To give a complete list of trusts, of their torturous workings, is impossible. . . . Let us glance, however, at a few of the articles known to be controlled by trusts. If a man desires to build a house he must obtain lumber from a lumber trust, nails from a nail trust, earthenware from an earthenware trust; the painter whom he employs gets linseed oil from a linseed oil trust and white lead from a white lead trust; if he puts a fence around his place he has his choice between patronizing the lumber trust or the barbed wire trust. The oil cloth for his floors is controlled by a trust; the stove for his kitchen comes from a trust. The slates and slate's pencils, the rubber shoes and castor oil for his children are under control of trusts. Trusts control the sugar and salt for his table, the paper bags for his business, if he be a retailer. If he be a farmer, he is affected by the plow-steel trust, the railroad that carries his produce is oppressed by the steel rail trust, the Bessemer steel trust, the iron nut and washer trust. He may, perhaps, avoid other trusts but he is in danger of coming under the influence of the jute bag trust, the cordage trust, the borax trust, the cottonseed oil trust, or the copper, lead, zinc, nickel or tin trust. And after having passed through life surrounded and hedged in by trust, he dies only to fall into the hands of the National Burial Case Association, or undertakers' trust." [6]

In the 1880's the foundation was also being laid for the domination of finance-capital in the twentieth century. Already giant banking houses such as J. P. Morgan & Co. were emerging, absorbing the properties of smaller banks and extending their control over railroads and industrial corporations.[7]

Monopoly, in short, was already becoming the dominant feature of American capitalism. The age of the small manufacturer, the age of free competitive enterprise was passing. It was being replaced by what was widely called in the 'eighties "The New Feudalism." Said President Grover Cleveland in a message to Congress on December 3, 1888: "As we view the achievements of aggregated capital, we discover the existence of trusts, combinations and monopolies, while the citizen is struggling far in the rear or is trampled to death beneath an iron heel. Corporations, which should be carefully restrained creatures of the law and servants of the people, are fast becoming the people's masters." [8]

ROLE OF THE MACHINE

The increasingly important role of the machine was among the most important developments of the 'eighties. During that decade the total horsepower employed in manufacturing establishments in the United States was augmented by 85 percent. Again, the number of patents issued increased from an annual average of about 13,000 for the 'seventies to about 21,000 for the 'eighties. This significant increase reverberated in industries which previously were never affected by the machine. "The displacement of labor by machinery in the past few years," Samuel Gompers solemnly asserted in 1887, "has exceeded that of any like period in our history." The New York Bureau of Labor Statistics summed up a nationwide trend when it pointed out in 1894 that although there had been a great growth in the use of machinery in New York State since 1880, the percentage of increase in the number of workers had been small. One labor spokesman in 1888 declared that it would be more accurate to call "labor-saving machines" "wage-saving and labor displacing machines." [9]

With the rapid spread of the factory system, large-scale methods of production, and the introduction of machinery, wage-earners discovered a radical alteration in their status. No longer employed as self-respecting handicraftsmen, more and more workers were becoming mere adjuncts to a great machine. Their working conditions were directed to a great extent by managers representing impersonal and absentee corporation owners. Workers all over the country complained that they had to "suffer under insolent, unscrupulous bosses, rapacious foremen, greedy and unsympathetic managers, wealthy and avaricious contractors, brutal and egotistical capitalists." [10]

It was not unusual to find that in many factories the men were looked upon as nothing more than parts of the machinery they operated. A New England clergyman deplored "the increasing tendency to regard the operative simply as a wheel, or a pin to a machine. He is, in the eyes of employers, very much what a mule or a spindle is, and no more. . . . They care not who or what the operative is, or where he lives, or what his character, except as any of these things bear on profit." There is ample testimony from employers themselves confirming this statement. Thus a Massachusetts manufacturer, a member of the Legislature, declared, according to Gompers: "I regard my employees as I do a machine, to be used to my advantage, and when they are old and of no further use, I cast them in the street." [11] And with increasing speed-up of the machines, young workers found themselves rapidly becoming "old and of no further use." A foreman in a Massachusetts shoe shop bluntly told a labor leader: ". . . I can take an able-bodied young man eighteen years of age, without a physical blemish, and put him to work at either one of those machines and bring gray hairs in his head at twenty-two." [12]

CONTRAST BETWEEN WEALTH AND POVERTY

"There are too many millionaires and too many paupers," declared the *Hartford Courant* in 1883. All of America was a land of contrast. At one end of the scale was magnificence unstinted. The "robber barons" who made up the new plutocracy consisted of an array of "millionaires whose riches," Engels noted, "can hardly be expressed in our miserable marks, guldens, or francs. . . ." Vying with each other in "conspicuous waste," the "monied aristocracy" of the Gilded Age—the Goulds, Vanderbilts, and others—accentuated the widening gap between "those who have but toil not and those who toil but have not." Their arrogant display of wealth caused even Henry Clews, a prominent Wall Street banker, to comment in his memoirs: "If any facts could be supposed to justify the doctrines of socialism and communism it would be the sudden creation of such fortunes as these which within a very few years have come into the hands of our railway magnates." [13]

What were conditions like at the other end of the scale? To answer this question we must turn to an examination of the wages, hours of labor, and living conditions of the American working class.

Reliable figures of aggregate wages in the 1880's are lacking, but there is much truth to Samuel Gompers' statement, in 1883, that "the wage of working men is less now than it was in 1870." The United States Census of 1870 estimated the average annual income at a little over $400 per capta; the Census of 1880 placed it at a little over $300 per capita. In Pennsylvania this downward trend was borne out in the wages paid by the largest mining companies in the Pittsburgh district; the miners were paid ninety-two cents per ton of coal mined in 1880; ten years later they were receiving seventy-nine cents for the same amount extracted. In the annual report of the Massachusetts Bureau of Labor for 1883, Commissioner Wright demonstrated that the workingmen's share of the return on their own labor from 1875 to 1880 "so far from increasing has decreased one-sixth." In Illinois, a study of the wage-records of 114 establishments from 1882 to 1886 revealed that of these, 71 showed a decrease, 23 an increase, and 20 no change. This downward trend was confirmed by *Bradstreets'* in a survey conducted in 1885. It found that wages had been cut 15 percent on the average, ranging from 40 percent in coal mining to a low percentage in the building trades. [14]

A variety of factors operated to force wages down.

The opening years of the 'eighties were marked by a depression from which the country did not fully recover until 1886. At the depths of this depressed period there were close to a million unemployed workers in the United States. Factories closed and wages were reduced. "We could not possibly print all the past week's reports of wage-cutting and discharging of hands in scores of industry all over the country. They would overflow this paper," *John Swinton's Paper* noted late in 1884. Every passing week brought fresh evidence of the truth of this journal's observation "that it is the unemployed who fix the rate of wages for the workers."

"I stand every morning in my factory," said a New England manufacturer in 1884, "and am obliged to refuse the applications of men who want to come to work for a dollar a day . . . and women begging for the opportunity to work for 50 cents a day. . . . It is evident . . . that there are a large number of men who desire to be employed at the low rate of wages now prevailing, and who cannot find employment." [15]

ROLE OF IMMIGRATION

As in the past, a major method used by the capitalists to force down wage scales was the creation of labor surpluses. The reservoir of labor was flooded by the shift of population from the country to the city. It was enormously increased by the huge wave of immigration. The total number arriving during the decade 1880-1890 was more than five and one-half million; two and one-half million more than during the previous decade, and one and one-half million more than during the 'nineties. [16]

To the discontented peasant in Italy, Hungary, Rumania, Germany, and the Scandinavian countries, to the Jews in tsarist Russia facing progroms and increased restrictions on their freedom to live and work, the glowing descriptions of life in America evoked eager responses. These descriptions were laid before them by steamship companies desirous of carrying full cargoes of immigrants on each trip to America and by commission agents working for industrialists seeking unskilled labor, for railroad land companies eager to settle prospective customers and land buyers along the lines of their roads, and for States seeking people to help develop their agriculture and industry. Circulars distributed by these agents told poverty-stricken European peasants that they could make from $2.50 to $3.50 per day in the Pennsylvania coal regions or in the New England textile factories. [17]

The average European immigrant staggering down the gangplank with a heavy pack on his shoulders faced the immediate and pressing problem of earning a livelihood in a strange land. In the vast majority of cases, he was taken over by labor bureaus and sent out to work on railroads, in factories, mines, lumber camps, etc. These labor bureaus sent out circulars to employers of unskilled labor offering to furnish large quantities of workers, and, in many instances, specifying that the labor could be obtained at very low wages, far below existing scales. Thus the New York City Italian Labor Bureau offered to furnish any number of workers at from 50 to 60 cents a day, and was even willing to stipulate "that the laborers will serve from one to five years without demanding an increase." [18]

All too frequently newly-arrived immigrants of every nationality made their first entrance into American industry as strikebreakers. Attracted by the glowing promises of agents in Europe, totally unaware of the uses they were to be put in the new world, they became, unwittingly, the tool of rapacious capitalists in the drive to cut wages and smash unions.[19]

To list the unions weakened or destroyed or the strikes broken in the 'eighties by industry's policy of introducing immigrant labor or strikebreakers would require many pages. The failure of a great number of strikes in the cotton textile, mining, iron and steel, cigar, railroad, and other industries must be attributed, in no small measure, to the ability of employers to make use of unskilled labor obtained from the labor exchanges and steamship companies as strikebreakers. These workers were rushed to the scene whenever a strike was in the offing or had already been declared. Often there was a simultaneous process: the moment it appeared that a union was being formed and a strike prepared, the employers would introduce machinery and import unskilled labor to operate the machines.[20]

Several common features emerge from the use of immigrants as strikebreakers during that decade. For one thing, in nearly every instance, the immigrants were completely unaware that a strike was taking place. As the Freighthandlers Central Union pointed out in the summer of 1882, during its strike against the five leading railroads in New York and New Jersey: "The raw immigrants from European cities are brought here by padrones, and others, and these poor creatures, unacquainted with our language or customs, are taken off the ship and put at work without being allowed to converse with anybody who would be likely to explain the real situation of affairs." [21]

Where the strikers could break through and establish contacts with the immigrants, strikes were successful. Unfortunately, in many cases the strikebreakers were guarded so carefully that the union men were unable even to see them. In these cases, the strikes usually failed.

When immigrant strikebreakers were informed of the real situation, they frequently left the scene immediately. In a number of cases, they even joined the strikers and became members of the union. During the freighthandlers' strike, for example Jewish and Italian branches of the

Freighthandlers' Central Union were formed. On July 14, 1882, five hundred Jewish immigrants, imported as strikebreakers, marched from the piers at the Battery to the union headquarters and joined the union. The following day, 250 Italians left the New York Central Yard to join the union.[22]

Frequently, too, immigrant strikebreakers went on strike after the strike they had been imported to break had been broken. The *American Iron and Steel Bulletin* acknowledged as early as August 23, 1882, that the immigrants, imported as strikebreakers, soon became a problem for the employers. "They are not content to live less handsomely than they see others live. They will take no lower wages. . . ." Three years later, the New York Bureau of Labor concluded that "when first brought here [the immigrants] were willing to work for very low wages, but after a few years residence they became sufficiently Americanized to strike." Even immigrants who were assisted to come to America "on condition that they did not join trade unions" were soon organizing and striking for higher wages. "In hundreds of cases," the New York *Tribune* lamented, "it has turned out . . . that the foreigners imported here because they were expected to work cheaply were presently engaging in a most desperate strike for the highest wages known in like employment anywhere in the country." [23]

By the summer of 1886, many of the same industrialists who had been the most active in sponsoring the importation of "cheap foreign labor" to reduce existing wage scales and to weaken the labor movement "grew alarmed at the idea that immigration itself was strengthening the labor movement . . . and suggested that aggressive unionism might be crippled if immigration were more rapidly supervised." [24]

Throughout most of the 'eighties, however, employers continued to draw upon Castle Garden in New York City and other labor exchanges and to rely upon fresh shipments of immigrants to replace strikers, many recent immigrants themselves. The union and the strikers might succeed temporarily in persuading the strikebreakers to leave the job and even to join the ranks of the strikers, but few indeed were the unions that had the strength to cope with the ability of employers to continue to import strikebreakers through the Labor Exchanges. The vice president of the Freighthandlers' Union in Jersey City summed up the cause of the defeat of this and other strikes in the 'eighties: "It's that —— —— Castle Garden that's killing us." [25]

There was nothing inherent in the immigrants from southern and eastern Europe which caused them to be used as wage-cutters. Soon enough, as we shall see, the immigrant workers began to make heroic contributions to the growth of an American labor movement that would battle for decent living standards for all workers. The vast influx of immigrant labor resulted in wage-cutting, lowered living standards, and threats to trade union organization not because of the inherent character of the new immigrants but because of the vicious system by which they were introduced into America, because of the conscious use made of them by industrialists to cut wages and destroy existing wage levels, and because of the penniless state of the immigrant workers when they landed in American ports which compelled them to obtain work at whatever wages were offered them, invariably much lower than those being received by the already underpaid workers in the field.[26]

LABOR CONDITIONS

A great number of the American workingmen lived as paupers. In Massachusetts, where statistics of labor are the most abundant, the average workingman was not in a position to support his family. Reverend Josiah Strong pointed out that "In 1883 the average expenses of workingmen's families . . . were $754.42, while the earnings of workingmen who were heads of families average $558.68. This means that the average workingman had to call on his wife and children to assist in earning their support. We accordingly find that in the manufactures and mechanical industries of the state . . . there were engaged 28,714 children under sixteen years of age. Of the average workingman's family 32.44% of the support fell upon the children and mother." * And when Dr. Strong continued with the words, "I am not aware that the condition of the working man is at all exceptional in Massachusetts," he was painting the national labor scene a much brighter hue than it actually was. In the same year, 1883, the average national per capita was estimated at "about $375 a year," which was closer to the correct amount than Dr. Strong's. The conservative M. Levasseur, a French observer of the American labor scene, who expressed the fear that his "picture of American industry and the condition of the American laborer is far too flattering," was compelled to admit that "*starvation wages*, that is to say, wages that will not enable the recipient to live as well as the common laborer, are found in America as well as in Europe." [27]

And such "starvation wages" were found in every industry. "I have a brother who has four children, besides his wife and himself," a New England workingman told a Senate Committee in 1883. "All he earns is $1.50 a day." "This," writes a labor historian, "was the abbreviated life history of thousands." [28]

"He works in the ironworks at Fall River," the workingman continued.

* In 1870 there were 739,164 children at work in America. By 1880, this number had risen to 1,118,000 or slightly less than one-sixth of all children in the United States. (*Proceedings,* A.F. of L. Convention, 1890, p. 4.)

"He only works about nine months out of twelve. There is generally about three months of stoppage, taking the year right through, and his wife and his family all have to be supported for a year out of the wages of nine months—$1.50 a day for nine months out of twelve, to support six of them. It does not stand to reason that those children and he himself can have natural food or be naturally dressed."

Asked by one senator whether there were many families living in this way in his community, the workingman replied: "I could not count them, they are so numerous. . . . They live on less than $150 a year. . . . I have heard many women say they would sooner be dead than living. I don't know what is wrong, but something is wrong." [29]

The highest daily wage in the 'eighties was $4.00. But this was enjoyed by only a small group of very skilled workers, particularly those in the building trades, and even in good years, such workers might be expected to be employed for thirty weeks or one hundred and eighty days. At $4.00 per day, the annual wage of the best-paid workers was $720.00. On the basis of the lowest estimates of living costs and allowing $204 per year for rent, the worker and his family could spend $516, or less than $10 a week, for food, clothing, fuel, and other necessities. This just about supported life on the subsistence level.[30]

And this conclusion is based on the highest wage received. What of the vast majority of workers throughout the United States whose average earnings in 1883, according to government statistics, came to slightly more than a dollar a day? [31]

With an average of 282 working days a year, these figures give the male workers an average annual income of less than $300. Since the annual living costs of a workingman's family in 1883, on the basis of the lowest estimate of living costs, was over $720, it is again clear that if the families of most of these workers were to maintain life on the subsistence level, the wages of the male workers had to be supplemented by the earnings of wives and children. In many industries whole families worked together at the job.[32]

In a report on their tour of the United States during the 'eighties, Eleanor Marx and Dr. Edward Aveling, daughter and son-in-law of Karl Marx, noted: "Everywhere we found women forced to work for wages because the husband's were insufficient for even bare subsistence, besides having to tend their children, and go the usual dreary round of endless household drudgery. We have lived in English factory towns and know something of English factory hands; but we may fairly say we have never in the English Manchester seen women so worn out and degraded, such famine in their cheeks, such need and oppression staring in their eyes, as in the women we saw trudging to their work in the New Hampshire Manchester. What must the children born of such women be?" [33]

In many industries the pitiful wages were reduced by excessive fines.

The system of deduction from wages for minor offenses grew rapidly during the 'eighties, and, in certain industries, particularly those employing large numbers of women and children, was the rule rather than the exception. Of 152 Southern mills investigated in 1885, 100 imposed fines on employees. The causes were lateness, absence from work, remaining too long in lavatories, opening windows without permission, singing or talking during working hours, imperfections in the work, and a general heading called "misconduct." In some mills, absence in the afternoon was punishable by deduction of the morning's earnings.[34]

In industries where the company store system prevailed, the workers were paid partly in cash and partly in goods or orders for goods.* (In some cases, the workers never received cash at all.) If a worker rebelled and bought from an independent store, he was immediately discharged. Employees of the H. C. Frick Coke Company in Pennsylvania complained that if they did not spend from $20 to $25 a month at the company store, they were told to look for work elsewhere. Yet goods at the company store sold at prices from five to 20 percent higher than those prevailing at independent stores in the same locality. It was estimated in 1881 that H. C. Frick Coke Company did an annual business of $800,000 at its company stores of which at least $160,000 represented clear profit.[35]

An investigation into the conditions of southern textile workers described them as "oppressed, abused, the victims of the [company] 'pluck-me-store.'" On many Southern plantations Negro workers were paid their meager wages in pasteboard tickets which were only transferable at the company stores, operated by the planters. John Swinton pointed out that the Negro's average wage in the South was from 50 to 75 cents a day, and after the company stores reaped a profit, there was nothing left.[36] After a tour of the South in 1888, Frederick Douglass, the great Negro leader and one of the outstanding personalities of the nineteenth century, reported bitterly:

"The same class that once extorted his [the Negro's] labor under the

* After an organizing tour through the Pennsylvania mining districts, a labor leader reported that most of the companies in the area "pay their hands only at the end of 30 days, and by this means the hands are forced to trade at the Company's Store."

"This is not all," he added. "The company pays the miner so much per bushell (*sic*) for coal, after it is screened and the screens are made so as to leave nothing but large lumps in the screen. All the screening are sold to the Smelters which brings 4 to 5 cents per bushel, the miner getting nothing for this." (Abner W. Dyer to Chris Evans, Feb. 9, 1891, American Federation of Labor Correspondence, A.F. of L. Archives, Washington, D. C. Hereafter cited as *AFL Corr.*)

Miners constantly complained that the operators changed the mesh size of the screen always to the disadvantage of the workers. The miner's car of coal was dumped to slide down the screen, and whatever went through the holes he was not paid for. By making the holes larger, the miners would be paid less. "Keep your eye on the screen," went a line in the song, "A Miner's Life."

lash, now extorts his labor by a mean, sneaking, and fraudulent device, which is more effective than the lash. That device is the trucking system, a system which never permits him to see or save a dollar of his hard earnings. He struggles from year to year, but like a man in a morass, the more he struggles, the deeper he sinks. The highest wages paid him are eight dollars a month, and this he receives only in orders on a store, which in many cases is owned by his employer. The scrip has a purchasing power on that one store, and that one store only. A blind man can see that by this arrangement the laborer is bound hand and foot, and he is completely in the power of his employer." [37]

Working conditions in most factories in the 1880's were unsatisfactory. Poor ventilation, poor lighting, inadequate sanitary conditions, and the horrible danger of fire to which many workers were exposed, were all causes of frequent complaints by witnesses before the Senate and state investigating committees. Dangerous machinery was often unprotected, and the number of industrial accidents was high. [38]

As for the physical well-being of the worker, Professor Richard T. Ely pointed out at that time that "No current fiction is more widely removed from the truth than the common assertion that workingmen and their families enjoy exceptionally good health. The exact opposite is the truth, and statistics have established beyond controversy that laborers are shorter-lived by many years than those who belong to the wealthier social classes." Mill operatives were described by a physician as "dwarfed physically" and "most of them are obliged to live from hand to mouth, or . . . they do not have sufficient food to nourish them as they need to be nourished." The Ohio Labor Statistics Bureau charged, and substantiated its charge, that "man must die that trade may thrive." [39]

Working hours were often 12 to 15 a day, and in many industries employees worked holidays and Sundays, the year round. It was not unusual to require laborers to work 24 hours consecutively when changes from day to night shifts were made. In the railroad industry, the hours were especially long. Many workers, including switchmen, telegraphers, trackmen and station men, were on the job 12 hours a day, and even from sunrise to sunset. [40]

The living conditions of the working class were notoriously bad. In the mining areas the workers were forced to live in overcrowded, poorly constructed, filthy company houses for which they paid exorbitant rents. Houses that cost only $50 to build were rented out at $2 to $2.50 per month The Pennsylvania Legislative Committee described the houses in the bituminous fields as being "in a very filthy and untenable condition, the miners being herded together like cattle and in many places wallowing in their own filth, breeding disease and affecting not only their own health, but that of the community in which they live." [41]

A glimpse into the living conditions of the wage-workers in urban centers may be gathered from a report of the investigation of the tenement areas in Chicago 1883-84, which speaks of the "wretched condition of the tenements into which thousands of workingmen are huddled, the wholesale violation of all rules for drainage, plumbing, light, ventilation and safety in case of fire or accident, the neglect of all laws of health, the horrible condition of sewers and outhouses, the filthy dingy rooms into which they are crowded, the unwholesome character of their food and the equally filthy nature of the neighboring streets, alleys and back lots filled with decaying matter and stagnant pools." For these "unwholesome dens," into which they were crowded, working class families paid extravagant rents in proportion to the wages they received. In many cases, they were "fleeced at a rate which returns 25 to 40 percent per annum of the value of the property." [42]

Yet Chicago, with an average of over eight persons to a dwelling, and with about 17 percent of the dwellings containing three or more families, appears to have had housing facilities which were superior to other urban centers. New York City's Tenth Ward, where the Jewish immigrants congregated, was said to be the most crowded district in the world. Here, investigations showed, about one out of every three persons "slept in unventilated rooms without windows." [43]

The so-called "homes" in the Tenth Ward were both homes and workshop, tenement house manufacture of men's and women's clothing and cigars being generally carried on in the living quarters of the immigrant families. The rooms inside these sweatshops were little more than cubbyholes, but rents were 10 to 20 percent higher than rents of similar apartments elsewhere. Provisions for adequate sanitation were non-existent, with water closets "in the back yard, around which a few boards were nailed." [44]

In the year 1885, wages for clothing workers in these hideous sweatshops were from $6 to $7 a week. The New York State Bureau of Labor Statistics reported that the "very best" workers were "getting $10 a week, while the women employed in the industry were earning from $3 to $6 a week." Furthermore, the report continued, "some even with the aid of their families and working 14 hours a day could earn only $12 and $15 a week. Others could only make $4 by working 10 hours a day." [45]

Morris Rosenfeld, himself a pants presser, captured the heartbreaking agony of the endless work day in the sweatshops in his famous poem, *My Boy*, parts of which went:

> *I have a little boy at home,*
> *A pretty little son;*
> *I think sometimes the world is mine*
> *In him, my only one.*

But seldom, seldom do I see
My child in heaven's light;
I find him always fast asleep ...
I see him but at night.

'Ere dawn my labor drives me forth;
'Tis night when I am free;
A stranger am I to my child;
And stranger my child to me....[46]

EFFORTS AT LABOR LEGISLATION

Callous exploitation of labor, especially of women and children, long hours and appalling sanitary conditions were typical of all of American industry in the 1880's. Attempts to remedy these conditions through legislation proved ineffective. Even in older industrial states like Massachusetts, Rhode Island, Connecticut, New York, and Pennsylvania, agitation for child welfare legislation, which began in the early part of the century, did not achieve results until the closing years of the century. At the national capital a Senate Committee, investigating industrial relations, reported:

"Time after time in each of these industrial states the sentiment of the public was aroused, organization was effected, and well-drafted bills were introduced only to be killed in committee, emasculated, or killed on the floor of the legislature, or passed with exceptions which rendered them entirely ineffective. Even the attempt to reduce the hours of children below twelve per day was bitterly contested and met by every known trick of legislative chicanery." [47]

As a result of labor pressure, social legislation of various kinds slowly started to emerge. In 1877 Massachusetts passed the first American law requiring factory safeguards, and by 1887, 15 states had passed laws providing elementary safety measures in factories. By the same time, several states had restricted the labor of women and children. It was also during this period that a number of states established bureaus of labor or bureaus of labor statistics. The United States Bureau of Labor was founded in 1884.[48]

It is not to be expected that those who were exploiting labor so profitably would accept without resistance these attempts to curtail their ruthless activities. Where possible, they got around these laws through a loophole or a legal technicality. Where no adequate enforcing agency was provided, they ignored the regulations. And in the vast majority of laws, no real enforcing agency existed. Few, if any, of the bureaus of labor statistics, for example, were equipped either with funds or personnel to function properly, and most of them were little more than names.* Again, most of the laws which set up standards of wages, hours, and working conditions were to prevail only if the employers and workers did not make an agreement to the contrary. Other laws made it possible for the worker to maintain his rights only if he brought civil suits against his employer. Even more widespread were the laws which made violation by an employer punishable by fine, but left it up to the worker, or some other interested party, to initiate proceedings by informing the prosecuting attorney.[49]

ROLE OF THE COURTS

Where labor succeeded in forcing legislatures to adopt social legislation, the courts weakened or entirely wiped out these gains by declaring the laws unconstitutional. Both the "iron-clad" oath which required a worker, as a condition of employment, not to join a union and the blacklisting of workers were sanctioned by the courts as a necessary protection of property rights. When legislation was obtained, after years of labor's pressure, which outlawed "iron-clad" oaths and forbade any corporation from firing a worker because he belonged to a union or was involved in an attempt to form one, the courts declared such laws unconstitutional.[50]

Although laws had been passed in several states prior to the 'eighties designed to legalize the normal functioning of trade unions, they contained provisions which prohibited the use of "force, threats or menace of harm to person or property." Employers were quick to take advantage of this loophole to secure convictions of trade unionists for criminal conspiracy. The courts, as usual, cooperated eagerly, defining intimidation so loosely that even if no interference with the right to work had occurred, the mere inducing of workers to break their contract with an employer was considered a conspiracy. Indeed, the mere presence of a large number of strikers outside a mine or factory often resulted in convictions for conspiracy. In nearly every case where such convictions were appealed to the state Supreme Courts, the judgments of the lower courts were sustained.[51]

Towards the latter part of the 'eighties, conspiracy indictments were replaced more and more by injunctions which the employers learned could be used to greater advantage in stopping union activity. Convictions for conspiracy depended on a jury, and as the hostility of farmers and small businessmen toward monopolistic corporations increased during the decade, the jury system became an unreliable instrument in the drive

* The same cannot be said, however, of the Federal Bureau of Labor Statistics. Under Carroll D. Wright, it won international renown and influenced the establishment of labor bureaus in every important European country and in Australia.

against unionization. Quite often local juries simply refused to return verdicts of guilty, and when they did convict, the sentences were usually very light and did not serve as a sufficient deterrent in preventing labor organization.*

As the decade advanced, dissatisfaction with the system of conspiracy indictments based on jury trials was voiced more and more in business journals. It was openly suggested that injunctions were a better means to curb trade unionism. Employers' associations hailed the injunction as a "new and highly efficient instrument" to prevent the organization of American industry. Soon injunctions were issued to prohibit boycotts and to prevent union leaders who were not employed by a company from approaching its workers for the purpose of organizing them.[52]

The view that the courts had been captured by the corporate interests and were their subservient tools was advanced by no less an authority than Samuel Freeman Miller, who had been appointed by Lincoln as Associate Justice of the Supreme Court. "It is in vain," wrote Justice Miller, "to contend with Judges who have been at the bar advocates for forty years, of railroad companies and all forms of associated capital, when they are called upon to decide cases where such interests are in contest. All their training, all their feelings are from the start in favor of those who need no such influence." [53]

The attitude of the courts towards legislation aimed at improving working conditions fully bears out Justice Miller's evaluation. Statutes imposing minimum wages or maximum hours were declared by the Supreme Court to be "mere meddlesome interference with the right of the individual." And any legislation limiting the power of the employer over the worker was no more than "an arbitrary interference with the liberty of contract which no government can legally justify in a free land." [54]

The state courts followed and expanded the arguments of the federal court and provided new rationalizations. A good example is the fate of a New York State law passed in 1885. It was designed to put an end to the "sweating system" by prohibiting the manufacture of cigars and other tobacco products in tenement houses in cities of first class. The New York Court of Appeals held the law unconstitutional, maintaining that it was "an abuse of police power and an infringement of the cigar-maker's liberties in that it sought to force him from his home and its hallowed associations and beneficent influences, to ply his trade elsewhere."

The same hypocritical concern for the liberty of the worker is revealed in the 1886 decision of the State Supreme Court of Pennsylvania declaring unconstitutional a law outlawing company stores. The court charged that

* In the Clearfield case in Pennsylvania, 1884, the fine was only six cents each. In the Jones conspiracy case of 1881 the sentence was one day in jail.

in the law "an attempt has been made by the legislature to do what, in this country, cannot be done; that is, to prevent persons who are *sui juris* from making their own contracts. The Act is an infringement alike of the right of the employer and the employee; more than this, it is an insulting attempt to put the laborer under a legislative tutelage, which is not only degrading to his manhood, but subversive of his rights as a citizen of the United States." [55]

Thus we find the ironical situation of the courts arguing that the very legislation the workers demanded and fought for to defend their freedom was inimical to their interests in that it deprived them of their freedom. Professor Morris Raphael Cohen put it well when he commented caustically that "the freedom to make a million dollars is not worth a cent to one who is out of work. Nor is the freedom to starve, or to work for subsistence, one that any rational being can prize—whatever learned courts may say to the contrary." [56]

CAPITAL JUSTIFIES MASS POVERTY

We have seen enough to understand why workers all over the United States bitterly resented their conditions. It is only natural that they should complain:

"Whereas labor produces all the wealth of the world, the laborer receives only as much as will keep him in the poorest condition of life to which he can be crowded down, for the shortest number of years; that he makes civilization possible, and is reduced to barbarism,—building houses not to own them, carriages not to ride in, growing food he may not eat, and weaving raiment he may not wear; that all of the arts and comforts that lift human life above the brute are present to tantalize him, and not to encourage him; that steam, electricity, chemistry and productive machinery are competitors and not co-operators, with him; that his conditions of employment are debasing and not elevating,—demoralizing and not self-controlling; and that, whereas he is the most important factor, he is treated as the least; that his home is in the tenement houses, back-slums and alleys of the city, or the unhealthy lowlands of the suburbs; that his wife is forced from home and his children from school; that he cannot, as a laborer, hope for thanks." [57]

When confronted with such a moving indictment of the existing social and economic system in the United States, the capitalist class and its allies hid behind the ideological concept of "social Darwinism." Darwin himself had made no effort to apply the principle of evolution to the study of the social structure. This task was undertaken by Herbert Spencer, the English philosopher and social scientist, in his *Study of Sociology* published in 1874 and widely reprinted and quoted in the

United States during the 'eighties. Spencer's application of the biological doctrine of the adaptability and survival of the fittest to society was seized upon by big business to justify the existing social and economic conditions and to prevent any efforts to change them as restraints upon the natural process of economic life.[58]

To the old notion that God rewarded the virtuous and punished the wicked was added the claim that the wealthy were the "elect" of the human race destined to be victorious in the contest for survival. The poorer classes, on the other hand, were "inferior" stock destined to a life of poverty. Those who were "blessed with property" were of the opinion voiced by John Hay: "That you have property is proof of industry and foresight on your part or your father's; that you have nothing is a judgment on your laziness and vices, or on your improvidence. The world is a moral world, which it would not be if virtue and vice received the same reward." [59]

University professors, clergymen, and newspaper editors, avid disciples of Spencer, wrote learned treatises and delivered lengthy sermons to prove that "Poverty is only a proof of indolence and vice. Wealth simply shows the industry and virtue of the possessor." "The impecunious condition of millions of the wage classes of this country," went the common refrain, "is due to their own improvidence and misdirected efforts. Too many are trying to live without labor . . . and too many squander their earnings on intoxicating drinks, cigars, and amusements, who cannot afford it." [60] The same theme was emphasized in Thomas Bailey Aldrich's novel, *The Stillwater Tragedy,* published serially in the *Atlantic Monthly* early in 1880. The factory workers at Stillwater, Aldrich wrote,[61] were poverty-stricken because "they squander a quarter of their week's wages at the tavern." *

Francis A. Walker, a leading economist, advanced the theory that the workers were themselves to blame for their inadequate wages and poverty

* Few things infuriated workers more than did this vicious propaganda of the ruling class and its agents. As one worker pointed out in a poignant letter to Henry D. Lloyd, a mid-western reformer: ". . . I have seen *my* babies cry for bread. I have seen *my* wife lie sick and hungry in a cold house; I have searched from early morn until driven in by the darkness in search of work, I have taken in and done washing to get the wherewith to feed *my hungry children.* I have got down on my knees and begged for work, and was *kicked in the breast* and kicked out of the shop for asking for work. I have never touched a drop of whiskey in my life, I have never spent a cent of money in my life for liquor or tobacco in any form, yet I have suffered this much, and I am not yet thirty years old. . . . Having the *Labor Question,* thus burned into my very life, do you wonder that I get mad and say mean things, and call men liars when they say that 'if workingmen would quit drinking whiskey there would be no labor question?'" (Bert Stewart to Henry Demarest Lloyd, Jan. 14, 1887, Lloyd Papers, Wisconsin State Historical Society, Madison, Wisconsin. Hereafter cited as *WSHS.*)

because of their "excessive reproduction, sexually." Others found it more useful to place the blame upon unalterable economic laws. Because of such laws, the political economists pointed out, the workers could not really improve their conditions. Under the wages-fund theory, widely advocated by the economists, any struggle by labor for higher wages was futile. That which was paid for labor in every country was a certain portion of the accumulated capital "which cannot be increased by the proposed action of Government nor by the influence of public opinion, nor by combination among the workmen themselves. There is also in every country a certain number of laborers and this number cannot be diminished by the proposed action of Government, nor by public opinion, nor by combinations among themselves." Thus it was impossible to blame the employers for the abject poverty of the working class.[62]

A huge conspiracy existed, in short, to convince the exploited workers that they had no just cause for complaint, that whatever poverty existed was due either to laziness or lack of restraint of the workers themselves or the operation of natural laws, and that they had better reconcile themselves to the fact that there was nothing they could do to change these unfortunate conditions. Labor was predestined to occupy its low station in life. "The rank and file are assigned their duties and places by the Captains of Industry," wrote a leading economist. "Men must be contented to work for less wages," the New York *World* declared. "In this way the workingmen will be nearer to that station in life to which it has pleased God to call them." [63]

Fortunately for themselves and for later generations of American labor, the vast majority of the workers were not "contented." "The laborer and capitalists are living in war relations," declared George E. McNeill. The feeling prevailed among workers that there is an ever-recurring conflict between the two classes, and it is succinctly expressed in the following excerpt from the preamble adopted by the Federation of Organized Trades and Labor Unions of the United States and Canada, later known as the A. F. of L., in November, 1881: "A struggle is going on . . . between the oppressors and the oppressed . . . a struggle between capital and labor, which must grow in intensity year by year, and work disastrous results to the toiling millions . . . if not combined for mutual protection." [64]

THE LABOR PRESS

Despite the seemingly insuperable obstacles placed in its way, labor was determined to organize. This determination was enforced by a growing labor press. It was estimated in January, 1885, that 17 monthly journals, published by as many unions and societies, 400 weeklies and a

handful of dailies * constituted the labor press.⁶⁵ Of these the most interesting and most influential was the weekly journal published and
edited by John Swinton.

On October 14, 1883, John Swinton resigned from his lucrative post
as managing editor of the New York *Sun* to start his four-page weekly
which he called *John Swinton's Paper.* "My objects in starting it," he
declared, "were to raise the social question, and to induce the working
people to bring their interests into politics." The paper's statement of
principles, carried in the first issue, were: "1.—Boldly upholding the
Rights of Man in the American Way. 2.—Battling against the accumulated wrongs of society and industry. 3.—Striving for the organization
and interests of workingmen, and giving the news of the Trades and the
Unions. 4.—Warning the American people against the treasonable and
crushing schemes of Millionaires, Monopolists and Plutocracy." ⁶⁶

The paper kept up the good fight for almost four years with the help
of its readers and local and national unions which endorsed it as their
official organ. But on August 21, 1887, the last number was published.
Swinton had put $40,000 of his personal savings into the project.⁶⁷

Swinton's paper had the faults of every free-lance enterprise, lacking
real organic links with the trade union organizations of the day. Nevertheless, the paper, well edited, excellently written and interesting throughout, was constantly responsive to the needs of the trade unionists of New
York and the rest of the country. It played a significant role in the upheaval of the American working class in the mid-'eighties, and, as we
shall see, was a force for miltiant trade unionism and independent working class political action.

It took great courage to publish a labor paper at that time.† The em-
ployers knew full well the importance of the labor press, and they sought
in every way to suppress these papers. The experience of J. P. McDonnell,
Socialist editor of the Paterson (N. J.) *Labor Standard* is a case in point.
In 1879, three years after the weekly was founded, McDonnell was fined
$500 and costs for denouncing the use of scabs in the Great Adams Strike.
A year later, he was indicted by the Grand Jury for publishing the letter

---

* Among the daily papers was the Socialist New York *Volkszeitung* and the
Irish World and American Industrial Liberator. During the eighties the latter
journal was transformed from a paper devoted almost entirely to events in Ireland
to a paper which devoted more than one half of its eight pages to labor affairs.

† It also took courage to read and subscribe to a labor paper. On February 1,
1885, *John Swinton's Paper* declared bitterly: "To get an idea of what things are
coming to in some quarters, take a few facts of this kind. There are American wage-
workers, descended from Revolutionary sires, who dare not take this paper for fear
of their employers. . . . Several men think it safer to get the paper in roundabout
ways or at post-offices distant from their homes. To be caught with it in some of
the slave-mills of New England would cost a man as much as his wages are worth."

of a brickmaker in which the terrible conditions in the brickyards were exposed.

The indictment aroused great indignation in labor circles. A circular issued by the trade unions of New Jersey asked, "Is American Liberty Dead?" and warned that if "the capitalistic power" succeeded in imprisoning the editor of the *Labor Standard,* there would be "No Free Labor Press." [68]

McDonnell went to jail, but the labor press was not so easily crushed. The labor journals, whether daily, weekly or monthly, kept alive the message that in organization lay labor's hope for the future. The labor press met red-baiting head on. As the *Irish World and American Industrial Liberator* put it in 1884: "The term 'communism' has for a long time served as a bludgeon in the hands of the enemies of Labor with which they have attempted to kill every reform movement that had any tendency to benefit American workingmen. As the slaveholders and their organs made the word 'Abolitionist' synonymous in the popular mind with all that was wicked, so capital and its organs have endeavored to prejudice public opinion with the free use of the epithet communism." [69]

Not the least of the contributions of the labor press was its role in instilling confidence in the workers that they could end the miserable conditions under which they worked and lived. When cynical commentators in the commercial press observed, at the opening of the decade, that the labor movement had been too seriously weakened by the depression which began in 1873 and lasted until 1879 ever to be able again to remedy the grievances of the working class, the *Labor Review* of Detroit wrote confidently on September 25, 1880: "Wait a little longer; have patience. Labor is waking from its long slumber. The rising giant is just now stretching and yawning. But his eyes are beginning to open and his sinews tightening; and soon he will make his strength felt in every phase of American life."

The history of the labor movement of the 'eighties, the growth of labor organization on a hitherto unknown scale during this decade, is testimony to the accuracy of this prediction.

CHAPTER 2

The Socialist Movement in the Eighties

In a previous volume we have traced the history of socialist movements in the United States from the Utopian stages of the 1820's and 1840's to the founding of the Socialist Labor Party in 1877 and its development to the opening of the decade, 1880-1890.* It is unnecessary in the present volume to recapitulate the history of American socialism before the 1880's, but certain facts are of importance as they relate to the development of socialism after 1880.

LASSALLEANS AND MARXISTS

American Socialists in the 1870's were divided into two groups: Lassalleans and Marxists. The former accepted Ferdinand Lassalle's belief in the "iron law of wages," maintaining that since there was always a surplus of labor under capitalism, wages were always forced down to minimum levels. Therefore, any economic action by labor aimed at raising wages or shortening hours was futile. The Lassalleans considered trade unions as doomed to failure, stressed the omnipotence of political action and the founding of government-financed cooperatives that would gradually replace the capitalist system.

The Marxists were not opposed to political activity.† In fact, they held that every class struggle was a political struggle. But they placed major

---

* See Philip S. Foner, *History of the Labor Movement in U.S.*, Vol. I, pp. 167-79, 205-07, 211-12, 230-34, 308-10, 448-53, 469-73, 487-88, 489-91, 493-99.

† Most American labor historians, following the lead of Commons and Associates (*History of Labor in the United States*, New York, 1918, Vol. II, pp. 449, 514-15) have oversimplified this conflict of theories and tactics in the American socialist movement by speaking of the "political socialists" versus the "trade union socialists." Actually, the issue revolved about the *relationship* between the trade unions and political action; both wings were part of a *political* party, and the Marxists never rejected political action.

emphasis upon building the trade unions to enable workers to fight for the improvement of their conditions, stressed the importance of combining trade union and political activities, and pointed out that a strong trade union movement was the necessary base for successful political action.

Although Lasalleanism remained influential in the Socialist Labor Party throughout the 'eighties, the Marxist position of combining trade union and political activity became the accepted doctrine of the party. With this outlook, the S.L.P. began to influence the formation of unions all over the country and to supply trade union leaders who exercised a militant influence in the labor movement.

In 1881 the party membership had dwindled to less than 2,600, but the influence of the S.L.P. in the labor movement far outweighed its numbers. Many of the unions of the late 'seventies and early 'eighties were of socialist parentage, outstanding examples being the organization of the carpenters and joiners, dress and cloak makers, seamen, cigar makers, furriers, and furniture workers.[1]

City central labor bodies all over the country were organized by the Socialists who continued to influence their policies throughout most of the 'eighties.[2]

THE CENTRAL LABOR UNION OF NEW YORK

The most important central labor organization in the country was the Central Labor Union of New York. It was formed at a conference held on February 11, 1882, attended by delegates from 14 unions. One of the addresses was made by Phillip Van Patten, national secretary of the Socialist Labor Party. Peter J. McGuire, leader of the English-speaking wing of the S.L.P. and founder and Secretary of the United Brotherhood of Carpenters and Joiners, was influential in drafting the platform of the Central Labor Union and in contributing "a strongly socialistic spirit" to the program. Although several sections of the platform were diluted with Lassalleanism—particularly the doctrine that producer cooperatives, financed by government credit, could ultimately eliminate capitalism—it did emphasize the Marxist idea that both trade union and political organization are necessary in the class struggle.[3]

The Central Labor Union of New York grew rapidly. By August, 1883, it had more than 60 affiliates, and three years later, 207 unions, representing about 150,000 members, were affilaited. The C.L.U. did a great deal in stirring up public interest in the land question, the money, transportation, and general labor questions by holding mass meetings, parades, and festivals. It initiated the practice of making the first Monday in September Labor Day. It fought conspiracy laws aimed at labor by going into political action. It developed the use of the boycott. It assisted trade unions in their strikes by raising contributions from labor organizations. Thus in July, 1882, in support of the freighthandlers' strike, the C.L.U. raised $60,000 for the strikers. In August, 1885, when a two-week general strike took place in the cloak trade, involving 1,500 workers, the majority Jewish immigrants, the "delegates of the Central Labor Union took an active part in helping to settle the strike." [4]

All in all, the C.L.U. illustrated the emergence of Marxism as an organic expression of the developing labor movement. It was the main stream of New York labor, a powerful organization of white and Negro workers, American-born and foreign-born. Its leadership was socialistic, its principles radical.

Other central trade councils in New York, organized and led by the Socialists, were the United German Trades, the Jewish Workingmen's Union, and the United Hebrew Trades. [5]

THE JEWISH SOCIALISTS

In the early 'eighties a small group of Jewish Socialist immigrants laid the foundation of what was later to develop into a strong socialist and trade union movement among the Jewish workers in this country. Many of these Jewish radicals were young people, who had participated or were sympathetic to the Russian revolutionary movement before coming to the United States. They had little experience in the trade union movement when they arrived here, and some even regarded the trade union struggle for working class improvements as a hindrance to the social revolution. [6]

Several workers' *vereins* were organized among the Jewish immigrants in 1882, 1884 and 1885, the most important being the Jewish Workingmen's Union, formed on April 19, 1885. The J.W.U. established a Yiddish labor and Socialist organ, The New York *Jewish Volkszeitung,* which appeared first on June 25, 1886, and lasted until December 20, 1889, reaching a peak circulation of 5000 copies. During these three-and-one-half years, the weekly contributed significantly to the development of labor and Marxist ideology among the Jewish workers. It reprinted Marx's classic pamphlet, *Wage-Labor and Capital,* and carried important theoretical discussions of Marxism along with announcements of all Socialist, anarchist, and trade-union gatherings. [7]

During its 27 months' existence, the J.W.U. did more effective organization work among the Jewish immigrant workers than all of the many previous *vereins* combined. By 1886, it had succeeded in organizing 14 unions with some 3,000 Yiddish-speaking members in such crafts as hat and cap blockers, shirtmakers, grocery clerks, pants makers, pocket makers, tailors, cloak operators, barbers, compositors, and peddlers. It gave valuable organizing assistance to the general strike of cloakmakers in the New York contracting shops in 1885, and in 1886, organized an anti-sweatsop league which agitated for the abolition of the sweatshop and the whole contracting system. It also helped organize the strikes of cigarmakers and furniture workers in June, 1886.

It is significant that every union organized by the Marxist J.W.U. contained a clause in its constitution calling for independent labor action in politics.[8]

The early unions of immigrant workers organized by the J.W.U. enjoyed but a short life. Born primarily in strikes, these unions would all too frequently fall apart once the struggle was over. In addition to relentless attacks by the employers, the unions suffered setbacks because of the lack of experience of the Jewish socialists in the trade union movement. If the strike was lost, the union seemed futile; if it was won, it was judged to be no longer necessary to maintain the organization since the workers had accomplished their aims through the strikes. Moreover, while the anarchists found it necessary, in order to reach the immigrant workers, to participate in the leadership of the strikes, they did little to encourage the building of stable unions. On the contrary, many of the Jewish anarchists emphasized that trade unions were mere palliatives which could divert workers from the important struggle for the complete emancipation of the working class.

THE UNITED HEBREW TRADES

The experience of the J.W.U. taught the Jewish socialists the importance of building strong, stable unions among the immigrant workers. This newly-acquired knowledge was reflected in the birth and growth of the United Hebrew Trades, the first permanent federation of Jewish labor organizations.

The United Hebrew Trades was organized on October 9, 1888, at a conference attended by ten delegates and individuals, representing three existing Jewish unions—the Hebrew-American Typographical Union, the Jewish Actors' Union, and the Jewish Chorus Singers' Union; two Socialist Labor Party Branches—No. 8 (Yiddish-speaking) and No. 17 (Russian-speaking), and the United German Trades, which lent aid and organizational support to the Jewish workers. Bernard Weinstein, a cloakmaker, was chosen as recording secretary and Morris Hillquit, a shirtmaker, the first corresponding secretary.

The conference adopted what was probably the clearest expression of Marxist theoretical doctrines in the labor movement of the 'eighties. In writing its own constitution, the U.H.T. took as a basis the constitution of the powerful Central Labor Union of New York, but changed many

Lassallean formulations in that document to Marxist ones with respect both to general principles and specific demands. The statement of principles called for the organization of the workers "for the purpose of mutual protection against the oppression of capitalism, and to make clear to the workers that they can free themselves from the yoke of capitalism through organization and trade unions on the one hand and through political struggle on the other." It went on to state that it was "clear and obvious that, with the accumulation or concentration of capital in a few hands, so-called political freedom becomes no more than an empty phrase. There can be no peace between capital and labor under the present social system for the simple reason that capital consists of interest, rent, and profit unjustly taken from the worker who owns no land, property, or means of production."

This statement of Marxian theory of value, price, and profit was reinforced by the paraphrase of another Marxist slogan: "The liberation of the working class can be brought about only by the workers themselves, because no other class has any interest in bettering their conditions." The declaration of principles also stressed that in working class hands "rests the future of our free institutions, and it is their destiny to replace the present iniquitous social system by a new order founded on justice, freedom, and the solidarity of all workers of the world." [9]

The three unions affiliated with the U.H.T. when it was founded had a total of 80 members. At its first meeting, the U.H.T. selected an organizing committee which immediately went to work to revive the dormant unions of Jewish workers and to build new ones where none existed. At its second meeting, the committee reported that the shirtmakers' union had been revived. Soon after this, a pants makers' union, a knee-pants makers' union, and a cloakmakers' union were organized to be followed by unions of Jewish musicians, bookbinders and purse workers.

Six months after the organization of the U.H.T., it had 11 affiliated organizations with 1,200 members and by 1890, it had 22 affiliated local unions with an estimated membership of 6,000. It was to continue to grow during the early years of the 1890's at which time, too, federations of Jewish workers, modelled after U.H.T. of New York City, were organized by socialists in Philadelphia, Chicago, and Boston. [10]

The role of the Socialist Labor Party in founding national unions, in organizing city central labor bodies, and in building local unions, especially among foreign-born workers—German, Jewish, Irish, Bohemian, Russian, Scandinavian, etc.—was an outstanding contribution to the developing American labor movement. Unfortunately, the influence of Marxist ideas in the labor movement was not reflected in the growth of the S.L.P. itself. Splits continued to plague and weaken the party. Thus an important section of the S.L.P. fell prey to the extreme leftist doctrines of the Anarchist school.

THE ANARCHISTS

From German immigrants who had experienced Bismarck's "Exception Laws" of 1878 which put all labor unions and radical political organizations under a ban, and from Russian and Italian immigrants who had experienced the repression of revolutionary activity in their own countries, numbers of American militant trade unionists and Socialists heard about the formation of self-defense corps, and secret preparation for the revolution in other countries. They could have learned from the futile assassinations of czars and kings that terrorism was a hindrance to a struggle for political and economic liberation. But they were not yet mature enough to understand this lesson from history.

As far back as 1875, a small group of German Socialists in Chicago had formed an armed club to protect workers against military assaults. This club came to be known as the *Lehr and Wehr Verein*. The attack on the workers during the great strikes of 1877 by the police, the militia, and the United States Army resulted in spreading the movement. Although most of the members of the armed groups belonged to the S.L.P.; the national executive committee denounced such organizations on the ground that they gave a false picture of the objectives and policies of the socialist movement. In 1878 all members of the S.L.P. were ordered to leave these clubs, but this order was resented by the Socialists in Chicago, and, together with other issues, led to a split in the party in 1880.

That same year, a group that had seceded from the S.L.P. in New York formed an organization known as the Social Revolutionary Club. Soon Social Revolutionary clubs sprang up in other cities—Boston, Philadelphia, Milwaukee, and Chicago—where there were large foreign populations and immigrants whose new and bitter experiences in the class struggle in the United States made them particularly receptive to anarchist ideas.[11]

The Chicago club, the most important in the movement, was led by Albert R. Parsons, and August Spies. Parsons was the outstanding native-American Socialist personality in the midwest. August Spies, a German-born worker who joined the Socialist movement after the 1877 Railroad strike, became one of America's leading Socialist orators and journalists, speaking and writing fluently in both English and German. Both Parsons and Spies were militant trade unionists who had run for office on the Socialist ticket in Chicago. But both had lost faith in political action and were searching for a new method to meet the attacks by the police upon the working class and their organizations, the most brutal of which had occurred in Chicago.[12]

"The police of Chicago," write Bogart and Thompson, "reflected the hostility of the employing class, regarding strikes *per se* as evidence that the men had placed themselves in opposition to law and order . . . it had become a pastime for a squad of mounted police, or a detachment in close formation, to disperse with the billy any gathering of workingmen. The billy was an impartial instrument; men, women, children, and shop-keeping bystanders alike composed its harvest. It was the police, aided by the 'Pinkertons,' who added the great leaven of bitterness to the con-test. To the workingmen they furnished concrete and hateful examples of the autocracy against which they protested." [13]

THE INTERNATIONAL WORKING PEOPLE'S ASSOCIATION

A national conference of Social Revolutionary clubs was held in Chi-cago in 1881. The meeting was called by the New York club, which had participated in a London congress, where efforts were made to revive the International Working People's Association—the so-called Black In-ternational—the organization of anarchists founded by Bakunin, who had brought disruption to the European labor movement and caused the split in the First International from which he was expelled by the Maxists. Returning from the London convention, where they had affiliated their club with the I.W.P.A., the New York Social Revolutionaries brought back with them the doctrine of "propaganda by deed." They advocated conspiratorial action and individual terror against the ruling class as the only way to rouse the masses to revolt.

The 1881 convention of the Social Revolutionary clubs did not result in a unified organization, but a name, the Revolutionary Socialist Party, and a platform were adopted. The platform urged the organization of trade unions on "communistic" principles and asserted that aid should be given only to those unions which were "progressive" in character. The platform also denounced the ballot as "an invention of the bourgeoise to fool the workers," and recommended independent political action only in order to prove to workers "the inequity of our political institutions and the futility of seeking to reconstruct society through the ballot." The chief weapon to be used in combatting the capitalist system were "the armed organizations of workingmen who stand ready with the gun to resist encroachments upon their rights." [14]

Not until the arrival of Johann Most in America in 1882 did the Social Revolutionary movement truly unite its ranks and become an active force. A powerful orator, a caustic and brilliant writer, temperamental and egotistical, he rapidly became the acknowledged leader of the American anarchists.

Following a tour of the country, Most helped pave the way for a congress of American anarchists at Pittsburgh in October, 1883. Twenty-six cities were represented at the convention where the International

Working People's Association was formed. Most, Parsons and Spies were the outstanding delegates.

Most dominated the convention. An ardent advocate of terroristic tactics, he opposed the struggle for immediate demands—shorter hours, higher wages, better working conditions—as mere sops thrown to the working class which only served to tie them closer to the capitalist system. The manifesto of the I.W.P.A., written in the main by Most, made no reference either to political action or to immediate demands. It emphasized the "destruction of the existing class rule, by all means, that is, by energetic, relentless, revolutionary, and international action," and "the establishment of a free society based upon cooperative organization of production." The manifesto ended with an appeal to one remedy for the evils of capitalism—*force!* [15]

Two distinct elements were present at the Pittsburgh congress—united primarily by their opposition to political action. The delegates from New York and other eastern cities, led by Most, favored individualistic acts of terrorism. The western delegates, led by Parsons and Spies, agreed with Most on the futility of political action and the value of force, but they believed firmly in trade union work. In theory, they now held the view that the trade union was not to contend for immediate demands; its sole function was to struggle for the complete destruction of capitalism and the formation of a new society. Basing itself upon the direct action of the rank-and-file, the trade union, as the "embryonic group" of the future society, would build the foundations of the free society. Its chief weapon as a fighting unit against capitalism would be force and violence. The manifesto called upon the workers to unite, to arm and to throw off the yoke of slavery: "Let the tryrants tremble! The Day of Judgment is not far!"

This mixture of anarchism and syndicalism came to be known as the "Chicago Idea." It was adopted by the Pittsburgh congress because the western faction had enough votes to push it through. Most and his faction were not interested in this phase of the manifesto, and only capitulated when it became obvious that a split might result of they rejected it. As far as they were concerned, it was purely a statement on paper, for they had little intention of concentrating on trade union organization aside from attempting to win the membership of the unions to the support of anarchist theory and practice.

Although the manifesto, in theory, emphasized that the trade union was not to contend for immediate demands, in practice, the followers of the I.W.P.A. were often compelled, in order to win a hearing from the workers, to support immediate demands. Consequently the I.W.P.A. made headway among trade unions, especially in the mid-west, where the Chicago section, led by colorful and militant personalities like Parsons, Spies, Michael Schwab, Sam Fielden, and others, penetrated deeply into the trade union movement. Many workers joined the International—Chicago alone had five to six thousand members—and the Social Revolutionaries in the Windy City published five papers: the *Alarm* in English, a fortnightly edited by Parsons with an edition of 2,000-3,000; in German, the daily *Arbeiter-Zeitung,* edited by Spies, with an edition of 3,600, the *Vorbote*; and a daily in Bohemian.

By staging impressive mass demonstrations and parades, conducting speaking tours all over the mid-west, the Chicago Social Revolutionaries were able to exert much greater influence than their numbers would indicate. They dominated the Central Labor Union of Chicago, which consisted of 22 unions in 1886, among them the seven largest in the city. They participated in most of the labor struggles of the mid-west and helped workers in their battles regardless of their affiliation or social philosophy, but they repeatedly made it clear that immediate demands were of no importance. Direct action—force, violence—these were the cure-alls. As the following resolution of the Chicago Central Labor Union, introduced by Spies in October, 1885, put it: "We urgently call upon the wage-earning class to arm itself in order to be able to put forth against their exploiters such an argument which alone can be effective: Violence. . . ."[16]

The S.L.P. lost many of its members in the anarchist split. Section after section seceded and joined the more militant International Working People's Association. By the end of 1883, the former had dwindled to 1,500 members, while by 1885 the latter boasted a membership of 7,000.[17]

This was the high point of the I.W.P.A.'s growth. The basic weakness of the anarchist position, the hysteria created after the Haymarket bombing in May, 1886, and the more militant position adopted by the S.L.P., re-established this party as the leading revolutionary organization in the United States.

MARXISTS AND ANARCHISTS

Conscious of the confusion in the public mind between anarchism and socialism,* the S.L.P. tried to make the fundamental differences clear. In April, 1883, Phillip Van Patten wrote directly to Frederick Engels, co-founder with Karl Marx of scientific socialism, pointing out that Jo-

* In their tour of the United States, Edward and Eleanor Marx Aveling went to great pains to show the difference between socialism and anarchism. "The mistake into which the Americans had fallen," they wrote, "was the common one, that anarchism is revolutionary. Anarchism is reactionary, and the Socialist Labour Party of America, like its most recent speakers, are not anarchists because they are revolutionaries." (*op. cit.,* p. 21.)

hann Most and his friends in the United States were boasting "that Most has stood in close relation to Marx . . . and that Marx had been in agreement with the propaganda which Most had conducted." Most's anarchist activities had "already done us [the Socialists] too much harm here," Van Patten emphasized; hence he felt that Engels' opinion "as to the attitude of Karl Marx on the question of anarchism versus socialism" would help the American Socialists overcome these effects. In his reply, Engels made it quite clear that the Marxism had nothing in common with "anarchist nonsense," * that Marx had opposed anarchism "from the first day it was put forward in its present form by Bakunin," † and that anyone who asserted that Most had any relations with Marx or received any assistance from the latter "has been deceived or . . . is deliberately lying." Van Patten was authorized to publish Engels' letter.

In 1886, the S.L.P. pamphlet, *Socialism and Anarchism, Antagonistic Opposites,* proclaimed its "protest against being confounded and in any way identified with Anarchists of any type; we are the implacable enemies of all anarchism." Commenting on the anarchist theory of force and violence, the pamphlet explained: "we may have to fight for the redemption of the working class from the threatening complete thraldom. But the war must be forced upon us—we must try our best efforts to avoid it, and though this may be impossible in most European states, we must and do consider it possible in the United States, and wherever freedom of speech and of the press, the right to peacefully assemble and organize, and universal suffrage (inclusive of the suffrage of women) are not curtailed by existing laws. We are fully outspoken in our ideas and aims, all our working for liberation is above board, we shun secret organization for our purposes." [18]

It was not enough, however, to distinguish between the theoretical confusion of the anarchists and the clarity of Marxism. What the S.L.P. failed to grasp was the real reason for the influence of the International Working People's Association in the trade unions. The Association did not devote itself exclusively to the propagation of its theories through lectures and literature, but also assumed leadership in strike struggles, especially, in the fight for the eight-hour day. Consequently, although the Association had its main membership among German immigrants, it had made significant inroads among American workers in the trade unions.

---

* In his letter to Van Patten, dated London, April 18, 1883, Engels briefly summarized the fundamental difference between Marxism and anarchism. *See* Karl Marx and Frederick Engels, *Letters to Americans, 1848-1895,* New York, 1953, pp. 137-38. Van Patten's letter to Engels is reprinted in *ibid.,* p. 137n.

† The reference is to Michael A. Bakunin (1814-1876) the Russian ideologist of anarchism who led a factional conspiracy in the First International and was expelled at the Hague Congress in 1872.

ROLE OF GERMAN-AMERICAN SOCIALISTS

In large measure, it was the influence of the German-American Socialists that retarded the S.L.P.'s development. Throughout the 'eighties,
Engels repeatedly castigated the German-American Socialists for their
sectarian approach to the American labor movement. He complained that
they did not appreciate the fact that "our theory" was not a credo but "a
guide to action," something that was living, not dead. Their refusal on
principle to learn English was to him not only an example of their
narrow-mindedness, but also of their political ineptitude. No wonder that
Engels, in a letter to Sorge, declared in exasperation that "if the whole
German Socialist Labor Party went to pieces . . . it would be a gain, but
we can hardly expect anything so good as that." [19]

Despite the hold of the German-Americans, the S.L.P. did take some
steps to Americanize itself. At the 1885 convention, attended by 33 delegates, representing 41 sections and about 4,000 members, it was decided
to establish an English "party organ." In addition, the party was divided
into sections by nationality in order to allow the establishment of purely
American sections. [20]

Although it praised this action, *John Swinton's Paper* pointed out correctly that the party's influence would never grow as long as the German-
American Socialists remained isolated from the mass labor movement.
They would continue to remain isolated, it emphasized, so long as they
refused to learn English and confined their activities to German-speaking
workers.

"The German-Americans of this city, or of the country at large, have
not one-tenth of the social, moral, or political influence they would have
if they would all learn to speak, read, and write the American language.
Multitudes of them are isolated from the general life of their community
by their inability to do so. What a stream of new thought they would
pour through the country if they commanded the country's tongue! We
are aware that the German is a rich, ripe, delicate, subtle and mellifluous
language, but so also is the American which is spoken by over fifty
millions of our progressive population white and black." [21]

Engels agreed wholeheartedly with this criticism. He believed that in
order for the Socialists to play an important role in America, "they will
have to doff every remnant of foreign garb . . . [and] to become out and
out American. They cannot expect the Americans to come to them, they
the minority and the immigrants must go to the Americans, who are
the vast majority and the natives. And to do that, they must above all
things learn English." [22]

Engels, of course, did not underestimate the enormous contributions the foreign-born, immigrant workers made to the growth of the American labor movement. He understood, too, that in encouraging since 1872 the formation of branches among foreign-born workers, the members of which conducted meetings and educational work in languages other than English, the S.L.P. was acknowledging a necessity that grew out of the diverse national group components of the American working class. As the *Arbeiter Zeitung,* organ of the Jewish Socialists, explained: ". . . because only we, the Jewish-speaking citizens, can succeed among Jewish immigrants, and because we speak their language—only for these reasons do we organize a special Jewish body. The Yiddish language is our material. To remove all division between Jew and Gentile in the labor world is one of our aims." [23]

As we have seen, the immigration of the 1880's had so changed the composition of the labor force that in many industries the foreign-born constituted the majority of workers. In recognizing the fact that the immigrant workers needed to be organized on a national group basis with the old language as the means of organization, the S.L.P. made an important contribution to the growth of the American labor movement. What was wrong with the work of the S.L.P. was not that it operated among the foreign-born workers and used their national and folk language, the only language understood by the immigrants, as a medium for organization. Rather it was that the Socialists did not understand that the extension of Marxist influence in the United States was intimately bound up with the spread of their message, as Swinton put it, to the "fifty millions of our progressive population white and black." They made no special effort, for example, to reach the hundreds of thousands of Negro workers; indeed, they completely neglected the vital problems facing this important section of the American working class such as discrimination in American political and economic life, deprivation of civil liberties, and lynchings. It is true that the 1885 S.L.P. convention came out for universal suffrage regardless of race, sex, and color, but no other specific demands of the Negro people were included in the platform.

On September 19, 1886, Dr. Edward Aveling, Eleanor Marx Aveling, and Wilhelm Liebknecht, German Socialist leader, came to the United States. Dr. Aveling, an English physiologist and Socialist, and his wife, Eleanor Marx, the daughter of Karl Marx, lectured at various places under the auspices of the S.L.P. They helped to sow the seeds of Socialist doctrine among English-speaking workers, and influenced the Socialists to play a leading role in the great mass political upheaval of the labor movement in the fall of 1886. This represented the first time in the 1880's that the S.L.P. became an integral part of the mass labor movement in the United States. [24]

But the Avelings were not too successful in their efforts to transform the S.L.P. into an American party. The influence of the German-American sectarian elements was still too pronounced. The Avelings left the United States convinced that there was fertile ground here for the Socialists if they worked correctly. They were impressed by the existence in this country of a "vast body of unconscious working-class Socialists," who, after hearing an exposition of Socialist doctrines, would exclaim, "Well, if that is socialism we are Socialists." [25]

The proof of the Avelings' observation that great masses of the American people were ready for the message of the Socialists is seen in the restless searching of Americans in this period to find something better than the existing unsatisfactory economic system, to replace competition with co-operation and private ownership with social ownership. This was reflected in the formation of the Society of Christian Socialists * in 1889 by ministers and professors, led by William D. P. Bliss, George D. Herron, and Richard T. Ely, with the aim of bringing all social, political, and industrial relations into harmony with "the fatherhood of God and the brotherhood of Man, in the spirit and according to the teachings of Jesus Christ." [26] It was also reflected in the appearance of some 40 utopian Socialist novels which pictured the glorious future awaiting all Americans if only they would replace the existing system with one based upon principles of common sense.

BELLAMY AND THE NATIONALIST MOVEMENT

The most influential of these utopian novels was the literary sensation of the 1880's—Edward Bellamy's *Looking Backward*. Public demand for the novel was so great that the printer could not keep up with it. Over a million copies were sold in a few years, and at one point it was selling at the rate of 1,000 per day.

Bellamy's main plank, the nationalization of industry, stimulated the growth of a short-lived socialistic movement, the Nationalist clubs, which began in Boston in 1888, and spread overnight across the country. Linked together loosely through correspondence and exchange of lectures, and recruiting their membership mainly from the urban middle class, the Nationalist groups sought to remedy the fundamental evils of capitalism by nationalizing the functions of production and distribution. When this was accomplished, a "true democratic and popular society will become

---

* The Christian Socialists emphasized municipal ownership of light, heating, and transit companies, the nationalization of the telegraph and railroads, and the establishment of postal savings banks as preparatory steps to the complete socialization of all industries. Meanwhile, taxes should be levied to reduce the glaring inequalities of wealth. (W. D. P. Bliss, *What is Christian Socialism?* 1890, pamphlet.)

possible as never before; for the first time in history, the world will behold a true republic, full-minded, full-ordered, complete—a republic, social, industrial, political."

This new society was to be instituted through a gradual reform process; the ends were to be sought by "rational, peaceful means." [27] The movement proposed to take over industry after industry as the public became prepared for it. Its first demands were for the nationalization of the telegraph, telephone, express service, railroads, and coal mines, the municipilization of local franchises, the equalization of educational opportunities, and civil service reform.[28]

Although the Nationalist movement had little in common with scientific socialism and Bellamy himself went to great pains to point out that he was no Marxist, it did contribute to the growth of socialist thought in this country. Despite its shortcomings, *Looking Backward* continued for many years to constitute for many Americans their first introduction to socialism.

It was the duty of the Socialists to reach the American workers and their allies who were restlessly searching for a remedy for the evils of developing monopoly capitalism. It was their duty to bring to them the message of Marxism, to encourage and deepen their resentment against the inequities in American life until it assumed mass proportions. In order to achieve these aims, the Socialists should have been in the very center of all agitation and movements to teach the workers that fundamental changes in their conditions could only come with a fundamental change in the social structure, and that this change could not come about as a result of the response of the capitalists to logical arguments. They should have been in the center of all movements that led in the direction of separating the workers from the two old parties and toward establishing an independent party for the working class and its allies.

CONTRIBUTIONS OF THE S.L.P.

The Socialist Labor Party did carry out some of these functions in the 1880's. In a decade of tremendous class struggles, the S.L.P. brought a stimulus and freshness of view and interest to the entire labor movement. It was instrumental in the formation and growth of important national trade unions, local unions and city central labor organizations, and its rank-and-file did heroic work in the Knights of Labor. It sharply differentiated socialism from anarchism, which in these years sought to penetrate the American labor movement. It led struggles of the workers which won for them important gains in higher wages, shorter hours, and better working conditions. Among the immigrant workers, the S.L.P. laid the foundation for militant labor organizations that were soon to assume major importance in the American trade union scene. All such unions of foreign-born workers were affiliated with and became a part of the general American labor movement.

Nevertheless, the Socialist Labor Party failed to develop a solid Marxist program and leadership, and those in the party who could actually be called Marxists were few and far between. During much of this period, Lassalleanism exerted too dominant an influence in the party * with results which, as we shall see, were disastrous for socialist influence in the labor movement, especially in the Knights of Labor. Finally, throughout this whole period, the S.L.P. retained its almost exclusive German composition with a scattering of Jews, Poles, Bohemians, and Italians. "The Socialist Labor Party of the 'eighties," observes Justus Ebert, "was a German party and its official language was German. The American element was largely incidental." [29]

Although the Socialists of the 1880's made important contributions to the development of the American labor movement, they were separated from the American workers by tradition, language, and experience. Consequently, they failed, in Engels' words, to "use their theory as a lever which could set the American masses in motion."

* It was not until September, 1889, that the national officers of the S.L.P. who still adhered to the Lassallean attitude of favoring political action at the total expense of trade union activity were deposed and replaced by men who emphasized the need to expand trade union activity. (Justus Ebert, *American Industrial Evolution, New York*, 1907, pp. 66-67.)

[Since this work was published, the writer has published *When Karl Marx Died: Comments in 1883* (New York, 1973). Of special pertinence to the chapter above is that part of the book dealing with the great Cooper Union Institute rally in New York City which mourned "the Teacher." This gathering of over 10,000 workers was the largest tribute to the memory of Marx in the United States or Europe at that time. The daily press reported that a hall twice the size would have been filled to overflowing, so great was the regard of the masses "for the memory of the great labor champion, Karl Marx." Among the speakers at the meeting were John Swinten and P.J. McGuire.]

CHAPTER 3

Rise of the Knights of Labor

The labor scene during most of the 'eighties was dominated by the Noble Order of the Knights of Labor. The meteoric career of this organization has had few if any parallels in the history of the labor movement of the world. Historians have differed more sharply in their interpretations of the rise and decline of the K. of L. than perhaps about any other phase of American labor history. On one point, however, all historians agree. All previous labor movements in the United States seem insignificant in contrast to the K. of L.[1]

We have described in a previous volume * the history of the K. of L. from its birth in 1869 to 1881 when the Order abandoned secrecy and voted to make the name of the organization public.† The real growth of the Knights dates from the year 1881.

GROWTH OF K. OF L. AFTER 1881

After a drop in membership in 1881, 1882 showed 42,519 and the next year 51,914 in the Knights. By September, 1884, when the Order celebrated "the fifteenth and most successful year of Knighthood," the membership rolls showed an increase of about 20,000, bringing the total to 71,326.[2] The membership had tripled in a period of three years, jumping from 19,000 in 1881 to over 70,000 in the summer of 1884. And this in the face of such discouraging factors as the industrial depression which began in 1883, a backlog of unsuccessful strikes, and the membership rivalry of another organization, the Federation of Organized Trades and Labor Unions of the United States and Canada.‡ The *Journal of United*

---

* See Foner, *History of the Labor Movement in the U.S.,* Vol. I; pp. 434-38, 477, 480, 484, 504-12.

† Many local asemblies maintained the most rigid secrecy throughout their existence, still fearing victimization by employers.

‡ See pp. 93-96.

Labor (founded in 1880 as the official organ of the society) declared gleefully on July 25, 1884: "The enemies of organized labor asserted last September that the Knights of Labor were breaking up and fast going to pieces. Well, we have broken up in this manner by organizing 561 new assemblies, reorganizing 34 old ones, establishing 12 new District Assemblies, and reorganizing two old ones. The Order was never in such good condition, both financially and numerically as at present."

But the period of the Order's greatest growth still lay ahead. Two developments occurred in 1885 that were to send the membership sky-rocketing. One was the success of the militant boycotts which the Knights conducted against many establishments hostile to union labor. The other was the successful strike which it led against three Gould railroads—the Wabash, the Missouri, Kansas and Texas, and the Missouri Pacific.

ROLE OF BOYCOTTS

Boycotts were not mentioned in the Order's Constitution and were not employed during the first years of its existence. But by 1885 the K. of L. had become the most successful boycotting agency in the history of the American labor movement. Boycotts were levied against newspapers, manufacturers and dealers in hats, cigars, clothing, carpets, dry goods, shoes, stoves, flour, beer, pianos and organs. Owners of hotels and theaters, and of excursion steamers, builders, coal mining companies, and many others felt the pressure of the boycott. In practically every case, the boycott was also a secondary boycott, the person or firm disregarding the boycott being boycotted in turn.

The term boycott become so common that it was frequently used interchangeably with strike.[3] So popular was the boycott by 1885 * that a good union man went to considerable trouble to study lists, and one union man complained in the summer of 1885 that "to be a sincere and systematic boycotter now, requires the carrying about of a catalogue of the different boycotted firms or articles; and, if you have a family, another catalogue is required for their use."[4] Notices of boycotts appeared in overwhelming numbers in the labor press, in public halls and in union halls. Circulars and handbills were posted even in workers' kitchens to make "your wives and all members of your families" aware of the names of the boycotted products.[5]

On being questioned about the principle on which boycotting was based, John Swinton replied: "It is 'an eye for an eye' and 'a tooth for a tooth'—the law as laid down by Moses. The employers say, 'we will

* *Bradstreets'* listed 196 boycotts as having taken place throughout the country in 1885, of which 59 ended successfully, 23 were failures, and 114 were still pending at the close of the year. (Dec. 19, 1885.)

blacklist you,' whereupon the men reply, 'we will boycott you.' That is the whole story." [6]

There was, however, more to the story. Boycotts were invoked by the Knights in three general cases: (1) as a means of organizing without the use of a strike; (2) to organize a shop or factory when a strike was proving unsuccessful; (3) to tieup plants of an anti-union firm in communities that could not be easily reached by the union.[7] In practically every case, however, the boycott was used in retaliation only when the employers locked out members of the union and replaced them with scab labor. As the power of the boycott became evident, some employers put signs in front of their plants on which was inscribed the notice: "The company prefers to employ organized labor." [8]

An energetic boycott was carried out in 1885 against the hats sent to the markets by the hat manufacturers in South Norwalk, Connecticut, who locked out members of the K. of L. in their factories. All over the country the cry to "boycott" the South Norwalk hats was heard, and thousands of workers intent upon getting new hats, looked under the "sweat band" of the merchandise offered them in the stores. If they found there the brand of any of the Norwalk firms, they refused to purchase. The boycott was so effective that many dealers cut out the brand. In the end, the protest of the customers forced the Norwalk firms to end their lockout and the boycott was withdrawn.[9]

An example of the perfect local boycott was one in Orange, New Jersey, against Berg's hat factory, the only "unfair" firm among the twenty hat factories in the town. The boycotting union had the local dealers so well under control that brewers refused to furnish beer to saloon-keepers who sold drinks to strikebreakers employed in Berg's factory. One manufacturer discharged an employee because he lived with his brother who worked for Berg's.[10]

The most famous boycott of the 'eighties was conducted by Typographical Union No. 6, with the aid of the Knights, against the New York *Tribune*. The dispute began in 1877 when Whitelaw Reid, its owner, declared his hostility to the printers by ordering a reduction in wages. The boycott was begun in 1883 and ended in 1892 when the officials of the newspaper announced that the *Tribune* "is now a strict union office." [11]

During the boycott of the *Tribune,* the union maintained its own weekly newspaper, *The Boycotter* (1884-1886), later called the *Union Printer* (1886-1887) to present its side of the controversy. Every subscriber of the *Tribune* who cancelled his subscription could receive a subscription to *The Boycotter*.[12] In its nation-wide campaign against the *Tribune* and its advertisers, the union used every kind of appeal including even verse in which it called upon workers to:

Buy not of those who patronize,
Who thus defer its certain doom,
And boycott those who advertise,
Their business in the "rat" Tribune.[13]

Over a score of newspapers were being boycotted in 1885-86, many of them because they refused to hire union printers and others because of their anti-labor views. The St. Louis *Post-Dispatch* was placed under a boycott at a meeting in the fall of 1885 of the various assemblies and trade unions of the city because this "Rat" paper had "time and again misrepresented the Knights of Labor, and heaped abuse and insult upon all who belonged to or favor labor organizations." [14]

THE GOULD STRIKE OF 1885

In spite of the hostility of its leadership to the strike as a weapon, the K. of L. attained its greatest membership as a result of the Order's role during strikes. Quite a few unions joined the Order during a strike. A strike would originate under the union's auspices and then become a concern of the Knights, with the union affiliating with the Order to gain from its growing influence and power.[15] Typical is the case of the Brussel Workers of Philadelphia who were locked out in 1884 by the manufacturers after they had refused to accept a wage cut. During the strike which followed, the workers voted to turn over their union in a body to the K. of L. When the manufacturers learned of this, they "sent for the committee and desired a compromise before they [the workers] entered the Order." But the committee "was inflexible." An assembly of the K. of L., No. 3266, was organized and on the very next day, "the manufacturers sent for the men to go to work on Monday at the old prices."

"So much for the K. of L. moral support," wrote the national Secretary of the Order jubilantly. "We are getting respected and feared." [16]

The K. of L. really became "respected and feared" when it won a tremendous strike victory against one of the greatest capitalists of the day.

Of all the "robber barons" of the post-Civil War era, the most hated by the people at large was the notorious Jay Gould, described by Karl Marx as "the Octopodus railway king and financial swindler." [17] Gould's labor philosophy was summed up in few words: "I can hire one-half of the working class to kill the other half." He also boasted that this policy enabled him to hire workers at starvation wages and to keep them at that level as long as he needed them.[18]

Early in the 1880's the Knights began organizing the miserably exploited workers of Gould's enterprises. The first national strike under the aegis of the Knights was called in the summer of 1883 in behalf of the telegraph operators, including those employed by the Western Union controlled by Gould.* The two eastern companies agreed to the demands of the strikers for higher wages and better working conditions, but the strike of the Western Union telegraph operators was savagely crushed. The workers were forced to disband their organization and to sign iron-clad oaths.[19]

Gould's victory over the Order was short-lived. The Knights turned their attention to the Gould railroad system in the southwest, concentrating on shopmen, trackmen, and other workers not included in the Railroad Brotherhoods which represented the engineers, firemen, conductors, and brakemen.

In October, 1884, the Missouri Pacific Railroad, the backbone of Gould's southwestern system, slashed the wages of the shopmen 10 percent.† Four months later, in February, 1885, a wage cut of five percent was added. A similar wage cut was handed out to the shopmen of the Missouri, Kansas and Texas and the Wabash Railroads.[20]

The showdown came immediately after the wage cut was announced. On February 27, 1885, the day after they received their wage cuts, the Wabash shopmen went out on strike, and were followed several days later by their fellow-workers on the Missouri Pacific and the Missouri, Kansas and Texas. On March 9, 1885, the strike became general on all points of the Southwestern railroad system, involving 10,000 miles of railroad and 4,500 workers in all the important shops of the Southwestern system in Missouri and Texas. The headline in the *New York Times* of March 9 read: "A Revolt Against Low Wages On The Gould System."

Local Assemblies of the Knights leaped to the support of the strikers. The first to act was L.A. 3218. This local of the Union Pacific employees had been organized during a brief but successful strike of shopmen in May, 1884, under the leadership of Joseph R. Buchanan, the militant, socialist editor of the weekly newspaper, *The Labor Enquirer,* published in Denver, Colorado. L.A. 3218 appropriated $30,000 and sent Buchanan to assist the strikers.[21]

Equally important for the striking shopmen was the fact that the four

* Prior to 1883, the Knights were involved only in local strikes, chiefly in the mining district.

† The wages of shopmen on the Southwestern system were $2.00 per day for a sixty hour working week. Actually, there was no limit on the working hours since the workers were often required to put in extra hours without extra pay. One shopman recalled later: "At this time there was no hour limit. I have been called time and again to go out with only an hour or two at the terminal and no sleep or rest at all." (Quoted in Ruth A. Allen, *The Great Southwest Strike,* Austin, Texas, 1942, p. 28.)

railroad brotherhoods also rallied to their support. As a result, all freight traffic was suspended on the Southwestern system. In vain, management tried to move about 1,500 freight cars tied up in the yards. When an engine was fired up, and attached to a train, the engineer was approached by a strikers' committee with the plea: "For the sake of your family and ours, don't take out that engine." The train did not move! [22]

Aware that popular sympathy was on the side of the strikers, the Gould management ordered the wage cuts rescinded. The wage scale was restored to its former level, and the company agreed that no worker would be dismissed for participating in the strike. On March 16, the strike was officially ended.[23]

The prestige of the K. of L. among railroad workers soared as a result of the victory. The influx of the shopmen into the Order, which had already begun in earnest during the strike, now became a flood as thousands more from the Southwestern system flocked to become Knights. The Knights also absorbed several existing lodges and unions of railroad workers, uniting skilled and unskilled workers on the Southwestern system into what promised to become a compact fighting body.[24] *

Jay Gould did not intend to allow that compact fighting body to exist without a struggle. The Gould management decided to destroy the local assemblies on the Southwestern system by discharging their leaders and the most militant rank-and-filers.

The Wabash Railroad management was the first to strike out against the Knights. The members of the Order were laid off by the railroad, and on June 16, the shops were closed down completely. The officers of the Knights correctly concluded that the shutdown was an effort to break the union, and declared that the men had been locked out. On August 18, the Knights declared a strike on the Wabash, and when this brought no response from the management, the General Executive Board of the Knights issued a general order to all assemblies on the Union Pacific and the Southwestern system directing their members to ". . . refuse to repair or handle in any manner Wabash rolling stock until further orders. . . ." [25]

Had this order gone into effect, a nationwide railroad strike on the order of the great strike of 1877 would probably have broken out. But Gould knew that the times called for a temporary retreat, and, acting upon a suggestion from the Knights, he called a conference of the railway officials and the General Executive Board of the K. of L. At the conference, Gould blandly assured the Knights that he was a very much misunderstood and maligned man; that he believed in labor organization, and the arbitration of all labor difficulties, and that he "would always endeavor to do what was right." [26]

* In September, 1885, District Assembly 101 was formed, comprising all the Local Assemblies of the Southwestern system.

The Knights demanded the dismissal of all scabs, and the reinstatement of all discharged men, with the leaders of the strike to be given priority. They also required assurance that in the future no discrimination would be shown against members of the Order by the railroads. These terms were presented by Powderly and Fred Turner, general secretary of the K. of L., to A. A. Talmadge, general manager of the Wabash, on September 3. The next day, Powderly and Turner received an urgent wire from R. W. Drew, K. of L. leader in Sedalia, Missouri: "Unless Wabash troubles are settled today I cannot hold south western system in longer." Informed of this telegram, Gould and the officials of the railway settled substantially on the terms presented by the Knights, and Gould personally declared his readiness to arbitrate all labor difficulties that might arise.[27]

UPSURGE IN MEMBERSHIP

When Jay Gould capitulated, it marked the high point in the power of American and, perhaps, world-wide labor organizations up to that time. "The Wabash victory," said the St. Louis *Chronicle,* "is with the K. of L. . . . No such victory has ever before been secured in this or any other country." [28]

The spectacular triumph over one of the greatest capitalists of the day brought thousands of new workers into the ranks of the K. of L. "All the pent-up feeling of bitterness and resentment which had accumulated during the two years of depression, in consequence of the repeated cuts in wages and the intensified domination by employers, now found vent in a rush to organize under the banner of the powerful Knights of Labor." [29]

Forgotten was the fact that most of the strikes conducted by the K. of L. up to this time were failures—the disastrous end of the telegraphers strike in 1883; the long, bitter and unsuccessful struggle of the Hocking Valley miners which began in June, 1884, and ended in March 1886, with the miners returning to work at a drastic wage cut of 70 cents a ton, and resigning from the union; the defeats sustained by the Fall River spinners in 1884, and the fatal ending of other strikes. A new day had dawned for American labor when Gould surrendered. What employer could now hold out against the Knights? Already the employers were learning the lesson of the victory over Gould. One month after Gould capitulated, the great lumber strike in the Saginaw Valley of Michigan which began on July 15 ended in a victory for the strikers. Thomas B. Barry, leader of the strike, was an outstanding figure in the Order.[30]

All at once the whole world of labor seemed to fly to the Knights. Workers began "rushing into the Order like prospectors to a reported gold rush." "The only trouble we have now," wrote one organizer, "is to keep men out of the Order." A member of the Order at LaCrosse, Wisconsin was besieged by hundreds of workers asking him to organize them. He wrote to Powderly in December, 1885: "I have been here for the last week. I have three assemblies ready to organize but there is no organizer here. I wish you would inform me of the nearest organizer there is to this place. I have in one place here 150 members and another 93 and another 56. . . ."[31]

It was a typical experience. New locals sprang up with lightning rapidity—700 in the three months ending January 25, 1886, as many as in all of the preceding years since the Order was founded; 515 in February; 417 in the first part of March; 690 in the last fifteen days of April, and 877 in May, 1886. Between July, 1885, and October, 1886, membership in the Knights of Labor jumped from 110,000 to over 700,000. "Never in all history," John Swinton joyfully declared, "has there been such a spectacle as the march of the Order of the Knights of Labor at the present time."[32]

The organization grew so rapidly during this period that the leadership became worried by exaggerated accounts published by newspapers which were seeking to magnify the "Menace of Organized Labor." The Knights' leadership took measures to curb what it regarded as a "too-rapid growth." When the figures for the month of February revealed that there had occurred an increase of more than 200 in the number of assemblies organized in January, the General Executive Board notified 600 organizers to stop organizing for 40 days from March 2, 1886. Charters to new locals were refused. But a great many organizers, dependent for their precarious existence upon the commission for each local organized, continued with their activity, holding back the fee until the 40 days had expired.[33]

Estimates of the actual membership of the Order at its peak in 1886 vary from 700,000 to over one million. Whatever the specific figure, the K. of L., at this time, had members in many parts of the world. Local assemblies were formed in Australia, New Zealand, Belgium, France, England, Ireland, and Italy. It was even reported that an organizer was making progress in India.[34]

Outside of the Untied States, the Order made the greatest headway in Canada. The first local assembly was established at Hamilton, Ontario, in the fall of 1881. By August, 1882, it had spread to Toronto. By September, 1884, the Knights had eight assemblies in Hamilton, nine in Toronto, three in London, and others scattered over a dozen more towns. However, in the Province of Quebec, it had only three assemblies and those all in the city of Montreal. The fact that the Order fell under the ban of the Catholic Church in Quebec accounts for the lack of strength in that Province. However, with the removal of the ban in the Spring of

1887,* the Knights made headway in this Province. By July, 1887, 38 local assemblies belonged to District Assembly 114, Montreal. A local assembly was formed in Winnipeg in 1884, and two years later, a District Assembly was organized in this region.[35]

From what groups did the K. of L. recruit its membership? Unfortunately, the official publications of the Order do not throw much light on the character of the membership. But enough evidence exists to enable us to draw a number of conclusions.

Originally only gainfully occupied workers were permitted to join the Order. With the organization of the General Assembly in 1878, membership qualifications were changed. Persons not workers were admitted to membership in a local assembly provided they did not constitute more than one-fourth of the membership. Lawyers, bankers, and those who lived in whole or in part by the sale or manufacture of intoxicating beverages were excluded. In 1884, professional gamblers and stockbrokers were added to the list of those excluded. Known enemies of labor such as scabs and labor spies were excluded from the beginning of the Order's career.[36]

With these exceptions, almost anyone might join the K. of L., and many non-working class elements did.†

Basically, however, the K. of L. drew the main bulk of its membership from the working class. The Order achieved what no other American labor organization before the 1880's had succeeded in doing—the organization and unification of the American working class. As Frederick Engels pointed out in his brilliant evaluation of the K. of L. at its height:

"The Knights of Labor are the first national organization created by the American working class as a whole; whatever be their origin and history, whatever their platform and their constitution, here they are, the work of practically the whole class of American wage-earners, the only national bond that holds them together, that makes their strength felt to themselves not less than to their enemies, and that fills them with the proud hope of future victories . . . to an outsider it appears evident that here is the raw material out of which the future of the American working-class movement, and along with it, the future of American society at large, has to be shaped." [37]

---

* See p. 90.

† In some assemblies the working class members were also small business men on the side. Describing such a situation in the Enterprise Assembly of North Danville, Virginia, a correspondent informed Powderly: "We have men in our midst who are engaged in a small business on their own account such as bakers, merchants, sewing machine agents, selling on commission or buying small lots and reselling them through the country, Dealers in [a] small way in leaf tobacco, contractors for building, Painting, etc." (R. P. Nichols to Terence V. Powderly, Jan. 13, 1886, Powderly Papers, Mullen Library, Catholic University of America, Washington, D. C. Hereafter cited as PP.)

CHAPTER 4

The K. of L. and Labor Solidarity

"An injury to one is the concern of all"—this great slogan of the Knights aroused thousands of workers all over the country. Martin Irons, the militant, Socialist labor leader in the West, told what the slogan meant to him:

"When that beautiful watchword, 'An injury to one is the concern of all,' resounded through my life, when I learned that Knighthood embraced every grade of honest toil in its heights and depths—when I learned that it meant broad and comprehensive union for labor on a basis that would counter-balance the power of aggregated and incorporated wealth and give to the creator of wealth the wealth he creates,—then I felt that I had reached a field in which I was ready to spend the remaining energies of my life." [1]

Whatever its shortcomings, the K. of L. did face resolutely the issue of labor solidarity. Before it came into existence, the American working class had never been unified; it had never presented a solid front against oppression. The K. of L. provided a form of organization and a common leadership for the American working class, skilled and unskilled, men and women, North and South, Negro and white, native-American and foreign-born, of all religious and political opinions.*

POSITION OF SKILLED WORKERS

As we have seen in the previous volume, the early locals of the Knights in Philadelphia were rigid craft unions. Although the strictly craft form

* The Knights of Labor was not the first organization in American labor history to emphasize the principle of labor solidarity. The National Labor Union had done so in the late 1860's and early 1870's, and in 1878, the International Labor union was formed by the Marxists and leaders of the Eight-Hour Leagues "to band together Jew, Greek, Irishman, American, English and German, and all nationalities in a grand labor brotherhood." The I.L.U. put special emphasis upon the organization of the unskilled workers. However, both the N.L.U. and the I.L.U. were short-lived, the latter lasting only until 1881. But both left their mark upon the K. of L. (Foner, op. cit., pp. 370, 433, 500-504.)

of organization broke down as the Order expanded, this did not mean that the trade unions of skilled workers had no place in the over-all structure of the Knights. The Window-Glass Workers' Association established a powerful and successful national union within the Order. The Association included about nine-tenths of the workers in the nation. Its strikes were uniformly successful, and were fully supported by the membership. In one strike, $100,000 was collected through members' contributions, and in another, $50,000.[2]

The spectacular success of the Window-Glass Workers' Association influenced the passage of laws by the General Assembly in 1882 and 1884 legalizing national trade assemblies.[3] Under these laws, a large number of national trade unions were chartered by the General Assembly. District Assembly 45, the telegraphers' national trade assembly, was formed in 1882. The Lithographers' International Union was formed in 1883, and the Miners' National Association, District Assembly 135, and District Assembly 247, the carriage workers' national trade assembly, were other examples of national trade assemblies in the K. of L.[4] While none were as successful as the Window-Glass Workers' Association, their existence indicated that unions of skilled workers could find a place in the Order.

Further proof of this is the extensive list of local craft assemblies in the Knights. Railroad and transit workers, textile workers, brewery workers, butchers and packing-house workers, carpenters, and many others organized trade assemblies in the Order. Some were even organized on a shop basis.[5]

Such names as LA 2878, Car Assembly of Brooklyn, Coopers' Assembly, K. of L. 1883, Boot and Shoemakers' Assembly 1794 K. of L., Plumbers, Gas and Steamfitters' Assembly 2292, K. of L., Carpenters' Assembly 2546 K. of L., all of Buffalo, New York, Can Makers' Assembly 1384 of Baltimore, Shoe Lasters' Assembly 2851 of New York City, and many other assemblies bearing similar names show clearly that the craft groups fitted very easily into the K. of L. which allowed local assemblies to make up assemblies selected on the basis of occupation.[6]

FOREIGN-BORN AND THE KNIGHTS

A common employer practice was to split the working force into many nationality groups—"judiciously mixing" so many workers from Hungary, so many from Austria, so many from Poland, so many from Russia, so many from Italy, so many Negro workers, and so many native-born white workers.[7] The division of the labor force into many nationality groups made the task of trade union organizers exceedingly difficult. As an organizer in the anthracite mining districts of Pennsylvania pointed out: "I find that literature must be in at least five different languages to wit: Slovak, Polish, Italian, Lithuanian, Hungarian, in order to become beneficial to educate them in regard to the benefits of organization." [8]

The Knights faced this problem as it grew. By 1885 the ritual had been translated into French, German, and Scandinavian tongues, and requests for Italian, Polish, and Bohemian translations were pouring into the national headquarters. There were continual requests of the General Executive Board to translate official documents into German, Spanish, French, Italian, Hungarian, Bohemian, Jewish, and other languages.[9]

Far from discouraging these requests, the leadership of the Knights repeatedly stressed the necessity of organizing workmen, regardless of nationality, bringing the message and educational material of the Order to them in their own languages, engaging organizers who would be able to speak to these workers in their native tongues, and forming assemblies based on nationality groupings. In forming "mixed" assemblies composed of workers of different nationalities, organizers were often required to be linguists. "The speaker," went a contemporary description of one such organizer at work, "would talk in Polish, Hungarian, German and English." [10]

Space does not permit a listing of all the assemblies formed by foreign-born workers on a nationality basis. Nevertheless, a number may be cited to indicate the trend. In Key West, Florida, there were four Cuban locals of cigar makers. In Minnesota, there were three Scandinavian local assemblies. In Montreal, of 20 local assemblies in 1886, 12 consisted of French Canadian members. A French speaking assembly was organized in Battle Creek, Michigan, in 1885. Italia Assembly 4236 was organized in Danbury, Connecticut. There were at least four Jewish assemblies, two in New York, and one each in Chicago and in St. Louis. All were organized by Jewish cloak and dress makers.[11]

The foreign-born members of these and other similar assemblies conducted their meetings and kept records of their proceedings in their native language.

THE CHINESE WORKERS

The chief blot on the K. of L.'s record on the issue of labor solidarity was in the case of Chinese workers.* Shortly after he became Grand Master Workman, Powderly ruled that Asians could not become members of the Order, and, furthermore, that they were unfit even to reside in

---

* For a discussion of labor's attitude towards Chinese workers before the 1880's, see Foner, op. cit., pp. 488-93.

the United States.* This reactionary, chauvinist viewpoint was also voiced by spokesmen for the Knights before Congress in urging the exclusion of the Chinese from this country, and the leaders of the Order boasted that the organization had played an important role in securing the passage of an anti-Chinese bill in 1882.[12] Some K. of L. leaders, particularly those on the Pacific Coast, even boasted of their work in mobilizing vigilante terrorism against the Chinese.[13]

Instead of denouncing the terrorists, Powderly and other leaders of the Order attacked the Chinese laborers and blamed them for the violence. In his opening address to the 1885 General Assembly, Powderly made mention of the Chinese massacre at Rock Springs, Wyoming, during which white miners, members of the Order, raided the Chinese section of the town, killed 28 Chinese, wounded 15, burned the homes of the Chinese laborers, and pillaged their possessions. But though Powderly admitted that "this act of inhumanity and butchery is inexcusable," he went on to blame "the Chinese and those who desired to employ them. Exasperated at the success with which the Chinese had evaded the law ... the white workmen became desperate and wreaked a terrible revenge upon the Chinese." [14]

Nevertheless, the Rock Springs massacre aroused considerable anger among members of the Order. Condemnation of the murderers who carried the banner of the K. of L. as they committed their crimes and of the officials who condoned their conduct was freely and widely expressed. A reevaluation of the whole policy of the Knights in relation to the Chinese was called for. "Already some want to know if we have not taken a bigger mouthful than we are able to chew in handling the Chinese riots," Powderly confessed in a private letter.[15]

Reflecting the rising protest against the prevailing policy towards the Chinese was the effort made to organize Chinese workers. Timothy Quinn, Socialist leader of District Assembly 49 of New York, organized two groups of Chinese in New York City. But when an effort was made

---

* Powderly used almost the same language in calling for the expulsion of the Hungarian workers from the region of the Pennsylvania mines because they were by nature "unfit" to enjoy decent wage standards or to become American citizens. A handbill issued by the Knights in 1883, "An Appeal to the Christian Public,"—the title also indicates anti-Semitic prejudices—referred disparagingly to the Hungarian's "uncleanliness" and to "their degrading influence on the community." (Powderly to Scranton *Truth*, June, 1884, cited in *Proceedings*, General Assembly, K. of L., 1884, pp. 576-77; *Journal of United Labor*, May, 1883, pp. 458-59; *John Swinton's Paper*, July 26, 1885.) Fortunately, the mass of the K. of L. rank-and-file did not swallow this chauvinist propaganda. By 1886 Hungarian assemblies were being set up in Pennsylvania and Hungarian organizers were traveling about recruiting men and women into the Order. (*See* the account in the Pittsburgh *Dispatch*, April 28, 1888.)

to secure charters for them as regular local assemblies, opposition arose, particularly among Knights on the West Coast. A majority of the General Executive Board was opposed to granting the charters, but a minority, composed of Thomas B. Maguire, Captain Mazzi, an Italian exile and Master Workman of an Italian local, Victor Drury, an active New York Socialist, and Frank J. Ferrell, also a Socialist and the most famous Negro in the K. of L., spoke out in favor of the request. In the minority report, Maguire pointed out that "the first and basic principles of the organization was the obliteration of all lines of distinction in creed, color or nationality." He further argued that the only remedy for the problem created by the use of the Chinese by employers to cut wages of other workers was to organize the Chinese. And, pointing to the fact that the Chinese had conducted a militant strike in California in 1884 for higher wages,* Maguire concluded that they could make valuable contributions to the American labor movement when organized.[16]

The opposition was too strong, and the charters were denied. A similar request for charters by two groups of Chinese in Philadelphia was also denied. Both the New York and Philadelphia Chinese assemblies were then dissolved and transferred to "mixed" assemblies. Thus Powderly was now able to inform the public that "we have some Chinese Knights of Labor." [17]

It is obvious that employer-sponsored chauvinist propaganda exercised influence in shaping the policies of the Knights. Although the record is seriously marred by the anti-Hungarian and anti-Chinese chauvinism, the general stand of the Order in relation to unity of workers regardless of national origin and language differences marked a real advance. The most famous of the songs written for the Knights of Labor, "Storm the Fort, Ye Knights of Labor," was translated into numerous languages and sung by workers of all nationalities. Out of the misery in America's coal mines and railroads, the oppression in the textile mills, the degradation of the men and women in the sweatshops rose the militant cry in English, German, Polish, Italian, French, Jewish, and other tongues:

> *Toiling millions now are waking,*
> *See them marching on;*
> *All the tyrants now are shaking,*
> *Ere their power is gone.*

* The strike involved a "large force" of hop-pickers in Kern County, California. The employers planned to replace the Chinese strikers with Negroes, but the scheme fell through largely because of the refusal of the Negroes to act as strikebreakers. (*See* Stuart Jamiesen, "Labor Unionism in American Agriculture," United States Department of Labor, Bureau of Labor Statistics, *Bulletin No. 836,* Washington, 1945, p. 46n.)

CHORUS:

> Storm the fort, Ye Knights of Labor,
> Battle for your cause;
> Equal rights for every neighbor,
> Down with tyrant laws! [18]

WOMEN AND THE ORDER

The preamble to the constitution adopted by the first national convention of the Knights in 1878 included a historic provision which asserted that one of the principle objectives of the Order was "To secure for both sexes equal pay for equal work." * But the constitution made no provision for the admission of women. The 1880 convention appointed a committee to prepare a ritual and regulations for the formation of special assemblies composed of women. But the committee never issued a report, and Powderly rendered the entire question academic by ruling at the 1881 convention that separate forms and rituals for women were unnecessary. Shortly after the convention adjourned, the first local composed entirely of women, the Garfield Assembly, 1684 (shoe workers) of Philadelphia, was organized. Bowing to the inevitable, the 1882 convention voted to permit the initiation of women.[19]

Once the doors were opened, the number of women's assemblies grew markedly. One other women's local was formed in 1881; three in 1882; nine in 1883; 13 in 1884; 46 in 1885, and 121 in 1886.† Figures on the number of women members in the Order vary. But it has been estimated that in 1886, when the K. of L. membership was at the highest point, there were about 50,000 women members, forming eight or nine percent of the total. The largest membership was in Massachusetts where in a year and a half preceding January, 1887, no less than 13,200 women were

---

* The K. of L. was not the first national labor federation in American history to come out for equal pay for equal work. In 1868, the National Labor Union had voted for equal pay for equal work. (Foner, *op. cit.,* p. 385.)

† A breakdown of the occupations of the women's assemblies in 1886 reveals the following information: 91 assemblies were listed as composed of various trades; 19 shoe workers; 17 mill operatives; 12 housekeepers; five each, sewing girls, tailoresses, laundresses; four each, knitters, collar and shirt ironers, dress and cloak makers; two each, hatters, weavers, paper-box makers; and one each, government employees (Washington, D. C.), bookbinders, carpet makers, cigar makers, farmers, feather curlers, gold cutters, lead pencil workers, and rubber workers. There was one assembly of Bohemian women in Chicago, and 15 of Negro women whose occupations were housekeepers, farmers, chambermaids, and laundresses. (John B. Andrews and W. D. P. Bliss, "History of Women in Trade Unions," *Senate Document No. 645,* 61st Congress, 2nd Session, Vol. X, pp. 130-32.)

admitted to the Knights. Four-fifths of the women members in the Bay State were in the shoe and textile industries.[20]

But the importance of the Order to women and of women to the Order cannot be accurately judged from statistics alone. Shut out from all but a few of the national trade unions,* women workers were at the mercy of the employers. Membership in the Order gave them a sense of courage and militancy which many heretofore had been afraid to assert. As early as 1882, an observer at a Chicago women's assembly reported that "timid young girls—girls that have been overworked from their cradles—stand up bravely and in steady tones, swayed by conviction and the wrongs heaped upon their comrades, talk nobly and beautifully of the hope of redress to be found in organization." [21]

WOMEN IN STRIKES

The women showed their spiirt in action as well as words. About a year after the Garfield Assembly was organized, a Philadelphia shoe manufacturer discharged the grievance committee and every officer of the local employed in the shop. The men in the Knights had encouraged the women to organize by assuring them that no officer would be victimized, but now they advised the members of the Garfield Assembly not to resist. The women correctly concluded, however, that unless they fought the issue through and established a precedent of opposing discrimination against militant union members, union organization of women workers would seriously suffer. They therefore called the shop on strike, and, after a bitter struggle, succeeded in reinstating every one of their members.[22]

During the general strike called in the New York cloak trade in August, 1885, involving several thousand cloak and skirt makers, the men and women strikers, members of the K. of L., met in separate strike halls. "But though meeting apart," the *New York Times* reported on August 15, "they were united in action." This unity resulted in a resounding victory for the workers, bringing wage increases and reductions in hours.[23]

The 1884 strikes of women members of the Knights in the textile mills of Fall River and Worcester and in the hat factories of South Norwalk were outstanding for the militancy and perseverance of the strikers. In 1885 one of the most memorable strikes of the decade was conducted by

* From 1860 to 1880 there were some 30 national trade unions, but women were admitted to membership in only two, the printers and cigar makers. (Report on Women and Child Workers in the United States," *Senate Document No. 645,* Vol. X, Washington, 1911, pp. 108-110.)

2,500 carpet-weaving women members of the Order employed by Alexander Smith's Sons in Yonkers, New York. There were some men involved in the strike, but nine-tenths of the strikers were women.[24]

The immediate cause of the strike was the firing of a group of women workers on account of their membership in the Knights. On February 20, 1885, 2,500 girls left their jobs and began picketing the mills. Only 700 were members of the union on the eve of the strike, but directly after the struggle began all 2,500 joined the Knights.[25]

Attacks upon the pickets mounted. Three of the women strikers, Ellen Tracy, Lizzie Wilson, and Mary Carey, were seized by the police and charged with "walking upon Nepperham Avenue" near the struck mills. The women were arrested, hauled into court in a police wagon, and held for trial.* Fearing that no jury would convict the women, the court ruled that the strikers could be tried without a jury. But an appeal to the higher courts forced the trial to be held before a jury.[26]

As a mark of admiration for the brave conduct of the three young women Knights and as a token of respect "for the whole striking sisterhood of Yonkers," the entire labor movement of New York City joined hands in a testimonial meeting sponsored by the powerful Central Labor Union and the Excelsior Labor Club. Delegates from every New York trade union were among the two thousand people of both sexes who packed the hall on the occasion. Seated on the platform were the honored guests, the three young women members of the K. of L. from Yonkers. Next to them was seated John Swinton who had been designated to present them with medals in honor of their militancy and courage.

The medals carried the words below the insignia of an American Eagle:

IN HONOR
of the
ARREST OF A PICKET
in the
YONKERS STRIKE
May 18, 1885.[27]

As the Yonkers officials had feared, the jury quickly acquitted the young women.

* The arrest of the women strikers aroused tremendous indignation in Yonkers. Thousands of citizens packed a mass protest meeting at Getty Square, music being supplied by the band of the Young Men's Catholic Association. Resolutions were adopted denouncing "the action of the police as being despotic," and pledging "moral support" to the strikers "until the strike is ended." Serge Schevitsch, editor of the Socialist New York *Volkszeitung,* was one of the chief speakers. (Yonkers *Statesman,* May 22, 1885.)

Although the strike ended late in August, 1885, without the union being recognized, the wage cut was rescinded, the fining system was completely revised, and several other grievances of the workers were remedied.[28] Equally important was the fact that the militancy of the strikers increased respect for women in the labor movement.

Women members of the Order were also of tremendous assistance to brother Knights engaged in strikes. They assisted on the picket lines; gave scabs the "ditch-degree" and "water-cure," * and rendered both moral and financial support.[29] Small wonder that Powderly observed that women "are the best men in the Order." [30]

OFFICES HELD BY WOMEN

The highest office held by a woman in the assemblies was the position occupied by Mrs. Elizabeth (George) Rogers who was, for several months, Master Workman of District Assembly 24 in Chicago. She presided over 600 Knights, men and women, who represented 40,000 members of the Order.[31]

Women first appeared as delegates to a national convention of the Knights in 1883. Mary Sterling, a Philadelphia shoe worker, was the delegate. The next convention saw two women delegates and the 1885 convention, three; there were 16 women delegates out of a total of 660 at the 1886 convention.

The 1885 convention appointed a national committee to collect statistics on women's work, and in the following year, it became a permanent organization, "the object of which will be to investigate the abuses to which our sex is subjected by unscrupulous employers, to agitate the principles which our Order teaches of equal pay for equal work, and the abolition of child labor." Mrs. Leonora M. Barry, a worker in a hosiery mill, was appointed a general investigator of women's wages and hours and conditions of work. She became a national organizer of women, devoting her entire time to the work.[32]

Throwing herself energetically into her work, Mrs. Barry conducted an extensive correspondence all over the country to discover the conditions and status of women workers. She travelled about the country, investigating complaints, visiting factories when she was not barred by the employers, speaking before trade unions and general meetings of working people, Women Temperance Conventions, and Women Suffrage Associations.† In her addresses to the Women Suffragettes, Mrs. Barry re-

* The scabs would be thrown into ditches and doused with dishpans of water.
† Mrs. Barry's presence at the suffrage conventions was in keeping with the friendly attitude of the Knights towards the woman suffrage movement. Not only did the Order endorse the demand for woman suffrage, but leading Knights often

peatedly emphasized that it was upon the working class that they should rely for their most consistent and effective allies. Moreover, she reminded the woman's rights advocates that it was not enough to battle for the suffrage and other legal advances: "Do not, I ask you, in the name of justice, in the name of humanity, do not forget to give your attention and some of your assistance to the root of all evil, the industrial and social system that is so oppressive, which has wrought the chain of circumstances in which so many have become entangled, and which has brought the once-tenderly cherished and protected wife, the once fondly-loved mother to the position of the twelve or fourteen-hour toiler of to-day. If you would protect the wives and mothers of the future from this terrible condition we find these in to-day, give them your assistance." [33]

Wherever Mrs. Barry went—in the course of which she visited hundreds of cities and towns from Rhode Island to Colorado, from Alabama to Toronto, Canada, delivered more than 500 lectures, organized half a dozen new women's locals as well as increased the membership in many old ones, and organized scores of men workers—the response was uniformly "loud and enthusiastic." [34] So too was the response to her spirited defense of her right to serve the labor movement. Her work aroused the opposition of several Catholic priests, one of whom, Father Peter C. McEnroe of Mahoney City, Pennsylvania, denounced her as a "Lady Tramp," and called the Order "a vulgar immoral society" for encouraging women to act as organizers. Mrs. Barry met the attack head-on in a stinging letter to Father McEnroe in which she denounced his "Slanderous attack upon my character and motives as a representative of a grand and Noble Order pledged to the service of humanity," and defended her right as "an Irishwoman, a Catholic and an honest woman" to serve the cause of her fellow-workers.

Mrs. Barry's defense aroused the admiration of many Catholics including even some of the priests. A Father Mahoney commended her for her work and contributed ten dollars to further her activity.[35]

Until 1890, Mrs. Barry continued to head the Department of Woman's Work. But there was little she could do. The Order was dying, and had neither the funds nor the energy to carry on much education and organization among women workers. During 1890, Mrs. Barry again married, and became L. M. Barry Lake. This was the name signed to her letter to the 1890 general assembly in which this outstanding woman organizer bade farewell to the labor movement.

An effort was made to continue the Woman's Department and the

spoke from the same platform with Miss Susan B. Anthony and Mrs. Elizabeth Cady Stanton, pioneer woman suffrage leaders. Miss Anthony was inducted into the Order in the early 'eighties. (Terence V. Powderly, *The Path I Trod*, New York, 1940, p. 389; Elizabeth S. Bryant to Powderly, Feb. 1st, 1883, *PP*.)

office vacated by Mrs. Barry was offered to the only woman delegate to the 1890 convention. When she declined the post, the Woman's Department of the Knights of Labor was abandoned.[36]

It is difficult to estimate accurately the effect of the Knights on the conditions of women workers. But the following observation by the New Jersey Commissioner of Labor in 1886 tells an important story: "Since the girls have joined the Knights of Labor here they make the same wages as the men." [37]

In summing up, we can say that the K. of L. boldly declared that women were entitled to the same pay as men for the same work, and that, after an early reluctance to accept women to membership, systematically encouraged the organization of women on an equal footing with men. "In all our assemblies, local, district, state, trade, and general," Mary Hanaflin, a Philadelphia saleswoman, told a woman's convention, "woman has an equal voice, when a member, with her brother trade unionist." [38] After a survey of the national labor scene in the mid-'eighties, the Los Angeles *Union* concluded: "The Knights of Labor is the only organization we know which encourages the membership of ladies, demands for women exact equality, and insists on equal pay for equal work." [39]

NEGRO MEMBERSHIP

Facing widespread hostility, fanned by employers, including even the threat of lynching,* organizers for the Order in the South found it necessary to organize secretly under different names such as "Franklin Lodge," "Washington Lodge," "Protective Lodge," etc., to post sentinels at meetings to protect members from a sudden raid, and to take every possible care to insure the greatest secrecy. But in spite of these difficulties and the great opposition to their organization, tens of thousands of Negro workers, who had never been brought into the trade union movement before, joined the K. of L. It is impossible, for lack of complete records, to determine accurately the number of Negro members or even to locate all of

---

* After a trip through Virginia, Georgia and the Carolinas, Thomas B. Barry, member of the General Executive Board, wrote: "It is as much . . . as a person's life is worth to be known as a member of the Knights of Labor there." (Sidney H. Kessler, "The Negro in the Knights of Labor," unpublished M.A. thesis, Columbia University, 1950, p. 16.) In 1885 a white organizer wrote to Powderly from Raleigh, North Carolina: "You have no idea of what I have to contend with (in) the way of prejudice down here. There is a continual cry of 'n——r,' 'n——r!!' . . . I believe that our Order is intended to protect all people who work, the poor ignorant underpaid and over-worked as well as the skilled mechanic, and have tried to act up on that principle. And for this alone I have incurred the abuse and social ostracism." (Jno. R. Ray to Powderly, June 22, 1885, *PP*.)

the Negro locals. (The Proceedings of the General Assembly do not distinguish between Negro and white delegates or local assemblies.) John H. Hayes, General Secretary, estimated that in 1886, when the membership of the Order exceeded 700,000, there were no less than 60,000 Negroes in the Knights. A year later, the New York *Sun* reported that there were over 400 all-Negro locals in the Order, estimated "the whole number of colored men in the Knights . . . at 90,000 or 95,000," and concluded that "they are growing at a rate out of proportion to the increase of white members." [40]

Whatever the exact number of Negro Knights, there can be no doubt that it indicates a high degree of organization, especially when one considers the rural nature of the Negro population at this time, the bitter opposition of the Southern ruling class, and the fact that their occupations were mainly restricted to farming and domestic service. Undoubtedly even this high degree of unionization of Negro workers by the Knights—practically ten per cent of the total membership—would have been still higher if the Order had fought persistently against anti-Negro elements in its ranks.

BACKWARD INFLUENCES

A major factor that retarded the further organization of Negro workers was the failure of the Knights' leadership to take firm action to root out the cancer of segregation. The problem arose in acute form as early as 1883 when Negro candidates for membership in several local assemblies in the North and South were turned down solely because of their color. In other assemblies by-laws were passed "excluding anyone from membership on account of color." [41]

These actions came to the attention of the Knights' leadership. In his decisions, Powderly ruled that while a local assembly could adopt by-laws, the constitution explicitly stated that local assemblies must not conflict with this document, a principle which had been reaffirmed by the Grand Master Workman and approved by the General Assembly. Since any exclusion of members because of color violated the constitution, such by-laws were illegal. Nevertheless, Powderly left a loophole by assuring a Southern local that had adopted discriminatory by-laws: "The best plan to adopt now is to organize a colored assembly in your city and turn all applicants of that kind over to them; then your by-laws will be binding." [42]

Powderly's vacillating position is also shown by the fact that while he did not approve of exclusion on account of color, he also made it clear that Negro workers could constitutionally be excluded from membership if a majority of members voted to do so. "The ballot is in reality the only means of settling who shall or shall not be members," he wrote to a Knight in Chattanooga, Tennessee, who objected strenuously to allowing Negroes to join assemblies of white workers.[43]

Protests from Negro and progressive white Knights, however, compelled Powderly in specific cases to oppose the tendency of local assemblies to keep out Negro candidates solely because of their color.[44] Early in 1886 he overruled the action of L.A. 2378 of Glen Cove, New York in excluding a Negro candidate, and read the assembly a sound lecture: "The objections presented were not sufficient to reject the candidate. If he is in other respects qualified to become a member his color cannot debar him. The employer of labor in reducing wages does so regardless of color. The men who work with colored men dare not find fault, they take their wages and abuse side by side and our Order will not recognize the right of any man to blackball another man on account of his race or religion." [45]

However, no sustained effort was made by the general officers to combat and eliminate discriminatory practices, and the local assemblies often ignored the rulings issued by the General Master Workman. Nor did the general officers regularly enforce their own forward-looking rulings. The 1887 convention received a communication from Negro members of a Harrisburg, Texas, assembly complaining of their treatment by their white brothers. The General Executive Board replied that the assemblies must "treat the colored members with respect." [46] But the Board did nothing to enforce its ruling.

Basically, Powderly (and most of the other white leaders of the Order) stressed that the solution of the problem lay in "patience." [47] In a letter to a Southern white leader of the Order who found that there was serious objection in his area to Negroes entering white assemblies, Powderly wrote: "I scarcely know how to advise you on so delicate a question. The color line cannot be rubbed out, nor can the prejudice against the colored man be overcome in a day. I believe that for the present it would be better to organize colored men by themselves. In the present instance you must act in strict accord with the law bearing on our organization, act as though you were in no way interested in the matter. I leave the matter in your hands." [48] This advice could be interpreted as the local Knights desired.

Had the position outlined by Powderly—"that for the present it would be better to organize colored men by themselves"—been linked to a persistent campaign to end the Jim Crow locals, the Negro workers would have been even more enthusiastic in their desire to join the Order. For the Negro workers bitterly resented the idea of segregated locals. "It would be plain sailing if we could induce the colored faction to form another assembly," the Master Workman of L.A. 2068, Richmond, Indiana, wrote to Powderly as early as May, 1883, "but they will not, at least they show no disposition so to do, for as one of them observed at a recent meeting: 'This is the only organization in which we stand on an equal footing with the whites, and it is a big thing, and unless we can work here we will work nowhere.' This equality is what seems to stick in their craw." [49]

While criticizing anti-Negro practices in some sections of the Order and the formation of segregated assemblies, the Negro press, in the main, insisted that the Negro people must not permit these defects to dominate their attitude toward the organization. To do so would be to play into the hands of the common enemy of both the Negro and the white workers. Whatever its shortcomings, declared the New York *Freeman,* a leading Negro journal, "nothing short of a potentiality like the Knights of Labor can ever force Southern capitalists to give their wage workers a fair percentage of their labor. If there is any power on earth which can make the white Southern employers of labor face the music, it is organized white and black labor, with the labor power of the nation to sustain it. . . ." [50]

The Negro people agreed! Their great numbers in the Order was achieved in spite of bitter organized opposition and a low standard of living which meant that in many cases even the payment of dues was a hardship. In Covington, Georgia, the Negro Knights had to travel on foot six miles to be present at meetings, but not only was there one-hundred percent attendance, but some members even paid their dues for months in advance. [51]

NEGRO-WHITE UNITY

While the Knights of Labor did not succeed in eliminating race prejudice in its ranks and in eradicating discriminatory practices against Negro members, it did establish a significant record of labor solidarity. For the first time in the history of the American labor movement, widespread Negro-white unity flourished as Negro and white members of the Order acted together for common purposes. In the South, race prejudice, built up assiduously for over a century by the ruling class, suffered serious setbacks at the hands of the fellowship of labor.

In Richmond and Norfolk, Negro and white Knights employed in some of the factories worked together cooperatively, and a reporter was amazed to find that "harmony prevails between white and black workmen." [52] A dispatch from Charleston, South Carolina in *John Swinton's Paper* of May 13, 1886, tells a significant story: "The white and colored mechanics and laborers of this city are working in great harmony as K. of L. This is a grand stride. The organization of the K. of L. has done this much for the South. When everything else had failed, the bond of poverty united the white and colored mechanic and laborer."

In many industries where the Knights exercised influence, Negro and white workers engaged in strikes together. Thus in Baltimore, Negro and white caulkers joined the Knights for mutual protection against a cut in wages. The men were on strike from August 3, 1885, to May 6, 1886, and throughout this prolonged period, they resisted every attempt by the employers and the press to drive a wedge between them by appeals to racial prejudice. One hundred and fifty strikebreakers were imported, but Negro and white caulkers united to drive them out of the shipyards. The strike was settled with what the United States Labor Commissioner referred to as "partial success" for the strikers. The caulkers' wages were reduced from $2.75 to $2.50 a day, and the working week remained at 60 hours.[53] The strike ended with the unity between Negro and white workers strengthened.

In Louisville, Kentucky, over 6,000 Negro and white marched together in a K. of L. parade. Louisville parks were closed to Negroes, but after marching through the streets, the parade entered National Park, and "thus have the Knights of Labor broken the walls of prejudice." In Birmingham, Alabama, over 5,000 Negro and white marched in a labor demonstration sponsored by the Order. After the parade, a Negro speaker and a white speaker addressed the workers from the same platform. The Knights of Dallas, Texas, held a Fourth of July celebration and a Negro local assembly marched with the white workers. After the parade, two of the speakers were Negroes. "This is the first time such a thing happened in Texas," observed a contemporary newspaper.[54]

At a great Labor Day parade in Baltimore in 1886, 25,000 persons, Negro and white, were reviewed by Powderly. A reporter noted the fact that Negro workers were "well mixed in and through the procession. In some instances, you would see an assembly composed entirely of colored Knights; another assembly would be perhaps half colored, and in some instances one solitary colored individual would be marching with any number of his white trades-brothers. The procession was a very orderly one, the colored and white fraternizing as if it had been a common thing all their lives."[55] The following year, one of the K. of L. recommendations to the Maryland legislature included the striking out of the word "white" wherever it occurred in the constitution and laws of the State.[56]

NEGRO OFFICERS

A Brooklyn Knight wrote to John Swinton: "I am connected with an Assembly of the Knights of Labor which contains 450 members, 25 of whom are colored, and there has not been a single outburst of feeling on account of color. I am a colored man myself, and am Worthy Treasurer, an office which was forced upon me for the third time." His case was not at all unusual, for Negroes were elected to positions of leadership on all levels of the Order, the local assemblies, district assemblies, state conventions, and the General Assembly, and in the vast majority of cases when the Negro members were a minority.[57]

At the famous Richmond Convention of October, 1886, many districts in various parts of the country sent Negroes to represent them. Of the 18 known Negro delegates, the best known was Frank J. Ferrell, the outstanding Negro leader in the K. of L., representing District 49 of New York. It was at this convention that Ferrell became the center of a series of significant incidents which were to affect the entire position of the Negro in the American labor movement, both inside and outside of the Knights of Labor.

A few months before the convention, an officer of District 49 went to Richmond to see which hotels would be available for the 60 delegates, including Ferrell, the only Negro delegate from the District. On the basis of this report, the District officers made arrangements for all the delegates to stay at the hotel of Colonel Murphy, a Confederate war veteran. When Colonel Murphy discovered that one of his guests would be a Negro, he cancelled the contract, arguing that Negroes would not be allowed into many Northern hotels, and asserting, "customs here must be respected." He offered to provide Negro delegates with quarters at a Negro hotel.[58]

When District 49 learned that they might have accommodations at the hotel only if Ferrell were excluded, the following resolution was unanimously adopted: "That no arrangements be made for hotel accommodation for the delegates from this district that excludes any delegate without regard to color, creed or nationality." * The delegates, most of whom were Socialists, came to Richmond carrying tents, as an indication that they would not under any circumstances abandon their Negro brother. "The delegates," wrote the *New York Times* correspondent from Richmond, "are determined to fight the battle on the color line right in the midst of that part of the country where race prejudice is the strongest, and they will insist on carrying on what they claim is a fundamental principle of their order—that the black man is the equal of the white socially as well as politically, and that all races stand upon an equal footing in all respects." [59]

* The New York delegation was not the only group to face and meet the difficulty of segregated quarters. When the proprietor of the St. Charles Hotel informed the Baltimore delegates that he would not provide accommodations for Joseph W. Edmonds, a Negro delegate, the white delegates resolved that the entire delegation would eat and sleep together. (Richmond *Whig,* Oct. 6, 1886; Cleveland *Gazette,* Oct. 9, 1886.

The delegates from District 49 proceeded immediately to prove that the *Times'* correspondent had quoted them correctly. They succeeded in engaging board with several Negro families, and a dozen delegates worshipped at the only Negro Catholic Church in Richmond. For another, they attended in a body a performance of *Hamlet* at the Mozart Academy of Music in Richmond, Ferrell seated between two of his white friends in the orchestra, thus becoming the first Negro in Richmond's history to occupy an orchestra seat in a theater.[60]

Before the Convention opened, Master Workman Quinn of District 49 approached Powderly, explained to him what had happened at Colonel Murphy's hotel, and requested that Ferrell be allowed to introduce the Governor of Virginia, Fitzhugh Lee, to the Assembly. Powderly objected on the ground that "it would not be pleasant for either the Governor or the convention to attempt to set at defiance a long established usage."[61] He suggested instead that Ferrell introduce him (Powderly) after the Governor had spoken. This was agreed upon.

To over 800 delegates, assembled in the Armory Hall of the First Virginia Regiment, the largest hall in the city, Delegate Ferrell introduced the Grand Master Workman. "One of the objects of our Order," Ferrell reminded the delegates and the Governor of Virginia who was seated on the platform, "is the abolition of those distinctions which are maintained by creed or color."[62]

The Negro question came up several times during the rest of the Convention. A resolution was adopted which asserted that the Knights of Labor recognized "the civil and political equality of all men and women in the broad field of labor, recognizes no distinction on account of color, but it has no purpose to interfere with or disrupt the social relations which may exist between different races in any portion of the country."[63] The last part of the resolution was a concession to a number of white delegates, particularly those from the South, who feared the serious repercussions of the events in Richmond upon public opinion in their own communities.* A resolution, sponsored by District 41 of Maryland, was passed urging the admission of Negro apprentices into the mechanical trades. Another resolution, introduced by District 1 of Pennsylvania, urged the formulation of a uniform scale of wages for workers throughout the country, so that the Middle States would not be brought into competition with the cheaper labor of the South. To accomplish this end, the resolution recommended that organizers be sent throughout the South "to organize all classes of laborers." The resolution was reported favorably.[64]

---

* It was reported that Southern delegates met with Powderly and threatened to secede and form an Order of white Southern labor. (New York *Tribune,* Oct. 14, 1886.)

The Convention closed with a parade and a picnic. The parade to the picnic grounds was headed by a squad of police, followed by Grand Marshal Lynch, with mounted Negro and white marshals riding at his side. A band followed, then the delegates from District 49, with Ferrell in the front rank. The rest of the delegates came next, and behind them the officers of the Order. Negro and white women in carriages brought up the rear of the procession. It was estimated that about 3,000 people marched in the parade, half of whom were Negroes. The entire Negro population of Richmond turned out to witness the proceedings. Several more thousands were at the fair grounds, where officers of the Order made addresses. Senator-elect Daniels, Mayor Carrington, and Governor Lee were scheduled to speak but did not appear. Their absence was attributed in the press to the Order's position towards Negroes.[65]

The prominent role played by Ferrell at the convention, the refusal of many white delegates to accept hotel accommodations and seats in the theaters because Negroes were excluded, the adoption of a resolution to admit Negro apprentices in shops, and the high degree of Negro-white solidarity displayed at Richmond brought down upon the Order a barrage of criticism from the Southern press.[66] The Negro press had only words of the highest praise for the Order. Negro newspapers which had earlier expressed distrust of unions were now specifically recommending that Negroes join the K. of L. "Taking all things into consideration, time, place, surroundings," editorialized the Cleveland *Gazette*, "it is the most remarkable thing since emancipation. The race's cause has secured a needed ally in the Knights of Labor organization." It urged all Negro newspapers, especially in the South, to spur their readers into joining the Knights since it was "generally seen and admitted that it is a grand organization and will do more for them than any other agency in existence.[67]

To white workers, too, the events that occurred at Richmond were highly significant. The white delegates obtained a first-hand glimpse of conditions confronting their Negro brothers and sisters in the South. "It opened their eyes to the true condition of affairs in the South as nothing else could have done," wrote a white member of the Order from Virginia. They realized as never before that "appeals to race prejudice" were part of the conspiracy against all workingmen. Finally, the Richmond Convention had taught the white workers (and others who were not members of the labor movement) that the suppression of Negro labor in the South meant lower living standards for workingmen everywhere, and that in the interest of all members of the Order, "a colored Knight of Labor must be placed on equal terms with a Knight of Labor who is white, so far as wages and political rights are concerned."[68]

The Order as it declined in power became more and more opportunistic and compromising in its attitude toward the Negro.* Nevertheless, we have shown enough to demonstrate that the K. of L. at the height of its power had learned what Frederick Douglass, the great Negro leader and former president of the National Colored Labor Union, told his people and the labor movement in 1883:

"Their [the Negro workers'] cause is one with the labor class all over the world. The labor unions of the country should not throw away this colored element of strength. . . . It is a great mistake for any class of laborers to isolate itself and thus weaken the bond of brotherhood between those on whom the burden and hardships of labor fall. The fortunate ones of the earth, who are abundant in land and money and know nothing of the anxious care and pinching poverty of the laboring classes, may be indifferent to the appeal for justice at this point, but the laboring classes cannot afford to be indifferent. . . ." [69]

* During an organizing tour in the South in February-March, 1889, Leonora M. Barry was shocked to learn that "in some places the white K. of L. would not allow the colored K. of L. to come into the Hall where I was giving a public lecture." She urged Powderly to take concrete steps to remedy this situation. Nothing was done. (Leonora M. Barry to Powderly, Feb. 13, March 5, 21, 1889, *PP*.)

[Since the present volume was published, the following publications dealing with the Knights of Labor have appeared which would be worth consulting for further details on the Knights: Philip S. Foner, "The Knights of Labor," *Journal of Negro History*, vol. LIII, 1968, pp. 70-77; Philip S. Foner, *Organized Labor and the Black Worker, 1619-1973*, New York, 1974, pp. 47-63; Gerald N. Greb, "Terence V. Powderly and the Knights of Labor," *Mid-America*, vol. XXXIV, 1957, pp. 39-55; Gerald N. Greb, "The Knights of Labor and the Trade Unions, 1878-1886," *Journal of Economic History*, vol. XVIII, 1958, pp. 176-92; Katherine A. Harvey, "The Knights of Labor in the Maryland Coal Fields, 1878-1882," *Labor History*, Vol. X, 1969, pp. 555-83; Irvin M. Marcus, "The Southern Negro and the Knights of Labor," *Negro History Bulletin*, vol. XXX, 1967, pp. 5-7; William B. Faherty, "Father Cornelius O'Leary and the Knights of Labor," *Labor History*, vol. XI, 1970, pp. 175-89.]

CHAPTER 5

Policies and Leadership of the Knights

As an organization which had marshalled the forces of the American working class from coast to coast, the Knights of Labor had within it great potential power. If it had been guided consistently by correct policies and wise counsels, the Order might have changed the course of American labor history in the past seven decades, and with it the course of American history as a whole.

Unfortunately, despite the Order's basically progressive stand on such issues as labor solidarity, many of the policies and most of the leaders of the Knights were so confused and so completely out of tune, and even in conflict, with the real needs and aspirations of the mass of the American workers that the potential collective strength of the organization was never fully realized. This situation had its roots in a basic conflict between the leadership and the rank-and-file on almost every issue facing the labor movement.

ROLE OF EDUCATION

"The fundamental principle of the Knights of Labor is *Education*," declared a leaflet issued by the Order. It was a basic tenet of the Knights that the workers would have to be educated before they could hope to assume the leadership in society which was their birthright. Since most of its members were "persons who, by circumstances not under their control, have been deprived of opportunities of knowledge as taught by schools." [1] and since even those who had gone to school had not learned the truth of social, economic and political issues, but only distorted, anti-labor, pro-capital interpretations, it was necessary for the Order to establish its own educational apparatus and program.

In the main, the educational activities of the Order consisted of lectures given by prominent men and women in the organization as well as friendly progressives on the outside, and the establishment of libraries and reading rooms.[2] The local assemblies heard discussions on a wide variety of topics at their semi-monthly meetings. "The local assembly," noted a contemporary labor paper, "became a school of practical economics in many localities and dispelled the fallacies which have so long prevented the people from knowing what hurt them." [3]

Libraries and reading rooms were established by many of the local assemblies and were usually located in the halls of the organizations. In several communities, Labor Temples, built and owned by the Order, became the center of all social and cultural life.[4]

Unfortunately, to the leaders of the Order education became a substitute for action. Operating on the theory that the members were not sufficiently educated on economic and political issues to act intelligently and effectively, they emphasized that strikes, boycotts and political activity be held in abeyance until the educational program had been fully developed. "Ours is essentially an educational body," went the argument. "To propagate sound economic doctrine is our holiest mission, and to which we should devote our best endeavors for years to come. . . . Let us ask of them [the membership] no more than to study the truths of social and economic science. When they have studied their lessons well, then action." [5]

But the rank-and-file viewed education as a guide to correct action not in some distant future but in the day-by-day struggles they faced.

The K. of L. leadership, however, shared none of the rank-and-file's concern with the day-by-day struggles. Powderly considered a wage program to be a "short-sighted work," involving merely "a few cents more in the day," and he emphasized that "to talk of reducing the hours of labor . . . is a waste of time. What men gain through a reduction of hours will be taken from them in another way." [6]

Instead of concerning themselves with such "petty questions" as higher wages and shorter hours, the K. of L. leadership urged the workers to direct all their energies to "banish the curse of modern civilization—wage slavery . . . by embarking on a system of cooperation, which will make every man his own master, and every man his own employer." Despite the failure of the producers' cooperative movement sponsored by labor in the years immediately following the Civil War,* the K. of L. leadership seized upon this utopian panacea and held it out to the workers as their only hope to end the evils of capitalism. The fact that the growth of monopoly capitalism in the 1880's had made it even more difficult for producers' cooperatives to exist successfully made no impression upon the leadership of the Order. Cooperation was "the lever of labor's emancipation," Powderly insisted. Upon this lever the hopes of all workingmen and women were centered.[7]

* See Foner, op. cit., pp. 178-81, 417-19.

The K. of L. were instrumental in establishing and maintaining for a short time many producers' and consumers' cooperatives.* But the wave of cooperation that swept the Order soon exhausted itself as experience proved that cooperation on a modest scale was doomed to failure. In every case the capitalist class fought the cooperatives tooth-and-nail and the labor projects faced interference by wholesalers who withheld supplies, and rank discrimination by railroads in rates and facilities and by banks in the matter of credit. In addition, the privately-owned companies cut prices and offered special inducements to kill off their cooperative competitors.[8]

Hasty action, inefficiency, dissension in the ranks, and lack of funds were also among chief causes of the failure of the cooperatives undertaken by the Knights. And if any cooperative had weathered all these trials, unscrupulous, aggressive capitalist enterprises, with the aid of railroads, middlemen and banks, blocked their growth and eventually made their existence impossible.[9]

Several of the cooperatives faced labor troubles of their own. A strike by teamsters who were forced to accept a wage cut brought an end to the cooperative bus company of the Toronto Knights of Labor. A somewhat similar situation hastened the death of the highly successful coopers' cooperatives in Minneapolis. The introduction of machinery into the barrel making process forced the coopers' cooperatives to spend a great deal of their funds to install expensive machinery in order to compete against private concerns. This, in turn, diminished the number of workmen that could be employed and led even to the use of boy labor at the machines at low wages. As a consequence, the cooperatives in Minneapolis faced strikes of their own workers. Within a few years, the projects had closed down.[10]

In directing the energies and funds of the Order towards the creating of producers' cooperatives,† the leaders of the Knights weakened the day-to-day struggles of the hard-pressed membership. For all the radical-sounding phraseology these leaders used in connection with the principles of cooperation, they were actually helping the capitalists by emphasizing that the workers should not bother to fight for immediate gains within the existing system.

* Most of the consumer cooperatives organized by the Knights were small grocery stores, and many of the local assemblies built halls with such stores on the first floor. (Edward W. Bemis, "Cooperation in New England," *Johns Hopkins University Study,* Baltimore, 1888, p. 69.)

† The Union Mining Company of Cannelburg, Indiana, the only instance of a cooperative established by the Order as a whole, was sold for $4,000, less than one-tenth of what the Order had sunk into the cooperative coal mine in hardly two years. (Frederick Turner to Powderly, April 18, 1885; Wm. T. Lewis to Powderly, April 15, 16, 28, May 11, 1885, *PP;* Powderly to Wm. T. Lewis, May 4, 1885, (Powderly Letter-Books, Mullen Library, Catholic University of America. Hereafter cited as *PLB.*)

ANTI-TRADE UNIONISM

Throughout most of the Order's early history, a see-saw battle took place between the pro- and anti-trade union elements, but, in the main, the trade union outlook triumphed. As we have already seen, the craft unions of skilled workers fitted very easily into the organization of the Knights which allowed each union to form an assembly on the basis of occupation. The formation of national trade assemblies closely patterned after national trade unions was encouraged, and many of the most powerful unions of the 'eighties occupied important places in the Order.

But the harmonious relationship between the Knights and the trade unions did not continue for long. By 1885 the leadership of the K. of L. had fallen into the hands of elements who were dominated by a backward anti-trade union ideology. Foremost among them were the Lassallean Socialists entrenched in the Home Club of District 49, the most powerful single body in the Knights of Labor and the second largest district in the Order. The District Assembly was organized in July, 1882, and took in most of the locals of New York and Brooklyn. It had a membership of 60,000 in the middle 'eighties.

Hostile to trade unions, indifferent or actively opposed to the struggle for higher wages, shorter hours, and better working conditions, champions of the program of establishing workers' cooperative enterprises as the method of alleviating the evils of the wage system, the Lassallean Socialist leaders of the Home Club strengthened the middle class tendencies of the Powderly leadership and contributed enormously to the disastrous conflict with the trade unions in and outside of the Order. In a short time, its anti-trade union outlook became the official policy of the General Executive Board. By 1886, the Home Club exercised considerable influence over the policies of the Order, and controlled most of its general officers.[11]

This is not to say that the only anti-trade union sentiment in the Order came from the Lassallean Socialists. It came from other sources too: farmers, storekeepers, rural professionals, businessmen, remnants of the Grangers and the Greenback Labor Party, and other non-working-class elements in the Knights. But the important things to note is that the anti-trade union attitude of the Lassallean Socialists coincided with the views of the non-working class elements in the Order and fitted into the program of Powderly and other leaders.

The anti-trade union elements in the Order argued that the trade unions were entirely outmoded by the widespread introduction of machinery and were totally incapable of combatting effectively the power of developing monopoly capitalism. The industrial revolution, they maintained, had, through specialization, so greatly diminished the number of skilled workers that there was no longer any need for craft unions. Furthermore, the isolated, individualistic policies of many of the trade unions rendered them ineffective in the struggle against anti-labor employers. Too frequently the employers were able to smash a strike called by a trade union because the members of other unions in the industry continued to work at their jobs and even did the work of the striking trade unionists. As Fred Turner, General Secretary of the Order and a member of the Home Club, put it: "Trade unions isolated from other trades are failures, and it is the duty and aim of the K. of L. to wipe out this trade union feeling and make one common brotherhood of man." [12]

Another criticism of the trade unions was that they were interested primarily in immediate improvements, such as higher wages, shorter hours, and better working conditions. In 1884, the General Assembly set forth what it regarded as an essential difference between the trade unions and the Knights: "that our Order contemplates a radical change, while Trades' Unions . . . accept the industrial system as it is and endeavor to adapt themselves to it. The attitude of our Order to the existing industrial system is necessarily one of war." [13]

In short, the anti-trade union elements believed that the reason for being for this "relic"—the trade union—had passed. It should be replaced by general labor bodies like the "mixed" assemblies in which all types of workers, skilled and unskilled, would be merged, and through which the workers would be educated regarding the fundamental principles of labor solidarity and the value of producers' cooperatives in ending the evils of wage slavery. "In comparison to isolated trade unions," Powderly thought that the "mixed" assembly of the Order "bears the same relation that the locomotive of to-day does to the stage-coach of half a century ago." [14]

Some of the criticisms levelled against the trade unions were justified. Too many of the craft unions were concerned only with getting as much as possible for themselves; they ignored the plight of the unskilled and semi-skilled; erected barriers against the admission of Negro, women, and foreign-born workers; maintained an isolated existence, indifferent even to the needs of fellow-trade unionists who were under attack, and operated on the theory that immediate improvements were the be-all and end-all of the labor movement. Nonetheless, there were serious defects in the reasoning of the anti-trade union elements, and their solution for the shortcomings of the craft unions was destined to affect adversely the entire working class, not merely the skilled workers.

Despite the fact that machinery had made serious inroads into the bargaining strength of the skilled workers of the 'eighties, it had not yet rendered obsolete the existence of craft unionism. To criticize the craft unions for their exclusive policies was correct, but to conclude that these unions should be destroyed and their members drawn into the Knights directly and united in "mixed" assemblies together with workers of different trades, unskilled workers and even non-working class elements, was to betray a woeful ignorance of strategy and tactics. While the skilled workers had problems and needs in common with the unskilled, they had problems and needs which were peculiar to themselves. It was the recognition of this fact that had led to the correct policy of establishing K. of L. assemblies organized along trade lines. The need of the day was not to unite the workers into a general, confused body regardless of the special requirements of the different categories of workers, but rather to build closer unity between the trade assemblies of skilled workers and the "mixed" assemblies. Already, as we have seen, the Knights had succeeded in establishing remarkable solidarity among all workers regardless of skill, color, sex, religious beliefs, and nationality backgrounds. When the anti-trade union elements declared war on the trade unions in the name of labor solidarity, they actually disrupted the advance of labor solidarity. For, as we shall see, they forced the skilled craftsmen, in self-protection, to break the links that bound them in the Knights to the unskilled workers.

The criticism that the trade unions were primarily interested in immediate improvements and accepted the existing industrial system would appear, at first glance, to be an extremely advanced declaration of principle. But it overlooked several vital facts. One was that not a few of the trade unions of the 'eighties, influenced by the Marxists, also contemplated a "radical change in the existing system," and labored "to bring about that change." But they did so by correctly linking the struggle for immediate demands with the movement for the abolition of wage slavery. This approach was infinitely more progressive than the radical-sounding but utopian doctrine of the anti-trade union elements who emphasized that the energies of the workers should be directed towards changing the industrial system through producers' cooperatives. When one realizes that the leadership of the anti-trade union elements was chiefly in the hands of those who rejected the class struggle, espoused the identity of interests between labor and capital, and were either indifferent or hostile to the struggle for immediate demands through which the working class could be organized and educated to advance towards the abolition of wage slavery, it is clear that fundamentally the doctrine was a backward one. Basically, it retreated to the labor philosophy of the 'sixties which was frequently characterized by middle-class panaceas.

ATTITUDE TOWARD POLITICAL ACTION

Writing in 1880, Powderly emphasized that most of the problems facing the working class required political action for their solution: ". . . the evils we now strike against are brought about by bad legislation, and, being corrected and reformed by wise legislation, the necessity for the strike ends." Political action was constantly linked by Powderly and other leaders of the Order with strikes to hammer home the point that strikes were unnecessary. This connection is clearly set forth in the 1884 constitution for local assemblies: "Strikes, at best, only afford temporary relief and members should be educated to depend upon thorough organization, cooperation, and political action, and through these the abolition of the wage system." [15]

A reading of this statement of principles would lead one to believe that the leadership advocated intense political activity for the K. of L. Yet in a number of his innumerable decisions, Powderly ruled that political action must not be discussed in local assemblies. "The Knights of Labor," he declared in typical mystical fashion, "is higher and grander than party. There is a nobler future before it." He was opposed to a labor party on the ground that it was not in "accord with the genius of American institutions." [16]

Thus the membership of the Order was placed in the confusing position of being told, on the one hand, that many of the most pressing problems facing the labor movement could only be solved through political action, and, on the other, that discussion of political action in the assemblies was a violation of the Knights' principles. Small wonder that Powderly was flooded with letters from assemblies asking for clarification on the question of "taking political action." Little wonder, too, that many assemblies, in taking a political stand, had to hide behind the subterfuge that their discussions and actions *will not be political.* [17]

Actually, despite continued warnings from Powderly and other national leaders, assemblies in a number of states were active politically.[18] In the fall of 1885, K. of L. tickets were nominated and elected in Michigan, Illinois, Connecticut, Massachusetts, New York, and Virginia.[19] Instead of hailing these labor victories, Powderly was furious. He issued a decree warning assemblies which nominated candidates for office "as Knights of Labor under the name of the Order [that] they have forfeited their right to membership in the Order." But the assemblies ignored the threat, and John Swinton chided Powderly for ignoring the facts of life: "The Order of the Knights of Labor is not a political party; but it cannot steer clear of politics. Its members must take part in governing the country." [20]

The futile platitudes and vacillations of the leadership weakened the political influence of the Order. With the exception of its successful lobbying activities in behalf of the anti-contract labor law adopted by Congress in February, 1885 (14 of the 16 organizations represented at the Congressional hearings were affiliated to the K. of L. and one of the petitions presented to Congress by the Order contained 50,000 names *), the political action of the Order as an integrated whole was negligible. The passage of the anti-contract labor law was but a meager windfall of what might have been a rich legislative harvest for the working class.

ATTITUDE TOWARDS STRIKES

In common with the leaders of other labor organizations of the 1860's and 1870's,† the men who founded the K. of L. were convinced that the strike was a hopeless weapon and should be abandoned in favor of arbitration and conciliation. These conclusions were influenced by the fact that many unions were still poorly organized and also by the unsuccessful strikes of the post-Civil War period. Underestimating the strength of organized labor, these men assumed that strikes would invariably end in defeat.

The K. of L. leadership clung to this approach even in the 1880's when labor's strength was growing rapidly and when many strikes were successful. Their position was that regardless of the outcome "strikes are as a rule productive of more injury than benefit to the working people." As Powderly put it: "A strike seldom fails of one result, that is, to create confusion and distrust, and finally breaks up the union. Whether the strike was successful or not, it generally breaks up the branch engaged in it." [21]

The policy of the national leadership on the strike question failed to impress the rank-and-file members who in their daily life knew intimately employer-worker relations, and a group arose which claimed that if the Knights were to gain anything "they must be prepared to strike even though they never do it." [22] This group did not contend that the correct approach to the policies of the national leadership was an irresponsible attitude towards strikes. They did not contend that strikes should take place under any and every circumstance, regardless of the hardship they would cause the workers and the possibility of victory. But they correctly accused the national leadership of playing directly into the hands of the employers. Apart from depriving the workers of a chief method of struggle, their policy completely overlooked the fact that most employers in the 1880's were not even willing to consider the idea of talking things

* Many of these K. of L. organizations represented trade unions within the Order, a fact which contradicts the thesis advanced by some historians that "the trade unions gave little support" to the campaign for the passage of the anti-contract labor law, presumably because the skilled workers were not menaced by the contract labor system.

† For a discussion of the attitude of labor leaders towards strikes in the 1860's and 1870's, see Foner, op. cit., pp. 374-75, 503-09

over with a union to conciliate differences with their workers. Also ignored was the fact that many of the strikes by members of the Order were called only as "a last resort," after all attempts at arbitration had failed.[23]

The members of the Order knew from experience that without the use of the strike as a last resort, employers would be uncompromising and their efforts to improve their conditions would be fruitless. Hence they paid little heed to pronouncements on the evils of strikes by the national leadership.[24]

Infuriated by the indifference of the rank-and-file to their frequent utterances emphasizing the futility of strikes, the Powderly leadership took steps in 1886 to render it almost impossible for the Knights to use the strike as an economic weapon. Striking was forbidden unless two-thirds of a secret ballot was voted in favor of it. No strike was to be entered upon when outside financial aid was required until a member of the general executive board had tried to arbitrate and then, if he were unsuccessful, the strike could be begun only by order of the general executive board. In short, the executive board had deliberately relieved itself of responsibility to heed the pleas of the hard-pressed membership.

The result of this bankrupt policy was disastrous for the members of the Order. "No sooner," Powderly himself admitted, "did our Order place a strong hand on strikes and boycotts than the employers of labor began to strike and boycott. Over two hundred lockouts have occurred since the employers got the idea that members of our organization could not strike without violating the laws of the Order.[25] *

BETRAYAL OF SECOND GOULD STRIKE

Powderly's conduct in the second Gould strike in the spring of 1886 and the battle of the packinghouse workers in the fall of that year intensified the conflict between the leadership and the rank-and-file.

It became clear soon after the settlement in 1885 that Jay Gould had no real intention of permitting a union to exist in his empire. In violation of the agreement, railroad workers who joined the Knights were fired; overtime work was not paid for; wages were not restored to the pre-strike level, and yardmen, bridgemen, sectionmen and other semi-skilled and "unskilled" workers were constantly being discriminated against in the matter of wages, hours, and working conditions.[26] It also soon became

* In the two years, 1886 and 1887, 161,610 workers (most of them members of the K. of L.) were thrown out of work by lockouts. This was 60.3 percent of all who lost work through this cause during the whole decade of 1881-1890. (Computed from U.S. Industrial Commission *Report*, 1901, Vol. XVII, p. 633.)

obvious that unless the Knights were recognized on the Southwestern system, the management could not be forced to obey the terms of the strike settlement.

At a convention of District Council 101 in January, 1886, a resolution was adopted almost unanimously calling for recognition of the Order by the Southwestern system, and a minimum wage of $1.50 per day for "unskilled" labor. The District Assembly's executive board began immediately to prepare for a strike if it should prove necessary to call one to force the acceptance of the demands for union recognition and a minimum wage.[27]

The showdown came on the Texas and Pacific Railroad, then in receivership. On February 18, 1886, Charles A. Hall, Master Workman of District Assembly 101 and a foreman in the Texas and Pacific shops, was fired for being absent from work without permission. Martin Irons, Socialist chairman of D.A. 101's executive board, anxious to achieve a peaceful settlement, appealed unsuccessfully to the receivers to reinstate Hall. When all attempts to confer with the receivers failed, the order to strike went out to the local assemblies of the Texas and Pacific. Coal heavers, miners, and telegraph operators joined the striking shopmen.[28]

When the Gould management rejected every overture to settle the strike peacefully, it spread to the entire Southwestern system. Between March 6 and 13, shopmen, switchmen, trackmen, and other railroad workers laid down their tools. Unfortunately, many of the engineers, firemen, brakemen, and conductors, who were so active and important in the 1885 strike, remained at work. The conservative leaders of the railway brotherhoods turned a deaf ear to appeals for labor solidarity.

The highly skilled railroad workers had received preferential treatment by the Gould management to separate them from the other workers on the lines, and the opportunistic leaders of the brotherhoods resolved not to jeopardize these gains regardless of what it might do to the strike. Gould's policy of dividing and conquering the workers on his railroads would now pay dividends.[29]

Despite terror, intimidation, an hysterical red-scare, and sabotage by the leaders of the railroad brotherhoods, the strikers held fast. Traffic was blockaded and business came to a standstill at St. Louis, Kansas City, and other points in the southwest.[30]

In its initial stages the strike was directed by Martin Irons. But his militant strategy and tactics frightened the top leadership of the Knights, and by the middle of March, Powderly decided to intervene. The Grand Master Workman immediately took steps to assure the railroad management that Iron's policies did not reflect those of the K. of L. and he appealed to H. M. Hoxie, managing vice-president of the Missouri Pacific, who had assumed charge of the management of the Southwestern system, for a conference to settle the strike by arbitration. Powderly got nowhere, ·

but undeterred he appealed to Gould himself. This time he appeared to be successful. Gould met with Powderly on March 28, and a basis for arbitration was reached. Gould informed Powderly that he had wired Hoxie ordering him not to discriminate against Knights in hiring men. The telegram also stated: "We see no objection to arbitrating the differences between the employees and the company, past or future." [31]

Powderly was jubilant. His policy of peaceful arbitration seemed vindicated. Without bothering to consult the strikers or any of their chosen strike leaders, Powderly wired Irons that Gould had consented to arbitration and ordered the strikers back to work. Joyfully he informed the press that Gould would arbitrate with the strikers and that the strike was over. [32]

The very next day Gould announced that he had never consented to arbitration! Hoxie was in charge of the strike, he declared, and he was the one to decide policy. [33] The agreement between Gould and Powderly was thus revealed at one stroke to have been a device by management to break down the morale of the strikers.

Powderly pressed for another conference, and this time he was told by Hoxie that management would deal only with a committee of workers who were actually at work. Even though this meant that the strike would have to be called off before the grievances of the strikers would be heard, Powderly ordered Irons to yield to Hoxie's terms. [34] Again Powderly had not bothered to consult a single representative of the strikers before announcing his order.

"Had Irons obeyed," writes a student of the strike, "the strike would have ended at this point, and the Knights of Labor would have suffered a crushing and humiliating defeat, for these were the terms of abject surrender." [35] But Irons refused to countersign Powderly's sell-out, and called upon the strikers to hold their ranks intact and prepare for a last-ditch battle. The response of the strikers forced Powderly to agree to a continuation of the strike. [36]

Although they gave lip-service support to the strike, Powderly and other top K. of L. leaders did little beyond issuing bravely-worded statements. Meanwhile, the attack upon the strikers reached new heights of fury. Seven workers were killed on April 9 during a battle between strikers and police, militia and deputy sheriffs in East St. Louis. Strikers were arrested daily and put in jail on such flimsy charges as contempt of court and inciting to riot. There were even indictments for communicating with individuals "requesting them not to work." [37]

While strikers were being shot down and arrested, Powderly confined himself to lecturing Gould on his duties as the head of a leading industry and to appealing to his better judgment to end the strike. These pitiful appeals were ignored. Gould made it crystal clear that he was determined to smash the union. [38]

On April 12, the House of Representatives ordered an investigation of the strike, and, three days later, a committee of seven Congressmen left for a tour of the strike area. Long hearings were held after which the committee wrote a report finding many of the strikers' grievances justified and admitted that "the concentration of wealth and power and the oppressions which have occurred as shown in the evidence taken may have promoted the unrest of labor." But the committee, having thrown a bone to labor, turned right about and asserted that the real cause of the strike was "Martin Irons, chairman of the executive board of District Assembly 101 (but for whom it is the opinion of your committee the strike would have been declared off at the request of Mr. Powderly, Grand Master Workman of Labor)." [39] The committee failed to explain why the great majority of the strikers felt that Powderly had betrayed them and why they had insisted that he rescind his order undemocratically calling off the strike.

By the end of April, it was clear that the strike was lost. The Southwestern system was almost in full operation, and only small bands of stalwarts reported for picket duty. The majority of the strikers were unable to hold out any longer against hunger, mass arrests, unprovoked attacks by police, sheriffs, troops, and vigilantes, and the vascillating policies of the top leadership of the Knights.

On May 4, the General Executive Board of the Order formally declared the strike ended. Powderly heaved a huge sigh of relief. "The strike in the Southwest will be over this evening and I am glad of it," he wrote privately.[40] The workers could not share Powderly's joy. The surrender was unconditional. No protection for the strikers was arranged; no consideration of grievances was even asked for. No member of the Knights was rehired.[41] Blacklisted on the railroads, many of the strikers faced a dark future. Irons himself was blacklisted in every industry, and deprived of any opportunity to make a living as a worker.*

BETRAYAL OF PACKINGHOUSE STRIKERS

Powderly's betrayal of the railroad strikers was followed a few months later by equally treacherous conduct in the battle of the packinghouse

---

* Misfortune hounded Irons's steps. His wife died during the strike and his furniture was seized for debts. Forced out of every job he tried his hand at, he attempted to lecture but failed, and during his last years was reduced to keeping a lunch counter in a small basement saloon in Missouri. But he remained a class-conscious, militant Socialist throughout these years of bitter privations. (See *Writings and Speeches of Eugene V. Debs,* New York, 1948, p. 42.)

Irons died in 1900, but his memory was kept alive by the workers of Missouri in 1910, under the auspices of the Missouri State Federation of Labor, erected a monument above his grave paying tribute to him as a "Fearless Champion of Industrial Freedom."

workers. In the summer of 1886, the Chicago packinghouse bosses reneged on their agreement of May First when the packinghouse unions had won their strike and gained an eight-hour day without a wage reduction. Repudiating the agreement, the Chicago packers reintroduced the ten-hour day. In October, 1886, 25,000 workers of the Union Stock Yards at Chicago went on strike for the eight-hour day. Thomas B. Barry, member of the K. of L.'s General Executive Board, was sent immediately by the Board to take charge of the strike.

The strikers had the stockyards completely tied up, and the bosses were on the point of yielding. Just when the workers were on the verge of victory, Powderly sent a telegram ordering the men to abandon their demands for an eight-hour day and return to work.[42]

The strikers were so dumbfounded by Powderly's strikebreaking order that at first they could not believe it to be true. But when they were assured that there was no mistake about the order, they refused to obey it. Thereupon, Powderly sent a message to Barry, directing him, if the men refused to obey the order to return to work, to take their charters from them. Since Powderly sent a copy of his message to Barry to the Associated Press, the packinghouse bosses knew immediately that with the Grand Master Workman's generous assistance, they had gained the upper hand in the struggle. They broke off negotiations with Barry and the strike committee, and, on November 8, 1886, adopted a resolution, signed by 24 packinghouse firms (among them Armour & Co., Swift & Co., John Cudahy, Nelson Morris & Co., Chicago Packing & Provision Co.), in which they denounced the stockyards assemblies of the Knights of Labor and told the strikers: "That we will not employ any man who is a member of said labor organizations. That all men employed will be required to resign from such labor organizations, and place such resignations in the hands of his employer." [43]

The strike ended a week later in a total defeat for the workers. The men returned to work, their faith in the Knights severely shaken. At a meeting of the strikers on the very eve of their return, they adopted a resolution in which they declared that the Grand Master Workman's action in ordering the men to return to work unconditionally proved "that T. V. Powderly was playing into the hands of the packers and not in the interest of the men." The late strikers also appealed to the Order to rebuke Powderly for his strikebreaking role at a special assembly called for that purpose. "Principles are what we contend for, not men, nor the dictation of any man," the embittered and disillusioned packinghouse workers declared.[44]

Pressed to explain his treacherous conduct, Powderly answered: "The laws of business cannot be lightly tampered with." And again: "Men who won capital are not our enemies. If that theory held good the workman of to-day would be the enemy of the fellow-toiler on the morrow. For after all, it is how to acquire capital and how to use it propertly that we are endeavoring to learn." [45]

ROLE OF CATHOLIC CHURCH

Added to Powderly's determination not to antagonize employers by labor militancy was his deep concern not to antagonize the Catholic Church. Actually, the two are intertwined, for prominent business men were continually urging the Church to condemn the Order on the grounds that it was plotting a socialist revolution. One industrialist warned a Catholic prelate as early as 1882 that the growth of the Knights of Labor led him to expect in the United States "scenes not less terrible than those committed by the Commune in Paris." By 1886 when the Order had reached a membership of over 700,000, these industrialists were look-ing to the Catholic Church as a major bulwark against the wrath of the miserably exploited workers.[46]

In September, 1884, instructions were issued by the Holy See at Rome condemning the Knights of Labor and directing every Catholic prelate in North America to stop their parishioners from belonging to the Order.[47] * Despite the fact that the Knights increased its membership tremendously after 1884, Powderly was convinced that unless the ban was removed, the Order was doomed. "With the christian church op-posed to us," he wrote in the fall of 1886, "we will make but little head-way. To have all forms of the Christian religion arrayed against us would no doubt give us the support of the infidel element and with these elements acting in sympathy with the Knights of Labor it is easy to judge the length of time our Order would remain a power for good." [48]

Powderly's formula "to win the benevolent forbearance of the American hierarchy" was a simple one: prove by words and deeds that the Order was a conservative influence in American life and that not only did it have no connection with radicalism in any shape or form, but that it was actually a bulwark against radicalism. Precisely for these reasons, more-

---

* The reaction of many of the 125,000 Catholics estimated to be members of the Order in the fall of 1884 was set forth by one of the Catholic members who wrote: "We cannot as Catholics refuse implicit obedience to the behests of the Church, but at what a cost would she exact that obedience if she commands us to resign our only hope of relief from the state of slavery to which the Vanderbilts, Goulds, Barretts, Perkins and other corporation magnates have reduced us owing to our hitherto isolated and consequently defenseless condition." (Jno. S. B. Coggeshell to Powderly, January 28, 1882, *PP*.) The figure of the number of Catholics in the Order, based on Powderly's estimate, is little more than a guess since the religion of the members was not asked. (*See* Powderly to Archbishop Patrick J. Ryan, Oct. 24, 1884, *PLB*.)

over, the Church should encourage Catholic workers to remain in the Order, for if they left, the control of the organization would fall into the hands of radical elements.[49]

While this formula may have appeared simple when set forth in well-rounded phrases, it was quite another matter to reconcile it with the militant activities of the rank-and-file Knights. When even strikes were being characterized as "limited revolution" by clergymen, it is easy to see that Powderly undertook no simple task when he set out to prove to the Church that the Order was a conservative body. Especially so since Powderly himself had to remove the impressions created by his own earlier associations with the radical elements in and outside the Order.

Although Uriah S. Stephens, the founder of the K. of L., bitterly opposed having anything to do with the socialists "either individually or as a body," [50] Powderly was for several years on good terms with the leaders of the Socialist Labor Party. He was eager to accept the support of the socialists in the campaign against the Order's absolute secrecy, and he even became a member of the S.L.P.[51]

But by the summer and fall of 1882, Powderly had reached the conclusion that he had to make a real effort to remove the suspicions his associations with the radical elements were causing among the clergymen. He privately acknowledged that he still entertained "socialistic ideas," and that "If socialism and communism means the restoration of man's natural rights I am a socialist and a communist. . . ." But he deliberately avoided appearing at meetings at which "prominent *Socialists*" would speak, convinced that if he did so, "it would be telegraphed to the four corners of the earth that the K. of L. was a socialist society." [52]

Powderly was to devote a large portion of his time, both in speeches and writings, to the repetition of the theme that neither he nor the organization he headed had anything in common with radicalism. He became almost hysterical as he denied that he had ever belonged to the Socialist Labor Party.[53]

There is no doubt that Powderly's conservative speeches and actions played a large role in the *rapprochement* between the Catholic Church and the Knights of Labor and helped to win favor for the Order in Rome. For one thing, the Catholic press in the United Press hailed Powderly's leadership as "conservative and intelligent," praised the Knights for having "put the right man in the right place when they chose him for their leader," and predicted that it would be an "almost irreparable loss" if he were ever unseated as head of the Order.[54] For another and more important thing, in his famous appeal to the Vatican to reverse its condemnation of the Knights which he delivered to the Holy Office personally on February 20, 1887, Cardinal James Gibbons of Baltimore placed considerable emphasis on Powderly's testimony regarding the inherent conservatism of the Order as well as the fact that the Knights' leadership discouraged violence and kept strikes within the limits of good order and legitimate action.

Powderly's champions have argued that the announcement in March, 1887, that the Holy Office objected to nothing in the K. of L. and the final decision a year and a half later in which the Holy See conditionally tolerated the Order * justified the Grand Master Workman's conservative policies.[55] But this ignores, first, that the removal of the ban on the Knights did not end the attacks on the Order by individual Catholic clergymen in the United States; second, that the removal of the ban came when the Order was declining rapidly, and, third and most important, that this decline was considerably hastened, as we shall see below, by these very conservative policies of the leadership that were so important in gaining for the Order the Church's conditional toleration. This is not to say that Rome's final decision was not to be of importance for the American labor movement, for it was a significant step in the transition from opposition on the part of Church leaders toward trade unions to conditional approval (the condition being that the unions must not become too radical). But the members of the Knights of Labor and the American working class as a whole paid a costly price for the decision from Rome in the form of a reactionary drive by the leadership of the Order against militant trade unionism and those who espoused this policy.

THE POWDERLY MACHINE

Had the other general officers displayed characteristics different from those of their superior, the unfortunate influence exercised by Powderly might have been nullified. But with the exception of a few men like Joseph R. Buchanan, many of the general officers showed the same ready capacity for the utterances of fine sentiments, while their acts bore no special relation to their verbal professions. Like Powderly, they were not well grounded in issues of major concern to the workers, and found it

---

* The decision of the Holy Office was "conditional toleration" not approval in the sense that "It certainly showed no outright approval of American labor organization," and that "Its emphasis was definitely anti-socialistic, rather than on the positive necessity and the good to be derived from such a labor association." The decision demanded that several of the statutes of the Knights of Labor should be corrected. "Especially in the preamble of the constitution for local assemblies words which seem to savor of socialism and communism must be emended in such a way as to make clear that the soil was granted by God to man, or rather the human race, that each one might have the right to acquire some portion of it, by use however of lawful means and without violation of the right of private property." (Henry J. Browne, *The Catholic Church and the Knights of Labor*, Washington, D. C., 1949, pp. 323-24.)

difficult to mingle with the rank and file. Like Powderly, they expressed contempt for the workers and blamed them for the attacks upon the Order by employers and their agents. Like Powderly, they engaged in red-baiting, charged that the opposition to the leadership's class collaboration policies was "all the work of the Socialists," and even egged on the Grand Master Workman to "bring on an issue between those who desire reform after the American idea or through the methods and treachery of importation," [56] thus echoing the cry of the employers and their agents that socialists and other radicals were "foreign agitators." In essence, the General Executive Board displayed many of the qualities exemplified by the Grand Master Workman. There is full justification for the statement that what was achieved by the Knights of Labor was achieved in spite of these leaders.

Although he resigned once (on January 5, 1883),[57] and threatened to resign many times thereafter, Powderly remained Grand Master Workman until 1893. The constitution gave him and his henchmen on the General Executive Board great power. As Joseph A. Labadie pointed out correctly in 1882: "It [the constitution] gives too much power to a few who are responsible to no one." [58] Powderly appointed most of the committees of the General Assembly, especially the powerful committee on credentials, and was thus able to dominate the seating of delegates, kill off resolutions to which he was opposed, and, in general, operate the conventions more or less as he wished. Moreover, the General Executive Board, controlled by Powderly and his lieutenants,* could suspend any local officer or member, revoke any charter, and, by a unanimous vote, terminate any strike, general or local.[59] Finally, through control of the official journal, Powderly and his henchmen were able to see to it that the membership heard only one (their) side of any conflict over policy.[60]

FAILURE OF S.L.P. TO CHALLENGE POWDERLY

Many of the local leaders and rank-and-file members of the Order (like Martin Irons and Frank J. Ferrell) were Socialists or were influenced by the Socialists, and they were instrumental in mobilizing the Knights for militant struggle, and in advancing the program of labor solidarity.[61] But the same cannot be said of the S.L.P. leadership, most of whom were German-Americans who concentrated on securing resolutions from labor organizations endorsing in general terms the desirability

---

* "My machinery is working very nicely through the country," Powderly wrote. "Someone will have to get off the [general executive] board soon or be expelled." (Powderly to John Hayes, Feb. 22, 1888, Powderly-Hayes Correspondence, Mullen Library of the Catholic University of America, Washington, D. C. Hereafter cited as *PHC*.)

of socialism, and who held the Knights in contempt for its failure to come out clearly and decisively for socialism.

Writing to his American friends, Engels criticized the German-American Marxists for remaining aloof from the K. of L. because it did not proclaim a clear-cut Marxist program. Engels pointed out that it was necessary for the Marxists "to work inside them (the Knights), to form within this still quite plastic mass a core of people who understand the movement and its aims," and who would be able, backed by the rank-and-file, to challenge successfully the class-collaborationist policies of the Powderly leadership.[62]

But with few exceptions,[63] the S.L.P. leadership remained on the sidelines during the crucial years of the internal struggle in the Order between the rank-and-file and the Powderly administration, and only abandoned this attitude in the early 1890's, when the K. of L. was a shell of its former self.*

In due time, the workers came to realize the utter bankruptcy of Powderly's policies. In battles with the employers, they found the head of the Knights and his lieutenants on the side of the enemies of the workers. By then, Powderly's machine was operating in high gear, and it was no easy matter to remove him from leadership and reverse his policies. But the struggle continued, and in 1893, as we shall see, the rule of the labor misleader, Terence V. Powderly, was brought to an end.

---

* While the Marxists remained aloof from the Knights, other wings of the Socialist movement, like the Lassallean Socialists, exerted increasing influence in the Order. An independent Socialist movement in the far west and the Rocky Mountain region, under the leadership of Burnette G. Haskell, captured the leadership of a number of local assemblies, and placed Joseph R. Buchanan on the Knights' General Executive Board. (Burnette G. Haskell Papers, Bancroft Library, University of California; Charles McArthur Destler, *American Radicalism, 1865-1901*, New London, Conn., 1946, pp. 79-103.)

[In the chapter that follows the discussion of the origins of Labor Day was written before the publication of evidence that it may have been Matthew Maguire, and not Peter J. McGuire, who was the father of Labor Day. In 1967, George Pearlman, a retired machinist of Paterson, New Jersey, began publishing articles setting forth evidence that his fellow machinist, Matthew Maguire, was the real Father of Labor Day. For a discussion of the controversy over who is the Father of Labor Day, *see* Jonathan Grossman's article on this subject, *Monthly Labor Review*, September, 1972, pp. 3-6.

Since the discussion of the Haymarket Affair in the same chapter was published, Henry David published a revised edition of his work, *The History of the Haymarket Affair* (New York, 1963), and the present writer published *The Autobiographies of the Haymarket Martyrs* (New York, 1969), making available for the first time since they appeared in the *Knights of Labor* and *Alarm* the autobiographies of all eight of the Haymarket Martyrs together with an analysis of the case by their attorney, William Perkins Black.

Songs of the Eight Hour Movement may be found in Philip S. Foner, "Songs of the Eight-Hour Movement," *Labor History*, vol. XIII, 1972, pp. 571-88, and reprinted in Philip S. Foner, *American Labor Songs of the Nineteenth Century*, (Urbana, Illinois, 1975).]

CHAPTER 6

The Federation, Labor Day, and May Day

Even while the Knights of Labor were achieving their greatest successes, an organization was emerging that was soon to supplant the Order as the leader of the American labor movement. This was the Federation of Organized Trades and Labor Unions of the United States and Canada, the name of which was changed in 1886 to the American Federation of Labor.

THE FEDERATION OF ORGANIZED TRADES AND LABOR UNIONS

In a previous volume we traced the forces that led to the formation of the Federation and described in detail its birth at a convention in Pittsburgh in 1881.*

From the very beginning, the Federation was brought under the control of the national trade unions by a provision which gave them representation in the annual convention according to the size of their membership, whereas the local councils were given only one vote regardless of membership. But, despite the prominent role assigned to them, the majority of the national trade unions did not for some years show much enthusiasm for the Federation, and those that did, confined it to "wordy endorsements" when the organization was desperately in need of funds.[1] The anti-trade union elements had not yet seized control of the K. of L., hence many of the leading national unions felt that their needs were being served by the Order. Others remained aloof from both the Knights and the Federation. The Amalgamated Association of Iron and Steel Workers represented by ten delegates at the Pittsburgh Convention in

* See Foner, *History of the Labor Movement in the U.S.,* Vol. I, pp. 512-24.

93

1881, withdrew from the Federation in 1883 because the organization adopted a series of resolutions condemning high tariffs.[2] *

Issuing no charters to its constituent organizations and hampered by lack of membership and funds, the Federation was rapidly reduced to the status of a resolution-passing body.† Between conventions, the Federation functioned only through its Legislative Committee set up in 1881 to organize a campaign to secure protective and other legislation favorable to the workers.‡ The Committee helped to secure employment for blacklisted workers, stimulated the organization of trade unions in several cities, and helped to strengthen a number of national unions. Although its work in the economic field was gradually expanded, the committee's activity was mainly political.[3] It maintained that during the first two years of its existence it had helped to bring about the general investigation of capital and labor by the Senate Committee on Education and Labor; aided in defeating a bill declaring unions of seamen to be conspiracies and mutiny, punishable by heavy fines and a long term of imprisonment; influenced the passage of a bill by the Ohio legislature to abolish the prison labor contract system, of another a bill by the New York legislature abolishing cigar-making in tenement houses, and the adoption of bills by several legislatures prohibiting the employment of children under twelve, and providing for compulsory education of children.[4] The Committee reported further that "In recent elections friends

---

* The loss of the union was a severe blow to the Federation. The Amalgamated membership was estimated in 1882 at between 50,000 and 60,000. (New York Sun, May 14, 1882; W. H. Foster to Gompers, Dec. 28, 1885, *AFL Corr.*) Years later, P. J. McGuire, leaders of the Carpenters' Union and A.F. of L. secretary-treasurer, wrote to Gompers: "We cannot afford to take a position on the tariff question, for our prior experience of the injury it wrought to the old Federation in 1882 is a sufficient lesson." (May 21, 1897, *AFL Corr.*)

† Among the resolutions adopted by the Federation between 1882 and 1884 was one at the 1882 convention extending an invitation to all women's organizations and assuring them that they would be represented at future sessions "upon an equal footing with trade organizations of men." (No such invitation went to organizations of Negro workers.) The 1883 convention followed up the invitation to women's organizations with a direct appeal to "Working Girls and Women," urging them to organize and unite with the Federation in establishing the principle that "equal amounts of work should bring the same prices whether performed by man or woman." The convention also appealed to factory workers to organize, and called upon its Legislative Committee "to devote its special effort, the ensuing year, towards organizing the factory operatives of the country." (*Proceedings,* Federation of Organized Trades and Labor Unions, 1882 Convention, pp. 16, 19, 20, 23; *Proceedings,* 1883 Convention, pp. 13, 19.)

‡ Samuel Gompers was chairman, Richard Powers, first vice-chairman, Gabriel Edmonston, second vice-chairman, W. H. Foster, secretary, and Robert Howard, treasurer of the Legislative Committee.

of labor have been elevated in several sections of the country to positions which give them a voice in the enactment of the laws which govern us, and, what is more gratifying, several office-holders notoriously hostile to our cause have been defeated by the unified efforts of trade unionists." [5] *

Whether or not the claims were justified—a point difficult to determine on the basis of the available evidence—the Legislative Committee was far from satisfied with its achievements. "It was our intention," it reported to the 1883 convention, "to circulate extensively during our term of office, tracts and brief pamphlets, with the object of educating the Toilers up to Trade Unionism and the aims of the Federation; but up to very recently we were without funds, and are consequently obliged to bequeath this work to our successors." [6]

But the "successors" were in no better position. In his report to the 25 delegates, representing less than 50,000 members of affiliated unions, at the 1884 convention in Chicago, Secretary Frank K. Foster admitted that the Federation was a failure. Its legislative achievements were hardly significant. Its campaign to organize the factory workers had scarcely begun. The attempt to unify the labor movement had produced no results. Most of the important national unions were still outside the Federation, and the few who were inside and sent delegates to its conventions, gave it little or no support. The chief bright spot in the gloomy picture, Foster announced, was the fact that it was his "pleasant duty" to inform the delegates of the opening of fraternal relations between the trade unions of France and the United States as a result of the Federation's work.† Otherwise there was little he could point to as a positive achievement. "In presenting my report as Secretary for the year past," Foster declared, "I am conscious that its chief interest will consist of future possibilities it suggests rather than its record of objects attained. The lack of funds has seriously crippled the work of the Federation, and this, coupled with an organization lacking cohesiveness, has allowed small scope for effective expenditure of effort." [7]

---

* On November 20, 1881, immediately after it was organized, the Legislative Committee unanimously adopted a resolution asserting that no member of the body "should publicly advocate the claims of any of the political parties; but this shall not preclude the advocacy to office of a man who is pledged purely and directly to labor measures." (Minutes of the Legislative Committee of the Federation of Organized Trades and Labor Unions of the United States and Canada, Nov. 19, 1881-Dec. 17, 1887, AFL Archives.)

† In correspondence with the trade unions of France, Foster Wrote: "The labor question is practically the same the world over; it varies in degree, not in kind. Labor knows no country, and the laborers of the world should clasp hands for their common weal. With industrial unity, barbaric war cannot exist." (Proceedings, 1884 Convention, pp. 12-13.)

FOUNDING OF LABOR DAY

Yet out of the 1884 convention of the dying Federation of Organized Trades and Labor Unions came two resolutions which were to have far-reaching effects on the American labor movement and the American people as a whole for generations to come. One resolution led to the establishment of Labor Day, and the other of May Day, as labor holidays.

On May 18, 1882, Peter J. McGuire, Socialist founder and General Secretary of the Brotherhood of Carpenters and Joiners, arose at a meeting of the Central Labor Union of New York City and introduced a resolution recommending that "a day should be set aside as a festive day [for] a parade through the streets of the city." He proposed the first Monday in September, since "it would come at the most pleasant season of the year, nearly midway between the Fourth of July and Thanksgiving, and would fill a wide gap in the chronology of legal holidays." [8]

The proposal was enthusiastically received and the labor body set September 5, 1882, as the date for its first parade. More than 30,000 men and women, bricklayers, freight handlers, printers, painters, blacksmiths, railroad men, cigar makers, furriers, seamstresses, and other workers lined up for the march on the morning of September 5. "LABOR WILL BE UNITED," "EIGHT HOURS FOR WORK—EIGHT HOURS FOR REST—EIGHT HOURS FOR WHAT WE WILL," "STRIKE WITH THE BALLOT," were some of the slogans on the placards carried by the workers as they proudly marched down New York's fashionable Fifth Avenue and into Union Square. [9]

When labor turned out again on September 5, 1883, there were 10,000 in the line of march and newspapers reported that "ten times that number lined the streets and cheered." Many of the marchers, Negro and white,* carried placards reading: "WE MUST CRUSH MONOPOLIES LEST THEY CRUSH US." [10]

In 1884 the New York Central Labor Union decided to hold the Labor Day parade on the first Monday in September, which was September 1.† It also communicated with central labor bodies in other cities to urge them to celebrate the first Monday in September as "a universal holiday for workingmen." Every worker who toiled for a living would be welcome. "No distinction of color will be made; race prejudice will be ignored; religious differences will be set aside; but all men will be on an equality provided he earns his daily bread." [11]

That year workers marched in Buffalo, in Cincinnati, and in Lynn and Haverhill, Massachusetts, as well as in New York City. More than

* The Wendell Phillips Labor Club, an organization of 150 Negro workers, headed the second division of the parade.
† The 1882 parade was held on a Tuesday and the one in 1883 on a Wednesday.

20,000, representing 50 trade unions, paraded in New York. The New York *Herald* headlined its account thus: "A GREAT OUTPOURING FROM THE CENTRAL LABOR UNION; A PROCESSION THAT FILLED THE STREETS—AND WAS RECEIVED WITH CHEERS." [12]

The first national organization to move that a day be set apart throughout the nation for labor to celebrate was the Federation of Organized Trades and Labor Unions. At the 1884 convention in Chicago, the veteran labor leader, A. C. Cameron, a member of Typographical Union No. 16, representing the Chicago Trades and Labor Assembly, introduced the following resolution: "Resolved, That the first Monday in September of each year be set apart as a laborer's national holiday, and that we recommend its observance by all wage workers, irrespective of sex, calling, or nationality." [13]

The resolution was unanimously adopted. In a call to workers all over the country to rally behind the resolution, the Federation urged "all connected with the grand army of labor, skilled or unskilled, to be ranged under one banner, and help to make this a day worthy of the cause they represent." [14] This call was supplemented by special resolutions adopted by local groups in many states. The Minneapolis Trades and Labor Assembly called on the workers to demonstrate:

"To capitalists, bankers and their hirelings the power you possess when you thoroughly understand how to think and legislate for yourselves. While you drudge and toil away your lives for a bare existence, these idlers and non-producers live in luxury and debauchery, squandering with a lavish hand that which belongs to you—that which your labor produces. . . .

"They have tried to deny us the right to organize—a right guaranteed by the constitution of this government. Therefore we call on you to show that we defy them; that you will organize; that you have organized; that the day of your deliverance is approaching. To do this we ask you to join in our ranks in celebrating the day.

"The Trades and Labor Assembly proclaims to be labor's annual holiday the first Monday of September. Leave your benches, leave your shops. . . ." [15]

The first nation-wide observance of the first Monday in September as a national holiday took place on September 7, 1885, on which day, a contemporary newspaper commented, "was inaugurated a national labor holiday which will be observed, probably, so long as labor organizations exist throughout the United States." [16] The first state in the Union to make Labor Day official was Oregon, in 1887. In 1894, Amos J. Cummings, a New York Congressman and member of Typographical Union No. 6, introduced a bill in Congress, drawn up by the A. F. of L., to establish Labor Day, the first Monday in September, as a national legal holiday. It was adopted by Congress on June 28, 1894, and signed on the same day by President Cleveland.[17]

THE EIGHT-HOUR DAY

In every Labor Day demonstration of the early 1880's, the leading slogan was "Eight Hours to Constitute a Day's Work." Hence it is not surprising that the same convention of the Federation which issued a call to the workers to celebrate the first Monday in September as labor's national holiday, should have taken the lead in a nationwide campaign for the eight-hour day. The Federation's 1884 convention adopted a historic resolution which read: "Resolved, By the Federation of Organized Trades and Labor Unions of the United States and Canada, that eight hours shall constitute a legal day's labor from and after May 1, 1886, and that we recommend to labor organizations throughout this district that they so direct their laws as to conform to this resolution by the time named." [18]

May Day as a day when the workers demonstrate their class and international solidarity thus has its origins in their efforts to achieve a shorter working day, particularly their struggles for the eight-hour day. In the previous volume, we traced the history of the battle for an eight-hour day before the 1880's.* This struggle produced some results. Six states adopted eight-hour laws by 1867. A number of city councils enacted ordinances extending the eight-hour day to its public employees. In June, 1868, Congress enacted the first federal eight-hour law in American history, granting the eight-hour day to government employees.

These laws, however, were ineffectual and are mainly significant for establishing a legal precedent and mirroring growing popular demand. The state laws did not provide any means of enforcement and usually contained a clause excepting employees from the provisions of the act if they had a special contract with their employers providing for longer hours. The federal law was subject to such varied interpretations that it did not secure an eight-hour day for all the workers who were supposed to be covered. It was accompanied, moreover, by a 20 percent wage-cut which remained in effect until 1872 and was only nullified by labor's persistent resistance. Finally, in 1876, the United States Supreme Court completely nullified the law by declaring that the federal government could make separate agreements with its employees.[19]

In the early 'eighties emphasis in the struggle for the eight-hour day was still on legislative action. But it soon became obvious that labor could

* See Foner, *op. cit.*, pp. 363-69, 371, 277-82, 500-04.

no longer depend upon legislative action to secure the eight-hour day.* "The way to get it," P. J. McGuire told a mass meeting of carpenters was "by organization. In 1868 the United States passed an Eight-Hour law, and that law has been enforced just twice. If you want an Eight-Hour law, make it yourself." Speaking for the Carpenters' and Joiners' Union, McGuire declared: "We want an enactment by the workingmen themselves that on a given day eight hours should constitute a day's work, and they ought to enforce it themselves." [20]

In 1884, McGuire's union, the Brotherhood of Carpenters and Joiners, instructed its delegates to the Federation's convention in Chicago to submit a resolution fixing May 1, 1886, as the time for a simultaneous establishment of eight hours as a legal day's labor for all workers. The resolution, introduced by Delegate Edmonston, and adopted after a lengthy discussion by a vote of 23 to 2, contained no provision indicating what methods should be used by labor to secure the eight-hour day on May 1, 1886. But that a strike was envisaged by the delegates is seen in the approval of a proposal by Frank K. Foster urging "that a vote be taken in all labor organizations, prior to the next Congress, as to the feasibility of a universal strike for a working day of 8 (or 9) hours, to take effect not later than May 1, 1886." [21] The delegates, wrote a correspondent who covered the convention for *John Swinton's Paper,* were convinced that "It is useless to wait for legislation. . . . A united demand for a shorter working day, backed by thorough organization, would prove vastly more effective than the enactment of a thousand laws depending for enforcement upon the pleasure of aspiring politicians or sycophantic department officials." [22]

Success or failure of its proposal, the Federation knew, depended upon the response of its more powerful and influential rival, the Knights of Labor. Hence a resolution was passed instructing the incoming Legislative Committee to extend an invitation to the Order "to co-operate in the general movement to establish the eight-hour reform." [23]

There was reason to believe that this invitation would not meet with a favorable response from the Order's officialdom. In 1884, the K. of L. declared it to be the aim of the Order "to shorten the hours of labor by a general refusal to work for more than eight hours." [24] But Powderly

* A committee appointed by the Federation and headed by Congressman Murch visited President Chester A. Arthur in 1882 to secure enforcement of the existing national Eight-Hour Law. The committee was received coldly at the White House and bluntly informed by the President: "I do not think the Eight-Hour Law is constitutional, and no power on earth can make me enforce an unconstitutional law." (*Proceedings,* 1882 Convention, Federation of Organized Trades and Labor Unions, pp. 2, 18.) It did not seem to occur to the President that his duty was to enforce and not to interpret laws.

and his colleagues on the General Executive Board made it clear that this did not mean support for a general strike movement for the eight-hour day. Instead of a mass demonstration, Powderly recommended that all members of the Order should simultaneously write letters to the newspapers on Washington's Birthday, February 22, 1885. After the letter-writing campaign was over, Powderly pronounced it a great success in "creating a healthy public opinion," for "manufacturers began to discuss the question and study its possibilities." [25] This was cold comfort, of course, to the hundreds of thousands of workers toiling long hours in the factories, shops, and mines.

It became clear by the summer of 1885 that the officialdom of the Knights was out to undermine the movement for the eight-hour day inaugurated by the Federation. Fred Turner, General Secretary of the Order, did not even bother to acknowledge the letter from the Federation's Secretary urging the Knights "to cooperate with us in establishing the Eight-Hour work day from May 1, 1886." At the General Assembly in 1885 the officials granted scant consideration to a resolution commending the Federation and urging support of the movement it was sponsoring. Moreover, in his annual address to the convention, Powderly went out of his way to condemn the May 1 plan of the Federation. Asserting that "the eight-hour question . . . is a political one," he recommended that "the proposition to inaugurate a general strike for the establishment of the shorter-hour plan on the first of May, 1886, should be discountenanced by this body. The people most interested in the project are not as yet educated in the movement, and a strike under such conditions must prove abortive. The date fixed is not a suitable one; the plan suggested to establish it is not the proper one." [26]

But the rank-and-file Knights thought differently. Assembly after assembly adopted resolutions requesting the general assembly to fix May 1 "as the day on which to strike for eight hours," and the K. of L. organizers utilized the eight-hour issue in establishing new assemblies. A number of the letters to Powderly from assemblies endorsing the eight-hour movement added that it should be coupled with a demand for a more thorough-going change in the economic system. "The time has arrived, fellow workmen," wrote one assembly in this connection, "when we should stop lopping off branches and lay the axe at the root. We must demand an entire change in the industrial system as well as an eight-hour day." [27]

It is significant that these letters did not call for abandonment of the fight for an eight-hour day until the whole social system had been revolutionized. Powderly, on the other hand, in typical demagogical fashion, took the view that the "advantage gained when the hours of labor are reduced to eight hours a day" could only be realized when "a just and humane system of land ownership, control of machinery, railroads, and telegraphs, as well as an equitable currency system" were achieved.[28]

THE FOUNDING OF MAY DAY

The enthusiastic response from the rank-and-file of the labor movement encouraged the delegates to the Federation's convention in 1885 to repeat the declaration that an eight-hour system was to go into effect on May 1, 1886. Furthermore, they requested that member unions and organizations not affiliated to the Federation which did not propose to strike for the shorter day should aid those which would "with all the power at their command." The Legislative Committee was entrusted with authority "to put the eight-hour-work-day in practical operation" on May 1, 1886, and was empowered to appeal for financial aid from all trade and labor unions.[29]

This time the officers of the Federation took some steps to make effective preparation for the impending struggle. Machinery was established by which the eight-hour day could be gained through negotiation with employers, and a form agreement was drawn up to be signed at conferences between the unions and employers. But if peaceful negotiation proved fruitless, the unions were to resort to the strike. Meanwhile, until May 1, 1886, the unions were to agitate for the eight-hour day through mass meetings, circulars and other means, and the workers were to be mobilized to take action at the proper moment.[30]

This program was submitted to the K. of L., which was again asked to cooperate. Once again, the leadership received the invitation coldly, and for the most part ignored the appeal. And once again the rank-and-file of the Order welcomed the plan with open arms, and an increasing number of local assemblies passed resolutions calling upon the leadership to support the Federation. "The rank-and-file of the Order," one historian points out, "was ready for militant methods, but its leaders were far too peace-loving to resort to widespread industrial action." [31]

When, despite admonitions from headquarters, the rank-and-file membership of the Knights began to make preparations for the first of May, 1886, Powderly, in one of his many secret circulars, remonstrated against the efforts of members to pledge the Order to support the eight-hour movement. In the well-known secret circular of March 13, 1886, Powderly wrote: "No assembly of the Knights of Labor must strike for the eight-hour system on May first under the impression that they are obeying orders from headquarters, for such an order was not, and will not, be given. Neither employer nor employe are educated to the needs and necessities of the short hour plan." [32]

While Powderly was powerless to stop the eight-hour movement, he did succeed in preventing effective and concerted action in labor's ranks. The March circular divided the members of the Order, and although thousands of Knights continued to play a conspicuous role at all meetings held to prepare for May First in New York, Philadelphia, Chicago, Louisville, St. Louis, Milwaukee, Boston, and other cities, they did so in the knowledge that they were going over the heads of their national leaders, a step which many Knights were not prepared to take.[33]

In Chicago, scene of the most aggressive effort to win the eight-hour day, the Social Revolutionaries threw themselves wholeheartedly into the movement, and were largely responsible for the tremendous upsurge in that city for the shorter working day. At the outset, the anarchist leaders of the International Working People's Association—the so-called "Block International"—did not look with favor on the eight-hour demand. "To accede the point that capitalists have the right to eight hours of our labor," declared the *Alarm*, "is more than a compromise, it is a virtual concession that the wage system is right." The movement for a shorter working day, even if successful, was trivial compared to the struggle to abolish the wage-system. It would be only a sop thrown to the workers to keep them satisfied and to divert their energies from the struggle to overthrow wage slavery.[34]

But when the Chicago anarchists saw how deeply the working class everywhere was stirred and how bitterly the industrialists opposed the movement, they understood that all-conscious laboring men and women had to join in a common front. As Parsons explained later, the left-wingers endorsed the eight-hour struggle, "first, because it was a class movement against domination, therefore historical, and evolutionary, and necessary; and secondly, because we did not choose to stand aloof and be misunderstood by our fellow workers." [35]

Once they entered whole-heartedly into the eight-hour movement, the Chicago Social Revolutionaries put real life into the struggle. Though they were ignored by the more conservative labor leaders, the radicals worked day and night for the cause, and the Central Labor Union, in which the members of the I.W.P.A. were active, gave full support to the Eight-Hour Association, the united-front organization which had inaugurated the campaign in Chicago. On the Sunday before May 1, the Central Labor Union organized a huge eight-hour demonstration in which 25,000 workers, representing over 25 unions, took part.[36]

Preparations for the nationwide May Day strike were most successful and aggressive in Chicago, the center of a militant left-wing labor movement. But also in New York, Cincinnati, Baltimore, Milwaukee, Boston, Pittsburgh, St. Louis, and Washington and many other cities, thousands of workers, skilled and unskilled, men and women, Negro and white, native and immigrant, organized and unorganized, were drawn into the struggle for the shorter working day. "There is eight-hour agitation everywhere," *John Swinton's Paper* exulted in mid-April, 1886. By that time almost a quarter of a million industrial workers were involved in the movement, and so powerful was the upsurge that about 30,000 workers had already been granted a nine- or eight-hour day.[37] *

Never before had a popular slogan gripped the hearts of American workers as did the eight-hour call. Newspapers and other spokesmen for the employers wailed that the eight-hour day was "Communism, lurid and rampant," that it would encourage "loafing and gambling, rioting, debauchery, and drunkenness," and would only bring lower wages, more poverty, and social degradation for American workers.[38] † But the workers were not impressed. They smoked "Eight-Hour Tobacco," purchased "Eight-Hour Shoes," and sang the "Eight-Hour Song"[39]:

> *We mean to make things over;*
> *we're tired of toil for naught*
> *But bare enough to live on: never*
> *an hour for thought.*
> *We want to feel the sunshine; we*
> *want to smell the flowers;*
> *We're sure that God has willed it,*
> *and we mean to have eight hours.*
> *We're summoning our forces from*
> *shipyard, shop, and mill:*
> *Eight hours for work, eight hours*
> *for rest, eight hours for what we will!*

THE FIRST MAY DAY

On the fateful first of May itself, workers in every industrial center downed tools in demand for the eight-hour day. About 350,000 workers in 11,562 establishments in the country at large went out on strikes. In Chicago alone, 40,000 workers went on strike, and more than 45,000 were granted a shorter working day without striking. "Every railroad in the city was crippled, all the freight houses were closed and barred, and

* Some unions began with the demand for the nine-hour day and then shifted to the eight-hour day in the course of the struggle. (*See American Federationist,* Vol. II, June, 1895, p. 61.)

† Here and there a labor leader echoed the employers' sentiments. Thus P. M. Arthur, conservative Grand Chief of the Brotherhood of Locomotive Engineers, denounced the eight-hour day because "two hours less work means two hours more loafing about the corners and two hours more for drink." (Charles E. Endicott, *Capital and Labor. Address before the Central Trades Union . . . at Boston,* March 28, 1886, n.d., p. 11.)

most of the industries in Chicago were paralyzed." A Chicago paper reported that "no smoke curled up from the tall chimneys of the factories and mills, and things had assumed a Sabbath-like appearance." The K. of L. meatpacking unions in the city joined the national eight-hour strike, and closed down the stockyards. The packinghouse unions won their strike, gaining an eight-hour day without a pay reduction.[40]

In Detroit, 11,000 workers marched in the eight-hour parade held under the combined auspices of the Detroit Council of Trades and Labor Unions and the K. of L.[41]

"HURRAY FOR SHORTER TIME," was the New York *Sun's* headline over the story on the New York May Day demonstration. It was estimated that there were close to 25,000 marchers in a torchlight procession through Broadway, swinging into Union Square on 17th Street past two stands— a German and English-language one. Over the former stand "the Red Flag flourished." The members of each local union marched behind their own banner, 3,400 bakers, members of Bakers Local No. 1, heading the demonstration, the likes of which had never been seen in New York.[42]

Altogether, it was estimated that 185,000 out of 350,000 workers who struck for the eight-hour day gained their demand on May 1 and the days following. Moreover, the eight-hour agitation was mainly responsible for reducing the daily working time of no less than 200,000 workers from 12 or more to ten and nine hours per day. In many trades in which the daily working hours were 14 or 16, a reduction took place to 12; not a few 12-hour industries were reduced, and scores of ten-hour trades, especially in the building line, were cut down to nine hours. In many places the Saturday half-holiday was adopted; there was an extensive movement for the early closing of stores, and the practice of Sunday labor was on the way out in most industries.[43]

It is true that many of these workers went back to a longer week-day again as a result of the employers' offensive against the labor movement immediately after May First, but Gompers was correct when he stated in 1899 before the industrial commission appointed by Congress: "I have no hesitation in expressing my conviction that the movement of 1886 resulted in a reduction of fully 1 hour's labor of the working people of the United States." [44] In a speech at the A. F. of L. Convention of 1889, a trade unionist declared: "It is popularly believed that the eight hours movement of 1886 was a complete failure. . . . Do you know of any one trade in which the working people are working as many hours today as they did before May 1, 1886? Look even not at the skilled but at the so-called unskilled laborers." [45]

The struggle for the eight-hour day led thousands of workers to affiliate with organizations of labor. It was a mighty organizing weapon.

CHAPTER 7

Haymarket

Terrified by the great power and solidarity of the workers on the first May Day, the Chicago capitalists gathered their forces to crush the labor movement. A huge police contingent, augmented by Pinkertons and special deputies, was ready. The state militia to the number of 1,350 men, was on hand. The "Citizens' Committee" of business men was holding continuous sessions.[1] The newspapers were hurling their heaviest propaganda blasts. The Chicago *Mail* on May 1 denounced Albert Parsons and August Spies as "two dangerous ruffians," who were "fomenting disorder." It concluded on an ominous note: "Mark them for today. Keep them in view. Hold them personally responsible for any trouble that occurs. Make an example of them if trouble occurs."

THE McCORMICK MASSACRE

Trouble occurred on May 3 at the McCormick Harvester factory where 1,400 locked-out workers, members of the L.A. 582, K. of L., were on strike for the eight-hour day and a $2 daily wage, for an end to wage-cutting and the foul piece-work system.

On May 3, 300 scabs, guarded by 350 to 500 police, had been put to work. When the strikers, aided by several hundred striking lumber-shovers, demonstrated against the scabs, the police fired without warning into the unarmed workers. At least four were killed and many wounded.[2]

This barbarous act, by a police force already sufficiently hated for its wanton savagery against labor, aroused wide indignation. Quickly circulars were printed and distributed calling for a meeting in Haymarket Square the very next day—May 4—to protest the brutality of the police.*

* Among the circulars issued was one which came to be known as the "Revenge Circular." August Spies was so incensed at the police brutality that he wrote a

HAYMARKET SQUARE

Attacks upon gatherings of strikers continued throughout the morning and afternoon of May 4. But when it was reported that Mayor Carter H. Harrison had given permission for the mass meeting that evening in Haymarket Square, workers began to assemble as early as 7:30. Within an hour, 3,000 persons, men, women, and children, had gathered at one end of the square. Spies, Parsons, and Samuel Fielden, in that order, addressed the crowd, condemning the police, warning against violence, and urging firmness and organization in continuing the strike for the eight-hour day. With Parsons were his wife and two children.

Mayor Harrison attended the meeting from its opening, listening to all three speakers, and he testified later that the meeting and the speeches were orderly. Toward ten o'clock, a threatening rainstorm began to disperse the gathering. Spies and Parsons had already left. Mayor Harrison, believing the meeting was over, left shortly after 10 o'clock, and called in at the Desplaines Street police station, a half-a-block distance from the Haymarket Square, to report that there had been no trouble, and, according to one account, ordered that the police should be "released for their ordinary duties."

When the mayor departed, Fielden was on the point of winding up his speech, and two-thirds of the crowd had left to go home. The mass meeting was within a few minutes of its end when the police appeared. Armed and marching in military fashion, 180 strong, they came on the scene a few minutes after the mayor was out of sight, under the command of Captain John Bonfield, hated throughout the city for his extreme brutality. Captain Ward, on Bonfield's order, commanded the dwindling crowd to "disperse." Fielden cried out that it was a peaceable meeting. As though by a signal a bomb was thrown toward the police, and its explosion killed one policeman instantly, wounded five others so severely that they died later, and inflicted less serious wounds on some half hundred more.

The police immediately opened fire on the crowd, chasing, clubbing and shooting down workers. Several were killed (how many is unknown) and at least 200 were wounded.[3]

handbill in the office of the *Arbeiter-Zeitung,* the paper he edited, in which he called upon the workers to "rise in your might ... and destroy the hideous monster that seeks to destroy you." The circular, printed both in English and German, was headed "Revenge! Workingmen! To Arms!" and closed: "To arms, we call you, to arms!" Spies later disclaimed authorship of the heading and closing, and insisted that they had been inserted without his knowledge. (Henry David, *History of the Haymarket Affair,* New York, 1936, pp. 191-94.)

The next day the capitalist offensive against the working class went forward rapidly. The anarchists had espoused the cause of the eight-hour day. The Haymarket tragedy afforded the capitalists and their hirelings an excellent opportunity to use the cry of anarchism to kill the eight-hour day agitation and weaken the entire labor movement. Newspaper headlines equated "Bomb Throwers" with belief in the eight-hour day and other labor demands.[4]

RED SCARE

Hundreds of workers in Chicago were arrested. Meeting halls, printing offices, even private homes were broken into and searched. "Homes were invaded without a warrant," writes Professor Harvey Wish, "and ransacked for evidence; suspects were beaten and subjected to the 'third degree'; individuals ignorant of the meaning of socialism and anarchism were tortured by the police, sometimes bribed as well, to act as witnesses for the state." [5]

Three years later, in an interview, the Chicago chief of police, Captain Frederick Ebersold, admitted that the police, led by Captain Michael J. Schaack, deliberately set about organizing anarchist societies and planted bombs and ammunition at these organizations. Every day the press headlined the raids on these police-instigated anarchist societies and listed the discoveries—ammunition, dynamite, bombs, shells, underground rifle ranges, bayonets, pistols, etc.[6]

Of the hundreds of workers arrested and taken into custody by the police, eight were finally selected for trial: Albert R. Parsons, August Spies, Samuel J. Fielden, Eugene Schwab, Adolph Fischer, George Engel, Louis Lingg, and Oscar Neebe. These men were most hated by the Chicago employers, not for the fact that they were anarchists, but because it was due to their militant spirit and organizing genius that Chicago was the outstanding labor center in the country and had made the greatest contribution to the struggle for the eight-hour day.

None of the eight was at the Haymarket meeting when the bomb was thrown, except Fielden, who was speaking. But this did not trouble the grand jury which quickly indicted the men for the murder of Mathias J. Degan on May 4 and set the trial for June 21.* The men were all accused of murder, but not of throwing the bomb; they were alleged to be murderers on the grounds that the unknown bomb-thrower was influenced by their speeches.[7]

* Actually, 31 persons were indicted, but several bought immunity by becoming State's witnesses; others were released on bail until the trial of the eight was over. One of the indicted prisoners, Rudolph Schnaubelt, left the country and was never found.

TRAVESTY OF A TRIAL

The trial opened at the criminal court of Cook County, with Joseph E. Gary as Judge, State's Attorney Grinnell as chief prosecutor, and William P. Black, a successful corporation lawyer of liberal beliefs, heading the defense. The jury was composed largely of foremen and superintendents of large factories. Not a single worker sat on the jury. The candidates for the jury were not chosen in the usual way by drawing names from a box. In this case, a special bailiff, nominated by the State's Attorney, was appointed by the court to select the candidates. A Chicago business man, Otis S. Favor, swore under oath that the bailiff had said to him in the presence of witnesses: "I am managing this case, and know what I am about. These fellows are going to be hanged as certain as death. I am calling such men as the defendants will have to challenge peremptorily and waste their time and challenges. Then they will have to take such men as the prosecution wants." [8]

Exactly what the bailiff predicted happened. After the defense had exhausted all its peremptory challenges, a jury, openly prejudiced against the defendants, was selected.[9]

Seven of the "suspects" were present when the trial got under way. The missing one was Albert R. Parsons, who had baffled a police search for six weeks, and, thoroughly disguised, was perfectly safe in a hideout removed from Chicago. Just as the preliminary examination of candidates for the jury began, Parsons walked into the courthouse and informed Judge Gary: "I present myself for trial with my comrades, your Honor." [10]

The trial was a travesty of justice. The jury was stacked. The witnesses for the State were the police and their tools who were paid for testifying. Years afterward, in attempting to defend himself against indignant critics, Judge Gary unwittingly condemned his own conduct of the trial in the words—"if I had a little *strained the law*. . . . I was to be commended for so doing."[11]

Actually, Judge Gary's confession was a masterpiece of understatement. The judge permitted men to serve on the jury who frankly admitted that they believed the defendants to be guilty and that this belief would strongly influence their verdict. He even ignored the fact that one juryman was actually a relative of one of the victims of the bomb. He forced the eight men to be tried together. He confined counsel for the defense, in cross-examining the state's witnesses, to the specific points touched on by the state, but in the cross-examination of the defendant's witnesses, he permitted the state's attorney to go into all manner of subjects foreign to the issues on which the witnesses were examined. He allowed the prosecution to drag in any and all questions associated with anarchism, but denied the defense the right to clarify the defendant's attitude towards the use of force and violence.* He permitted the police to display all types of dynamite and bombs, in order to strike terror among the jurymen, and his insulting remarks about the defendants made throughout the trial within hearing of the jury, revealed his deep hatred of these men.[12]

That the eight men were being condemned for their ideas and not for any deeds was made clear from the outset. The trial closed as it had opened on this note, as witness the final words of State's Attorney Grinnell's summation speech to the jury: "Law is on trial. Anarchy is on trial. These men have been selected, picked out by the grand jury and indicted because they were leaders. They are no more guilty than the thousands who follow them. Gentlemen of the jury; convict these men, make examples of them, hang them and you save our institutions, our society." [13]

Parsons himself summed up the nature of the frame-up in a notebook, hitherto unpublished, which he kept during the trial. "According to the instructions of the court to the jury they were to consider labor agitation in organizing labor in defense of its rights as murder." Parsons added: "These men had an interest in finding us guilty. We the defendants held opinions that the working class were being wronged by the monopolies, capitalists, etc. The employers of labor held the opinion that laborers had no right to such an opinion." [14]

As was predicted by the press and even by the defendants themselves, who were under no illusions as to the class character of the trial,† the jury on August 20, brought in a verdict of guilty. Seven of the defendants were sentenced to be hanged, and the eighth, Oscar Neebe, was sentenced to 15 years imprisonment.

After a motion by the defense for a new trial was denied by Judge Gary, the convicted men were called upon to speak before sentence was pronounced. Their speeches, lasting three days, are imperishable classics of proletarian literature, and reveal these high-minded and courageous men as true heroes of the working class.

"Your Honor," began Spies who spoke first. "In addressing this court I speak as the representative of one class to the representative of an-

---

* "It can & must be shown to the jury that all this arming was for resistance not for attack," Parsons wrote in his notebook. (Manuscript notebook of Albert R. Parsons, containing notes taken during the trial, *WSHS*.)

† "As well put the fugitive slave before his master for endeavoring to gain his liberty," Parsons wrote in his notebook. "These men [the jurymen] were not & could not be impartial & they confessed they were not. They believed us to be guilty when the trial began & not being able to establish our innocence beyond the shadow of a doubt, this class jury were only too eager to convict & punish us. The interests of their class so found." (WSHS.)

other. . . ." He spoke for hours, refuting the charges of murder and conspiracy, charging the state with deliberately plotting to use the Haymarket tragedy as an excuse to assassinate the leaders of the working class, accusing the employers of using the same episode to destroy the eight-hour movement by murdering those whom the workers looked up to as their leaders. But he was confident that this conspiracy would not succeed: "If you think that by hanging us you can stamp out the labor movement . . . the movement from which the downtrodden millions, the millions who toil in want and misery—expect salvation—if this is your opinion, then hang us! Here you will tread upon a spark, but there and there, behind you and in front of you, and everywhere, flames blaze up. It is a subterranean fire. You cannot put it out." [15]

WHO THREW THE BOMB?

In his speech, Parsons indicted the press of his day, quoting from editorials in the Chicago *Tribune, Frank Leslie's Illustrated Newspaper,* and the New York *Herald,* to prove that these papers, as spokesmen for the employers, advocated open violence against the working class—"the killing of people, when they protested against wrong and oppression." He charged the employers with the bomb-throwing crime, which he said had been committed for the purpose of discrediting the eight-hour movement.[16]

No one knows even to this day who threw the bomb. But there is much evidence to bear out Parson's statement. The suspicious conduct of the police after Mayor Harrison's departure, the total lack of motive for the dispersal order, the entire setting and background of the deed, indicate that an *agent provocateur,* working for the police, was involved in the crime. The Avelings, who visited the United States during the trial, reported in the English workers' organ, *Today,* that among the workers of Chicago "the feeling was very general that it [the bomb] was thrown by an agent of the police." [17]

Even more conclusive is the testimony of Chief of Police Ebersold concerning Captain Schaack, one of Captain Bonfield's closest co-workers on the police force, given in an interview with the Chicago *Daily News* May 10, 1889: "After we got the anarchist societies broken up, Schaack wanted to send out men to organize new societies right away." This incontrovertible testimony concerning a member of the police force reveals how the police officials acted as provocateurs. Certainly, men like Bonfield and Schaack, in collaboration with the Pinkertons, were fully capable of plotting the throwing of a bomb.* When one realizes that Schaack, as is

---

* "The police officials in Chicago were at this time quite equal to such a thing," writes Samuel Yellen (*American Labor Struggles,* New York, 1936, p. 56.)

now known, was being paid extra money by Chicago employers to watch the anarchists, the meaning of Parson's charge becomes quite clear.

There is much evidence to show that Rudolph Schnaubelt, an anarchist, was the *agent provocateur* used by the police. Schnaubelt was twice arrested and both times released, and was permitted by the police to make his escape to the Mexican border. In short, at a time when the police were rounding up and imprisoning all anarchists and their sympathizers, Schneubelt was released twice and allowed to make his escape without the slightest interference by the police officials in Chicago. On August 6, 1900, the Chicago *Daily Intelligencer,* in a careful review of the Haymarket affair, pointed out that all evidence "proved that Rudolph Schnaubelt was the miscreant who threw the bomb." Hence it was significant that of all the men arrested during the period of wholesale arrests, Schnaubelt was the only one "immediately turned loose." It was also significant, the paper concluded, that "he was frequently heard from in foreign countries years later, but was never arrested."

Seven years after the trial, Judge Gary, reviewing the case, admitted that Schnaubelt was probably the person who had thrown the bomb. He added: "But whether Schnaubelt or some other person threw the bomb, is not an important question." [18]

In this instance, Judge Gary spoke the truth. The actual throwing of the bomb was not important to the employers and their henchmen. What was important was that the Haymarket affair provided a good excuse for the destruction of the movement for the eight-hour day and the labor movement as a whole. A partner in a large Chicago clothing firm was reported to have said: "No, I don't consider these people to have been found guilty of any offense, *but they must be hanged. . . .* I'm not afraid of anarchy; oh, no, it's the utopian scheme of a few a *very* few philanthropic cranks, who are amiable withal, but I do consider that the *labor movement must be crushed*! The Knights of Labor will never dare to create discontent again if these men are hanged." [19]

THE DEFENSE MOVEMENT

The employers had spoken—"*they must be hanged!*" The higher courts hastened to comply. The defense appealed, and the State Supreme Court, unable to ignore completely the trial's open irregularities, pointed out to the lower court what these "irregularities" were and how to correct them, and then confirmed the verdict. In ruling on the appeal, the Illinois Supreme Court defined Socialist principles as the advocacy of theft of property, hence a juror was entitled to prejudice against Socialists! [20]

The defense tried to appeal the case to the United States Supreme Court, but that august tribunal, as it did later in many cases involving frame-ups of Negro and white workers, refused to review it. In this final appeal for a new trial, the Honorable Leonard Sweet, the old law associate of Abraham Lincoln, joined the defense attorneys, but even this distinguished sponsorship made no impression upon the Supreme Court.

Meanwhile, the defense efforts in behalf of the eight men swelled into an international movement. Immediately after the verdict was announced, the movement to save the condemned men flamed into life. Many who were at first blinded by hysteria to the real significance of this classic anti-labor frame-up had had their eyes opened during the trial. Some workers had been intimidated by the reign of terror; but many were stirred to resistance, and as the trial proceeded, more and more sections of the labor movement came to understand that the real target of the employers and their henchmen was not the anarchists but the organized strength of the working class.

After the Supreme Court had refused to review the case, the defense efforts in behalf of the eight men gathered momentum. The United Trades of New York passed a resolution urging organized labor all over the country to hold protest mass meetings. The powerful Central Labor Union of New York endorsed a similar appeal, signed by 14 well-known labor leaders, including Samuel Gompers and Frank Ferrell, Negro leader of the Knights. The document urged that a great public demonstration be held simultaneously throughout the country by all representative labor organizations to "save our country from the disgrace of an act that can be considered in no other light than as a judicial murder, prompted by the basest and most un-American motives. . . ." [21] In answer to this appeal, mass meetings were held in cities all over the country.*

The A. F. of L. at its convention passed a resolution pleading for clemency.[22] "In the interests of the cause of labor and the peaceful methods of improving the condition and achieving the final emancipation of labor," wrote Gompers, the A. F. of L. president, "I am opposed to the execution. It would be a blot on the escutcheon of our country." [23] In his autobiography, written in the 1920's, Gompers advanced the following significant reason to explain his action in behalf of the framed Haymarket martyrs: "Labor must do its best to maintain justice for the radicals or find itself denied the rights of free men." [24]

The victims of Haymarket were supported, morally and financially, by many locals of the K. of L. However, the opportunist national leadership of the Order took no part in the defense movement, and actually threatened to suspend or even expel a district assembly taking action. Resolutions expressing sympathy for the Haymarket victims and demanding action in their behalf poured into the Richmond Convention in 1886. But

* Peter J. McGuire, James E. Quinn, and Samuel Gompers were among the speakers at a mass meeting in New York City.

they were rejected by the conservative leadership. Powderly even said that rather than a vote of sympathy, the Order owed the condemned men "a debt of hatred. . . ." [25]

Among the prominent Americans who protested against the verdict and petitioned for a commutation of the sentences were William Dean Howells, Robert G. Ingersoll, Daniel De Leon, Lyman Trumbull, who had been a judge of the Illinois Supreme Court and 18 years a U. S. Senator, Henry Demarest Lloyd, the noted liberal writer, Stephen S. Gregory, later president of the American Bar Association, Murray F. Taley, then chief justice of the Illinois Circuit Court, Lyman Gage, later Secretary of the Treasury, John Brown, son of the great emancipator, and Moncure D. Conway, the biographer of Thomas Paine. Howells, a distinguished novelist and editor and dean of American letters, summed up the feelings of the entire group when he called the frame-up "the greatest wrong that ever threatened our fame as a nation." [26]

The defense movement transcended national boundaries. Eleanor and Edward Marx Aveling called upon the British workers to "strengthen the hands of their American brethren by holding meetings and passing resolutions," and at scores of mass meetings English workingmen and women voted in favor of "a protest against the murder of the labor leaders." [27]

On October 14, 1887, Southplace Institute in London was crowded to the doors, and beyond, by an enthusiastic audience which unanimously resolved:

"That the English workers in this meeting desire earnestly to urge on their fellow workers in America the great danger to Public Liberty that arises from suffering citizens to be punished for resisting attempts to suppress the right of Public Meeting and Free Speech, since a right that the people are punished for enforcing is evidently thereby made no right at all, but a crime.

"That the fate of the seven men now under sentence of death for holding a public meeting in Chicago at which certain policemen were killed for attempting forcibly to disperse the people and silence the speakers, is of deep concern to us as English workers, because their case is the case of our comrades in Ireland to-day, and is likely to be ours tomorrow unless the workers from both sides of the Atlantic declare with one voice that all who interfere with the rights of Public Meeting and Free Speech act unlawfully and at their own peril. . . ." [28]

William Morris and the young George Bernard Shaw were among those who addressed this meeting. The account in *The Commonweal* of October 22, 1887, states: "George Bernard Shaw (Fabian) disclaimed any sympathy with Anarchism or Anarchists, but emphatically supported the view that this was a question alone of freedom of speech and opinion.

The case of these men today, tomorrow might be any of us, of any political sect or party, who made himself obnoxious to the Government of the Day." [29]

A group in the French Chamber of Deputies, on October 29, telegraphed protests to the Governor of Illinois, as did the Municipal Council of Paris and the Council of the Department of the Seine. The petition called the impending executions a "political crime" which would be an "everlasting mark of infamy upon republicanism." [30]

Meetings of workers were held in France, Holland, Russia, Italy, and Spain, and many contributed out of their scanty wages for the Haymarket defense fund.[31]

As the execution date, November 11, 1887, drew near, a flood of resolutions, letters, and memorials poured in upon Governor Oglesby urging a reprieve. They came from workers, liberal intellectuals, trade unions and radical societies all over the world.[32] But these voices of hundreds of thousands of workers and their allies were drowned out by the cry of the employers: *"They must be hanged!"*

Still the huge defense movement did have its effect. Governor Oglesby commuted the sentence of Fielden and Schwab to life imprisonment.

One of the younger defendants, Louis Lingg, committed suicide (or was murdered by police guards). Parsons, Spies, Engel, and Fischer were hanged on November 11, 1887.

The struggle for amnesty for Fielden, Schwab, and Neebe continued, and many thousands from all over the world urged clemency upon Oglesby, and upon his successor, Governor Joseph Fifer. But it was not until John Peter Altgeld, fearless and honest young liberal, became governor of Illinois that a victory was at last won.

On June 26, 1893, Altgeld issued his famous pardon message in which he showed "that the defendants were not proven to be guilty of the crime." In pardoning the imprisoned labor leaders, Altgeld stated bluntly that they were completely innocent and that they and the hanged men had been the victims of packed juries and a biased judge.[33]

Although the capitalists raged at the pardon and the *Chicago Tribune,* the *New York Times* and other newspapers heaped invective on Altgeld's head, the workers and their allies rejoiced. The A. F. of L. convention in December, 1893, praised the pardon message as "an act of justice." The trade unions and Populists distributed 50,000 copies of the pardon message.[34]

A monument to the martyred labor leaders was unveiled June 25, 1893, nearly six years after their judicial murder. But a greater monument to their memory is the fact that the words "Haymarket Martyrs" have become a symbol of May Day.

CHAPTER 8

The Political Upheaval

The eight-hour movement, May Day, and the Haymarket Affair of 1886 were followed by one of the most significant events in American history: the memorable campaigns conducted by an aroused working class which sought through independent political action to stem the reactionary drive of capital and its agents in the government, and to secure the passage of laws which would improve labor's status in society. The labor parties formed in industrial centers throughout the country during the fall campaign of 1886, marked the emergence of what many contemporary observers recognized as "a new force in our politics." [1] It also marked a sharp change in labor's whole approach towards political action.

From November, 1884, to the middle of 1886 the dominant trend in the labor movement was away from political action. The disappointing results of the campaign waged by some labor groups in the presidential election of 1884 were important in shaping this trend.* But primarily it was due to the growing feeling in trade union circles that labor could secure more through strikes and boycotts than through legislation. The case of the New York car conductors and drivers was frequently cited in the labor press to justify this outlook. For several years these workers had failed in their efforts to obtain a shorter working day through legislation. But in January, 1886, they won their demand through unionization and a strike.[2]

---

* Labor forces favoring independent political action, led by John Swinton, rallied behind the third party movement represented by the People's Party (the union of the Anti-Monopoly and National parties) and headed by Benjamin F. Butler, its presidential nominee. Most trade unions, however, refused to endorse Butler, and supported the candidates of the major parties. Butler polled only 18,000 votes in New York State. (See *John Swinton's Paper*, May 18, June 8, July 6, Nov. 9, 16, Dec. 14, 1884; *New York Times*, May 15, 19, July 9-11, 1884; *The Boycotter*, May 31, June 14, 28, 1884.)

Even that staunch advocate of independent political action, *John Swinton's Paper,* reflected the new trend. "It is now apparent to everybody," it declared on March 21, 1886, "that they [the working classes] only need to be aroused, enlightened, and organized to enable them to achieve a hundred desirable objects for which they have appealed in vain to politicians, legislatures, and Congress." Other labor papers echoed the viewpoint that by organization and strikes labor could obtain improvements which it could never hope to secure from capitalist dominated legislatures.

With such an attitude prevailing in labor circles, it is not surprising that the third party movement completely disappeared from the horizon by the spring of 1886.[3] Yet within three months, independent political action underwent a complete rejuvenation and by October, workers in almost every part of the country had organized independent political parties and nominated candidates for office.

THE EMPLOYERS' OFFENSIVE

Immediately after the victories of May 1, 1886, the employers' offensive began in earnest. The Haymarket bombing was followed by a reign of terror against the labor movement. The lockout, the "iron clad" oath, the Pinkerton detectives, the blacklist, and the red-scare were the answer of the employers to the militant labor movement. Employers formed associations * to wrest the eight-hour day from workers who had gained it on and immediately after May First, and "to break up labor organizations."[4] The police and the courts were assigned an important role in the employers' counter-offensive. Strikes were broken largely because of police interference with picketing. Police activity was matched by judicial tyranny. Arrests and imprisonment of strikers and boycotters on the spurious charge of "conspiracy" occurred all over the country.[5]

"New York is now under a reign of terror," declared John Swinton during the employers' offensive. "Corrupt judges and police who are slaves of monopoly now drag citizens to prison by wholesale." Probably the most vicious activity of the police occurred during the Third Avenue street car strike. On June 5, the managers of the line determined to run out a car. A squad of police was on the spot near Fourteenth Street, the most densely inhabited part of the city. The New York *Sun* reported that "there was a crowd of about 10,000 counting the women and children

---

* Among these employers' associations one of the most important was formed by the managers of the railroads which had terminals in Chicago. Most students of labor history place the beginnings of this powerful employers' association anti-labor activities in 1893 and particularly in connection with the Pullman Strike of 1894. The manuscript records of the Association's proceedings in the John Crerar Library in Chicago reveal clearly that the organization's anti-labor activities originated during the 1886 employers' offensive.

blocking up Avenue B and flowing over into Tompkins Square." Into this peaceful crowd, the police suddenly dashed, and began to club right and left under orders of Captain McCullagh. Said the conservative *Sun*: "Men with broken scalps were crawling off in all directions and squabbling children were knocked every way by their daddies who were flying from the clubs." [6]

Police brutality and interference was not restricted to the Third Avenue strike. It was a general phenomenon in New York in the summer and fall of 1886. Police interfered in a private meeting of the K. of L., at which Powderly spoke, and forced its adjournment. On September 18, 1886, Dr. Edward Aveling, Eleanor Marx Aveling and Wilhelm Liebknecht, German Socialist leader, arrived in New York City. On the following day, they were welcomed at a grand reception attended by thousands of workers and intellectuals. The reception was marred by a brutal attack upon the audience by the New York police, and even two of the honored guests were struck by the police. In a letter sent to all New York newspapers, under their signature, Liebknecht and the Avelings wrote: "We have never seen in Europe such wanton interference on the part of the police with the liberty of the subject as we saw today in a country proverbially known as the land of the free." [7]

Numerous arrests were made for picketing and boycotting and for "unlawful assemblages and unlawful Words." In one case, Judge Power warned: "I hold that any man who walks up and down in front of a man's place of business commits a species of assault. I intend to hold such men hereafter on bond to keep the peace."

In two months in New York City, there was a "legal roundup" of some 100 strikers and boycotters under the charge of "conspiracy." Men who distributed circulars advising the boycott of a bakery got ten days. For boycotting Cavanagh, Sandford and Co., 47 tailors were indicted. In the Gray Boycott case, the Secretary of the Bakers' Union, the walking delegate, sandwich men, and circular distributors were indicted for conspiracy. [8]

THE THEISS BOYCOTTER'S CASE

The issue came to a head in the famous Theiss boycotter's case. In March, 1886, the Carl Sahm Club (K. of L. musicians) declared a boycott, after an unsuccessful strike, against the "concert saloon" of George Theiss. The Waiters' Union, which also had a grievance against Theiss, joined the boycott and soon a general boycott was declared by the Central Labor Union. Pickets were arrested, but the boycott continued until Ehret, the brewer and Theiss' backer, fearing the sales of his beer would fall off, persuaded Theiss to reach an agreement with the boycotting committee which included the payment of $1,000 for the expense of the boycott.

Soon Theiss brought suit against the members of the union committee. They were charged with extortion and intimidation. But the District Attorney stated the real issue of the case: ". . . this boycott business must be annihilated and stopped. These men of the Central Labor Union and the other Unions that have shown themselves opposed to the common good are like the Algerine pirates who extorted moneys and tributes without reason. This must be stopped at once."

In his charge to the jury, Judge George C. Barrett held that striking, picketing, and boycotting were lawful, provided that no force, threats, or intimidation were used. But he defined "intimidation" to include the action of pickets in advising passers-by not to patronize the concert saloon, and the issuance and distribution of boycott circulars. Moreover, the $1,000 which Theiss gave the union in the settlement was ruled to be a case of extortion, for the money had been obtained by fear induced by a threat to continue the "unlawful injury" to his property.

The jury, which was composed entirely of employers (the property qualification required a trial juror to own real or personal property worth $250), found all five defendants guilty. They were sentenced to State Prison at hard labor—two for two years and ten months; two for one and one-half years, and one for three years and eight months.

The purpose of this outrageous decision was to paralyze labor's activity. But it had precisely the opposite effect. "The sentence passed on the boycotters," *Der Sozialist,* official organ of the S.L.P. reported, "has poured flaming fire into the hearts of the workingmen in New York, and has driven into the background all differences in labor's camp. It has united the many-voiced choir of the organizations in a single powerful cry of indignation." [9]

Swinton called for a rapid reevaluation of labor's strategy and tactics. The employers' offensive proved that reliance on strikes and boycotts was not enough. To stem the reactionary drive, it was necessary for labor to enter the political arena. On June 13, 1886, he wrote: "One right however remains to the working classes; the right of voting as they please—at least in some states; and if they do not by this means drive from power the parties which are upholding the widespread conspiracy of capitalists against public liberty, we will very soon not have much of it to boast of." [10]

On July 2, 1886, the day Judge Barrett passed sentence on the Theiss boycotters, delegates from the Cigarmakers', Bakers', Bartenders', and Waiters' unions, the Carl Sahm Club, and the Socialist Labor Party met to call a mass meeting to denounce the decision. Three days later, the Central Labor Union endorsed the protest meeting, condemned the trial and sentence, and warned: "That the insidious attempts of the prosecuting officers . . ., of the packed juries and servile judges, to stamp out boycotting will only serve to make it more effective and unrelenting in the future." [11]

At the mass meeting held at Cooper Union, speaker after speaker insisted "on the necessity of organizing labor politically to crush its would-be-oppressors." Boldly the meeting passed resolutions supporting the "Theiss Heroes," and pledging to continue the boycott movement, "undismayed by arbitrary judicial decisions." [12]

FORMATION OF LABOR PARTY IN NEW YORK

On July 11, four days after the Cooper Union meeting, the regular weekly session of the Central Labor Union met. A motion was introduced early in the meeting urging that a committee be appointed to devise a plan to take independent political action in the fall elections. It was greeted with cheers, and, after excited discussion, adopted. A week later, the committee presented a resolution to the Central Labor Union calling for the organization of the wage workers of New York "in one grand political organization" to redeem the city "from the hands of the plunderers." The Central Labor Union adopted the report of the Committee on Political Action and called a conference of every trade and labor organization at Clarendon Hall on August 5.[13]

That day 402 delegates representing 165 labor organizations with a membership of 50,000 met in Clarendon Hall. A motion in favor of independent political action was introduced by Ludwig Jablinowski, a member of the Progressive Cigarmakers' Union and the S.L.P. A long and exciting debate followed; after which the motion in favor of independent political action was carried by a vote of 296 to 40.[14]

Before adjourning to August 19, a committee of 17 on permanent organization was elected. The committee comprised a cross-section of the labor forces in New York, including leading figures in the K. of L., the Federation, and the S.L.P.

At the second Central Labor Union Political Conference held on August 19, the number of delegates increased to 508. The committee on permanent organization suggested a new political party, to be known as the Independent Labor Party of New York and Vicinity.[15]

ROLE OF HENRY GEORGE

The name most constantly mentioned as a possible labor candidate for mayor was Henry George. His international reputation as an author and lecturer was regarded as assuring wide-spread support for the new party.

He was popular with the Irish because he had worked as the correspondent for the *Irish World* in Ireland, and was noted for his pro-Irish sentiments. His book, *Progress and Poverty,* published in 1879, had appealed in a remarkable way to the masses of the American people, and in 1885 Professor Ely wrote that "tens of thousands of laborers have read *Progress and Poverty,* who have never before looked between the two covers of an economic book. . . ." in all he was regarded by many labor leaders as "the greatest of living Americans." [16]

Although the Socialists did not block the move to nominate George as labor's candidate for mayor, they made it clear that they were not in sympathy with his theory that the "single tax" was the solution of all social ills. As Marxists, the S.L.P. members criticized the Henry George single-taxers for ignoring the exploitation of labor by the industrial and financial capitalists. The single-taxers found the root of evil in capitalist society in private ownership of land, while the Socialists opposed private ownership of all means of production, machinery as well as land. "What the Socialists demand," wrote Engels, "implies a total revolution of the whole system of social production; what Henry George demands, leaves the present mode of social production untouched." [17]

In short, the Socialists joined the independent political movement to participate in a struggle of labor against capital and, as the New York *Volkszeitung* put it, accepted George "not on account of his single tax theory, but in spite of it." [18]

The stand of the Socialists was in sharp contrast to the sectarian position taken by the anarchists who declared that it made no difference whether the labor party won or lost the election. "A man who desires to bring about an improvement," declared an anarchist spokesman,, "must proclaim the *overthrow of all existing laws,* and not promise to carry them out as George has done. . . . Only look at the gang who are supporting him: social quacks, K. of L., Trades Unionists, school teachers, priests." [19] The fact that the groups mentioned as supporting George constituted the vast majority of the workers of New York apparently made no impression upon the anarchists.

After a number of visits by the Committee of the Political Conference, Henry George was persuaded to accept the nomination for mayor pending the guarantee that at least 30,000 votes would be cast for him. Although the national organ of the Socialists, *Der Sozialist,* complained that by accepting George's condition, "we are creating a Henry George party and that is not a labor party," the Political Committee sent out 1,000 petitions to the trade and labor organizations and the campaign for 30,000 signatures began in earnest.[20] Nearly a month was spent in this petition drive and by the middle of Septemebr it was completed.

THE CLARENDON HALL CONVENTION

On September 23, the nominating convention was held at Clarendon Hall, attended by 409 delegates from 175 trade and labor organizations representing a membership of 60,000 workers. John Casserly of the United Order of Carpenters nominated Henry George. This was seconded by Frank Ferrell, Negro K. of L. leader, who said: "Our political movement will work a peaceful revolution—a revolution as decisive as that which John Brown preached. It means industrial emancipation and Henry George is the man to lead us to the consummation of our hopes."

James J. Coogan, a furniture merchant, was also nominated, but George received 360 of the 409 votes on the first ballot. No other candidates were nominated, it being "left entirely to the individual voter to cast his vote for any candidate outside of Mr. George." [21]

The convention adopted a resounding statement of social and economic principles known as the Clarendon Hall platform. The document announced boldly that the third party movement aimed "at the abolition of the system which makes such beneficent inventions as the railroad and telegraph a means for the oppression of the people and the aggrandizement of an aristocracy of wealth and power." Specifically, the platform demanded the abolition of property qualification for trial jurors; the ending of the practice of drawing Grand Jurors from one class; the simplification and reform of court procedure so that "the rich shall have no advantage over the poor;" the end of "officious intermeddling of the police with peaceful assemblages"; the enforcement of sanitary inspection of buildings; the abolition of contract labor in public works; the granting of equal pay for equal work without distinction of sex in public employment, and the municipal ownership and operation of the means of transportation. A single tax provision was also included in the platform, calling for the abolition of all taxes on buildings and improvements and the levying of taxes on the land irrespective of improvements "so that those who are now holding land vacant shall be compelled either to build on it themselves or to give up the land to those who will." The platform closed on a stirring note:

"And since in the coming most important municipal election, independent political action affords the only hope of exposing and breaking up the extortion and speculation by which a standing army of professional politicians corrupt the people whom they plunder, we call on all citizens who desire honest government to join us in an effort to secure it, and to show for once that the will of the people may prevail even against the money and organizations of banded spoilsmen." [22]

Apart from the single tax plank, included at George's insistence, the Clarendon Hall platform most clearly expressed the aims of the labor movement. Many workingmen expected that George's victory would bring about an extension of political and industrial democracy, and were confident that by showing its voting strength, labor would force the politicians to grant its just demands. *Der Sozialist* pointed out that the Clarendon Hall platform was "not socialistic," but hastened to add that if this program were "carried out, it would be an advantage for the workers and a heavy blow for capitalism." [23]

THE LABOR PARTY'S CAMPAIGN

For a new political organization, the Labor Party carried on a magnificent campaign. The unbounded enthusiasm of the laborites made 1886 one of the liveliest, if not the liveliest mayoralty campaign in New York history. This enthusiasm was reflected in the new song written for the campaign to the tune of the K. of L.'s famous "Storm the Fort."

> *See the workmen now advancing*
> *George is leading on!*
> *Politicians now are falling*
> *They will soon be gone!*

CHORUS

> *Fierce and long the campaign rages*
> *But our help is near*
> *Onward comes the labor hero*
> *Cheer, ye workmen, cheer!* [24]

Most of the New York trade unions were active in the campaign. Not only did the vast majority of the unions give George their endorsement, but "hundreds of unions of the trades and assemblies of the Knights of Labor" held nightly meetings in which the ordinary transactions were ignored for political business. And this was the regular procedure throughout the campaign even though most of the unions had clauses in their by-laws forbidding the discussion of politics.[25]

Two outstanding national labor leaders supported George: Samuel Gompers, president of the Federation of Trades and Labor Unions, and Terence V. Powderly, General Master Workman of the K. of L. At the very outset of the movement in New York for independent political action, Gompers had attempted to prevent the formation of a labor party by recalling previous failures of labor as an independent force in politics. His argument, however, was brushed aside, Swinton observing: "Let the dead past bury the dead. The world is whirling. Now is on the march.

Time is telling. Things ride mankind. Today is not yesterday and to-morrow will be different from both." [26]

Either Gompers was convinced or, more likely, he was shrewd enough to realize that it would not be wise to buck the swelling tide. At any rate, Gompers became active in the campaign. He headed the city organi-zation of George clubs, and as the person in charge of the speakers' bureau, spoke daily, addressing labor meetings throughout the city, appealing to workers to support "the new party of equal rights, social reform, true republicanism and universal democracy." [27]

Powderly held back from participating in the campaign until the very eve of the election. Meanwhile, he was subjected to increasing pressure from members of the Knights to endorse George publicly. On October 7, a Knight wrote to Powderly from New York City: "This Henry George movement in New York would were you here be a revelation to you. All the discord has ceased and as one man all are working shoulder to shoulder. Not only can George be elected but the influence for good cannot in my judgment be measured. . . . I know you are very busy but I think there is no more important work that you can do in the little time that it will take than the writing of this letter (publicly endors-ing George)." [28]

Unable to withstand this type of pressure, Powderly came out for George on October 30. Although they spoke together at the largest meeting ever held at Cooper Institute, there were many workers who felt that Powderly had injured the third party campaign by withholding his endorsement until the very end. All in all, his conduct in the campaign was, as Frederick Engels correctly characterized it, "sheer trickery." [29]

No treatment of George's supporters among the working class is com-plete without referring to the immigrant workers. The foreign-born were assisted to become citizens by the naturalization bureau established by the labor party. Of the 9,000 people naturalized in New York as of Sep-tember 1, it was estimated that seven-eighths of them were George supporters. Over one-half of the new citizens were Germans who gave the third party powerful support; indeed, about one-fifth of the signers of the George petition were German-Americans, many of them So-cialists. [30]

Many of the Irish-Americans rallied to George's support. The Irish-American Independent Democrats endorsed George, and the *Irish World* supported the labor party candidate. At the beginning of the campaign, it was reported that 40 of the 61 parish priests of the Catholic Church in New York supported George. They were led by Father Edward McGlynn, pastor of the St. Stephens Church. [31]

George made a special appeal to the Negro people, and at least four campaign clubs, composed of Negroes, were organized. The Rossmore

Association, a K. of L. assembly of Negro waiters, officially endorsed the labor party candidate. Several Henry George campaign clubs were organized by the Negro people, and the New York *Freeman,* a leading Negro journal, reported that "colored men do not hesitate to say that Henry George's party is the party of the colored man." Commenting on this report, another Negro journal observed: "The poor man's interests and the colored man's interests are identical. That must be apparent to the most prejudiced. Let us vote together." [32]

Jewish workers were especially active in the campaign, and the Jewish Socialists were in the thick of the political upheaval. The New York *Yidishe Volkszeitung,* organ of the Jewish Workers' Verein, carried the picture of Henry George under the headline, "Our Future Mayor." The Socialist weekly featured the slogan, "Jewish immigrants become citizens," urging all "who are already five years in the country" to take out their citizenship papers to enable them to fight, in common with all other workers, for their freedom." [33]

As the campaign developed, many people broke old party lines to support George. Indeed, even old-line politicians, amazed at George's increasing popularity among workers and professionals, supported the labor party condidate.[34]

Thus the third party was more than a single movement. It represented mainly the organized workers who wanted social reform, but it also represented middle class people who wanted good government, and it attracted politicians who sought individual betterment. The intrusion of this last group alarmed some of the labor party leaders, and led Swinton to issue the following warning: "The time is short but it is long enough to keep such creatures from mischief. After election it will be too late to find them out." [35]

Although the campaign of 1886 was not completely in the hands of the workingmen, they represented, for the first time in American history, the dominant group in the leadership of the third party movement. John McMacklin of the Operative Painters was chairman of the Executive Committee of the Political Conference; the Secretary of the Committee was George Block, the founder and Secretary of the National Bakers' Union, and the founder and, for a long time, corresponding secretary of the Central Labor Union. Other members of the committee occupied similar important positions in the trade unions.[36]

There were many other trade unionists who were active in the campaign even though they were not members of the Executive Committee. Only a small fraction of these labor leaders had had any previous experience in American politics. Though inexperienced, they brought a new and fresh spirit to the American political scene and the organization they set up behind George was the envy of the older politicians. Within two days after the nomination of George, assembly district organizations were formed in five districts. By October 3, a little over a week after George's nomination, the party had clubs in 22 of the 24 assembly districts with over 7,750 members. On October 10, the membership had increased to 10,000, and six days later it was almost 15,000. Three types of Henry George campaign clubs were formed: 7 trade union legions (tobacco workers, printers, building trades, longshoremen, butchers, clerks, and salesmen), 30 national campaign clubs (3 Italian, 4 Negro, 1 French, 7 Bohemian, 6 German, 9 Jewish), and numerous assembly districts and trade union campaign clubs.[37]

Campaign funds for the labor party were raised by assessments of 25 cents per capita upon members of each union, and by contributions from unions, individual workers, and sympathizers among professional and business people. Scores of labor unions emptied their slender treasuries into the campaign funds, sending from $25 to $100 each. Money was collected by "passing the hat" at street meetings and in halls, an innovation for a political party. Moreover, unions and workers from coast to coast sent letters of congratulations to George with small contributions enclosed. From Ontario, Canada, District Assembly 7814 of the K. of L. sent $25.[38]

Despite these contributions, the labor party did not have sufficient funds. "Our only difficulty is the shortness of money," George wrote on October 8. It was a serious difficulty since it became clear early in the campaign that money would "flow like water" to beat George.[39] Big business was thoroughly alarmed by the strength of the new party and it quickly marshalled its forces and allies to defeat the workers' candidate.

RED SCARE

When the Democrats split over the nomination of a candidate, the business interests forced Tammany to agree to the nomination of Abram S. Hewitt, a large iron manufacturer and son-in-law of Peter Cooper, to meet the need for "a representative of the conservative interests" who would be acceptable to both factions. At a convention presided over by Elihu Root, the corporation lawyer, Theodore Roosevelt, then a New York Assemblyman, was nominated by Chauncey M. Depew, a railroad magnate, as the Republican candidate for Mayor.[40]

In his letter accepting the Democratic nomination, Hewitt raised the issue most prominently featured by both old parties against the labor party—red-baiting. "A new issue has suddenly sprung upon the community," he wrote. "An attempt has been made to organize one class of the citizens against all other classes. . . ." He went on to charge that the labor party embodied "the ideas of Anarchists, Nihilists, Communists, So cialists. . . ." "The demon of discord, hate, anarchy, and the enemy of all mankind threatens," Hewitt cried at a mass meeting, "and the anarchists are rearing their heads." [41]

The commercial press became more and more hysterical as the campaign advanced. On October 5, a cartoon was published in the *Daily Illustrated Graphic,* entitled, "The Pirate Ship—Will the Socialists Capture the City Government?" On board the pirate ship which is approaching New York City are Henry George and his clergymen, but hidden behind them are men with beards and gruesome faces, armed with swords, bombs, rifles and cannon, whose names are "anarchist," "socialist," "striker," "boycotter," and "delegate.' The newspapers charged that George had really been nominated by the Socialists and that the Clarendon Hall convention merely endorsed the Socialist candidate.[42]

To the credit of the labor party, instead of retreating from the red-baiting issue, it took "the bull by the horns." James Casserly, the Treasurer of the Central Labor Union, gave the answer of his powerful organization: "We are here tonight to hurl back the foul slander that none but Anarchists, Communists, and Socialists are supporting Henry George for Mayor. We are trade unionists and Americans, and our organization holds a charter from the State. If it is Socialism to see our wives and children properly housed and clothed, and to strive for better conditions, then we are Socialists. If it is Socialism to elect Henry George on November 2, then we are Socialists." [43]

Having failed to break the ranks of the labor party through lies, slanders and red-scares, the Democrats, realizing the need to claim labor support, hired W. A. Carsey, a "professional labor leader," who formed labor clubs and trade unions to order. Carsey organized a fake Independent Labor Party which issued an address to the workers to oppose George, the "social revolutionists" and the "anarchists from Europe," and to stand by the Democratic party, "champion of the laboring classes." [44]

When this device failed,* the anti-labor party forces adopted coercive tactics. At the beginning of the campaign, many, if not a majority, of the Catholic priests supported George. But as the campaign advanced, "at the suggestion" of the "higher Catholic powers," all Catholic priests except Father McGlynn withdrew from active participation in behalf of the labor party candidate.[45]

When he was warned by Archbishop Corrigan not to speak for George, Father McGlynn wrote: "Most Reverend and Dear Archbishop: I, in view of my rights and duties as a citizen, which were not surrendered

---

* Only one real trade union leader, the very conservative P. M. Arthur, Grand Chief Engineer of the Brotherhood of Locomotive Engineers, spoke against George. (New York *Commercial Advertiser,* Oct. 24, 1886.)

when I became a priest, am determined to do what I can to support Mr. George; and I am also stimulated by love for the poor and oppressed laboring classes, which seems to be particularly consonant with the charitable and philanthropic character of the priesthood, by virtue of which it has gained everywhere its greatest triumphs." [46]

McGlynn was temporarily suspended from his priestly functions for refusing to obey his superior and to desist from aiding the labor party candidate.

Other forms of coercion were used. Several city employees were discharged because they supported George. The street car companies warned their drivers and conductors of the necessity of defeating the labor party ticket if they wanted to be sure of their jobs. A business man inserted a note in his workers' pay-envelopes warning that if "Mr. George and the Socialists" were victorious "a great part of the wealth of New York would vanish into thin air, business would be suspended and workmen would be unemployed." [47]

THE ELECTION RESULTS

The outpouring of workers at the October 30 parade, the culmination of the George campaign, proved that the terror had not weakened the labor party. Beginning at 8:10 in the evening, over 20,000 people marched for one hour and forty minutes in a drenching rain to Union Square. "The heavy rain storm no doubt interfered with it seriously," the *World* commented, "but that from 20,000 to 25,000 men should turn out to march on such a night shows a power and a spirit in the movement that cannot be winked out of sight." [48]

Power and spirit the new party had in full measure. But this could not overcome the effect of lack of experience in politics and the widespread bribery by the old machines. Nevertheless, when the election returns were in, the workingmen of New York learned that they piled up 68,110 votes for George or 31 percent of the total votes cast. The winner, Abram S. Hewitt, had failed to receive a majority, but obtained 90,552 or 41.4 percent of the total. Roosevelt ran third with 60,435 votes or 27.6 percent of the total.

The belief that George had been "grossly counted out" was widespread, and many agreed with the labor party candidate when he said after it became known that Hewitt had won: "Under a fair vote of the people of New York I would be tonight elected Mayor of New York. . . ." Two months later, George wrote to a friend: "They were determined that I should not be elected and nothing was spared to beat me; on a square vote I would undoubtedly have been elected." [49]

The labor press hailed the result of the election as a great victory. The *Irish World* congratulated the workers upon having made a wonderful beginning of a great movement. It predicted that in time to come, labor's first fight would become as famous as Bunker Hill. "The new Political Forces," exclaimed John Swinton, "largely made up of raw recruits, struck a blow truly astounding under the circumstances. They were confronted by the huge machines of both parties—by the monopolies that shadow the city—by Wall Street and all that the term implies, by the press that enters into every mind, by the City, State and National Government. . . . The campaign was by all odds the most formidable demonstration yet made by the forces of organized labor in the United States." [50]

The commercial press viewed the huge labor vote with consternation. But the New York *World* observed soberly: "The deep-voiced protest conveyed in the 67,000 votes for Henry George against the combined power of both political parties, of Wall Street and the business interests, and of the public press should be a warning to the community to heed the demands of Labor so far as they are just and reasonable—and that is much further than the majority of citizens have thus far been willing to admit. . . ." [51]

It was Frederick Engels, however, who best recognized the significance of the campaign. Closely following the events in the United States, he wrote to F. A. Sorge three weeks after the election:

"The Henry George boom has of course brought to light a colossal mass of fraud, and I am glad I was not there. But in spite of it all it was an epoch-making day. . . . The first great step of importance for every country newly entering into the movement is always the constitution of the workers as an independent political party, no matter how, so long as it is a distinct workers' party. And this step has been taken, much more rapidly than we had a right to expect, and that is the main thing. That the first program of this party is still confused and extremely deficient, that it has raised the banner of Henry George, these are unavoidable evils but also merely transitory ones. The masses must have time and opportunity to develop, and they can have the opportunity only when they have a movement of their own—no matter in what form so long as it is *their own movement*—in which they are driven further by their own mistakes and learn through their mistakes." [52]

LABOR PARTIES IN OTHER COMMUNITIES

Among the most significant effects of the New York mayoralty campaign was the stimulation of labor to independent political action throughout the entire nation.* The Central Labor Union's announcement that it intended to support Henry George on a labor party ticket aroused labor groups elsewhere to nominate independent labor candidates. From the St. Louis labor movement, the Clarendon Hall Convention which nominated George received the following telegram: "Organized working-men of the West congratulate you on your first independent movement. Your success is ours. Henry George and Labor will be the battle cry for all the enslaved toilers from the Atlantic to the Pacific." [53]

A wave of independent political action swept the entire labor movement. Labor candidates were run for Congressional positions in Maine, Connecticut, New York, New Jersey, Pennsylvania, Ohio, Kentucky, Michigan, Illinois, Wisconsin, Missouri, Arkansas, Kansas, and Washington; for positions in the state legislature in Maine, Connecticut, New York, New Jersey, Pennsylvania, Georgia, Tennessee, Indiana, Michigan, Wisconsin, and Colorado. State labor tickets were run in Illinois, Connecticut, and Wisconsin, and municipal tickets in Rutland, Vermont; Lynn and Boston, Massachusetts; South Norwalk and Naugatuck, Connecticut; Newark, New Jersey; New York City; Baltimore, Maryland; Chattanooga, Tennessee; Key West, Florida; Richmond, Virginia; Bradford, Pennsylvania; Eureka and San Francisco, California; Chicago and Springfield, Illinois; Indianapolis, Indiana; St. Louis, Missouri; Milwaukee, Wisconsin; and Des Moines, Iowa. Most of these labor party platforms were similar to the one adopted in New York with one important exception: outside of New York, few of the labor parties showed much interest in George's doctrines, and the "single tax" was not included in their demands.

The results astounded the old line politicians. The laborites of Chicago won 25,000 out of a total of 92,000 votes, and elected a state senator and seven members of the lower house. The Labor Party candidate for Congress narrowly missed election by only 64 votes. The People's Party of Milwaukee carried the county with 13,000 votes, and elected the mayor of the City, a state senator, six assemblymen, and one Congressman. The K. of L. in Leadville, Colorado, elected a state senator and three assemblymen. An assemblyman was elected in Newark, New Jersey. In the Sixth Congressional District of Virginia, a K. of L. candidate was elected. In Fort Worth, Texas, and Eaton, Ohio, most of the labor candidates were elected, with the Knights playing the outstanding role. Victories by labor

* This effect was international in its impact. "In Europe the effect of the American elections in November was tremendous," wrote Engels on November 29, 1886. "The very fact that the movement is so sharply accentuated as a labor movement and has sprung up so suddenly and forcefully has stunned the people completely." (Marx and Engels, *Letters to Americans,* p. 164.)

were also recorded in Lynn, Massachusetts; Nagatuck and South Norwalk, Connecticut; Key West, Florida; and Richmond, Virginia. Moreover, in many areas, the Democrats and Republicans were forced to run pro-labor candidates, and the two old parties were forced in other communities to combine or merge for the election to defeat the unprecedented labor bid for political power.[54]

POLITICAL ACTION IN CHICAGO

Next to the campaign in New York City, the battle in Chicago aroused the greatest interest. While the Haymarket Affair, as we have seen, was used to unleash a reign of terror and intimidation against the labor movement in Chicago, it also produced a unity within it that was unprecedented. Conservative, radical, and "pure and simple" trade unionists all joined in a huge protest movement which was expressed especially in the political arena.

Preliminaries for the independent political movement having been thrashed out during the early summer, a provisional committee called a conference on August 21, 1886. Approximately 51 delegates representing 47 trade and labor organizations, 41 K. of L. assemblies and an organization called the People's Party Club, responded to the call and formed a "federation for independent political action." At a later meeting on September 23, the federation took on the name "United Labor Party," and at the same session purged all delegates who were not distinctly representatives of labor organizations in an effort to keep out "reformers" and "old party adherents." [55]

On September 27, the United Labor Party reconvened and nominated a state and county ticket with the greatest emphasis on positions in the state legislature. One of the candidates nominated for the state senate was William Bruce, a Negro barber active in the organization of Negro barbers and waiters into the Knights. "A man of unusual intelligence," commented the Chicago journal of the Order, "he is eminently qualified to discharge faithfully the trust to be placed in him this fall, as a representative of an abused people in the state senate." [56] *

The demands of the United Labor Party included planks calling for the defeat of the "power of aggregated wealth," for an eight-hour day, government ownership of all means of communication, anti-contract labor laws, a national monetary system, tax reform, forfeiture of unearned land grants, reservation of public lands to actual settlers, abolition of private police, weekly wage payments, and employers' liability laws.[57]

The success of the campaign was second only to the mark set by the

---

* Bruce was not elected but he polled 28,000 out of the 92,000 votes cast.

labor party in New York. The United Labor Party's candidate for county treasurer, Frank Stauber, polled the surprising vote of 24,845 out of a total of 92,000 votes cast. The party actually elected one state senator and six members of the lower house of the state legislature. In addition, they placed four judges of the Superior Court in Cook County and one county judge, and came within 64 votes of electing a Congressman.[58]

Labor had good reason to feel jubilant over the results. "No party," a contemporary labor journal commented, "ever polled so large a vote nor made itself so generally felt at so young an age as the United Labor Party."[59]

Even as death approached, the Haymarket martyrs could taste the workers' victory. "The direct result of our persecution," wrote August Spies in his *Autobiography,* taken down in prison, "has been general activity in labor circles, great progress in organization and, particularly, in ideas. . . . The Political Party which cast over 25,000 votes last fall is also one of the many good results of [State Prosecutor Julius S.] Grinnell's revolutionary propaganda."[60]

The amazing sweep of the campaigns of 1886 carried the labor movement on to a new high of enthusiasm for independent political action. In 1885 the Federation of Organized Trades and Labor Unions had defeated a resolution in favor of the formation of an independent labor party which would sponsor trade unionists as candidates. But after the elections of 1886, the Federation unanimously adopted a resolution on "Political Action" which hailed "the remarkable and extraordinary demonstration made by the workingmen of New York, Milwaukee, Chicago, and other places," and concluded: *"Resolved, That the Convention urges a most generous support to the independent political movement of the workingmen."*[61]

It appeared certain that labor, united and with the experience of 1886, would go on to greater victories.

CHAPTER 9

The American Federation of Labor

Anyone studying the tremendous sweep of independent political action in the fall of 1886 would conclude that there was a high degree of unity in labor's ranks. All types of labor groups were united in the political campaigns—conservative, liberal and radical, trade unions affiliated with the Federation and the Knights, local and district assemblies of the Order, and independent labor organizations.

Actually, the labor movement was anything but unified. Precisely at the height of the political campaigns, the leadership of the Knights and of the trade unions were engaged in a conflict that shook the entire labor movement and ended disastrously for hundreds of thousands of workers who had hoped to see their dreams of a unified, powerful labor movement realized. While there was blame on all sides in the conflict, the major share must be placed on the shoulders of the anti-trade union elements in the Knights.* Basically it is the tragic story of how the conservative, vacillating leadership of the Order, together with the small clique of Lassallean Socialists in New York City and the non-working class elements, fought the trade unions to the finish—to the finish, to be exact, of the Knights of Labor, not the trade unions.

ANTI-TRADE UNION ELEMENTS

Complaints against the anti-trade union elements in the Order were registered by the trade unions as early as the spring of 1883. Henry C. Cole, president of the Bricklayers' and Masons' International Union of North America, angrily informed Powderly of a plot engineered by the Home Club in District Assembly 49 to induce local unions to withdraw from the International and affiliate with the Knights directly through "mixed" assemblies. "I do not think it will be to the interest of the K. of

* See pp. 78-80 for a discussion of anti-trade unionism in the Order.

L. to antagonize trades unions," Cole continued. "That in my opinion is not the purpose for which the Order was established. Its aim and purpose should be to promote organization, and any of its members who advocates disorganization of trade unions for the purpose of swelling the members of the Order should be severely dealt with, and such a man is more of a detriment than a help to the cause of honest labor reform." [1]

In the next two years, complaints similar to those voiced by Cole came from the Printers, the Car Drivers, the Plumbers, Shoemakers, Cigar Makers, Jewelers, Furniture Workers, and scores of unions in and out of the Order. The Plumbers complained that after District 49 had compelled them to leave the Order by its anti-union policies, it had called strikes against them. The Furniture Workers complained of numerous, specific instances where representatives of the Knights were trying to win members away from the union and to initiate them directly into the Order on the plea that their dues would be lower. The Printers, Carpenters, Molders and Cigar Makers also complained that the Order was initiating men branded by these unions as unfair, scab labor. [2] In November, 1885, a group of trade unionists asked the K. of L. general executive board:

"Is this what the K. of L. is for—to burst up organizations or locals because they cannot control them?

"Is that what D.A. 49 is for—to defend the bosses' rights?

"Is the K. of L. to organize scabs who have always fought unions? . . .

"We leave the decision of this to you. If you decide that is what the Order is for, we want no more of it." [3]

THE KNIGHTS AND THE CIGAR MAKERS

By 1886 nearly every trade union in America had complaints against the dominant clique which ran the K. of L., but it was the conflict over the cigarmakers which led to a complete break. While one can agree with Professor Ware that "in the accepted story of the conflict between the Knights and the trade unions, too much attention proportionately has been given to the Cigar Makers," yet the story of the Cigar Makers' International Union is typical. For not only did the Home Club control the local situation in New York, where District Assembly 49 came into conflict with the cigar makers; through its control of the general officers, it dictated the attitude adopted toward the trade unions throughout the land. It must also be remembered that the nation-wide publicity devoted to the Order's relations with the Cigar Makers' International Union influenced to a great degree the position of other trade unions.

In the early 'eighties, harmony between the C.M.I.U. and the Order prevailed. In New York and other cities, local unions of the International Union formed assemblies of the Knights "with a view of helping along the general movement of labor reform." The official journal of the Order urged that "if our members cannot get K. of L. cigars, take those made by the C.M.I.U. just as freely, and assist that organization . . . in trying to protect the product of union labor." * In 1883, the *Journal of United Labor* boasted that the C.M.I.U. was having "a great success with their union label, with the aid of the K. of L. We have manufacturers in this city [New York] that have paid the initiation fee for their workmen in the union, simply to be able to get the label, for without it they could not sell their cigars." [4]

As the attitude of the leadership of the Knights became hostile towards the trade unions, the cigar makers and the Order came into conflict. In New York, where the conflict started, the situation was aggravated by the the presence of a rival to the C.M.I.U., the Progressive Cigarmakers' Union, formed by a group of Lassallean Socialists who had split from the International Union.† As soon as the split occurred, the Lassallean Socialists appealed to District Assembly 49 for support for the Progressive Cigarmakers' Union. Even though there already existed in New York a local assembly of cigar makers who were members of the International Union as well as of the Knights of Labor—L.A. 2458—D.A. 49, dominated by the Home Club, chartered the Progressive Cigarmakers' Union as L.A. 2814. [5]

The Progressive Union organized members expelled or suspended from the International Union. By offering a lower scale of wages than the International, the Progressive Union won agreements with manufacturers who heretofore had recognized the C.M.I.U. When members of the International—who were also members of the Knights—went on strike, the Progressive Union offered to fill (and did fill) their places with cigar makers at lower wages. [6]

The conflict between the two cigar makers' unions first came to the attention of the leadership of the Knights in the spring of 1884 as a result of a petition from D.A. 47 of Cleveland, urging Powderly to investigate the conduct of the Progressive Union. "It being the opinion of this Assembly that if all is true that is laid to the 'Progressives' it would hardly be consistent with our obligation as K. of L. to countenance their pro- ceedings," the Cleveland Knights declared. Powderly asked Fred Turner for enlightenment, whereupon the Grand Secretary, himself a member of the Home Club, dismissed the entire issue as "purely a fight of the

---

* In advertising its label which was of a light blue color, the Cigar Makers' Inter- national Union called attention to the fact that it was endorsed "by a large number of Local Assemblies and Districts of the Knights of Labor." (*John Swinton's Paper*, May 16, 1886.)

† For a discussion of the split, see Foner, *op. cit.*, pp. 517-18.

leaders of the two organizations and has no business to be brought into the K. of L. Let the two unions fight it out."[7]

While the two unions were fighting it out (to the glee of the anti-trade union elements in the Order), the employers in the cigar making industry were enjoying a field day. The employers naturally availed themselves of the opportunities afforded by the dissenion in labor's ranks to fix rates and conditions as it pleased them. Referring to the formation of manufacturers' associations in New York, Detroit, Cincinnati, Chicago, and Milwaukee, the New York Times reported early in 1884 that "these bodies are naturally not anxious to see the restoration of complete harmony between the factions of journeymen Cigarmakers."[8]

Matters came to a head in 1886. In January, the Cigar Manufacturers' Association of New York City announced a wage cut of 20 percent in the industry. When the local unions of the International Union (which were also affiliated to the K. of L.) refused to accept the wage cut, 6,000 of its members, men and women, in 19 factories were locked out. In the strike that followed the lockout, the union demanded the restoration of the wage cut and the abolition of the filthy sweatshops in the tenement houses.[9]

After a four-week struggle it appeared as if the strike was won. The manufacturers were making overtures for a conference with the union, and victory seemed to be in the workers' grasp. Just at this crucial point, District Assembly 49 jumped into the breach, and contracted with the manufacturers' association to supply labor at rates lower than those offered by the International on condition that the employers promised to employ none but members of the Progressive Union. The employers readily agreed, and D.A. 49 promptly set about organizing men who had replaced the locked-out cigar workers into the Progressive Union—"thus presenting," L.A. 2458 complained bitterly, "the novelty of the age, Knights of Labor being victimized by Knights of Labor in collusion with grinding, grasping bosses."[10]

The International retaliated with a boycott on all cigars which did not bear its own label, and Adolph Strasser, president of the International Union, sent Powderly a stinging letter demanding that he take steps to stop the strikebreaking activities of D.A. 49 in New York: "I consider the action of your organizers in New York City and of District No. 49 of the Knights of Labor a bold and unscrupulous attack upon recognized trade union principles and as hostile to the Cigar Makers' International Union in particular. Should you fail to denounce the action of your organizers in New York City you will merit the condemnation of the Cigar Makers' International Union and of every national trade union in the country. I now demand action on your part."[11]

The General Executive Board, headed by Fred Turner, came to New York to investigate the charges made against D.A. 49. Since the members of the Board were controlled by the Home Club, the decision was a foregone conclusion. They suspended L.A. 2458 for "violating the laws," exonerated D.A. 49, and flatly refused to grant the request of the C.M.I.U. to be allowed to enter the Order as a national trade assembly.[12]

In an editorial entitled, "A Dangerous Difference," the *Irish World* observed: "The trouble which has broken out between the Cigar Makers' International Union and the Knights of Labor . . . bids fair to result in a *serious rupture which may cause a formidable split in the labor ranks*." [13] This prediction was soon realized. The trade unions were quick to see that at a time when employers' associations were springing up to profit by dissensions within labor's ranks, they could be seriously injured by the practice of the anti-trade union elements in the Order of organizing suspended and expelled members of the unions and negotiating agreements with employers providing for lower wages and poorer working conditions than those already in existence. It was natural that an effort should be made to solidify the trade union ranks for an effective defense against the hostile elements in the leadership of the Knights.

CONFERENCE OF NATIONAL TRADE UNIONS

On April 25, 1886, a call was issued to all national trade unions to meet in Philadelphia on May 18, 1886. The letter stated that the conference was being called to protect the trade unions from the "malicious work of an element who openly boast 'that the trade unions must be destroyed.'" This element, operating through the K. of L. "is doing incalculable mischief by arousing antagonisms and dissensions in the labor movement. . . . Rats, scabs, and unfair employers are backed. . . . Suspended or expelled members of trade unions are welcomed into their ranks." The aim of the conference was to devise a plan for submission to the general officers of the Order for preventing the hostility of those who would destroy trade unions "under cover of the K. of L., and so far as we can learn, without authority from that body." The circular was signed by Peter J. McGuire, General Secretary of the Brotherhood of Carpenters, Adolph Strasser, President of the Cigar Makers' International Union, Josiah Dyer, General Secretary of the Granite Cutters' International Union, P. J. Fitzpatrick, President of the Iron Molders' Union of North America, and W. H. Foster, Secretary of the Federation of Organized Trades and Labor Unions.[14]

Twenty delegates, representing 367,736 organized workers, met in response to the call. All had the same tale to relate, all stressed the necessity for action to be taken against the anti-trade union elements who dominated the Knights. The Order was charged with conspiring with scab bosses; initiation of scabs and defaulters; working below the union scale; infringing upon the hours of labor, and a host of other labor crimes. The delegates agreed that the solution of the entire matter lay in the establishment of the following principles: the distinct and individual autonomy of each trade union; the avoidance of the hazards of dual unionism; the belief that trade unions are best qualified to regulate their own internal affairs. To attain this end, the convention drafted a six-point "treaty" which was to be submitted to the special general assembly of the K. of L. that was to convene at Cleveland on May 24, 1886. Inasmuch as this document was the basis for all future negotiations, it is given in its entirety:

"First, That in any branch of labor having a national or international organization, the K. of L. shall not initiate any person or form any assembly of persons following said organized craft or calling without the consent of the nearest national or international union affected.

"Second, That no person shall be admitted to the K. of L. who works for less than the regular scale of wages fixed by the union of his craft, and none shall be admitted to membership in the K. of L. who have ever been convicted of scabbing, ratting, embezzlement, or any other offense against the union of his trade or calling, until exonerated by the same.

"Third, That the charter of any K. of L. Assembly of any trade having a national or international union, shall be revoked, and the members of the same be requested to join a mixed assembly, or form a local union under the jurisdiction of their respective national or international trade unions.

"Fourth, That any organizer of the K. of L. who endeavors to induce trade unions to disband, or tampers with their growth or privileges, shall have his commission forthwith revoked.

"Fifth, That whenever a strike or lockout of any trade union is in progress, no assembly or district assembly of the K. of L. shall interfere until settled to the satisfaction of the trades unions affected.

"Sixth, That the K. of L. shall not establish or issue any trade mark or label in competition with any trade mark or label now issued, or that may hereafter be issued by any national or international trades union." [15]

At first glance it would appear that if this "treaty" were accepted, the trade unions would have been in sole possession of the field of organization, with the Knights reduced to an educational institution. But this presupposes that the national trade unions were altogether outside of the Order, and that the K. of L. was just a heterogeneous mass of unassimilated workers. Actually, many of the trade unions who made the proposals were part of the Knights, and even if most of the provisions of the "treaty" had been accepted, they could have continued to function and grow within the Order. It would have meant, however, that the trade unions inside the Order would have to be given their own autonomy, and that the leadership of the Knights would not engage in jurisdictional disputes and battles for membership with the national unions that remained outside of the Order.

At the same time, however, the first two points in the "treaty" would have made it impossible for the Knights to organize workers who were kept out of the existing unions by such barriers as high initiation fees and discriminatory clauses against unskilled, foreign-born, Negro and women workers. Referring to these workers, Powderly asked pertinently: "Must we close the door against them in order that the International Union may take them when it gets ready? Are we to understand that every man who is not in the International Union is a scab? If so why do they take in new members at all, for if all men not in unions are scabs the doors of all unions must in all consistency be closed against all men who are not at this time in the organization?" [16]

It is clear that the labor leaders who drew up the "treaty" were insisting on concessions that went counter to the fundamental concept of the Knights—labor solidarity. Nevertheless, the basis for negotiations did exist. As far as the rank-and-file of the labor movement was concerned, they were interested only that a peaceful settlement of the conflict be achieved as quickly as possible, and they were convinced that "there need be no difficulty in establishing an agreement by which the rights claimed by the Trade Unions can be fully maintained in accordance with the principles and policies of the Knights of Labor."

As *The Boycotter* put it, in an editorial calling for peace and unity in the labor movement: "The enemies of organized labor throughout the country are shouting and rubbing their sordid hands in glee over the rumors of an approaching conflict between the K. of L. and the Trades Unions. There is not the slightest occasion for any clash or conflict between the unions and the Knights. All that is necessary is for each to let the internal affairs of the other alone, and both work together in unity, amity and cooperation. Everybody knows that we are all working for a common end, wherefore then, the occasion for conflict?" [17]

THE CLEVELAND GENERAL ASSEMBLY

In letters to Powderly, members of the Order echoed the sentiments of *The Boycotter*. George Blair, head of the Workingmen's Assembly of the State of New York and an important figure in the Order, assured Powderly that the trade unions had justifiable grievances against the anti-trade union Home Club. "I think for the interest of the Order this NY clique

should be shown up [at the special session of the General Assembly]. . . .
I think the rule or ruin men should be relegated where they belong." [18]

Powderly was momentarily impressed by the growing demand for
peace and unity in labor's ranks. He invited the trade union committee
to come to Cleveland to present the "treaty" to the General Assembly.[19]

The trade union committee departed for Cleveland in an optimistic
frame of mind. But the events at the special General Assembly proved
that the Home Club and the other anti-trade union elements were in the
saddle. The trade union committee bearing the "treaty" was not permitted
to present it to the General Assembly. Instead, they were given a hearing
by the General Executive Board, dominated by the Home Club. The
conferences were brief. Powderly refused to enter into lengthy discussions with the leaders of the trade unions. Several weeks later, in answer
to critics, who accused him of torpedoing the negotiations by his curt
behaviour, the Grand Master Workman defended himself with the
comment: "Whenever the officers of the Int. Union came to call on us
one or more of them was so drunk that they could not transact business.
I will speak plainly—Mr. Gompers never came near me only when he
was drunk and *I will not transact business with a drunkard at any time
or place.*" [20]

Two days later, Powderly acknowledged that he may have been mistaken in his estimate of the sobriety of the trade union committee. "There
was not a drunken man present at any of the sessions," he admitted.[21]
At any rate, while Powderly's approach to labor problems may have
endeared him to the Woman's Christian Temperance Union, it only
served to widen the breach with the trade unions.

Following the brief and fruitless conferences between the trade union
committee and the K. of L. leaders, the terms of the trade unions were
laid before the General Assembly. Although fully one-third of the delegates at the extraordinary session were trade unionists, the anti-trade
union Home Club clique and their allies managed to dictate its policy.
The assembly did not act upon the "treaty," claiming that since it was
in special session it had no power to legislate upon the matter (an obvious
subterfuge since one of the reasons for calling the special session was the
relations of the trade unions to the Order). The Home Club did maneuver the assembly into declaring open hostilities against the trade unions
by successfully instructing the General Executive Board to "issue a
command to the Order, instructing our members to support and protect
all labels or trade marks issued by the Knights of Labor in preference to
any other trade mark or label. Any member who refuses to obey shall
be guilty of violation of obligation." [22] Violators of the obligation were
subject to summary expulsion from the Order.

The action taken by the special assembly brought the conflict between the Knights and the trade unions to a head. Powderly feebly extended the olive branch to the national unions, inviting them to enter the Order, and promising that "no interference in the management of your crafts or their affairs will result." [23] But Powderly's subservience to the anti-trade union elements at Cleveland and the patently hostile acts of the special assembly rendered his words meaningless.

The trade unions throughout the country were enraged by the brusque treatment of their representatives at Cleveland. Their journals abounded with fulminations directed against the Order. The Knights were painted as "traitors to the labor cause" and "Knights of Cheap Labor." Amalgamation with the Knights, a real possibility before the Cleveland assembly, was formally rejected by the coal miners, the iron and steel workers, the telegraphers, the plumbers, steam and gas fitters, and the typographical unions. All expressed to a degree the sentiment that it "would be suicidal in the extreme to affiliate with the K. of L.," and that they were "totally opposed to combining with an organization composed of wage-workers, shopkeepers, employers, manufacturers, professional men, and a heterogeneous medley of elements, who have not the same interests as we have." [24]

THE RICHMOND GENERAL ASSEMBLY

The regular General Assembly of the Order in October, 1886, at Richmond, witnessed a crucial struggle over the future policy to be pursued in relation to the trade unions. Here, as in Cleveland, the trade union delegates were a significant group, but the majority of the delegates, newly organized, were attending a convention for the first time. Without parliamentary experience and lacking cohesiveness, the delegates were easily led by the anti-trade union District Assembly 49 of New York. D.A. 49 had 61 delegates of its own, bound by the unit rule. As in Cleveland, Powderly lined up with the Home Club.

Fully 14 resolutions aimed at the formation of trade assemblies and the restoration of peace between the Knights and the trade unions were killed in committee by the Home Club. The "treaty" and grievances which the trade unions had presented were ignored.

Drunk with its power, D.A. 49 dealt irreparable injury to the Order when it submitted and forced through "Document 160." This resolution asked: "That the General Assembly be petitioned to indorse the order issued by D.A. 49, to the effect that cigar makers, packers or who so ever are employed in the cigar trade who are members of the K. of L. and also members of the International Union to withdraw from said Union or leave the Order." [25]

Joseph R. Buchanan of Denver, the leader of the minority delegation which favored friendly relations with the trade unions and one of the wisest men in the entire labor movement, described accurately the significance of the ill-advised action at Richmond: "It was at Richmond that the seal of approval was placed upon the acts of those members who had been bending every energy since the Cleveland special session to bring on open warfare between the Order and the trades unions. . . . The majority by which the resolution was adopted was not, comparatively, large, but it was enough; and the greatest labor organization up to that time known in this country received its mortal wound at Richmond." [26]

The command to choose between the Knights and the Cigar Makers was not rigidly enforced throughout the Order. D.A. 89 of Denver refused "to endorse and carry out the unconstitutional order requiring the expulsion of the International Cigar-Makers' Union who had committed no crime that we were aware of," and D.A. 79 of Minnesota demanded exemption of the Minnesota assemblies from the edict on the ground that dual allegiance had not been causing trouble in the state. Several Detroit assemblies officially condemned the action of the Richmond Assembly, and stated unequivocally that they would not tolerate any spirit of antagonism toward the trade unions.[27]

Regardless of how widely the command of the Richmond Assembly was enforced, it had its telling effect nevertheless. While only the cigar makers had been singled out in the edict, the trade unionists knew that this was but the beginning of an all-out attack. Faced with the immediate prospect of having to choose between membership in their trade unions and the Order, many Knights who were also enrolled on the books of trade unions, preferred to leave the K. of L. It was because it had forced the trade unionists to reach this decision that Buchanan felt that the Richmond Assembly had inflicted a "mortal wound" upon the Order.

THE AMERICAN FEDERATION OF LABOR

Aroused by the attitude of the leadership of the Knights, the trade union committee of five labor leaders (McGuire, Strasser, Dyer, Fitzpatrick, and Foster) who had sponsored the Philadelphia conference in May, issued a call to all the trade unions of the country to send delegates to a convention to be held at Columbus, Ohio, on December 8, 1886. The purpose was to draw "the bonds of unity much closer together between all the trades unions of America" by means of "an American federation of alliance of all national and international trade unions." The Federation of Organized Trades and Labor Unions decided to hold its convention at the same time and place.[28]

Forty-two delegates from 25 labor organizations, 13 national unions and 12 local unions and city centrals assembled at Columbus on December 8, and agreed to form themselves into an American Federation of Labor. At the same time, 20 delegates to the convention of the Federation of Organized Trades and Labor Unions, representing seven national unions and five city centrals, met at Columbus and decided to merge with the newly-formed A. F. of L. The older Federation turned over all its property including a balance on hand of $284.97 to the new organization, and it resolved to request all affiliated unions "to connect themselves with the American Federation of Labor." After this, the Federation of Organized Trades and Labor Unions of the United States and Canada passed out of existence.[29] *

CONSTITUTION OF THE A. F. OF L.

The constitution of the A. F. of L. embodied a number of the features of the Federation of Organized Trades and Labor Unions. The preamble was carried over to the new organization with its militant statement: "Whereas, a struggle is going on in all the nations of the civilized world, between the oppressors and the oppressed of all countries, a struggle between the capitalist and the laborer. . . ." When the preamble was first adopted in 1881, its class conscious character had evoked unfavorable comment in the general press, and the Pittsburgh *Telegraph,* noting that it "breathes a spirit of conflict rather than pacification," had expressed the hope that it would be replaced by a new document which breathed "the spirit of concord with capital." [30] But the trade unionists who gathered at Columbus in December, 1886, knew from bitter experience, particularly from the Haymarket Affair and the employers' offensive following it, that a class struggle existed, and they voted unanimously to incorporate the preamble of the earlier Federation in their new constitution.

The objects of the A. F. of L., as set forth in the constitution, were "the encouragement and formation of local Trades and Labor Unions, and the closer Federation of such societies; The establishment of National and International Trades Unions, based upon a strict recognition of the autonomy of each trade; The Federation of all National and International Trades Unions, to aid and assist each other . . . and to secure National Legislation in the interests of working people. . . ." Another object was "to aid and encourage the labor press of America."

* Although the American Federation of Labor was considered a new organization at the time it was formed, it actually was recognized as a continuation of the earlier Federation of Organized Trades and Labor Unions. In 1889 the A.F. of L. decided to consider the Federation of Organized Trades and Labor Unions as part of its own history, and it dates its origin from 1881.

The direction of the new organization was placed in the hands of an annual convention, the basis of representation in which was specifically set forth,* and in an executive council, composed of five officers—a president, two vice-presidents, a secretary, and a treasurer. This council was empowered "to watch legislative measures directly affecting the interests of the workers; to organize new National or International Trades Unions" as well as local trades unions; "to secure the unification of all labor organizations"; to assist in boycotts, and extend voluntary financial aid in the event of a strike or lockout. The Federation's revenue was to be raised from a per capita tax of one-half of one cent per month, or six cents per year, and from charter fees. Membership in the organization was through the national and international unions, but any seven wage workers "of good character and favorable to Trades Unions, and not members of any body affiliated with this Federaiton," could form a local body, to be known as a federal labor union, and obtain a charter from the president. Through the federal labor union provision was made for the organization of mixed bodies of skilled and unskilled labor in localities where there were not sufficient workers to form a distinct trade union. In larger centers, unskilled labor could affiliate with the Federation through the federal labor union.[31]

The constitution emphasized that the objects of the A. F. of L. included the securing of legislation in the interests of the working people. In addition, a declaration was adopted by the convention which stated "that the time has come for the working people to act independently in politics." No action was taken at Columbus to form a distinct labor party, but it was clearly understood that the trade unions could not support the political parties of the employing class. As one delegate expressed it: "Why should we fight 364 days in the year for Wages, and on the 365th lose all our victories by voting for our enemies?"[32]

The president of the Federation was made a full-time officer with a salary of $1,000 a year and traveling expenses. Samuel Gompers was elected President, Peter J. McGuire, Secretary, and G. Edmonston, Treasurer.

There were at least two provisions in the constitution which reflected the struggle between the Knights and the trade unions. One was the statement that the national and international trade unions to be established would be "based upon a strict recognition of the autonomy of each trade," and the other was the reference to the fact that a candidate for

* The basis for representation in the convention was: from national or international unions, for less than 4,000 members, one delegate; 4,000 or more, two delegates; 8,000 or more, three delegates, 16,000 or more, five delegates, and so on; from each local or district trade unions, not connected with or having a national or international union, affiliated with the Federation, one delegate.

membership through a federal labor union had to be a wage worker "favorable to Trades Unions." The intention was clearly to avoid the mistake of the Knights of permitting non-working class elements to belong to the Order.

Impressed by the unity demonstrated by the trade unionists at Columbus, Powderly consented to meet with the trade union officials and act upon their "treaty." The trade unionists accepted the invitation and met with the K. of L. committee in Columbus on December 10 while the delegates to the convention were still in session. But they quickly discovered that Powderly had made an empty gesture. His committee did not have the power of recommendation, nor was it willing to discuss the terms of the "treaty" or any modification of these terms. "We cannot guarantee anything definite," the trade unionists were told whenever they asked the Knights what could be done to reconcile the differences between the Order and the trade unions. After much ambiguous discussion, the trade unionists reported back to the A. F. of L. convention "that no settlement could be arrived at unless the K. of L. Committee were clothed with power to settle, and give us proper guarantees for the future." [33]

Convinced that peace was no longer to be considered when dealing with the leaders of the Knights, whom they regarded as men crazed with power and blinded by ambition, the trade union delegates at the convention formally condemned the Order for "conspiring to pull down the Trades' Unions which it has cost years of work and sacrifice to build," called upon "all workingmen to join the Unions of their respective trades, and urge[d] the formation of National and International Unions and the centralization of all under one head, the American Federation of Labor." [34]

CHAPTER 10

The Decline of the Labor Parties

Already by the winter of 1887 it was evident that the 60,000 votes cast for Henry George—labor's "Triumph in Defeat"—were producing results. In his message to the New York State Legislature, Governor David B. Hill pointed to the votes for George as proof of "the fact that there seems to be a growing discontent among the industrial classes." "What the thoughtful workingmen of the State want is not glittering generalities or fine-spun theories, but practical measures of relief," the Governor warned the Legislature.

The legislative session showed the effect of labor's political influence. The State Board of Arbitration was extended for three more years with increased powers. Legislation was enacted providing for stricter regulation of tenement houses, the institution of Labor Day and Saturday half-holidays, stricter regulation of women and child labor, the abolition of contract labor in relation to state prisons, the ten-hour day for all railroad workers, and the prohibition of "iron-clad" contracts. After passage of the law providing for eight additional factory inspectors, Governor Hill appointed eight prominent union leaders to these offices.[1]

Proudly recording the triumphant march of labor reform, John Swinton pointed out that one show of the independent strength of the workers had brought more results than years of "balance of power" politics.[2]

LABOR IN ELECTIONS, 1887

Inspired by the victories scored in New York, the independent political movement of labor gained impetus. Labor tickets were nominated in the municipal campaigns of some 60-odd cities scattered through 21 states. In 20 cities, mostly in the Middle West, the labor tickets won victories, and in several, notably Cincinnati, Ohio and Paterson, New Jersey, they fell short of victory by only a few hundred votes. A victory that aroused considerable interests was the election of Dr. Isaiah S. Tuppins, a Negro physician, as the mayor of Rendville, Ohio, the first Negro north of the Mason-Dixon line to hold that office.* In Selma, Alabama, where the labor ticket emerged victorious in the municipal contest, it was reported that "the 'Negro' and the 'Jew' and the poor 'white trash' are running things down here." [3] Translated into more meaningful English, the comment meant that the working class and its allies were gaining their rightful political place in the community.

In evaluating the gains scored by the labor parties in the spring elections, the New York *Herald* conceded that the working class was a factor to be reckoned with in American politics. "A million and a half men count for something in a country like this, especially if they all think one way," it observed on April 10, 1887.

Within a year, the independent political movement of labor had collapsed, and most of the labor parties were on the verge of disappearing if they had not already disappeared.

DISRUPTIVE ROLE OF HENRY GEORGE

The factors responsible for the decline of the labor parties varied to some degree from community to community, but the basic ones are clearly demonstrated in the history of the labor party movement in New York.

"No man," declared the *Knights of Labor* on January 15, 1887, "has exercised so great an influence upon the labor movement of to-day as Henry George, although never himself connected as a leader with any of the labor organizations of the country." That influence at the time this editorial was written was already proving to be very unfortunate for the labor movement.

As soon as the exciting mayoralty campaign of 1886 was over, a group of Henry George's close friends called a mass congratulations meeting at Cooper Institute. It was decided to organize the independent political movement on a permanent basis with the aim of replacing the Republican and Democratic parties by "an organization which shall be . . . a real party of the people."

A committee consisting of John McMackin, Rev. Dr. Edward Mc-

---

* Dr. Tuppins, the son of free Negroes in Nashville, won considerable fame as a teacher, lawyer, and medical practitioner. In addition to nominating Negro candidates, a number of the labor parties took a stand in support of the political freedom of the Negro people. In the labor party formed in Topeka, Kansas, "a particular emphasis was placed on the right of the Negro to representation, and it was pointed out that the workingmen's ticket was the only one which recognized this right." (Edith Walker and Dorothy Liebengood, "Labor Organizations in Kansas in the Early Eighties," *Kansas Historical Quarterly*, Vol. IV, Aug., 1935, p. 289.)

Glynn, and Professor David Scott was appointed to take charge of the educational work of "lectures, discussions, and dissemination of literature" in behalf of "land reform, ballot reform, and lesser principles," and to prepare for "the formal organization at the proper time of a national party."[4] The committee opened an office, and, with Gaybirt Barnes, George's publishing agent, as executive secretary, began the organization of "Land and Labor Clubs" throughout the country.

The formation of this group had greater significance than was realized at the time. *The Leader,* a daily labor paper founded during the mayoralty campaign, commented later: "At this point began the work of side-tracking the movement from the whole issue of Labor to the one question of a single land tax."[5] The meeting had been called without the advice of the trade unions; only one of the three members of the executive committee was a labor representative, John McMackin; a publishing agent was put in charge of the organization, and George tried to side-track the labor emphasis by changing the name of the organization to the Progressive Democracy and later to the Land and Labor Committee. He even established his own weekly, *The Standard,* to advance the cause for a new party based only on a single-tax platform.

The Land and Labor Clubs set up by the Henry George committee included a few workers, but they were dominated by professional and business men—lawyers, ministers, doctors, and small employers. The sole issue for the clubs was the George single tax program. The struggle, in the eyes of George and his disciples, was not one between labor and its allies against their common exploiters. They held that it was a struggle between the masses and the classes, and by "classes" they meant political corruptionists of all kinds.[6] In this crusade, they insisted, the business and professional men had even more at stake than the workers and were entitled to a more influential role in the movement.

In addition to the Land and Labor Clubs, George and his disciples established the Anti-Poverty Society with Father McGlynn, excommunicated from the Catholic Church because of his support of the single-tax, as President, and George as Vice-President. The Society's platform offered the single-tax "as an all-inclusive panacea."[7] Using biblical language to denote the work in which it was engaged, the Anti-Poverty Society gave the Henry George movement a religious tone which appealed to the middle class elements. The trade unionists and the Socialists were not impressed by this type of appeal, and they became more and more concerned as they saw the growing influence of middle class elements in the labor party.[8]

The Socialists favored the maintenance of the labor party on a labor platform and opposed the infiltration of the party with middle class elements espousing the single tax issue as the "be-all and end-all." While criticizing the single taxers for attempting "to emasculate the platform of the labor party," the Socialists declared that they were ready to unite with George and his followers in building the independent political movement on the basis of the Clarendon Hall platform. Although some members of the S.L.P. wanted the "Labor party to adopt a Socialist program immediately," the leaders of the Socialist party, on the advice of Frederick Engels, refused to force their program on the independent political movement and repeatedly emphasized that they were eager to maintain unity with the labor party. But that unity, they insisted, must be based on a labor party platform not one dedicated solely to the single tax and appealing solely to the middle classes.[9]

Trade union leaders who had been active in the 1886 campaign joined the Socialists in criticizing the attempts of George and his disciples to convert the labor party into a single tax party. Indeed, union leaders, including Gompers, A. F. of L. President, openly voiced the opinion that George's reform program was of little value to the workers. The official organ of the International Cigar Makers' Union declared forcefully: "Henry George's theory that the taxation of land values will relieve the work-people employed in factories, mines and mills of their present misery and poverty is a snare and a delusion. No sensible trade unionist will take any stock in George's patent medicine. . . . No financial scheme or novel plan of taxation will shorten the hours of labor." The same journal reminded George and his disciples: "The votes for the labor parties were for higher wages and shorter hours, not taxation of land values." [10]

While the differences between the Georgeites and the Socialists and trade unionists were becoming sharper, another conflict arose within the labor party. John McMackin and several of his associates began to maneuver to become the "bosses" of the United Labor Party, hoping to use the organization for their own personal advantage. They refused to publish a financial statement of the 1886 mayoralty campaign, and violated the labor party's constitution by not publishing a regular monthly financial report of the general executive committee. It was evident that McMackin and his cronies—called the "labor politicians"—were attempting to build a personal machine which they could then surrender to the Democrats or Republicans and thus "destroy the influence of the new Labor Party." [11]

SYRACUSE CONVENTION, 1887

During these conflicts, the United Labor Party called a state convention at Syracuse on August 17, 1887. The representation at the convention was to be three delegates and three alternatives from each assembly district, and one delegate from each Land and Labor Club in districts where there were no Assembly District organizations.

The call for the convention revealed that the middle class elements were gaining control of the United Labor Party. It was a document remarkably different from the old Clarendon Hall platform. The evils of society were supposedly due to "the making of the land on which all must live the exclusive property of but a portion of the community." Three remedies were suggested for the solution of the problem: the tax on land values; the Greenback currency demand, the government ownership of railroads and telegraphs. The call ended with a condemnation of the "monopoly controlled" and "shamelessly corrupt" old parties. *Labor demands and an appeal to labor were entirely left out of the call.*[12]

In the election of delegates to the state convention, the assembly district organizations made their dissatisfaction with the call clear. The Eighth A.D., the Tenth A.D. and the Fourteenth A.D. denounced the "reactionary tactics of the platform" embodied in the call, and in the instructions given to delegates by many of the assembly districts, they were urged to defend the term "labor" in the party's name, to nominate "a straight labor ticket," to emphasize "labor demands," and to preserve unity.[13]

The instructions of the delegates were also aimed at the "labor politicians." The Tenth A.D. instructed its delegates "to ask for a regular monthly financial report of the General Executive Committee, which has so far been omitted contrary to the constitution." [14]

The crisis had come for George and the "labor politicians." They united to meet the challenge of the rank-and-file members of the labor party by red-baiting and splitting tactics.

EXPULSION OF SOCIALISTS

In the middle of July, 1887, rumors were afloat that the United Labor Party would oust the Socialists because they were members of another political party.* But when the Socialists insisted that the County Executive Committee issue a ruling on the eligibility of Socialists for membership in the United Labor Party, that committee announced "that membership in the Socialist Labor Party does not disqualify a citizen for membership in the United Labor Party." [15]

Nevertheless, the single taxers and the "labor politicians" moved swiftly to rescind the action of the County Executive Committee. When the County General Committee met on August 5, a motion was made to approve the report except that part which included the ruling upholding the right of the Socialists to membership in the party. This motion aroused considerable excitement which finally quieted down, and the chair was asked for a ruling. John McMackin, leader of the "labor poli-

---

* As early as April 23, 1887, Engels had predicted this development. ". . . the latter [George]" he wrote to Sorge, "grows more and more set on his land fad, and must suppress all that is socialist." (*Letters to Americans*, p. 184.)

ticians," ruled that under the labor party's constitution there was no room in the organization for another political party which nominated and ran candidates. Any action "in which the Socialists had a voice was null and void," he announced.[16]

McMackin's ruling was sustained. Thus the Socialists, who had opposed George's maneuvers to convert the United Labor Party into a single tax movement, and who had blocked the attempts of the "labor politicians" to turn the independent political movement over to the old party machines, were expelled.

The expulsion of the Socialists aroused bitter feelings among rank-and-file members of the United Labor Party. The Eighth, Tenth, Fourteenth, and Twenty-second A.D.'s protested the "Henry George decree" expelling the Socialists as an "attempt to steer the working people away from the object of the labor movement in the line of a middle class tax reform swindle. . . . " In an article prophetically entitled, "A Fatal Mistake," *The Leader* denounced the expulsion, pointing out that the Socialists had been an integral part of the United Labor Party from the beginning, had done everything to advance the interests of the independent political movement, and were interested in its continuation as a "labor party."[17] In Chicago, the militant labor leader, Joseph R. Buchanan, warned the laborites of New York: "Look out for the paid agents of the republican and democratic parties! . . . The bosses of the old political machines are determined to strangle the embryonic political giant before 1888 if possible. . . . They would have you quarrel among yourselves and thereby scatter your forces. Have some sense and don't do it."[18]

But Henry George refused to heed the appeals for unity. He openly stated in *The Standard* that the expulsion of the Socialists was an essential part of his attempt to win over the middle class and even the big capitalists since these elements would never support an independent political movement which embraced the Socialists and their doctrine of the class struggle.[19] The most important task before the United Labor Party convention in Syracuse, George argued, was to "firmly and clearly define the position of the party in relation to socialism." By clearly stating its hostility to the Socialists and rooting them out of the independent political movement, the labor party would merit the support of the middle class, of employers and farmers, and would deprive "its enemies [of] a specious pretext to make the charge [that] it does [endorse the views of the Socialists]."[20]

On August 17, 1887, the State Convention of the United Labor Party met, with the fate of the New York political labor movement in its hands. The major issue confronting the 177 delegates was the exclusion of the Socialists. The composition of the delegates foreshadowed the tragic outcome of the gathering. The convention was "packed" by the single taxers and the "labor politicians" who controlled the Land and Labor Clubs. Although many of these clubs had only two or three members, they sent delegates to the convention who were promptly seated by the Executive Committee dominated by the single taxers and the "labor politicians." Louis F. Post, George's lieutenant, had been defeated in his own district by the workingmen members of the Party. He was promptly chosen to represent the Albany Land and Labor Club. The fact that he lived in New York City and was not even a member of the Club which elected him was ignored by the Executive Committee.[21]

By packing the convention with paper delegates and representatives from the middle-class-dominated Land and Labor Clubs,[22] the coalition of single taxers and "labor politicians" were able to control the proceedings. After the speeches of several delegates, Sergius E. Schevitsch, the recognized leader of the Socialists, was allowed 15 minutes to address the convention. His speech, delivered with much feeling, has lost none of its significance even today almost seventy years later: ". . . It is with sadness that I speak, because having studied the labor movement, as a somewhat intelligent observer of events, I tell you that by doing what you are about to do you are ruining your party past all possible redemption for the present. In the course of time the great movement of wage workers will again evolve and take the upper hand, but for the present your party will go to pieces.

"You have shown today the true intent of the leaders of your party. It is their intention to oust the most honest, the most self-sacrificing, the hardest working elements of that party. . . .

"Last summer it was the Socialistic workingmen of New York who first started the ball rolling which afterward became the avalanche of November. After the infamous boycott trials in New York it was the Socialistic party that aroused the workingmen to a sense of the invasion of their rights and started that movement which has developed into this party.* These reviled, despised Socialists were those who took up the banner and led in the fight, saying to the members even of New York, 'Now is the time to protest, to unite, to organize and show your strength at the ballot box.' It was out of that movement that the United Labor Party grew. . . .

"I say to you, beware of what you do. I am not a Cassandra, but the consequences of what you are about to do will be more dangerous than you think. . . . Catch as many men as you can, but beware of widening the breach you have already made in New York. I know full well that anything I can say here today will be of no avail. I am here only to make

---

* See p. 117. Engels also referred to the Socialists as "the founders of the [United Labor Party] movement." (Letter to Sorge, Sept. 16, 1887. Marx and Engels, *Letters to Americans*, p. 192.)

the declaration that I stand on this platform not as a Socialist, but as a member of the United Labor Party.

"Expel me; brand me as something I have never been in my life, but you cannot take from me that I am a member of the United Labor Party because I accept its principles, for every action I take is for the benefit of that party and I have no personal motives. Have we sunk so low as to grasp at names instead of at principles? Take the thing as it is and then you will see it will be as absurd, as criminal for the United Labor Party to expel us as for the Republican party to expel the Abolitionists from their ranks." [23]

Moved by Schevitsch's stirring address, T. B. Wakeman, a delegate from the Central Labor Union, spoke out for compromise. He recommended that the Socialist delegates be granted a half vote for each delegate and that the S.L.P. be called upon at its convention in September to disavow the claim of being a political party in competition with the United Labor Party.[24]

As soon as he observed the sentiment growing for compromise, Henry George took the floor and said: "The greatest danger that could befall the party would not be the separation of its elements . . . but would be a continuance within its ranks of incongruous elements. . . . This is the question we must settle." The signal given, the single tax and "labor politicians" machine went into action. The vote 91 to 54 against the compromise resolution. The Socialist delegates were then rejected by a vote of 91 to 86.[25]

The single tax—"labor politician" coalition, having rid itself of its major obstacle, proceeded to "steamroll" its platform and candidates through the packed convention. The single tax was made the main issue, and not one of the candidates nominated for office was a workingman or a trade unionist. George was nominated for secretary of state; Thomas Wilder, the candidate for controller was treasurer of the Railroad Supply Company, with an office on Wall Street; John Cummins, candidate for state treasurer, was a boot and shoe dealer; James Feely, candidate for attorney general, was a wealthy lawyer, James Sweet, nominated for surveyor, was a wealthy farmer. Except for George none had been active in the 1886 campaign, and several were politically active in the Democratic and Republican parties.[26]

Thus ended the Syracuse Convention and with it ended the bright promise of the great upheaval in the fall of 1886. Having received detailed reports of the convention from its American correspondent, *Freedom*, the British radical journal, commented that George's followers in England "will be grieved to see the man whom they considered as an earnest champion of the oppressed, now turning his back on the workers and entering into a union with the middle class.

"For a union with the middle-class it was, this Syracuse Convention of the United Labour Party, at which Labour was *not* represented, even by a feeble minority; while lawyers (fourteen lawyers!), doctors, parsons, employers, and grocers fully represented all factions of the middle-class. Its platform is a middle-class platform throughout." [27]

THE PROGRESSIVE PARTY

Protest meetings against the destruction of the labor party held by the Socialists and their sympathizers led to a call for a conference to be held at Webster Hall on September 4. Approximately 200 delegates, representing 78 bona fide labor organizations, met to decide upon concrete action to make certain that labor was politically represented in the forthcoming state election. In comparatively short order, they came to agreement, and reaffirming the original purposes of the United Labor Party which "has been perverted in its aims, adulterated in its composition and converted into a despotic ring by the very candidate whom it had most honored and trusted," they "Resolved, That for the furtherance of the great American movement of the masses against the classes upon its natural lines, we constitute ourselves into an independent political party under the name of Progressive Labor Party." [28]

At a state convention of the Progressive Labor Party on September 28, approximately 100 labor organizations combined to pick a slate to represent labor. The ticket included John Swinton, candidate for state senator, J. Edward Hall, H. A. Barker, and T. B. Wakeman. The last three candidates were all trade unionists. [29]

Outside of New York the precise details of the split in the United Labor Party were not too clearly understood. But to the Chicago *Labor Enquirer,* among many others, this much was evident: "There are now in that state two full fledged labor political camps. The effect is to rejoice the enemies of organized labor and to discourage, enervate, and humiliate its friends. . . . The time has come to put an end to all this. . . . 'Unite or die!' " [30]

But it was too late. Hopes that a "deal" between the two labor parties might materialize continued throughout the campaign, but it was never realized. On the contrary, bitter wrangling featured the campaign. Swinton assailed the "jobbery and corruption" of the United Labor Party, and George condemned the Progressive Labor Party as a "Socialist tool." Condemnations of both labor parties continued in the commercial press. Although George was praised for having expelled the Socialists, he was still attacked for arousing class hatred, and was characterized as a threat to the existing economic system and a champion of "anarchy." [31]

The net effect of all the disruption, splitting and vituperation was to alienate the great bulk of the workingmen. A general decline in enthusiasm for independent political action was noted in the trade unions. The Central Labor Union just barely rejected endorsement of the Progressive Labor Party by a vote of 55 to 54 with about 50 abstaining.[32]

In the election itself, George polled a mere 72,000 as against 459,000 for the Republicans and 480,000 for the Democratic Party. (His vote in New York City was one-half of his 1886 total.) The Progressive Labor Party polled approximately 10,000 votes.[33]

It was indeed a dismal showing for labor. The contrast of the elections of 1886 and 1887 in New York showed more clearly than ever the dangers of red-baiting and splitting tactics, and the need for labor unity as a prerequisite for successful independent political action by the working class. The election results in 1887 proved that red-baiting and splits in labor's ranks not only antagonized the workers but alienated the middle class allies of the working class. Only the capitalists and their political parties had benefited by the split in labor's ranks.

DECLINE IN CHICAGO

Chicago witnessed a similar tragic development in the months following the great political upheaval in the fall election of 1886. Preparations were begun for the spring municipal elections. In February, 1887, a plan for the organization of ward and town clubs was instituted. Qualifications and rules for membership were set forth, primarily by a declaration of non-affiliation with either of the old parties and the provision that a majority of members of all ward and town clubs had to be wage workers.* Candidates specifically had to belong to the K. of L. or some other labor organization. The Chicago Central Labor Union then unanimously endorsed the declaration of principles, platform, and nominations of the United Labor Party.[34]

Despite a violent attack in the commercial press on the labor party as being dominated by "red flag communists," spirit continued to run high.[35] Difficulties, however, arose in the course of the campaign. Frightened by the red-baiting attacks in the commercial press on the labor ticket, Powderly declared invalid the action of Chicago's District Assembly 24 in donating $50 to the United Labor Party. "No money can be voted from an assembly, district or local for political purposes," was his arbitrary dictum.[36] The circular, read to all the local assemblies in the city, was particularly harmful to the labor party campaign inasmuch as its candidate for mayor was none other than Robert Nelson, Master Workman of D.A. 24. The action of the top leadership of the Knights in

* Farmers were considered wage workers.

specifically forbidding assemblies to assist in any way Nelson's election caused confusion in labor's ranks. Many Knights were undoubtedly frightened away from activity in support of the United Labor Party by Powderly's splitting tactics.[37]

The Democratic and Republican parties, fearing the possibility of a labor victory, fused for the purpose of the election and ran a "law and order" campaign. Under the brunt of this attack, Nelson polled about 25,000 votes and the labor party was able to elect only one alderman.[38] In the fall of 1886, the labor party had elected a state senator and several assemblymen.

Repercussions followed. Complaints were raised by the middle class and professional elements in the labor party that the reason it had not made a better showing was that it had failed to attract the small businessmen and farmers, and that this, in turn, was due to the influence exerted on the independent political movement by the "tainted Red Leadership" of Thomas J. Morgan and other members of the S.L.P.. The middle class and professional groups threatened to leave the labor party unless there was an immediate end to "the red flag influence." [39]

In Chicago, too, the "labor politicians" played their part in splitting the independent political movement. In collaboration with the Democratic Party, William Gleason managed to organize a party and appropriated, by a state charter, the name "United Labor Party." The original labor party was forced to change its name to the Radical Labor Party.[40]

Despite these attacks, sentiment in favor of the Radical Labor Party still appeared in labor circles. A mass meeting of carpenters in September, 1887, unanimously resolved "that each and every voter who shall neglect or refuse to work and vote for all the candidates of the labor party ... will be traitors to their fellow workingmen." The Central Labor Union also endorsed the Radical Labor Party.[41]

Still, as in New York, the red-baiting, the splitting, and the confusion resulting from the existence of two organizations bearing the name, labor party, had inflicted irreparable damage to the cause of independent political action. In the Spring election of 1888, the Radical Labor Party was able to poll only some 7,000 scattered votes.[42] Once unity had been lost and the red-scare penetrated its ranks, in a futile effort by the middle class elements to appease the reactionary enemies of the labor movement, the labor party in Chicago (as in New York) disintegrated at a rapid pace.

The disintegration of the labor parties in New York and Chicago discouraged the adherents of independent political action in other parts of the country. In many states and cities, the labor parties declined, and by the spring of 1888, the tidal wave for independent political action had completely subsided.[43]

The disappearance of the local and state labor parties doomed the movement to unite the independent forces nationally. Momentum for such a movement generated rapidly after the elections of 1886 and bore fruit in the formation of the National Union Labor Party. Born in February, 1887, it absorbed the remnants of the Greenback Labor Party and gained the allegiance of farmers' groups, anti-monopolists, and Knights of Labor.[44]

In 1888 the Union Labor Party proposed to amalgamate with Henry George's United Labor Party, but since it declined to make the single tax the major demand in its platform, George's party refused to have anything to do with it.[45]

Both parties nominated presidential candidates in 1888, but the United Labor Party garnered the grand total of 2,808 votes nationally, and the Union Labor Party, now composed largely of farmers, attracted a negligible labor vote.[46]

The rapid waning of the strength of the Knights was an important factor in the disappearance of the labor parties. Although the leadership of the Order did little to encourage and much to discourage support of the labor parties, in many communities the local and district assemblies provided the mass base for independent political action, and when these organizations disintegrated, the labor parties received a serious blow. And, as we shall now see, many of the same factors responsible for the decline of the labor parties—autocratic leadership, red-baiting, expulsions, futile efforts of the leadership to appease reaction, splits and divisions, and indifference of the leadership to the real needs of the workers—were also extremely important in the decline of the Knights of Labor.

CHAPTER 11

The Decline of the K. of L.

The unparalleled growth of the K. of L. in the decade beginning with 1880 to a dominant position in the American labor movement was followed by an equally spectacular decline. The ranks of the Order thinned out from the maximum of over 700,000 in the summer of 1886 to 510,351 by July, 1887.[1] A year later, the membership had sunk to 221,618. In an article entitled, "Decay of a Great Order," the New York *Tribune* pointed out in August, 1889: "The dissolution of assemblies has taken place by the hundreds almost everywhere, and in the former strongholds of the once all-powerful Knights the name and purpose of the organization are like a song of the past."[2]

What brought about this transformation in the Knights of Labor?

CAUSES OF DECLINE

The causes of the decline of the Order are numerous and varied. Among the reasons most commonly advanced by contemporaries and by later historians are: (1) the bitter opposition of the employers who were determined to wipe out labor organizations in general and especially one, like the K. of L., which sought to bring together in one body all the workers of the country, skilled and unskilled, native and foreign-born, Negro and white, men and women; (2) the unwieldiness of an organization composed of peoples of all kinds of trades and occupations, many assemblies consisting of members following a hundred or more avocations; (3) the poor organizational structure of the Knights, suited for united action of many workers in many industries and trades, but which could not be adapted to meet the daily problems of workers in specific industries and trades; (4) the struggle between the anti- and pro-trade union elements within the Order and the open warfare between the Knights and the rising of A. F. of L.; (5) the conflict between the rank-

and-file and the leadership of the Order over policies, tactics, and strategy.[3]

All of the above factors played their part in hastening the disintegration of the Order, though some have been overemphasized by labor historians.* But the basic cause was the breach between the leadership and the rank-and-file, a conflict already present in the K. of L. at its height in 1886.

Already in 1885 and 1886 working class Knights were complaining of the ease with which non-working class elements joined the Order, and that it was more difficult for workers than owners of small businesses to join certain assemblies. "There has been to[o] much effort made in our assembly to get in business men and shut out laboring men on trifling excuses," wrote a Knight from Canton, Pennsylvania in January, 1886.[4]

The chief complaint, however, was that the non-working class elements were beginning to dominate the policies of the assemblies and direct them against the interests of the vast majority of the K. of L. membership. A Michigan Knight pointed out: "No employer should be admitted to membership in the Order, for under their auspices there will be nothing but milk-and-water work." A report from a Boston assembly offered concrete evidence on this point, revealing that the working class members "were obliged to smother their grievances in the meeting because of the fact that their bosses held the offices, and that they would be discharged if they complained. They also assert that they were prevented [from] asking for wage increases and sick benefits for the same reason." [5]

Powderly readily conceded that in not a few assemblies, employers had a controlling influence, but he welcomed this development, for he counted heavily upon the non-working class elements as allies in the conflict emerging in the Order between the leadership and the rank-and-file. It was a conflict between two ideologies: the first of these based itself on the class struggle and the second on class collaboration.

The pattern of betrayal unfolded in the Gould and meat-packing strikes † was to be repeated time and again as Powderly and his associates on the General Executive Board threw their influence on the side of the employers. It was evident in the winter and spring of 1887 during the bitter battle waged by 7,000 Knights in the Massachusetts' shoe towns against an employers' association lockout; again in September, 1887, during the strike of 60,000 Knights on the Reading Railroad, and again

---

* The major reason advanced by the Commons-Wisconsin school of labor historiography for the failure of the Knights was that the Order's structure could not be adapted "to the practical needs of job-conscious workers." As we have seen above, this idea is erroneous since the Order was actually highly flexible in meeting the organizational requirements of its varied membership. Actually, it was not so much a structural as it was an ideological issue—pro versus anti-trade unionism—that was involved in this question.

† See above, pp. 83-88.

during the strike of K. of L. workers at Andrew Carnegie's Edgar Thompson Steel Works at Braddock, Pennsylvania, in April, 1888. In each case, Powderly and the General Executive Board refused to answer the appeals of the hard-pressed strikers for funds to help them meet their most urgent needs; in each case, Powderly urged the strikers to abandon the struggle, to oust the "radical elements" whom he blamed for the workers' difficulties, and to assure the employers that henceforth they planned to live in peace and harmony with capital. And in each case, Powderly earned the gratitude of the employers.* But the results were disastrous for the rank-and-file Knights who, if they were not blacklisted, returned to work on the bosses' terms which required them to renounce their membership in labor organizations before going back to work.[6]

While the terror against the Order was mounting, Powderly was busy lecturing on what he called the "two great questions" facing the organization: "education and temperance." While employers were posting notices in their shops and factories warning their workers to sign "iron-clad" oaths, Powderly was assuring these employers that "their interests (and those of the Knights of Labor) are identical, and they should strengthen the Knights of Labor as the surest antidote to anarchy." While members of his organization were being locked-out and blacklisted, Powderly was telling newspaper reporters in an interview:

"Mr. Powderly, do you concede the right of an employer to employ and discharge whom he pleases?

"I do. I know there are many in the Order who do not. This has been one of the knottiest questions we have had to contend with. If I was an employer I can see I would strive to make the most money out of the work done by my employees."[7]

It is no wonder that the Order lost 600,000 members in four years! Many of these workers were forced out of the organization by the employers (the entire D.A. 33, composed of Illinois coal miners, was forced to leave the Order), but a great many left the organization in sheer disgust. "The members are dropping away like the dead leaves before an Autumn wind," K. of L. organizers informed Powderly in the spring of 1887. Furious over the failure of the General Executive Board to come to their assistance during a lockout, hundreds of rubber workers in New Brunswick, New Jersey, left the Order. The obituary notice of their local assembly was posted in the K. of L. hall in New Brunswick: "On Friday

---

* Hailing the K. of L. Grand Master Workman for having condemned the strike at the Edgar Thompson Steel Works, Carnegie told a Pittsburgh *Dispatch* reporter: "Mr. Powderly seems to me to be one of the wisest counsellors that labor ever had." He only regretted that the rank-and-file Knights paid little attention to Powderly's wise counsel which was based, he pointed out, upon "a close alliance and harmonious relation with capital." (Pittsburgh *Dispatch,* May 7, 1888.)

Evening April 29, [1887], Local Assembly No. 3,354 K. of L., killed by the General Executive Board. Funeral ceremonies at Rahway on Saturday Evening, April 30. Please omit flowers."

A few days later, a newspaper carried the following report from New Brunswick: "The withdrawal of the hundreds of rubber workers in this city from the Knights of Labor seems to be the beginning of a stampede from that order, and of the disintegration of other assemblies." [8]

CONFLICT WITH THE TRADE UNIONS

As was to be expected, defection from the K. of L. ranks was accelerated by the conflict between the Order and the trade unions. The action taken at the Richmond Convention compelling members of the Order who were also enrolled on the books of the Cigar Makers' International Union to leave the latter, accounted to a high degree for the distintegration of the Knights. The International Cigar Makers were backed up not only by the leading trade unions of the country, by the New York Central Labor Union, the Boston Central Labor Union, the Newark Trades and Labor Assembly, and other organizations, but by many of the Districts in the K. of L. itself. Scores of assemblies remonstrated against the enforcement of the circular of expulsion. [9]

In Baltimore, where the command was strictly enforced, 30 locals left the Order in 1887.* In Chicago, the powerful D.A. 24 ordered all locals to withdraw from the Chicago Trades and Labor Assembly and the Illinois State Federation of Labor because both had endorsed the Cigar Makers' International's label. Some assemblies acceded to this order, but a great number gave up their charters and reorganized into independent unions so that they might remain within the Trades and Labor Assembly. The membership of D.A. 24 fell off from 25,000 in 1886, to 3,500 in the following year.† As early as February, 1887, Newark, one of the largest cigar centers in the United States, reported that there was not one K. of L. cigar maker in the entire city. [10]

Although the decrease in membership was assuming gigantic proportions—over 2,600 assemblies were suspended in 1887 for non-payment of dues—the K. of L. leadership persisted in its policies throughout the better part of the year. A number of local and district assemblies openly endorsed the light blue label of the International Cigar Makers' Union. They were promptly expelled from the Order. [11]

* By January 1, 1890 only ten locals with 489 members remained.
† The membership was a bare 500 in 1889. On May 24, 1890, the *Knights of Labor*, official publication of the Chicago Assembly, observed sadly: "There are no Knights of Labor in Chicago worthy of consideration. There may be 500 that pay dues . . . but we doubt it."

On the eve of the Minneapolis convention in October, 1887, a great tidal wave of opposition to the general officers poured in from local and district assemblies in all parts of the country. Some district assemblies went so far as to withhold credentials from several members of the General Executive Board. In fine, the members were anxious to be represented by something more substantial than bombast.[12]

In speeches and interviews prior to the convention, Powderly dismissed the criticism of the general officers with the observation that it came only from the Socialists and anarchists. "Labor was never so much respected as at present," he declared.[13]

ATTACKS ON MEMBERS IN SOUTH

While Powderly was speaking, the members of his organization were being locked-out, blacklisted, lynched, even massacred. In the summer of 1887, a K. of L. organizer, H. F. Hoover, was "shot down like a dog by the 'best citizens of South Carolina' because he was organizing the laborers, Negroes as well as whites, in that labor-hating country."[14] During a strike of Negro Knights on the sugar plantations of Louisiana in the fall of 1887, armed deputies opened fire on the strikers and killed four Negro workers on the spot. Later, a mob of armed whites, headed by the local military unit, numbering from two hundred to three hundred men, attacked the Negro settlement where the evicted strikers and their families were living. The attackers went from house to house, firing at all Negroes who made their appearance. Reports differed on the number of people killed, but the New Orleans *Times-Democrat,* a spokesman for the planters, admitted that the number of Negroes slain might reach 30 when all the corpses were found. The *Irish World* reported that 30 Negroes were massacred.

Not content with this mass lynching, a mob of whites, with the cooperation of the sheriff and his deputies, took George and Henry Cox, two Negro strike leaders who were arrested * and jailed at the beginning of the strike, from their cells and lynched them.[15]

In an angry editorial, the Detroit *Advance and Labor Leaf* condemned the leaders of the Order for failing to speak out against the massacre and lynching of Negro Knights in the South. "As yet our general officers have nothing to say about it," it declared bitterly, "and if the officers of the Order are to stand by with folded arms, see their organizers butchered in cold blood, and make no protest, it is time the rank and file of the Order took the means to defend their noble and self-sacrificing organizers even in the South." The rank-and-file agreed with this criticism. Letters

---

* Other strike leaders were also arrested. They were defended before the Louisiana Supreme Court by a Negro state senator, Henry Demas.

to Powderly expressed horror at the leadership's indifference to the massacre of the Negro Knights.[16]

THE MINNEAPOLIS CONVENTION, 1887

These stirring appeals had no effect. Powderly was too busy telling reporters how the Order had earned the respect of employers and how it was building "harmonious relations" with the Catholic Church as a result of its bold stand against the radical elements. True, the Order had lost members, but "the reason for the falling off in members is to be found in the persistent efforts of the Anarchists and their friends to get control of the Order." At any rate, the Knights would be stronger with "one hundred thousand men in the Order, who were thoughtful men, men who would study well their duties to their families, the principles of organization and their allegiance to the country" than with "one million men" who were continually stirring up strife with the employers and antagonizing the public by their radical activities. In the long run, "the hundred thousand men will do more good for humanity than a hundred million of the other class." [17]

The Minneapolis Convention was packed with pro-administration delegates,* and the administration machine, through its control of the credentials committee, indiscriminately excluded delegates who were known to be championing the cause of the condemned men. Thus Powderly saw to it that Joseph R. Buchanan, the militant member of the General Executive Board, was debarred from the General Assembly on the ground that his local had failed to pay its dues. When Buchanan offered to pay the sum in arrears, the offer was rejected by the credentials committee. The administration machine sustained the report of the credentials committee, and Buchanan was denied his seat.[18]

At the General Assembly, Powderly dedicated a considerable portion of his address as General Master Workman to the question of "anarchy within the order" and his attitude toward the "Chicago anarchists." He roundly denounced assemblies which had passed resolutions of sympathy for the condemned Haymarket martyrs, accusing them of placing the entire Order in jeopardy.[19]

When a resolution was introduced, urging the convention to vote a petition of clemency for the condemned men, Powderly pulled out all the stops in demanding its rejection. He denounced the radical elements within the Order, blaming them for the employers' offensive against labor, and, in an effort to stampede the delegates, deliberately invented

---

* In a letter to John W. Hayes, Feb. 22, 1888, Powderly admitted that he had "packed the last G.A. [at Minneapolis]." (PHC.)

two attempts on his life by "anarchists." The administration machine promptly sustained Powderly, and the resolution was rejected. The true sentiments of the delegates were clearly revealed by the fact that nearly all of them signed a petition, circulated at the convention, asking Governor Oglesby to commute the sentence to life imprisonment.[20]

As soon as they learned of the action taken at Minneapolis on the Haymarket question, scores of district and local assemblies condemned Powderly's "moral cowardice" and censured the General Assembly for having failed to pass the resolution calling for the commutation of the sentence of death. But to Powderly the sentiments of the rank-and-file Knights did not matter; one letter like the following carried more weight with Powderly than dozens of resolutions adopted by district and local assemblies: "Your speech of Monday night [denouncing the resolution on behalf of the condemned men] has awakened comment and sympathy in a quarter of the K. of L. has never reached before namely among the business men and their assistants." [21]

Most of the remaining days at Minneapolis constituted a nightmare for organized labor, and a windfall for organized capital. The only note of sanity struck was the conciliatory attitude adopted towards the trade union element. Recognizing at last the tragic consequences of the expulsion of all cigar makers who adhered to their International union, Powderly rescinded the circular which had ordered all members of the C.M.I.U. out of the Knights. The assembly voted that "members of the Cigar Makers' International Union, expelled by reason of the law enacted by the G.A. at Richmond, be reinstated without paying initiation fees or back dues, provided they express a desire to be so reinstated." [22]

But this note of reason was drowned out in an orgy of red-baiting. Any effort to purge the Order of its ruinous practices was met with the charge that the change was being sought by the "anarchistic element." "This is the whole programme," sadly wrote the American correspondent of the British journal, *The Commonweal*, "of one of the largest labour organizations in the world. Oh shame upon such spoilers of healthy movements." [23]

It was a program, however, dear to the heart of the employers. A leading employers' journal expressed the joy of the American capitalists in its keen evaluation of the convention: "The general assembly of the Knights of Labor, which has been in session in Minneapolis for the greater part of the past two weeks, has contributed much to the good opinion entertained of the order, and done little to cause the men who are large employers of labor ... to apprehend a great deal of danger from the order so long as its control is in the present hands. . . . So long as the Powderly element is dominent [sic] in the order there is little to fear from the Knights." [24]

Small wonder Joseph Labadie predicted upon his return from Minneapolis that the Order had reached "its greatest number of members and that its decline is certain. Too many have used it for immediate personal gain, and too many have been entrusted with its guidance who are not well grounded in the science of social order and industrial economy." [25]

EXPULSION OF POWDERLY'S CRITICS

At the Indianapolis convention in the fall of 1888, the remains of what was once hailed as "the most grandiose culmination of the American labor movement" was given another wound. General Secretary Charles Lichtman was forced by Powderly to resign because of his opposition to the administration's policies. [26] Two members of the General Executive Board, Thomas B. Barry and A. A. Carlton, critics of Powderly and his policies, were expelled from the Order. Powderly then placed in nomination the names of eight cronies as candidates for the General Executive Board. From these the new Board was elected. Powderly had stated publicly that he did not intend to run for General Master Workman again, but he changed his mind. As one newspaper pointed out: "Mr. Powderly is looked upon with favor by the manufacturers generally and this fact may go far to induce him to change his mind. He is known as a conservative labor leader and as long as he is at the head of the order the radicals must keep in the background." [27]

After he had been ousted from the K. of L. because of his opposition to Powderly and his policies, Barry addressed a circular to the workingmen and women of America in which he pointed out that the Knights had been virtually destroyed by an autocratic leadership which had deserted the cause of the working class. He accused Powderly of extravagance, of the usurpation of power, of rewarding men who worked for the administration's benefit, and of sacrificing the interests of the rank-and-file Knights in order to appease the employers and the Catholic Church hierarchy. He suggested the formation of a new labor orgainzation, to be called the Brotherhood of United Labor, which would lead the workers in a dual struggle: for immediate improvements and for more fundamental reforms. It would maintain friendly relations with "all legitimate organizations of labor," but would "draw the line clearly on scabs and scabbism." Individuals not in good standing with their own trade unions were not to be initiated by the Brotherhood until a settlement had been affected with their trade organization. [28]

For a brief period, Barry succeeded in associating groups of former Knights from different states with him in the undertaking, and state and local branches were established. But the Brotherhood was unable to compete with the rising A. F. of L. in the campaign to attract present and former members of the Order. It had a fairly strong base in Michigan, Barry's own state, but with the growth of the A. F. of L., even this nucleus was wiped out. After 1890, the Brotherhood passed from the labor scene.[29]

One by one the national trade assemblies within the Knights became convinced that their destiny lay not with the Order but with the A. F. of L. In February, 1889, the Shoemakers' National Trades Assembly 216 left the Knights and formed the Boot and Shoe Workers' International Union, affiliated with the A. F. of L. National Trades Assembly 198, composed of machinists, blacksmiths, foundrymen, and boilermakers, seceded from the Order in 1889 and formed the National Association of Machinists. That same year the Mule Spinners Association, the miners attached to District Assembly 135, the iron workers, included in District Assembly 217, and the Philadelphia and Reading Railroad Workers, in District Assembly 214, abandoned the Knights. In January, 1890, newspapers carried the reports of a joint convention at Columbus, Ohio, of the National District Assembly 135 of the K. of L. and the National Progressive Union. The new organization, named "The United Mine Workers of America," was chartered by the A. F. of L. on January 25, 1890.[30] Eventually, all of the K. of L. miners went over to the new organization.

These and other national trade assemblies, who were gradually to cut loose from the Knights pointed out that they had been reduced by the administration's suicidal policies to a "handful of members," and that only by breaking away from the Order could they even maintain their existence.

The secession of the national trade assemblies was a severe blow to the Order. "These secessionist groups were strong," one student notes. "They left within the Order national bodies of one of two types: those not strong enough to stand by themselves, and those so strong that being in or out of the fold made little difference. Of the latter group, the Window-Glass Workers was almost the sole example." [31]

Since the national trade assemblies were "the backbone of the K. of L." in many of the industrial areas, their exodus from the Order hastened the disintegration of other assemblies within the region. In Michigan, for example, the transfer of the shoe workers from the K. of L. to the A. F. of L. was largely responsible for the rapid disappearance of the Order from the state. The Grand Rapids labor directory for 1891 had no reference to Knights at all, and in Detroit the last active assembly had officially disappeared before 1892. In some instances, the Michigan assemblies transferred their allegiance as a body to the A. F. of L. Others simply went out of existence.[32]

Powderly shed few tears over the departure of the national trade assemblies. He informed Hayes that he had made up his mind to tell the trade union assemblies "to go to the devil out of the Order ... damned if I don't drive them out this time and then tell the world that we don't want any more trades unionism in the Order, I am tired of them." [33] *

It is clear that the administration welcomed the exodus of the trade union assemblies and was only too anxious to hurry it along. The entire trend now was to surrender the "great or large cities," and to base the K. of L. on the rural elements—the farmers and "the village blacksmith, the village carpenter, shoemaker, and the other laboring men of the place as well as the village painter and paper hanger." [34]

K. OF L. BECOMES RURAL

Reports of the state assemblies to the Atlanta Convention of the General Assembly in 1889 disclosed that the K. of L. was becoming increasingly rural in make-up. Only 40 new local assemblies had been added during the year and these were recruited from the agricultural class exclusively. Two hundred and twenty local assemblies had withdrawn from the Order during the year while 60 had failed to report for months.

In keeping with its rural make-up, the Order now made the land question the key issue in its program. Powderly came out with an enthusiastic endorsement of the single tax idea, and, in his presidential address to the Atlanta assembly, recommended its adoption as part of the official program of the Knights. The constitution was amended to include a clause which emphasized that "occupancy and use should be the only title to possession of land," and affirmed the principle of the single tax. [35]

The action at Atlanta was hailed in the rural press and joyfully greeted by Henry George as the "most important event" of the era. [36] In working class circles, however, the action was regarded as acknowledgement of the fact that the K. of L. had lost its base in the industrial areas, and that the leadership had given up all hope of regaining it. "A glance at the labor field," wrote a contemporary observer, "will reveal the general situation. The ranks of the Knights in the industrial and manufacturing centres throughout New England, New Jersey, Baltimore, Wilmington, this city [Philadelphia], Pittsburgh and the West, have been depleted to an extent that is disheartening." [37]

Membership statistics after 1889 mirror the decay of the once-powerful Order: 100,000 in 1890, a loss of 100,000 members in a year; no figures for 1891 and 1892, and 74,635 in 1893. Even in Canada, where the decline

---

* So vicious was Powderly's language when he referred to the trade unionists that many of his expressions are unprintable. In one letter he referred to Gompers, Strasser and other trade union spokesmen as "the damn Jews" and "these Christ sluggers." (Powderly to John W. Hayes, December 19, 1889, PHC.)

of the Order had been much slower than in the United States, the Knights had shrunk considerably by 1892. In many Canadian cities and smaller urban centers, the Order had disappeared.* Only three district assemblies and seven local assemblies answered a questionnaire issued by the Canadian Bureau of Industries in 1892.[38]

THE OUSTING OF POWDERLY

In November, 1893, at the Philadelphia General Assembly, Powderly was ousted as Grand Master Workman of the tottering Order. The action was long overdue. As the *Industrial Tribune,* a mid-western labor paper, pointed out in the summer of 1891: "There has existed for several years a deep-seated hatred against Powderly and his mismanagement of the Order which he has reduced to a pitiable wreck." [39] But as long as Powderly's machine remained intact, the opposition to his misleadership made little headway. Those who opposed his bankrupt policies were either expelled or forced to resign.

The move which ousted Powderly from office resulted from an alliance of members of his machine, the western agrarian elements, and the Socialists, the latter led at this time by Daniel De Leon.† His chief accuser was his former lieutenant, Secretary-Treasurer John W. Hayes whom Powderly had called "my main dependence on the [General Executive] Board." The main charges against him were those of blocking the will of the majority, using the Order for private gain, and destroying the organization's militancy in order to win favor from the employers and the Catholic Church hierarchy.[40]

The new General Master Workman was James R. Sovereign of Iowa, and his election identified the Order more and more as a farmers' movement. Sovereign was elected with the support of the Socialists in return for his promise to appoint a member of the party as the editor of the Knights' official publication. Hayes continued as General Secretary-Treasurer.

The new administration issued optimistic statements promising that soon the Order would be "booming with all the vigor of its youthful days." [41] But the mass of the workers who had left the organization were not impressed by verbal exhortations. They had had more than their

---

* An expansion in membership took place in 1892 in Kingston and Quebec through the recruiting of lumbermen, but this temporary growth did not compensate for the losses which the Order suffered elsewhere in Canada. (Douglas R. Kennedy, "The Knights of Labor in Canada," unpublished M.A. Thesis, University of Western Ontario, 1945, pp. 134-36.

† For a discussion of the role of the Socialists in the Order in the early 1890's, see p. 294-96.

share during Powderly's regime. Moreover, they knew that the men who replaced Powderly had no tactical or theoretical difference with him; indeed, all had been part of the Powderly machine, and were among his loyal supporters until they decided that they could better serve their own personal interests by breaking with him.[42]

In many of the small towns and urban centers in rural areas, the Order continued to hold its own. It still maintained a vigorous life among government employees in the nation's capital, and it kept a foothold in some industries through the old device of organizing suspended and expelled members of trade unions and signing agreements with employers which included a scale of wages considerably lower than those demanded by the unions outside of the Order.[43]

The Order uttered one of its last vigorous gasps in the early months of 1895 in the Brooklyn trolley strike, a bloody industrial struggle that raged over the entire area of that sprawling city.* The defeat of the 6,000 trainmen, members of D.A. 75, meant that the most important remaining District Assembly had been destroyed.[44]

"No sadder chapter in the history of the world's labor movement has been written than that which records the decadence of this once and great powerful organization," commented the Boston *Labor Leader* on December 7, 1895. "In the short space of nine years its membership has decreased from over 750,000 until its present strength, liberally estimated, is not over 20,000 in the entire country."

One after another the magnificent temples of the Knights were taken over by their creditors.[45] By 1900 the Order had ceased to be even a memory for most workers in the United States. In its report in that year the Industrial Commission placed the K. of L. membership at "a few thousand." [46]

The K. of L. was still alive in Boston in 1932. The Order had assemblies among Boston's city employees, among some of the Boston and Albany Railroad workers, and other trades. The last local, 3030 in Boston, consisting of 50 motion picture operators, finally gave up the ghost by merging with an A. F. of L. union in October, 1949.[47]

THE TRAGEDY BEHIND THE DECLINE

Speaking of the decline of the K. of L., George E. McNeill correctly pointed out: "The story of the heroism of the rank and file will live in history, and the responsibility will not rest upon them." [48] The tragedy of the decline and disappearance of the Knights has been repeated too

---

* The strike was for an increase of wages from $2 a day for 18 hours work to $2.25. It was broken by the National Guard. (Brooklyn *Daily Eagle,* Jan. 27, 28, 1895.)

many times in American labor history. That tragedy was due to the rise of a "rule or ruin" leadership which became corrupt and lost contact with the fundamental problems of the workers, a leadership that was more concerned with winning respectability and of earning applause from the employers and their allies than in gaining basic improvements for the workers.

The rise of the K. of L. was a period of the greatest militancy in the ranks of the workers. A crusading spirit swept the working class. The unity of all workers, Negro and white, men and women, native-born and foreign-born, against their common exploiters fired the imagination, aroused the initiative, and inspired the confidence of the great masses in the Knights to accomplish remarkable deeds. The army of labor was surging forward. It was winning important victories. Its spirit and morale were high.

But the leadership of the Order destroyed this unity and this marvelous militant morale. The enemy the workers were asked to fight was no longer their exploiters but the militant elements who had made such a vital contribution to the growth of the organization. The radicals in the labor movement and not the employers were made the enemy. More attention was paid to destroying the trade unions than in completing the great task of the organization of the unorganized. More concern was expressed for winning the applause of the employers than for winning gains for the workers.

In such an atmosphere it is not surprising that the crusading spirit that had accompanied the rise of the Knights disappeared. It was too much to expect workers to become excited over the prospect of expelling the radical elements who they knew were self-sacrificing, militant fighters, and to shout with joy over the prospect of fighting other unions. Slowly but surely the Order found itself shorn of its former vitality and strength.

Privately, Powderly acknowledged that a labor policy based on gaining respectability and winning the applause of the employers must of necessity destroy the militancy of the labor movement. "There is no objection to the labor organization," he wrote in September, 1892, "if it would only organize and do nothing more, but if it attempts to win an advance in wages and strikes then its members are communists, anarchists and loafers. If on the other hand, they do not strike but take political action then the same bedeviled press howls them down for meddling in politics." [49] Later, Powderly also admitted that a labor policy geared towards appeasing the Catholic Church hierarchy was not one that was suited to advance the workers' interests.*

* In 1917, when he penned this observation, Powderly confessed that his experiences as leader of the Knights "shook my belief in the Catholic Church. . . ." (*The Path I Trod*, pp. 371-75.)

It was precisely because the leaders of the Order reduced the organization to one that served the employers and their allies that they earned the scorn of the rank-and-file. Buchanan points out that "the circulars of the Master Workman prohibiting strikes, political action, assessments in aid of brothers in need and the like, had raised the query, 'What are we organized for?' and no satisfactory answer being forthcoming, the unanswered left the Order." [50]

In short, the working people had become tired of paying dues to an organization which did nothing to help them in their struggles against the employers and which maligned and expelled all who championed the cause of struggle. Those who were not driven out dropped out of an organization which had given such great promise, but whose destinies were controlled by men who had no interest in and no plans for realizing that promise.

Yet that promise was to remain. For, despite its inglorious end, the K. of L. did make a number of very important contributions to the American labor movement. As heirs to the best traditions of the National Labor Union, the Knights established a magnificent record of labor solidarity, of a workers' unity strong enough to surmount differences of race, creed, sex, national origin, and skill. It was the first organization to unify large sections of the working class and present a solid front against the oppressors. At its height, with its organization of skilled and unskilled, men and women, North and South, Negro and white, of all religious and political opinions, the Knights of Labor gave the modern American labor movement a democratic tradition to live up to, greater and more important than that of any other labor body of the nineteenth century. Despite its conservative leadership, it challenged, at its height, the rising might of monopoly capitalism through strikes, boycotts, and political action.

These were no small achievements, and although the Order did not last long after it reached its height in 1886, American labor has benefitted from its contributions ever since.

CHAPTER 12

The Formative Years of the A. F. of L.

The boom in labor organization in the mid-'eighties was bound up with the meteoric rise of the Knights of Labor, but it did not follow that organization in its rapid descent into oblivion. On the contrary, while the K. of L. was disintegrating, the American Federation of Labor was experiencing a slow but steady growth. Membership figures furnished by the Federation and its leaders during these early years need to be heavily discounted because of an overzealousness to prove the organization's strength.* However, the number of national unions affiliated with the Federation increased. By 1892 the 13 national unions which founded the A. F. of L. in 1886 had grown to 40 national unions. Most of these unions had small membership, but a number had come out of the 'eighties with a fairly substantial body of members. Among the stronger unions affiliated with the Federation were the United Brotherhood of Carpenters and Joiners with a membership of about 57,000; the Cigar Makers' Union with some 27,000 members; the Iron and Steel Workers' Union with over 24,000 members; the Iron Molders' Union with a membership of about 23,000, and the Typographical Union with 28,000 members.[1]

The slow progress of the A. F. of L. during its formative years did not, of course, equal the phenomenal growth of the Knights during the mid-'eighties, and some contemporary labor spokesmen predicted that the Federation would soon be a thing of the past. In June, 1891, Robert Schilling, the veteran labor reformer, assured Powderly that he was expending too much time and energy worrying about the A. F. of L.

---

* According to the figures officially given by the A.F. of L., its membership increased from 138,000 to 225,000 between 1886 and 1890. Yet in December, 1886, P. J. McGuire placed the membership of the Federation at 316,782, and, in his testimony before the Joint Congressional Committee on Immigration in 1890, Gompers said that the A.F. of L. membership was 630,000. (*John Swinton's Paper*, Dec. 19, 1886; New York *World*, April 11, 1890.) The knife should be applied even to the official figures given by the Federation for these years.

The Federation was "traveling to oblivion as fast as hell," and "in two years . . . will be forgotten." Gompers was finished! "I think he will find it very difficult to be reelected, if his federation should last much longer." [2]

Schilling lived to eat his words. Yet there was much truth in his characterization of the A. F. of L. during these early years as "his [Gompers'] federation." For the youthful Federation was practically the "personal organization" of Samuel Gompers. [3]

ROLE OF GOMPERS

After adjourning the A. F. of L. Convention at Columbus, Ohio in December, 1886, the delegates left the work of the organization entirely in Gompers' charge. He was to devote his entire attention to the advancement of the Federation, and was to receive, if the organization had the money, a salary of $1,000 annually. With an empty treasury, in an office eight by ten feet, equipped with a kitchen table, a child's writing desk, some crates to be used for chairs and empty tomato boxes for filing cases, Gompers set to work to build the Federation.

Whatever his faults, lack of energy and enthusiasm and of a selfless devotion to the youthful A. F. of L. were not among them. He worked tirelessly, day and night, doing every conceivable job including that of errand boy. He wrote in March, 1887: ". . . my official duties are taking up my entire time and energy. You may readily form an idea of the truth of this when I tell you that I have not had the pleasure of partaking of afternoon or evening meals (Sunday included) with my family for months and that although my aged parents live within a quarter of a mile from my 'residence' I have been to their house but twice in six months and then only on a flying visit." [4] *

Money for the Federation came in so slowly that Gompers was compelled to insert a public appeal in the labor press during the spring of 1887, calling upon the affiliated unions to pay their charter fees and per capita taxes. "If the principles which the Federation was organized to contend for, are of any moment," he pleaded, "they are worth paying a trifle for it." The response was so discouraging that Gompers was faced with the decision of "giving up the position, take a job at my trade, or starve." "If the unions of the country don't want a Federation they don't

---

* Evidently, there were other reasons for Gompers' failure to be with his family more often. George Edmonston, one of the leaders of the Carpenters' and Joiners' Union and a member of the A.F. of L. Executive Council, wrote: "I am rather inclined to think Sam is a model husband as the haunts that used to know him now mourn his absence; his favorite pool room has closed up doors." (Edmonston to "Dear Friend," Aug. 11, 1892, *AFL Corr.*) The convivialities of the saloon were always welcome to Gompers.

and that settles it," he raged. "With a large family depending upon me for support, I cannot give my *entire time* without recompense." [5]

THE EARLY A. F. OF L. ORGANIZERS

Gompers was by no means the only one to make personal sacrifices to build the early A. F. of L. Organizers for the Federation, most of them doing voluntary work without pay,* faced extreme hardships. "The undersigned," went a typical letter from an A. F. of L. organizer to Gompers, "has been driven to the very lowest ebb financially as he has been boycotted & blacklisted, & he & family have had to live this winter on the charity of relatives and friends." Another wrote: "I have a wife and three children to look after and they all have me spotted. . . . I have been discharged, Blacklisted, Spotted, and every thing else on account of my principles as a union man."

Despite these terrible hardships, most of the early A. F. of L. organizers persisted in their work of building the Federation. "I will speak my sentiments live or Die, Sink or Swim," wrote an organizer who had been discharged and blacklisted, "for all this is only evidence that I am doing good work and it is a great encouragement to me." Another in a similar position wrote: "I have made up my mind some years ago that the ballance [*sic*] of my life should be devoted to the elevation of mankind and the emancipation of the Laborer." [6]

In later years, many of the A. F. of L.'s organizers like many of the leaders of the Federation and the unions affiliated with it, were men who regarded the labor movement simply as a lush business through which they could enrich themselves. But most of the organizers for the early A. F. of L. were men and women who were consumed with zealous determination to improve the conditions of their fellow workers. Dominated solely by a hatred of exploitation and of the system which produced such widespread misery and poverty, these men and women, Negro and white, worked themselves to the bone for a mere pittance, contacting workers and exhorting them to unite against their exploiters. Eugene V. Debs wrote accurately in describing these unsung heroes and heroines of the American working class: "The labor agitator of the early day held

---

* Organizers for the A.F. of L., unlike those in the K. of L., received no commissions for the unions they organized. Some received a small salary and expenses, but most were volunteers who worked without compensation. When their personal funds ran out, they would return to their jobs, if they could still hold on to them. "I have been doing no work for a few weeks, that is my regular work that I make a living at," wrote an organizer from New Orleans. "My money is nearly run out now so if you do not hear from me in organizing other unions just conclude that I have gone to work and have to make a little money to support myself for a while." (J. W. Callahan to Gompers, June 28, 1892, *AFL Corr.*)

no office, had no title, drew no salary, saw no footlights, heard no applause, never saw his name in print, and fills an unknown grave. The
labor movement is his monument, and though his name is not inscribed
upon it, his soul is in it, and with it marches on forever." [7]

There was little that Gompers could do for the persecuted organizers
other than wish them better luck in the future.[8] But there can be little
doubt that these moving letters were largely responsible for the fact that
though he continued to suffer privation,* he did not relinquish his position as president of the Federation. He scraped together enough money
from the trade unions to meet office bills, and he even raised the necessary
funds to launch a journal, *Th Union Advocate,* which the A. F. of L.
Executive Council established as the Federation's official journal.[9] †

GOMPERS ON THE A. F. OF L.'S OBJECTIVES

Gompers once proudly reported: "At no time in my life have I worked
out definitely an articulated economic theory." [10] Yet in the late 'eighties
and early 'nineties, he did "work out" the tactics and strategy of the
youthful A. F. of L., many of which continued to influence the Federation
for years to come.

Despite his awareness that there was a long and varied history of the
American labor movement from colonial times to the last quarter of the
nineteenth century, Gompers believed that trade unionism in the United
States at the time the A. F. of L. was founded was "practically in its
infancy." By this he meant that the bargaining power of the workers w s
still puny in a period when the tendency was towards greater and greater
"concentration of wealth and power" in industry. Compared with the
"lightning rapidity" with which power was concentrating in the hands
of the capitalist class, the labor movement had been moving "with the
gait of a stage coach." [11]

To bring the labor movement to a level where it could cope with the
growing power of capital, it was essential, Gompers argued, that the
A. F. of L. should avoid the errors of the past that had largely been
responsible for preventing organized labor from emerging from its
infancy. "We do not wish to raise a structure," he wrote in June, 1887,
"whose foundations are rotten, being built up by repeating the errors of
others who have preceded us." [12]

* On November 17, 1888, Gompers wrote to the A.F. of L. Executive Council:
"I had travelled in midwinter nearly 10,000 miles made about 50 speeches with the
greatest success and came home about $90.00 out of pocket." (Gompers Letter-Books,
Samuel Gompers Memorial Room, A.F. of L. Building, Washington, D. C. Hereafter
cited as *GLB.*)

† *The Union Advocate* had a brief existence. The A.F. of L. convention in 1887
voted to abandon publication of a journal, and it was not until March, 1894, that an
official organ was again published. This was the *American Federationist,* under
Gompers' editorship.

What were the errors of the past that Gompers sought to avoid in building the Federation on a foundation which would make it possible both to survive and to forge ahead?

One was the practice, seen clearly in the case of the K. of L., of permitting all sorts of non-working class elements, including even employers, to belong to a labor union. Specifically criticizing the K. of L.'s policy of permitting employers to become members, Gompers pointed out that this "very frequently deterred working men from seeking an improvement in their condition by reason of fear in giving offence to such employers." [13]

In dozens of letters, Gompers emphasized that "the members of Unions affiliated with the American Federation of Labor must be exclusively wage-earners. None other can be admitted." There was room for non-working class elements, even employers, to work jointly with the trade unions in broad, progressive movements, but the unions must be reserved for the worker, whom Gompers defined as "one who receives wages for his work as in contradistinction to the wage payer." He had learned from "the honored dead Karl Marx," whose works he had read in German,* the all-important significance of this principle in labor struggles. In a letter, dated October 8, 1890, Gompers, paraphrasing Marx, stated the case succinctly: "The A. F. of L. holds it as a self-evident maxim that the emancipation of the working class must be achieved by the working classes themselves. There is no doubt that men with the best intentions outside of the ranks of labor can aid in the movement. We court their co-operation, their sympathy and their advice but cannot give into their hands the direction of the affairs which rightfully belong to and must be exercised by the wage workers." [14]

Another danger arising from allowing non-working class elements to enter the trade unions was that they tended to divert the workers' organizations from the immediate problems facing them. A major error of the past which flowed from this, in Gompers' judgment, was hitching the labor movement to the wagons of different panacea-peddlers who promised an easy solution to all of the problems of the working class. In this category he placed such utopian nostrums as the single tax, currency reform, producers' cooperatives, and other enticing all-embracing plans to lift the working class out of wage slavery by a short-cut route. "The ills of our social and economic system," Gompers wrote, "cannot be cured by patent medicine." [15]

One of Gompers' chief objections to the middle class reformist panaceas was that they tended to push the class struggle out of the minds of the

---

* In his autobiography, *Seventy Years of Life and Labor,* Gompers asserts that he studied German with special diligence so that he might read Marx. In an interview with a reporter for the Detroit *Free Press* in 1896, he emphasized the same point, and added in his own handwriting to the printed report of the interview that he did this "to be of greater service to the [labor] movement." (Detroit *Free Press,* Oct. 18, 1896, and copy with Gompers' handwritten additions in *AFL Corr.*)

workers by spreading illusions that they could be transformed into farmers, independent business men or cooperative self-employers in an economic system under which workers were likely to remain workers throughout their lives. "When the laboring man becomes an investor even in a small way he is less liable to engage in a conflict between labor and capital," Gompers wrote in 1892. Regarding trade unions as only a temporary necessity until he became an entrepreneur, the worker who was influenced by the panacea-peddler would not make the necessary contributions and sacrifices to build stable unions capable of combatting the "avarice of the capitalist classes." [16]

In later years, Gompers denied the existence of the class struggle, but not so in the period when the A. F. of L. was taking form. In the initial number of the *Union Advocate,* June, 1887, Gompers wrote: "Life is at best a hard struggle with contending forces. The life of the toiler is made doubly so by the avarice of the arrogant and tyrannical employing classes. Greedy and overbearing as they are, trying at nearly all times to get their pound of flesh out of the workers, it is necessary to form organizations of the toilers to prevent these tendencies more strongly developing, as wealth is concentrating itself into fewer hands to prevent engulfing and drowning us in an abyss of hoplessness and despair." [17]

Gompers had only scorn for the doctrines spread by Powderly and other leaders of the Knights which proclaimed that the interests of labor and capital were identical and harmonious. He stated flatly, at this time, that it was impossible to have harmonious relations with "cruel and iniquitous employers and companies who think more of dividends than of human hearts and bodies." "The production of profits," Gompers emphasized, "is the primary and constant object of the capitalistic system." Under this system, the blood of the workers was "being used as the lubricating oil for the machines that grind their very bones into cash to gratify the wishes of the insatiable monsters whose only deity was the almighty dollar." To think of harmonious relations between labor and capital under such a system was the height of folly. "I think that the struggles of labor cannot be obviated in the future," Gompers stated categorically in 1892. He set forth his "credo" for this period in the following statement: "From my earliest understanding of the conditions that prevail in the industrial world, I have been convinced that I have asserted that the economic interests of the employing class and the workers are not harmonious. . . . There are times when for temporary purposes, interests are reconciled, but they are temporary only." [18]

Disagreeing sharply with those leaders of the Knights who regarded strikes as an outmoded "relic of barbarism," Gompers gave unswerving support to labor's right to strike. In an interview in the New York *World* in April, 1890, Gompers declared that the A. F. of L. had found through experience that strikes were often "the only means whereby the rightful demands of labor can be secured." As he saw it, "the strike is the most highly civilized method which the workers, the wealth producers, have yet devised to protest against wrong and injustice. . . ." [19]

The emancipation of the working class from the capitalist system, Gompers announced, was one of the objectives of the youthful A. F. of L. Gompers' letters of this period contain frequent references to this theme. "I believe with the most advanced thinkers as to ultimate ends including the abolition of the wage system," he wrote in 1887. He was to repeat this sentence in many of his letters during these early years of the A. F. of L., always being careful, however, to link together the struggle for immediate demands and the ultimate goal of emancipation from wage slavery under the capitalist system. He insisted that only through the day-to-day struggles around "conditions that prevail in the shop, the factory, the mill and the mine; the question of higher wages, less hours of labor, less obnoxious rules and conditions," could the working class be effectively mobilized for the final emancipation from wage slavery. As he put it, once again paraphrasing Marx: * "Out of the improvements in these respects are evolved the necessary stamina, manhood, independence and intelligence which prepare the workers for a higher and nobler civilization, but without these elementary improvements disaster is the result." [20]

During these years, Gompers frequently evaluated issues and demands in terms of the relationship between the immediate struggles and the ultimate goal of the working class. Thus he objected to Henry George's single tax theory on the ground that it "does not promise present reform, nor an ultimate solution." He suggested to an organizer about to set out on an educational tour among A. F. of L. unions that the single tax was an issue be omitted from the discussion since it was "not a living material issue upon which the workers depend for amelioration and final emancipation." [21]

In his correspondence with European Socialist and labor leaders,† Gompers made it clear that the A. F. of L.'s ultimate aim was the emancipation of the working class from capitalist wage slavery. One of his letters to Victor Delahaye, to be read to a gathering of French workers, opened: "Comrades, Though oceans divide us, the same spirit and purpose prompts us to seek in organization and the final emancipation of the Proletariat of the World." Another letter to the French Socialist leader concluded:

* For Marx's statement on this issue, see Karl Marx, *Value, Price and Profit*, New York, 1930, p. 16.

† Gompers kept up a vast correspondence with labor and Socialist leaders abroad. He received letters from Tom Mann, John Burns, Eleanor Marx Aveling, Victor Delahaye, Wilhelm Liebknecht, and scores of other European labor leaders as well as from labor leaders in Japan. There is a huge collection of these letters, most of them unpublished, in the A.F. of L. Correspondence. Gompers' replies are in the Gompers Letter-Books.

"Convey to the organized wage-workers of France and yourself as well as the men and women who strive and struggle for the improvement of the condition and final emancipation of the toiling masses the kindest wishes of,

Yours, sincerely,
Samuel Gompers." [22]

THE EIGHT-HOUR MOVEMENT, 1889-1891

As in previous years, the issue that solidly welded the bonds of international labor solidarity was the struggle for the shorter work day.

The employers' counter-offensive following the May First, 1886, general strike halted but did not end the struggle for the eight-hour day. Within two years the workers had reformed their lines and were in a position to actively renew the movement. At the convention of the A. F. of L., held in St. Louis in December, 1888, it was decided that all efforts of organized labor should be concentrated for the inauguration of the eight-hour workday on May 1, 1890. The Executive Council was instructed to issue pamphlets and arrange mass meetings to advance the movement. Four days were set apart upon which the working people of the country were to hold eight-hour mass meetings: Washington's Birthday, February 22, 1889 and 1890; Independence Day, July 4, 1889, and Labor Day, September 2, 1889. The movement was to be climaxed with a great general strike on May 1, 1890.

The A. F. of L. convention called upon all labor bodies to perfect their organizations, and to urge every man and woman who worked at the trades over which they had jurisdiction to join the unions so that they might be better prepared on May 1, 1890, to enforce eight hours as a day's work.* Where no local unions or central labor bodies existed, Eight-Hour Leagues should be formed to further the movement. The watchwords of the struggle were, "Eight Hours! Firm, Peaceable and Positive"; the slogan, the familiar: "Eight hours for work, Eight hours for rest, Eight hours for what we will." [23]

It is clear that the A. F. of L. regarded the eight-hour movement as a great organizing issue, a conclusion justified by the experience of the movement during the years, 1884-1886. Regardless of the outcome on May 1, 1890, Gompers pointed out early in 1889, "the agitation will do us good. It will wake up the millions of workers from their present lethargy.

---

* The emphasis throughout the eight-hour movement of 1888-1891 was on obtaining and enforcing the shorter work day through the organized strength of the workers in their unions. "Eight-Hour Laws made by politicians," said the *Carpenter*, expressing a typical point of view, "will never be observed by the employers. The only eight-hour law that will ever have binding force in this country will be made and enforced by the workingmen." (Jan. 20, 1891.)

Upon it all men of labor, however much they may differ upon other matters, can unite upon this." In short, the eight-hour day was "a watchword and a movement around which all sincere men in our cause should rally." [24]

The campaign inaugurated by the A. F. of L. was militant and aggressive. On Washington's Birthday, 1889, 240 mass meetings were held simultaneously in as many cities, and resolutions, prepared and submitted by the A. F. of L. Executive Council, were adopted endorsing the action of the Federation's St. Louis Convention, the participants pledging themselves "individually and collectively, to aid to the full extent of our ability regardless of all minor considerations, this grand and determined movement of the American people for the Eight-hour Workday, and to conquer, in spite of all opposition." [25]

The second series of simultaneous demonstrations, held on July 4, 1889, took place in 311 cities and towns throughout the country. On Labor Day, September 2, the number of meetings to agitate the eight-hour question, held simultaneously, had grown to more than 420. By November 9, 1889, over 300 general organizers of the A. F. of L. had held meetings and delivered addresses in their respective cities and towns, and several special organizers and lecturers had been placed in the field to travel throughout the country to address working people on the eight-hour question. By this time, too, more than 50,000 pamphlets had been distributed; more than half a million circulars issued, and 1,200 personal letters sent to prominent leaders throughout the country.[26]

Across the Atlantic, meanwhile, the determination of the American workers to gain the eight-hour day was hailed, and labor organizations in England, France, Germany, and other European countries instituted steps to advance the movement. The international aspect of the eight-hour struggle was stressed in the A. F. of L.'s literature. Thus a widely-distributed pamphlet, published in 1889 under the title, *The Economic and Social Importance of the Eight-Hour Movement,* pointed out: "Although there is no international organization, there is a manifest international movement in this direction. Even in Germany the demand for eight hours has been voiced by a strike of nearly a hundred thousand laborers. . . . In England they have already reached nine hours and a half, and are now asking for the next step towards eight. The same movement is taking definite form in France and Belgium." [27]

On July 14, 1889, the hundredth anniversary of the fall of the Bastille, the leaders of organized Socialist movements of many lands met in Paris at the founding congress of the Second International. Although the A. F. of L. was not represented at the convention, Gompers sent a message to the Paris Congress informing it of the contemplated action for May 1, 1890, urging unity of action internationally for the eight-hour day and proposing that May 1 be celebrated "as an International Labor Day." As a result, a French delegate, Lavigne, introduced a resolution favoring an "international manifestation" for May First in support of the eight-hour day. Accordingly, the Paris Congress resolved

"To organize a great international demonstration, so that in all countries and in all cities on one appointed day the toiling masses shall demand of the state authorities the legal reduction of the working day to eight hours. . . .

"Since a similar demonstration has already been decided upon for May 1, 1890, by the American Federation of Labor at its Convention in St. Louis, December, 1888, the day is accepted for the international demonstration.

"The workers of the various countries must organize this demonstration according to conditions prevailing in each country." [28]

The last paragraph in the Paris Congress' resolution was already being discussed in the United States. For a while Gompers felt that by winning public support through a mass agitational campaign and by organizing labor's ranks thoroughly, "the employing class as an advantageous alternative will concede the Eight-Hour rule rather than risk the loss consequent upon a strike for it." At the same time, however, he made it clear that a strike would be resorted to if necessary. Surveying the state of the labor movement in 1889, Gompers reached the conclusion that it would be a serious mistake for a union to go out on strike on May 1, 1890 "whether prepared for it or not." By February, 1889, he had decided that the best strategy to be followed in the May Day effort at obtaining the eight-hour day was to have it undertaken by a few unions at a time. "It does not necessarily follow that because we are agitating the subject that all unions must strike for it [on] May 1st, 1890. . . . I am aware that many organizations will not be able to enforce the demand but if we succeed in a few instances, those who have achieved the victory can after that aid those left behind to reach the goal." [29]

In short, there was to be no general strike for the eight-hour day. Instead, one or two unions, capable of waging a successful struggle, would lead the way, and with the aid of the rest of the labor movement, including the K. of L.,* establish the eight-hour day in their respective trades.

* The A.F. of L. Executive Council sent an open letter to the K. of L. General Assembly at Atlanta, Georgia, November, 1889, outlining what steps had already been taken in preparation for the May 1, 1890, demonstration, and appealing to the Order to join in the common fight for the eight-hour day. Urging the K. of L. not to be concerned over who started the movement, the letter stressed the need for cooperation between the Order and the A.F. of L. in the struggle since "the interests of the toiling masses are identical." (Gompers to the officers and delegates of the General Assembly of the Knights of Labor, assembled, at Atlanta, Georgia, Nov. 9th, 1889, GLB.) Unfortunately, the leadership of the Knights rejected the proposal, branding the May 1, 1890 demonstration as an alien and radical undertaking. (Powderly to John W. Hayes, Dec. 16, 1889, PHC.)

Every year thereafter another union (or several unions) would follow this pattern on May First until the employers generally conceded the eight-hour day.

In March, 1890, after polling all of the affiliated unions as to whether they wished to be selected to make the demand for the eight-hour day on May 1, 1890, the A. F. of L. Executive Council selected the United Brotherhood of Carpenters and Joiners to lead the way for the eight-hour demand in 1890, to be followed by the United Mine Workers whenever this union's executive board should decide to take the step.* The choice of the Carpenters and Joiners was a good one; the union had built up a big strike fund for the eight-hour struggle, and was fully prepared to battle it out with the employers with the assistance of the rest of the labor movement. While the union would depend primarily upon its own treasury, the A. F. of L. raised a fund through an assessment on its affiliates to assist the Carpenters. Furthermore, on the eve of May 1, 1890, Gompers issued an appeal to "The Toilers of America," urging them to "aid the Carpenters and Joiners to win in the contest." [30]

The appeal was heeded, union after union resolving that, since they could not participate in the struggle directly, they would aid the Carpenters and Joiners with all the means at their disposal.† At the same time, these unions called on all workers to participate in the May First demonstrations.[31]

May First, 1890, brought one of the most powerful demonstrations of labor the world had yet seen. The New York *World* on May 2, 1890, devoted almost its entire first page to coverage of "Labor's Emancipation Day" in the United States and throughout the world. "PARADE OF JUBILANT WORKINGMEN IN ALL THE TRADE CENTRES OF THE CIVILIZED WORLD," read one of the headlines. "EVERYWHERE THE WORKMEN JOIN IN DEMANDS FOR A NORMAL DAY," read another.

Tens of thousands of workers demonstrated throughout the world—in

* The miners were scheduled to make the demand on May 1st, 1892, but they decided that conditions did not warrant their acting and called it off. However, 25,000 miners, principally in Iowa and Pittsburgh, went on strike for higher wages and shorter hours. The A.F. of L. contributed $2,000 to the strikers, mainly to those in Iowa, but the strike failed.

This represented the last significant attempt of the A.F. of L. to provide central direction of the movement for shorter hours. After 1891, the movement was left to the individual unions themselves. In 1895 Gompers proposed that the Federation select another union to strike for the eight-hour day on May 1, 1896, and a year later, he recommended that preparations be made for a general strike on May 1, 1898. But nothing came of these proposals. (*Proceedings,* A.F. of L. Convention, 1895, pp. 30, 61-62, 1896, pp. 23, 68.)

† Gompers was able, through these contributions, to turn over $12,060.64 to the Carpenters to further their efforts to attain the eight-hour day. (Gompers to P. J. McGuire, May 8, 1890, *GLB*.)

Australia, Austria, Belgium, Chile, Cuba, Denmark, England,* France, Germany, Holland, Hungary, Italy, Peru, Switzerland, and the United States. Wrote Frederick Engels: "the proletariat of Europe and America is holding a review of its forces; it is mobilized for the first time as One army, under One flag, and fighting for One immediate aim: an eight-hour working day. . . . The spectacle we are now witnessing will make the capitalists and landowners of all lands realize that today the proletarians are, in very truth, united. If only Marx were with me to see it with his own eyes!" [32]

In a similar vein, Samuel Gompers wrote: "The demonstration of the toilers of Europe proves the universality of our movement and is a ray of hope for the attainment of the poet's dream, 'The Parliament of Man,' 'The Federation of the World!'" [33]

In many industrial centers in the United States, the May First demonstrations were under the joint sponsorship of the A. F. of L. and the S.L.P. In Chicago, 30,000 workers marched under this joint sponsorship. One hundred trade unions were represented in the line of march, led by the 6,000 striking Carpenters and Joiners. "WE LIVE BY LABOR NOT BY WAR," read one of the signs carried by the Carpenters. "ABOLISH WAGE SLAVERY," was another.[34]

Seventy trade unions marched in the New York demonstration, many of them carrying red flags along with American flags. The slogans on the banners carried by the demonstrators reflected the Socialist influence: "No More Bosses—Wage Slavery Must Go—The Present Industrial System Means Robbery—The 8 hour day is the Next Step in the Labor Movement. The Socialistic Commonwealth is the final aim."

After P. J. McGuire, vice-president of the A. F. of L. and Secretary-Treasurer of the Carpenters and Joiners, had spoken, the demonstrators adopted a resolution hailing both the A. F. of L. and the Paris Congress of the Second International for having inaugurated "a new and final eight-hour movement not to be relaxed until its complete triumph is achieved." Another resolution declared that "owing to the workings of capitalism the eight-hour demand can be but a measure of temporary relief for the exploited masses and nothing short of the abolition of the wage system and the reorganization of society on a socialist basis can effectively solve the labor problem." [35]

* In England, some workers marched on May First; but the vast majority turned out on May 4, 250,000 in London alone. Of particular importance in organizing this tremendous outpouring of British workers was Marx's daughter, Eleanor Aveling Marx. She was active in the Legal Eight Hours and International Labour League which mobilized the eight-hour movement in England. The League was in close touch with developments in the United States. George Copsey, its Honorary Secretary, corresponded with Gompers in order "to strengthen each & every organization having the same aims & objects." (*See especially* Copsey to Gompers, Feb. 1, 1890, *AFL Corr.*)

The success achieved by the Carpenters and Joiners far exceeded the expectations of the most optimistic labor leaders. The union reported that it had won the eight-hour day for 46,197 workers in 137 cities and nearly 30,000 had reduced their hours from 10 to 9 hours. The movement had also brought an influx of new members. Between March 14 and July 14, 1890, 132 new locals were formed; in all the Carpenters gained more than 22,000 new members in 1890, as compared to an increase in the organization's membership of 3,078 in 1889.

Nor was the effect of the eight-hour movement confined to the Carpenters. Other building trades succeeded in reducing hours in many communities. The German-American Typographia won the eight-hour day in nearly every German printing office in the nation. The Granite Cutters' National Union won the nine-hour day for its members, and the Bakers and Tailors won the ten-hour day in many cities. In short, hundreds of thousands of workers secured increases in their wages and reduced their hours of labor in the strikes on and around May 1, 1890.[36] *

To Gompers these victories offered decisive proof of American labor's "determination to work more energetically in the contest for the improvement and final emancipation of labor." Writing to a French Socialist on May 9, 1890, he declared: "The agitation for the Eight-Hour movement not only has had the effect of gaining this immense advantage for the Carpenters and Joiners of America, but it has given courage and hope to the working people who for years were disheartened and acting on the defensive against the encroachments of the employing classes. Every trade and labor union of the country has vastly increased its membership." [37]

Reports from the A. F. of L. organizers corroborated Gompers' conclusion. They emphasized that the Federation and its affiliates had gained enormous prestige as a result of the A. F. of L.'s militant activity in sponsoring and mobilizing the movement for the eight-hour demonstration while the K. of L. had suffered a serious blow to its prestige because of its leadership's sabotage of the struggle. As one organizer in Michigan noted: "The position of affairs is at present such that we are crowded with the work of organizing. Every branch of labor wants to know if they can come in with us." [38]

Internationally, too, the A. F. of L. gained prestige. At a gatheirng in London late in 1890 on the occasion of Frederick Engels' 70th birthday, Wilhelm Liebknecht, August Bebel, Eleanor Marx Aveling, Tom Mann, William Thorne, and other Socialist and labor leaders, praised the A. F. of L. for its work in advancing the international struggle for the eight-hour day. When many of these same figures took steps to establish a

* According to *Bradstreets'*, more strikes were initiated on May 1, 1890, than on any other single day in the history of the United States up to that time. For the month of May, 1890, 243 strikes were reported involving 67,507 workers. (*Bradstreets'*, May 3, 10, 31, 1890.)

series of international bodies to prevent the export of strikebreakers from one country to another, the A. F. of L. was chosen as the body to represent the United States, and Gompers was appointed one of the International Secretaries of Labor. Gompers accepted the honor on behalf of the A. F. of L. He hoped, he informed Eleanor Marx Aveling, that "this movement as well as the aspirations of labor may tend to the closer international Alliance to crystalize and attain the fondest hopes of laborers; their amelioration and final emancipation." [39]

GOMPERS STRESSES SOLIDARITY

In sending fraternal greetings to the International Labor Congress held at Brussels, Belgium, in August, 1891, Gompers stressed the importance of strengthening the ties of international labor solidarity: "It appears to us that notwithstanding the difference in the character of the Labor Movement in our respective countries, caused by conditions possibly beyond our past control, we should endeavor to inculcate the knowledge and recognition by our fellow-toilers of the interdependent internationality and identity of the interests of the wage-earning masses." [40]

The phrase—"the identity of the interests of the wage-earning masses" —appears frequently in Gompers' writings and speeches during these early years. There was a good reason for this. From its very inception, the Federation was confronted with the accusation that it was interested solely in the organization of the skilled craftsmen, and actually "objected to the organization of unskilled workmen." The A. F. of L. was often characterized in labor circles during these years as "a business organization of the skilled mechanics of the country." [41]

Gompers frequently and vigorously challenged this interpretation of the A. F. of L.'s objectives. He pointed out that the Federation always maintained that a trade union could be organized "from all classes of wage workers of any particular trade or calling, whether skilled or unskilled," and he warned unions affiliated with the A. F. of L. that it would be dangerous to follow a course of neglecting the welfare of the unskilled workers who, feeling a natural resentment at being neglected, could be utilized as strikebreakers by the employers. "The effort of organized labor," he stated, "is not simply to protect skilled labor. The effort of organized labor is to protect and advance the interests of every wage earner, and to secure justice for all; and experience has demonstrated that these can be best attained by a broad and comprehensive organization of workers of all branches, in any given industry, under one jurisdiction."

Basically, Gompers pointed out, it mattered little to the employer what color, sex, religion or nationality the worker belonged to; his sole concern was to obtain the cheapest labor. "The Protestants, the Catholic, the Jew and the free thinking unfair employers are all besmirched by the same tar. Religious professions or the absence of them count for naught when the question of the interests of the toiling masses are at stake. Their sole aim is to obtain labor at the lowest possible wage that the toilers are willing to work for and as a rule they do not ask what a man's religion is but how cheap and how long he will work."

Whatever prejudices workers might have on questions of religion, race, color, nationality, they must surrender them at the door of the union.* "Coming into the meeting of the Union," Gompers repeatedly emphasized, "the question of labor's interests and the interests of our families and our fellow men should be uppermost in our minds. All other divisions and causes for antagonism should be left on the outside." [42]

GOMPERS' POSITION

Gompers' statements on labor solidarity like those on the class struggle, the emancipation of labor from wage slavery, and others of his militant and radical utterances which are quoted above will certainly sound startling to those who know that Gompers spent much of his time during his long career as A. F. of L. president in combatting these very principles. The question naturally arises: Was there a fundamental difference between Gompers of the early Federation and Gompers after the late 1890's?

Before answering this question it is important to note that at least in one respect Gompers remained consistent throughout his tenure as A. F. of L. president. Consistently and bureaucratically he ignored the constitution of the A. F. of L. as well as the specific instructions of the conventions whenever he opposed the policies they advocated. In the majority of instances, as we shall see, he defied the will of the A. F. of L. membership, as expressed in conventions, when it favored a radical and militant program. One example during the early years of the Federation will illustrate this point. When the Federation convened a few days after the Henry George mayoralty campaign of 1886, it will be recalled, the

* Gompers, however, did see religion introduced into unions where no such thing occurred. Thus he objected in 1891 to the United Hebrew Trades on the ground that it was organizing Jewish workers "in unions of their religion rather than of their trade." (Gompers to W. C. Owen, July 10, 1891, *GLB*.) Actually, this criticism was completely unjustified. There was nothing religious about the United Hebrew Trades nor about the unions to which the Jewish workers belonged. The U.H.T. organized the Jewish workers according to their trades, not their religion. It is significant that in his autobiography, written years later, Gompers reversed his earlier attitude of hostility to the U.H.T. and conceded that its formation marked an important advance for the Jewish-American labor movement. In a large measure, as his letter to Owen makes clear, Gompers' earlier hostility to the U.H.T. stemmed from his objection to the Socialist principles of the organization.

delegates enthusiastically adopted a resolution declaring that the time had arrived for the working people to decide on united action at the ballot box and also resolved to urge a most generous support to labor's independent political movement. But Gompers deliberately sabotaged the convention's decision. Instead of carrying out the mandate of the Federation, he "stood back and watched" and "did not let the A. F. of L. become entangled in any partisan activity. . . ." He even belittled the entire movement for independent political action in a letter to the United Labor Party's journal, and refused to say a word for its candidates during the 1887 campaigns, declaring that the questions involved did not affect labor's interests.[43]

The incident is significant in at least two important respects. For one thing, it reveals that for all of his progressive and militant utterances, Gompers actually lagged behind the A. F. of L. membership and even the leaders of the craft unions on the crucial issue of independent working class political action. For another, it discloses that from the very outset of the Federation, Gompers was a bureaucratic leader who had not the slightest hesitation in defying the will of the membership.

In addition to being fundamentally a labor bureaucrat, Gompers was also basically an opportunist who knew how to trim his sails to the particular situation he faced Writing to an International Socialist Congress Gompers could sound very radical indeed; addressing a gathering of business leaders he could sound very conservative. Expressing views at a time when the workers were becoming more radical under the impact of the growing power of monopoly and its domination of the government, Gompers could voice radical sentiments. At a time when many of the mass movements of the workers had been defeated and when the leaders of the craft unions were yielding to the monopolies, he could easily repudiate each and every one of his earlier progressive utterances. In short, Gompers was moved at all times by one consideration only: What would advance the interests of Samuel Gompers and further his career as president of the A. F. of L. In the early years, advancing the career of Samuel Gompers meant building the Federation since obviously unless the organization he headed attracted workers his position as president meant nothing. And from the very outset of the Federation, Gompers adopted the attitude that he had a vested interest in his job as president.

Gompers was shrewd enough to understand that during the early years of the A. F. of L. he was addressing workers who had gone through the militant struggles of the 'eighties and were deeply influenced by Socialist thought and by the principles of labor solidarity emphasized by the K. of L. To attract these workers to the A. F. of L., it was necessary to convince them that the Federation did not reject the class struggle or the ultimate goal of a new social system and that it continued the finest traditions of the Knights while disposing of those features which were hastening the

Order's decline.[44] To be sure, Gompers knew how to keep his radical utterances sufficiently vague and general as to render them often meaningless.* Nevertheless, he knew enough to advocate radical principles when these would advance his own position in the labor movement, and he was fully prepared to abandon them the moment he felt that they were proving to be an obstacle to his career.

Gompers had risen to leadership in his own organization, the Cigar Makers International Union, by advocating the principles of industrial unionism and by combatting the exclusive admission requirements under which the International not only refused to admit the unskilled and semi-skilled workers in the trade, but forbade its members to work in the same shop with them. Realizing that the union was doomed if it did not abandon its restrictive policies and that industrial unionism was growing more and more popular among the cigar makers, Gompers stressed the importance of uniting all the workers, skilled and unskilled, and permitting all branches of the industry to be eligible for membership, whether they worked by hand, mold, or machine.[45]

Gompers understood that many workers had been deeply influenced by the K. of L.'s emphasis upon industrial unionism as opposed to craft organization of the skilled workers only. Hence he began to champion a form of industrial unionism during these early years. In 1888 he recommended to the Federation that in the near future the basis of the A. F. of L. should be modeled on industrial divisions which would hold their own conventions, legislate on subjects that affected the general interests of their particular trades and industries, and would, in turn, be represented by their proportionate number of delegates in the conventions of the A. F. of L. With each industrial division having a representative on the Executive Council, the Federation would become a federation of industrial federations rather than a federation of trade unions.[46]

Gompers' proposal ran into the solid opposition of the trade union leaders in the Federation, and he quickly realized that he would never advance his career as A. F. of L. president if he advocated the principles of industrial unionism. He swiftly abandoned the plan and became a staunch defender of craft unionism. In short, Gompers was ready to support a progressive program as long as it would advance his career; the moment he saw that this would actually be an obstacle to his career he not only abandoned the program but became the leading opponent of what he previously had championed.

In abandoning so quickly the proposal for industrial federations, Gom-

* His statements about the "future development" of society and "emancipation of "labor" were extremely vague, and he never really specified the nature of the future society. The closest he came to it was to express the view, privately, that the trade unions were "the germ of the future state." (Gompers to George W. Perkins, Mar. 22, 1894, GLB.)

pers became a stalwart supporter of trade autonomy. This, of course, made a mockery of his lofty, militant statements. However progressive Gompers sounded in proclaiming what he represented were the principles of the Federation, they had absolutely no binding effect upon the affiliated unions which could and did violate these principles with impunity. Most leaders of the trade unions in the A. F. of L. were prepared to endorse Gompers' lofty statements on labor solidarity as long as they were couched in general terms. They agreed verbally with "the broad and liberal sentiments" he expressed, and that, as P. J. McGuire, second in command of the A. F. of L. put it, "the interests of the working classes are everywhere identical, and we should do all in our power to organize all trades and callings in every city, town and hamlet of the country." But they also made it clear that they regarded the interests of the skilled mechanics as paramount, that they would not consider jeopardizing the craft unions of skilled workers by organizing the unskilled in their trades, and that they did not expect the A. F. of L. to repeat the "tragic mistake" of the K. of L. by uniting skilled and unskilled in the same union.[47]

From the outset, therefore, a conflict developed in the youthful A. F. of L. between the principles of labor solidarity and that of craft narrowness, between the principles enunciated in statements affirming that the Federation sought to organize all workers regardless of skill, race, creed, color, sex or national origin and those enunciated and practiced by the leaders of the craft unions which emphasized primarily the interests of the skilled mechanics, most of whom were male, white, and native-American. The nature of this conflict is clearly set forth in the policy of the A. F. of L. during its formative years towards the organization of women, Negroes, and foreign-born workers.

CHAPTER 13

Early A. F. of L. and Labor Solidarity

The census statistics for the decade 1880-1890 revealed that the number of women workers had increased at a greater rate than that of men. There had been an increase of 4,076,008 males engaged in gainful occupations, or 27.64 percent, and of females, 1,267,554 or 47.88 percent.[1] These statistics alone gave validity to the statement of Eva McDonald-Valesh, a woman labor leader of the 1890's, who told the A. F. of L. membership: "If men seriously expect higher wages or shorter hours they must, for their own self-preservation, organize the women, making them valuable allies instead of a source of danger." [2]

WOMEN WORKERS

Officially the A. F. of L. understood the significance of the above statement. Women were eligible to membership in the Federation under the same conditions as men, and in his report to the 1888 Convention, Gompers recommended that the A. F. of L. "aid and encourage with all the means at our command the organization of trade unions among women and girls." Two methods could be used to organize women: (1) they could be brought into the Federation as members of existing unions, affiliated to the A. F. of L., and (2) they could be organized into separate unions.[3]

A few A. F. of L. unions, at this time, admitted women to membership,* and many of the Federal Labor Unions chartered by the Federation

* In March, 1892, the General Secretary of the United Garment Workers informed Gompers "that three fifths of the Garment Workers of America consist of women, two Locals No. 8 & 16 are entirely composed of young girls, and No. 18 of Newburgh, N. Y., which is mixed has about 400 women in good standing. . . ." (Chas. F. Reichers to Gompers, March 26, 1892, *AFL Corr.*) No other A.F. of L. union which allowed women to become members had such a high percentage of women members.

included women as well as men. In the main, however, women workers, being relatively unskilled, did not fit into the craft unions of the A. F. of L., and to the degree that they were organized into the Federation, the tendency was to set up separate unions for women workers. Indeed, it was not uncommon for A. F. of L. organizers to form two unions in a shop or factory, "one for women and one for men," and to arrange for negotiations with employers to be conducted by a joint committee representing both unions. The women workers frequently complained that they got the worst end in such an arrangement, since "the men think that the girls should not get as good work as the men and should not make half as much money as a man." [4]

Several Federal Labor Unions composed solely of women workers were chartered by the A. F. of L. in the late 1880's and the early 1890's. Among them were the Working Girls' Protective Union No. 5633 of Toledo, the Working Woman's Federal Labor Union No. 5542 of Terre Haute, Indiana, and the Ladies' Federal Labor Union No. 2703 of Chicago. [5] The Chicago union was the most important organization of women workers affiliated to the early A. F. of L. This mixed union, composed of typists, seamstresses, dress makers, clerks, music teachers, candy makers, gum makers, etc., was organized in June, 1888, "to prevent, to some extent, the moral, physical and mental degradation of women and children employed as wage workers in this city [of Chicago]." [6] The union was led by its militant secretary, Hannah M. Morgan, the wife of Thomas M. Morgan, the leading spirit in Chicago's Socialist movement.

"My education is but poor," Mrs. Morgan modestly informed Gompers, "but I will do the best I can as I like many other children had to work when but 11 years old. I went to work in a Mill and worked from 10 to 16 hours a day and for that reason I am not very good to write. . . ." But she was a splendid organizer. By February, 1892, the Ladies' Federal Labor Union had brought into being 23 women's organizations including unions of bookbinders, shirt makers and cloak makers, watchmakers, and shoe workers. These unions had all started out from the federal labor union. When ten women of one craft had been recruited into the federal union, they set up a union of their own, received a charter from the A. F. of L., and began to organize other women in the trade. [7]

In November, 1888, the Ladies' Federal Labor Union organized the Illinois Women's Alliance. The Alliance did splendid work in advancing the cause of woman suffrage, [8] a policy endorsed by the national A. F. of L.* But its special work was the protection of women and children in the

---

* The 1891 A.F. of L. Convention endorsed woman's suffrage and called upon the entire membership to support the campaigns organized by the various suffrage associations. The Woman's Suffrage Association adopted a special resolution thank-

various relations of industrial and social life, and in this work, the activities of the Alliance included the school, the tenement house, the factory,
the store, the hospital, the asylum, the poorhouse, the police station, the
courts, and the various departments of the city government. With Mrs.
Morgan as chairman and with members of the Ladies' Federal Labor
Union as active participants on all committees, the Women's Alliance
chalked up an impressive record of achievement. It completely exposed
the weakness of Illinois' Compulsory Education Law under which children were required to attend school only 16 weeks in the year; obtained
the passage of an improved law, and saw to it that the law was strictly
enforced by obtaining the appointment of truant officers and factory
inspectors who, assisted by members of the Alliance, took thousands of
children from the streets and factories and placed them in the schools. The
Alliance proved that the insufficient number of public schools in Chicago
was responsible to a large degree for the failure to enforce the Compulsory
Education Law. "Children cannot be driven into schools which have no
existence," it pointed out. The Alliance led the mass campaign which
resulted in the construction of new schools.[9]

In August and September, 1891, committees of the Women's Alliance
and the Chicago Trades Assembly conducted a thorough investigation of
the sweating industries of Chicago. The report, drawn up by Mrs. Morgan, head of the investigating body—10,000 copies were printed and
distributed by the Chicago Trades Assembly—completely disproved the
statements of wholesale clothing manufacturers who denied that there
was such a thing as a "sweating system" in Chicago. It disclosed reduction
of wages to the starvation level; showed that men, women, and children
were forced by the "sweaters" to work in vile dens in defiance of every
law of decency and in violation of city ordinances which required ventilation, access to water, and other accommodations for health and decency.
Finally, it disclosed that thousands of children under 14 years of age—
"some of these children are as young as 5 years"—worked in miserable
tenement houses sewing on buttons and picking out basting.[10]

In March, 1892, Mrs. Morgan learned that Congress was preparing to
investigate the "sweating system." She sent a copy of the 1891 report of
the Woman's Alliance and Trades' Assembly investigation to Senator
George F. Hoar and to the Committee of Congress that had been appointed to conduct the inquiry. The report made such an impression on
the Congressmen that they decided to start their inquiry in Chicago and

ing "the [American] Federation of Labor for their practical service to our cause . . .
by their hearty declarations in favor of woman suffrage." (*Proceedings*, A.F. of L.
Convention, 1891, p. 16; Francis Dickinson to Gompers, Jan. 21, Feb. 4, 1891; Susan
B. Anthony to Gompers, Dec. 11, 1892, *AFL* Corr.)

invited Mrs. Morgan to be the first witness. Her testimony, it was acknowledged in the press, "was listened to with a great deal of interest by the Congressmen." [11]

To the A. F. of L.'s Ladies' Federal Labor Union and its offspring, the Illinois Women's Alliance, must go the credit for stimulating public opinion in favor of better conditions for women and child workers, and, as a result of their constant agitation, the abatement or abolition of many of the existing evils confronting these workers. It is obvious, too, that Mrs. Morgan deserves a high place among those women who have made distinguished contributions to the development of the American labor movement.

The A. F. of L. also directly chartered unions of women workers in a specific industry. The most important of these was the union of collar and shirt workers in Troy, New York.

On January 6, 1891, the collar, cuff and shirt workers employed at the Lansingburgh factory of the United Shirt and Collar Co. at Troy struck against systematic wage cuts which had reduced wages to an average of 50 cents a day. Within a few days the strike spread to other factories in Troy, and with 500 girls on strike the entire shirt and collar industry was tied up. The State Branch of the A. F. of L., answering an appeal from the strikers, sent several representatives to the area. The strikers then formed a union under the A. F. of L., and elected Miss Mary S. Evaline, the 23-year-old-strike leader, as president and Miss Dora Sullivan as vice-president.[12]

When the powerful United Shirt and Collar Co., a concern doing a business of close to one million dollars annually, refused to discuss a settlement with the strikers, the State Branch of the A. F. of L. issued a boycott against its products. No sooner was the notice of the boycott released, than the company capitulated. A committee, composed of the strike leaders and the State A. F. of L., drew up a new scale of wages for the company. This scale served as a basis for other companies involved in the strike, and it was to serve similarly for all shirt and collar establishments in Albany and Glens Falls. For the State Branch of the A. F. of L. resolved "to ask all members of labor organizations to withhold their patronage from such firms who fail to pay their employees such reasonable rates of wages as they may demand in accordance with the scale of prices accepted by the United Shirt and Collar Co." [13]

On February 1, 1891, *The Northern Budget* of Troy, announcing the end of the strike, described it as having "perhaps attracted more attention . . . than any fight which has occurred between capital and labor in this vicinity for many years. . . . The girls go to work under an increased schedule of prices and they have won a victory." [14]

On the same day, H. J. Ogden, A. F. of L. general organizer in Utica and first vice-president of the New York State Branch, wrote jubilantly to Gompers: "You have no doubt learned the result of the collar girls strike at Troy. It was a great victory for the girls and the Federation. . . . We expect to have seven thousand of them organized in the very near future under the Banner of the Federation." To achieve this goal, the State Branch immediately engaged Mary S. Evaline as a special organizer with power to establish local unions of collar and cuff workers. In the fall of 1891, the national A. F. of L. commissioned Dora Sullivan as a special organizer to assist in organizing the working women of Troy and vicinity. By November, 1891, there were six unions in the collar, cuff and shirt industry of Troy, all affiliated with the A. F. of L. Several unions in the industry, composed of female operatives, were also organized in the principal shirt manufacturing centers at Albany, Cohoes, Glens Falls, and Greenwich, New York.[15]

The appointment of special women organizers by the A. F. of L. grew out of several years of experience. Women workers complained to Gompers that male organizers were often ineffective because they "used strong language," and were "guilty of Drunkenness." Male organizers themselves conceded that they had trouble in reaching women workers after working hours. "If a girl is living at home, it is not quite so awkward, but if she is in lodgings, I can't possibly ask to see her in her own room. If I talk to her at all, it will be out in the street, which is not pleasant, especially if it is snowing or freezing or blowing a gale. It is not under these conditions that a girl is likely to see the use of an organization or be attracted by its happier or more social side." [16]

There were women in different localities who, unofficially, did organizing work for the A. F. of L., the outstanding examples being Ida Van Etten, a leader of the Working Women's Society of New York City,* and Mrs. Eva McDonald-Valesh, editor of a fortnightly paper published for the Trades Assemblies in the twin cities of St. Paul and Minneapolis.[17] In addition, the A. F. of L. commissioned some women to serve as organizers for a particiular area or industry, as in the case of Miss Dora Sullivan of Troy. But the first woman general organizer commissioned by the Federation was Miss Mary E. Kenney, a leader of the Chicago Bindery Workers' Union, one of the offsprings of the Ladies' Federal Labor Union No. 2703.

Appointed by Gompers in April, 1892, Miss Kenney began work as an organizer in New York City where she spent the months of June and July setting up unions of garment workers and of bindery girls. From New York City, she moved up-state to Albany and Troy, holding mass

* The Society, organized on January 14, 1888, collected statistics and published facts on conditions of women workers, aided strikes of women workers, and fought for legislation in their behalf. The Society was largely responsible for the passage of a law in 1890 providing for women factory inspectors in New York State. (Alice Henry, *Women and the Labor Movement,* New York, 1923, pp. 43-44.)

meetings of women workers and establishing unions among the shirt makers and bindery girls. In September and October, she moved about Massachusetts, addressing tailoresses, women printers and bindery girls in Boston, and shoe workers and women carpet weavers at Middleboro and Haverhill.[18]

When Gompers recommended that Miss Kenney be allowed to continue as General Organizer, he was voted down by the other members of the Executive Council. Chris Evans bluntly informed Gompers that the Federation "is not in a condition financially to keep a woman organizer in the field without better hope of success than at present indicated." Miss Kenney's efforts were "worthy of commendation, yet the fact remains that they have proved futile."[19]

The A. F. of L. remained without a woman General Organizer until December, 1893, when Gompers commissioned Miss E. E. Pitt, a member of the Typographical Union in Boston who had done considerable work in her spare time organizing the women garment workers. At the request of the Boston A. F. of L. office, which urged that Miss Pitt be empowered to "extend her field of operations . . . among the women of other trades," Gompers commissioned her to begin "organizing women regardless of their trades or callings."[20]

In January, 1894, Gompers recommended to the A. F. of L. Executive Council that four additional women organizers be appointed, but that body voted: "That on account of the present depression in trade that action on the appointment of four female organizers be deferred until a more propitious time." Due to lack of funds, Miss Pitt was allowed to carry on only for a few months, so that by the summer of 1894, the A. F. of L. was again without a woman General Organizer. The "more propitious time" did not come until 1898 when only one woman was appointed as organizer and made assistant editor of the *American Federationist*.[21]

It is clear from the above that the early A. F. of L. did make some significant contributions to the organization of women workers in a number of localities. But it is also evident that it did not add a conspicuous number of women to the labor movement. Gompers himself freely admitted in November, 1892, that "as yet we have not met with the success which is necessary to place the working women in a position to occupy the proper place among the working men of the land."[22]

Good intentions of a few leaders could not overcome the basic fact that the vast majority of women in industry were unskilled and semi-skilled workers, and, in common with other workers of the same type, their needs were neglected by the craft unions who comprised the bulk of the A. F. of L., and who ignored the resolutions adopted at conventions of the Federation which called for the organization of women workers.

Precisely the same problem arose in connection with the organization of Negro workers, although here the record of achievement by the early A. F. of L. was better than in the case of women workers.

THE NEGRO WORKERS

The 1890 A. F. of L. convention announced to the world that it "looks with disfavor upon trade unions having provisions which exclude from membership persons on account of race or color." The same convention was faced with a test of this principle when the question arose of the affiliation of the National Association of Machinists. Having learned that the union's constitution limited membership to white persons, the convention refused to grant it a charter and instructed the Executive Council to request the organization to strike out the constitutional provision excluding Negroes from membership.[23]

Gompers visited the 1891 convention to persuade the machinists to remove the constitutional ban against Negroes. When the delegates refused, and insisted on their discriminatory policy, the A. F. of L. sponsored the formation of a new union, the International Machinists' Union. In the call for its founding convention, the new union emphasized that it would seek to unite the machinists into an organization "based upon the principles which recognize the equality of all men working at our trade regardless of religion, race or color." [24] On the basis of this principle, the new Machinists' Union was admitted to the A. F. of L.

A similar policy was adopted at this time by the A. F. of L. toward the Brotherhood of Boiler Makers and the Iron Ship Builders of America. When these two national organizations consolidated their forces in 1893, a color line was inserted into the constitution limiting membership to "white" workers in these trades. The A. F. of L. not only refused to grant the union a charter, but assisted in organizing an independent union of Boiler Makers which opened its ranks to Negroes as well as whites. The union promptly received a charter from the Federation.[25]

Throughout the late 'eighties and early 'nineties, Gompers was constantly being asked by the A. F. of L. organizers and representatives in the South: (1) what to do about organizing the Negro workers; (2) what to do about the city and state A. F. of L. bodies that refused to admit Negro delegates and even to admit delegates from unions which permitted Negroes to become members; (3) what to do about local unions that barred Negroes, and (4) whether it was in accord with A. F. of L. policies to charter separate unions of Negro workers when they were barred from the existing organizations.[26] To these questions, Gompers replied: (1) that Negroes should be organized and that special efforts should be made by A. F. of L. representatives to organize the Negro workers; (2) that city and state A. F. of L. bodies must not bar Negro delegates and delegates from unions that admitted Negroes since the fact that "a local union may be opposed to the ridiculous attempt to draw the color line in our labor organizations and because they stand right is no reason why they should be treated wrong upon it;" (3) that wherever local unions barred Negroes, an effort should be made to eliminate such anti-labor barriers, and (4) that, meanwhile, the Negro workers should be organized into separate locals "but attached to the same national organizations with the same rights, duties and privileges" as all other locals. "In other words, have the Union of white men organized and have the Union of colored men organize also, both unions to work in unison and harmony to accomplish the desired end." [27]

The policy of organizing separate locals was thus part of the early A. F. of L.'s approach towards Negro workers. But it is significant to note that, at this time, it was only one feature of the approach, emphasis being placed upon the fact that separate locals were to be organized only when no other method could be used to bring Negro workers into the Federation, and that these separate locals were to be temporary only. In later years, however, as the A. F. of L. itself became a Jim Crow organization, separate locals were regarded by the A. F. of L. leaders as the preferred way of permanently organizing Negro workers.

The main point stressed in Gompers' replies to all inquiries was that the Negro workers *must* be organized. Humanity demanded it, but it was not a question of humanitarianism alone. Basically, it was a practical trade union question, for the A. F. of L. could not succeed unless it waged a relentless struggle "in order to eliminate the consideration of a color line in the country."

"If we fail to organize and recognize the colored wage-workers," Gompers wrote to an A. F. of L. organizer, "we cannot blame them very well if they accept our challenge of enmity and do all they can to frustrate our purposes. If we fail to make friends of them, the employing class won't be so shortsighted and play them against us. Thus if common humanity will not prompt us to have their cooperation, an enlightened self-interest should." [28]

This theme found expression in all of Gompers' responses to the queries raised by A. F. of L. organizers, in the South as well as in the North. A letter to an organizer in Forth Worth, Texas, which stressed the above theme, closed: "Sincerely hoping that if humane considerations are left out of sight the practicability of the suggestions made will commend themselves to the consideration of our fellow workers of Fort Worth and the entire country." [29]

Gompers' sound advice did not sit too well with many A. F. of L. representatives in the South. They bluntly informed him that under no circumstances would they heed his advice to organize the Negro workers. To do so, wrote C. C. Tabor, general organizer in the South, in a viciously chauvinistic letter, would be fatal to the Federation. "If you organize them [the Negroes] they will compete with White Labor so strongly they will be compelled to give up the shops as they will stand much more abuse than the whites. The Negroes in the South are not like they are in the North. . . . Hoping you will not take exception to it, but I will do all in my power in the field of white labor." [30]

It is to the credit of the youthful A.F. of L. that they did "take exception" to these statements and refused at this stage to base their program on the white supremacy ideology of these Southern organizers. In the face of those threats, the Federation took steps to organize Negroes into unions and to charter these organizations. To carry out this program, the A.F. of L. leaders also relied on Negro organizers.

On July 9, 1891, Gompers commissioned George L. Norton, Negro Secretary of the Marine Firemen's Union No. 5464 in St. Louis, as an A.F. of L. general organizer. Norton who was "well-acquainted along the [Mississippi] river," set up unions of longshoremen, engineers, and firemen from Cairo, Illinois, to Vicksburg, Mississippi. "My trip to Memphis and Vicksburg was all that I could wish for," he wrote to Gompers, "and I only hope that I may be as successful elswhere. I have got a good many men, known as deckhands on steamers, that will, I think be ready to send for its charter before long. I don't intend to stop as long as there is anything [to be] organized." [31]

Norton had been appointed general organizer at the request of A. S. Leitch, A.F. of L. general organizer in St. Louis. Leitch praised Norton's work as Secretary of the Marine Firemen's Union, and described this A.F. of L. union of 140 Negro firemen as one of the most influential in the city. "They have won all demands for wages so far without recourse to strike and with but little trouble," he wrote to Gompers in June, 1891. "They are working harmoniously with the other trades here, especially the Electric Wiremen and Linemen's Union, whom they can materially assist as firemen at the electric plant." [32]

The first strike in which the Marine Firemen were engaged was one of the most stirring in St. Louis' labor history, involving nearly all of the waterfront workers, Negro and white. The strike started on March 30, 1892, when the owners of the steamers on the levee rejected a demand by the marine firemen that the union scale of wages be paid and that none but union men be employed on the boats. The marine firemen struck and were followed by members of the longshoremen and roustabout unions who also raised the demands for union recognition and higher wages. "As the men on strike are all Afro-Americans, thoroughly organized, and members of the American Federation of Labor," reported the Cleveland *Gazette,* a Negro journal, "it is believed that they will force the companies to accept their request." [33]

White workers joined the strike in response to a call issued by the A.F. of L. headquarters at St. Louis to all unions "at points up and down the river where organizations exist." Describing a procession on April 4, of the thousands of strikers, Negroes and white, the St. Louis *Globe Democrat* observed: "Numerous banners were carried by the men on parade these being among them: 'Equal Rights for all!' 'Fair Wages and Union Men only!' 'Monopoly caused this Strike!' 'We want Living Wages!', etc. After parading the principal downtown streets and visiting the Levee, the men went to Union Hall, on Christy Avenue, where they were addressed for nearly two hours by labor agitators, white and colored." [34]

In the face of such unity, the importation of scabs and the shooting down of strikers by police, who were described by George L. Norton as "acting in the interests of the employers as usual," could not break the strike. The struggle ended on April 6, 1892, in a partial victory for the strikers. Although the employers refused to grant union recognition, the wage demands were conceded and incorporated in the new schedules. The St. Louis press admitted that this gain had been made possible by the unity of Negro and white strikers under the banner of the A. F. of L. [35]

Gompers urged Norton to furnish him with all press reports of Negro-white unity during the strike so that he could send the clippings to every A. F. of L. organizer in the South. "The men engaged in this contest," he added, "have demonstrated in the plainest possible manner . . . that the sprit of freedom, independence and emancipation is dawning, and the progress for the improvement and final emancipation of the wage worker will be contested by the white and black laborer shoulder to shoulder." Gompers was delighted to receive letters from A. F. of L. organizers in the South admitting that the press reports of Negro-white unity during "the strike on the Mississippi river" were making a great impression upon white workers in the South, and were opening up possibilities for organizing Negro workers without imperilling the Federation. [36]

Impressed by these reports, the A. F. of L. executive council sent Norton on a mission to organize Negro workers along the Ohio and Mississippi Rivers for a month, and appropriated $200 for salary and expenses. On May 3, 1892, as Norton was about to depart on his organizing tour, Gompers gave him the following message for the Negro people: "Convey to our brothers that you may meet and those whom you may convert to become brothers in this grand American Federation of Labor my earnest sentiments that they should bear in mind that there is only one way in which they can hope to attain improvements in their condition to realize that freedom which has been promised them to secure these comforts of home and independence—through organization." [37]

Without reading too much into this statement, it is significant to note that Gompers found it expedient at this time to emphasize the relationship between the Negro people's movement for freedom and the efforts of organized labor to unite Negro and white workers.

Gompers was satisfied with the results of Norton's month-long organizing tour which had brought several hundred Negro workers into the A. F. of L., and he wrote to the Negro organizer upon his return to St. Louis: "As an evidence of my confidence in you, I reissue and extend your commission to June 1st, 1893." The A. F. of L. president was convinced that in due time even the most backward white workers in the South would come to realize the importance of what Norton was doing to advance the interests of white workers as well as those of the Negroes.[38] *

Events quickly justified Gompers' confidence. Before Norton's visit to New Orleans, John M. Callahan, the A. F. of L.'s general organizer, was convinced that "it would be almost impossible for them [Negro and white workers] to commingle in one union," and he had expressed bitter opposition to having a Negro organizer function for the Federation in New Orleans. Yet on June 12, 1892, shortly after Norton's departure, he forwarded to Gompers an application for a charter from one of the unions Norton had organized—the Journeymen Horseshoers.

"The union is composed of both white and black men. I am sure that in the course of a few months they will have by far the greater number of the men employed at that calling within the ranks of their union. The Horseshoers are pretty well divided as to color and at my request they made a nearly equal division of officers. . . .

"There is an energetic very intelligent colored man down here who is Financial Secretary of Longshoremen's Ass'n and takes a great interest in the labor movement. He is not in any union connected with the Federation but I am sure if it is not against the rules to issue him a commission as an organizer he would render a good account of himself. He materially assisted in organizing the horeshoers and I am pretty certain he could get several of the strong colored labor organizations to enlist under the Banner of the A. F. of L. He also was one of the Arbitration committee of the Car Drivers' Union. . . .

* Norton continued to do work as general organizer for the A.F. of L., but most of his activities were directed towards building the Marine Firemen's Union in St. Louis of which he was Secretary. (*See* his letters to Gompers, March 5, May 5, 9, June 20, July 13, 1893, Feb. 7, 1894, *AFL Corr.*)

"I find I have been giving his good qualities and have not yet given his name. His name is James E. Porter." [39]

Porter was commissioned and did such excellent work that Callahan praised him as the most effective organizer for the A. F. of L. in the deep South. "I can assure you that there is none better than Porter," he wrote to Gompers on August 3, 1892. [40]

THE GENERAL STRIKE IN NEW ORLEANS

How deeply the progressive concept of labor unity had sunk into the unions affiliated to the A. F. of L. in the South is illustrated in the November, 1892, general strike in New Orleans. In this strike called by unions affiliated to the A. F. of L. and described by one historian as "the first general strike in American history to enlist both skilled and unskilled labor, black and white, and to paralyze the life of a great city," about 25,000 workers stopped work for four days. These workers represented 49 unions affiliated to the A. F. of L., many of them organized during the summer of 1892. The unions were united in the Workingmen's Amalgamated Council, to which each union sent two delegates. [41]

Among the recently organized unions in New Orleans were the Teamsters, Scalesmen, and Packers which made up the so-called Triple Alliance. Many of these workers were Negroes, mainly members of the Teamsters' Union. On October 24, 1892, between two and three thousand workers, members of the Triple Alliance, left their jobs, because the Board of Trade refused to grant them a ten-hour day, overtime pay, and a preferential union shop.*

The strikers relied upon the support of the Workingmen's Amalgamated Council to win out against the merchants and their allies: the four railway systems entering New Orleans, the cotton, sugar, and rice exchanges, the clearing house, and mechanics' and dealers' exchange. This support was immediately forthcoming; if necessary, declared President Leonard of the Council, every A. F. of L. union in New Orleans would go out in sympathy with the strikers. [42]

The employers then tried a splitting maneuver. The Board of Trade announced that it would sign an agreement with the Scalesmen and Packers' unions, but not with the third group in the Triple Alliance—the Teamsters' Union—for under no circumstances would they "enter into any agreement with 'n——rs'." To sign an agreement with the Triple

---

* Under the preferential union shop, the employer, whenever he needs additional workers, must first make application to the union, specifying the number and kind of workers needed. If, after a reasonable time, the union is unable to furnish the required number of persons, the employer is allowed to secure them in the open market.

Alliance including the Teamsters, the Board declared, would be to place the employers under the control of Negroes, for soon the man who would control the Alliance "would be a Big Black Negro." [43]

The press joined in attempting to divide the strikers by fanning anti-Negro prejudice. The papers featured terrifying accounts of "mobs of brutal Negro strikers" moving freely about the city, "beating up all who attempted to interfere with them." *"Negroes Attack White Man,"* the New Orleans *Times-Democrat* shrieked in its headlines on November 2. *"Assaulted by Negroes,"* was its headline two days later.[44]

Not only did the ranks of the strikers remain solid in the face of the lynch spirit aroused by the employers and their agents, but the Scalesmen and Packers publicly declared that they would never return to work until the employers signed up with all three members of the Triple Alliance. Moreover, the rest of the A. F. of L. rank-and-file began to call for a general strike to show their solidarity with the strikers, Negro as well as white. At various meetings, the unions polled their members on the question of a general strike, found uniform enthusiasm for the proposal, and went on record for it.[45]

The New Orleans *Times-Democrat* accused the white trade unionists of lunacy for considering a general strike in order to assist the Negro trade union of the Triple Alliance win an agreement. It charged that the decision proved that the Negroes had gained a dominant position in the New Orleans labor movement. "The very worst feature, indeed, in the whole case seems to be that the white element of the labor organizations appear either to be under the dominance of Senegambian influence, or that they are at least lending themselves as willing tools to carry out Senegambian schemes." [46] *

On November 8, after two postponements, the general strike went into effect. Each of the 49 unions on strike demanded union recognition and a closed shop, and in many cases, added special demands for shorter hours and higher wages. Several of the unions, including the street car drivers and printers, broke their contracts to join the general strike.

The general strike was under the leadership of a Committee of Five: John Breen, representing the Cotton Screwmen's Union; John M. Callahan, A. F. of L. general organizer and representative of the Cotton Yardmen; A. M. Kier of the Boiler Makers' Union; James Leonard of the Union Printers, and James E. Porter, the Negro labor leader who was the assistant state organizer of the Car Drivers' Union and had recently been commissioned as an assistant organizer for the A. F. of L. In addition to Porter, J. Madison Vance, a Negro lawyer, played a prominent part in the strike.[47]

"Tie the town up," was the cry of the 25,000 strikers and for three

* The reference was to the inhabitants of Senegambia, a region of West Africa.

days they succeeded in doing just this. Business was at a standstill; cars stopped running; the gas supply was discontinued; light and power was cut off, and the city was in total darkness. "There are fully 25,000 men idle," Callahan wrote excitedly to Gompers on November 7. "There is no newspapers to be printed, no gas or electric light in the city, no wagons, no carpenters, painters or in fact any business doing. . . . I am sorry you are not down here to take a hand in it. It is a strike that will go down in history." [48]

Once again the press tried to break the strike by Negro-baiting. The papers shrieked that the Negro strikers would take advantage of the crisis to seize control of the city, and reported that there were already "instances where ladies and school children had been insulted by the blacks." But once again the divisive appeals to race prejudice were in vain; the strikers' ranks remained solid. B. Sherer, financial secretary of the New Orleans Marine and Stationary Firemen's Protective Union, assured Gompers that the Negro and white workers had answered the divisive propaganda of the press by resolving "to cement the Bonds of Brotherhood and Fraternal ties that will stand before the world an ever-lasting monument of strength, and show to the world at large that in unionism there is strength, and that our order [the A. F. of L.] stands preeminently at the head of the human Race." [49]

The press deliberately pictured the existence of a state of anarchy to justify the use of armed military might to break the strike. Actually, however, the strike was conducted so peacefully that the employers sought frantically and "in vain for some act on the part of the men to justify Capital calling upon its allies, the militia and the law." Even after Governor Foster of Louisiana called out the militia, in response to pleas from the employers, the conduct of the strike was so orderly and peaceful that he was compelled to remove the troops. The employers then finally agreed to arbitrate the strike. The unions consented, and after a few conferences, at which the employers sat down with Negro and white representatives of the strikers, the Triple Alliance, including the Teamsters' Union, gained most of its original demands—a ten-hour day, overtime pay, and adjusted wage schedules. Other unions also obtained increased wages and reduced hours by reason of the strike. Although the settlements did not include the preferential union shop, there was to be "no discrimination against union men." [50]

Existing unions increased their membership and new unions were formed during the strike. "Yesterday," the New Orleans *Times-Democrat* reported on October 30, 1892, "there were three new unions formed and admitted to membership. The names of the unions were not given to the press, but it was intimated that every man in the Federation of Labor was actively engaged in furthering the interests of the order, and in getting together as many bodies of organized labor as possible."

Thus ended what this newspaper described as "the most colossal strike that this country has even seen."[51] The failure of the strikers to win a preferential union shop did not detract from the significance of the struggle. It revealed the militant, class-consciousness of the American Federation of Labor in its formative years.*

The outstanding feature of the strike was its great demonstration of labor solidarity in action. Thousands of workers in the deep South had shown that they could unite in common struggle, Negro and white, skilled and unskilled, and that they could stay united despite the efforts of the employers and their agents to divide them by appeals to anti-Negro prejudice. With good reason a strike leader wrote to Gompers: "It was the finest unification of Labor . . . ever had in this or any other city." In a letter to Callahan, Gompers himself underscored the very same point:

"To me the movement in New Orleans was a very bright ray of hope for the future of organized labor and convinces me that the advantage which every other element fails to succeed in falls to the mission of organized labor. Never in the history of the world was such an exhibition, where with all the prejudices existing against the black man, when the white wage-workers of New Orleans would sacrifice their means of livelihood to defend and protect their colored fellow workers. With one fell swoop the economic barrier of color was broken down. Under the circumstances I regard the movement as a very healthy sign of the times and one which speaks well for the future of organized labor in the 'New South' about which the politicians prate so much and mean so little."[52]

Had the A. F. of L. adhered to the policies and practices set forth during its formative years, Gompers' prediction would have been fully realized. For it is clear that the early A. F. of L. made important contributions towards building the unity of workers regardless of color. It

---

* Practically every study of the history of the American labor movement, including the exhaustive work by John R. Commons and Associates, fails to mention the New Orleans general strike of 1892 and the role played in it by the A.F. of L. In fact, one student of the A.F. of L. has written: ". . . the Federation does not endorse all strikes undertaken by union organizations. The general strike has been disapproved since 1886." (Mollie Ray Carroll, *Labor and Politics: The Attitude of the American Federation of Labor Toward Legislation and Politics,* Boston and New York, 1923, p. 68.)

The absence of discussions of this strike in labor histories is especially surprising when it is realized that it stimulated the first application of the Sherman Anti-Trust Act to labor unions. Following the general strike, at the instance of the New Orleans employers, a suit was entered in the Federal Circuit Court against 44 union leaders on charges of violating the Sherman Anti-Trust Act by a conspiracy to restrain trade. A temporary injunction was granted by a Federal Judge, but the Workingmen's Council of New Orleans appealed the case to a higher court. The case was indefinitely postponed, and eventually quashed. (*See* Circular issued by Workingmen's Amalgamated Council of New Orleans, *AFL Corr.;* New Orleans *Times-Democrat,* Nov. 14-16, 1892.)

laid down as a cardinal principle the policy of organizing and uniting Negro and white workers "for the purpose of elevating the condition of both black and white;" it pointed with pride to the fact that international unions which barred Negroes as members were, in turn, barred from becoming affiliated with the Federation, and it boasted that within its ranks "the colored man and his white brother are joined by the fraternal hand of fellowship." [53]

Despite these progressive policies, the early A. F. of L. could not succeed in laying the foundation for the effective organization of the Negro workers. Gompers himself unwittingly gave the main reason for this when he wrote in the Spring of 1891: "There are not many skilled mechanics among the colored workmen of the South." [54] Yet the A. F. of L. from the beginning adopted a form of unionism, based primarily on the skilled workers, which by its very nature excluded the vast majority of the Negro workers. Thus while the Federation at this time stood for organization without regard to race or color, it also added the qualification that the worker must be skilled, when, for the most part, the Negro workers were unskilled and opportunities for advancement in the skilled trades were denied them in industry, as well as by the policy of most craft unions. As with many other questions, the craft organization of the A. F. of L., based essentially on the skilled workers, shunted the Federation away from the progressive road.

THE FOREIGN-BORN WORKERS

Candidates for the youthful A. F. of L. were required to take the following pledge: "I promise never to discriminate against a fellow worker on account of color, creed or nationality." One group, however, was not included within the scope of this pledge—the Asian workers. Gompers conceded that the employers played Asian workers against white workers, particularly in cigar making and in the shoe and textile industries, but his solution for this problem was entirely different, and unlike his approach to the Negro workers at this time, basically reactionary. Negro and white workers could and must unite, he said repeatedly, but the barrier between Caucasian and Asian workers was unsurmountable. The Asian workers must not only be kept out of the unions; they must be excluded from the country. Either they would be excluded by law or they "will be driven out by force of arms." [55]

Gompers' statements dealing with the Asian workers during these early years of the A. F. of L., when the emphasis generally was on labor solidarity, reeked of the most vicious racism. They were filled with references to the so-called "Yellow Menace," to the "inborn inferiority" of the Asian peoples, and are replete with other racist epithets. He took pride in the fact that he had led the movement to influence Congress to pass the Exclusion Act of 1882, which suspended the immigration of Chinese workers for ten years. He pressed for renewal of the law when its time was up, dispatching dozens of letters to government officials, demanding, as President of the A. F. of L., the total exclusion of Chinese immigrants.[56]

This racist approach to the Chinese workers was all too soon to be applied in full force to many immigrant workers from Southeastern Europe. But in its early years, the A. F. of L. adopted a fairly progressive approach to European-born workers. The Federation received many requests for the appointment of organizers who spoke Italian, Bohemian, Spanish, Swedish, French, German, Jewish, and other foreign languages, and for the publication of organizing literature and union constitutions in these languages.[57] Despite a serious lack of funds, most of these requests were fulfilled. A contemporary report noted that a feature of the A. F. of L. was its "cosmopolitan character," which was "illustrated by the fact that many of them [the affiliated unions] have their constitutions printed in four or more languages." [58]

In large measure, the policy of the A. F. of L. leadership was motivated by the understanding, developed from reports from organizers in the field, that if they did not fulfill these requests for foreign-language speakers and literature, the influence of the K. of L. among the foreign-born would revive.[59] As long as the K. of L. was still a threat to the Federation, the A. F. of L. leadership was compelled to pay attention to the special needs of the foreign-born workers, including the immigrants from Southeastern Europe. Within a few years, as we shall see, when the threat from the K. of L. had disappeared and when the immigration from Southeastern Europe began in earnest, the policy of the A. F. of L. leadership towards these foreign-born workers underwent a sharp change.

Yet even during those early years, the degree to which the A. F. of L. could organize the foreign-born workers was sharply limited, as in the case of Negro and women workers, by the fast that the bulk of these workers were unskilled. Essentially, for all the emphasis on unity of the working class and on organization of the unorganized regardless of race, creed, color, sex or nationality, the craft union form or organization, coupled with high dues and initiation fees, led inevitably to the neglect of the needs of the unskilled and semi-skilled, particularly the Negro, women, and foreign-born workers, and to the creation of a virtual aristocracy of skilled craft workers. Already in 1892, Frederick Engels noted that while American labor was organizing "on trade-union lines . . . it still occupies an aristocratic position and wherever possible leaves the ordinary badly paid occupations to the immigrants, only a small portion of whom enter the aristocratic trade unions." [60]

CHAPTER 14

The Homestead Strike

Eighteen hundred and ninety-two was the year of some of the most bitter class conflicts in American labor history. The year witnessed the general strike in New Orleans, the Switchmen's strike at Buffalo, New York, the coal miners' strike in East Tennessee, the copper miners' strike in Couer d'Alene, Idaho, and the steel workers' strike in Homestead, Pennsylvania. The last-mentioned struggle was one of the bloodiest clashes between capital and labor in American history and aroused nationwide and international attention.

THE BACKGROUND

In 1889 the skilled workers at Carnegie, Phipps and Company's Homestead plant were organized into six lodges of the Amalgamated Association of Iron and Steel Workers, with 800 members out of a working force of 2,500. A national organization in the iron and steel industry, the Association's membership was restricted to skilled workers in the rolling mills and puddling furnaces and did not include the laborers who increasingly were an important part of the labor force. In 1891, the Association claimed 290 lodges and 24,068 members. But even at this time, the period of its greatest strength, fully three-fourths of the iron and steel workers eligible for membership did not belong to the Association. Not even in Allegheny County, the heart of the Amalgamated stronghold, did the Association have much more than half of the workers in the union.[1]

In 1892 the workers at Homestead were operating under an agreement signed by the Carnegie Company and the Amalgamated Association in 1889. Wages were to rise and fall in accordance with the market price *

---

* In the iron trade the scale was based on the market price of the muck bar, the product of the puddling furnace; in steel, on the steel billet, the product of the converter. Wages were adjusted at intervals of three months, and wages for the next period were based on the average price of the preceding period.

of 4 x 4 standard Bessemer steel billets, except that a minimum of $25 per ton of steel billets was set as the point below which wages were not to fall even though the market price sank lower. The agreement was to expire on June 30, 1892.[2]

On April 4, 1892, almost three months before the contract with the Amalgamated was to expire, Carnegie wrote to Henry Clay Frick, the notorious anti-union manager of the steel company,* outlining his policy for the future. The letter, which remained unpublished until 1903, read in part: "As the vast majority of our employees are Non-Union, the Firm has decided that the minority must give place to the majority. These works, therefore, will be necessarily non-union after the expiration of the present agreement."[3]

Frick called the committee of the Amalgamated lodges into his office, and handed the men a scale which called for average reduction in wages of 22 per cent,† and for a change in the date for the termination of the contract to January 1, 1894, instead of June 30, 1894. In addition, some men were to be displaced and others were to be put on a salary basis instead of tonnage rates.

Frick gave the men until June 24 to accept. The company did not care whether the workers belonged to a union or not, he declared, "but we think our employees at Homestead would [be] far much better working under the same system in vogue at Edgar Thomson and Duquesne."[4] The system referred to was non-union!

The committee asked for an explanation of the company's proposals, but none was forthcoming. It was understood, however, that the company regarded "the present wages as a relic of the war, which, now that thirty

* Frick had only recently assumed control over the Carnegie Steel Company. He had already stamped out unionism in the coke regions, ruthlessly crushing strikes by means of the Coal and Iron Police, the Pinkerton guards, deputy sheriffs, and the state militia. (George Harvey, *Henry Clay Frick—The Man,* New York, 1928, pp. 83-86.)
Even before the strike started at Homestead, Frick began preparations to crush it by force and violence. He literally turned the steel plant into an armed fortress. As a contemporary bit of verse put it:

THE FORT THAT FRICK BUILT

Twixt Homestead and Munhall
If you'll believe my word at all
Where once a steel works noisy roar
A thousand blessings did pour
There stands today with great pretense
Enclosed within a whitewashed fence
A wondrous change of great import
The mills transformed into a fort.

† Under the new scale proposed by the company, a worker who earned $179.55 in May, 1892, would have his wages reduced to $84.04 for the same amount of work. A heater's helper would have his tonnage rates reduced from $3.00 to $2.13 a hundred tons.

years have passed, should be wiped out." This prompted the *National Labor Tribune* to remark: "So is the protective tariff a war relic. So are the laws that admit of the immense concentration of wealth which places the workman at so marked disadvantage. So is monopoly. So are all the devices that are building up a snide aristocracy of wealth."[5] Actually, the wage reductions and the other company proposals were part of the basic program set forth in Carnegie's letter—the smashing of the union.

THE STRIKE BEGINS

Although the workers had rejected the company's proposals, they believed that further conferences would be held out of which a compromise agreement might possibly emerge. But on the evening of June 29, and the morning of the 30th, the great mill at Homestead was shut down, hours before the contract expired, thereby making it a lockout and not a strike.

Even before the shutdown occurred, the day laborers had been contacted by the union and assurances received that they would not work unless the union was recognized. On June 30, a mass meeting of the mechanics and transportation departments was held, and, despite their signed agreement, they, too, voted to stand by the Amalgamated Association. Immediately, the eight lodges went into secret session at which an Advisory Committee of 50 members, headed by Hugh O'Donnell, was elected to handle all aspects of the strike.[6]

Antagonism between the highly skilled men and the lesser skilled men had existed at Homestead as a result of the exclusive character of the Amalgamated Association. But all differences vanished during the strike of 1892 when the entire labor force of 3,800 men, skilled and unskilled, union and non-union, native and foreign-born, joined hands against the company. The union was the hope of all the workers. It might restrict its membership and bar the less skilled workers, but every worker in the mills knew that if the union was smashed he would be completely at the mercy of the company.

Steps were speedily taken to assure that the company could not put men into the mill by any surprise move. The steam launch *Edna,* along with a number of skiffs, was secured to patrol the river and warn of any move in that direction. The men were divided into shifts, and picket lines were thrown about the mill and town 24 hours of the day. The ferries were watched and all trains met in anticipation of a move by the firm. Strangers were challenged, and anyone who could not give a satisfactory explanation for his presence was promptly hustled out of town. Headquarters for the Advisory Committee were established and telegraph communications were set up so that they might be warned of any attempt by the firm to secure strikebreakers elsewhere. Special arrangements were made to preserve order; saloon keepers were visited and their cooperation was asked to prevent excessive drinking.[7]

The Advisory Committee exercised complete control during the strike, even to the extent of issuing special badges to newspaper men, allowing them to enter the borough. They expelled any reporter who issued erroneous news to his home office.[8]

Throughout the first week of July, the Company remained silent. But it was not inactive. It was making extensive preparations to recruit scabs. Ads for strikebreakers were placed in newspapers in Boston, St. Louis, and Philadelphia. Steps had even been taken to import iron workers from Europe.[9]

THE BATTLE AGAINST THE PINKERTONS

Even before the deadline for the acceptance of the scales had expired, negotiations were opened with the Pinkerton Detective Agency. It was agreed that the Agency should furnish 300 guards for which the Carnegie Steel Company would pay $5 per day per man. It was planned to start up the mills on July 6, and the guards were to be brought in the night before.[10]

The Pinkerton Agency collected a force of three hundred men from Philadelphia, New York, and Chicago, and united them at Ashtabula, Ohio, on July 5. They were then whisked on a special train, coaches darkened, to Davis Island Dam, five or six miles below Pittsburgh. Here they were transferred to two barges, and while the crafts proceeded silently up the river, the guards put on the blue Pinkerton uniforms and armed themselves with Winchester rifles.

Despite all the efforts at secrecy, the strikers learned of the movement of the flotilla even before the barges had left Pittsburgh. The alarm was sped to Homestead. Immediately the steam whistle on the electric plant shrilled the news to the strikers and their allies that the hour had come, and the streets soon filled with townspeople hurrying to the river bank. The *Edna* paddled down the river to meet the foe, and trailing after her came the smaller craft of the strikers' navy. Meanwhile, a crowd of men, women, and children lined the river bank.

The crowd on shore had kept pace with the boats as they passed the town, but were stopped momentarily by the fence around the mill which had been brought down to the water mark so as to cut off all access by land. When the strikers saw that the Pinkertons intended landing, they broke down the fence and swarmed through the mill yard to the landing. The workmen warned the Pinkertons back, but Captain Heinde, in charge of the guards, stepped out of the barges, announcing they were there to take over the works and that the crowd must leave. Shouts of defiance greeted him from the strikers massed several deep on top of the embarkment. A gangplank was shoved out and several Pinkertons started down it.

A shot rang out, closely followed by another. Then came a volley into the crowd from the Winchester rifles which brought down several workers. The firing was general on both sides for several minutes. The Pinkertons retreated to their barges, but since the steamboat which had towed the barges had departed to take the wounded detectives up the river to Braddock, the invaders were left without means of escape. While awaiting the return of the steamer, the besieged guards cut holes in the sides of the barges, and rifle men awaited the next move of the strikers.

Who fired the first shot is not known, both sides later claiming that the other fired first. But it was the Pinkertons who fired into the crowd of women and children and brought down several.

For some hours the besieged guards and the strikers exchanged continuous rifle fire. At one point, the steel workers loaded a flat car with oil-soaked boxes and barrels; set them on fire and pushed them down a siding toward the barges. When this effort to destroy the barges failed, a tank of oil was pumped into the river and attempts were made to set it on fire. But a contrary wind rendered the attempt useless, and the battle of the Monongahela settled down to an exchange of rifle fire between the Pinkerton sharpshooters and the steel workers.

The battle lasted from 4 o'clock in the morning of July 6 until 5 o'clock that afternoon. At least nine workers were killed,* and three of the Pinkertons paid with their lives for their attempt to take over the mill.[11]

Terms of surrender of the Pinkertons were arranged. Shortly after five in the afternoon, the "Pinks" marched from the barges to the skating rink of the town where they were kept. Oil was poured on the barges and they were set on fire. The battle of the Monongahela ended amidst the roaring blaze.[12]

The blaze swept the entire country. The dramatic events of July 6 were headlined in the press from New York to San Francisco. The editorial writers in the commercial press wept bitter tears for the Pinkertons, and denounced the strikers as "savage beasts who deserve no pity."[13] But the workers shed no tears for the hated Pinkertons. "They [the Homestead strikers] have the sympathy of all the laboring men down

---

* An eight-foot stone shaft stands today at a street intersection in Homestead and carries this inscription: "Erected by the members of the Steel Workers Organization Committee Local Unions, in memory of the Iron and Steel workers who were killed in Homestead, Pa., on July 6, 1892, while striking against the Carnegie Steel Company in defense of their American rights."

here," wrote the A. F. of L. organizer in New Orleans, "and the only fault I have heard expressed is that they left a living Pinkerton man get away." [14]

The events at Homestead brought to a boiling point labor's long-seething hatred of Pinkertonism. Mass protest meetings, sponsored by the A. F. of L. central bodies and individual unions, were held all over the country. Indignant resolutions were adopted denouncing "the outrages recently committed by the 'Pinkerton Detectives,' the hired thugs of the many times millionaire Carnegie," protesting "against the Employment of such Ruffians in the future," and calling upon Congress "to take prompt measures for the suppression of this vast army of the capitalist class." Besides adopting resolutions, the meetings raised funds for the "Homestead widows and orphans deprived of their supporters by the bullets of hired assassins." "Your fight is our fight and victory for you means victory for us all," the meetings declared in telegrams to the locked-out workers at Homestead.[15]

THE STRIKE CONTINUES

Meanwhile, at Homestead, the battle continued. The Amalgamated once more took over command of the city. Order was completely restored, the union working in intimate cooperation with the borough government.[16]

The company, meanwhile, was issuing statements to the press asserting that the battle of the Monongahela had settled "one matter forever, and that is that the Homestead mill hereafter will be run non-union, and the Carnegie Company will never again recognize the Amalgamated Association nor any other labor organization." [17] But the strikers were not disturbed. They were convinced that their effective system of patrols and guards, coupled with the activity of the A. F. of L. Executive Council in organizing picketing of the labor recruitment agencies in New York, Brooklyn, and other cities, would render it impossible for the company to run strikebreakers into the plants. Moreover, with reports filling the press that the situation at Homestead was peaceful, and with Governor Robert E. Pattison receiving information that there was no need for troops, the strikers began to feel certain that the militia would not be called out.[18] Finally, the strikers were heartened by support they were receiving from Amalgamated members in other Carnegie plants. The workers at the Union Mills declared a strike and shut down the plant, despite the agreement they had signed. The workmen at the Beaver Falls plant went out on a sympathetic strike on the same day. In explanation of their action, a worker from Union Mills said: "It is not our battle we are fighting, but for organized labor. They signed our scale, but we knew we would be the next victim. . . . Homestead is the stronghold and should Mr. Frick win the strike there nothing will be left for us but to fall in line." [19] *

On July 10, Governor Pattison, who had turned down previous requests for troops, suddenly reversed himself and ordered Major General George R. Snowden to assemble the National Guard of Pennsylvania, numbering 8,000, and move to Homestead. It later became clear that the Governor's decision was due to his concern over the complete control by the union of the borough's affairs. The success of the Advisory Committee posed a future danger that similar union control might help labor win out in other industrial cities. These threats had to be nipped in the bud and General Snowden was the man to do it.[20] His attitude towards the strikers is illustrated in his statement: "Philadelphians can hardly appreciate the acutal communism of these people. They believe the works are their's quite as much as Carnegie's." He characterized conditions at Homestead in three words: "revolution, treason, and anarchy." [21] †

Under the guns of the militia, the steel company prepared to secure outside labor to set the mills in operation. Bunk houses, dining halls, and kitchens were built in the mill yard and equipped to provide living accommodations for a large number of men.

Thus prepared, and assured of military protection, the steel company began to recruit strikebreakers. Employment agencies the country over were contacted and at least 70 labor agents scoured the principal cities for men to work at Homestead. Skilled workers in the non-union iron mills of the eastern states were offered special bonuses and furnished railroad tickets to Pittsburgh.

With the National Guard escorting the strikebreakers into the mill, the strikers could do little to stop the company from starting to operate again. Undoubtedly, the company reports of the number of men at work were exaggerated, and certainly the quality of the work produced by the strikebreakers was poor. The fact that the company was unable to

* Unfortunately, the union did not succeed in shutting down all of the Carnegie mills. The workers at the Edgar Thomson mill at Braddock refused to heed the appeals for assistance, and while the Duquesne workers went out, their picket lines were broken by the militia and a number of strikers were promptly arrested. Losing heart, the workers, who had never been organized before, returned to work. This was an important victory for the company, since the pig iron from the Duquesne blast furnaces was essential to the operation of the Homestead converters and rolling mills. (Wm. Weihe to Gompers, July 24, 1892, *AFL Corr.*)

† At first the attitude of the Homestead strikers towards the National Guard was friendly, but after Snowden's comments were publicized it changed rapidly. It was replaced by a feeling of anger and hate as the guardsmen helped the company break the strike. Cooks and servant girls refused to prepare food for and wait upon the company command. (*See* "The Girls for Union," Pittsburgh *Press,* July 17, 1892.)

fulfill its armor plate contracts with the government was proof that its was having difficulty starting the mill.*

Although the company had been successful in starting up the mill with scab labor, it knew it could not operate with these men for any length of time. The training of a new force would be a slow and costly process. What the company wanted was to rehire the men outside the gates—but on its own terms. How to break the spirit of the strike was the question. In some way the leaders must be intimidated or bought off in the hope that the rank-and-file would abandon the struggle.

The legal prosecution of the Homestead men, long threatened by the company, became a reality on July 18 when seven strike leaders were charged with the murder of a Pinkerton detective. Warrants were immediately sworn out for their arrests. Within the next few days the men surrendered themselves, and after spending a night in jail, all but one were released on $10,000 bail each.

The strikers retailed by preferring murder charges against officials of the Carnegie Steel Company and their Pinkerton allies. The defendants were admitted immediately to $10,000 bail each, without being required to spend a night in jail before obtaining a hearing in court. The difference in the treatment reinforced what the workers had already learned about the nature of capitalist justice.[22]

THE BERKMAN EPISODE

On July 23, while the legal battle was in progress, Alexander Berkman, a young anarchist from New York, entered the company office in Pittsburgh, shot and stabbed Frick, wounding him seriously. Berkman instantly surrendered himself and was jailed.†

Although the Advisory Committee took steps immediately to dissociate itself from Berkman's irresponsible action, denouncing and condemning "the unlawful act of the wounding of Henry Clay Frick," the anti-labor press just as quickly associated Berkman with the cause of the strikers.[23] The red-scare was exploited to the full; after the assault the Pittsburgh and Allegheny police began an investigation of the "anarchists" in those cities with the obvious aim of linking their so-called findings to the strike. As was to be expected, they found the region "full

* When the Navy Department granted the Carnegie Steel Company an exemption from penalty as a result of the delay in fulfilling its contract, labor loudly denounced the government for this favoritism to big business.

† Berkman spent 14 years in jail, being released in May, 1906. A campaign for his pardon started in the late 1890's in which Gompers himself participated. (*See* Gompers to Senator Boies Penrose, April 19, 1899 and Boies Penrose to Gompers, April 22, 1899, *GLB* and *AFL Corr.*)

of men with Anarchist principles." Arrests were made, and Chief O'Mara reported: "I am now satisfied that there was an organized movement against Frick, and Berkman was only the tool of a number of conspirators. . . . There were more Anarchists here than people supposed and they were getting ready to carry out some gigantic schemes."[24]

At Homestead, meanwhile, the strike continued. Weekly rallies were held in the skating rink and the spirit of the strikers remained unbroken. The arrest of 16 of their number for murder had not frightened them. In the face of repeated threats of mass prosecution they refused to capitulate. "The men at Homestead I am pleased to say are still holding the fort, and are confident that victory is not far off," Stephen Madden, the Amalgamated's Secretary wrote to the A. F. of L. national office on August 26.[25]

It was obvious that further intimidation was necessary. On August 30 the company exploded its second bombshell in the form of informations against the Advisory Committee on charges of conspiracy* and riot. When the grand jury met on September 22, it returned 167 true bills against the Homestead men. There were six different indictments: three for murder, two for aggrevated riots, and one for conspiracy. This time O'Donnell and other strike leaders were refused bail and remanded to prison to await trial. The others who gave themselves up had to put up huge bail; a satisfactory bond of over a half million dollars being required. This was obviously an impossibility, and some of the accused men went into hiding.[26]

The strikers again retaliated by charging Frick and his associates with riot and conspiracy. It was of slight importance; the steel magnate and the detectives had no difficulty in procuring bail from the Pittsburgh bankers, Andrew and Richard Mellon.[27]

But the company was not finished. The charge of treason was not brought against the harrassed Homestead strikers. The charges of murder and riot based on the events of July 6 and against the strikers in general. This new accusation was against the Advisory Committee and was based on the "usurpation of civil authority" in Homestead before the arrival of the National Guard. Thirty-four warrants were issued, and with the exception of O'Donnell, in prison on a charge of murder, all were freed on $10,000 bail each on October 4.[28]

In all there were about 185 separate indictments against the strike leaders, often three or four against the same men. "It appears," President Weihe wrote to Gompers, "the company intends to get the leaders all

---

* The charge of conspiracy was in total disregard of a Pennsylvania statute of 1891 making it lawful for workmen to quit work "without subjecting them to indictment for conspiracy at common law or under the criminal laws of this commonwealth." (See Laws of the General Assembly of the State of Pennsylvania, Passes at the Session of 1891, Harrisburg, Pa., 1892, p. 300.)

arrested on different charges so that they cannot secure the bondsmen to be released. . . . It just keeps us going to get bondsmen." [29] Not a single leader of the strike escaped arrest on one charge or another.

In his charge to the Grand Jury of Allegheny County, Judge Edward Paxson of the State Supreme Court based the entire treason indictment upon the activities and character of the Advisory Committee. He placed the blame for conditions at Homestead upon "the addition of large numbers of foreigners to our laboring population. Many of them are densely ignorant, as well as brutal in their dispositions. They have false ideas of the kind of liberty we enjoy in this country. It is needed that all such persons should be taught this lesson that our liberty is the liberty of law and not the liberty of license." "We have reached a point," he concluded his vicious address, "where there are but two roads left for us to pursue; the one leads to order and good government, the other leads to anarchy." [30]

Although the company lost in the courts, not a single worker being found guilty by a jury, the legal victories were exceedingly costly to the strikers. The leadership had been forced to devote much of its time to legal maneuvers and defense; the funds of the strikers, inadequate at best, had been seriously drained by bail requirements and legal expenses, and many of the most militant strikers had been forced into hiding to escape arrest.

THE PLIGHT OF THE STRIKERS

"We are badly in need of shoes and wearing apparel," Thomas J. Crawford of the Advisory Committee informed Gompers on October 13. The strikers were "suffering for lack of things," and finding it difficult to feed and clothe themselves and their families. With 1,600 men on the relief rolls costing the union $10,000 a week, and with outside contributions dwindling, the locked-out men began to realize in mid-October that their cause was doomed. Reports of strikers leaving Homestead to look for other jobs and of some applying for and receiving positions in the mill began to fill the press.[31]

On November 5, the Amalgamated's Advisory Board met at Pittsburgh to discuss the question of applying to the A. F. of L. Executive Council to issue a boycott order against the material manufactured by the Carnegie Steel Company. The Board decided that "under existing circumstances it would not be advisable . . . to make such application at the present time." Instead, it voted to request the Executive Council to issue a circular in conjunction with the iron and steel union for financial aid for the locked-out men at Homestead, Pittsburgh, and Beaver Falls.[32]

It is evident that the leadership of the strike lagged behind the rank-and-file in militancy. Indeed, unknown to the strikers, Hugh O'Donnell had gone to New York late in July in an effort to get Whitelaw Reid, publisher of the New York *Tribune,* to contact Carnegie and inform him that the strikers were ready to settle on any terms so far as wages, hours "or anything else" were concerned, provided that the settlement included recognition of the Amalgamated Association. Nothing came of the effort, but it revealed a lack of faith in the workers that paved the way for the refusal to call for a boycott of material manufactured by the Carnegie Company.[33]

Gompers and the other members of the A. F. of L. Executive Council were considerably relieved by "the very sensible conclusion they [the union leadership] arrived at in regard to the Boycott." The Council discussed the proposal to issue a circular for financial aid, and concluded that the best step would be to appeal for contributions to a special defense fund for the support of the men who had been arrested on "alleged offenses" in connection with the strike. This special defense fund should be used to procure eminent attorneys and other legal talent, and to raise the fund a special day should be set aside and designated as "Homestead Day." Workers all over the country would be urged to devote some part of their earnings on "Homestead Day" towards this fund; theatres and other places of amusement would be asked to give benefits on that day, the proceeds to go to the defense fund.[34]

The appeal, dated November 12, 1892, and signed by the A. F. of L. Executive Council, the President and Secretary of the Amalgamated Association, and by the Advisory Board, was addressed "To the American Public." It designated Tuesday, December 13, 1892, as "Homestead Day," and called upon the wage workers and all liberty-loving citizens of the country to make a contribution of a portion of their earnings on that day to aid the struggling workers of Homestead in their efforts to defend themselves before the courts.[35]

Scattered contributions to the defense fund began as early as November 16. About the same time, numerous messages began pouring into the A. F. of L. headquarters endorsing the plans for "Homestead Day," and guaranteeing that it would be widely observed.[36] Unfortunately, none of this altered the fact that the men at Homestead had reached the limits of their endurance. It was clearly a case of too little and too late. The A. F. of L. Executive Council, in the opinion of many strikers, had thrown its full weight behind the embattled workers when it could no longer decisively influence the outcome.*

---

* On June 9, 1893, Gompers wrote to the A.F. of L. Executive Council: "During the past week a committee came especially from Homestead in reference to the matters connected with their late difficulty. They called attention to the wide-spread belief among the Homestead men that the Executive Council of the A.F. of L. did not perform their full duty towards the men engaged in that trouble as well as [towards] the Amalgamated Association." (*AFL Corr.*)

On November 18, four and one-half months after the struggle began, the first real break in the strikers' ranks occurred. The mechanics and day laborers met and appointed a committee to submit to the Amalgamated men the proposition that the strike be declared off and also asked release from further obligations. The unionists met that evening and voted to continue the strike, but notified the others to do as they liked. Released from their obligations, the mechanics and day laborers voted unanimously to return to work, but not to take tonnage jobs. Immediately the rush for jobs began. The men were forced to line up before Charles M. Schwab, the new company superintendent, who sadistically chose a number for work and told the others that their jobs were filled.

The Homestead lodges of the Amalgamated Association met for their weekly meeting on November 20. No more than a third of the membership of 800 was present; O'Donnell and a number of the men were still in jail; others had left Homestead to seek jobs elsewhere, and still others were too discouraged to appear. When the question was put to declare the strike off and the Homestead mill open, it was carried by the close vote of 101 to 91.[37]

The next morning the second rush on the mill gates began. Again the men were forced to line up before Schwab who checked off the names, referring to a book in which the list of the most active strikers were kept.[38] Some were given work at considerably reduced wages,* but many were turned away.

At the same time the lodge at Beaver Falls declared the strike off and the mill was reopened. The lodges of the Union Mills held out much longer, maintaining the strike until August 14, 1893. But it was a strike in name only, for only 53 men were left to vote and the firm had had the mills in operation since September, 1892.[39]

RESULTS OF THE DEFEAT

Thus ended the great struggle which at its height involved 8,000 workers, practically ending also the career of the union in the iron and steel industry for many years to come. From 1892 onward, not a single union man was ever employed in a Carnegie mill. In 1895, there was an attempt made by some skilled workmen to organize at Homestead, but

---

* Men who earned $4 for an eight-hour day were forced to work twelve hours for half of that sum. (*National Labor Tribune*, Jan. 12, 1893.) The eight-hour day disappeared in the steel industry shortly after the Homestead defeat. By the beginning of 1894 the 12-hour shift became the rule in the Carnegie mills, and others soon followed. Up to the time of the strike little Sunday work was done in mills under contract to the Amalgamated Association, but after the strike it became a common practice in the industry.

the company broke up the lodge in short order and dismissed 35 of the more prominent organizers. Another attempted organization in 1900 was similarly frustrated by the company.

The Amalgamated Association continued to exist for years after the Homestead strike, but as an effective organization it was shattered. The Carnegie Steel Company dominated the industry, and set the pattern for other mills. The defeat at Homestead not only meant the end of unionism at the Carnegie plants, but led to the downfall of unionism in the entire industry. The Amalgamated Association had reached its peak in 1891 with 24,068 members. Thereafter its decline was rapid; membership dropped to 10,000 in 1894; 8,000 in 1895; remained at that level by the end of the century, and reached in 1909 a low of 6,295 members.[40]

The solidarity and tenacity of the Homestead strikers, union and non-union, skilled and unskilled, are a high point in the development of American labor militancy and unity. None of the Homestead men "scabbed" on their fellow-strikers. Even Frick grudgingly admitted this. "The firmness with which these strikers held on is surprising," he wrote to Carnegie.[41]

The unity of skilled and unskilled during the strike indicates that the failure of the Amalgamated Association to open its membership to the rank-and-file of the day laborers and mechanical departments was not a decisive factor in the defeat of the strike. But it cannot be denied that had this unity existed prior to the strike and had it been developed as the basic program of the union, the Amalgamated would have been in a better position to move forward after the setback. As it turned out, however, the solidarity of the steel workers ended with the strike, and the union made no effort to retain and develop this unity and to use it as a power with which it could gradually regain its position in the steel industry. It continued after 1892 to adhere to the policy of excluding Negroes from membership.[42] In short, while the steel workers, skilled and unskilled alike, had demonstrated tremendous militancy and unity during the Homestead struggle, the leadership of the union did nothing to use these great qualities of the steel workers to build a new type of organization, an industrial union, which alone could challenge the power of monopoly capitalism.

[Since this chapter was published only one important work on the Homestead strike has appeared: Leon Wolff, *Lockout, the Story of the Homestead Strike of 1982.* (New York, 1965). Several songs of the Homestead strike apppear in Philip S. Foner, *American Labor Songs of the Nineteenth Century,* (Urbana, Illinois, 1975).]

CHAPTER 15

Coal Creek and Couer d'Alene

While the nation was concentrating on the terrific labor struggle in the steel industry, it was aroused by tremendous battles between capital and labor in two sections of the mining industry: the struggle of the coal miners in eastern Tennessee and that of the copper miners in Idaho. Like their brothers in the steel industry, the miners, both eastern and western, faced bitter employer opposition, and like them, they were forcd to meet the full might of the state power arrayed on the side of the employers.

THE CONVICT LABOR SYSTEM IN TENNESSEE

A labor song of the 1890's, entitled "Buddy, won't you roll down the line," contained the lines:

> *Way back yonder in Tennessee*
> *They leased the convicts out*
> *Put them working in the mine*
> *Against free labor stout.*
> *Free labor rebelled against it*
> *To win it took some time.*
> *But while the lease was in effect*
> *They made 'em rise and shine.*[1]

The uprising referred to in the song was the "Coal Creek Rebellion," the great struggle in eastern Tennessee against convict labor, which is scarcely mentioned in most histories of the American labor movement, despite its dramatic and significant episodes. It was a revolt against the vicious system under which the state rented convicts to private businessmen who guarded, disciplined and worked them as they saw fit with no supervision by the state authorities. The supplying of convicts to plantation owners, construction contractors, and mine owners was so profitable a business that innocent men, many of whom were Negroes, were railroaded to jail to furnish convict labor to employers.

By 1891, public opposition, spearheaded by labor organizations, had compelled a large number of states to abolish the use of prison labor for profit.[2] But in Tennessee, Georgia, Alabama, Texas and other Southern states, the system still continued.

Since 1889 convicts in Tennessee had been contracted out to the Tennessee Coal, Iron and Railroad Company which owned and controlled nearly all the mines in eastern Tennessee and also operated mines in Alabama with convicts.* The company paid the state about $60 per head for convicts, and since it had a monopoly of all the men imprisoned during the life of the contract, it sub-leased its excess convicts to other companies at a profit.[3]

The great struggle in Tennessee against contract prison labor began in April, 1891 when the miners of Briceville, a short distance from the village of Coal Creek in the northeast part of the state, went out on strike against the Tennessee Coal and Mining Company. The contract with the K. of L. having expired, the company had set out to break the union. Only miners who signed an "iron-clad" agreement that they would not join a union would be given employment. The company demanded that the men agree not to employ their own checkweighman to weigh the coal—a right granted to them under the state law—but to have "implicit confidence in the integrity" of the company. Having been systematically robbed for years by the company's checkweighman before they had compelled it to accept one of the union members in the post,† it is not surprising that the miners refused to sign the proposed agreement.[4]

The company promptly locked out the miners and evicted from company houses all who refused to sign the agreement. B. A. Jenkins, president of the company, signed a five-year contract with the Tennessee Coal, Iron and Railway Company to supply him with contract convict labor.

From April to July, 1891, the miners kept the mines shut down. On July 4th, Independence Day, the Tennessee Coal and Mining Company announced that convicts were to be imported to break the strike at Briceville. The next day, 40 convicts were brought in, leased from the

* Thomas C. Platt, Republican boss of New York State, was president of the company, and many of the biggest stockholders were northern capitalists. In 1907, the company became a subsidiary of the United States Steel Corporation.

† After the law was passed in 1887 giving miners the right to elect their own checkweighmen, the Briceville miners had selected one of their own members. But it took a strike to compel the company to recognize him. In other mines, too, it was found that the law could be enforced only where there was a strong union to police it.

Tennessee Coal, Iron and Railway Company, and put to work tearing down the houses formerly inhabited by the evicted strikers. The lumber from the houses was used to build a stockade to keep a group of 150 convicts expected to arrive on July 15.

RELEASE OF THE CONVICTS

The company's action in importing convict labor aroused the entire community. A citizens' mass meeting was held on July 14, and the miners, merchants and other property owners, all of whom stood to lose from the importation of convict labor,* unitedly decided to march on the stockade and demand the release of the convicts.

Shortly after midnight, a determined band of about 300 miners and other citizens, armed with shot guns, revolvers, rifles, and army muskets appeared before the stockade. Far outnumbered, the guards turned the convicts over to the crowd. Convicts and guards were marched to Coal Creek, a distance of five miles. There they were loaded on a train for a 32-mile journey southeast to Knoxville. The entire incident was well organized and went off without the slightest confusion or violence.[5].

After they had released the convicts, the miners and their allies sent a telegram to Governor John P. Buchanan explaining their action as a necessary step to defend their families from starvation and their property from ruin. In appealing to him to prevent the return of the convicts, they emphasized that only bloodshed would result if the company persisted in using convict labor to take away the free miners' livelihood.[6]

Governor Buchanan's reply to the committee's telegram was to call out three companies of the state militia.[7]

Organized labor in Tennessee came to the support of the miners. Mass meetings were held in the principal cities, and resolutions were adopted by the assembled unionists condemning the Governor and demanding that all union men in the militia return home at once.[8] The Chattanooga Federation of Trades sent a representative, H. H. Schwartz, to express solidarity and to bolster up the spirits of the locked-out workmen. Much to his surprise, he discovered that they needed little encouragement. He sent back this report:

"I should like to impress upon people the extent of this movement. I have seen the written assurance of reinforcements to the miners of fully 7,500 men, who will be on the field in ten hours after the first shot is fired. But the time for action has not arrived. There is no division of sentiment. The entire district is as one over the main proposition, 'the

---

* Since the convicts who bought nothing from them were replacing their major customers, it is not surprising that the merchants and other property owners should have joined the miners in the protest action.

convicts must go.' I counted 840 rifles on Monday as the miners passed, while the vast multitude following them carried revolvers. The captains of the different companies are all Grand Army men.* Whites and Negroes are standing shoulder to shoulder." [9]

THE MARCH ON THE STOCKADE

On Sunday afternoon, July 10, a miners' committee called upon Colonel Sevier, commander of the militia, with a proposal for a peaceful solution. The troops and convicts were to depart retaining their arms. The miners would assist with their transportation and baggage. The Colonel's reply was that if the miners attempted to enter the camp they would be fired upon.

At a mass meeting that evening, the miners drew up plans to move upon the stockade the following morning. Before daybreak, miners converged on Briceville from all the mining camps of northeast Tennessee. They came on foot, trains, and mules, armed with rifles, shotguns, Colt pistols, and old squirrel guns. Eugene Merrell was in command. The miners were organized in strict military discipline, prepared for whatever might happen. A roll call was drawn up listing each man, with a note as to his arms. Those who had been drinking were ordered to fall out. Marching four abreast, in two columns, two thousand miners and farmers started out on their two-mile hike to the stockade. "Their organization was complete," said a contemporary newspaper, "and their leaders placed them along the hills with military precision." [10]

As they approached the camp, situated on a knoll in a valley ,the miners occupied the hills and completely surrounded the stockade. A column of miners marched to within 200 yards of the camp when Merrell gave the signal to halt. A committee of three, under a flag of truce, called for Colonel Sevier and went to meet him. When the Colonel made a move as if to take the committee captive, Merrell waved his handkerchief, and at once 1,500 miners sprang from the hillside and made their way towards the stockade. Impressed with the strength of the miners and considering resistance futile, Colonel Sevier surrendered. The miners agreed not to injure company property and to assist in guarding the convicts. Then Merrell and his committee waved their hats and swords, a signal of success. There was a tremendous cheer from the miners.

In high spirits the miners started the convicts, guards, and militia on the march to Briceville. At the town they boarded a train of flat cars waiting for them. While waiting for a special train at Coal Creek, the miners invited the soldiers into their homes for lunch. The troops,

* The reference is to the Grand Army of the Republic, the Union Army during the Civil War.

many of whom sympathized with the miners, departed in good spirits, and as the train left Coal Creek there were reciprocal cheers by soldiers and miners. When they arrived at Knoxville, the soldiers gave the press a statement in which they thanked the miners for the "many courtesies and kindness extended to us during our stay in camp." [11]

Meanwhile, the miners released 125 convicts being used at the Knoxville Iron Company mine and placed them on a train for Knoxville. Then at a closed meeting, the miners took an oath not to molest state or company property and to remain quiet and orderly. Guards were placed around company property to prevent injury, for the miners were familiar "with the old tactic of coal companies of planting a charge of dynamite in time of strike to incite public opinion against the miners." [12]

The discipline and organization of the miners in the second release of the convicts aroused admiration in many parts of the state. "The capture of the Tennessee militia was one of the most amazing things in military tactics," declared the Louisville *Times*. The conservative newspapers, spokesmen for the mine owners, carried screaming headlines denouncing the strikers: *"Anarchy, Law of Tennessee Set at Naught. Organized Mob of Miners Defy and Override the Power of the State."* Taking his cue from these headlines, Governor Buchanan, after consulting T.C.I. officials, issued an order mobilizing the full military strength of the state, 14 companies of militia, and prepared for war. Troops were ordered out from six cities and placed under the command of General Samuel T. Carnes of Memphis. As Gompers correctly put it in denouncing the Governor's action: "The state of Tennessee really converted itself into a bureau to supply scab labor. [13]

On July 25, the convicts were returned under military escort accompanied by Governor Buchanan. They were received in silence by a crowd in Coal Creek. Thirty-six convicts were delivered to the Tennessee Coal and Mining Company, and 125 to the Knoxville Iron and Mining Company. A speech announced by the Governor had to be cancelled when no one turned out to hear him. [14]

THE LEGISLATIVE SESSION

Yielding to pressure from labor and its allies, Governor Buchanan had agreed to call a special session of the legislature to consider the miners' demand that "The convicts must go!" But in the very proclamation calling for the session, the Governor made it even more clear than before that he was a servant of the corporations. The first item on the agenda was to be conferring upon the governor greater authority over the militia, and an increase of its strength. His final betrayal of the people came in his message to the legislature, in which he advocated the continuance of the convict lease system in the face of the clear desire of the majority of the people to be rid of that iniquitous evil. Modification perhaps, but no repeal, said the Governor, and he cited as his main reasons for retaining the system that it would be too expensive to consider building a new prison to house 1,500 convicts and that the state would lose $100,000 a year, the sum received from the convict contract.

The legislature refused to repeal the convict lease system by a vote of 59 to 23, and passed laws which made the convict lease system even more obnoxious. Interference with the labor of a convict was made a felony punishable with five years' imprisonment. Leading a protesting group—"mob" was the word used in the law—was to be punished by seven years in prison. And the sum of $25,000 was appropriated for the maintenance of the militia with which to further intimidate the miners, while $14,458.13 was set aside to pay the bill already incurred by the militia at Briceville. Finally, the Governor was commended by the legislature for his firm and prompt action in restoring order in the mining district.[15]

The Governor could now do legally what he had been pleased to do illegally.

Not only the miners but the entire state was shocked by the legislature's action. Senator Woodlee, a Farmers' Alliance Democrat from Grundy County, declared: "It is a disgrace to have been a member of this general assembly." [16]

At a mass meeting on October 28, the miners' committee made its final report and tendered its resignation in these words: "As the state had willed it, and is prepared to enforce its will with bayonet and Gatling gun, that you peacefully give up your work, your homes, and your sweet memories that around them cling, and like Hagar did, find a protection in a Divine Providence, for surely you can find none elsewhere, with sorrow too deep to express, we ring down the curtain on the last act in the Briceville drama by tendering our resignation." [17]

THE STORMING OF THE STOCKADE

However, the last and what was by far the most dramatic act in that drama was just beginning. Convicts had been used in the mines since 1871 and the miners had waited patiently for 20 years for the law to redress their grievances. They had refrained from resorting to extra-legal methods until they had exhausted every possible legal instrument. Now the miners were prepared to use much more drastic action.

On the last day of October, word was passed around announcing a meeting in each mine. As the men approached, all lights were extinguished so that no one could be recognized. "Jack-in-the-box" spoke, advising all miners to disguise and arm themselves, and gather together that night at Rock Bottom Hall.

From the hall the miners marched 1,500 strong to the stockade which was quickly surrounded. The leaders, with handkerchiefs across their faces, demanded of the warden that the convicts be turned over to the miners. The demand was met at once. After furnishing each convict with civilian clothes, they were set free. The stockade was burned to the ground. This was the first violence to property in the long struggle. It was clear that ,whatever the cost, the miners did not intend to permit the convicts to return again.

The convicts at the mine of the Knoxville Iron Company were also freed, though here the stockade was not burned, for the warden's wife was seriously ill in an adjoining house. The guardhouse and the office, however, were destroyed. Convicts were supplied with clothing before they were set free.[18]

The release of the convicts had been conducted with the utmost secrecy and with no shots being fired. Everything had gone off with military precision.

Newspapers sympathetic to the miners compared the attack on the stockade to the storming of the Bastille in the French Revolution. When the Nashville *Banner* asked, "Shall Tennessee allow a gang of thieves, robbers, ruffians and outlaws to trample with impunity upon the law?" the Chattanooga *Republican* replied:

"They are not ruffians and they are not cut-throats. Rather call the legislature robbers. . . . Rather call the legislature inhuman because they refused to listen to the appeals of the miners; and when they asked for the right to labor and earn bread for their families, received in answer the contemptuous reply: we not only make it a crime for you to interfere with state convicts, but we send more convicts in your midst to show you that the power of the state is supreme." [19]

A reward of $5,000 was offered by the governor for the arrest of the leaders of the miners and of $250 for each additional member of the miners' union who participated in the attack on the stockade. But no one was arrested and no legal action was taken against the miners. It was impossible to proceed legally against an entire county. No one knew who was responsible, at least no one would talk. As for the convicts, most of them were rounded up by railroad and company detectives.[20]

For several months following the attack on the stockade, peace reigned in the area between Coal Creek and Briceville. Most of the companies decided that it was the better part of wisdom to deal with the union on reasonable terms. They met with committees representing the United Mine Workers to which organization the miners, formerly affiliated with the K. of L., now belonged, and agreed to permit the miners to select their own checkweighmen, and to desist from importing convict labor. In Briceville the company finally decided that it had had enough. In spite of pressure from Godwin, agent of the Tennessee Coal, Iron and Railway Company, the Briceville mine owners refused to bring back the convicts. Convicts were never again used in Briceville.[21]

On July 15, 1892, the first anniversary of the freeing of the convicts at Briceville was celebrated. Eugene Merrell made the welcoming address, and Billy Webb, president of the United Mine Workers in the district, was the principal speaker. During the afternoon and evening there was dancing on a platform constructed from the old timber of the convict stockade. "It's funny what a little organization will do," Webb wrote in the *United Mine Workers' Journal,* describing the celebration.[22]

The miners' rejoicing was premature. The Tennessee Coal, Iron and Railway Company was determined that the state of Tennessee should have convicts mine its coal, regardless of what the miners and the rest of the population thought about the matter. It proceeded to buy out a number of companies that had signed agreements with the miners' union, rebuilt the stockades that had been burned, built new ones, and brought in convicts. In these mines, convicts worked full time while the free miners received only one or two days a week. The best places in the mines were given to scabs and blacklegs. Miners who had been active in the convict fight were discharged and blacklisted.[23]

Trouble was in the air. Once more the miners began to hold secret meetings.

THE BATTLE OF OLIVER SPRINGS

This time the explosion burst in Tracy City in the southeastern part of Tennessee. Although the miners at Tracy City had suffered under the convict lease system longer than any other group (it was here in 1871 that the Tennessee Coal, Iron and Railway Company had first introduced the use of convict labor in the mines), they had not taken part thus far in the war to end the system. Then in July, 1892, the Tennessee Coal and Iron Company cut the free miners to half time, while the convicts were working full time. A committee of miners asked that as soon as work picked up, they should be given more time instead of giving it all to the convicts. The company replied that they would give the request consideration, but promised nothing.

Soon more orders came in. Instead of heeding the miners' request, the company imported more convicts, and increased the number of guards at the stockade, located at Oliver Springs, several miles to the north of Tracy City. It was this action that caused the pent-up resentment of years to explode.[24]

About five o'clock on the morning of August 13, 1892, a committee of miners called on Superintendent Nathrust. They demanded employment on equal terms with the convicts. He made a vague promise to take up the matter with the company officials. When the miners received this report, they decided to take action. They were fed up on promises.

At nine o'clock in the morning, 150 miners approached the stockade at Oliver Springs, while three miners covered each guard. With drawn guns, the leaders, Berry Simpson, Bob Vaughn and Jim Frazier, demanded the keys to the stockade. All personal property of the convicts and the company were carefully removed. The stockade was burned and the convicts placed on the train for Nashville.[25]

The next day the conservative press demanded that the Governor take immediate action to preserve "the dignity of Tennessee." "There must be a stop to this," raged the Nashville *American*. "We point to anarchism and communism in other states, and at the same time are nurturing them in our midst." [26]

The Governor did act. Troops were sent in, the convicts were returned, and the stockade was rebuilt. More and more free miners' jobs were taken by the convicts. A permanent armed garrison was now stationed at Coal Creek.

On August 14, the story of the battle of Oliver Springs was related to a mass meeting of miners at Coal Creek. Full approval of the miners' action was voted. Resolutions were also adopted hailing the Homestead workers for their courage in battling the Pinkertons employed by the Carnegie Steel Company. There was a demand for new action to rid the entire area once and for all of convicts.[27]

On August 16, miners from all parts of eastern Tennessee and southern Kentucky poured into Coal Creek. Everyone realized that the final showdown was at hand. Freight trains were taken over by the miners as a small army of miners, 3,000 strong, moved in the direction of Oliver Springs. At 4:30 am. they arrived before the stockade.

Under a flag of truce the miners agreed not to injure company property, guards or militia, provided that the convicts were released. In the face of such odds, the guards and militiamen surrendered. As the guards and militia marched out between a double file of miners, they were disarmed and permitted to leave unharmed. For the third time in a year, a carload of convicts moved toward Knoxville. Again the stockade at Oliver Springs was burned.

Before the Oliver Springs battle began, word of the miners' plans had reached the authorities and a regiment had been sent to the area from Chattanooga. A train was waiting to convey the regiment to Oliver Springs, but the railroad engineers and train crews refused to move the train. In spite of the raging and threats of the officers, the men stood their ground. The train did not move.[28]

Invited to a conference by the miners, the Governor replied evasively, advising them to remain quiet and satisfactory arrangements would be made. He was merely stalling for time, for he had already set about mobilizing the entire military power of the state. Regiments of troops were ordered to Coal Creek, and, acting under the new legislation passed at the special session, the Governor ordered the sheriffs in all the neighboring counties to furnish large forces of men for duty. Volunteers, "all belonging to the best families," responded to the sheriffs' appeals for forces. Arms and munition were supplied by the United States War Department. The armed force, which included, according to a Knoxville newspaper, "some of the most prominent citizens of the place . . . Good representatives of the class of men who favor the maintenance of law and order," started for the front at Coal Creek.[29]

The miners entrenched themselves on Walden's Ridge opposite Fort Anderson. Pickets were posted on the surrounding mountain top to prevent a surprise attack, for word had reached the miners that thousands of soldiers were on their way.

On August 19, however, trainloads of soldiers arrived in Coal Creek. With the large number of soldiers came field guns and Gatling guns.

Greatly outnumbered and unable to withstand the artillery shelling, the miners were driven from their positions commanding the fort. Coal Creek was in the hands of the militia. Troops continued to pour in, and as soon as it was known that armed resistance had been broken, large numbers of volunteers turned up eager to fight the dispersed miners.[30]

THE REIGN OF TERROR

The war turned into a mad man-hunt. Revenge and terror were the order of the day. The troops combed the hills and mining towns taking custody of hundreds, not only miners but ordinary citizens, regardless of whether they had been participants in the war. Hundreds were arrested and prisons soon overflowed.* The village schoolhouse was converted into a prison, and when that was filled, the Methodist Church was used for the same purpose.[31]

On August 20, General Garnes announced that he had 300 miners in custody and was continuing the reign of terror with zeal. "Soldiers have been engaged all day arresting miners and the work is to be prosecuted with vigor. Houses are to be searched and all arms and ammunition in them will be confiscated. No quarter will be given miners who resist." [32]

A Negro, Jake Witsen, who was alleged to have "resisted," was shot and killed, his body being pierced with a dozen bullets. Witsen, described

---

* There would have been even more miners imprisoned if the citizens of the area had not hidden and fed them. Even though they knew that if they were discovered they would be arrested, these citizens hid the miners in cellars and attics.

in the conservative press as a "desperado," had been one of the leaders in the revolt. His body was carried to his home at Clinton and a funeral was held which was attended by several thousand white fellow-workers and neighbors.[33]

Three hundred miners were indicted for conspiracy, carrying of arms, murder and many other "crimes." Nothing was said at their trials about the lawless acts of the companies nor of the soldiers and how they had terrorized women and children. After long drawn-out trials, a number of miners were sentenced to the penitentiary. D. B. Monroe, one of the leaders of the battle, was given seven years in the penitentiary. He served only two years, and, after his release, was again in Grundy County organizing the miners.[34]

Following the battle at Coal Creek in August, 1892, there was comparative quiet in the mountains until the spring of 1893. Then the miners of Tracy City staged the final pitched battle of the convict wars. The stockade near Tracy City had been burned in the August battle. A short time later it had been rebuilt. The new structure was a real fortress, complete with portholes from four to six inches in diameter, and block houses on the corner. Miners continued to drill in secret against the day when they would fight again for their jobs.

On the evening of April 19, 1893, 150 miners approached the stockade. Coats were thrown over their heads for disguise. For several hours a battle raged. As soon as the news of the battle reached Nashville, five cannon shots were fired from Capitol Hill, the signal for the troops to take off. A special train carried four companies of the First Regiment of the Militia, a cannon and Gatling gun. At Murfreesboro further reinforcements were picked up. Adjutant-General Fytte and Captain Henry Ward of the United States Army were in command.

With the arrival of the troops, the outnumbered miners dispersed and a hunt began for their leaders. Most of them took to the woods. They were hidden and cared for by hundreds of friends and sympathizers who wanted to see the convict lease system abolished. Thus ended the final battle in the great convict war.[35]

While apparently defeated in their long struggle, the miners were the final victors in the fight over the convict lease system. Their struggles had aroused the state to the point where public opinion demanded an end to the convict lease system in the mines. In response to the continued pressure from the miners, their union, the United Mine Workers, and their supporters throughout the state, the contract with the Tennessee Coal, Iron and Railway Company was not renewed when it expired in 1896. After exactly 25 years of suffering and struggle, and two years of pitched battles, the miners rid themselves of this yoke and wiped from the slate a disgraceful mark against the state of Tennessee.[36]

CONDITIONS OF WESTERN MINERS

At the very same time that the miners were waging their historic struggle in eastern Tennessee, another battle was occurring in the western mine fields at Idaho. A common bond of oppression linked the eastern coal miner and the western metal miner.

By 1890, the great majority of the western miners were dependent upon corporations, dominated by absentee owners, for their livelihood. Gone was the independent miner of the early "rushes" into the mine fields. In his place were strictly wage earners, working for corporate organizations under a whole new set of restrictions and regulations, and piling up profits for absentee owners in what was easily the most dangerous of America's major industries. As William D. (Big Bill) Haywood, the militant leader of the western miners, wrote in his description of a typical mining town: "Human life is the cheapest by-product of this great copper camp."[37] And as a miner himself put it, the worker in the mines was treated as:

> Only a man in overalls—a very good man as a rule—
> But a man with us is rated as a farmer rates a mule,
> One is as good as the other, but the long eared slave's the best,
> He's a little rougher, decidedly tougher,
> And doesn't need half the rest.
>
> Only a man in overalls, lay him anywhere—
> Send for the company doctor—we have not time to spare;
> Only a little misfire, only a miner crushed.
> Put another one on, from dark till dawn
> This smelter must be rushed. [38]

THE WESTERN MINERS ORGANIZE

In the face of the evils growing out of corporate mining, the majority of the miners in the camps came to realize that only through organization, through cooperation together, and through united opposition to exploitation could their conditions be improved. Although it was not until 1893 that a federation of western miners' unions was formed, local unions had been in existence long before then. During 1880-90, the K. of L. were able to absorb most of the ore miners' unions, and by 1888 had established 43 assemblies in Colorado as well as a number of assemblies in Montana.[39]

A number of local unions of silver and lead miners were formed in the Couer d'Alene area of Idaho in the late 1880's, and in 1890 they came together to form the Consolidated Miners' Union.* A Central Executive

* The union included almost all of the underground workers in the Couer d'Alene camps.

Committee was set up to coordinate the activities of the local unions, and to manage all common enterprises, such as the administration of sick benefits, and the establishment of a union hospital.* The committee was also empowered to direct activities during a strike or lockout.[40]

In the summer of 1891, the Miners' Union laid siege to the Bunker Hill mine, reputedly financed by Standard Oil, and the citadel of anti-unionism in Couer d'Alene. After a two-week strike, the company capitulated, agreeing to pay the union scale, to rehire strikers without discrimination, and to pay the hospital fees as the men desired. With this victory, the entire Couer d'Alene area came under union control; every mine in the region now paid the union wage scale.[41]

Up to now the mine owners had been fighting unionism tooth and nail individually, but in 1891, they formed the Mine Owners' Protective Association of the Couer d'Alene or, as generally known, the Mine Owners' Association and abbreviated M.O.A. In January, 1892, the mine owners shut down their mines and the M.O.A. announced a new wage scale in the district which would wipe out many of the previous gains won by the union. The association offered $3.00 per day for carmen and shovellers and $3.50 per day for miners, a wage reduction averaging 25 percent.[42]

The Miners' Union refused to accept the wage cut, recognizing that this was but the first step in the association's drive to wipe out unionism in Couer d'Alene. Thereupon, the M.O.A. locked out the members of the union, and announced that "the association has resolved never to hire another member of the miners' union." [43]

With the entire community, including some of the papers and the police, friendly to the miners, the employers were unsuccessful in even a limited attempt to work the mines. However, on May 4, they were able to secure a court injunction restraining the miners from interfering with work at the mines, or from discouraging workers from entering the region for the purpose of replacing locked-out miners.[44]

Gradually the mines resumed operations, 300 scabs being brought from Duluth under 53 armed guards. Armed guards travelled about the Idaho countryside, rounding up farmers who were told that they would be paid three dollars a day in the mines and additional money for serving as deputized U.S. marshals.[45]

"PEACEFUL PERSUASION"

"Peaceful persuasion" was the union's answer to the owners' importation of strikebreakers. Pickets met all the trains entering the district, swarmed around the scabs, isolated them, and lectured to them as they

* The project to set up a union hospital was dear to the heart of the miners. There were no workmen's compensation laws in existence and the company's medical assistance was completely inadequate to meet the needs of the miners.

marched to the company boarding houses on why they should not take the jobs of the locked-out workers. This method of meeting the employers' offensive achieved remarkable success. Many of the scabs were induced to quit their jobs or to abandon their efforts to seek work. Out of the 74 men brought in on the first train in May, about 30 quit work as strikebreakers, went down to union headquarters and joined the Miners' Union. It has been estimated that "at least fifty per cent of the men who came into the district seeking work were taken into camp by the Union." The men who had been induced to stop strikebreaking and join the union received the same strike relief as the locked-out workers.[46]

Two small mines yielded to the union's successful "peaceful persuasion" early in July, but the M.O.A. remained firm. It was almost six months since the January shutdown and over three months since the April lockout. "Peaceful persuasion" had been successful in interfering with the attempt to run the mines with strikebreakers, but it had not yet brought recognition of the union and elimination of the proposed wage cut.

On July 7, the locked-out miners learned that the locked-out steel workers at Homestead, Pennsylvania, had given battle to two barge-loads of Pinkerton detectives coming up the Manongahela river from Pittsburgh to act as strikebreakers. The action of the steel workers in beating back the Pinkertons and defeating the strikebreaking attempt impressed the miners in Idaho, especially when they discovered that their recording secretary was a Pinkerton spy planted in the union by the M.O.A.[47]

On July 11, a large group of armed miners gathered outside of the Frisco mine, and a fight between them and the Pinkertons, armed deputies, and the strikebreakers inside ensued. The miners loaded some "giant powder" on a rail car and sent it down the track, where its explosion demolished the Frisco mine and compelled the surrender of the strikebreakers. The strikers then compelled the non-union men to leave the region.[48]

Open warfare between armed strikers and armed strikebreakers, Pinkertons and deputies continued for a few days and resulted in the death of three union men. Non-union men were forced to quit. The armed battle stopped strikebreaking at two or three mines, but as one student of the strike points out: "The union's conquest of the rest of the district was bloodless, achieved without firing another gun, but always backed by the threat of further violence in case resistance was offered. . . ."[49]

THE ARMY MOVES IN

Recognizing that without the aid of the state and federal authorities, they would lose out, the mine owners appealed frantically for such assistance. It was immediately forthcoming. On July 13, Governor Willey declared that a state of insurrection existed, and requested and received

Federal troops to restore order. Close to 1,500 soldiers, members of the National Guard and the United States Army, commanded by Major General J. M. Schofield, moved into the Couer d'Alene district.[50]

With the open aid of the troops, the strikebreakers were brought back, the mines resumed operation, and 600 men were thrown into "bull pens" at Kellog and Wallace. With the exception of those who fled to Montana, all the union leaders, practically all the union membership, and a considerable number of union sympathizers were taken prisoners.

"The arbitrary and mendacious conduct of some of the U.S. Army officers," wrote an A. F. of L. organizer who visited Couer d'Alene, "was never equaled in Russia, Siberia or by a plantation Slave-Driver for cruelty towards those arrested or came under the displeasure of the mine-owners." One striker testified later: "I have been shut up in a small cell without ventilation and with little light except what comes through the bars. No friends have been permitted to see me. We could not get permission to have a barber shave us. The soldier barbers are not permitted to work among us. Each one was obliged to eat alone." [51]

Organized labor stood loyally behind the imprisoned strikers.* Miners' unions in Montana and other states helped to raise a defense fund for the men in Idaho. The A. F. of L. announced full support of the miners, appropriated $500 for their defense, and called for a Congressional investigation of the whole Couer d'Alene affair.[52]

THE TRIAL

The trials of the imprisoned men opened on August 2 before a jury composed almost entirely of farmers. Twenty-one of the defendants were charged with contempt of court for having violated a court injunction. Nine were found guilty and sentenced to six to eight months in prison. The others were dismissed. In a trial for conspiracy, growing out of the Frisco mine explosion, four of the miners were found guilty and sentenced to between 15 months to two years in prison. They were later released on appeal to the United States Supreme Court. At the same time, 480 indictments returned by the federal grand jury were quashed.[53]

No sooner were the miners released from the prison pens than they picked up the strike where it had been left off. The men who were forced to remain in jail as a result of the convictions learned the happy news that despite military suppression, the miners had won the strike, forcing the mine owners to rescind the wage cut and to recognize the Union. "Most all the men working in the Couer d'Alene country are now union men," P. J. McArthur, recording secretary of the Butte Miners' Union wrote to

---

* The trade unions of Chicago refused to participate in a Columbus day parade because the military heading the procession had been used against the miners in Couer d'Alene. (*Army and Navy Journal*, Oct. 15, 1892.)

Gompers on February 19, 1893. "We have two unions there notwithstanding the temporary injunction that is standing over them. We think before six months we will have better unions than ever before and the wages is the same as before the trouble." Thus, as a contemporary reporter correctly concluded: "with all the Federal and state troops, with all the corrupt officials, with all the enormous wealth of the association, with the car-loads of non-union men, still the companies could not operate the mines. The mine owners, after months of persistent effort to train the new men, gave up in despair, and discharged them. They were again compelled to employ all the old Couer d'Alene men who made application. . . . The union was victorious." [54]

FORMATION OF THE WESTERN FEDERATION OF MINERS

"We have made a fight that we are proud of and propose to continue it to the end," a spokesman for the victorious strikers wrote to Gompers.[55] The fight did continue. The men sentenced to prison on contempt were quartered in the Ada County jail. They spent part of their time discussing labor strategy and tactics. It was during these discussions that the idea of a federation of western miners' unions was conceived. Reviewing the events since the shutdown in January, 1892, the imprisoned miners reached the conclusion that better organization and more complete unity among the workers were essential for continued advances. All recognized the importance of the aid they had received from the miners' unions in Montana and from other labor organizations, and they thought long and hard about the way "to organize labor's forces more effectively in the whole mining West." [56]

At Butte, Montana, too, discussions were taking place on the need to unite the various miners' unions into one powerful federation. In February and March, 1893, the contempt prisoners were discharged from the Ada County jail. Three of them went directly to Butte and conferred immediately. The result of these conferences was the issuance of an invitation in April by the Butte Miners' Union to all miners' unions in the west urging them to send delegates to a convention at Butte on May 15, 1893.[57]

From May 15 to 19, 1893, 43 delegates gathered at Butte to form a federation of all the miners' unions of the west. The delegates were unanimous in their approval of the plan to form a federation whose purposes were to "unite the various miners' unions of the West into one central body; to practice those virtues that adorn society and remind man of his duty to fellow man; the elevation of the position and the maintenance of the rights of the miner." The Western Federation of Miners was chosen as the name of the organization.[58]

CHAPTER 16

The Economic Crisis of 1893

On May 4, 1893, the National Cordage Company, which only five months before had declared a stock dividend of 100 percent, failed. A general break in the stock market followed, and soon the country was passing through the severest economic crisis U. S. capitalism had yet experienced, with runs on the banks, thousands of business failures, and severe unemployment following in its wake. During 1893, 642 banks failed and 22,500 miles of railway went into receivership.[1] More than 16,000 business firms went into bankruptcy. Thousands of shops and factories shut down; more thousands worked part time only.

THE UNEMPLOYED

Hundreds of thousands were thrown out of work. In the summer of 1893, *Bradstreets'* reported that 119 cities of the country showed 801,000 unemployed upon whom 1,956,000 persons depended for bread. This made a total of 2,757,000 persons without visible means of support in these cities alone. In its report for the week ending December 23, 1893, *Bradstreets'* admitted that returns from the same 119 points showed 3,000,000 people without means of earning a livelihood. These 119 points, of course, by no means covered the whole country. With at least three million out of a total labor force of five million unemployed, and with two to five times as many people dependent on these workers for their existence, it is clear that by the end of 1893 a large percentage of the population were unable to procure the necessities of life.[2]

Wherever the unemployed turned there were more applicants for jobs. Large numbers of idle workers, desperately searching for a means of livelihood, traveled long distances looking for work, only to find upon their arrival that there was not enough employment for the workers already there. Without visible means of support, these itinerant workers were immediately classified in the press as "tramps" and "hoboes" who had no real desire to work. But a study of homeless workers in 14 cities revealed that these men were only too eager to work; that more than half the men had "trades, employments or professions requiring more or less skill." Three-fifths of the men were under thirty-five, and three-fourths under forty—in short, in the prime of life.[3]

The burden of providing some measure of relief to enable the hundreds of thousands of jobless men and their families to keep body and soul together fell upon charitable organizations, municipalities,* and a number of stronger trade unions. In large cities, these trade unions—typographical, cigar makers, carpenters, shoe workers, building trades—were able to care for their own unemployed members, so that these workers were not compelled to resort to outside relief. Several unions, notably the printers and cigar makers, had established permanent out-of-work funds long before the crisis, and were able to use them to assist unemployed members. But most unions had not accumulated enough reserves in prosperous times, and they relied mainly upon emergency contributions or assessments upon employed members. In general, the unions that gave relief furnished weekly benefits of between $3.00 to $5.00 for unmarried men, with additions of coal, flour, meat, and other provisions for men with families. In some cases, relief was extended as loans to members. Occasionally union relief funds were dispensed not only to members but to all who applied.[4]

DEMANDS FOR PUBLIC RELIEF

Although the economic crisis of the 'nineties marked "the first widespread contribution to unemployment relief by trade unions,"[5] the trade union relief affected but a very small proportion of the total number of the unemployed. The trade unions themselves were among the first to recognize this fact, and demanded public aid for the unemployed. Following a meeting of trade unionists in New York City, a call went out to the trade unions to send delegates to a conference to be held on August 20 at the hall of the International Labor Exchange:

"A fearful crisis is upon us; countless thousands of our fellow men are unemployed; men, women and children are suffering the pangs of hunger! The present indications are, that the poverty and misery of our people will not be diminished, but on the contrary intensified for some time to come.

"We cannot allow by our indifference hundreds or even thousands to die of starvation. . . . The wants of the needy must be supplied, the hunger of our brothers and sisters *must be* satisfied.[6]

* No state appropriated money for relief purposes during the depression, 1893-97.

One hundred delegates representing about 100,000 organized workers were present at the trade union conference on August 20. Among the speakers were George E. McNeill, the veteran labor leader, Herbert Burrows, and Victor Delahaye. The last two were the delegates of the workingmen of England and France to the International Labor Conference at Chicago.

Gompers, as chairman, made the major address. He presented a moral indictment of the ruling class, avoiding an attack upon the capitalist system. He placed the blame for the economic crisis squarely upon the shoulders of "the wealthy possessors of our country." Since they were quite content to let the unemployed starve to death, it became the duty of government to "provide the means by which the manhood and womanhood of our country may be maintained." Gompers set forth a number of relief measures. He called upon the cities of the nation to inaugurate movements for public improvements; the states should improve their roadways, deepen their canals and make them available for larger ships, and the Government of the United States should construct a Nicaraguan Canal and improve the Mississippi River. Such public works would give the unemployed something useful to do, would stave off starvation for hundreds of thousands, and would cause an upturn in business conditions.[7]*

Three committees were set up by the conference: one to visit public officials to demand relief for the unemployed and a program of public works; another to solicit contributions for unemployment relief, and the third to draw up a proclamation. The proclamation was issued the next day. It called upon the Mayor and the Board of Aldermen of New York City to convene a special session to devise means of commencing public works for the unemployed, and urged the State Governors and the President of the United States to call a special emergency convention by public proclamation, and take such legislative action as would relieve the widespread distress.[8]

The New York Organized Labor Conference for the Relief of the Unemployed revealed that the trade union movement was alert to the dangers facing the working class early in the crisis, and that it did not intend to wait for the "wealthy possessors of our country" to starve American labor into submission.[9] The conference, moreover, had an important effect throughout the land. Writing to Gompers after a tour of several states, McNeill observed: "The result of that meeting cannot be judged by the measure of relief received by those dependent upon the charity of the world. The voice of that meeting was heard throughout

* In an article especially written for the New York *World* of Jan. 14, 1894, Gompers advanced these and other proposals. In all, he listed 22 propositions for relief.

our broad land, and the attention of thinking people brought to a closer examination of causes and conditions." [10]

MASS DEMONSTRATIONS OF UNEMPLOYED

The Organized Labor Conference had shunned mass activity, relying instead on the work of its committees. But it soon became clear that resolutions adopted at labor conferences were meaningless if they were not backed up by mass demonstrations.* Fruitless visits to the Mayor of New York City and the Governor of the State convinced even Gompers and other top A. F. of L. leaders that mass activity was necessary to give substance to the program adopted by the Conference. Denouncing these officials for having "failed to do anything in response to the direct appeals of organized labor for the relief of the workers in distress," the A. F. of L. leadership began to call for mass demonstrations of the unemployed. Federation organizers were instructed to devote themselves to organizing meetings of the unemployed in their communities, and many spent most of their time in this work. Several even organized the unemployed into federal labor unions which were promptly chartered by the A. F. of L. [11]

The A. F. of L. national office sent McNeill on a tour as an official spokesman for the Federation to rally the unemployed. He helped to organize and addressed gatherings of the unemployed at Albany, Buffalo, Toledo, Detroit, Owosso, Michigan, Indianapolis, Cincinnati, Columbus, and Chicago. At each of these meetings, he reported to Gompers, "the leading labor men of the cities were present." [12]

The mass meeting in Chicago, sponsored by the trade unions, was held on the Lake Front late in August, 1893. The resolutions adopted demanded, among other things, that Congress should issue a circulating medium direct to the people; that idle men should be employed on roads and other public improvements where convict labor had been used, and that the hours of labor should be reduced until all could be employed. After the meeting, the workers paraded through the streets, carrying the

* Before the Organized Labor Conference took place, Joseph Barondess, head of the Socialist Jewish Clothing Workers' Union, affiliated to the A.F. of L.'s United Garment Workers, urged Gompers to call a demonstration of the unemployed of New York City, organized and unorganized, to bring pressure upon the public officials. Gompers was opposed to the suggestion, privately informing Chris Evans, A.F. of L. Secretary-Treasurer, that it would not be "the wisest thing" for the Federation to sponsor a demonstration of the unemployed. Instead, it was decided to call a conference of trade unionists. (Joseph Barondess to Gompers, Aug. 15, 1893; Gompers to Chris Evans, Aug. 17, 1893, AFL Corr.; GLB.)

Rebuffed by Gompers, the Jewish Clothing Workers' Union called a mass demonstration of the unemployed at Union Square on August 19, the day before the Organized Labor Conference met. It attracted thousands of workers. (New York Sun, Aug. 20, 1893.)

banners of various trade unions and of the Socialist Labor Party, and demanding work of the city government.

Early in the fall of 1893, another mass meeting of 10,000 workers was held in Chicago, addressed by Gompers and Henry George. A committee of trade unionists, elected by the meeting, assisted a Mayor's committee in putting 1,400 men to work for a month on the Chicago drainage canal, and in arranging for street repairs that would employ 2,000 men at $1,000 per day.[13]

Demonstrations in cities by labor groups resulted in clashes with the police whose solution for the problems of the crisis "was to club and brutally maltreat all unemployed who gathered to express their demand for relief and work." But these demonstrations also forced the municipal governments to provide some measure of relief for the jobless. Soup kitchens were established in dozens of cities; many municipalities provided work in the improvement of streets or parks.

But the unemployed received bare subsistence wages. Heads of families in some cities received ten cents an hour, but the average was much lower. Single men worked for meal and lodging tickets only. Destitute men, however, rarely were permitted to work for more than a day at a time. In San Francisco some of the unemployed were permitted to sweep streets for two half-days each week at a wage of a dollar and forty cents— "enough to keep them alive for a week at the Salvation Army 'Life Boat.'"[14]

THE MILLIONAIRES PROTEST

Yet even these meager disbursements for the unemployed aroused irate cries of "communism" and "waste" from the wealthier classes. In Cincinnati a committee of businessmen protested vigorously against the city's providing work for the unemployed, insisting that it was solely a problem for private charity. The committee listed three objections to public works to aid the unemployed:

"1. That it is not necessary, and that it is a waste of tax-payers' money.

"2. That it is communistic in principle.

"3. That it demoralizes those who receive it."[15]

It is hardly surprising that when the unemployed read such reports[16] that they should ask in the words of a moving poem, written during the crisis by a Chicago trade unionist, "why then should we be"

Starving in a land of plenty,
In a great and growing nation.
Men and women—little children crying out in desolation.
Harvests rich, and ripe, and golden,
Leaping forth from fruitful acres—safely stored in vaults that hold them.

Starving in a land of plenty,
Workless, where real work is needed....
Smokeless mills, and factories closing;
Labor's legions standing idle, idle without wish or choosing.

Starving in a land of plenty
Hunger-lines on haggard faces.
Thousands tramping on and on—in search of work in far-off places....[17]

Gompers reiterated this theme at a great mass meeting of New York's unemployed held at Madison Square Garden on January 30, 1894. So carried away was he by the terrible fact that "in a country such as ours, rich as a nation could be . . . large masses of our citizens were forced to endure hunger because unemployed," that he threw caution to the winds and cried out in bitterness:

Let conflagration illumine the outraged skies!
Let red Nemesis burn the hellish clan
And chaos end the slavery of man! [18]

Although Gompers speedily regretted the vehemence of his language,* his fiery call adequately reflected the sentiments of hundreds of thousands of workers. All over the country there arose a wail of hunger of men, women, and children calling upon the national government to step into the unbearable situation and provide for the needs of the unemployed. At its convention in Chicago, December, 1893, the A. F. of L. resolved forcefully that "the right to work is the right to life," and declared that "when the private employer cannot or will not give work the municipality, state or nation must." In advocating passage of the resolution, Gompers went beyond the moral indictment of the capitalists to launch an attack on the capitalist system itself: "In a society where such abnormal conditions prevail there must of necessity be something wrong at the basic foundations, and it requires but little study to come to the conclusion that the ownership and control of the means of production by private corporations which have no human sympathy or apparent responsibility, is the cause of the ills and wrongs borne by the human family." [19]

Under these circumstances it was necessary for government to intercede and provide for the welfare of the hundreds of thousands of workers who were facing starvation through no fault of their own.

---

* The radicalness of Gompers' speech was probably influenced by the fact that members of the S.L.P. in attendance at the meeting greeted his appearance with jeers and cat-calls. At any rate, in his autobiography, published in 1925, Gompers states that he was horrified by the thought that his speech might well have led the audience, which was "in an ugly frame of mind," to take extreme steps. (Samuel Gompers, *Seventy Years of Life and Labor*, New York, 1924, Vol. II, pp. 4-7.)

But in Congress, as in the state legislatures, there was no awareness that the problem of unemployment and relief was any concern of the government. B. O. Flower, editor of the liberal magazine, *The Arena,* complained bitterly in the spring of 1894: "Millions for armories and the military instruction of the young but not one cent to furnish employment to the able-bodied industry in its struggle to escape the terrible alternative of stealing or starving—such seems to be the cry of government in the United States today." Flower suggested an extensive program of public works to relieve unemployment, authorized under the general welfare clause of the Constitution.[20]

ON TO WASHINGTON

While these ideas were being discussed in newspapers and magazines and at labor conventions, masses of unemployed workers were making their way by foot, rail or water to Washington, there to register emphatic dissatisfaction with the conditions of the country and to demand redress of the grievances of a whole people. From hamlet and city, the armies of the Commonweal were recruited, and the spring of 1894 saw them marching down from New England, straggling in from California, Arizona and Texas, and tramping through the late snow storms in the Alleghenies. All told about 10,000 men were on the march throughout the country with Washington as their destination.

The originator of the descent upon Washington was Jacob Sechler Coxey, a wealthy manufacturer of Massillon, Ohio, who formulated a plan under which the unemployed would be put to work on public work projects, which would be financed by issues of greenbacks. Any state, county or town which would undertake such a public improvement program would receive greenbacks from the federal government in return for its own bonds. These non-interest-bearing bonds would be repaid at the rate of 4 percent per annum. In addition, the federal government would issue $500,000,000 in greenbacks to be expended for the employment of citizens on a huge nationwide road-building program.[21]

"As you know," a leader of the Commonwealers wrote to Gompers, "the Coxey movement is made up of men of all labor unions and may therefore properly ask the sympathy and cooperation of all organized labor in this struggle for relief." The A. F. of L. responded quickly to the appeal. Its executive board expressed sympathy for the Coxey movement, and the *American Federationist,* its official organ, noted that "the fact that in all the cities and towns throughout the country a feeling exists to respond to the call, 'On to Washington,' is the best evidence that hundreds of thousands of our fellow human beings are suffering the pangs of hunger and smarting under the lash of injustice." Several leaders of the Commonwealers, like Lewis C. Fry, Carl Browne, and Arthur

Vinette, were also general organizers of the A. F. of L. They were in close touch with A. F. of L. headquarters during the march on Washington, and, as a result of this correspondence, arrangements were made for the armies to hold conferences with local organizations affiliated to the Federation.[22]

A considerable number of central labor bodies, affiliated with the A. F. of L., endorsed the Coxey movement, characterizing it, in the words of the Central Labor Union of New York, as "the forerunner of a great uprising of the toilers of America in the near future." The Central Labor Council of Richmond, Indiana, sponsored and distributed copies of a song entitled, "Marching with Coxey," written by an A. F. of L. member. The price of the printed copy was "One loaf of bread to feed Coxey's army." Sung to the tune of "Marching through Georgia," the song went in part:

We are marching to the Capital, three hundred thousand strong,
With live petitions in our boots to urge our cause along,
And when we kick our congressmen, they'll feel there's something wrong.
As we go marching with Coxey.

CHORUS
Hurrah! hurrah! for the unemployed's appeal!
Hurrah! hurrah! for the marching commonweal!
Drive the lobbies from the senate,
Stop the trust and combine steal,
For we are marching with Coxey.

We are not tramps nor vagabonds that's shirking honest toil,
But miners, clerks, skilled artizans, and tillers of the soil
Now forced to beg our brother worms to give us leave to toil,
While we are marching with Coxey.[23]

Although the General Executive Board of the K. of L. expressed sympathy for the Coxey movement and local assemblies sponsored meetings to assist the Commonwealers, the work of the Order in behalf of the cause was hampered by the fact that Grand Master Workman Sovereign publicly denounced the march on Washington as foreboding "both insurrection and rebellion." "It is likely to create a spirit such as that which John Brown brought to life at Harper's Ferry," Powderly's successor told the press which promptly headlined the fact that "Sovereign Says Coxey's Methods Are Full of Great Peril." [24]

On May 1, 1894, Coxey's army arrived in Washington. They were given permission to parade, with the warning that the passage of processions or the carrying of banners through the Capitol grounds was forbidden by statute. If Coxey or his men attempted to hold mass meetings or make speeches on the Capitol grounds, they would be promptly arrested.[25]

In defiance of the warning, Coxey paraded his men through the Capitol grounds. For this offense, he and Browne were arrested and punished by a 20-day imprisonment and, in addition, were fined $5 each for walking on the grass.[26]

The police brutality and the arrest of the leaders of the unemployed produced tremendous protests from trade unions, Populists and other sympathizers. The Executive Board of the K. of L. demanded that Congress begin an immediate investigation of the outrage, and scores of labor organizations sent similar protests to Washington. Calling the action of the police "A Crime Against Freedom," the *American Federationist* denounced the brazen attempt "to crush out the constitutional and natural rights of free speech, free assemblage and freedom of petition." "If history teaches anything aright," it warned, "it wholly and conclusively demonstrates that bludgeons and prison walls have never yet prevented truth from becoming generally accepted, recognized and established." [27]

Despite the protests and warnings, the Senate refused to interfere, and the penalties of the court were duly paid.

Coxey could not obtain hearings before Congressional Committees to present the relief program. By August 15 the army was dissolved. The "On to Washington" movement had proved ineffective in forcing legislation to provide for the unemployed, but the industrial army processions had thrust before the eyes of the country the stark and naked fact that there was something basically wrong in the nation, and this was something that jokes and quips in light-hearted newspaper accounts of the movement could not altogether conceal.

As the depression continued, agitation for the eight-hour day increased in crescendo. At every unemployed demonstration, street corner meeting, and workers' lecture, the eight-hour day was pressed and arguments were brought forward to support it. The eight-hour day would create more work and reduce unemployment; "it will set millions of men and women at work who are now idle, it will infuse new life into those now at work and send hope into the hearts of young men and women everywhere of higher wages and better things." "Were the eight hour system now in vogue," wrote a trade unionist in August, 1894, "it would require five men to perform the labor done by four men under the present ten hour system. This would reduce the recruits of Coxey's army and the idle men in every community." [28]

EMPLOYERS SEEK TO WIPE OUT LABOR'S GAINS

The demand for the eight-hour day was also pressed as an answer to attempts by employers "to take advantage of the necessities of the workers to extend the hours of labor," destroy wage standards, and wipe out all past improvements in working conditions. The financial crisis had barely descended upon the country when the A. F. of L. national office was deluged with letters from unions in all parts of the country telling of the attempts being made by employers to use "the industrial stagnation . . . to fasten upon us onerous conditions, and to deprive us of the rights and benefits it has cost us years of work to secure." The Lumber Shovers' Union in up-state New York reported in June, 1893, that a thousand of its members had been "locked out by the capitalistic lumber kings" who had informed the workers as soon as the depression started: "You must disband your union and come to work as individuals, otherwise you cannot work." The American Flint Glass Workers' Union reported that in the summer of 1893, the Associated Manufacturers, composed of the vast majority of employers in the industry, announced "that no members of the union would be employed in the future." As the union president noted: "The panic had come, and the time was now propitious to fight the Union." [29]

Reports to A. F. of L. headquarters pointed out how difficult it was for the unions to combat the employers' offensive. With 50 to 75 percent of their members unemployed and income consequently seriously curtailed, the unions were hardly in the position to render considerable financial aid to the victims of the employers' attacks. "There is probably not more than two National Unions affiliated with the American Federation of Labor," Gompers wrote on September 28, 1894, "which have not had their resources greatly diminished and their efforts largely crippled by reason of trade struggles, and the enormous number of members who have suffered through lack of employment.[30]

Nevertheless, American workers were not intimidated by the fury of the employers' drive to rob them of their hard-won gains nor by the incredible obstacles and hardships caused by the depression.

When the owners of the gold mines in Cripple Creek, Colorado, took advantage of the crisis to lengthen the working day from eight and nine hours to ten hours, members of the Western Federation of Miners, voted to strike for a uniform eight-hour day. Early in February, 1894, they went out on strike. In the face of the most disheartening conditions—with thousands of men in the area unemployed, with a meagre union treasury— the miners fought the employers, the strikebreakers, the 1,300 armed deputies and the entire state militia, and won their fight. After a five months' struggle, the miners returned to work in mid-June, 1894, with the eight-hour day fully established.[31]

Contemporaneously with the Cripple Creek strike came a great strike in the bituminous coal industry. Wage cuts began immediately after the panic of 1893 and further slashes in the miners' wage scales were threatened. Conditions became so intolerable by the spring of 1894 that the

United Mine Workers, with a treasury of only $2,600 and a membership of not more than 24,000 (of whom only 13,000 were paid up members), decided to call a general strike in the bituminous coal industry. No coal was to be mined for any purpose after noon on April 21, 1894, until wages had been restored to where they were on May 1, 1893.[32]

Responding to the call, the members of the union refused to enter the pits on April 21, and they were joined by miners throughout the country. In all 180,000 miners in Pennsylvania, Illinois, West Virginia, and Ohio struck—thousands more than even the leaders of the United Mine Workers had expected—and the production of bituminous coal almost completely ceased.[33]

The strike lasted eight weeks, and ended in a defeat for the miners. Although some adjustments in wages were made, the mine owners refused to rescind most of the wage cuts, and the strikers, with meagre resources at their disposal, were unable to hold out longer. They returned to the pits, once more at the mercy of the operators. Their union, the United Mine Workers, was practically shattered. A year after the strike, Patrick McBride, U.M.W. National Secretary-Treasurer, wrote to the A. F. of L.: "The National is busted we will have to suspend the Journal, and tax to the Federation is an impossibility. . . . I cannot for the life of me see what course we can persue [sic] other than throw up the sponge. . . ."[34]

LABOR UNITY CONFERENCE

However strong the determination of workers to resist the employers' drive might be, it was clear that the best defense of labor's past gains could come through unity of action. With this in mind, Joseph R. Buchanan, the militant labor editor, sought during the winter of 1893-94 to achieve a closer union of labor forces to resist the employers' offensive. When his efforts produced enthusiastic responses from labor leaders throughout the country, Buchanan issued a call for a conference to be held in Philadelphia on April 28, 1894.

"Organized capital," he appealed, "has sent forth the edict that wages must come down, and every opportunity is being seized to utilize the present depression to force labor nearer the brink of pauperism and to strangle the labor movement, which is the toilers' only protection. . . .

"If the workers are not to be crushed down to the position of slaves then they must act, and act quickly. First there must be a thorough unification, a close alliance of all organized workers without regard to creed, occupation, sex or nationality. The toilers must combine for protection. . . ."[35]

A large and representative group of labor men and women met in

Philadelphia in response to the call. Among them were Gompers and Chris Evans, representing the A. F. of L.; J. G. Schonfarber and Powderly, representing the K. of L.; Chas. A. Wilson, A. H. Hawley, and P. H. Morrisey, representing the Railroad Brotherhoods, and prominent leaders of international unions such as P. J. McGuire of the Carpenters and Joiners, John B. Lennon of the Tailors, George W. Perkins of the Cigar Makers, Charles F. Reichers of the United Garment Workers, C. L. Drummond of the Printers, and M. M. Garland of the Iron and Steel Workers. Rarely had so many different groups of labor organizations been represented at a general conference.[36]

On the second day, the conference adopted a report in which it hailed the gathering as "a living evidence that the organized labor sentiment of the country is a unit on the fundamental truths that underlie the labor problem;" urged the A. F. of L., the K. of L., and other national and international organizations to "take such steps as will lead to an agreement for united action of labor's forces in the industrial and legislative fields;" recommended the end "of strife and antagonism between labor organizations, for strife and antagonism in labor's ranks is fratricidal and ruinous to the best interests of the working people," and called upon "the labor forces to unitedly resist any further reduction of wages, and to energetically renew our efforts for the reduction of the hours of labor."

Buchanan was disappointed that nothing more concrete emerged from the conference. He had hoped that the demand for greater unity, expressed in letters he had received from workers the country over, would lead to a definite plan of action. Still, he felt confident that the conference had taken an important step towards solidifying labor's ranks and would strengthen the ability of workers to resist the employers' attacks. Such solidarity, Buchanan felt, was more necessary than ever before. As he informed the conference when it was about to adjourn, the labor movement was still to feel the full impact of the employers' drive.[37]

At the very moment that the conference of labor representatives was being held to discuss the need for labor unity, American workers were seeing living proof of the benefits that flowed from united action. A new union of railroad workers—the American Railway Union—had come into being based upon the principle of unity of all workers in the industry, and within a short time it had achieved victories hitherto undreamed of by the railroaders. Although Buchanan had not spelled it out at the conference, he had made it clear elsewhere that it was this industrial union, uniting skilled, semi-skilled, and unskilled workers in an entire industry, which should serve as the model for a unified American labor movement: "With the necessary changes to fit the situation, I want to see the principles of the American Railway Union adopted by the great national labor movement [in the United States]." [38]

CHAPTER 17

The Railroad Brotherhoods and the American Railway Union

Except for those in the K. of L., the railroad workers of the 1880's and early 1890's were organized into five brotherhoods: the Brotherhood of Locomotive Engineers (founded in 1863), the Order of Railway Conductors (organized in 1868), the Brotherhood of Locomotive Firemen (founded in 1873), the Brotherhood of Railroad Brakemen (founded in September, 1883, changing its name in 1890 to the Brotherhood of Railway Trainmen), and the Switchmen's Mutual Association (launched in 1886).* Only the Engineers had started as an organization for collective bargaining; the others, from their inception, were secret fraternal societies, emphasizing primarily insurance systems to protect members and their families from the hazards of the very dangerous occupation of railroading. Gradually, all of the brotherhoods became organizations for collective bargaining.

CHARACTERISTICS OF RAILROAD BROTHERHOODS

The brotherhoods made the transition from fraternal societies to trade unions, but they had no common fraternity, no common confederation for mutual protection and for the advancement of their general interests,†

* For the history of organization and struggles among railroad workers before 1880, see Foner, *op. cit.*, pp. 464-74, and George E. McNeill and others, *The Labor Movement: The Problem of To-Day*, New York, 1888, Chapter XII, "The Rise of Railroad Organizations," pp. 312-20. For discussions of the railroad workers in the K. of L., *see* pp. 50-53; 83-86.

† The brotherhoods also pursued the policy of remaining aloof from the rest of the labor movement, desiring no alliance with militant unions either in the K. of L. or the A.F. of L. A strong anti-strike sentiment among the brotherhoods' leaders deepened the gulf separating them from other unionists.

a policy which enabled the corporations to deal with each union separately, playing one against the other. The brotherhoods represented only a tiny fraction of the railroad workers. Regarding themselves as composed of the "aristocrats of labor," the brotherhoods ignored the great mass of unskilled and semi-skilled workers on the railroads, and, in the case of Negro workers, deliberately sought to drive them out of their jobs.* Not only were the unskilled and semi-skilled unorganized, but even among the engineers, firemen, conductors, and trainmen, many were non-union. Altogether in 1893, the combined membership of the brotherhoods was less than one hundred thousand—one-tenth of the railroad workers in the United States. Small wonder that Fred Anthony, Grand Master, Brotherhood of Railway Shop Employees, wrote early in 1893: "Every trade and occupation in the country is better equipped for defense than the railway men." [1]

The conditions of the railroad workers reflected the weakness of their unionism. The annual wages for various railroad workers in the year 1890, according to the fifth annual report of the Commissioner of Labor, were: engineers, $957; conductors, $575; firemen, $337; brakemen, $212; switchmen, $264; flagmen, $224; baggagemen, $311; laborers, $124, and telegraph operators, $235.[2] The wages of the engineers, because of their superior bargaining power, placed them among the aristocracy of labor. But the vast majority of the railroad workers in the country received wages below the level required for subsistence.

These miserably low wages were paid for many of the most dangerous jobs in all of American industry. According to the Interstate Commerce Commission's reports, there were 2,070 workers killed and 20,148 injured on the railroads for the year ending June 30, 1888; 2,554 killed and 28,267 injured for the year ending June 30, 1892, and 2,727 killed and 31,729 injured for the year ending June 30, 1893. This meant one railroad worker killed out of every 115 employed and one injured out of every ten employed!

The railroad corporations either attributed the accidents to carelessness of the workers or called them "acts of God." Challenging this cynical interpretation, the *Locomotive Firemen's Magazine* declared: "It comes to this: While railroad managers reduce their force and require men to do double duty, involving loss of rest and sleep, they will continue to lament the occurrence of accidents, involving the loss of life and maiming. The accidents of which they complain in numerous instances are chargeable to the greed of the corporation." [3]

---

* In 1867 the Engineers changed its membership requirements so as to prevent Negroes from becoming members. The Firemen excluded Negroes from its very beginning as an organization. (*See* William W. Bennett, "The Railroad Brotherhoods and Collective Bargaining," unpublished Ph.D. thesis, Princeton University, 1932, p. A-39.)

DEBS CALLS FOR UNITY

Since 1885 the editor of the *Locomotive Firemen's Magazine* had repeatedly emphasized that the only way to curb the greed of the railroad corporations and improve the conditions of the railroad workers was by achieving joint activity by the railroad unions. The editor was Eugene V. Debs. In stirring editorials, in which he quoted with approval the K. of L.'s slogan, "an injury to one is the concern of all," Debs repeatedly pointed out that a single union was powerless against a giant railroad, and that the only way for the railroad workers to win out was through "federation between engineer and fireman, switchman and brakeman." Just as the individual workers had combined for mutual protection, the brotherhoods should combine on matters of common concern.[4]

Debs' outspoken advocacy of federation took root. It won little support among leaders of the brotherhoods who feared it would be followed by a reduction in the number of office-holders, and it encountered the bitter opposition of P. M. Arthur, conservative, arrogant Grand Chief of the B. of L. E., an outspoken advocate of class collaboration who believed that he could win gains by siding with employers against the other brotherhoods and the rest of the labor movement.[5] Despite Arthur's opposition, the engineers and firemen began working together in 1886. Victories were won over the New York City Elevated Railways, controlled by Jay Gould, and the Ohio & Mississippi Railroad. The New York Elevated contract, gained after a strike in the opening months of 1886, provided for a pay increase, extra pay for overtime work, the nine-hour day, a half day's pay for reporting to work, strict seniority, and reinstatement of all men who had been fired during the struggle. Debs hailed the victory in the *Locomotive Firemen's Magazine:* "The incident supplies abundant proof that the two great Brotherhoods are necessary to each other."[6]

Joint action by the firemen and engineers was an important step forward in building a united front of all railroad workers against the corporations, but by itself it could not accomplish too much. This was fully demonstrated in the strike of the engineers and firemen, beginning February 27, 1888, against the Chicago, Burlington & Quincy Railroad. The switchmen and brakemen refused to quit work. Moreover, the K. of L. railroad workers, incensed by past strikebreaking by the engineers in K. of L. strikes, took the places of the striking members of the brotherhoods. Although the brotherhood leaders, particularly Debs, influenced many of the switchmen to support the walkout, and, with the assistance of Joseph R. Buchanan, convinced many K. of L. strikebreakers to respect the strike, the absence of real organic unity among the brotherhoods made the failure of the strike inevitable. The Burlington strike, Debs pointed out, could have been won in a day "if from the first there had been federation between engineers and firemen, switchmen and brakemen on the C. B. & Q." The April, 1888 issue of the *Firemen's Magazine* featured an editorial headed, "Federation, the Lesson of the Great Srike." [7]

The loss of the strike taught the members of the brotherhoods an important lesson. "This," wrote Thomas Neasham, leader of the K. of L. employees of the Union Pacific Railway, "has taken all the aristocratic feeling out of them, and it has got through their heads that they are only men like ourselves. This is a great revelation, to some of these fellows, and I think it best to strike the iron when it is hot or in other words to lift up the standard of Federation." [8]

In editorial after editorial in the Firemen's magazine, Debs lifted "the standard of Federation." The cry met with powerful support from the rank-and-file members of the brotherhoods—so powerful, indeed, that even the conservative leaders of the crafts were unable to withstand the unity movement. [9]

Meeting in convention in the fall of 1888, the Firemen drew up a plan of federation which provided for the establishment of a board of federation on each system of railroads to be composed of representatives from each of the grievance committees of the brotherhoods which joined. If after all efforts to settle a dispute with management by a member organization on its own had failed and it had decided that a strike was necessary, the board, by a two-thirds vote, might order all the member organizations to join the walkout. The Switchmen endorsed the plan, and the Brakemen also announced their approval. But when the Engineers met in convention, Grand Chief Arthur and his conservative supporters came out against federation. With the aid of "some shrewd parliamentary maneuvering," the conservatives carried the day. Federation was turned down by the convention. [10]

SUPREME COUNCIL OF UNITED ORDERS OF RAILWAY EMPLOYEES

Although the refusal of the Engineers, the strongest organization of railroad labor, was a severe blow to the supporters of federation among the brotherhoods, the Firemen, Switchmen, and Brakemen decided to proceed. The highest officers of the three brotherhoods met in Chicago on June 3, 1889, and established the Supreme Council of the United Orders of Railway Employees under the motto "Mutual Justice," and with Frank P. Sargent and Eugene V. Debs of the Firemen as president and secretary respectively. Unlike the Firemen's plan, which was based on federations on each railroad system, the Supreme Council consisted of a centralized authority made up of representatives from each member organization—the chief executive and two associated grand officers chosen for the purpose.* Grievances were to be handled by this group of high officers. After a member organization had exhausted its own grievance procedures, and decided to strike, it could, with the consent of its chief executive, refer the dispute to the Supreme Council. A unanimous vote of the Council was required before the strike could be endorsed, and, after such a vote had been secured and the company still refused to settle the dispute peacefully, the Council would order all its members to strike. However, the Council was also empowered to prevent strikes as well as to declare them; no strike was to begin until the Council authorized it, and any constituent organization violating this rule might be punished.[11]

The Brotherhood of Locomotive Engineers and the Order of Railway Conductors, under ultra-conservative leadership, remained aloof from the Supreme Council. But the Brotherhood of Conductors, a new organization formed in November, 1888, in opposition to the conservative, strikebreaking Order of Railway Conductors, joined the Council. The sole holdout was the Engineers whose membership, President Sargent of the Supreme Council correctly pointed out in his first annual report, "are in favor of federation as now in effect, but ruled by despotic power they are for a time held back. . . ." He predicted, however, that the rank and file would soon make their desires felt.[12]

In his report, President Sargent pointed out that during its first year of existence, the Supreme Council had won every battle without being forced to resort to a strike. In the four threatened strikes in which it had intervened (involving the Erie, the Pittsburgh yard men, the conductors on the Queen and Crescent, and the engineers and firemen on the Ohio & Mississippi) the corporations, faced for the first time with a united movement of railroad workers, had been forced to settle peacefully and to grant improvements in conditions—wage increases, seniority, reduction in working hours, etc. The Supreme Council was more than satisfied with these results, and in its greetings to the membership it declared: "we are happy to say after a year's experience as a federated organization, that our expectations have been more than realized, that every pledge had been redeemed and that we reaffirm our faith in the federation of the members of the several organizations of railway employes, as now established, as the redeeming and emancipating power of our age." [13]

The record of the Supreme Council influenced the Engineers at their convention, over Arthur's objection, to set up a committee to study the question of federation.[14] †

Just when it seemed that Debs' dream of a merger of the brotherhoods

* The Firemen's plan was called the "local" or "system" plan and the Supreme Council's plan as "general federation" or "the association plan."

† The committee produced a plan of federation similar to that of the Supreme Council, but nothing came of it.

into one organization would be realized, factional strife, a bitter jurisdiction dispute among the Trainmen, Switchmen and Conductors over
membership,* and petty quarrels broke out among the leaders of the
brotherhoods and gradually reduced the Supreme Council to a paper
organization. The Council's prestige was further reduced by two unsuccessful interventions: one in the case of the strike of the K. of L. on the
New York Central and the other in a dispute between a member of the
Council and the Houston & Texas Central Railway.

In the case of the K. of L. and the New York Central, the Supreme
Council acted in keeping with the fundamental principle of labor solidarity,† but in the dispute with the Houston & Texas Central, it completely
violated that principle.

In September, 1890, the officers of the Brotherhood of Railway Trainmen complained to the Houston & Texas Central Railway that Negro
switchmen were being hired in the Houston yard and demanded that
they be discharged. The complaint was filled with chauvinistic statements
such as: "Observation, deep and honest conviction, has taught us that we
degenerate in the eyes of all, when we acknowledge them [the Negroes]
our equals, which we are compelled to do, as the position they occupy is
on a par and must necessarily be recognized as equal to ours, and compels
us to associate with them to an unbearable extent." When the company
refused to discharge the Negroes, the brotherhood called upon the Supreme Council to intervene, and a special session of the Council was held
at Houston on October 9, 1890.

The session was marked by a total absence of understanding of the
need for unity between Negro and white workers. President Sargent
proposed that the Council prove to the company "that the amount and
character of the labor performed by them [the white workers] was in
every way superior to that of the colored man." Grand Master Wilkinson
of the Railroad Trainmen applauded the proposal, and added that the

---

* The Brotherhood of Railway Trainmen changed its name from Brotherhood of
Railway Brakemen and took in conductors, switchmen, and other railroad workers.
The Switchmen and Conductors insisted that the Trainmen should include only
Brakemen. For details of the jurisdictional disputes, see "Report of Evidence Given
in the Trial of the Brotherhood of Railroad Trainmen Before a Committee of the
Supreme Council of the United Orders of Railway Employes," in *Proceedings of
the First and Second Annual Sessions and Intervening Special Sessions of the
Supreme Council of the United Orders of Railway Employes*, Galensburg, Ill., 1890.

† The Supreme Council visited Vice-President H. Walter Webb of the New York
Central in an effort to persuade him to negotiate with the K. of L., but failed to
gain any concession. At a special session following this visit, the Supreme Council
adopted a resolution endorsing the course of the Knights and condemning Webb,
but pointing out, at the same time, that it had no power to intervene officially
because the Knights was not a member. (*Ibid.*, "Special Session at Terre Haute,
Indiana, August 23-25, 1890.")

Council should demand the removal of the Negro workers on the same principle as it "would ask for the removal of an obnoxious yardmaster or a 'scab.'" After the discussion, during which Debs was not present, the Council voted to ask the railroad to discharge the Negroes. It met with a flat refusal.[15]

It was hardly to be expected that an organization whose slogans were "Mutual Justice" and "Each for all and all for each" could gain respect in the labor movement when it practiced discrimination against an important section of railroad workers and cooperated with the corporations' policy of pitting Negro and white workers against each other.

When the annual session of the Supreme Council was convened in Chicago, June 20, 1892, only the Firemen and Switchmen were present. Upon a motion by Debs, the organization was dissolved.[16]

THE BUFFALO SWITCHMEN'S STRIKE

Upon the heels of the dissolution of the Supreme Council came the great switchmen's strike at Buffalo, New York—a strike that more than any other previous struggle pointed up the glaring weaknesses of the separatist policies followed by the brotherhoods.

On August 12, 1892, the switchmen on the Lehigh Valley, the Erie and the Buffalo railroads went out on strike to enforce the recent New York State law establishing the ten-hour day in all industries and to secure an increase in wages from 19 to 23 and 25 cents an hour for day work and from 21 to 23 and 25 cents an hour for night work. When the sheriff's deputies, sympathetic to the strikers, refused to help the companies break the strike, the Governor called out the militia, commanded by General Doyle, in civilian life General Freight Agent of the Lehigh Valley Railroad, and sent 8,000 state troops to crush the walkout. The switchmen on the New York Central and the Nickel Plate joined the strike in sympathy with their brothers.[17]

The hard-pressed switchmen, battling scabs, police, and militiamen, called on the officers of the other brotherhoods for assistance. They emphasized the urgent necessity of calling a general strike on the railroads involved in the dispute. Debs endorsed the switchmen's appeal, but he was convinced that the heads of the brotherhoods, hiding behind constitutional provisions which forbade sympathetic strikes, would do nothing. "I am in full and hearty sympathy with the switchmen," he told the press on August 23, "but in my opinion it will be the same old story. Justice to labor will never come in my judgment until labor federates and wields its united power for the good of all." [18]

Debs was correct. It proved to be "the same old story." At the request of Grand Master Frank Sweeney of the Switchmen, the leaders of the conductors, the firemen, and the trainmen came to Buffalo. (Arthur of the engineers refused to appear.) The conference was brief. A general strike, Sweeney was informed, was impossible. Sweeney's response was equally brief: "We can't fight 8,000 militia, a dozen or so railroad corporations and the other brotherhoods at the same time." [19]

On August 25, the Buffalo *Express* headlined the news: "STRIKE OFF." The sub-headings told the full story behind the complete defeat for the switchmen:

THEY THOUGHT THE SWITCHMEN'S GRIEVANCE JUST BUT COULD NOT COME TO THEIR RELIEF.

THE OTHER GRAND MASTERS TOLD HIM A GENERAL STRIKE WAS IMPOSSIBLE.

SWEENEY HAS SUCCUMBED TO THE INEVITABLE.

THEY HAD BUT SYMPATHY.

The switchmen, Debs pointed out, had appealed "for support in a just cause." Instead of practical help they had "secured oceans of sympathetic drool. Like a man in the parable the switchmen asked for bread and were given only stones or peanut shells. Bayonets and bullets, scabs and capitalists won a victory, rode rough shod over a principle which must eventually triumph or labor's emancipation day will never dawn." The principle was labor unity, or as the *Trainmen's Journal* put it in commenting on the lost strike: "If the injury to one is not the concern of all, the history of organized labor will soon be of the past." [20]

Before he left Buffalo, Grand Master Sargent of the Firemen predicted that the strike "will do more than anything to bring the railroad men together." "The rank and file," he told a reporter, "want union, and if the leaders will not consent they will choose new ones who will." [21]

THE AMERICAN RAILWAY UNION

The spokesmen for the rank-and-file acted even more swiftly than Sargent expected. On September 5, less than two weeks after the disastrous defeat of the Switchmen, George W. Howard * informed Gompers that

* Howard headed the Brotherhood of Conductors, formed in September, 1889, in opposition to the conservative Order of Railway Conductors, until the fall of 1891, when the organization was merged with the Order of Conductors. He had advanced the plan of uniting all railroad workers into one organization as early as the summer of 1891 in discussions with Gompers. Once the united organization was achieved, it would seek a charter from the A.F. of L. Gompers approved the project and encouraged Howard to sound out others who might support the project.

Thirty years later, in his autobiography, Gompers wrote that he did not encourage Howard in his enterprise, and, in fact, tried to dissuade him from going ahead because he "felt that it was better to let the brotherhoods correct their own mistakes rather than to foster a dual organization with the hope of bringing the railroad secret meetings were being held in Chicago for the purpose "of getting the Railroad men into *one* organization." It was to be "an organization built up of *all 'classes'* of R.R. men from the Trackmen & Car Greaser, Wiper, etc., & including the Conductor & Engineer etc.—a Tree complete with all its branches." [22]

At Cincinnati in September, 1892, Debs told the national convention of the B. of L. F. that he was resigning as grand secretary and treasurer and editor of the magazine in order to devote himself to establishing one great union to which all railroad workers, skilled and unskilled, would be admitted. When the delegates refused to let him resign, Debs agreed to retain the editorship of the union's magazine. Since Debs had boosted its circulation from 1,500 when he became editor in 1878, to 37,000 copies per month in November, 1892, it is easy to understand why the Firemen were so anxious for him to retain the post. [23]

In June, 1893, the press headlined the sensational news that "a compact organization of all the various classes of railway employees has been established." [24] On June 20, 50 railroaders had met at Ulrich's Hall in Chicago and officially launched the American Railway Union.* Membership was open to all white employees, men and women, who served the railroads in any capacity,† except superintendents and other high officials. Even coal-miners, longshoremen, and car-builders, in the employe of a railroad, were invited to join. Dues were small—a dollar initiation fee, a dollar a year to the national union, local dues to be decided by each lodge.

The aims of the organization were to maintain a living-wage scale and satisfactory working conditions, to lobby for favorable legislation for workers such as the eight-hour day, safety applications for trains, restriction of

---

unions into the Federation." The correspondence between Howard and Gompers in the A.F. of L. archives proves conclusively that Gompers' recollections were not accurate, and that he encouraged Howard to organize an industrial union of railroad workers which would be brought into the A.F. of L. (*See* G. W. Howard to Gompers, Nov. 6, 10, Dec. 17, 1891, Sept. 5, 1892; Gompers to G. W. Howard, Nov. 6, 1891, *AFL Corr.*, Gompers, *Seventy Years of Life and Labor*, Vol. I, pp. 404-05.)

* Final plans to establish the organization were drawn up at a meeting in Chicago on February 7, 1893, where representatives of the engineers, firemen, conductors, and carmen appointed a committee to draw up a constitution consisting of Debs, S. Keliher and Louis W. Rogers. Originally the name selected was "The United Railwaymen of America."

† Women were not only admitted to membership, but the A.R.U. insisted "that when a woman performs a man's work, she ought, in all justice, to have a man's pay." (*Railway Times,* June 15, 1894.)

The ban against Negro members, the one blot on the A.R.U. constitution, was a backward carry-over of practices in all of the brotherhoods which denied membership to Negroes and attempted to drive them out of the railroad service. The first annual A.R.U. convention voted down a proposal to admit Negroes by 113 to 102.

Sunday work, employers' liability laws, etc., to provide cheap insurance, and to publish a daily newspaper. In its declaration of principles, the new union expressed the belief that labor and capital could, if each acted fairly and honorably toward the other, adjust differences without recourse to lockouts, strikes, blacklists, and boycotts. To achieve this peaceful relationship, however, the railroad workers had to be "thoroughly organized in every department. . . ."

Although preferring the old brotherhood policy of avoiding strikes and boycotts, the A.R.U. permitted branches engaged in disputes to sanction local walkouts if all efforts at mediation had failed. National headquarters could not call a strike without the approval of local unions whose interests were involved.[25]

The structure of the A.R.U. was that of a modified industrial union. Its locals were organized on a craft basis, and these craft locals were organized into a federation on each major railway system. The system federations, in turn, were unified in the national organization. The distinctive feature of the new organization was its policy of united action whenever the rights of any members were threatened. This policy had been adopted, Debs noted because, "in the one towering, pivotal and essential feature, that of protection against corporate power, all the organizations of railway employees hitherto known have been failures."[26]

With Debs as president, Howard as vice-president, and Kelihler, secretary-treasurer of the Railway Carmen, as secretary, the American Railway Union got under way. "The new organization," the *Machinists' Journal* noted, "starts out with brilliant prospects ahead and under one of the brain[i]est men of the present age. We feel safe in predicting for it one of the grandest victories that labor has yet achieved."[27]

It proved to be an accurate prediction. The first A.R.U. lodge was organized on August 17, 1893, at Fort Madison, Iowa. By November 15 charters had been issued to 86 lodges; at the end of the year the Union Pacific, the Denver & Rio Grande, the Rio Grande & Western were solidly organized. There were 22 A.R.U. locals on the Northern Pacific and more than 40 on the Southern Pacific. All told, there were 125 locals in the union when the year 1894 opened.[28]

January 1, 1894, marked the appearance of the first number of the *Railway Times,* the new union's official organ. The four-page, six-column bi-weekly, edited by Louis W. Rogers, former editor of the *Railroad Trainman,* pledged, in its opening editorial, to fight to better the conditions of at least 800,000 railroad employes who had hitherto "been overlooked, left out in the cold . . . and abandoned to their dismal fate" by the brotherhoods. The editorial, the Chicago *Intelligencer* reported, "has created a great deal of interest among railway men and the labor field at large."[29]

The rank-and-file railroad workers eagerly read and discussed each issue of the *Times*. And thousands rushed to join the new movement. Entire lodges of the Railway Carmen and Switchmen transferred to the A.R.U. Firemen, conductors, even engineers, hastened to sign up with the industrial union; in St. Louis a local was composed exclusively of engineers. But these recruits from the older brotherhoods were the minority of the new members. The vast majority were from the ranks of unorganized labor, the unskilled workers and the young workers,* who had been for so long a time exploited by the railroads and kept out of the brotherhoods either because of their deliberate policy of exclusion or because they had been unable to pay the high monthly dues and special fees. Membership dues in the A.R.U. were $1.00 a year.[30]

THE GREAT NORTHERN STRIKE

The membership drive received tremendous impetus from the great victory of the industrial union in its first real struggle—the strike on the Great Northern Railroad in the spring of 1894. The line was a transcontinental one, having its headquarters in St. Paul, Minnesota. It was 2,500 miles in length and it had 9,000 workers on its payroll. Wage cuts on the Great Northern in August, 1893, and again in January and March, 1894, had brought wage levels to an average of less than $40 a month.

In April, the workers voted to strike unless James J. Hill met their representatives to set up a new wage scale. When Hill refused to respond and ignored a letter from the American Railway Union informing him of his employees' decision, the men struck.

The strike began on the Montana division. It spread rapidly, both east and west, until the tie-up of the giant railroad was complete.

The strike made labor history. The 9,000 employees of the Great Northern—engineers, conductors, switchmen, truckmen, roundhouse workers, firemen, section hands, etc.—were completely united in support of the struggle. Even the station agents, operators, yard masters, and similar type of employees, usually loyal to the railway companies, struck with the others and remained out until the settlement.

Every train was stopped except mail trains which were allowed to move on Debs' explicit orders. A few local trains were run, but not a single transcontinental train went through.

Strikebreakers, imported by the company, were on hand, but, faced

* Commenting on the composition of the more than 400 delegates to the first convention of the A.R.U., the Chicago *Times* observed: "They are young men generally, but young men whose words and actions show that their minds have been as active as their hands and that wisdom does not always wait on years." (June 13, 1894.)

with such a solid, united front of railroad workers, no attempt was made to use them to fill the strikers' places. Probably the fact that farmers and business men in towns and villages along the line wholeheartedly supported the strikers and passed resolutions in sympathy with the men and in denunciation of the corporation, contributed to Hill's decision not to use the imported scabs. The company had expected that the paralysis in business during the strike would turn public opinion against the workers. But the farmers and business men had been victimized too often by the Great Northern to fall prey to its propaganda. They stood firm behind the strikers.

Eighteen days after the strike began, the company gave in. The strikers won practically all their demands, an aggregate wage increase of $146,000 a month.[31] "That a corporation of so gigantic proportions had to yield so quickly to their men," commented the Salt Lake *Tribune*, "indicates that the day has already come when the voice of united labor has to be heard in the matter of wages." [32]

The smashing victory in the midst of the great depression was also proof of the strength of the industrial union idea. Hill had not been able to set one brotherhood against another, as the railroads had usually done. Unity had paid off, and it convinced thousands upon thousands of railroad workers not only that they too could win out under the leadership of the new union, but that they could do so even without a strike. The A.R.U. was proving itself to be so powerful an organization that no railroad would dare to resist its just demands. At any rate, so the railroad workers felt and they joined the new union in increasing numbers.[33]

In the weeks following the Great Northern victory, the A.R.U. gained members at the rate of 2,000 a day. A year after the union was founded it was the largest trade union in the United States with 425 locals. The 50 original members had increased in one year to 150,000. The combined brotherhoods, in existence for years, had only 90,000 members, and their membership was steadily declining because of the inability of the workers to pay the high dues. Many members of the brotherhoods, reported the Columbus *Dispatch*, "have been out of work and could not pay their dues, and accordingly have been dropped from the rolls." [34]

In observing the first anniversary of the American Railway Union, the Chicago *Times* commented editorially: "The new general organization in a surprisingly short time has developed greater strength than any other labor alliance ever projected which took its members from the workers in one single line of industry. The American Railway Union today represents the interests, sympathies, ambitions, and in some degree the politics of a majority of the employes of whatever class and in whatever department of most of the great trunk line systems of America." [35]

In certain quarters the first birthday of the A.R.U. aroused anything but enthusiasm. The new union emphasized that it did not ask the railroad men to leave the older brotherhoods and that it was possible for those who decided to belong to the organization of their craft and to the industrial union to be "loyal to both." But the craft union leaders of the brotherhoods were both enraged and frightened by the new union's phenomenal success.[36]

EMPLOYERS UNITE AND ATTACK

Yet the alarm in the headquarters of the brotherhoods was as nothing compared to the concern registered by the railroad corporations. The growth of the A.R.U. was the greatest threat the railroads had ever faced.

Addressing a secret gathering of railroad managers from all parts of the country in August, 1893, J. T. Odell, General Manager of the Baltimore & Ohio, warned his colleagues that the day they had all dreaded had already arrived. "For years," he cried, "we watched with fear and trembling, so to speak, the inevitable coming of the time when demands would be made which were thoroughly disastrous and absolutely inimical to the interests and property in our charge." That time had come with the formation of a "perfect organization" of the railroad workers—the American Railway Union. No longer could the railroad corporations divide and conquer their employees with the aid of "the wise men of the organizations [the Brotherhoods] who proclaimed their loyalty to their employers." They were now confronted by new forces who had ended many of the divisions among the railroad crafts, forces which "not only seek to determine the amount of wages [paid to the railroad workers], but practically to determine also the management and control of the parties seeking the wage." From there it would be only a short time before these new forces would seek to take over "the management and control" of the railroads themselves.[37] *

What really concerned the railroad managers was that these new forces threatened to destroy their carefully-laid scheme to add to "our treasuries thousands upon thousands of dollars" by cutting wages of all railroad workers. This scheme, developed over a period of years, was to be put into effect by an employers' association encompassing all the railroad

* Confirmation of this warning appeared in reports in the press that "one of the objects of the newly formed American railway union is an aggressive agitation for making the railroads of this country the property of the American people. The railroad employees are becoming sick and tired of being squeezed and tyrannized by corporations organized for private gain." (Seattle *Evening Telegram,* July 3, 1893.)

At the first convention of the A.R.U. Debs came out for government ownership of the railroads, saying, "the change would be of incalculable benefit" to the railroad workers. (*Railway Times,* June 15, 1894.)

managers in the country.[38] The organization was the General Managers' Association.

In March, 1893, the G.M.A. set up the "Chicago scale" for switchmen. In August, the Association, asserting "that a reduction of wages of employees, however much to be regretted, is imperative," worked out an elaborate schedule of wages paid upon the line of its 24 members.* As a result, during the fall reductions in wages were made on a number of roads. The whole tendency was to "equalize" wages on all lines at the lowest level.[39]

The objective of the G.M.A. was clear. It was to establish a uniform scale on all railroads throughout the country by reducing wages to the level of the lowest paid workers. With this in mind, the Association invited lines not running into Chicago into membership. At a meeting in Chicago in August, 1893, 58 leading roads were represented. The meeting urged all general managers to adopt the anti-labor policies so effectively worked out and put into effect by the Chicago Association. A plan for an organization of all the general managers of the United States was set up.[40]

The chief, and in fact, the sole obstacle to the plans being worked out by the Managers' Association of Chicago and its allies throughout the country was the new, united movement of railroad workers represented by the A.R.U. To eliminate that obstacle, the Association laid plans to organize a powerful onslaught on the new industrial union. "Corporations have and are scanning the field of railway," Debs warned early in 1894. "They know just when to attack." [41]

The attack came while the industrial union was celebrating its first birthday. It originated in the town of Pullman, 12 miles south of Chicago. From there the struggle spread until it enveloped two-thirds of the United States.

* The 24 lines which made up the General Managers' Association in 1894 represented 410,000 miles of railroad, $818,000,000 in capital stock, and about 221,000 workers. Among the members were such giant roads as the Atchison, Topeka & Santa Fe; the Baltimore & Ohio, the Chicago & Northwestern; the Illinois Central; the Chicago, Rock Island, & Pacific, etc. Debs estimated that of the 870,000 American railway workers, some 50 percent were employed by the roads belonging to the Association. (Chicago Herald, Feb. 7, 1895.)

CHAPTER 18

The Pullman Strike

More perhaps than any other industrial clash since the Civil War, the Pullman strike, or the "Debs Rebellion" as it was named by the newspapers, shook the nation to its very depths, bringing to the surface all the pent-up bitterness of exploited labor, and exposing the role played by the federal government as the agent of the capitalists in their drive to crush completely the aims and activities of the labor movement.

STRIKE BEGINS AT PULLMAN

For years before the spring of 1894, employees of the Pullman Company had found the almost feudal paternalism of George Pullman, founder and owner, an intolerable burden. Forced to live in over-crowded tenements in the so-called "model company-owned town of Pullman, Illinois," compelled to pay exorbitant rents, often 25 percent higher than in adjoining communities,[1] and even more exorbitant utility rates, and subjected to innumerable shop abuses—blacklisting, arbitrary dismissals, and favoritism—the workers became increasingly restive when the panic of 1893 brought wholesale dismissals and cut wages. Wages were cut by 25 to 33⅓ percent, and, in some cases, as much as 50 percent—the company, meanwhile, continued to pay eight percent dividends to its stockholders—but rents and other living costs were not reduced. In defiance of law, rent was withheld from salaries, and one employe framed his weekly pay check of two cents.[2]

In March and April of 1894, the workers began to organize branches of the American Railway Union to which they were eligible because the Pullman corporation owned and operated a few miles of railroad. So successful was the unionization drive that 19 local unions were founded at Pullman with a total membership of 4,000 men.[3]

Early in May, 1894, the workers at Pullman selected a grievance committee of 46 members to present their demands for reduction in rent, an investigation and correction of shop abuses, and the restoration of wages to the pre-depression level. On May 7, the committee called on Thomas H. Wickes, second vice-president of Pullman, and presented their demands. Wickes told the committee to return two days later with their grievances in writing. At the second conference, Pullman himself was present, but he unequivocally refused to talk about wages or rents, agreeing only to investigate the shop complaints. George W. Wickes, vice-president of the A.R.U. was also present, and while he did not participate in the negotiations, he did seek assurance, which was granted by management, that members of the grievance committee would not be discriminated against.

Pullman's refusal to make any real concessions increased the determination of the workers to strike. And when they learned that three members of the grievance committee had been discharged, in violation of the company's pledge,* the workers were ready for action. In an all-night meeting, the grievance committee debated the question of calling a strike. Officials of the A.R.U. who were present, at Debs' advice, counselled against hasty action, urging caution until the union could learn the facts. But the workers were determined to act, and, on the third ballot, the grievance committee voted unanimously to strike.

At noon of May 11, 4,000 workers left their jobs at the Pullman shops, and the remaining 300 were immediately laid off. In the evening the corporation posted the following notice on the entrance gate of the plant: "The works are closed until further notice." [4]

A central strike committee, composed of members elected from the local unions, was set up, and 300 strikers were posted as guards around the plant to protect the shops from vandals.

The strikers believed that with the powerful A.R.U. behind them and with labor in Chicago rallying magnificently to their support, their chances of victory were fairly good. The A.R.U. had neither called nor authorized the strike; nevertheless, since the Pullman strikers were members of the union, Debs took immediate steps to investigate the situation at first hand. He visited Pullman, spent several days and nights in the model town talking to the workers, and reached the conclusion that the strike was completely justified.

When the first national convention of the A.R.U. met in Chicago on June 12, 1894, the Pullman strike was already a month old. After listening to several workers from Pullman describe in moving language their plight and the "justice" of their cause, the convention proposed that a

---

* In his study of the Pullman Strike, Almont Lindsey asserts that the men were not fired for their part in the protest. (*The Pullman Strike*, Chicago, 1942, p. 122.) This may or may not be true, but the fact remains that the Pullman workers believed that the men were discharged because they served on the Committee.

boycott be declared on Pullman cars. But Debs, still trying to avoid a major strike, suggested that a committee be appointed to confer with the Pullman company and attempt to adjust the difficulties peacefully. Several committees went back and forth from the convention to the Pullman corporation, proposing arbitration of the strike, but each time the company refused to yield an inch. "We have nothing to arbitrate," the various committees were told.

On June 22, a special committee, which had been appointed to recommend a plan of action, proposed that unless the Pullman company agreed to begin negotiations to adjust grievances within four days, the members of the A.R.U. would refuse to handle Pullman cars and the Pullman shops at St. Louis, Missouri, and at Ludlow, Kentucky, would be struck. Three members were immediately sent to notify the Pullman company of the convention's decision. Wickes informed the committee that the company would neither submit anything to arbitration nor have any dealings with the union. When the convention learned this, the delegates voted unanimously to begin the boycott at noon on June 26 unless the company changed its mind. Then the convention adjourned.[5]

THE BOYCOTT BEGINS

At noon on June 26, as scheduled, the boycott became operative as Debs ordered all sleeping cars cut from the trains and sidetracked. The response surprised even Debs himself. Their wages slashed since the start of the crisis, suffering from blacklisting, long hours, arbitrary treatment, and discrimination of one form or another, the railroad workers, especially the switchmen, trackmen and common laborers, were only too ready to champion the cause of the Pullman strikers. In a few days the boycott had spread over the entire central and western United States, and nearly 125,000 men had answered the union's call.

When it became apparent that the railroads would refuse to detach Pullman cars, the boycott developed into a strike, since the railroad workers refused to operate the trains if the Pullman cars were attached to them.

On the day after the boycott was announced, the General Managers' Association declared publicly that it would act to maintain existing contracts with the Pullman company. When the boycott commenced on June 26, the Association assumed control for the railroads. "All efforts of the general managers," writes Almont Lindsey in his authoritative study of the strike, "were directed toward one end—the complete annihilation of the American Railway Union. At no time was the association prepared to negotiate for an amicable solution of the dispute or to make even the slightest concessions in the interest of peace."[6]

One June 29, the Association let it be known that any worker who was discharged for refusal to perform his duties or quit work at the order of the A.R.U. would never again be eligible for employment on any railroad represented by the General Managers. Moreover, the man replacing the strikers would be given special protection and permitted to retain their positions permanently. This order converted the boycott automatically into a strike, for as each switchman was fired for cutting out Pullman cars the rest of the crew stopped work in a body.

RAILROAD LINES PARALYZED

The Association imported strikebreakers from 'all parts of the country and from Canada. But they could not prevent the A.R.U. from halting a vast amount of railroad traffic. By June 28, the Pullman traffic out of Chicago was completely paralyzed, and 11 roads were tied up by the automatic strikes that followed the Associations' decree. With remarkable speed the boycott and the ensuing strike spread west and south, covering almost the entire country. This was the first truly nationwide strike. It stretched from the West Coast to northern New York, and involved more than 150,000 workers in hundreds of local lodges.[7]

The A.R.U. leaders were not particularly worried about the efforts of the railroads to recruit strikebreakers, for as Debs wired to one local leader early in July: "Not enough men in world to fill vacancies, and more occurring hourly."[8] The strike was winning popular support everywhere it spread. In California traffic was completely halted and business paralyzed. So deep was the hatred of the Southern Pacific Railroad on the coast that nine out of ten people, including even businessmen who bitterly resented the exorbitant traffic rates, were in sympathy with the strikers. Deputies at Oakland, where one-half of the population was employed by the Southern Pacific, sat on the tracks, and were reported to have said: "Don't mind us, boys, we're blind." In Sacramento, members of the militia were seen wearing the white ribbon badges of Debs' followers.[9]* From Chicago William Boas, A. F. of L. organizer, wrote to Gompers on July 4: "The sympathizers of the strikers in Chicago are wearing white ribbons in their coats and you can not go a block without you see some people wearing a white ribbon."[10]

With more than 150,000 men on strike, the prospects for the railroad workers and their industrial union looked promising indeed. The union ranks were solid at every point, and organized labor was rallying to its support all over the country. True, the officials of the Railroad brotherhoods had refused to endorse the boycott and actually engaged in strikebreaking. P. M. Arthur not only announced publicly that unemployed

---

* In order to distinguish the strikers from elements hired by the railroads to foment violence as well as from hoodlums who were looking for loot, the A.R.U. arranged to have every striker wear a white ribbon badge.

Engineers would be permitted to fill the vacancies left by the strikers, but in a letter to the B. of L. E., he wrote: "If the company furnishes switchmen and firemen, whether they be union or non-union, it is the duty of the engineers to run their engines. Any member refusing to do so lays himself liable to dismissal, and will not receive any support from the brotherhood." *

The chief of the Conductors took the same position, and denounced the boycott as wrong "no matter what the conditions at Pullman were." The other brotherhoods announced clearly that they would do nothing to help the strikers.[11]

But the rank-and-file of the brotherhoods, agreeing with organized labor in many parts of the country that their leaders were "the Benedict Arnolds of the labor movement," were sympathetic, and many lodges not only participated in the strike, but actually turned in their charters and joined the A.R.U. All over the country, trade unions and central labor bodies were endorsing the boycott and urging the people not to ride in Pullman cars until the company accepted arbitration.[12]

THE FEDERAL GOVERNMENT INTERVENES

On July 2, John Egan, who was appointed to coordinate the anti-strike activities of the General Managers' Association, admitted that the railroads had been "fought to a standstill." He conceded that by themselves the corporations could not defeat the strikers and their union. "It is the government's duty to take this matter in hand," Egan declared. Two days later, on July 4, the Association jubilantly announced: "So far as the railroads are concerned with this fight, they are out of it. It has now become a fight between the United States Government and the American Railway Union, and we shall leave them to fight it out."

Two days after the strike began, the Post Office Department at Washington was informed that the mails were obstructed at some points in the West, and that the strikers were refusing to permit trains to which Pullman cars were attached to move over the lines. The federal government, of course, could very well have announced through the Postmaster General that until the strike was over, only passenger trains unattached to Pullman cars, could be used for the transportation of mail. But the government was determined to render immediate and decisive aid to the railroad corporations in their drive to smash the new union of railroad workers.

* Arthur sent a copy of his letter to the General Managers' Association. At a meeting of the Association, on July 5, 1894, it was read and greeted with thunderous applause. (*Proceedings of the General Managers' Association of Chicago, June 25, 1894 to July 14, 1894*, bound volume in John Crerar Library, Chicago, p. 159, marked "Confidential.")

Richard Olney, Attorney General of the United States, was the man in charge of the government's campaign against the A.R.U. Having served the railroad corporations for years as a lawyer and having been a railroad director and a member of the General Managers' Association before becoming a member of Cleveland's cabinet, Olney's interests were closely linked to those of big business. Moreover, Olney had sizeable financial investments in the railroads. He was a director of the Burlington, which was involved in the dispute, and he was also a co-director with George M. Pullman of the Boston & Maine.[13]

As soon as the boycott started, Olney deliberately set out to utilize the total machinery of the federal government to defeat it. He authorized that the U. S. marshal at Chicago employ special deputies to protect the mail, and he appointed Edwin Walker, a well-known railroad attorney, then Illinois counsel of the Chicago, Milwaukee & St. Paul and general counsel for the General Managers' Association, to conduct the government's case against the strikers. The special attorney for the federal government at Chicago had been recommended by the General Managers' Association, was still on the payroll of the railroads, and continued to remain so during the entire dispute.[14] *

THE INJUNCTION

But even this outrageous action was not enough for Olney. In a wire to Walker, he recommended that an injunction, based on the general principles of law and upon the Sherman Anti-trust Act of 1890, be obtained against the strikers. The fact that the Sherman Act had been passed by the Congress as a result of pressure by labor, small businessmen, and farmers to curb the evils of monopolistic control by big business, was of slight interest to an Attorney-general with a railroad corporation background. Olney refused to apply the law to illegal business combinations,[15] but he did not hesitate to use it as a weapon to destroy organized labor.

* The unpublished records of the General Managers' Association, in the John Crerar Library at Chicago, clearly reveal how closely Walker and the Association worked together. The report of the meeting held July 3, 1894, reads:

"Mr. Walker, Assistant to the United States District Attorney, was here introduced and spoke at length in reference to the injunction, asking that members furnish the United States officials with evidence of its violation.

"He also stated that Government troops would be ordered out and that when they arrived they would undoubtedly be distributed under the direction of the United States Marshal, who would be glad to have suggestions from the railways, as they would be better advised than anyone else of the necessities.

"The Association tendered its thanks to Mr. Walker and expressed the hope that he would be able to come daily to the meetings and give his advice and suggestions." (*Proceedings of the General Managers' Association of Chicago, June 25, 1894 to July 14, 1894,* p. 151.)

After several conferences with a number of lawyers for the railroads, the attorneys for the government drew up a bill in equity based upon the law prohibiting obstructions to the mail, and upon the Sherman Act. The restraining order, as originally planned, was based almost exclusively on damages to interstate commerce. But the G.M.A. determined to take no chances. At the behest of Edwin Walker, interference with the mails became a permanent feature of the complaint. An injunction would merely enjoin or lead to a minor sentence. Criminal conspiracy to block the mails meant the penitentiary for the strike leaders.

Upon Olney's authorization, the lawyers for the railroads presented a petition for an injunction to the federal district court in Chicago on July 2. Judges William A. Woods and Peter S. Grosscup immediately issued the most sweeping injunction ever handed down by a federal court up to that time. The injunction order prohibited Eugene Debs and other officers of the A.R.U., and "all other persons whomsoever ... from in any way or manner interfering with, hindering, obstructing, or stopping" any of the business of the railroads entering Chicago, and "from compelling or inducing or attempting to compel or induce by threats, intimidation, persuasion, force or violence, any of the employees" of the railroads to refuse to perform their duties as employees. Any "act whatever in furtherance of any conspiracy or combination to restrain" the railroad companies in the "free and unhindered control and handling of interstate commerce" was also prohibited.[16]

This sweeping injunction took from the railroad workers the right to strike. For there was little that the strikers could do to press their cause. They were even denied the right to peacefully appeal to railroad workers not to scab. It was, as even the Chicago *Times* was forced to admit, "a menace to liberty ... a weapon ever ready for the capitalist."[17]

THE FEDERAL TROOPS

Meeting in special session immediately after the injunction was served, the executive board of the A.R.U. debated their next step. It was clear that any attempt to violate the writ would mean a citation for contempt and summary punishment by the judges issuing the order. The accused would even be denied the benefit of jury trial. Yet obedience to the order would mean the crushing of the strike and the destruction of the union, and would cause thousands of strikers to lose their jobs, since the railroads had agreed among themselves not to rehire any strikers. The A.R.U. Executive Board, after carefully considering the alternatives, decided to ignore the injunction.[18]

On July 2, Edwin Walker informed Olney that he thought it would require troops to enforce the injunction. On the same day, when the

United States marshal attempted to read the injunction to a crowd of strikers in a Chicago suburb, he was hooted down. He, too, immediately reported to Olney that Federal troops were needed. Olney took his telegram to President Cleveland, and at four o'clock in the afternoon of July 3, the President ordered Colonel Crofton, in charge at Fort Sheridan, to move his entire command to Chicago to enforce the orders of the courts, protect Federal property and prevent obstruction of the U.S. mails and interference with interstate commerce.*

Cleveland and Olney had not bothered with the legal aspects of their action in sending federal troops. Under the United States Constitution, the President had the authority to send the army into a state to protect it against domestic violence upon request for such aid by the legislature or, when the legislature was not in session, by the governor. Cleveland, however, relied for authority on two Civil War statutes which had never been used in time of peace.[19] He sent troops to Chicago in complete disregard of the Governor of Illinois, and he did so because he was aware that Governor John Peter Altgeld believed that the situation did not warrant such drastic measures.

Altgeld was quite prepared to dispatch Illinois militiamen to those areas which he believed required military protection; indeed, at the time Cleveland ordered out the federal troops, militiamen were in Decatur, Cairo, and Danville to restore order. But Altgeld would not stand for military intervention where it was unnecessary, and in the course of the strike, he had recalled the militia from areas where the sheriff's alarm had no basis in fact. To prevent these false alarms, the Governor issued General Order No. 7 in which he said: "It is not the business of the soldiers to act as custodians or guards of private property."

Altgeld was justifiably indignant when Federal troops entered Chicago, and in a telegram to President Cleveland he protested that neither he nor the legislature had applied for assistance. He pointed out that there were three regiments of militiamen in Chicago that could have been ordered into service, but "nobody in Cook county, whether official or private citizen, had asked for their help," and for a good reason: ". . . our railroads are paralyzed not by reason of obstruction, but because they cannot get men to operate their trains." The newspaper accounts were "pure fabrications." [20]

Cleveland replied briefly that he was satisfied that conditions were actually as represented. Altgeld sent another telegram of protest to the president, and was answered in a brief, sharply-worded memorandum.

Newspapers, both Republican and Democratic, joined in labeling Gov-

* The attempt of many historians to picture Cleveland as the dupe of his Attorney General has no basis in fact. Cleveland was well aware of every development in the strike, and though Olney may have master-minded the plan for federal intervention, the President was acquainted with every detail.

ernor Altgeld an "anarchist," a "hater of society," and a menace to the American Republic.[21]

RED-SCARE

On Independence Day, the federal troops arrived in Chicago. They were greeted with boos and hisses by crowds gathered around the railroad property. Among the crowd was a large number of hoodlums who had remained in Chicago after the close of the Columbian Exposition of 1893. It was this semi-criminal element, not a few of whom were hired by the railroads for the purpose, and the U.S. deputy marshals assigned to strike duty, who were largely responsible for the violence and destruction of railroad property during the four days following the arrival of the federal troops. It is significant that newspaper reporters who covered the events in Chicago and mingled with the rioters were almost unanimous in their opinion that the strikers had very little part in the disturbances. But the newspapers ignored this evidence. Typical headlines in the press screamed:

FROM A STRIKE TO A REVOLUTION.

MOB BENT ON RUIN—DEBS' STRIKERS BEGIN WORK OF DESTRUCTION.

WILD RIOT IN CHICAGO—HUNDREDS OF FREIGHT CARS BURNED BY STRIKERS—THE TORCH IN GENERAL USE.

ANARCHISTS AND SOCIALISTS SAID TO BE PLANNING THE DESTRUCTION AND LOOTING OF THE TREASURY.

ANARCHISTS ON WAY TO AMERICA FROM EUROPE.[22]

Economists, ministers and other shapers of public opinion joined in the hue and cry against the strikers, their union and its president, Eugene Debs. They called openly for force and violence against the strikers, quoting approvingly Napolean Bonaparte's statement: "Shooting down one at the right time is saving the lives of tens of thousands in the future." Said Dr. Herrick Johnson, professor at the Presbyterian Theological Seminary in Chicago. "The soldiers must use their guns. They must shoot to kill."[23]

The soldiers did use their guns and they did shoot to kill—25 workers were killed and 60 badly injured—yet the strike remained unbroken. Thus the Associated Press reported: "Despite the presence of United States troops and the mobilization of five regiments of state militia; despite threats of martial law and bullet and bayonet, the great strike inaugurated by the American Railway Union holds three-fourths of the roads running out of Chicago in its strong fetters, and last night traffic was more fully paralyzed than at any time since the inception of the tie-up."[24]

EFFECT OF THE INJUNCTION

The intervention of federal troops did not halt the spread of the strike; "Troops cannot move trains," Debs wired the striking locals.[25] Nor did the sabotage of the strike by the officials of the railroad brotherhoods. The Pullman strike was broken, not by the U.S. troops, not by the opposition of the leadership of the brotherhoods, but by the action taken by the federal courts. The sweeping injunction made "the very command" of the union leaders "to their striking men . . . an open defiance of the courts." As a result of the injunction, it became literally impossible for the strike leaders, centered in Chicago, to coordinate the striking groups scattered from Michigan to California. When the leadership of the strikers even urged workers to join the struggle, they were cited for contempt and arrested. Moreover, throughout the country, grand juries, hastily impaneled by the government, indicted hundreds of strikers and their leaders for conspiracy.

On July 10, the federal grand jury at Chicago returned indictments against the officers of the union, charging them with complicity in obstructing the mails and hindering interstate commerce. Debs and his fellow officers were arrested on the same day and were released on bail.* While Debs and his associates were in the custody of the court, the union headquarters were raided and ransacked by a squad of deputy marshals and deputy postoffice inspectors.[26]

With the strike leaders removed from the scene of action, the strike headquarters in Chicago ransacked and abandoned, with all contact among the various local organizations of the union cut off, with the newspapers printing false reports of a sweeping back-to-work movement, it is not surprising that most of the strikers became confused and uncertain as how to act. Frantic telegrams poured into the strike headquarters in Chicago, but there was no one there to reply. Small wonder that demoralization spread rapidly among the strikers.[27]

GENERAL STRIKE IN CHICAGO

It was obvious by the second week in July that only a miracle could save the strike. Some labor leaders and many members of the trade unions felt that a general strike in Chicago might convert the doomed strike into a victory. On July 8, a mass meeting was held to which every local union in the city sent three representatives with full instructions

* So poor was the A.R.U. that the bail for the arrested union leaders had to be furnished by two Chicago saloonkeepers. (Florence Kelley to Henry Demarest Lloyd, August 1, 1894, Lloyd Papers, *WSHS*.)

and authority to act. Throughout the night until dawn, the trade unionists, representing over one hundred unions in Chicago and seven national labor organizations, debated the question: "Shall the trade-unions of Chicago strike in sympathy with the Pullman boycott, to the end that the principle of arbitration may win?" The vote was practically unanimous for a city-wide strike, but before taking that step, the trade unionists decided to make one last effort to persuade Pullman to accept arbitration. A committee was appointed for that purpose, and it was agreed unanimously by the delegates that if the strike was not settled by four o'clock in the afternoon of July 10, a general strike would start the following morning.[28]

Once again the Pullman company declared that there was nothing to arbitrate, and the committee appointed by the Chicago trade unions was forced to acknowledge failure. As soon as this report was turned in, the chairman of the Trades and Labor Congress issued a proclamation calling upon all trade unions in Chicago to launch the city-wide strike as planned. The response was disappointing. The local lodges of the remnants of the K. of L. turned out, as did several other unions. But in all, not more than 25,000 workers walked out. Even though the workers in Chicago were in favor of the general strike, the majority felt that with Debs and other officials of the A.R.U. arrested, and with the city of Chicago virtually under martial law, a sympathetic strike at this point could not save the sinking ship. They preferred to await the outcome of the A. F. of L. executive conference scheduled to meet in Chicago on July 12 before joining a general strike.[29]

THE BRIGGS HOUSE CONFERENCE

A call to Gompers, urging him to come to Chicago immediately, had been issued by the trade union conference on July 8. Since many of the trade unions that joined in the request belonged to the A. F. of L., Gompers decided to appear. After consulting his close advisers, he sent the following wire to members of the Federation's Executive Council: "Extraordinary industrial situation compels some action by Executive Council, hence you are urgently requested to meet with us at ten o'clock Thursday morning July 12th at Briggs House, Chicago, Ill. Don't fail to attend." [30]

We do not know just what was in Gompers' mind as he set out for Chicago; indeed, to avoid meeting reporters, he refused to reveal the exact time of the train's departure from New York. Nevertheless, some of Gompers' associates on the Executive Council were worried about the course he would follow in Chicago, fearing that he might be carried away by contact with the strike leaders. McGuire was particularly concerned, and on July 10 he wired Chris Evans, A. F. of L. Secretary-Treasurer, to persuade Gompers to "go slow on Chicago meeting of Council." McGuire was anxious to talk to Gompers before he left for Chicago to advise against precipitate action.[31]

There is no record of what transpired in the discussions between Gompers and McGuire, but six years later, the latter boasted, in an address before the Masters' Builder's Exchange of Philadelphia, an employers' association, that he had influenced Gompers to oppose the movement for a general strike in 1894 and that "he and Samuel Gompers fought and defeated the purpose in the Executive Council of the Federation."[32] It is likely that McGuire exaggerated his influence in the matter since there is little evidence that either he or Gompers had to struggle hard to defeat the proposal for a general strike at the Chicago conference.

The response to Gompers' telegrams was excellent; 24 high union officials, including representatives from two of the railroad brotherhoods, were present when the Briggs House conference convened.* With Gompers in the chair, the trade unionists turned immediately to a consideration of the status of the great strike. Early in the first session, a committee from the Cigarmakers' Union of Chicago advanced the proposal for a general strike. Pointing out that the welfare of all workers, organized and unorganized, was at stake in the battle of the railroad men, the committee expressed confidence that a nationwide work stoppage would force Pullman to arbitrate. The majority of the union leaders at the conference were more cautious, emphasizing the dangers of a sympathetic strike and expressing doubt that it could be effective. Therefore, no action was taken immediately on the proposal, and it was left for further consideration.

Meanwhile, the conference sent a wire to President Cleveland asking him to come to Chicago at once and attend the conference, and urging him to "lend your influence and give us your aid so that the present industrial crisis may be brought to an end." Cleveland did not bother to acknowledge or answer the telegram.

In the evening, Debs appeared at the conference. When asked by Gompers to offer a course of action, he suggested that the A. F. of L. president carry to the General Managers' Association an offer from the A.R.U. proposing the end of the boycott on the sole condition that all of its members be permitted to return to their jobs. Debs' statement

---

* P. M. Arthur of the Locomotive Engineers sent a telegram stating that it was impossible for him to attend. P. H. Morrisey, 1st Vice-Grand Master, Brotherhood of Railway Trainmen, and F. W. Arnold, Grand Secretary and Treasurer, Brotherhood of Locomotive Firemen, were the representatives of the two brotherhoods at the conference. (For a complete list of the trade union delegates to the conference, see American Federationist, Vol. I, Aug., 1894, pp. 131-33.)

killed off any hope that the conference would adopt the proposal for a general strike. It convinced the majority of the labor leaders that the A.R.U. conceded defeat, and that the union was no longer concerned with the issues that had caused the boycott.

With the strike apparently irretrievably lost and the sole question involved being the reinstatement of the strikers, the labor leaders were not willing to risk the future of their unions in a clash with the federal government. The army and the courts would move in swiftly to crush any organization that sought to spread the strike.

The conference advised Debs that he could select any one or more members of the gathering to act with him, and any other committee of citizens, to present his proposition to the Railway Managers' Association. The railroads obviously would not meet with Debs, and the A.R.U. president declined the offer.

To show its sympathy for the strikers and their leaders, the conference recommended that the A. F. of L. Executive Council contribute $1,000 to Debs' legal defense. As its final act, the conference issued a statement of policy. It came out unequivocally against a general strike, arguing that the situation in the country made the odds against the success of such a movement overwhelming. The document closed with an appeal for continued labor organization, and for the settlement of the issue at the ballot box so that the workers could take the government "from the hands of the plutocratic wreckers and place it in the hands of the common people.[33]

As soon as the statement was released, the Chicago Building Trades Council called off its city-wide strike, and other unions followed suit.

The press praised Gompers for "saving the people of this country from a most far-reaching and bloody revolution." But most members and officers of the A.R.U. felt that Gompers and others at the Briggs House conference "weren't radical enough." Still others bluntly accused Gompers of having deliberately betrayed the strikers, "sold out to the capitalists, and . . . [along with] Arthur should be driven out from all labor unions."[34] *

* Thomas J. Morgan, Chicago Socialist, publicly arraigned Gompers for having conspired to defeat the strike, and quoted the A.F. of L. president as having said when he left New York to come to Chicago: "I am going to the funeral of the American Railway Union." The issue was taken up at a meeting of the Chicago Trades and Labor Assembly on August 5, 1894, where a communication from Gompers denying the charge was read. Gompers, in his letter, stated that Morgan had based his charge on a report in an anti-labor paper which was utterly and completely false. At first Morgan refused to retract his charge, "but when the case was put to him whether he would take the report of the capitalistic press against the positive denial of Mr. Gompers he finally weakened and agreed to accept Mr. Gompers' statement as a vindication." (Chicago Times, Aug. 6, 1894.) The matter did not die there, for another delegate at the meeting arose and said that she had

One cannot avoid the conclusion that the Briggs House conference could have done more for the hard-pressed strikers than issue lofty statements to the press. The truth is that the A. F. of L. top leaders were not too eager to to come to the assistance of the A.R.U., and that they were not sorry to see the new union of railroad workers defeated. They saw in the A.R.U. a direct threat to the principle of craft unionism upheld by the Federation as well as the embodiment of the evil of dual unionism. The A. F. of L. leaders had been dismayed by the fact that so many members of the railroad brotherhoods had joined the ranks of the A.R.U., and they were apparently more concerned with keeping the brotherhoods alive than with preventing the destruction of the new union. In his autobiography published years later, Gompers coolly admitted that this was one of the motives for his stand at the Chicago conference in opposing a general strike: "The course pursued by the Federation was the biggest service that could have been performed to maintain the integrity of the Railroad Brotherhoods. Large numbers of their members had left their organizations and joined the A.R.U. It meant, if not disruption, weakening to a very serious extent." [35]

On June 14, 1894, the very next day after the Briggs House conference adjourned, McGuire wrote excitedly to Gompers from Chicago: "Sovereign and Debs have joined hands; the K. of L. and A.R.U. are one in method and now one in fact.* It is very significant. Yes, it indicates a joint warfare is to be made against the older railway Orders. The scheme is worthy our closest attention." [36] † To expect men like McGuire to go out of their way to prevent the destruction of a union whose principles and methods they feared and detested was to expect the impossible!

There is little doubt, too, that the leaders of the railroad brotherhoods who attended the Chicago conference sought to convince the A. F. of L. leaders that it would be better for the type of unionism represented by the Federation and the brotherhoods if the A.R.U. were destroyed. With the A.R.U. out of the way, plans to federate the brotherhoods

been informed by the vice president of the American Railway Union that he had a letter in his pocket from a New York trade unionist who asserted that he heard Gompers make the remark attributed to him. After considerable debate, the Trades and Labor Assembly decided "to receive Mr. Gompers' statement as the truth and let the matter go at that." (*Ibid.*) The charge, however, continued to be hurled at Gompers for many years thereafter. (See *Bill Haywood's Book: The Autobiography of William D. Haywood,* New York, 1929, p. 77.)

* In August, 1894, A. Strasser, one of the important A.F. of L. leaders, referred privately to the A.R.U. as "the second edition of the K. of L. movement, as managed by Debs and others." (Strasser to Gompers, August 9, 1894, *AFL Corr.*)

† Plans for an alliance of the A.R.U. and the K. of L. were actually drawn up at the union's convention before the boycott was ordered, but they were not adopted. (See Chicago *Tribune,* Jan. 28, 1895.)

under the A. F. of L. could be achieved.[37] The conclusion is thus inescapable that the leading labor officials at the gathering welcomed the defeat of the A.R.U. which they regarded as a definite menace to the trade union principles and practices they upheld and that this outlook was responsible for the failure of the conference to pursue a more vigorous course in behalf of the strikers. The motives behind this failure struck an ominous note for the future well-being of American labor.

TRIAL OF STRIKE LEADERS

On July 14, Mayor John P. Hopkins of Chicago carried to the General Managers' Association Debs' offer to call off the boycott if all strikers, except those, if any, who had been convicted of crime, were rehired. The offer was promptly rejected.

On July 17, Debs and the other strike leaders were again arrested and charged with contempt of court for having violated the injunction of July 2. Refusing to offer the bail fixed at $3,000, they were committed to jail. Explaining their refusal to accept bail, Debs remarked: "The poor striker who is arrested would be thrown into jail. We are not better than he." [38]

Debs and his fellow-officers were not tried on the contempt charge until the middle of the following December. They were then found guilty of contempt of an injunction issued on July 2 by the Federal District court in Chicago. (Judge William A. Woods, who presided over the contempt case, was along with Judge Peter S. Grosscup, responsible for the issuance of the restraining order.) The labor leaders were sentenced to jail for terms varying from three to six months.* Sixteen days after the defendants started serving their sentence for contempt, the trial for criminal conspiracy to obstruct and retard the mails began in the federal court of Judge Grosscup, one of the two promulgators of the injunction. From the Woodstock jail some 50 miles northwest of Chicago, Debs and his fellow prisoners were taken daily to that city for the trial which opened on January 24, 1895. The illness of a juror during the trial caused the case to be dropped.† Debs went back to Woodstock to finish his six months' sentence.

In January, 1895, the strike leaders who were in jail for contempt appealed to the United States Supreme Court for a writ of habeas corpus. On May 27, 1895, Justice Brewer, speaking for the Supreme Court, de-

---

* Defense counsel in the contempt case were the yet little-known Clarence Darrow and Stephen S. Gregory, a former president of the American Bar Association.

† Debs pointed out that the "trial . . . closed abruptly because the parties chiefly interested knew it would result in our complete vindication. There is not the slightest testimony against us and the only purpose they ever had was to destroy our organization." (Eugene V. Debs to August McCraith, Feb. 25, 1895, *AFL Corr.*)

nied the appeal. In upholding the Woods-Grosscup injunction which had been predicated on the Sherman Act, the Supreme Court did not rule on the applicability of that law, saying instead that "the jurisdiction of courts to interfere in such matters by injunctions is one recognized from ancient times and by indisputable authority." [39]

The decision of the Supreme Court in the famous Debs case was wholly irrelevant to the outcome of the Pullman strike. Long before the decision was handed down, the strike had ended in defeat. On July 18, 1894, 24 hours after the A.R.U. leaders were sent to jail, a large notice was posted on the gates at Pullman: "These gates will be opened as soon as the number of operatives is sufficient to make a working force in all departments." Two days later, the United States Army left Chicago. The Pullman strike was over. It remained only for the shattered union to make it official. At a hastily summoned convention in Chicago on August 2 the A.R.U. recommended to its local members that the strike be called off at once. [40]

The American Railway Union never recovered from the disastrous defeat. Its leaders in jail, its members completely demoralized, unemployed, and blacklisted out of whatever jobs they could obtain, [41] * the Union rapidly disintegrated. When the A.R.U. held its convention in Chicago in June, 1897, the 400 delegates of three years before had dwindled to a mere two dozen. From these shattered remnants of the once powerful industrial union was organized the Social Democratic Party —one of the forerunners of the Socialist Party of the United States.

SIGNIFICANCE OF PULLMAN STRIKE

Although some workers, especially in Chicago, wrested gains from their employers during the great labor upheaval accompanying the Pullman strike, all of organized labor, along with the A.R.U. suffered an overwhelming defeat. Nevertheless, many American workers gained rich experience and more valuable lessons from the struggle about "the underlying wrongs of modern society than all the lectures and publications could secure in a decade." [42] Many workers now saw clearly that the government was the tool of corporate interests, a conviction that was

---

* The railroads adopted the very simple method of requiring men to produce clearances before they would be given work; or they required them to sign applications stating when they had worked and the date they had quit their last employment. They then wrote each other asking information, and if the answer came back that the applicant had participated in the Pullman strike, he was denied employment. (Chicago *Tribune,* June 27, Oct. 25, 1899; U.S. Industrial Commission, *Report,* Washington, 1900, Vol. IV, pp. 503-25; Samuel Gompers, "Blacklisting Means Industrial Slavery," typewritten copy, *AFL Corr.*)

to intensify the feeling for independent political action in labor circles.* They also saw that only through powerfully organized unions and the utmost of solidarity could labor effectively challenge the might of corporate monopolies. As Debs pointed out in a letter to American workers, from Woodstock jail: "The recent upheaval has demonstrated the necessity for the solidarity of labor. Divided and cross purposes, labor becomes the sport and prey of its exploiters, but united, harmonious and intelligently directed it rules the world." [43]

Yet there were elements in the labor movement who drew precisely the opposite conclusion from the "recent upheaval." Many craft union leaders of the A. F. of L. and the railroad brotherhoods saw in the defeat of the strike a justification of their own conservative policies. The ferocity with which the corporate monopolies, the government, and the judiciary struck back at the railroad workers convinced these craft union leaders that any attempt to build trade unions along the lines of the A.R.U.— the lines of industrial unionism—would bring forth similar opposition from this alliance of big business and the government. The only type of unionism that would be tolerated was a unionism which did not seriously threaten the absolute control of the corporate monopolies over the economic and political machinery. To attempt to unite the workers into powerful industrial unions, the craft union leaders argued, was to court the destruction of the existing labor organizations and to doom the trade unions to the fate of the A.R.U.

The essence of this trade union strategy can be stated simply: Labor must never seriously challenge big business and the government. Avoid head-on collisions with big corporations and with government. Team up with these industrialists and politicians who seem inclined toward a live-and-let-live policy with the craft unions. Make peace with the employers on certain terms which would keep the craft unions alive even if this meant increased victimization of the unskilled and semi-skilled workers. This policy was soon institutionalized in the National Civic Federation.†

---

* European trade union and Socialist leaders, who followed the strike closely, predicted that it would bring American workers close to the thinking of European workers on such issues as independent political action. (Tom Mann to Gompers, July 25, 1894; Vicomte de Meaux to Gompers, July 17, 1894, *AFL Corr.*)

Typical of the support the strikers received from workers all over the world is the resolution adopted by the Social Democratic Federation of England on July 25, 1894, and forwarded to Gompers in which it "tenders its sympathy to the workers of America in their rising against the tyrannous monopolists who oppress them, and trusts that little time will elapse before the people on both sides of the Atlantic will join hands in an organised effort to emancipate themselves from the yoke of capitalist domination." (*Ibid.*)

† *See* pp. 384-87.

The progressive forces in the labor movement challenged the conclusions the conservative, craft union leaders drew from the Pullman strike. Had all organized labor been united and active in the support of the strikers from the beginning of the boycott, they argued, had it sought militantly to keep the courts and the federal government from entering the dispute, had it tried to restrain the strikebreaking activities of the leaders of the brotherhoods, the final outcome might have been different. At any rate, the lesson of the Pullman strike, as Debs so cogently pointed out, was the crying need for greater not less unity and solidarity in labors' ranks.

From 1894 on the progressive forces in the American labor movement strove diligently to apply this lesson. The odds against them were great. The corporate monopolies fought tooth and nail to prevent the rise of a labor movement that would unite all of labor in struggle against its exploiters. The monopolists had the ready assistance of the leaders of the craft unions, the press, large sections of the clergy, and, of course, the government, local, state, and federal. But the progressive forces persisted, keeping alive the policy pioneered by the A.R.U.—the policy of working class solidarity and for a new organizational form that led toward industrial unionism.

In 1905, a delegate to the founding convention of the Industrial Workers of the World characterized the great Pullman Strike as "a battle that in spite of the fact that it apparently ended in Woodstock jail, is not ended yet, but is going on today." [44] That battle continued until the cause for which so many workers had sacrificed in 1894 was crowned with success. The ultimate victory, it is significant to note, was predicted in the course of the great strike itself; indeed, at the very point when it appeared almost certain that labor's struggle was lost. On a large canvas strip, prominently displayed in Cooper Union Hall, New York City, on the evening of July 12, 1894, where a mass meeting of workers in support of the Pullman strikers was being held, was the following legend:

> *They hanged and quartered John Ball*
> *But Feudalism passed away.*
> *They hanged John Brown, but Chattel*
> *Slavery passed away.*
> *They arrested Eugene Debs, and may kill him,*
> *but White Slavery will pass away.*
> *Such souls go marching on.*[45]

CHAPTER 19

The Socialists and the Labor Movement, 1890-1896

In the summer of 1895, an article appeared in the *American Federationist,* entitled, "Socialism in the United States." The writer, after a careful survey of the labor scene in the country, concluded: "The feeling of wage-earners, i.e., of the vast majority of the people is growing more favorable toward socialism. The attitude of dislike and intolerance towards the idea is passing away, and they are becoming more willing to listen. The increasing power of great combinations of capital, and the increasing hopelessness of the wage-earners ever becoming an employer is rapidly bringing about this change of heart. He is now ready to listen to anything that promises to deliver him from the ever-narrowing walls of his prison-home." [1]

Yet in 1896, the Socialist Labor Party, although some 20 years in the field, was more isolated from the American workers than ever before in its history.

DE LEONISM

To a very large degree, the S.L.P.'s isolation in the years immediately preceding 1896 was due to its complete capitulation to the sectarian policies of the former Columbia University lecturer in international law, Daniel De Leon, who joined the party in 1890, and almost immediately assumed leadership of the socialist movement in America. He became national lecturer of the S.L.P. in 1890 and editor of its English-language weekly, *The People,* in January, 1892, after Lucian Sanial, the former editor, had to resign because of failing eyesight.

Sharp of tongue and caustic in his writings, De Leon possessed a supreme confidence in himself and his views. He was highly impatient with those who could not see matters in the same light as he saw them. To this arrogance and dogmatism was added a sectarian trade union policy, an indifference to immediate demands, a deliberate fostering of dual unionism in the labor movement, and a deep-seated hostility to any and all alliances between workers and non-working class elements. By this combination of incorrect policies, intransigence, and inability to work with anyone who did not unreservedly accept his doctrines, De Leon made it impossible for the S.L.P., under his leadership, to fulfill the historic task of guiding the American workers in the intensely sharpening class struggles of the 1890's.[2]

To Daniel De Leon the work of the Socialist unions in leading the workers in their day-to-day struggles was of slight importance. DeLeon insisted that the aim of a trade union of workers must be "the abolition of the wage system of slavery." Unions which concentrated on immediate demands—"pure and simple" unionism—were impeding the historic mission of the trade unions—the overthrow of capitalism. Hence no matter how militant a union was, no matter how progressive it was in its approach towards the organization of the unskilled and the semi-skilled, the Negro workers,* women and foreign-born workers, unless it endorsed a socialist program, it was a reactionary organization.[3]

De Leon labelled his trade union program "the new trade unionism" as opposed to the "pure and simple" unionism of the A. F. of L. He borrowed the name of the English movement, ushered in by the tremendous dock strike of 1889, led by Tom Mann, John Burns, and Ben Tillett, but none of its fundamental principles. For one thing, unlike the British "new unionists" who fought effectively inside the older unions to reform and revitalize them, De Leon was convinced that the existing trade unions in this country were so completely dominated by reactionary leaders, the "labor fakers" being so completely in the saddle,

---

* Requests to De Leon to make the Negro question a special feature of *The People* came from members of the S.L.P. One member wrote to De Leon indicating his desire to go South to organize Negroes into the S.L.P. to make "the Negro at the south . . . the ally of Socialism in America. . . ." He planned to concentrate on distributing *The People* among Negroes in the South, and he pleaded: "We should make the expression of southern and the worse known American oppression of the Southern Negro a special feature of the *People*. . . . This attitude of the S.L.P. and the People will give us and the paper not only a stronghold on the southern Negro population but in the colored population of the North. I believe it . . . alone [will] add 10,000 names to your subscription list. In addition it will give us the support of the Negro all over the North." (C. G. Baylor to De Leon, Providence, R. I., Dec. 8, 1895, De Leon Correspondence, *WSHS*.) De Leon did not even bother to answer the writer. To De Leon the Negro question did not exist. He reduced it to a class question. The only program he had for the Negro people was eventual socialism. "*The People* did not at any time make the Negro question a 'special feature,'" notes James Benjamin Stalvey in his unpublished biography of De Leon. (Ph.D. thesis, University of Illinois, 1946, pp. 193-94.)

that it was hopeless to attempt to reform and revitalize these unions. For another, unlike in England, where the "new unionism" signified the organization of the unorganized, class conscious, militant campaigns for higher wages, shorter hours and other improvements, the "new trade unionism" of De Leon and his followers was limited to propaganda activity for socialism and to attacks on union leaders who opposed the endorsement of socialism.[4]

De Leon's "new trade unionism" placed considerable emphasis upon the unity of the economic and political forces of labor for the achievement of socialism. Apart from the fact that there was no mention of using these forces in the everyday campaigns for immediate improvements, it is important to note that De Leon did not think in terms of an independent labor party. For to De Leon and his followers all efforts to build a labor party, based upon the trade unions, were "futile and in reality a betrayal of the movement for socialism." The only real labor party was "the Socialist Labor Party, the only party, which free[ly] and sincere[ly] proclaims that the liberation of the working class must be [by] the action of the working class itself."[5] No demand, however progressive it might be, could be supported by the S.L.P. and its members, according to De Leon and his followers, if it was initiated or advanced by any group but the working class or by any party but the Socialist Labor Party.

The story of how De Leon and the Socialists under his influence fell afoul of the two branches of the organized labor movement in the United States—the A. F. of L. and the K. of L.—is a tragic one. For it is basically the story of the self-isolation of the Socialists from the mainstream of the American labor movement precisely at a time when they had a full opportunity to stand in the vanguard of the whole movement.

BATTLE BETWEEN A. F. OF L. AND S.L.P. LEADERS

The story begins with the dispute between the A. F. of L. leadership and the New York Central Labor Federation.

Late in 1888, as a result of the unfriendly attitude of the Central Labor Union, affiliated with the A. F. of L., toward the S.L.P. in the New York City campaigns of 1887 and 1888,* the Socialist trade unionists organized the Central Labor Federation of New York. In March, 1889, after a thorough investigation, Gompers and the A. F. of L. Executive Council granted the new Federation a charter. Sometime in the latter part of 1889, the C.L.F. decided to amalgamate with the C.L.U. A Harmony Committee was elected by both bodies, and, among other things, it was decided to return the C.L.F.'s charter to the A. F. of L.

* See pp. 154-55.

President. The charter was delivered to Gomepers in December, 1889.

Another quarrel soon arose between the two organizations. The Socialists, under De Leon's leadership, withdrew from the C.L.U., reorganized the C.L.F. and, in July, 1890, asked Gompers to return its charter.[6]

Gompers had played a large part in the reconciliation of the quarrel between the Socialists and the Central Labor Union, and it was at his suggestion that the C.L.F. had resolved to merge with the C.L.U. When the C.L.F. applied for the return of its charter, Ernest Bohm, its corresponding secretary, sent Gompers a list of organizations represented in the Federation. Among the organizations represented was the American Section of the Socialist Labor Party. Gompers rejected the application for the charter on the ground that "as a political party the American Section of the Socialist Labor Party should not be entitled to representation in a Trade Union body." It was perfectly acceptable to the A. F. of L., he pointed out, for the members of the S.L.P. to be represented in the Central Labor Federation as representatives of their trade unions, but since the A. F. of L. was a federation of trade unions, the S.L.P. "could *not* properly be represented in a Trade Union Central Organization."[7]

This then is the background for the conflict between the Socialists and the A. F. of L. leadership. The wise and proper thing for the S.L.P. to have done at this point was to have withdrawn from the C.L.F., and to have instructed its members to join the organization as individual members through their trade unions. But De Leon and his followers refused to drop the issue, and instead launched a bitter tirade against Gompers, accusing him of collaborating with the employers against the Socialists and of seeking to weaken the labor movement by opposition to political movements. Rather than prolong the controversy and allow the anti-labor press to use the issue to weaken the A. F. of L., Gompers decided to refer the entire subject to the Federation's convention scheduled to meet at Detroit in December, 1890. In announcing his decision to Ernest Bohm, secretary of the C.L.F., Gompers made a pertinent point: "It seems to me that men in the labor movement can honestly differ with each other without finding it necessary to indulge in abuse and I cannot for the life of me understand why an expression of opinion should call forth the spleen manifested by you in your official journals, and which was given out officially by you for publication in the public press."[8]

One whole day and one-half was consumed at the A. F. of L.'s 1890 convention in consideration of the question: "Should a Charter be issued to a Central Labor Union which had a Political Party represented therein." The debate opened when Lucien Sanial presented his credentials from the S.L.P., which had sent him to Detroit to contest Gompers' decision. The matter was referred to a special committee which, in its report, denied Sanial his seat. The committee held that "a political party of whatever nature is not entitled to representation in the American Federation of Labor." [9]

The delegates debated the committee report back and forth. Some of the delegates blamed the Socialists for having raised an issue which could only cause dissension in the Federation at a time when unity was essential for the purpose of carrying through organizing drives. "It is the business of our organization to debate matters of practical policy," it was pointed out, "rather than to fling this bone of contention between the radical and conservative wings of the movement." To all this, Lucien Sanial, who was allowed to speak on the issue, replied that "we socialists will force socialism down the throats of the American workingmen." [10] * It was hardly the type of remark to influence the delegates to reject the special committee's report.

Not only was the committee report sustained, but by a vote of 1,574 to 496 the delegates decided not to grant a charter to the Central Labor Federation of New York "so long as they have the Socialist Labor Party, as a Party, represented therein." [11]

Following the convention, Gompers asked the Central Labor Federation whether the S.L.P. had withdrawn or intended to withdraw "in order that the charter may be issued to you." He was convinced that "the S.L.P. could do a great deal for the Trade Union movement in the City of New York by withdrawing," and instructing its members to join the C.L.F. through their trade unions. He argued that the way the Socialists could make their best contribution to the development of progressive ideas among American workers was as members of the trade unions. Socialists in Europe, Gompers pointed out, had followed this course of action with effective results both for the trade unions and the Socialist movement. Thus the British Socialists "never made so preposterous a claim to represent the Social Democratic Federation of England in the Trade Union Congress of that country. They came there as representatives of the Trade Unions and that is what I claim." [12]

Outside of New York, members of the S.L.P. tended to support Gompers in the charter dispute. The Detroit Socialists assured Gompers that they were "in accord with the action of the convention in the Socialistic matter." Thomas J. Morgan, the Welsh-born machinist and leader of the Chicago Socialists, even sent a letter to the New York branches of the S.L.P. urging the withdrawal of the party from the

---

* Several years later, the *Volkszeitung* conceded that Sanial's remark had not been wise and expressed regret that it was ever uttered. (*New Yorker Volkszeitung*, March 28, 1894. *See also American Federationist*, Vol. I, April, 1894, p. 30.)

Central Labor Federation and the reentrance of its delegates as representatives from their respective unions. The letter was read at a meeting of the New York Socialists by Ida M. Van Etten, a leading figure in both the S.L.P. and the A. F. of L., who strongly endorsed Morgan's suggestion. Since Morgan had supported Sanial at the A. F. of L. Convention, his letter carried considerable influence in Socialist circles.[13] *

Having won the support of many Socialists outside of New York, Gompers sought to enlist the backing of leading European Socialists. He felt this to be important because De Leon and his followers were busily engaged in circulating reports in Europe that the A. F. of L. at the Detroit Convention had condemned the principles of Socialism.[14] Of the several letters Gompers sent to European Socialists in connection with his dispute with the De Leonites in New York, the most important was the one he addressed to Frederick Engels on January 9, 1891. This letter, never before published, opened: "I make so free as to write you upon a question which I know you to take a deep interest in, and from the further fact of having been a life-long thinker and writer to and for the labor movement." Gompers then outlined the whole story of the dispute over the Central Labor Federation's charter including the action taken by the A. F. of L. convention.

"I am free to say," Gompers continued, "that in the discussion of the subject I took decided grounds that the Trade Unions were the natural organizations of the wage-workers, under present economic and social conditions to secure present amelioration and final emancipation of the wage-workers; that as a federation of Trade Unions the condition necessary to representation in a convention of Trade Unions is good standing membership in a Trade Union. This is the kernel of the whole dispute, and upon which I am willing to abide.

"There has never yet arisen a question in our councils whether a man was a socialist or not, whether he was an anarchist or not, in fact the greatest freedom and latitude of thought have been not only permitted but encouraged. Some of our best men and staunchest in holding as I do are well-known and avowed socialists. . . .

"Our movement is anxiously endeavoring to keep in touch with the wage-workers, to help organize them, to make them self-reliant; to coalesce them into one grand whole struggling against the unjust conditions that exist, and to supplant them with such that the noblest aspirations of mankind has conceived or can conceive."

Apologizing to Engels for troubling him with the entire subject, Gompers noted that "I do so because as I have said I have respect for your judgment, and as a student of your writings and those of Marx and others in the same line I would not have your judgment formed upon

* Morgan ran against Gompers at the Convention for the A.F. of L. presidency and was defeated 1,716 to 194.

the base of erroneous information." In concluding, he asked Engels "to favor me in the interest of our great cause, with an expression of opinion upon the above at your earliest convenience."[15]

Engels was not in London when Gompers' letter arrived, and he did not receive it for some time afterwards. By then it appeared that Gompers might be coming to Europe to visit the International Labor Congress in Brussels, and Engels thought he might have an opportunity to discuss the issue with him in person. Consequently, the co-founder of scientific socialism never answered Gompers' communication.[16] But he made his position clear in a letter to Hermann Schlüter, an editor of the *Volkszeitung* and a frequent correspondent of Engels:

"Nor do I understand the quarrel with Gompers," Engels wrote on January 29, 1891. "His Federation is, as far as I know, an association of trade-unions and nothing but trade-unions. Hence they have the *formal right* to reject anyone coming in as the representative of a labor organization that is *not* a trade-union, or to reject delegates of an association to which such organizations are admitted. I cannot judge from here, of course, whether it was *propagandistically* advisable to expose oneself to such a rejection. But it was beyond question that it had to come, and I, for one, cannot blame Gompers for it."

Engels was critical of the S.L.P. for failing to see the dividing line between party and trade union, and was strongly of the opinion that the Socialists should have made every effort "to keep on good terms with Gompers, who has more workers behind him at any rate, than the S.L.P. . . ." By playing a constructive role in the A. F. of L., the Socialists would be able to prove that a "narrow-minded trade-union standpoint" was insufficient in the struggles against capitalism. At the same time, they would contribute to the growth of their own movement, for, as Engels pointed out, "where do you find a recruiting ground if not in the trade unions?"[17] *

But De Leon and his followers showed that they had not the slightest understanding of the correct tactics to be followed in relation to the American labor movement. In May, 1891, August Delabar, the Socialist secretary of the Bakers' and Confectioners' International Union, anxious to heal the breach between the A. F. of L. and the S.L.P., asked Gompers point-blank "whether if the Socialistic Labor Party were to withdraw from the Central Labor Federation would you issue a charter from the American Federation of Labor to the C.L.F.?" Gompers replied that the moment the S.L.P. withdrew, the charter would be issued. He was ready to let bygones be bygones, and he sought no personal triumph in the matter. "There is no question of either a victory on one side and

* F. A. Sorge, another frequent correspondent of Engels, endorsed Engels position and supported Gompers in the controversy with the S.L.P. leadership. (*See* Samuel Gompers, *Seventy Years of Life and Labor*, Vol. 1, pp. 380-88.)

humiliation on the other. In this great labor movement of ours, sincere men should be above personal glorification. . . ." [18]

Impressed by the resonableness of Gompers' proposal, Delabar carried it to the Central Labor Federation. The overture was rejected. De Leon and his followers refused to let the charter dispute die. They seized upon it to drive a deep wedge between the S.L.P. and the A. F. of L., and advanced the thesis that there was no longer any point for Socialists to remain in the A. F. of L. The Federation had lost all significance for the working class, they argued, hence it was a waste of time for Socialists to play any role in its operations:

"What excuse has it now for existence except to furnish offices for a few men and opportunity for several more to pose as labor leaders or manufacture political capital? . . .

"It has become a whited sepulcher, a living lie, a petrified mummy galvanized into life once a year when certain eminent individuals pull the strings and cause it to dance before our wondering eyes and gaping mouths." [19]

De Leon kept up a steady attack on the A. F. of L. and its leaders, particularly Gompers. He condemned the Federation for its craft separation, its indifference to political action, and its concentration on immediate demands. He accused Gompers and his colleagues on the Executive Council of being "ignoramuses," "weaklings," "labor fakers," "agents of the capitalists inside the trade unions," and "traitors to the cause of labor.' They were guilty both of corruption and lack of vision. The organization they headed was ineffectual and hopeless, and it was a waste of time for Socialists to try to transform it.[20] "The dry-rot has set in the American Federation of Labor. As an organization the A. F. of L. is at best a cross between a windbag and a rope of sand; it has no cohesion, vitality or vigor worth mentioning. . . ." [21]

DE LEON URGES SOCIALISTS TO LEAVE A. F. OF L.

The effect of De Leon's bitter denunciations were felt by the A. F. of L., especially in New York. On April 16, 1892, Hugo Miller, New York organizer, informed Gompers privately that due to the activity of De Leon and his followers, "already there is a strong feeling amongst quite a number of our members, that the A. F. of L. is inactive, that it is useless to pay dues to the organization." Quite a few workers, especially in the unions affiliated to the United Hebrew Trades, where De Leon's influence was now considerable, were seriously discussing the value of being affiliated with the Federation.[22]

A little more than a year later, De Leon decided that the time had come for a complete break with the A. F. of L. *The People* of August

13, 1893, featured a clarion call to the Socialists in the Federation to quit the organization. "The pure and simple have been found out," De Leon wrote. "Some are ignorant, others are corrupt, all are unfit for leadership in the labor movement. To civilize and unite them is out of the question. The social revolution must march over the bodies of each and every one of them. . . ."

Thus at a time when the Federation had just begun to assume a definite shape and form, at a time when it was still possible for the Socialists to work inside the movement to rally affiliated unions, state federations, and city centrals to continue and develop many of the progressive policies of the early A. F. of L., De Leon called upon the militant elements to abandon what Engels reminded the American Socialists was their chief "recruiting ground" in the country.

To advance the march of the "social revolution," De Leon now turned his attention to the rapidly declining K. of L. He urged his followers to join the Order, appealing particularly to the Jewish unions in New York, associated together in the United Hebrew Trades. It was through the U.H.T. that De Leon hoped to win control of the once powerful and still influential New York section of the Order, District Assembly 49.

The U.H.T. responded favorably to De Leon's appeal, and approximately 12 to 15 of its affiliates joined the K. of L. and sent delegates to D.A. 49. Supported by the Jewish, German, and other non-English speaking Socialist-led unions in New York, the S.L.P. rapidly won leadership of D.A. 49.[23]

Outside of New York, the Socialists ignored De Leon's appeal and continued to function in the A. F. of L. The impact of the economic crisis of 1893, the anti-De Leonites argued, opened up vast opportunities for Socialist influence in the Federation. Hence to abandon the organization precisely at this time was to compound the evils inherent in De Leon's program.[24]

THE "POLITICAL PROGRAMME"

The 1893 A. F. of L. convention held in Chicago, in the midst of the great depression, saw a tremendous victory for the Socialists who upheld the policy of working inside the A. F. of L. On December 13, Thomas J. Morgan, Socialist delegate from the Machinists' International Union of Chicago, introduced the famous "Political Programme" of 1893. The preamble of the "Programme" took cognizance of the advanced political status of the labor unions of Great Britain, and recognized such independent labor politics to be based upon a platform substantially made up of eleven points adopted in January, 1893, by the Independent Labor Party in England: compulsory education; the initiative;

a legal eight-hour day; inspection of mines and workshops; abolition of the contract system in all public work; abolition of the sweating system; municipal ownership of street cars and gas and electric plants for public distribution of light, heat, and power; nationalization of telegraphs, telephones, railroads, and mines; the collective ownership by all the people of all means of production and consumption; the principle of referendum in all legislation.

The resolution called for the Convention's endorsement and provided that the program be favorably recommended for action by the local unions with the request that their delegates to the next annual convention be instructed on the matter. The opponents of the program succeeded in having the word "favorable" stricken out by a close vote of 1,253 to 1,882, but the program itself without recommendation was approved by the overwhelming vote of 2,244 to 67.[25]

What was surprising was the ready acceptance of the plank calling· for the collective ownership of all means of production and distribution by the people—Plank 10. The large vote revealed the radical temper of the delegates and caused considerable alarm in the press. The New York *Herald* noted: "It will be seen on reading the platform that the tenth plank contains in a nutshell the whole essence of the socialist creed, and that the platform all through is that of moderate collectivism or socialism."[26]

Interviews with delegates to the A. F. of L. Convention on the meaning and significance of its stand filled many columns in the press.[27] Gompers told a reporter in a discussion of the "Political Programme": "Personally I approve of nearly everything in the platform, and so do most of the delegates who were in Chicago, and I believe it will be adopted by the organizations." Gompers did not spell out just what he meant by "nearly everything," but, at the same time, he said nothing in opposition to Plank 10. Moreover, he put himself on record as completely in favor of independent political action: "I believe that the time has come for independent action on the part of organized labor. The industrial depression has been caused by a false system of economics and can only be righted by such action. . . . The people are now beginning to see how insincere and shallow the old parties and politicians are, and that the time has come to take independent action."[28]

When it came to being "insincere," Gompers could show the politicians a trick or two. There is not the slightest doubt that his remarks were part of a carefully calculated scheme to appear to be supporting the program of the progressive forces representing the rank-and-file in order to be in a position to sabotage it, a strategy Gompers was to resort to again and again in his career as A. F. of L. President. The strategy was not to oppose the "Political Programme" at this stage: "We must hold on to every inch we've got till matters resolve themselves into a condition of stability. In revolutionary times it is little use to preach conservatism—better go out of the way than try to stem the torrent." Rather than try to "stem" the torrent, divert it into meaningless channels. [29]

This strategy was unfolded at the 1894 A. F. of L. Convention.

REFERENDUM ON "POLITICAL PROGRAMME"

As the "Political Programme" of 1893 went the rounds of the affiliated unions,* events strengthened the arguments of the Socialists. The misery of the unemployed and the callousness of the capitalists and government towards the hundreds of thousands out of work through no fault of their own; the brutal treatment of the Coxeyites; the defeat of the Miners' strike, and, most important of all, the crushing of the Pullman strike by the alliance of monopoly corporations and the government—were all, as Tom Mann put it, "serving to teach the workers deep lessons." [30] Sentiment in favor of the entire "Political Programme," including Plank 10, increased enormously in labor circles. "The wage-earners should lose no time in voting themselves into the possession of all the tools of production—beginning with the railroads and telegraphs," a group of Philadelphia trade unionists wrote to Gompers in September, 1894. [31]

Only the Bakers' Union rejected the "Political Programme" in toto. The Typographical and Web Weavers' unions struck out Plank 10. The Carpenters and Joiners adopted Plank 10, but added the supplement "as the people elect to operate." The entire platform was upheld by the Mine Workers, Iron and Steel Workers, Cigar Makers, Lasters, Flint and Glass Workers, Tailors, Woodworkers, Brewery workers, Painters, Electrical Workers, Furniture Workers, Street Railway Employees, Waiters, Textile Workers, Shoe Workers, Mule Spinners, Machinists, the German-American Typographers and others. The state federations of Maine, New York, Ohio, Rhode Island, Missouri, Kansas, Nebraska, Montana, Michigan, Illinois and Wisconsin also approved it. City Centrals in Baltimore, New Haven, Cleveland, Toledo, Lansing, Saginaw, Grand Rapids, and Milwaukee endorsed it as well. [32]

It appeared certain by the fall of 1894 that a majority of the Federation members had instructed their delegates to adopt the entire "Political Programme" at the 1894 convention. At any rate, the A. F. of L. leader-

---

* At its meeting on January 13, 1894, the A.F. of L. Executive Council submitted the "Political Programme" to the affiliated unions and advised them to vote on all the eleven propositions separately and instruct their delegates to the 1894 Convention on each of the planks. (Minutes of the A.F. of L. Executive Council, Jan. 13, 1894, AFL Corr.; American Federationist, Vol. I, March, 1894, p. 19.)

ship was definitely alarmed by the radical stand of the rank-and-file—so alarmed, in fact, that early in November, 1894, plans were laid to override the decision of the majority of the Federation members. P. J. McGuire, himself a former socialist, was the chief plotter in this conspiracy whose objective was the defeat of the entire "Political Programme." "More than ever," McGuire wrote to Chris Evans on November 3, "it is now important that the political questions which have been thrust on the Federation should be disposed of in such a way that the A. F. of L. may be perpetuated and strengthened and not destroyed." [33]

McGuire's plan, as outlined to Gompers, was, first, to challenge the right of the radical delegates to the 1894 Convention to be seated on the ground that the organizations they represented had "failed to fulfill their financial duties regularly to the A. F. of L." With these delegates out of the way, it would be possible for the Federation's leadership "to take a most decided and positive stand at the next Convention against the introduction of distracting political issues in the A. F. of L." Meanwhile, McGuire would work upon the delegates from the Brotherhood of Carpenters and Joiners to make sure that "they are not likely to be carried away by any sentimentalism." [34] Since the Carpenters and Joiners had instructed their delegates to vote for the entire "Political Programme," it is clear that McGuire was planning to persuade them to violate their instructions.

1894 CONVENTION

In response to an invitation from McGuire, a number of top A. F. of L. leaders met in Chicago during the first week of December and discussed the strategy to be employed to defeat the "Political Programme" at the forthcoming Convention to be held in Denver. Present at the conference was William C. Pomeroy, head of a racketeering clique in the Illinois State Federation of Labor and the Chicago Trades Assembly,*

---

* In three to four years, they stole over $100,000. Direct theft from the treasuries of unions was perpetrated by labeling such withdrawals as "lobbying" and "committee work." "The conditions here," wrote a trade unionist from Chicago in September, 1896, "is enough for one to lose heart in the labor movement. Personal aggrandizement seems to rule the day." (Eugene Staley, *History of the Illinois State Federation of Labor*, Chicago, 1930, pp. 87-88; Lee M. Hart to Gompers, Chicago, Sept. 25, 1896, *AFL Corr.*) For a time, Pomeroy was the leader of the clique. Pomeroy gained a notorious reputation for selling out strikes for a payment from employers. (John Mulholland to Gompers, Oct. 22, 1900, *AFL Corr.*) Another leader of the clique was Edward M. Carroll, president of the Building Trades Council of Chicago, who had a record of six arrests for larceny, assault and battery, and drunkenness. (Chicago *Times-Herald*, April 25, 1900.)

who had already gained notoriety in labor circles because of his corrupt leadership and the unscrupulous methods he used in fighting the Socialists in the mid-West. It was decided at the conference to abandon the plan to challenge the right of radical delegates to be seated—probably because too many of the affiliated unions were behind in their payments to the Federation due to the widespread unemployment of their members—and to rely instead upon persuading delegates to ignore their instructions and vote to defeat Plank 10. Following the conference, McGuire let it be known privately that "Plank 10 will be defeated." [35]

Thus it was that even though the vast majority of the affiliated unions had ratified the "Political Programme," including Plank 10, the A. F. of L. leadership, determined to do "anything to beat socialism" and keep the Federation on a conservative path, set about to defy the will of the rank-and-file.

Discussion of the "Political Programme" was made the special order of the morning session of the fourth day at Denver. The convention refused to consider the program as a whole but voted on it piece by piece. The first casualty was the preamble which praised the action of the British trade unionists in adopting the principle of independent political action. The attack was led by Adolph Strasser, a former Socialist, whose union, the Cigar Makers, had endorsed the entire "Political Programme," including Plank 10, by a four-fifths majority and had instructed its delegates to the convention to take a similar stand.[36] Thomas J. Morgan led the defense, but Gompers used his power as chairman autocratically to crush the opposition. (When it was objected that the preamble was part of the program and could not be taken out, Gompers overruled the objection.) The vote revealed that the A. F. of L. leaders had been successful in persuading many of the delegates who had come instructed to accept the "Political Programme" to ignore their instructions. By a vote of 1,345 to 861, the Convention struck out the preamble.

When the discussion reached Plank 10, Strasser moved to amend the proposition so as to read: "The collective ownership by the people of all means of production and distribution without confiscation and with compensation." The discussion went on, other amendments were proposed, discussed, voted down. Finally, on the afternoon of the fifth day, the following substitute proposed by Delegate McGraith of the International Typographical Union was adopted: "The abolition of the monopoly system of land holding and the substitution therefor of a title of occupancy and use only." This was carried by a vote of 1,217 to 913.[37] Here, as in the vote on the preamble, delegates whose unions had instructed them to vote for the entire "Political Programme," particularly those from the painters, miners, iron and steel workers, tailors, and lasters, cast their ballots for the substitute.[38]

Each of the other ten planks in the "Political Programme" was voted upon, and none was materially changed, except that a declaration in favor of the repeal of the conspiracy law was added. But a motion to endorse the amended platform as a whole was voted down, 735 to 1,173. It was not made clear at the convention whether the amended "Political Programme" had been adopted, when each plank in turn had been approved. Later, the proponents of the Programme claimed that the Convention had adopted it in amended form, but the opponents construed the Convention's action as a rejection of the entire Programme. In any event, the Socialists complained bitterly that the heart had been taken out of the Programme by the elimination of all reference to independent political action and by the emasculation of Plank 10.

The strategy of the A. F. of L. leadership to defeat the will of the Federation's membership emerges clearly from the debate. Since the preamble had been declared not part of the "Political Programme," the delegates who had come from unions which had endorsed the program felt free to vote it down. When the Programme itself came up, it was claimed that it had been mutilated and therefore these delegates could reject it since they had been instructed to vote for it as it was. Still others simply claimed that they were free to vote it down on the ground that their constituencies did not fully understand it.[39]

The plot engineered by Gompers, McGuire, and other Federation leaders to defeat the "Political Programme," particularly Plank 10, made a mockery of the A. F. of L. President's repeated assurances that the organization he headed was one which insisted on "giving every shade of thought, opinion, and expression full play, where every member or union enjoys the utmost freedom of expression, whether of the most radical or conservative character. Through this liberty of thought, expression, and action we expect to maintain a strictly working class movement, and to extend to the fullest development, keeping pace, yes making the pace, which will evolve the freedom of labor from wage slavery."[40] These were fine words indeed, but the events at Denver indicated that the practice was a far cry from the principle. To be sure, the fullest freedom of expression was extended to the advocates of the "Political Programme," but the A. F. of L. leadership saw to it by undemocratic, bureaucratic procedure that the expression of the majority of the membership should not be translated into concrete action.

REACTION OF SOCIALISTS

Infuriated by the duplicity of the A. F. of L. leadership, the Socialists struck back by joining with other delegates who resented Gompers' high-handed tactics, and helped to defeat him for re-election. John McBride of the Mine Workers was elected to replace Gompers as president of the A. F. of L.

Shortly after the Denver Convention, President McBride urged the Socialists in the A. F. of L. to forget the defeat of Plank 10 and other changes in the "Political Programme," and to join hands with non-Socialist trade unionists to build a more powerful Federation.[41] It was important advice, but, unfortunately, too many Socialists were unwilling to accept it. Thomas J. Morgan emphatically rejected the suggestion; under no circumstances would he consider an alliance with conservative elements in the A. F. of L. who had been responsible for defeating Plank 10 and emasculating the entire "Political Programme":

"I would not play the part of a Gompers or a McGuire for all the world, he wrote to McBride. "Nothing can be greater treason than to lull the worker to sleep with the old trade union melody.

"My dollar and cents interests prompt me to be diplomatic, to talk of harmony between Capitalists & Laborers, etc., etc. No I shall still talk war, that there is not and cannot be peace, and that the old must give way to the new even in the labor movement. That the revolution comes nearer every year, and that our best efforts will fail to fully prepare us to meet it. . . . The old world is up and doing, why not us. They will not let even a Burns fool them,* why should we, John?"[42]

Although Morgan rejected McBride's appeal, he, at least, did not believe that the events at Denver had conclusively demonstrated that it was useless for the Socialists to continue to fight for their program inside the A. F. of L. Other Socialists, however, drew this conclusion, and, as early as March, 1895, began an exodus from the Federation. On March 5, 1895, Charles Rawhone, who occupied the strategic post of A. F. of L. general organizer for New England, handed in his resignation.

"Permit me to say," he wrote to President McBride, "that I cannot continue the office of organizer from this date for the following reasons. I am a Socialist and have been one for a number of years. I thought the time would come when the A. F. of L. would take independent political action but I was doomed to disappointment. The defeat of plank ten was a great disappointment to me in view of the disasters and defeats the Trades Unions have met with from their strong opponents the Capitalist Class. I am fully convinced that there is only one way to emancipate the toiling millions of [the] earth is through the collective ownership by the people of all means of production and distribution and the Co-opera-

* Morgan was referring to Burns' developing conservatism after the dock strike of 1889 of which he was one of the chief leaders. Engels observed this tendency as early as December 7, 1889, writing to F. A. Sorge: "I am not at all sure . . . that John Burns is not secretly prouder of his popularity with Cardinal Manning, the Lord Mayor and the bourgeoisie in general than of his popularity with his own class." (*Letters to Americans*, pp. 220-22.)

tive Commonwealth and in view of the fact that the A. F. of L. is to continue on trade union lines is my reason for resigning my position as organizer. Please discontinue sending the *American Federationist* to my address. It is not the kind of reading I want on the labor question." [43]

The very fact that a majority of the Federation membership had supported the entire "Political Programme," including Plank 10, should have convinced the Socialists that they should intensify their efforts among the rank-and-file, exposing the betrayal of the membership by the A. F. of L. leadership. Instead, as the above letter by the Socialist organizer for the A. F. of L. makes abundantly clear, many abandoned the rank-and-file, and surrendered them completely into the hands of the conservative leadership.

With Socialists voluntarily relinquishing important positions in the A. F. of L. and resigning in disgust from the organization, it is scarcely surprising that the conservative forces were in complete control at the 1895 Convention. The Socialists, outnumbered three to one, could do nothing to stem the tide in favor of Gompers' election as President. Instead of adopting a resolution urging the unions to organize an independent labor party, as proposed by the Socialist delegates, the convention by a vote of 1,460 to 158, passed a resolution which acknowledged that "it is clearly the duty of union workingmen to use their franchise so as to protect and advance the class interests of the men and women of labor and their children," and recommended "to the workers more independent voting outside of party lines." [44] The adopted resolution was little more than a gesture.

DE LEON AND THE K. OF L.

De Leon greeted the reports of the A. F. of L. Convention as conclusive proof of the bankruptcy of the policy advocated by the Socialists who had remained in the Federation. Not only had the Socialists failed to capture the Federation, but with each passing year, the A. F. of L. was proving itself an organization that was not even worth controlling. What point was there for Socialists to remain any longer in an organization that was "fossilized, useless and out of date," led by "labor fakirs, doing picket duty for Capitalism," an organization made up of craft unions which, as a whole, were little more than a "conspiracy of the capitalists and conservative labor leaders against the working class." With increased vigor, De Leon ordered all Socialists "to abandon the American Federation of Labor to the sure death which awaited it under the command of the labor fakirs." [45]

While the Socialists in the A. F. of L. had been attempting to obtain the adoption of their program, De Leon had been seeking to gain control of the K. of L. In 1893, due to the combined efforts of the Jewish unions and other Socialist-led unions in District Assembly 49, he was elected as a delegate to the national convention. There he led the Socialist forces into an alliance with Sovereign, and, together with other elements, they ousted Powderly from his 14-year leadership of the Order. Sovereign was elected Grand Master Workman in his place.[46]

At the New York State Convention of the S.L.P., held at Syracuse in June, 1894, De Leon predicted that it was only a matter of a short time before the Socialists would take over the leadership of the K. of L. His followers echoed his refrain. "The Knights of Labor are getting into line with the Socialists," one delegate announced joyfully, "and are openly expressing sympathy for our principles." [47]

There seemed to be grounds for the Socialist rejoicing. Sovereign was extremely anxious to obtain De Leon's support at the 1894 K. of L. Assembly. This support was crucial, for with Powderly's friends trying to restore him to power and with the Powderly-Sovereign forces evenly divided, the block of eight socialist delegates, led by De Leon, held the balance of power. De Leon agreed to support Sovereign for Grand Master Workman on condition that he would appoint Lucien Sanial editor of the *Journal of the Knights of Labor*.

When Sovereign was elected, De Leon was jubilant. In his presidential report to the General Assembly, Sovereign had called for the abolition of the "wage system" and the establishment of a "co-operative industrial system." With Sanial as editor of the Knights' official journal, the Order, with full Socialist support, could begin to take the necessary steps to emancipate the American people from the "yoke of capitalism." [48]

It was all wishful thinking. The Sovereign-De Leon alliance did not last long. The victorious Grand Master Workman disregarded his political bargain, and refused to reward the Socialists by appointing Sanial editor of the *Journal*. He was willing, he wrote to De Leon in January, 1895, to do something about giving "brother Sanial a position on the Journal" even though the financial difficulties of the Order made it hard to add new personnel. But he said nothing of the editorship. In a blistering reply, De Leon told Sovereign off: "In asking that Bro. Sanial be made the editor of the Journal, our purpose was not to give him a job but to have him turn the Journal into what it should be, & what it has not been, especially during the last year, to wit, a source of instruction to its readers."

When Sovereign refused to budge, De Leon declared war. *The People* now featured editorials excoriating the Knights' leadership as vigorously as it did the A. F. of L. leadership. The officers of the K. of L., De Leon charged, had "degenerated into a band of brigands no better than those of Powderly's old regime." He was confident, however, that they would not remain leaders long, for they were now in "desperate straits," and "ripe to be kicked out." [49]

The final break came at the 1895 General Assembly. By a narrow vote, the convention, controlled by Sovereign and his machine, denied the validity of the credentials held by De Leon and other representatives of D.A. 49, and refused to seat the Socialists.* In December, 1895, a month after the General Assembly, De Leon and his followers were expelled from the Order.[50]

The expulsion order was an academic gesture. Even before it had been announced, De Leon ordered the Socialists to break with the Knights and called upon "all self-respecting members of the Order to do the same." The whole organization was "rotten to the core," and had been reduced to "a nest of crooks," who had "prostituted it to their own base ends." The Socialist-led unions accordingly withdrew their 13,000 members from the Knights, and "left the remaining seventeen thousand to find their own way to oblivion."

Both the A. F. of L. and the K. of L. were now, in De Leon's eyes, "corrupt and decadent." Both were asking for mere crumbs for labor rather than working for an entire change in the industrial system. Both had "fallen hopelessly into the hands of dishonest and ignorant leaders." [51]

SOCIALIST TRADES AND LABOR ALLIANCE

Having already taken the disastrous step of persauding the small minority of Socialist-minded unions to secede from the A. F. of L. and the K. of L., De Leon now compounded the tragedy by embarking on a policy of dual unionism. On December 8, 1895, a call, signed by District Assembly 49, was issued urging "all K. of L. Assemblies and all progressive organizations to join with us in establishing a national body, on the natural class lines of the lines of the labor movement, the lines plainly marked out by the class struggle, in a word, the lines of International Socialism." Then on December 15, 1895, *The People* carried the news that at a joint conference of representatives from D.A. 49 of the K. of L., the Central Labor Federation of New York, the Central Labor Federation of Newark, and the United Hebrew Trades, the rough outlines had been drawn up for the establishment of a "national body that, on the economic field, shall stand toward the corruptionists of the fake K. of L., on the one hand, and the played out scare crow of the A. F. of L. on

* As early as the summer of 1894, some Knights had protested the validity of De Leon's membership in the Order, contending that he was a lawyer and that under the constitution "no lawyer can be admitted to the Order." (New York *Herald*, July 29, 1894.)

the other, in the same uncompromising attitude as the S.L.P. stands on the political field towards all the parties of capital—and the name proposed is the Socialist Trade and Labor Alliance." The new organization would be based on the principle that "the political and the economic movement must go hand in hand," and it had been brought into being because the experience of the past few years had proved that it was impossible to advance this principle in the existing labor movement. "Every endeavor to carry this principle into the old national organizations has failed and all future ones are bound to fail. By the light of this experience, the proletariat of the East has taken courage and set up a national organization that corresponds with the needs of our time—the Socialist Trades and Labor Alliance." [52]

The formation of the Socialist Trades and Labor Alliance struck consternation in the ranks of many Socialists who still advocated the principle of continuing to work inside the A. F. of L. They were infuriated by the fact that De Leon had staged the formation of the new organization with the aid of his few special lieutenants, but without the knowledge or consent of the Socialist membership. Moreover, they viewed with alarm the "unsocialistic" actions of De Leon and his associates in issuing appeals to workers in the national unions affiliated with the A. F. of L. urging them to withdraw their organizations from the Federation and bring them into the Alliance. [53]

Throughout the West many Socialists papers condemned both the formation of the S.T. & L.A. and its attempts to disrupt the existing unions. The *Brauer Zeitung,* official organ of the Socialist-controlled National Union of the United Brewery Workmen, *The Printer,* official journal of the Socialist-controlled German Printers' Union, and a number of other trade union journals, edited by Socialists, bitterly denounced the S.T. & L.A. The National Executive Board of the Brewery Workers' Union condemned the formation and actions of the Alliance "as a disgraceful treachery against the holy cause of Labor and the fundamental principles of Socialism." [54]

The Socialists who remained in the A. F. of L. looked forward eagerly to the forthcoming 1896 S.L.P. Convention in the hope "that the socialists throughout the country will rise and stop the wrongs committed in New York under the name of Socialism by a number of unscrupulous people." Some of the A. F. of L. leaders shared this hope; writing in February, 1896, McGuire reported that opposition to De Leon's policies was making itself felt in Socialist circles all over the country, and he predicted "that the next convention of the S.L.P. will be full of music for the New York gang." Gompers was less optimistic. He felt sure that the S.L.P. convention would be dominated by De Leon and the Alliance. [55]

Gompers proved to be correct. De Leon and his lieutenants were fully aware of the rising tide of resentment in the party over the formation of the S.T. & L.A. Hence when the Convention met in July, 1896, they cleverly concealed the real dual union purposes of the Alliance and presented it to the delegates "as a revolutionary union whose main purpose was to organize the unorganized." * Then De Leon introduced the resolution which endorsed the Alliance and called upon the Socialists of the land "to carry the revolutionary spirit of the S.T. & L.A. into all the organizations of workers. . . ." The resolution was endorsed 71 to 6 after which the National Executive Committee urged Socialists who had not thus far supported the Alliance to change their "faint and non-committal attitude," and recommended to all sections of the party to affiliate with the organization.[56]

A bitter dispute arose immediately as to the meaning of the endorsement. Although De Leon had assured the delegates that the Alliance would confine itself to organizing the unorganized, he and his followers insisted after the convention that endorsement was given with the "clear understanding . . . that it meant a declaration of war against the 'pure and simple' trade unions of the land, typified by the American Federation of Labor." Hence all Socialists who refused to support the Alliance, and especially all those who continued to work within the A. F. of L., were defying the will of the 1896 Convention and were traitors to the cause.[57]

The advocates of "boring from within" challenged De Leon's interpretation. They insisted that the 1896 Convention would never have endorsed the Alliance if it had been understood that it would seek to destroy the A. F. of L. and other craft unions. They asserted emphatically that the endorsement had been obtained "on the express promise given by its founders that it would not interfere with the existing trade unions, but would devote itself to organizing the unorganized."[58]

While the interpretation of the meaning of the endorsement was raging in the ranks of the S.L.P., the Alliance was issuing charters and recruiting membership from unions affiliated with the A. F. of L. It began and ended as a dual union.

The total result of De Leonist socialism, for all its sharp and unrelenting criticism of the rising labor bureaucracy, was the isolation of militant workers from the main body of organized labor, thereby strengthening the hold of the conservatives. The continuing rank-and-file pressure against bureaucracy and class collaboration was deprived of

* De Leon even went so far in his attempt to hide the true purposes of the Alliance from the delegates as to offer no objection to the passage of a resolution urging all Socialists "to join the organizations of the trades to which they respectively belong." (*Proceedings of the Ninth Annual Convention of the Socialist Labor Party, July 4, 1896*, pp. 28-29.)

its actual and potential leaders precisely at a time when it was possible for the Socialists to supply such leadership. The men who should have been organizing internal opposition to conservative leaders and their policies on the basis of the day-to-day issues related to the needs of union members, and who should have been demonstrating the connection between the economic and political struggles of the working class and the connection between the battles for immediate gains and the ultimate emancipation of labor, were busy passing revolutionary-sounding resolutions at gatherings attended only by those who were already full-fledged Socialists. Meanwhile, the conservative labor leaders, no longer forced to face effective opposition, hastened their march down the path of class collaboration.

All in all, as Fred E. Martin pointed out in resigning his office as member of the National Executive Committee and his membership in the New York Section of the Socialist Labor Party, De Leon's policies had "hopelessly estranged the hundreds of thousands of organized American workingmen, whose close relations with machinery, the greatest modern factor of production, make these bodies [the trade unions] logically, the most prolific field in this country for the propagation of the truths of Socialism." [59]

[Since this chapter was published a number of works have appeared which attempt to present a revisionist view of Daniel De Leon and assert that his positive contributions to the Socialist and Labor movements outweighed any negative factors. None of these works in the present writer's judgement are truly convincing and do not persuade me to change the presentation above set forth. But the reader can judge for himself by consulting the following: Carl Reeve, *The Life and Times of Daniel De Leon,* (New York, 1972), an uncritical biography which rarely proves its assertions; L. Glen Seretan, "The Personal Style and Political Methods of Daniel De Leon," *Labor History,* vol. XIV, Spring, 1973, pp. 163-201, which tends to view the opposition to De Leon's policies as primarily a matter of differences in personality and methodology, and Paul Buhle in John M. Laslett and Seymour Martin Lipset, editors, *Failure of a Dream: Essays in the History of American Socialism,* (New York, 1974), pp. 635-45 which views De Leon's contributions as primarily positive ones.

My evaluation of the negative effect of De Leon's influence on the labor movement has been criticized by John Laslett in his *Labor and the Left: A Study of Socialism and Radical Influences in the American Labor Movement, 1881-1924,* (New York, 1970). For my response, *see* my piece in Laslett and Lipset, *op. cit.,* pp. 233-43.

Insufficient attention was paid in my discussion of De Leon to his contributions on the Negro question, but this is developed in my work, *Black Protest and American Socialism,* (New York, 1975), vol. II.]

CHAPTER 20

Labor and Early Populism

Come join the Alliance to battle we go;
Labor united we'll conquer the foe! [1]

So went a Farmers' Alliance song appealing to organized labor to unite with the farmers against the common enemy, the monopolists.*

THE K. OF L. AND THE FARMERS' ALLIANCE

The response from the declining K. of L. was immediate and enthusiastic. In the local campaigns of 1890, the Farmers' Alliance and the K. of L. united to launch reform tickets. Labor demands, such as enforcements of laws establishing the eight-hour day, opposition to the use of Pinkertons in labor disputes and to the use of convict labor, were incorporated into the platforms, and labor representatives were nominated for office.[2] Outstanding successes were recorded in Nebraska, Kansas, and Colorado, and in the last-named state, the movement boasted that all of the elected officers were members of the K. of L.[3]

K. of L. delegates were present at the convention of farmer and labor representatives which met at Cincinnati in May, 1891, to launch the People's Party (56 of the 1,400 delegates represented the Order). These delegates exerted some influence in the shaping of the new party's platform. In addition to the traditional demands for free coinage of silver,

---

* The Farmers' Alliance movement arose out of the discontent of the farmers over steadily declining prices for farm products, high prices for everything the farmers had to buy in a highly monopolized market, excessive railroad rates, usurious interest rates on loans and mortgages, loss of farms through foreclosures of mortgages, and a rapid increase in farm tenancy. An official estimate in 1891 placed the total membership of the three Farmers' Alliances—the National Farmers' and Industrial Union, or Southern Alliance, the National Farmers' Alliance, or Northern Alliance, and the Colored Farmers' National Alliance and Cooperative Union—at three million members.

abolition of national banks, and regulation of railroads, the planks included demands for a graduated income tax, direct election of President, Vice-President and Senators, universal suffrage, and an eight-hour day.[4]

The platform adopted at Cincinnati by the People's Party was reaffirmed at a convention in St. Louis in February, 1892.* Nearly two-thirds of the 860 delegates at the St. Louis convention were representatives of farmers' organizations. Still, 29 percent of the delegates came from labor organizations: the K. of L. with 82 delegates, and from the A. F. of L., the International Association of Machinists, the Paper Hangers' National Union, the International Wireworkers' Union, the United Mine Workers, as well as delegates from the central labor bodies of St. Louis and Springfield, Missouri, Kansas City, Kansas, and Memphis, Tennessee.[5]

FARMER-LABOR UNITY ON THE ECONOMIC FRONT

Simultaneously with the developing unity between farmers and workers on the political front came examples of such unity on the economic front.† The November 1, 1890, issue of the *National Reformer* carried an appeal from the Gambrinius Assembly 7503, K. of L., urging all Alliance officers and members to boycott the beer of the Anheuser-Busch and Wm. J. Lemp Brewing Associations, two brewery firms guilty of denying their workers the right to organize and of blacklisting those "who they suspect of having joined a labor organization." Fifty thousand copies of the Alliance's official organ were specially printed and sent to 22,000 different local farmers' organizations. The Secretary of the K. of L. Assembly acknowledged that it was largely due to the Farmers' Alliance

* Prefixed to the platform drawn up at St. Louis was a militant preamble, the work of Ignatius Donelly, which presented a powerful appeal to the working class: "The urban workmen are denied the right of organization for self-protection; imported pauperized labor beats down their wages; a hireling army, unrecognized by our laws, is established to shoot them down, and they are rapidly degenerating to European conditions. The fruits of the toil of millions are boldly stolen to build up colossal fortunes, unprecedented in the history of the world, while their possessors despise the republic and endanger liberty." (Cleveland *Citizen*, Feb. 27, 1892.)

† Such unity emerged frequently during the 1880's. An outstanding example occurred during the second Gould strike in 1886. A K. of L. striker who had visited the Farmers' Alliance in Forth Worth, Texas, to obtain assistance reported: "They fully recognize that the fight of the K. of L. against Jay Gould was also their fight, and that it was suffering humanity's fight against monopoly oppression. Support was promised by every Alliance member who was spoken to, and our Relief Committee has begun to receive contributions of money and provisions." (Ruth A. Allen, *The Great Southwest Strike*, Austin, Texas, 1942, pp. 129-30; *John Swinton's Paper*, May 13, 1886.)

support of the boycott that the union had "succeeded in reducing their [the brewer bosses] sale of beer to a great extent," and had forced the breweries to withdraw their blacklists.

In Arkansas a campaign against convict contract labor was initiated in 1891 by the Farmers' Alliance. In Kansas the Alliance demanded that members should purchase only goods with a union label. In Indiana, South Dakota, and other states, the Alliances denounced "Pinkertonism." In the state of Washington, the Alliance helped the locked-out miners of the Oregon Improvement Company and condemned the use of scab labor and Pinkerton thugs. The national Alliance officially declared its support of a number of important labor boycotts.[6]

The spring and summer of 1892 were marked by even more numerous examples of such support for labor's struggles. The Farmers' Alliance in New York endorsed labor's boycott of the Rochester open-shop clothing firms. The People's Party in Michigan declared that it endorsed all K. of L. and A. F. of L. labels, and urged the adoption of an eight-hour day in all factories, mines, and shops.[7] In Congress, Thomas E. Watson, Populist leader in Georgia, spearheaded a drive to have the Pinkerton Detective Agency investigated and regulated by the federal government. He appealed to labor leaders to support his move by furnishing him with facts about its vicious work, and with this information, Watson was able to force Congress to agree to investigate the Pinkerton Agency.[8]

Especially impressive was the action of the Populists in support of the Homestead strikers of 1892. "The supporters of the People's Party in Kansas are warm and earnest in their sympathy for the Homestead workers," a K. of L. organizer wrote to Powderly from Eureka, Kansas. The shipment of two carloads of flour by the Nebraska Alliance to the strikers received wide publicity and "did much to unite the mechanic and agricultural classes." Populist rallies all over the country adopted resolutions extending "to organized labor at Homestead our heartfelt sympathy in its present struggle."

These pro-labor activities of the Populists made a deep impression in working class circles. Many who had previously argued that labor could gain nothing from the agrarian revolt began now to shift their position. Labor journals which had formerly been indifferent or hostile to the People's Party now declared that the "serious revolt of the farmers" appeared to bode well for "a speedy union of the workers' forces alike in factory and farm, city and village." [9] *

Events in the spring and summer of 1892 showed that labor support

* After the Homestead strike, the *Labor Leader,* organ of the Central Labor Union of Lancaster, changed its tone of hostility towards the People's Party and began to boom the Populist movement. (Reprinted in Cleveland *Citizen,* July 23, Aug. 13, Oct. 8, 1892.)

of the People's Party was not strictly limited to the declining K. of L. Under the leadership of the Cleveland Central Labor Union, People's Party clubs were set up throughout the city by the early summer. Populist clubs were also set up in Toledo, Columbus, and Zanesville, Ohio, and the printers at Cleveland and Akron, usually indifferent to political action, endorsed the People's Party. Following a conference of 81 trade unions at San Francisco in the early summer of 1892, the Populists were able to organize a network of party clubs. Similar clubs were set up by trade unions at Los Angeles and Sacramento.[10]

The *Northwestern Labor Union*, official organ of the Minneapolis Trades Assembly, came out strongly for the People's Party. At Tacoma, Washington, the Trades Council called for complete support for the new party. The Federated Trades Council of San Francisco, the central labor body of the A. F. of L. unions, endorsed the People's Party as did the A. F. of L. central labor body of Sacramento. The Denver Central Labor Union also endorsed the new party. The fact that the usually non-political typographical and machinists' unions, as well as the miners' organizations, which favored free silver, had taken the lead in booming the People's Party, was considered highly significant.

In the spring of 1892, some 300 delegates from farmers' and labor organizations met at Lansing and organized a state People's Party for Michigan. In the early summer, in accordance with resolutions adopted by trades and labor unions, K. of L. Assemblies and the German Arbeiter Bund, a conference of 50 labor organizations met at St. Louis and formed a state People's Party. With the inclusion of eight important labor planks in the platform, the Missouri Federation of Labor officially endorsed the party.[11]

THE S.L.P. AND PEOPLE'S PARTY

With such encouraging news pouring in from the labor front, the People's Party felt that it could count on fairly widespread labor support in the presidential campaign of 1892. The People's Party's convention at Omaha, Nebraska, on July 2, 1892, had adopted four resolutions directed towards gaining labor support,* and following the gathering the Populists issued an address warning that "labor organized and un-

* These resolutions condemned unrestricted immigration and denounced "the present ineffective laws against contract labor"; expressed sympathy with the efforts of organized labor to shorten the hours of labor and demanded "a rigid enforcement of the existing eight-hour law on government, and ask that a penalty clause be added to the said law"; characterized the maintenance of a "large standing army of mercenaries, known as the Pinkerton System, as a menace to our liberties," and demanded its abolition; and endorsed the boycott imposed upon the clothing manufacturers of Rochester by the K. of L.

organized, cannot resist the onslaughts of millions of dollars of capital working for the disintegration of organized labor." The People's Party, the address continued, "is in full sympathy with organized labor," hence workers were invited to vote for the Populist presidential candidate, James B. Weaver, and to support all other third party nominees, thereby insuring to "industrial workingmen as well as to agricultural laborers the full fruit of their labor without the necessity of strikes." [12]

The appeal left the leaders of the Socialist Labor Party and of the A. F. of L. cold.

From the birth of the People's Party, the S.L.P., dominated by Daniel De Leon, refused to see anything of value to labor in the new movement. De Leon argued that the farmer and the political expression of his discontent, the People's Party, was essentially reactionary. The farmer did not desire any change in the structure of society, even though, like the worker, he was "robbed" by the capitalist. The farmer's real aim was to maintain his bourgeois position, hence the worker, who had nothing to gain under capitalism, could gain nothing from an alliance with the agrarian reformers. Therefore, De Leon urged all local sections of the S.L.P. to have nothing to do with the "middle class corruption" of the Populist Party. Justifying the refusal of the S.L.P. to endorse the People's Party, De Leon declared: "Could the American Socialists, then, win the support of the rest of the American workingmen by supporting the Presidential candidate of the People's Party? No. Any other reply would be an insult to the intelligence and honesty of American labor." [13]

The issue raised by De Leon was not a simple one. Engels, for example, expressed the opinion at this time that the small farmers, business men, and professional people of the United States were incapable by themselves of organizing a third party because they consisted of elements that changed too rapidly, and because they were easy marks for politicians who used their discontent "to sell them out to one of the big parties afterwards." Nevertheless, Engels' approach was a far cry from the sectarian position De Leon adopted by labelling the whole Populist movement as representing only "middle class corruption." Much closer to Engels' position was that of the Socialists who insisted that it was the duty of the radicals to work inside the Populist movement in order to shape a program that would be capable of redressing the grievances of the farmers, the workers, and the common people generally.

"By working with them [the Populists] to the extent I have," a member of the S.L.P. wrote to De Leon from Independence, Kansas, "and at the same time preaching the truth as I see it, I have, I think, converted most of the populists who were not already socialists, to the true faith, and lots of my old democratic friends besides. If I had commenced by denouncing the populist organization, nothing I could ever have said or done would ever have availed to convince the populists here that I was anything but a wolf in the fold, trying to divide them that I might aid the old parties in conquering them. To make the populists of this section true socialists by building on the foundation of socialistic teaching they had already received in the Alliance, was to promote the spread of socialism more than I could in any other way." [14]

De Leon dismissed these arguments in typically arrogant fashion, accusing the writers of being dupes of the bourgeoisie. To cooperate with a movement that was interested solely in immediate improvements was to endanger the approaching social revolution. "Not immediate but safe ultimate victory should be the aim of the social reformer," De Leon editorialized. "Nothing short of Socialism" must be the slogan. [15]

In spite of De Leon's injunction, several sections of the S.L.P. began to cooperate with the People's Party.* In the main, however, De Leon's stand helped to isolate many militant workers from the natural allies of the working class and to isolate the S.L.P. from the emerging mass movement to fight monopoly.

GOMPERS' POSITION

Although he would probably have shuddered if the fact had been pointed out to him, in reality Gompers' approach both to the Farmers' Alliance and Populist movements was one of deep hostility, rivaling in sectarianism, despite the soundness of some of his arguments, the approach of Daniel De Leon.

At the 1890 convention, the A. F. of L. adopted a resolution instructing the president to forward the organization's "good will" to the officers of the Farmers' Alliance. Gompers refused to carry out these instructions, maintaining that the trade unions and the "employing farmers" who made up the bulk of the farmers' movement had nothing in common, and that the Federation should devote itself to aiding the farm laborers to organize thus building an alliance with the workers on the farms rather than with those who were their employers.

Spokesmen for the farm laborers informed Gompers of efforts to organize unions and of the bitter opposition they had encountered from "prominent members of the Farmers Alliance." The leaders of the "Farm Hands Labor Union of Ohio" wrote to Gompers in the summer of 1892:

"Ever since our first meeting [two years ago] we have met with the stubborn and selfish opposition of the wealthy farmers and Alliance men throughout the county. We have borne every discouragement that could be heaped upon us.

* From 1891 to 1893 the S.L.P. took no official position towards the Populists. Individual sections were permitted to act as they saw fit.

"We have no means to push our organization, and after two years of persecution we have accomplished nothing. But we still believe we have the last link to organized labor and our faith has not been diminished in the least, in the Belief that we must prohibit, by organization, the supply of Farm Laborers, from taking the places of union men, in the mills, workshops, mines, etc.—whenever a strike, or lock-out occurs." [16]

Such letters convinced Gompers that "the opinion I have always held in reference to the Farmers Alliance and kindred organizations of Farmers, is more than verified." These men exploited their farm laborers as much "if not worse than the employers of labor in the Industrial centers. . . . They have antagonized every effort on the part of the Farm Laborers and Farm Hands to organize a union for their own protection," he wrote to John McBride, president of the United Mine Workers, "so much so even that where the Farmers' Alliance exists they hold their meetings in the school houses, and refused the use of the school rooms for the Farm Laborers Union. Whenever it is possible, they discharge and blacklist a man who is known to belong to the Union." [17]

A number of reports Gompers received from A. F. of L. organizers in key Populist states also deeply influenced his stand towards the movement. These emphasized that many Populist leaders were "endeavoring continually to discourage the trades-union movement by pointing to and commenting on its failures and declaring that the 'strike at the ballot box' is the only strike that will succeed. . . . These people seem to think that if a strike succeed[s] it decreases the necessity of their party and if one fails it makes it so much more necessary." [18]

Gompers agreed with this criticism. All discussions he had had on "the trade union and strike question with our populist friends," had convinced him that "they simply do not understand and are woefully ignorant upon the underlying principles, tactics and operations of the trade unions. The strikes that are won, the advantages that are gained every hour and minute of the day by the wage-workers and which are unnoticed and unheralded, escape the notice of the men who superficially examine into the laws of our present societary system." [19]

All of Gompers' detailed criticism of the Populist movement, quoted above, were set forth in private correspondence. Its gist was embodied, however, in an article in the *North American Review* for August, 1892, entitled, "Organized Labor in the Campaign." After pointing out that the Populist movement was composed of "*employing* farmers without any regard to the interests of the *employed* farmers of the country districts or the mechanics and laborers of the industrial centers," Gompers concluded that the People's Party could not be considered as a "Labor Party" or "even one in which the wage workers will find their haven." [20]

Gompers' article aroused widespread discussion in Populist, labor, and general reform circles. Populist papers replied sharply that the People's Party was not a trade union and that even in a strictly labor party there was room for non-working class elements; that the agrarian reformers had already demonstrated their interest in "the mechanics and laborers in the industrial centers" by the pro-labor stand they had taken in resolutions, party platforms and concrete action in strikes and boycotts, and that the active stand taken by the Southern Populists in behalf of Negro tenant farmers, sharecroppers, and farm laborers proved that the movement was not indifferent to the needs of the "employed farmer of the country districts." * Some Populist papers accused Gompers of raising spurious arguments against labor support of the People's Party in order to prevent the organized workers from taking any action on the political front.[21]

Evidently the Populist replies to Gompers' article expressed the sentiments of sections of the A. F. of L. membership. Several A. F. of L. organizers, while agreeing with some of Gompers' criticism of the Populist movement, expressed concern that his approach would antagonize local unions affiliated with the A. F. of L. who were cooperating with the Populists and Farmers' Alliance and thus enable the K. of L. to win their allegiance. E. H. Cherry, general organizer of the A. F. of L. in Michigan, reported in alarm that K. of L. members in Lansing who were also active in the Farmers' Alliance had made effective use of Gompers' article to get the Lansing Trades and Labor Council to return its charter to the Federation. "We will try to have the Lansing Council again become attached to the A. F. of L.," he assured Gompers. But he was not confident that this would be easy to accomplish as long as Gompers' maintained so deeply hostile an attitude towards the People's Party. W. A. Kolley, A. F. of L. organizer in Kentucky, reporting the serious effects of Gompers' article in his state, urged the A. F. of L. president to issue a statement assuring the Federation's membership that "even if you were against the action of the 3rd party . . . you would not do anything to antagonize their interests." [22]

Gompers was forced to admit that his stand on the Populist issue did

* "In their platforms," writes C. Van Woodward, "Southern Populists denounced lynch law and the convict-lease and called for the defense of Negro political rights." (Origins of the New South, Baton Rouge, La., 1951, p. 250.) The contributions of Southern Populism to the establishment of unity between the exploited Negro and white masses were especially evident in Georgia where Congressman Tom Watson, campaigning for the third party, and for his own reelection to Congress, built a remarkable alliance of the Negro people, the white farmers and the urban workmen. (See Tom Watson, "The Negro Question in the South," Arena, Vol. VI, October, 1902, pp. 540-50; C. Van Woodward, Tom Watson, Agrarian Rebel, New York, 1938, pp. 220-30.) In later years, however, Watson became a vicious foe of the rights of the Negro people.

not win universal support even in A. F. of L. circles. This is not surprising, for though there was agreement with many of the arguments Gompers advanced, there was, at the same time, a strong feeling that his total attitude towards the Populist movement was entirely too negative. For one thing, the issue involved was political cooperation with the farmers' movement, not economic alliance. There was nothing inherent in this political cooperation that ruled out A. F. of L. activity in the economic organization of farm workers. The Populists did not raise as a condition of cooperation that the A. F. of L. should abandon its work in helping the farm workers to organize and chartering their unions. Indeed, even though the Populists were fully aware that the A. F. of L. was engaged in such activity, they were eager for a political alliance with the Federation.[23] *

There was reason for criticism of the attitude of important elements in the Populist movement towards trade union activity in general and strikes in particular. Yet the enthusiastic support by the Populists of the Coeur d'Alene, Homestead, and other strikes, and their campaigns against the use of Pinkertons, convict and contract labor in breaking strikes revealed that there was widespread support in the movement for labor's struggles against industrial despotism, and that this was the main reason for the endorsement of Populism in local labor circles, including A. F. of L. circles.

A positive position which would have met with almost unanimous support in labor circles would have been one which, while pointing, as Gompers did, to serious shortcomings in the Populist movement from labor's standpoint, would have, at the same time, stressed the need for unity between farmers and workers against their common foe—monopoly capitalism—and would have called on labor to work for the adoption of a program that would truly reflect the needs of both classes.

Henry Demarest Lloyd, the noted reformer and friend of organized labor, informed Gompers that he had read his article in the *North American Review* "with great interest." He went on: "You put your finger on the same weak point in the People's Party movement that I have often commented upon. I was deeply offended by the failure of the St. Louis and Omaha conventions to say a word of any value for the workingmen's movement—nothing in favor of trades' unions or the Eight-Hour Day."†

Lloyd then proceeded to advance a position that went beyond Gompers' negative criticism of the Populist movement, emphasizing that it

---

* In September, 1892, the A.F. of L. chartered the Farm Laborers' Protective Union of Bellaire, Ohio.

† Lloyd must have been aware that the Omaha platform did advocate enforcement of existing eight-hour laws. What he probably was referring to was the failure to speak out for the eight-hour day in all industries.

was the duty of organized workers, who "today are far ahead of the farmers in their comprehension of our social and economic drift," to assume a leading role in the movement and guide it in the direction that it should move against monopoly capital. "It is of the highest importance to the workingmen that the farmers should be made their allies, and of equal importance to the farmers. It is precisely the same pressure which the farmers feel in low prices for produce and high prices for tools, etc. that makes the laborers wages low and living poor. Every great social change has been led by the artisans, but has been also fed by the farmers." [24]

ELECTION RESULTS

The total results of the election must have startled both old parties. Though Cleveland was elected, Weaver polled over a million votes and received 22 electoral votes. It was the first third party to break into the electoral college since the Civil War. In addition, the People's Party sent ten Representatives and five Senators to Congress.[25] It is clear that the new party had made a profound impression upon the voters.

A break-down of the election returns reveals that the Populist Party had its greatest support in western rural communities. But it also discloses that working people in the cities of the West were voting Populist. A study of the votes by counties in Kansas, Iowa, and Colorado reveals that the "city communities furnished a considerable share of the Populist vote," and in Minnesota the votes by counties proved that "the cities were going Populist at almost the same ratio as the farming districts." [26]

Nevertheless, only a sprinkling of votes were cast for Populist candidates east of the Mississippi River, where labors strength was concentrated. In five states of the East, the Populists polled slightly over 20,000 votes while the S.L.P. in these states polled 21,000 votes and the Prohibition Party polled over 83,000 votes. In the urban centers of Illinois the Populist vote was less than half of one percent of the total. In New York only some 16,000 votes were polled and in Pennsylvania only 8,000. In the entire city of Pittsburgh only 578 votes were cast for Weaver. Undoubtedly, the Democratic Party's attack on Frick and the Carnegie Steel Company and its support of the Homestead strikers cut seriously into the Populist vote in Pennsylvania. In general, there is little doubt but that the intensive Democratic campaign to win the labor vote cut into the Populist vote in the eastern urban areas.[27]

Nevertheless, the total vote cast for the Populists impressed labor leaders, and it is significant that Gompers sought to gain credit for the labor movement for the results achieved by the third party. Writing to the newly-elected Populist Governor of Kansas, Lorenzo D. Lewelling, Gompers boldly asserted. "Throughout the country wherever a fair opportunity was presented the trade unionists were a part of and cooperated with the 'People's Party.' I have no doubt that the gratifying results attained in the recent elections were largely attributed to them." [28]

FARMER-LABOR UNITY AFTER THE ELECTION

Within a month after the election, the A. F. of L. convention met at Philadelphia. The aging John Swinton, addressing the delegates, received an ovation when he declared: "It is time for the struggling work people of the Eastern cities to link arms with the advancing farmers of the resurgent West." [29] As its contribution to the movement for unity, the convention adopted two of the planks in the Populist platform—the initiative and referendum and government ownership of the telegraph and telephone systems—and instructed the Executive Council "to use their best endeavors to carry on a vigorous campaign of education . . . in order to widen the scope of usefulness of the trade union in the direction of political action." [30]

Reports of the proceedings at Philadelphia were featured and hailed in Populist journals, and produced an enthusiastic response from the leaders of the farmers' movement. Noting "with much interest and pleasure" the "proceedings of your late meeting in Philadelphia," Ben Terrell, national lecturer for the Farmers' Alliance and an editor of the *National Economist,* wrote to Gompers: "I am more convinced than ever from the way in which things are shaping themselves, that there is a great need that the farmers and laborers of the country should be a unit upon such political demands as we may see proper to make upon the country." [31] James B. Weaver, the Populist presidential candidate, visited the A. F. of L. national headquarters upon his return from a gathering of People's Party representatives from 20 states held in December, 1892, and informed Gompers that the delegates had voted to organize a subsidiary Industrial Legion which would concentrate on building closer cooperation with the trade unions, including the craft unionists. He spent two days discussing with Gompers "a number of matters in connection with the labor movement and the People's Party."

Gompers felt that much had been accomplished during the discussions. He had conveyed to Weaver the feeling of many labor leaders that the Populists were not sufficiently sympathetic to trade union activities, such as strikes, and were not sufficiently supporting labor's key demands. He had obtained from Weaver the assurance that the Populists would support the A. F. of L. in its organizational campaigns. "He fully concurred," Gompers wrote jubilantly, "with my view of organization for less hours being essential for every reform movement to uplift the toiling masses." [32]

CHAPTER 21

The Rise of Labor-Populism

"I believe that the present industrial depression will have the effect of turning the thoughts of the workingmen of America toward independent political action," Gompers predicted in a press interview shortly after the outbreak of the economic crisis.[1] It was an accurate prediction. Local branches of the Industrial Legion appeared everywhere. Individual unions endorsed political action by the hundreds. At mass rallies of the unemployed in Chicago, New York, Cleveland, Los Angeles, and San Francisco, great emphasis was placed on the need for political action. As the *Western Laborer* noted in September, 1893: "By laying off some men and curtailing the time of some others the employers are setting labor unions an example worthy of emulation. Now let the laboring men unite at the polls and lay off a few capitalists." [2]

FARMER-LABOR UNITY

As the sentiment for political action began to mature in labor circles, the Populists intensified their efforts to convince the workers that it was through the People's Party that this sentiment could best be expressed. The farmers' organizations hailed the news that the delegates to the 1893 A. F. of L. convention had approved by an overwhelming vote the famous "Political Programme" which endorsed the principle of independent political action.* In a letter to Gompers, the Farmers' Alliance in Nebraska urged the Federation to supplement the convention's decision by joining hands with the farmers in furthering the Populist cause: "That it is a matter of great pleasure to us and we accept it as a sign of encouragement that the American Federation of Labor . . . have resolved with such unanimity and enthusiasm to carry the matter of capital

* *See above*, pp. 287-89.

and labor to the ballot box and we openly declare as we have always declared that the farmer and mechanic and wage laborer have one and the same cause—one interest." [3]

Whatever form the discontent the workers assumed during the difficult crisis year, the Populists were quick to lend it their support. They characterized the "enforced idleness upon several millions of workingmen throughout our land" as "the direct and inevitable consequences of legislation in favor of monopolies;" they supported the demands of the unemployed for relief and public works; they denounced the disruption of unemployed demonstrations by the police, and they condemned "the unlawful practice of our officers of arresting workingmen whose only crime is poverty." [4]

It was the Populist Senators who introduced Coxey's bill into Congress, and advocated its passage, who protested most vehemently the arrests of the Coxeyites for "stepping on the grass" while at Washington, and introduced resolutions in Congress to that effect.[5] It was the Populist Governor of Colorado, David H. Waite, who aided the miners at Cripple Creek win their strike for the eight-hour day in the spring of 1894, and won the distinction among workers "of being the only governor in the United States who had ever called out the soldiers to protect the workers." [6] It was the Populist Governor of Kansas, Lorenzo D. Lewelling, who won the title "Champion of Labor" when he demanded during the Pullman strike that the railroad companies remove 60 strikebreakers from the state and send them back to their homes in Philadelphia.* It was the Populist Senators who voted against the resolution in the Senate commending President Cleveland for his action in using federal troops to smash the strike. In every state, the Populists endorsed the strike, denounced the railroad magnates as "Anarchists and Nihilists," and gave material aid to the strikers.[7]

Even the leaders of the A. F. of L.'s Farm Laborers' Protective Union reported that a remarkable change had taken place in the attitude of the farmers' movement towards the organization of farm workers—a change from hostility to support. "Our enemies a year ago," Alonzo Crouse, president of the union, wrote to Gompers in September, 1894, "are now among the warmest supporters and advocates of the rights of labor." [8]

In the years 1891 and 1892 many in the labor movement were still skeptical of the value of joining the Populists. But, as one student of the period has pointed out, "after the panic descended and the Pullman strike came to pass with its injunction, U.S. troops, and the imprisonment of strike leaders, labor changed its mind and joined the Populists." [9]

* "It was the R.R. Company and the Republican Party on one side and the Populist Party and organized labor on the other," was the way an A.F. of L. organizer summed up the strike in Kansas. (M. C. Whelan to Gompers, Argentine, Kansas, Oct. 12, 1894, *AFL Corr.*)

FREE SILVER

In at least one other important respect the crisis of 1893 had the effect
of bringing labor closer to the farmers' movement. Before the panic,
workers, apart from those directly engaged in the silver mining industry,* had not been greatly interested in the currency reform aspect
of the agrarian revolt.[10] To be sure, as early as 1890 the K. of L. had
gone on record in favor of free coinage of silver, and between 1890 and
1893, a number of state and city central labor organizations had done
likewise.[11] But, in the main, it was not until the panic descended that
the issue aroused much comment in labor circles. On September 2, 1893,
a few weeks after the crisis began, the Boston *Labor Leader* predicted
that "the silver issue is liable to do what has not before been accomplished—weld together the farmers of the West and the mechanics of the
East."

The way out of the crisis and mass unemployment was through the
free coinage of silver, declared the free silver advocates. Free silver,
Ignatius Donnelly cried, "means work for thousands who now tramp
the streets . . . not knowing where the next meal is coming from. It
means food and clothes for the thousands of ill-clad women and children.
It means the reopening of closed factories, the relighting of fires in darkened furnaces." [12]

Searching desperately for a solution to the pressing problem of unemployment, a large section of the working class fell prey to this propaganda. Mass meetings of the unemployed echoed the "free silver" cry,
and resolutions were adopted asserting that through the free coinage of
silver, the industries of the nation would be brought into immediate
activity.[13]

Just how many workers understood the long-winded economic analysis
of the currency reformers that began to appear in many of the labor
newspapers after the panic, it is difficult to determine. Very likely the
bulk of the workingmen did not concern themselves with the intricacies
of the problem.† The only thing that appeared to matter was that here

* These workers were not insignificant, however, for silver mining was one of
the most important industries in the United States. "Between 35-40,000 men
worked in the mines and at least twice this number were dependent on them,
for example, the laborers in the reduction works. . . ." (Philip F. Buckner, "Silver
Mining Interests in Silver Politics, 1876-1896," unpublished M.A. thesis, Columbia
University, 1954, p. 16.)

† The Cleveland *Citizen,* one of the staunchest supporters of free silver among
the labor papers, admitted as much. "Don't understand this 'money question' is
often heard nowadays. Most men knowing that hundreds of thousands of columns
have been written on the subject can hardly be blamed for showing a lack of
interest in the subject which is dry at best." (Sept. 2, 1893.)

seemed to be a plan which offered a speedy solution to the ills of a society in the throes of a depression. Nor did these workers appear to be impressed by the argument that inflation would only bring higher prices for the goods they purchased. Union spokesmen hammered at the theme that the slide in farm income was hurting city workers as well as the farmers. They gave the names and locations of companies which had laid off thousands of workers as a result of the farmers' widespread inability to buy farm equipment and other goods. Free silver, by increasing the farmers' purchasing power, would restore work to thousands of the unemployed. In short, jobs were more important to the workers than high prices for the goods they purchased, and since the free silver crusaders offered a simple program to assure full employment, it is hardly surprising that so many half-starved, unemployed workers should have joined their crusade.[14]

The Socialists decried the entire stress placed upon the silver issue. They pointed out that "whenever the currency is debased, prices rise but their [the workers'] wages do not rise in proportion to the amounts they have to pay for rent, food, clothing." [15] They argued that since free silver did not strike at the system of capitalist exploitation and could not end the control of the economy by the capitalist class, it was of little use to the workers. In fact, by fostering illusions that it would solve labor's problems, it was a real menace to the best interests of the working class. In an election *Manifesto to the Toiling Masses of America,* the Socialist Labor Party warned the workers to beware of the free silver panacea "through which aspirant capitalists, bankrupt speculators, indebted skinners of labor, and designing politicians would rise upon your shoulders to wealth and power, leaving you forever in wage-slavery." [16]

But these appeals to logic availed little in producing any change in the general attitude among workers, organized and unorganized, favoring free silver. The majority of organized labor enthusiastically supported the free coinage of silver. Delegates from the K. of L., the A. F. of L., and the Railroad Brotherhoods attended the convention in Chicago in August, 1893, sponsored by the American Bimetallic League, and voted in favor of free coinage of silver. In 1894, a circular entitled, "Demands of Organized Labor for the Free Coinage of Silver and the Restoration of the Money of the Constitution," was signed by the heads of the A. F. of L., the K. of L., the Carpenters' and Joiners' Union, the United Mine Workers, the Railroad Brotherhoods, the National Farmers' Alliance and Industrial Union, and the Farmers' Mutual Benefit Association. The circular called upon the members of organized labor and all other producers and toilers throughout the United States to adopt a resolution demanding that Congress immediately restore "the free and unlimited coinage of silver at the present ratio of 16 to 1. . . ." [17]

It is difficult to evaluate to what extent these leaders reflected the sentiments of the rank-and-file of their organizations. But the circular certainly demonstrated that on the issue of free silver, the leaders of the farmers' movement and the leaders of the labor movement were seeing eye-to-eye.

LABOR-POPULISM IN ILLINOIS

In September, 1893, the Wisconsin Labor Congress endorsed independent political action and the platform of the People's Party. As the depression deepened and neither of the major parties did anything to relieve the suffering of the people, this trend became nation-wide. Many labor leaders cast in their lot with the Populists, and, speaking of the K. of L., one organizer noted that "they are nearly all Populists." [18] By the summer of 1894, this characterization could be applied to nearly all of American labor. As one student of the People's Party writes: "Everything pointed to the almost universal conversion of labor to Populism." [19]

The consummation of a labor-Populist alliance in Illinois, the leading industrial and farming state in the Northwest, was the outstanding event in this emerging coalition of farmers and urban workers. Nowhere was the influence of organized labor in the alliance as clearly seen as in Illinois. Willis J. Abbott, a contemporary observer, pointed out: ". . . in all essentials the movement was a labor movement, having its first inception in a labor union, supported throughout by the effort of organized labor and drawing its principal support at the polls from the manual working class." [20]

The developments in Illinois were not unexpected. Here was a powerful organized labor movement, coordinated through the State Federation of Labor, that could be expected to exercise considerable influence in the political campaign. (In Chicago, alone, the voting strength of labor was estimated at 235,000.) Here, too, one of the after effects of the Pullman strike was a new militancy in the unions, and labor organizations, including those affiliated with the A. F. of L., were thoroughly embittered by the Republican and Democratic parties, and were ready for a real labor-Populist alliance. In Illinois, moreover, were a group of professional men, long sympathetic to both labor and the farmers, who understood that an effective labor-Populist alliance would build the foundation for a truly progressive national third-party movement. Clarence Darrow, Lyman Trumbull, and other prominent men were included in this group, but the most important was Henry Demarest Lloyd, the prominent publicist, champion and spokesman for organized labor, and author of an important work, *Wealth Against Commonwealth,* a 600-page carefully documented attack on the trusts, especially the Standard Oil Company.[21]

Lloyd had followed the rise of the People's Party with great interest, and had made a careful study of its composition and platform. In 1892, it will be recalled, he had agreed with Gompers and other labor leaders who had criticized the farmers' movement for its hostile attitude towards the organization of farm laborers and its lack of sympathy for trade union activities. Nevertheless, he had urged organized labor to build an alliance with the People's Party, and by working inside the movement, to influence its policies in a radical direction. After the election of 1892, Lloyd continued to advance this program, emphasizing the importance of building an alliance between labor and the poorer farmers, and "in that way the more conservative farmers would in time be won over to us. . . ."[22]

Lloyd also felt that the Socialists should enter the Populist movement and work towards building a labor-Populist alliance that would be based on the city workers and the poorer farmers. His plan was to make the trade unions and the Socialists a decisive influence in the labor-Populist alliance, and beginning on a local and state-wide basis, gradually build the alliance into a nationwide movement. In this movement there would be no room for red-baiting, for Lloyd had learned from the history of the independent political parties of the 'eighties that this resulted in tragedy for the progressive forces and only benefitted the major parties representing the capitalist class. Thus Lloyd wrote: "To shut them [the Socialists] out would be to repeat the blunder Henry George made at the State convention in Syracuse some years ago.* They were willing to cooperate with him, but to save himself from the odium of 'socialistic' affiliations he excluded them from the convention—and he has never been heard of since as a political force. . . . If we begin to read each other out of the ranks for difference of opinion we are lost."[23]

In the late spring and early summer of 1894, steps were taken in Illinois to achieve the type of labor-Populist alliance Lloyd envisaged. On May 28, the Populists met at Springfield together with representatives of the K. of L., the Illinois State Federation of Labor, the Socialist Labor Party, various local trade assemblies, and general reform groups. The conference adopted a platform urging a union of "urban industrialists and agriculturists in one harmonious political party." Such a union was recommended to the Populist state convention to be held on the following day, and to this gathering the conference recommended "the favorable consideration" of the A. F. of L.'s political program.[24]

A bitter conflict arose at the Populist state convention which was to rock the emerging labor-Populist alliance for months to come. The Socialists in Chicago, under the leadership of Thomas J. Morgan, had ignored the official stand of the S.L.P., and had accepted the invitation

* *See above*, pp. 148-53.

to attend the Populist gathering at Springfield.* Apart from the fact that Morgan was critical of De Leon's intransigeant, sectarian approach to the farmers' movement, a decisive factor in his determination to lead his followers into an alliance with the Populists was his conviction that the People's Party was an important avenue through which to agitate for "Plank 10" of the A. F. of L.'s political program which, it will be recalled, demanded "the collective ownership by the people of all means of production and distribution." Since agitation for "Plank 10," in Morgan's eyes, was essential to the propagation of socialism, he regarded it as the heart and soul of any movement for independent political action.[25]

In taking this stand, however, this highly-respected mid-West labor and Socialist leader did not seem to understand that important elements in the emerging labor-Populist alliance were not yet prepared to endorse and commit themselves to socialism, and that to insist that they should do so was to endanger the prospects of realizing such an alliance. Indeed, rather than endorse "Plank 10," the more conservative Populists in Illinois, led by Herman E. Taubeneck, chairman of the National Committee of the People's Party, and the conservative labor forces, led by the corrupt, racketeering William C. Pomeroy, were prepared to oust the Socialists from a labor-Populist alliance. At the Populist State Convention, Taubeneck told Morgan bluntly when the latter carried the fight for "Plank 10" to the convention floor after it had been struck out of the program by the resolutions committee: "If this is what you came to the people's party for, we don't want you. Go back from where you came with your socialism." [26]

The convention defeated "Plank 10" by a vote of 76 to 16. But it did adopt every other demand proposed by the labor delegates, placing special emphasis upon the demand for the adoption of a state constitutional amendment for the abolition of payment in truck and enforcement of "weekly pay"—a demand extremely important to organized labor. But Morgan does not seem to have been impressed by this action; the fact

* At its national convention in July, 1893, the S.L.P., for the first time, took an official stand on the question of the relation of the Socialists to the Populist movement. Under De Leon's prodding, it attacked the People's Party as one based on a "hybrid and transitory class" doomed to dispossession, and charged that the farmers and small traders were appealing to the wage workers in order to prevent their falling into the ranks of the proletariat. A resolution was adopted which asserted that "the wage working class cannot possibly support this movement," and a clause was added to the party's constitution which stated: "No section shall enter into any compromise with any other political party." (*The People,* July 24, 1893.) The National Executive Committee, having but very limited power, could not do much to enforce the constitutional provision. It did suspend the weak sections in Cleveland and Toledo for having violated the provision by working actively with the Populists, but when the powerful sections in Chicago, Milwaukee, and St. Louis did the same, it could do nothing.

that the Populist convention had rejected "Plank 10" was enough to convince him that it was a failure.[27]

Early in July, a conference was held at Springfield under the auspices of the Illinois State Federation of Labor to consider the A. F. of L. political program and to discuss measures necessary for "independent political action." "The repeated deception of the laboring people by the Republican and Democratic parties emphasizes the necessity for independent political action on the part of the producers," the Federation declared in calling the conference.[28]

The conference was practically disrupted by the conflict over "Plank 10." Although the platform submitted to the delegates by A. L. Maxwell, the Populist leader, was "the product of an earnest effort to conclude a working agreement between the different schools of radical thought represented at the conference," and included, in order to placate the Socialists, planks advocating government ownership of mines and municipal ownership of public utilities, it did not endorse "Plank 10." (Every other proposal of the A. F. of L.'s ten-point political program was endorsed.) Morgan, however, refused to be placated, and insisted, in a minority report, upon the inclusion of "Plank 10." A bitter debate ensued which resulted in twice adjourning the conference, and, finally, on a roll call, in a defeat of Morgan's minority report by the vote of 59 to 49.

Just when it seemed that the Socialists would bolt the gathering and the conference be disrupted, Henry D. Lloyd, in an hour-long speech, introduced a compromise program. It recommended independent political action by the organizations represented at the conference; urged their officials to take immediate steps to hold a national convention "to perfect plans for such political action," and to establish a political party espousing the principles of labor-Populism. Pending the organization of such a party, the representatives at the conference and the members of the organizations should vote at the forthcoming election "for those candidates of the People's Party who will pledge themselves to the principles of the collective ownership by the people of all such means of production and distribution as the people elect to operate for the commonwealth." Lloyd's resolutions were added to the majority report, and after their adoption the conference adjourned on a harmonious note.[29]

A labor-Populist alliance had now at last been consummated in a key industrial and farming state. Although it had not been easily achieved, the alliance was a tremendous step forward for the people's movement. It was based, moreover, on a platform far in advance of anything thus far achieved in the rise of Populism. The Springfield conference had endorsed nine of the ten planks of the political program of British labor and of the A. F. of L. 1893 convention: it was pledged to nationalization of the mines; municipal ownership of street railways, gas, and electric plants; employers' liability for occupational injuries and diseases; abolition of the sweating system; sanitary inspection of mines, factories, and homes; compulsory education, a legal eight-hour day, and confiscatory taxation of speculative land holdings. Furthermore, the conference had adopted a modified version of "Plank 10," which endorsed the extension of collective ownership of the means of production and distribution as far as the voting public should approve. While there was considerable difference between the Populists and the Socialists as to whether the People's Party in Illinois was now committed to socialism,* there was complete agreement among all groups that the Springfield conference had adopted a program that went far beyond the Omaha platform of 1892.

The Springfield platform was endorsed at a great ratification meeting in Chicago, on July 12, 1894, attended by 2,500 A. F. of L., A.R.U., K. of L., Socialist, Single-Tax and Populist delegates. The gathering also renounced allegiance to old parties, and, declaring itself for independent political action, pledged itself to make "a straight fight under the banner of the people's party." [30]

Despite frantic efforts of corrupt labor leaders and Democratic politicians who feared the loss of the labor vote to disrupt it, the labor-Populist alliance in Illinois pushed ahead to nominate a county ticket. On August 25, 1894, a convention was held at Chicago's Ulrich Hall which was attended by 313 delegates, the vast majority of whom were representatives of organized labor. The Springfield platform, including "Plank 10," was endorsed, and, apart from three important offices, the nominations of the county ticket went entirely to labor representatives. Louis W. Rogers, leader of the American Railway Union, was made county chairman. The objective of the labor-Populist alliance, Rogers declared, was to "turn upside down our whole industrial system," and the ticket nominated by the convention was pledged to accomplish this objective. Rogers, one of the A.R.U. leaders imprisoned during the Pullman strike, was nominated for Congress in Chicago's 6th District on the People's Party ticket under the slogan, "From prison to Congress." [31]

LABOR-POPULISM SPREADS

Illinois paved the way for labor-Populist alliances in other parts of the country. The State Federations of Labor of New York, Ohio, Indiana,

---

* Many Populists argued that the clause in Lloyd's compromise, "as the people elect to operate for the commonwealth," meant a popular mandate attained through the initiative and referendum. The Socialists denied this and claimed the compromise platform committed the party to socialism.

Minnesota, Massachusetts, Wisconsin, Nebraska, Montana, Texas, and California sponsored conferences attended by trade union and Populist delegates at which many of the principles of the Springfield platform were endorsed, including, in the case of Wisconsin and New York, "Plank 10." The conferences issued declarations of support of the People's party that were ratified, in turn, by the sponsoring federations of labor.[32]

City central labor bodies followed the lead of the State Federations of Labor and combined with the People's Party in Cleveland, Cincinnati, and Tifflin, Ohio; New Haven and Bridgeport, Connecticut; Jersey City, New Jersey; Saginaw, Michigan; New York City; Springfield and North Adams, Massachusetts; Omaha, Nebraska; St. Louis and Kansas City, Missouri; Dallas, Texas; Alemeda, California, and Butte, Montana.[33] Little wonder that William V. Allen, a Populist Senator, declared jubilantly: "I think I might say that we can reckon upon the organized workingmen." [34]

GOMPERS OPPOSES LABOR-POPULISM

The spread of the labor-Populist alliance caused discussion of establishing it firmly on a nationwide basis.[35] Late in July, Henry D. Lloyd made an attempt to get Samuel Gompers to take the initiative in extending the labor-Populist alliance to the entire nation. In telegrams and letters, Lloyd urged Gompers to call upon the Populist Governors to join with him in convoking a national, delegate convention which should unite trade unionists, Socialists, Single-Taxers, and Populists in a common front in the autumn state and congressional elections. "You have in your place at the head of the workingmen the key to the future," the midwestern reformer pleaded.[36]

Governor Waite of Colorado and Laurence Gronlund, Danish-born Socialist writer and editor, endorsed Lloyd's appeal and pleaded with Gompers to give it serious consideration. The labor-Populist alliance, Gronlund wrote, held out the only hope for a progressive America, for "only in a union of wage-workers and farmers can there be success and there never was so good an opportunity as now." [37]

Gompers did not even bother to answer the appeals. Nothing was further from Gompers' plans than to sponsor a convention to advance the alliance between organized labor and Populism. If anything, Gompers was determined to restrict and end this developing alliance which, as he saw it, was completely subordinating the trade unions to party politics. Letters from A. F. of L. organizers during the spring and summer of 1894 strengthened Gompers' determination to do nothing to advance labor-Populism, for they emphasized that many unions were so preoccupied with building the labor-Populist alliance that they had abandoned all other activities. Criticizing the Central Labor Union of Indianapolis, an A. F. of L. body that was working closely with the Populists, the organizer in the area wrote to Gompers: "For months the officers have neglected real labor interests to work for the Populist Party. The result is that unions which might have been saved have been permitted to droop and die without one effort on the part of the C.L.U. to succor them." [38]

There is no question that disheartened by lost strikes, not a few trade unionists were falling prey to the arguments of some of the Populist leaders who, somewhat like the Lassallean Socialists, emphasized that the strike was a useless weapon and urged that organized labor should abandon the economic struggles in favor of political action as the sole solution of the problems of the working class. The *Railway Times,* official organ of the American Railway Union, reflected this tendency when, in urging labor to turn to independent political action and unite with the Populists, it argued that "nineteen out of twenty strikes fail," that the Pullman struggle had "clearly demonstrated that the strike cannot protect labor from the robbing corporations, now solidly united," and that the ballot pointed the only way out for the workers. [39]

Gompers was correct in being concerned over the fact that there was a tendency among trade unionists who were active in building the labor-Populist alliance to practically dissolve their unions as working class organizations in the economic field. At the same time, he refused to see that independent political action and the economic struggles were inseparable parts of the fight against the employers. The only good Gompers saw in the labor-Populist alliance was that it would convince the trade unionists, through first-hand experience, that they had nothing to gain and everything to lose by becoming involved in the bitter rivalries of different factions associated with independent politicial action. In this way, he prophesized, the emergence of labor-Populism would prove "not an unmixed evil" since the disillusioned trade unionists would come to the A. F. of L. Denver Convention in December, determined, on the basis of their own experience, to "save the general movement" from further involvement in independent political action. [40]

ELECTION OF 1894

On September 24, 1894, Gompers circularized the entire A. F. of L. in an effort to obtain a list of all union men who had been nominated for public office in the autumn state and congressional elections, the union of which they were members, and the party which had nominated them. [41] Letters in response to the circulars came from A. F. of L. officials all over the country. Heretofore unpublished, they throw considerable light on the cordial relations between the trade unions and the Populists,* as well as on the extent to which Gompers' opposition to independent political action was ignored by trade unionists affiliated with the A. F. of L.† The following are typical:

"In answer to your letter of inquiry in regard to candidates on the several tickets affiliated with Labor Unions," wrote an A. F. of L. official in Kansas, "I find them all on one ticket namely the Populist. This alone should be conclusive evidence as to the standing of the two old parties in this State and county."

"The People's Party ticket for the State of Ohio is composed of Union men and Farmers' Alliance," an A. F. of L. organizer in the state reported. "The laboring men predominate in the People's Party here," wrote the Secretary of the San Diego [California] Federated Trades and Labor Council, "and we have very good prospect of electing four or five of the principal officers on our ticket." The Secretary of the Sacramento Federated Trades Council, listing four trade unionists nominated for office, added: "These candidates are all good union men, and are all running on the People's Party ticket."

"We are working hard here, for the success of the People's Party," an A. F. of L. official wrote from Belleville, Illinois. "The old Partys don't know what to think. They can not draw voters to their meetings, with music and free Beer, they are badly demoralized. If we don't defeat them in our National Strike on November 6th [election day] we will have the satisfaction of knowing that we had them awfully frightened." [42]

So the story went as the reports poured in from the A. F. of L. officials. Even before all the reports were in, the *American Federationist* published a partial list of 300 union men who had been nominated for public office, and concluded that even this incomplete list was "a sufficient indication that the trade unionists are actively participating in the political campaign in their own interests." Although the journal failed to indicate the parties which had nominated the unionists, the correspondence on which the list was based reveals that the vast majority ran on the People's Party ticket. When to this is added the number of candidates nominated by the People's Party who, though not members of trade

* Of the hundreds of letters received by Gompers in answer to his circular, only one was critical of the People's Party. This came from William P. Daniels, Grand Secretary and Treasurer of the Order of Railway Conductors, who had been nominated for Congress by the Democratic Party in Iowa. (W. P. Daniels to Gompers, Sept. 28, 1894, *AFL Corr. See also* Cedar Rapids (Iowa) *Evening Gazette,* Aug. 28, Sept. 1, 1894.)

† Most certainly, the correspondence should cause one to question Professor Hicks' conclusion that the labor movement especially the A.F. of L., had nothing to do with the Populists in the 1894 campaign. (John D. Hicks, *The Populist Revolt,* Minneapolis, 1931, p. 35.)

unions, were recognized as "champions of their cause," [43] it is clear that a nation-wide labor-Populist alliance was beginning to emerge.

The People's Party campaign in the hard-fought elections of 1894 was waged intensely in working class districts. Debs and Ignatius Donnelly, symbolizing the unity of workers and farmers, spoke on the same platforms to packed meetings in a swing around industrial areas. Candidates nominated on the third party tickets spoke to workers at mass meetings, and many labor bodies welcomed them to their sessions. Leaflets and circulars addressed to the workers emphasized: "The People's Party is the great coming party of the United States; its platform represents the various political demands advocated by labor organizations. The People's Party has in many parts of the country nominated candidates selected only from the ranks of labor, and surely such a party deserves your confidence and support." Handbills reminded the organized workers that "the time to strike is the present, and the place to strike is the ballot box." [44]

The third party's campaign in Illinois' Cook County was correctly characterized by Willis J. Abbott as "a model for all independent movements." People's Party Clubs, Industrial Legions, and an active Women's Auxiliary were established in Chicago's wards and precincts. Thousands upon thousands of leaflets containing the platform and ticket were distributed, as was a pamphlet drawn up by Thomas J. Morgan, describing the history of independent political action of British labor. Apart from contributions from a few wealthy people, most notably Henry D. Lloyd, the funds for these and other campaign activities came from "workingmen, the clerks and small business men." [45]

A. F. of L. trade unionists, Socialists and Single-taxers worked wholeheartedly for the labor-Populist cause, each ignoring the warnings of their top leaders, Gompers, De Leon, and George, to remain aloof from the third party movement.[46]

Henry D. Lloyd, Lyman Trumbull, Clarence Darrow, Thomas J. Morgan, Eugene V. Debs, Ignatius Donnelly, Governor Waite of Colorado, Father McGlynn, Thomas I. Kidd, leader of the Woodworkers' Union, and other prominent trade union representatives of the A. F. of L. were among the brilliant array of speakers for the Populist cause in Illinois. They addressed monster mass meetings in Chicago's Central Music Hall, and so great were the throngs that frequently overflow rallies were held.[47] Three thousand supporters of labor-Populism packed the hall on October 6, 1894, and listened attentively as Lloyd analyzed "the evils of concentrated wealth," and predicted that the labor-Populist alliance of workers, farmers, Socialists and reform groups, would provide the forces to batter down "the inner citadel of monopoly and 'plank 10' is the battering ram which will bring down its walls." [48]

While the most conservative sections of organized labor in Chicago regarded Lloyd's emphasis upon "Plank 10" as much too radical, the viewpoint of the majority of the workers was expressed by Thomas I. Kidd when he endorsed Lloyd's address as embodying the hopes and aspirations of organized labor in America, adding: "We are not afraid nor ashamed to advance principles which must eventually bring about industrial emancipation to the masses." [49]

ELECTION RESULTS

The election results were a bitter disappointment to those who had looked forward to a sizeable representation of labor-Populists in Congress and the state legislatures. Despite the most strenuous efforts, only six of the trade unionists nominated for office were elected, all on the People's Party ticket. James Brettell, A. F. of L. third vice president and People's Party candidate for Congress from Ohio, wrote bitterly to Gompers: "I presume it is not necessary for me to tell you that I've got left in the late election. 'The people' are not yet ready for workingmen as members of Congress to make laws for workingmen. They do not understand their needs like the lawyers, bankers & millionaires." [50]

The disillusioned trade union candidate failed to understand that it was not a simple matter for the third party, with an empty treasury, to defeat the major parties with their experienced, well-financed machines. It is significant that many of the A. F. of L. officials who had replied to Gompers' circular of September 24 had cautioned against over-optimism, pointing out that the labor-Populist candidates were "to a very large extent handicapped for want of funds to make an aggressive campaign." [51]

There were other factors that were responsible for keeping the labor-Populist vote from rising to the strength anticipated by its followers. Throughout the campaign, the conservative press worked sedulously to precipitate a split between the trade unionists and the Socialists in the third party. Special emphasis was placed upon turning the Catholic workers against the independent movement by exaggerating the role played by the "atheistic Socialists" in the campaign. Some labor leaders were weaned away from the labor-Populist alliance in the closing weeks of the campaign by promises from the major parties of appointive offices in government and of special favors to their unions.

In response to the rise of the labor-Populist alliance, the Democrats in a number of states adopted a fairly progressive position in the campaign. Wherever the labor-Populist alliance was consummated, the Democrats embodied some of the third party's demands in their platforms. The Illinois Democrats, for example, adopted a militant anti-trust stand and advocated municipal ownership of electric light plants. This, in addition to the progressive administration of Democratic Governor John P. Altgeld, distinguished by unprecedented legislation and actions friendly to labor, made it difficult to draw the bulk of the labor vote from the Democratic Party.[52]

The Republicans also staged an aggressive campaign in 1894, placing great stress on the protective tariff as the solution for the hard times. This propaganda won over sections of the working class.[53]

Notwithstanding these numerous obstacles, the labor-Populist alliance made a very creditable showing in the elections. The returns revealed that in the urban areas a considerable increase had occurred in the People's Party vote over that of 1892. The vote in Illinois' Cook County increased from 2,000 to between 34,000 and 40,000, and it was widely conceded that the returns were falsified and that at least 25 percent of the labor-Populist vote was not recorded. Outside of Cook County, there was also evidence of strong labor support for the People's Party in Illinois. In Bureau County, 700 of the 973 votes cast came from the mining region of Spring Valley, scene of a recent strike in which two miners had been shot by U.S. troops. In Will County, most of the fairly large Populist vote was credited to the "railroad men of Joliet." The railroad workers were also responsible for the large vote of the third party in Peoria and Rock Island Counties.[54]

Coxey, labor-Populist candidate for Congress in Ohio, polled 24 percent of the votes cast in his district, mainly industrial in composition, and received more than five times as many votes as the Populist candidate two years before. In the entire state, the Populist vote increased from 15,000 in 1892 to approximately 50,000 in 1894. The vote of 1,286 cast in Milwaukee for the third party in 1892 was now 9,479, and in the state the vote was almost quadrupled, reaching a total of 45,000. In Minnesota the vote was increased 167 percent to reach 80,000, with St. Paul and Minneapolis (the industrial centers) polling 25,000—more than Weaver had polled in the entire state in 1892. Pennsylvania's Populist vote was doubled (from 8,000 to 16,000) with the city of Pittsburgh increasing its vote from 578 in 1892 to 3,000. The Populist vote in New York rose from 16,000 to 30,000. In Texas, where the State Federation of Labor, the Federated Trades, and the Farmers' Alliance had amalgamated, the labor-Populists elected the peak number of representatives to the legislature, having 22 successful candidates. California saw a great increase in the third party's vote, especially in the industrial sections of the state. "The People's Party have elected the Mayor of San Francisco," the *Coast Seamen's Journal* reported joyfully on November 14, 1894, and the victorious candidate was quoted as attributing his victory mainly to organized labor's support for the third party.[55]

Nationally, the Populist vote in 1894 was 1,471,590, an increase of close to one-half million votes over 1892. The People's Party elected six Senators and six Congressmen, besides several hundred state officers.[56] But the outstanding feature of the 1894 election was that the largest Populist gains were made in the industrial states, with the increased vote being largely attributed to labor's support for the movement. The following table prepared by Professor E. E. Witte in his unpublished study, "Organized Labor in Politics since 1880," shows this trend most strikingly. The table compares the percentage of the Populist votes in the cities to the state vote.[57]

	1892	1894
Minnesota	11	30.0
Minneapolis	5	35.0
Wisconsin	2.3	7.0
Milwaukee	2.5	19.0
Illinois	2.6	7.0
Chicago	.6	12.0
Michigan	4.3	7.0
Detroit	1.0	3.0
Pennsylvania	1.0	2.1
Pittsburgh	.8	4.0
Ohio	1.8	6.5
Cleveland	2.0	8.0
Massachusetts	.8	2.7
Boston	2.0	6.0

On the basis of this evidence, one can understand Henry Demarest Lloyd's conclusion, made in a letter to President Benjamin Andrews of Brown University shortly after the elections, "that all this shows that the workingmen are rapidly coming to the conclusion to have nothing more to do with the old parties, that they will work with the People's Party if it goes their way, and . . . their way grows more radically socialistic every day."[58]

But would it go "their way"? This crucial question was to be decided in the next two years.

CHAPTER 22

Labor-Populism and the Election of 1896

The campaigns of 1894, featured by the labor-Populist alliance in a number of key states, marked the achievement of the long sought unity between agrarian and urban labor. But already a conflict was in the making that was to disrupt the alliance and hasten the decline of labor-Populism.

SPLIT IN PEOPLE'S PARTY

It was not a new conflict. As early as 1892 a split within the People's Party between conservative and progressive forces was emerging. While most factions within the third party were in favor of free coinage of silver, many were opposed to turning the Populist movement into a Silver Party. On the other hand, there were strong forces operating within the third party—especially at the top—who were in favor of a "one plank party." These elements represented the wealthier farmers and the millionaire silver mining interests who were primarily concerned with using the Populist revolt to secure the passage of a law for the free coinage of silver.* In order to prevent these forces from dominating the Omaha Convention where the People's Party was to draw up its platform and nominate its candidates for the presidential campaign of 1892, Thomas E. Watson had strongly urged organized labor to be well represented. "Free silver," he wrote to Powderly in May, 1892, "is one of our demands . . . but we never thought it more important than many others." [1]

* Among these millionaire Populist mine owners were Wm. M. Stewart of Nevada ($40,000,000), Senator John P. Jones (Comstock lode—$25,000,000), the Hearst interests in California ($75,000,000) and Chas. E. Lane of California ($20,000,000). (Philip F. Buckner, "Silver Mining Interests in Silver Politics, 1876-1896," unpublished M.A. thesis, Columbia University, 1954, pp. 63-65.)

To the disappointment of the silver advocates, the delegates at Omaha decided to hold tightly to their original list of reforms with free silver being only one of the many planks in the platform. But the silver propagandists did not abandon their efforts to influence the People's Party to concentrate on the money question. In 1893, Herman E. Taubeneck, chairman of the National Executive Committee of the People's Party, relied heavily upon the western silver miners for financial aid in campaigns. He soon established close connections with the American Bi-Metallic League, sponsored mainly by the western mine owners, and its president, A. J. Warner. Joining in this alliance was James B. Weaver, the third party's former presidential nominee, and Senator William A. Peffer of Kansas.[2]

Talk for a new silver party spread rapidly from out of the West. Populism as a whole was declared to be unacceptable to many "conservative elements," and thus needing a strong "silver transfusion." Progressive Populists who attended conferences of the People's Party observed a "big plot" being engineered by the silver men of the West, led by Taubeneck, Weaver, and Peffer, to replace the "overly broad" Omaha platform with a new program emphasizing only one demand—free silver.[3]

The emergence of the labor-Populist alliances, the adoption of the Springfield platform and other progressive platforms drawn up by the state and local Populist parties during the 1894 campaign, the number of trade unionists nominated on the People's Party tickets, the activity of organized labor and the Socialists in the third party movement—all combined to convince the conservative elements that Populism was assuming too radical a hue. Henry D. Lloyd had been particularly impressed by the contributions made by the Socialists who cooperated with the People's Party. "They are the most intelligent, most energetic, most reliable workers we have," he wrote to Clarence Darrow a few weeks after the 1894 elections. But the conservative Populist leaders did not share Lloyd's views. On the contrary, they claimed that the slow growth of the third party vote in the rural areas was because the farmers and small businessmen "were affrighted by the apparent domination of the party by the socialists." "We could have had a bigger vote had the socialists been less prominent in the campaign," one Populist leader declared.[4]

Even during the 1894 campaigns, a number of Populist leaders went out of their way to deny that the third party movement was in any way committed to the ideas of the radical labor and Socialist elements. Immediately after the elections, the conservative mining and wealthy farmer group in the leadership of the Populist movement set out to nullify the influence of the labor and Socialist forces and to develop a new base for the People's Party with free silver as "the single issue." To offset the influence of organized labor and the Socialists in the third party movement, these elements sought energetically to attract more and more middle class forces, appealing openly that "Merchants are wanted; lawyers are wanted." They warned the farmers that the greater the influence exerted by organized labor, including the unions of farm laborers, in the People's Party, the greater the danger they would have to pay higher wages and extend shorter hours to their farm hands ."The whole influence and trend of their appeal," wrote a Kansas farm laborer, "is toward cheap labor." [5]

DEFEAT OF THE CONSERVATIVES

In extending invitations to a mass conference at St. Louis in December 28-29, 1894, the People's Party's National Executive Committee deliberately excluded the more radical elements, especially representatives of organized labor and the Socialists. As Henry D. Lloyd pointed out as soon as he became aware of this maneuver, the People's Party's leadership intended to "throw the radicals in the party overboard" at St. Louis. If successful, he warned, they would doom the third party. "Revolutions never go backward. If the People's Party goes backward it will prove that it is not a revolution, and if it is not a revolution, it is nothing." [6]

Alerted by Lloyd's warning, the progressive forces in the People's Party, including Debs and other spokesmen for organized labor, met before the St. Louis Conference and drew up plans to prevent the conservative leadership from shelving the program of labor-Populism and concentrating on the silver issue. Following the meetings, Lloyd, Thomas J. Morgan, J. Z. White, W. H. Madden, Thomas I. Kidd and other founders of the labor-Populist alliance in Illinois, issued a declaration predicting dire results to the third party cause and to the prospects of developing a full alliance between the labor and agrarian forces "if the silver barons are allowed to have their way [at St. Louis]." [7]

The result was a stunning defeat for the conservatives. Representatives of the mining and wealthier farm groups spoke up at St. Louis in favor of ridding the Populist movement of the "cranks and socialists," and urged that "a pure silver party [be] organized at once." But the resolutions adopted by the 250 delegates, drawn up by Lyman Trumbull and introduced by Henry D. Lloyd, reaffirmed the program of labor-Populism. They called for the ending of government by injunction and of the use of federal troops in labor disputes, for the limiting of the size of fortunes that could be acquired through inheritance; for public ownership and operation "under civil service rules" of all monopolies "affecting the public interest," and free silver. Free silver was mentioned, but it was subordinated to the struggle against the monopolists and their agents in the government. "Down with monopolies and millionaire control. Up with the rights of man and the masses!" was the slogan of the triumphant advocates of labor-Populism at St. Louis.[8]

EFFECT OF 1894 A. F. OF L. CONVENTION

But the victory for labor-Populism at St. Louis was overshadowed by the defeat it received at Denver. Here, at the 1894 convention of the A. F. of L., the delegates were to decide whether or not to adopt the 11-point political program which had been submitted to the Federation's membership for referendum. As we have seen above, the supporters of the political program, including "Plank 10," had won the referendum in advance of the convention, and the majority of the delegates came to Denver instructed to vote for the entire program. Moreover, quite a few delegates were specifically instructed to champion the cause of labor-Populism and to advance the slogan: "Boom the People's Party." Adoption of the political program, the *Eight-Hour Herald* predicted, would give a "powerful impulse to the third party movement."[9]

In his presidential address, Gompers tried to stem the tide in favor of independent political action and the labor-Populist alliance by pointing to the fact that few of the trade union candidates had been elected in November, 1894.[10] But the delegates were evidently not impressed by this argument, for the A. F. of L. leaders had to resort to trickery, dictatorial and despotic methods to defeat the will of the membership. As we have seen, by piecemeal consideration of the political program and by persuading delegates to violate their instruction, Gompers and his lieutenants succeeded in striking out the preamble, and in substituting a vague anti-land monopoly plank for "Plank 10." Finally, after all the remaining planks had been approved separately, a declaration to endorse the amended program was voted down.*

The "treachery" of Gompers and his lieutenants, to use the term employed by Henry D. Lloyd in describing their conduct at Denver, could not entirely obscure the fact that the bulk of the A. F. of L. membership favored independent political action. Nevertheless, the action at Denver was a severe set-back to the labor-Populist alliance. The defeat of the political program, especially "Plank 10," Lloyd observed in February, 1895, "threatens to make it impossible to get our workingmen into any kind of political action outside of the old parties."[11] Moreover, it encouraged the conservative leadership to renew their opposition to labor-Populism and to an alliance with organized labor and the Socialists. Why bother to advance the demands of labor-Populism when even the American Federation of Labor was not ready to endorse independent

* *See* pp. 290-92.

political action? Why run the risk of losing the support of farmers and businessmen when organized labor could not be counted upon to build the third party? [12]

In February, 1895, the *National Watchman,* the official Populist organ, featured an editorial which showed clearly which way the wind was blowing: "The time for Populism and Socialism to part has come. . . . Let us be conservative, in order to secure the support of the business men, the professional men, and the well to do. These are elements we must use if ever success comes to our party. For every loud voiced socialist who declares war on us we will get a hundred of the conservative element in our society." [13]

It was clear that by "Socialist" the Populist leadership meant anyone who supported the progressive planks adopted in the various state platforms during the 1894 campaign and reaffirmed at the St. Louis Conference after the elections. [14]

ELECTION OF 1895

With the trade unions affiliated to the A. F. of L. disinclined to play an active role in the independent politics following the stand taken at the Denver Convention, [15] the third party's base in the cities was considerably narrowed. The results of the Spring municipal elections of 1895 were disappointing to the supporters of the labor-Populist alliance. In a few cities, aldermen were elected by the Populists, but the vote generally was far below that cast in November, 1894. [16]

Disappointing as the results of the campaign were to the friends of the labor-Populist cause, they were received with joy by the Populist national headquarters. The election returns were hailed by the Populist leadership as proof that a labor-Populist coalition could get nowheres at the polls, and had vindicated those who wished to narrow the Populist platform to the silver issue. "The Platform of 1896 will not be broadened to meet socialist ideas," the *National Watchman* rejoiced. "Populism and socialism have parted company." [17]

Thus the crisis within the third party was officially proclaimed, and throughout the remainder of 1895 it became clearer and clearer that the Populist leaders were not eager for labor support and would accept it only on their own terms. But the majority of the workers who had voted Populist in 1894 were not willing to see the demand of the "extreme silver faddists" made the central slogan of a independent political movement. To these workers, the positive labor planks of the Omaha platform as well as those added in the summer and fall of 1894, were and should be, along with free silver, the basis of a great people's movement that "would revolutionize the politics of the country." As one worker put it in a letter to the *Railway Times* in the spring of 1895: "I am a Populist from core to rind, and the Omaha Platform is good enough for me. I do not believe that free coinage of silver and gold is all that the working millions want in this land of the poor and the home of the slave."[18]

The election returns in the fall campaigns of 1895 clearly revealed the effects of the conflict that was tearing apart the labor-Populist alliance. In the industrial areas, the People's Party polled about half as many votes as in the fall elections of 1894.[19] Only in the South, where the Populists as a whole fought the efforts to concentrate on the free silver plank to the practical exclusion of all other issues and went before the electorate on platforms embodying a wide list of reforms, did the third party increase its vote.[20] Unlike other sections of the country, the election campaign in the South was highlighted by effective unity between organized labor and the farmers, Negro and white.[21] *

The election figures for the industrial areas outside of the South were easy to explain, wrote the editor of the *Union Workman* when asked by a liberal reformer to account for the decline of the Populist vote in the urban centers: "There is no question in the minds of thinking workingmen of the industrial centers that the present leaders of the People's Party have none other than a commodity use for them. . . . If the state and national committees do not come to their senses soon—if they have any senses to come to—they will find themselves generals without an army. The mechanics of the city who take part in politics are not fools and they cannot be fooled with."[22]

POPULISTS FUSE WITH DEMOCRATS

The answer would be given conclusively at the national convention of the People's Party to be held on July 22, 1896, at St. Louis. Months before the convention opened, those who were still working for a labor-Populist alliance began to rally around the standard of Eugene V. Debs.[23] They argued that if the People's Party would nominate Debs as their candidate for the presidency on the original Omaha platform plus the added planks incorporated in subsequent state platforms, it would be an expression of good faith to the labor supporters of the

* The A.F. of L. general organizer in Texas wrote to August McCraith, the Federation's Secretary, in September, 1895: "I am a very strong Third party man and am doing good work in that direction. I have found a colored man here who is a Leader and Stump Speaker among the Colored. . . . He can do a great deal with his Race for us, he is Educated & Intelligent. . . . The Farmers seems to have awake up, and the Populist Party seems to be advancing nicely. . . ." (W. E. Cannon to August McCraith, Sept. 7, 24, 1895, *AFL Corr.* The A.F. of L. Correspondence contains a number of letters from organizers in the South describing their work in the campaign for the third party.)

movement and would rekindle enthusiasm for a labor-Populist alliance in working class circles.[24] While it was admitted that Debs was "too near the rank of the wage workers" to be acceptable to the conservative leadership of the People's Party,[25] it was also argued that because of his stand on the silver issue and his popularity among the farmers as well as workers, he would be the ideal standard-bearer. At any rate, it was around his candidacy that it was hoped that the People's Party could be salvaged.[26]

Starting in the summer of 1895, the boom for Debs spread rapidly in labor circles. Workers were warned that "the enemies of labor in the Populist movement are laying their plans for '96," and were urged to send penny postcards to the leaders of the People's Party insisting on Debs' nomination on a truly progressive platform. "It will cost you but one cent to express yourself. . . . Besides it will force his nomination on the platform that labor has been fighting for, for the last twenty years." By the winter of 1895-1896, labor papers all over the country placed Debs' name at the banner-head of their journals, and a number of trade unions passed resolutions favoring the Debs' candidacy.[27]

But the leaders of the People's Party had other plans. They decided to hold the national convention after those of the two major parties for the purpose of laying the groundwork for fusion with the Democratic Party. When the Democratic convention met at Chicago, the leading figures of the People's Party were on hand to work out the plans for fusion. The possibilities for fusion became greater when the Democrats endorsed free silver and nominated William Jennings Bryan, the young ex-Congressman from Nebraska, who, even though a Democrat, had long "flirted" with Populist doctrines, and whose famous "Cross of Gold" speech, which had won him the nomination, was filled with Populist ideas.* These possibilities were further advanced by the fact that the Democrats adopted a progressive platform, authored by Governor Altgeld, with planks for free silver, strict control of monopolies, a graduated income tax, a reduced tariff, and a sharp denunciation of Cleveland's action in the Pullman strike which attacked "government by injunction as a new and highly dangerous form of oppression." [28] Thus many of the strongest Populist demands had been taken over by a rival organization.

On the first day of the Populist convention, an informal poll showed that a majority of the delegations of 22 states favored Debs, including

* Bryan's speech which electrified the convention closed with these words: "You shall not press down upon the brow of labor this crown of thorns; you shall not crucify mankind upon a cross of gold." For 15 minutes after he finished, the Coliseum was a pandemonium, and the next day he was made the Democratic nominee.

entire delegations from Ohio, Indiana, Illinois, Texas, Georgia, and Missouri. Henry Demarest Lloyd, who had for almost two years been hoping to see Debs chosen as the Presidential nominee of the People's Party,[29] wired to Debs in Terre Haute informing him that he had a wide lead and would probably win the nomination if he wanted it.[30]

But Debs, fearing that his nomination would disrupt the Populist movement, withdrew his name, and ordered Lloyd not to "permit use of my name for nomination." When this was announced to the convention, the left-wing movement collapsed.[31]

Now the National Committee leadership was able to swing the convention to its desires. By a vote 758 to 564, the delegates, after hours of debate, supported fusion. The convention endorsed Bryan for President, and accepted silver coinage as the dominant issue in the campaign. The anti-fusionists gained a small consolation in the rejection of Sewall, a rich Easterner, and the substitution of Tom Watson for vice-presidential candidate.[32]

The St. Louis convention sounded the death knell of the People's Party. Without a clear program, without adequate leadership, torn apart into conflicting factions, it was impossible for the party to exist as an autonomous political organization. "The labor of many years is swept away and the hopes of thousands of good people are gone with it," Tom Watson wrote bitterly.[33]

Actually, though the People's Party had been "wounded unto death" at St. Louis, all this had been planned long before by the conservative leadership. Lloyd was correct when he observed: "Every development shows that the disintegration of the People's Party [was] planned two years ago by Taubeneck, Weaver et al and [was] given its great impulse at St. Louis. . . ."[34] Fear of organized labor, the Socialists and other radical forces in the labor-Populist alliance, and a determination on the part of the conservative leaders to eliminate the pro-labor, anti-monopoly demands from the Populist program and leave only the free silver plank —these factors were the root causes of the St. Louis debacle.

S.L.P. AND FUSION

When the Populists at St. Louis endorsed Bryan and went over to the Democratic camp, Daniel De Leon and his followers were overjoyed. Now their arguments against Populism were fully justified; now the People's Party stood out clearly as "a middle class movement." Moreover, "stripped of its Socialistic pretensions . . . it will cease to stand in our way and hinder the growth of our party in Western States, where the allurements held out by Populist politicians served to give them quite a large following from among the working class."[35]

With complete optimism, the S.P.L. proceeded to nominate presidential and vice-presidential candidates. Organizers were sent into the midwest to wean disillusioned Populists away from their party into the Socialist fold. The national S.L.P. convention, in a resolution entitled, "To the thinking and socialistic members and friends of the Populist Party," urged all earnest reformers, especially the organized workers, in that "middle class party" to support the party which aims to remove the cause of all class struggle—"the profit and wage system that underlies the present capitalist system of exploitation of the masses by the few." [36]

The response dashed the bright hopes of De Leon and his followers. Although the cause which Bryan championed in 1896 was essentially that of the farmers and the middle class, organized labor, with very few exceptions, supported the Democratic and Populist presidential candidate. Indeed, instead of the adherents of labor-Populism supporting the S.L.P. candidate in 1896,* not a few Socialists supported Bryan.[37] †

LABOR SUPPORT FOR BRYAN

The reasons for the widespread support for Bryan in labor circles are not difficult to discover. Large sections of the labor movement were still staunch in their support of free silver, even though they did not believe that this issue alone was of concern to the workers and their allies.[38] Throughout the spring, summer, and fall of 1896, trade unions, city centrals, and State Federations informed the A. F. of L.'s national headquarters that their members "are almost unanimous for the Free and Unlimited coinage of Silver at the Ratio of 16 to 1 regardless of former party affiliations, believing that by increasing the volume of Money it will help bring about a revival in business and thus again bring prosperity to our country." [39]

Debs expressed the views of many in the labor movement when he

---

* Although it was on the ballot in at least 16 states, the S.L.P. polled only 36,000 votes for its presidential candidate, C. H. Matchett. (*The People*, Nov. 17, 1896.)

† On October 22, 1896, Henry White wrote to Gompers from New York City: "Some of the principle Socialists are out for Bryan and are members of the Independent Bryan League. . . ." (*AFL Corr.*)
There would have been even more Socialists "out for Bryan" in New York City had not the Jewish Socialists been antagonized by the anti-Semitic propaganda associated with the Bryan campaign. The Jewish Socialists, like all Jews in the United States, were furious when they read in the New York *Sun's* report of the Democratic Convention that delegates screamed: "Down with gold! Down with the hook-nosed Shylocks of Wall Street! Down with the Christ killing gold bugs." (September 16, 1896. Edward Flower, "Anti-Semitism in the Free Silver and Populist Movement and the Election of 1896," unpublished M.A. thesis, Columbia University, May, 1952.)

declared it as his belief that "the triumph of Mr. Bryan and free silver would blunt the fangs of the money power." [40]

Yet most of the organized workers who supported Bryan did so not primarily because of their belief in free silver but because of their conviction that William McKinley, the Republican nominee, was the candidate of the anti-labor monopolist forces in the country, and that "every power and every interest bent on crushing labor and cutting down wages was united on the side of McKinley." They supported Bryan also because they believed that the Chicago platform of the Democratic Party, with its protests against industrial despotism, its support of the income tax, and its condemnation of government by injunction, reflected the principles of labor-Populism. "The issue of 16 to 1 is not the only issue of the campaign," declared the *Labor Advocate,* organ of the Troy (N. Y.) Central Federation of Labor. "The other planks in the Chicago platform are of greater importance than even the money clause." [41]

The unprecedented furor of the conservative attack on the Chicago platform led many workers to line up behind Bryan.* For the workers were convinced that the attack on the platform was caused not so much by the free silver plank as by the fact that the program had spoken out against government by injunction. This conviction was borne out by a survey made by the labor press during the campaign which pointed out: "No plank in the Democratic Platform . . . has been more fiercely denounced than the declaration against Government by Injunction. This declaration has been denounced as being anarchistic in its tendency and utterly subversive of law and order." [42]

Both the K. of L. and the American Railway Union went over completely to Bryan's standard, and from the beginning to the end of the campaign, their leaders devoted themselves to convincing the rank-and-file of labor that its welfare was linked to a Democratic victory. [43] Support for Bryan was also widespread in the A. F. of L. "It is a fight between the masses and the classes," observed James O'Connell, president of the International Association of Machinists, as he endorsed Bryan. [44] John McGrath, A. F. of L. organizer for the Southern district of Ohio, reported on July 14: "I found sixteen to one laboring men who are thoroughly dissatisfied with the Republican and Democratic parties, and who will vote the Democratic ticket this Fall, simply because they regard the situation so changed that it is now the masses against the classes." A week

* "No wild-eyed and rattle-brained horde of the red flag ever proclaimed such a specific defiance of law, precedent, order, and government," was the comment of the New York *Mail* on the Chicago platform. (Reprinted in *Public Opinion,* Vol. XXI, July 16, 1896, p. 75.) "Considering the platform," declared E. Ellery Anderson of New York, "it may be as well that a revolutionist like Bryan stands upon it. We want them with red flags so there will be provocation for shooting them down." (*Literary Digest,* Vol. XIII, July 18, 1896, p. 357.)

later, an A. F. of L. organizer wrote to Gompers from California: "All the unions are with an almost unanimous sentiment for Bryan as choice for president of the U.S. This is a golden opportunity to gain a step toward the objective point we have been battling for years to reach. I wish to say I was requested by a number of union men to write to you & we hope you will do your best to wheel organized labor into line for Bryan. Do your best as the situation is desperate, it is the classes for McKinley & I trust the masses for Bryan." [45]

This appeal to Gompers was one of hundreds that flooded his office from A. F. of L. unions and members during the summer of 1896 with demands that he abandon his attempt to keep the Federation neutral in the campaign, and officially endorse the Democratic-Populist candidate.

GOMPERS' ROLE

On June 27, 1896, even before the various national conventions met, Gompers issued a general circular to all A. F. of L. unions warning them against the dangers of political action. Of the 12-section manifesto, section three was the most important: "Whatever labor secured now or secured in the past is due to the efforts of the workers themselves in their own organizations—the trade unions on trade union lines, on trade union action." The problem was "to vanquish the political intruder at the doors of our meeting rooms, [to] compel him to turn about and take his departure." Then the happy day would be in sight "when there will be few if any of our fellow toilers outside the beneficent influence of organized labor." [46]

The manifesto did not have its intended effect. In many A. F. of L. unions it was either condemned on the ground that it violated local autonomy or quietly ignored, and Gompers was bluntly told "to mind his own business." [47] So hostile was the reaction to the circular that early in August, Gompers was compelled to issue a public statement in which he claimed that he had been misinterpreted: "By no amount of sophistry or distortion of language can any word used in the circular be construed to deny the right of the workers to take such political action as they may deem most advisable and even so far as the trade unions as such are concerned, there is not a word in the circular which even advises them to refuse to take political action." [48]

Since Gompers' modification of the circular was not accompanied by an endorsement of the Democratic and Populist candidate, it failed to satisfy his critics. Throughout the A. F. of L. the charge of insincerity and inconsistency was hurled at Gompers. It was inconsistent and insincere for Gompers to announce publicly that he was absolutely in favor of free silver, but was opposed to the Federation taking any position that would affiliate it with any political party. How could the A. F. of L. be in favor of free coinage and not place itself on record as in favor of the only man and party which represented the issue in the campaign? Logic alone should compel Gompers to follow the lead of many A. F. of L. officials and members and "support the candidates of that political party which favored the economic measure [free silver] which had been endorsed [by the A. F. of L.] in preference to the candidate, who, with his party, was pledged to defeat their will." [49] As John B. Lennon, a member of the A. F. of L. Executive Council and a supporter of Bryan, put it bluntly to Gompers: "To me it is indeed strange how a man can believe in a question as an economic demand and be opposed to the same principle as soon as it becomes a political question." In answer to Gompers' charge that labor's activity in the campaign would lead to a neglect of trade unionism, Lennon replied: "Trade unions will not be forgotten. My correspondence shows that the activity in politics of the public at large has awakened renewed interest in the union by the workers. I suppose this comes from the great amount of talk as to the effect on labor of the different Policies advocated, and the workers are more and more coming to realize that under any and all policies they will need the union." [50]

As the campaign drew to its close, the pressure upon Gompers to declare himself mounted. Hundreds of letters and telegrams poured into the A. F. of L. headquarters from affiliated unions, their officials and members pleading for Gompers "to come out flat-footed, in common with all the leaders of organized labor, against the common enemy."

"The plain people who have kept you at the head of the Federation are incensed at your silence," went a typical letter. "Before long there will be a protest sent up that will take you a lifetime to recover from. . . . Act now, and 'get off the fence.' If you value your position as a leader of the common people, lead them when they most need you." [51]

But Gompers refused to budge. He was aware that the course he was taking was exceedingly unpopular in the labor movement, but he agreed with P. J. McGuire that a basic issue was at stake that went beyond the campaign itself. That issue was stated bluntly by McGuire in a "confidential" letter on September 9, 1896, in which he warned Gompers to ignore the rising demand for him to endorse Bryan. "That is the trap, for if you declare for Bryan or anyone else it will be a pretext for the Socialists to drag in their politics." Agreeing that to endorse Bryan "will re-open the doors" to the Socialists, Gompers continued to turn a deaf ear to the appeals from the A. F. of L. membership, and refused to declare for any party in the contest. [52]

Although Gompers' refusal to speak out sowed some confusion in the labor movement, it had no appreciable effect in deterring the vast majority of A. F. of L. affiliates from declaring their position in the campaign. International and national unions, city centrals and State Federations of Labor openly endorsed and supported Bryan and sponsored the formation of Workingmen's Bryan Clubs. Not all members of these organizations saw eye-to-eye on the free silver issue, but they were all united in support of the other planks in the Chicago platform—its aggressive attitude towards trusts, its endorsement of an income tax, and, most important of all, its opposition to government by injunction. As Henry White, Secretary of the Bryan Campaign Club of the United Garment Workers and a leader of the Independent Bryan League, formed by the Central Labor Union of New York, pointed out to Gompers: "The political campaign is peculiar in that it does not in any way cause dissension within the unions and even those favoring sound money (?) do not object to the active work being done by the union officials on behalf of Bryan." [53]

PRO-McKINLEY REIGN OF TERROR

A handful of labor leaders, most of them like Powderly ex-labor leaders, spoke out for the Republican candidate. But even the Republican campaign managers agreed that these men spoke only for themselves. "The labor organizations are against us to a man," wrote one campaign manager to Mark Hanna. "Impossible to teach them. They are more interested in the question of Federal jurisdiction over strikes than the money question." [54]

Republicans like Theodore Roosevelt felt that there was only one way to deal with the problem: "The sentiments now animating a large proportion of our people can only be suppressed, as the Commune in Paris was suppressed, by taking ten or a dozen of their leaders out, standing . . . them against a wall and shooting them dead." [55] * Hanna and other Republican leaders decided on a different strategy which they felt would be even more effective—the use of economic pressure, intimidation and terror. On September 13, Theodore Nelson, Secretary of the Democratic State Central Committee of Illinois wrote in a "confidential" letter to Gompers: "We are daily in receipt of information at this office of a disposition on the part of employers to compel their men to vote for McKinley. To our certain knowledge many men who favor Mr. Bryan are compelled to wear McKinley buttons, and enroll themselves as mem-

* This was not the first time Roosevelt had offered such advice. On December 9, 1894, he wrote to a friend: "I know the populists and the laboring-men well, and their faults; I like to see a mob handled by the regulars, or by good State guards, not over-scrupulous about bloodshed." (*The Letters of Theodore Roosevelt*, selected and edited by Elting E. Morison, Cambridge, Mass., 1951, Vol. I, p. 412.)

bers of 'McKinley Clubs.' I have been informed from what I regard as reliable authority that the workingmen after enrolling in these clubs are watched by detectives." [56]

This "disposition" on the part of the employers was by no means confined to Illinois. As the campaign advanced, the labor press carried a constant stream of reports to the effect that "attempts are being made in different parts of the country to intimidate or coerce workingmen into voting as their employers wish." Mills and factories in every part of the country were shut down with the public announcement that operations would not be resumed until after the election, and then not unless the results were a Republican victory. Railroad employers, owners of textile and carpet mills, lumber companies, steel corporations, indeed every type of manufacturing concern, were found guilty of such intimidating tactics. Manufacturers received letters from dealers stating that they would cancel orders if Bryan were elected, and these were posted in conspicuous places in factories for the workers to see. One employer told his workers that if Bryan were elected he would pay them only $10 per month, whereas if the Republicans were victorious they would receive $26. The 3,000 employees of the Jones & McLaughlin iron works at Pittsburgh were forced to contribute one dollar each to the Republican campaign fund. The workers employed by the Goodyear Rubber Company were bluntly informed: "The stockholders and officers of the Goodyear Rubber Company wish to have it distinctly understood that a vote for Bryan and Sewall on the part of any of its employees will be regarded as an act committed directly against the welfare of the company and its employes, and any employe working for or voting the above mentioned ticket in the coming election may expect to be regarded by the officers as antagonistic to the company." [57]

Small wonder that Professor E. A. Ross commented: "Never since the days of the slavocrats has there been shown the ruthless determination to beat down, bulldoze or throttle opposition that is shown at the present time. . . . The brutality of the methods is almost incredible." [58]

EFFECTS OF THE TERROR

In many parts of the country, organized labor voiced its resentment against the intimidation of workers and affirmed its determination not to bow before it. Typical was the stand of the A. F. of L. City Central Council of Meriden, Connecticut, which expressed "its most solemn protest against such encroachment on the rights of labor, and pledges itself to resist by every means within its power such unjust and un-American conduct, and stamp it out as deserving the resentment and rebuke of all organized labor." In an article entitled, "Political Intimidation," the *American Federationist* published the above statement which it characterized "as a fair expression of the feeling of resentment felt by organized workers of this effort of many of the employing class to control, and unduly and unfairly control, the votes and political rights of the workers as men—as American citizens." [59]

It is questionable whether the Republican campaign of terror and intimidation had too much of an effect upon the organized workers. In coming out for Bryan early in October, the United Labor Conference of New York, representing nearly every union in the city, declared: "Intimidation of the most flagrant character has failed to swerve those of our people who believe in exercising their God-given right of casting a free ballot, and it is the unanimous opinion of the undersigned (executive committee)* that Organized Labor now has a splendid chance to show that they believe in the people being the true rulers, and not the paid attorneys of Trusts and Syndicates." [60]

Undoubtedly, the well-organized campaign in behalf of Bryan conducted by the trade unions and their leaders went far in counteracting Republican terroristic tactics among members of these unions. But this could not offset its effect upon the great mass of unorganized workers. More than any factor, Republican-employer-sponsored intimidation nullified the efforts organized labor made to win the support of the unorganized workers for the Democratic-Populist ticket. Following the election, the *Journal of the Knights of Labor* observed correctly: "The unorganized toilers of the great cities, terrified by the prospect kept constantly before their eyes of less work and lower wages, were led to desert their organized brethren and helped to bring about defeat." [61]

ELECTION RESULTS

All evidence leads to the conclusion that the vast majority of the organized workers supported Bryan at the polls. But this could not cope with corruption, threats, intimidation, and the endless supply of money the Republicans collected from corporations, individual industrialists and bankers, and poured into the battle. "We have carried the middle West by main strength and by an unprecedented use of money," one Republican campaign worker wrote frankly after the election. He estimated that three and one-half million dollars had been raised in New York City alone. One student of the campaign concludes that "in all probability some ten millions were used to further the candidacy of William McKinley." [62]

The vote Bryan polled in the election was a sharp disappointment to his supporters. Yet even though he did not win a single state from Maine to Minnesota and lost California, the loss may not be completely at-

* The Executive Committee was made up of representatives from the Bricklayers', Coach Drivers', Box Makers', Printers', Tile Layers', Helpers', and Waiters' Unions.

tributed to a lack of support from the urban industrial centers. As one historian points out: "The fact Bryan carried a number of the agricultural states of the West in 1896 while the East voted against him has obscured the further fact that he received strong support in many of the eastern urban centers while heavy majorities were in many cases rolled up in rural sections of the East." This conclusion has been substantiated in a statistical analysis of the election returns published in the *American Historical Review* in January, 1941, under the title, "Urban and Rural Voting in 1896." William Diamond, the author, points out in his conclusion that "Bryan, relative to his rural vote, did better in the cities of the more urbanized states or those most rapidly moving in that direction, than in the cities of the less populous and more agricultural states." [63] And, as an A. F. of L. leader pointed out to Gompers two days after the election: "In the cities Bryan's vote was largely the labor vote." [64]

Despite the defeat in the election, some of Bryan's labor supporters entertained hope for the future. The secretary of Local No. 1 of the American Railway Union wrote the defeated candidate to express the sorrow of the entire organization and to pledge continued support. "The American Railway Union voted solidly for you and ask you to keep up the good work. Your cause is just; success is certain." James R. Sovereign, K. of L. Grand Master Workman, sent similar assurances. "We will," he wrote to Bryan, "continue to fight for American financial independence together with the other important issues of the platform." The General Secretary of the A. F. of L.'s United Garment Workers wrote optimistically: "All active union men knew only too well that a movement represented by the Chicago platform could not succeed in one contest. It had to meet all the powers of darkness—the opposition of the church, the press, the organized money power. . . . I consider that the strength the movement showed to be a great gain." [65]

ANTI-POLITICAL ACTION TREND

But these were voices crying in the wilderness. Feeling that the election results had fully justified the role he had played in the campaign, Gompers laid down the course the labor movement should now follow. The time had come, he declared shortly after the election, for "the workers of this country to sever their connection with *all* political parties," and get down to the real business of trade union organization.[66] Or, as Andrew Furuseth, leader of the Sailors' Union of the Pacific, one of the most active supporters of Bryan, put it in a letter to Gompers three days after the election: "Our policy as organized labor seems to be plain. Organize, educate and get such legislation on conservative lines as we can." The Federation should draw up a limited legislative program and seek to achieve its passage by "lobbying" activities at the nation's capitol, confining itself to obtaining the enactment of laws favorable to the A. F. of L. and blocking the passage of bills harmful to the organization. Furthermore, the A. F. of L. should refrain from active participation in election campaigns, and, under no circumstances, should it support a movement for independent working class political action.[67]

In the face of this attack, even the staunchest supporters of independent political action in the labor movement weakened.[68] When the Chicago Labor Congress and the Trade and Labor Assembly amalgamated in December, 1896, to form the Chicago Federation of Labor, both organizations acceded to Gompers' demand that they insert a "no-politics" clause in the constitution. When one considers that the Chicago Trade and Labor Congress had been formed in December, 1894, precisely to advance the cause of independent political action and that its program reflected some of the most advanced thinking in the labor-Populist alliance *—it is clear that the conservative forces in the labor movement had temporarily carried the day.[69]

CAUSES OF DECLINE OF LABOR-POPULISM

Thus labor-Populism passed into political oblivion. Actually, the election of 1896 was only the final chapter of its decline. The People's Party had failed to wed labor and the farmer in a permanent alliance even before its surrender to the Democrats. The conservative leadership of both the Populist and the organized labor movements was not really interested in such an alliance. Henry D. Lloyd accused the conservative trade union leaders of being "henchmen" of the major political parties, and charged that their function was to make sure that "the trades-unions are kept in dependence upon the capitalistic parties." These labor bureaucrats, he pointed out, received rewards from the "capitalistic parties" in the form of appointive places in city, state, and national administration. "These leaders," Lloyd wrote in the London Labour Leader, "are given these positions as bribes to play the bell-weather to prevent the body of working men from leaving them." [70]

While large sections of organized workers were attracted to the People's Party and in several localities were the decisive force in it, organized labor had not been strong enough or united enough to attain leadership

---

* In addition to specific labor legislation, the Congress demanded abolition of the United States Senate, direct election of President and Vice President, nationalization of railroads, telegraphs, telephones, municipal ownership of public utilities, judicial reform, the initiative and referendum, abolition of stock speculation, and the ultimate establishment of the "co-operative commonwealth." (Destler, American Radicalism, p. 235.)

of the movement on a nation-wide basis, and, together with the small farmers, sharecroppers, and agricultural laborers, to build a real anti-monopoly party. The conservatism of the leadership of the People's Party, the strength of the silver miners and wealthier farmers in the Populist movement, the weakness of the silver panacea as an issue around which to build an effective farmer-labor alliance, the lack of unity in the labor movement, the influence of "pure and simple" trade unionism, and, of course, the attacks of big business and its allies which pictured Populism as an alien, un-American plot engineered by foreign-born Socialists [71]— in which attacks the leadership of the People's Party joined—all con-tributed to the downfall of labor-Populism.

Yet the fact that the Populist movement after 1896 was dissipated as an organized force * did not mean that the labor-Populist alliance had not left its mark upon American life. Measure after measure advocated by labor-Populist alliance—such as the eight-hour day, the institution of more adequate mine and factory inspection in industrial areas, and other specific labor legislation, direct election of U.S. Senators, the initiative and referendum, the Australian ballot, municipal ownership of public utilities, etc.—were to be included in the platforms of one or the other of the major political parties and to be enacted into legislation.[72]

The great social unrest that had swept so many farmers, so many organized workers, intellectuals and professional people into the Populist movement and led to the building of a labor-Populist alliance, did not die with the election of 1896. It was to revive again and to gather strength with each succeeding year of agitation against monopoly capitalism.

* After 1896 the People's Party gradually declined and soon passed out of existence. Returning prosperity, the phenomenal increase in the production of gold ending the monetary stringency, along with the effects of fusion with the Democrats, hastened its demise.

[Since this chapter was written, the following works have appeared which deal with labor and populism and are worth consulting: Norman Pollack, *The Populist Response to Industrial America*, New York, 1966; Gerald N. Greb, "The Knights of Labor, Politics , and Populism," Mid-America, vol. XL, 1958, pp. 3-21; Eli Goldschmidt, "Labor and Populism: New York City, 1891-1896," *Labor History*, vol. XIII, 1972, pp. 520-32. No-thing in these publications changes the basic approach in the chapters of the present volume dealing with labor and Populism.

Since the following chapter was published, the following works have appeared which should be consulted with respect to the issue of the early A.F. of L. and labor solidarity: Paul B. Werthman, "Black Workers and Labor Unions in Birmingham, Alabama, 1897-1904," in Milton Cantor, editor, *Black Labor in America* (Westport, Conn., 1969), and Herbert Gutman, "The Negro and the United Mine Workers," in Julius Jacobson, editor, *The Negro and the American Labor Movement*, New York, 1968. However, the reader should also examine my criticism of the Gutman thesis in my *Organized Labor and the Black Worker*, 1619-1973, New York, 1974, pp. 95-100.]

CHAPTER 23

The A. F. of L. and Labor Solidarity, 1896-1901

The *American Federationist* of October, 1897, featured the news: "Miners' Victory Encourages All Workers." And so it did! Reports from the A. F. of L. corps of 430 organizers in the United States and Canada, covering the period October 1, 1897, to April 1, 1898, revealed that the victory of the coal miners in their great strike of 1897, in which they secured a wage increase of 33 percent over the wages of 1893 and established the eight-hour day, was an important factor in the determination of workers to organize and present a more formidable front to employers.[1] *

But the leaders of the A. F. of L. showed little enthusiasm. In February, 1898, United Mine Workers' President Michael D. Ratchford complained to Gompers that the A. F. of L. leadership seemed lukewarm about the miners' victory. He politely asked if this was "due to indifference," and pointedly referring to Gompers himself, noted: "The president

---

* The strike of 1897, called "The spontaneous uprising of an enslaved people," was the first successful strike conducted by the United Mine Workers as a national organization. Over 200,000 men in the mines in Pennsylvania, Virginia, West Virginia, Ohio, Indiana, and Illinois, went out on July 4, 1897, paralyzing about 70 percent of the soft coal production in the United States. For twelve weeks, the miners stood firm. On September 4, 1897, the struggle ended in a resounding victory for the miners, and, at a meeting in Chicago on January 18, 1898, the coal operators and the union signed the first national agreement any important industry had reached with its employees.

The victory stimulated the growth of the U.M.W. In April, 1897, there were only 10,000 nominal members in the Union. On April 12, 1900, John Mitchell, successor to Ratchford as U.M.W. president, wrote jubilantly to Gompers: ". . . I am pleased to inform you that the United Mine Workers organization has a paid up membership for this month of one hundred and seventeen thousand (117,000), and we are seriously contemplating the absorption of the American Federation of Labor." (*AFL Corr.*)

of the American Federation of Labor, an organization which has struggled for years to gain the advantages for the workers that the miners have recently achieved should in our opinion not hesitate in voicing his approval of the work accomplished by the miners' organization. The reduction of the hours of labor from ten to eight hours per day with the other conditions mentioned for the miners of the five states can do much to open the way to all other trades to gain a short work day." [2]

It is not difficult to discover the reason for the lack of enthusiasm in top A. F. of L. circles. The Federation leaders were concerned lest the dramatic struggles and gains of the miners would highlight the fact that the miners' union represented industrial unionism, a unionism that united skilled and unskilled—workers of all creeds, colors, and nationalities.* John B. Lennon, head of the Journeymen Tailors' Union and A. F. of L. Treasurer, privately pointed out to Gompers that the proponents of this type of unionism were already making use of the miners' victory to advance their cause. He was "convinced that they will continue to do so in the future." [3]

The unionism that characterized the miners' union and was so largely important in aiding them to gain their victory, was not the type of unionism that was characteristic of the A. F. of L. as a whole. Precisely at this time, the A. F. of L. was moving more and more in the direction of an opposite type of unionism, a unionism that sought to organize primarily the skilled workers, that built its structure on a craft rather than an industrial basis, and was indifferent and even hostile to the needs of the unskilled and semi-skilled workers, of the Negro, foreign-born and women workers.

In the eyes of the A. F. of L. leaders, the history of the American labor movement during and immediately after the crisis of 1893 conclusively proved that a successful labor federation must be built on a foundation of craft unions, binding together primarily the most skilled, the steadiest of union men, who would stay organized in boom or depression. These men scoffed at the idea that craft unionism was obsolete. If anything, they insisted, the depression years and the years immediately following had proved that it was the type of unionism represented by the K. of L. and the American Railway Union that was obsolete. This type of unionism, based on the concept of bringing together in one union all workers in one industry regardless of skill, race, creed, color, sex or nationality, had proved inadequate to weather the economic crisis. On the other

---

* One of the objects of the U.M.W. was "to unite in one organization, regardless of creed, color or nationality, all workmen . . . employed in and around coal mines." The U.M.W. Constitution contained a clause which stated: "No member in good standing who holds a due or transfer card shall be debarred or hindered from obtaining work on account of race, creed or nationality." (Frank Julian Warne, *History of the United Mine Workers of America*, New York, 1905, p. 35.)

hand, craft unionism had proved that it could survive such a crisis and forge ahead when it was over. As P. J. McGuire put it in a letter to Gompers, the stability of the A. F. of L. during the crisis years and its growth immediately after the crisis, tripling its membership between 1897-1901 (264,825 to 787,537 *), "are a convincing evidence of the utility of wisely directed trade [craft] organizations." [4]

Millions of unorganized workers bore the brunt of the type of unionism practiced by these so-called "wisely directed" unions affiliated with the A. F. of L. Three groups of workers, in particular, were tragically affected by it: Negro workers, foreign-born workers, and women workers.

COMPLAINTS OF NEGRO WORKERS

In 1896, Gompers received complaints from a number of Negro correspondents who charged that they and other Negroes were kept out of A. F. of L. unions and "discriminated against simply because they are colored." White correspondents reported to Gompers that Negro workers in their region were complaining publicly and bitterly that unions affiliated to the A. F. of L. "had Barred the Door of their Unions against colored men."

The issue aroused nationwide publicity in 1897 when Booker T. Washington, head of the Tuskagee Institute, attacked the A. F. of L. for placing obstacles, through discriminatory practices, to the material advancement of the Negro people. Although Washington was not at all anxious to advance the cause of trade unionism among the Negro people,† his charge stung the A. F. of L. leadership. The A. F. of L. convention of 1897 passed a resolution condemning Washington's statement, and reaffirmed its declaration adopted at previous conventions "that it [the Federation] welcomes to its ranks all labor, without regard to creed, color, sex, race, or nationality and that its best efforts have been, and will continue to be, to encourage the organization of those most needing its protection, whether they be in the North or the South, the East or the West, white or black." Gompers was even more emphatic. When Delegate Jones of Georgia declared that the white people of the

* The total membership of all trade unions increased in the same period from 447,000 to 1,124,000, reaching the million mark in 1901 for the first time since 1886.

† In later years, Washington actually appealed to employers to use Negro labor on the ground that the Negro worker "is almost a stranger to strife, lock-outs and labor wars; labor that is law-abiding, peaceable, teachable . . . labor that has never been tempted to follow the red flag of anarchy." (Booker T. Washington, *The Negro in Business*, Boston, 1907, p. 317.) Washington argued that the Negro was not inclined toward trade unionism. ("The Negro and the Labor Unions," *Atlantic Monthly*, June, 1913, pp. 756-57.)

South would not submit to the employment of Negroes in shops, mills, and factories, and that the union of which he was a member did not admit Negroes, Gompers rebuked him, saying that "a Union affiliated with the American Federation of Labor had no right to debar the Negro from membership. . . . If we do not give the colored man the opportunity to organize, the capitalist will set him up as a barrier against our progress." [5]

These were fine words and certainly no Negro could quarrel with the declaration of policy adopted by the A. F. of L. convention. But in actual practice, exclusion and separation of the Negro workers were already in operation, and the A. F. of L. leadership capitulated to the actual practice and even advanced it.

JIM CROW UNIONISM IN THE A. F. OF L.

For the first few years after its formation, the A. F. of L. insisted that unions desiring to affiliate must eliminate the color clause from their constitutions. The 1890 convention refused to sanction the admittance of the National Association of Machinists because the union's constitution limited membership to white persons. The A. F. of L. even set up a rival national union, the National Machinists' Union, which drew up a constitution that extended membership to Negro and white machinists, and then received a charter from the Federation. A similar policy was pursued by the early A. F. of L. towards the Brotherhood of Boiler Makers and Iron Ship Builders of America.*

This progressive practice, however, was of short duration. In late 1894, the National Association of Machinists and the National Machinists' Union amalgamated to form the International Association of Machinists. In March, 1895, James O'Connell, head of the amalgamated union, reported that he had discussed the question of the constitutional ban against Negroes with Gompers, McGuire "and many other leading lights" in the A. F. of L.; that they had suggested that the union remove the color ban from the constitution, transfer it to the ritual, and then apply for membership in the Federation. O'Connell was assured that rejection "would not stare us in the face." This is precisely what happened. The I.A.M. removed the color bar from its constitution, transferred it to the ritual, applied for membership in the A. F. of L. and was allowed to affiliate. Thereafter, the union effectively excluded Negro machinists.[6]

Appealing to the Brotherhood of Locomotive Firemen in 1896 to affiliate to the A. F. of L., Gompers suggested that the organization should follow the same course as the Machinists, remove the lily-white clause

* See pp. 195-200.

from its constitution, and accomplish the same purpose by allowing each lodge to regulate its own membership. But the Brotherhood refused to heed Gompers' advice, informing him that the membership would not affiliate with the Federation because, among other reasons, "they do not care to belong to an organization that is not honest enough to make public its qualification of membership." [7]

Other unions were not so sensitive. One year after the Machinists affiliated, the Boiler Makers and Iron Ship Builders were welcomed into the A. F. of L., despite a similar method of excluding Negroes. A year later, the International Brotherhood of Blacksmiths changed their constitution which drew the color line, transferred the restriction on membership to the ritual, and were admitted to the Federation. [8]

With the admission of the Machinists, the Boiler Makers and Iron Ship Builders, and the Blacksmiths, the early A. F. of L. policy of equality of all workers regardless of color came to an abrupt end. To be sure, the A. F. of L. still insisted that no unions could affiliate if their constitutions banned Negroes, but they were accepted if this practice was accomplished through the rituals. After a while, the A. F. of L. officials did not even bother to insist on the elimination of constitutional barriers to Negro membership, but admitted as affiliates organizations which excluded Negroes by constitutional provision. When the Order of Railroad Telegraphers and the Brotherhood of Railway Trackmen, both of which restricted membership to whites in their constitutions, affiliated with the A. F. of L. in 1899 and 1900, Gompers reported their action "with much pleasure," and expressed the hope that the other railroad brotherhoods would follow suit. [9] It was clear that they could join the Federation, like the Telegraphers and the Trackmen, without altering their constitutional ban against Negroes. In 1902, the stationary engineers, a national union already affiliated with the A. F. of L., amended its constitution so as to exclude Negroes. Not a word of protest came from Gompers and the Federation. [10]

The absence of specific clauses barring Negro members did not mean that Negroes were admitted to other A. F. of L. unions. Many unions whose constitutions or pledges did not specify membership in the "white race" as a prerequisite for admittance and even some whose constitutions proclaimed the principle of equality of all workers, kept Negroes out by tacit agreement. Others achieved this objective by such practices as requiring high initiation fees which Negro workers could not pay; requiring special licenses which Negroes could not obtain; prohibiting Negroes from becoming apprentices, etc. [11] Basically, however, the fact that the vast majority of the Negroes were unskilled workers excluded them from the craft unions of the A. F. of L. which sought primarily to organize only the various skilled trades.

In 1902 an investigation as to the number of Negroes who were members of trade unions was conducted by Atlanta University under the supervision of Dr. W. E. B. DuBois. Correspondence was carried on with trade unions, and the results disclosed that 43 national organizations, including the railroad brotherhoods, had no Negro members and that in 16 of these this was due to the discriminatory policies of the unions. Twenty-seven other unions had very few Negro members, partly due to the refusal of the organizations to train Negro apprentices. The report estimated that there were altogether only 40,000 Negroes in the A. F. of L., and that half of this number were in the United Mine Workers.* The report revealed further that in some of the unions affiliated with the A. F. of L. a decrease had occurred in Negro membership during the decade, 1890-1900.[12]

It was impossible for the investigating committee to discover the Negro membership of the A. F. of L. The Federation's leaders proudly announced that since the A. F. of L. drew no "color line," it could not determine which of its members were white and which Negroes.[13] What the A. F. of L. leaders did not say was that the vast majority of the Negroes in the Federation were organized on a Jim Crow basis. Evidently to Gompers and his associates, the fact that few of the A. F. of L. unions admitted Negroes on an equal basis with white members and, instead, separated them into Jim Crow locals, did not constitute drawing the "color line." In the Southern organizing drive launched in 1898-1899 by the A. F. of L., the small number of Negro painters, barbers, carpenters, quarrymen, wheelwrights, etc. that were brought into unions were organized almost exclusively into separate Jim Crow locals.[14] Still, in announcing the affiliation of Jim Crow locals to the Federation, the A. F. of L. leaders took care to point out that this was not drawing the "color line." Thus, the following report submitted by an A. F. of L. organizer in Galveston, Texas, was published in the Galveston *Daily News* of September 6, 1898:

"There is no color line.

"'The colored labor union' of Galveston is no more. In joining the American Federation of Labor it was rechristened. The Federation has no color line. That matter was discussed at the Nashville meeting [1897 convention] a year ago and settled. The federation recognizes no 'white'

---

* Dr. Du Bois also prepared a study of the history of the A.F. of L.'s policy with regard to Negro workers in which he concluded that the Federation's policy had retrogressed from its earlier stand. He submitted the report to Gompers for his comment before publishing it. Gompers replied that the study was "neither fair nor accurate," and concluded coldly: "Let me say further, that I have more important work to attend to than to correct 'copy' for your paper." (Gompers to W. E. B. DuBois, Jan. 5, 1903, *GLB*; W. E. B. Du Bois, *The Negro Artisan*, Atlanta, Ga., 1902, pp. 169-70.)

unions, no 'colored' unions, as such. Consequently, when the Galveston colored union made application for a charter, it was told that it would have to change its name. It did so. The union is now known as 'Federal labor union No. 7147."

To the Negro workers, however, the question of whether or not the A. F. of L. drew the "color line" was more than a matter of semantics and names of unions. A union organized on a Jim Crow basis discriminated against Negro workers whether its title was "Colored" or "Federal."

The Negro workers were further discriminated against when, in many parts of the South, the Jim Crow locals were not permitted to send delegates to A. F. of L. central labor bodies. Gompers washed his hands off protests from Negro workers on this issue, maintaining "that a Central Body was the sole judge of the eligibility of a Delegate being seated therein." This, of course, resulted in an almost total ignoring by the A. F. of L.'s central labor bodies of the grievances of Negro locals, to say nothing of hampering whatever attempt was being made to organize Negro workers.* But when, in an effort to at least partially remedy this situation, the Negro locals set up their own central labor bodies and asked for an A. F. of L. charter, it was only granted when and if the Federation's leadership received the consent of the white central labor body in the area. Such consent was frequently not forthcoming, since the local central body raised the argument that the Negro central labor unions, if chartered, "would be entitled to seats in the State Federation [of Labor]." [15]

In March, 1900, the Central Trade and Labor Council of New Orleans, set up by seven A. F. of L. Negro unions who were not permitted to send delegates to the official central labor body in the city, applied to the Federation for a charter, promising to work in harmony with the council of white unions. The Executive Council turned the matter over to Gompers for investigation. He informed the Negro trade unionists that he must first obtain the consent of the white central body. When he learned from James Leonard, A. F. of L. general organizer in New Orleans, that "in the matter of organizing a C.L.U. of colored workers, the feeling against a project of this kind is so great that it would cause a great deal of trouble at this particular time," Gompers refused to grant the charter. Moreover, he added insult to injury by telling the Negro unionists in New Orleans that "there is no use kicking against the pricks and we cannot overcome prejudice in a day." To this James E. Porter, secretary

---

* "I could, I believe," wrote an A.F. of L. organizer, "organize 1,000 or over Negroes in this city working in cotton oil mills, lumber yards, laborers, etc., but the central body's delegates seem to be opposed to admitting delegates from colored organizations. I have, therefore, refrained from organizing them. . . ." (Henry M. Walker to Gompers, Nov. 4, 1899, Houston, Texas, *AFL Corr.*)

of the Negro Central Trades and Labor Council, replied bitterly but correctly: "I did not understand that there is prejudice when the wages and interest are the same and can only be upheld by concert[ed] action." [16]

Gompers referred the matter of the New Orleans Central Councils to the 1900 A. F. of L. convention. In his annual report, he came out strongly for a policy of segregation, and proposed that the Federation allow the formation of separate trade councils for Negro workers. The convention adopted the suggestion, and official sanction was given to a Jim Crow policy of organization. Article 12, Section 6, of the A. F. of L. constitution, as revised in 1900, reads: "Separate charters may be issued to central labor unions, local unions or federated labor unions, composed exclusively of colored workers where in the judgment of the Executive Council it appears advisable." [17]

Thus the A. F. of L. let it be known that affiliated national and local unions could continue to refuse admission to workers because of their color. The Federation and its leaders had settled into a fixed policy of Jim Crowism. Segregation, Gompers declared, was the best settlement of the problem; the separation of Negro and white workers was best for both groups and for the entire labor movement, for it would avoid "arousing bitterness." [18]

A. F. OF L. LEADERS JUSTIFY JIM CROW UNIONISM

The action of the 1900 Convention brought so many protests from Negro organizations that the A. F. of L. Executive Council issued a statement in April, 1901, defending the Federation's Jim Crow policies. The statement, signed by Gompers on behalf of the Council, was replete with double-talk. For years, it declared, the A. F. of L. had favored the organization of all workers without regard to creed, color, sex, nationality or politics, but the Federation "does not necessarily proclaim that the social barriers which exist between the whites and blacks could or should be obliterated." The formation of separate unions for white and Negro workers was only a recognition of existing prejudices and by no means evidence that the A. F. of L. was opposed to granting the Negro the right to organize. The absence of Negro membership in most of the trade unions affiliated to the A. F. of L. was no indication of their hostility to organizing Negro workers. The real blame rested upon the Negro workers themselves, for "the colored workers have allowed themselves to be used with too frequent telling effect by their employers as to injure the cause and interests of themselves, as well as of white workers." The statement concluded with a warning to the Negro workers not to frustrate the efforts of the A. F. of L. and its affiliates to organize them by scabbing and otherwise serving the interests of the employers. [19]

The statement clearly revealed that the A. F. of L. leadership fully approved of Jim Crow unionism and hypocritically sought to justify the shameful neglect of the needs of Negro workers by placing the responsibility upon Negro workers. That the issue upon which this conclusion was based—so-called Negro strikebreaking—was a mere subterfuge is demonstrated by the fact that most Negroes imported by employers to break strikes did not know the purpose for which they were to be used, and many refused to take the jobs when they learned that a labor dispute was in progress. Thus the United Mine Workers, learning through experience that the solution for so-called Negro strikebreaking was to inform the Negroes that they were being used without their knowledge to break strikes and assist them in their predicament,* successfully adopted this practice. When the union attempted to organize in the states of Arkansas, Kansas, and Oklahoma in 1899-1900 and Negroes were imported to be used as strikebreakers, the striking white miners met the Negroes and informed them that a strike was taking place. The vast majority of the Negroes refused to work. Some had to be sent back to their homes; others, assured of the union's support, remained to join the strikers.[20]

Despite such evidences of solidarity of Negro workers and white strikers, the craft union leaders of the A. F. of L. continued to point to "Negro strikebreaking" as proof that Negroes were themselves to blame for Jim Crow in the Federation.[21]

JIM CROW IN EMPLOYMENT

Jim Crow in the labor movement led inevitably to Jim Crow in employment. Not only did the craft union leaders condone the racism revealed so arrogantly in the hiring policy of most employers; they actively participated in a conspiracy against the Negro workers.

During the 1880's and early 1890's, Negro labor in Southern cities was important in railroading, shipping, and building. Beginning in the late

* Its most important experience was the bloody skirmish at Virden, Illinois, on October 12, 1898, in which 14 persons were killed and 50 wounded. During the strike, the coal operators sent agents to Alabama who engaged a thousand Negroes to come North and work in the mines. When the Negroes arrived and learned that a strike was in effect, they "complained that they had been deceived by the operators, and most of them refused to work. Deputies stationed on the grounds are charged with threatening to shoot Negroes who attempted to leave." (*The Public*, Aug. 27, 1898.) Unfortunately, the striking members of the U.M.W. made no effort to assist the Negroes or even to involve them in their struggle. Instead, they fell prey to "the anti-Negro spirit" fanned by the operators and their allies. In reporting the battle at Virden on October 12, *The Public*, an independent weekly, correctly emphasized: "The anti-Negro spirit must be looked for higher-up." (Oct. 22, 1898.) For further discussion of this event, see Ray Ginger, "Were Negroes Strikebreakers?" *The Negro History Bulletin*, Jan., 1952, pp. 73-74.

1890's, the Negro workers in Southern cities were steadily eliminated from skilled jobs as a result of a deliberate conspiracy between employers and the craft unions. By refusing to admit Negro members and by preventing union members from working with men who were not in the union, these organizations gradually pushed Negro workers out of skilled positions they had held formerly. Where Negro craftsmen were organized in separate, Jim Crow locals, they received little or no assistance from the city central labor bodies, composed of white men drawn from white locals. The skilled places held by the members of the Negro local were eyed jealously by the white craft unions which waited only for an opportunity to displace the Negro workers. Smaller and therefore less powerful, the Negro local was severely handicapped. The national unions to which the Jim Crow Negro locals were affiliated, refused to protect their jobs or wage scales.[22]

The substitution of formal apprenticeship training, controlled by the craft unions, for "picking up" the trade was an important factor in limiting the opportunities for Negroes in the skilled trades. Employers and unions conspired to confine apprenticeships to whites, and with vocational training closed to most Negroes in the South, the Negro was not only excluded from certain occupations he formerly had held, but given little or no opportunity to mount higher on the economic ladder.[23]

Some Negro spokesmen felt that the way to circumvent the conspiracy between empoyers and unions that was depriving the Negroes of opportunity even to learn skilled trades was to establish trade and industrial schools. But this by itself, it soon became evident, was no solution. At a conference held at the Hampton (Virginia) Industrial School in the summer of 1898, it was clearly established that "it was quite impossible for colored people to rise as long as the trades unions so generally excluded colored workmen. Some of the graduates at Hampton who had learned there, complained that they had not been able to work at their trades because [of being] excluded from the union."[24]

The employer-union conspiracy narrowing the field of industrial occupation open to Negroes existed also in the factory industries of the South which used white labor almost exclusively. The few Negroes in the cotton mills had lowly jobs, lived apart from the white workers, and were excluded from the A. F. of L. union in the field as well as from whatever limited plans this organization made to advance the status of the workers in the industry. In the tobacco factories of Virginia and North Carolina, the machine jobs were reserved for white workers, and the Negro workers were confined to the least desirable and most unhealthy jobs. Here too, the Tobacco Workers' International Union, affiliated to the A. F. of L., scarcely reached the Negroes in its feeble efforts to organize the industry.[25]

The total result of this conspiracy between the employers and the craft unions was to bar Negro workers from participation in a great portion of America's industrial life. Through the conspiracy between employers and many A. F. of L. unions (as well as between employers and the Railroad Brotherhoods), "white only" signs were placed upon such trades as electricians, plumbers, gas and steamfitters, railroad engineers and firemen, stationary engineers, cranemen, hoistmen, machinists, and hundreds of other skilled and semi-skilled occupations.

By the turn of the century, the Negro's place in industry, as a result of this conspiracy, was at the bottom of the scale. No matter where they were employed, they received lower wages than whites for the same job, and usually were limited to the hardest and dirtiest tasks. Negroes who managed to join craft unions found that they had gained little protection. White members received preference for jobs, and several A. F. of L. unions allowed Negro members to work longer hours than white workers and at a lower wage scale.

JIM CROW UNIONISM AND WHITE WORKERS

The explanation offered by the A. F. of L. leaders for the decision to accept the color line in the labor movement was spelled out time and again. The Southern white workers, and some of the Northern ones, would not accept Negroes in their unions or even work in the same shops and factories with them, and to insist upon a policy of integration of Negro and white workers would doom the chance of building the A. F. of L. In the face of the widespread prejudice against Negroes, went the explanation, to adhere to a policy of labor solidarity and unity would be suicidal. "This is *not* trades unionism as I have learned it," W. E. Klapetzky, Secretary-Treasurer of the Journeymen's Barbers' International Union, confessed to Gompers in August, 1897, announcing the decision to break up a union of Negro and white barbers in Galveston, Texas, into separate unions for Negroes and whites. But there was no alternative. To do otherwise, according to him, was to risk the entire future of the International.[26]

There is no doubt that there were white workers in many parts of the South, as well as in the North, who were filled with anti-Negro prejudice and would fight bitterly any and all efforts to unite Negro and white workers. Undoubtedly there were Southern white workers who were under the illusion that they benefitted from the Jim Crow practiced by industry and the A. F. of L. unions, and deluded themselves with the view that being white and "superior," they were able to command higher wages. But there was ample evidence to prove that the policy of discrimination practiced by the A. F. of L. affiliates injured the white workers as well as the Negro, and that because of the low wages received by the Negro workers, the wages of white workers could not rise much above the wage scale for Negroes.[27] Witness after witness told the Industrial Commission of 1900 that the unorganized status of the Negro working class was "a drag on the white laboring class in the South, and tends to cut down their wages." "The white journeymen bricklayer in our section," a Southern employer testified, "gets $2.50 a day, and we are able to employ a colored bricklayer for $1.75." Asked how this affected the wages of the white bricklayer, the employer replied frankly: "If a white bricklayer . . . asks for employment and makes known his rate of wages, which is $2.50 a day . . . the employer may say to him in return, I can employ a Negro bricklayer who has as much skill as you, and will do as good service for $1.75. Now, I will put you on at $2.25."

After a careful investigation of conditions in all Southern trades, C. C. Houston, editor of the Atlanta *Journal of Labor,* told the Industrial Commission: "My observation of colored labor in the South, so far as it relates to the trades where skilled labor is required, is that it is held over the head of white labor to the extent of holding down wages. . . . In the building trades, for instance . . . the wages paid to white labor are based primarily on the wages paid to colored labor; and in every instance in which an increased wage scale has been secured, with one or two exceptions, it has been reached only after the colored man was organized and a combined effort of the two was made."[28]

In an appeal to white workers in the A. F. of L., Houston reported that his investigation had convinced him that "the white man in order to retain his wages and in the hope of increasing his wage scale, has not only to recognize but to assist the black man, and unless you do assist him, and raise him up, he is going to pull you down to his standard." He bitterly condemned the fact that certain trade union officials justified discriminatory practices against Negroes on the ground that Negro workers were not really interested in bettering themselves. "They have an ambition to receive a wage equal to that of the white man and to live on a plane relatively equal to that of the white man."[29]

There were many Southern white workers who, like C. C. Houston, understood that they could not raise their living standards while the Negro workers remained on the lowest rungs of the economic ladder and that to make distinctions among workers as to color was to play into the hands of the employers, the common foe of both Negro and white workers. F. A. Davidson, secretary of the Atlanta Federation of Trades, criticizing an agreement which discriminated against Negroes drawn up by James Duncan, second A. F. of L. vice-president, and a Southern firm, protested to Gompers:

"I wish to say, emphatically, that it is our settled policy to recognize unions regardless of color. This policy is not wholly the outgrowth of the growing sentiment of the Brotherhood of Man but it is forced upon us by the fact of the invasion of all avenues of employment by the black man, and unless they are organized with us it can only result in a deadly competition. Taking into consideration these facts and conditions we are compelled to except to the spirit conveyed by Duncan." [30] *

In February, 1898, the Southern press announced the formation of "The Southern Confederacy of Labor" in Atlanta, Georgia, which aimed to establish an independent Federation of Southern white workers.† "The reason for the scheme," the Augusta (Georgia) *Banner* pointed out, "is that Northern organizations persist in admitting Negroes into their trade unions, something that is very distasteful to the working people of the South." But even more significant than this news was the fact that "The Southern Confederacy of Labor," set up to bar Negroes from the trade unions, gained little support among Southern workers. Many Southern labor organizations denounced the Confederacy as an employer-sponsored movement to split Negro and white workers and thereby increase their profits by intensifying their exploitation of both groups, and rejected invitations to attend its founding convention. The A. F. of L.'s Federal Labor Union in Augusta voted unanimously to have nothing to do with the Confederacy on the ground "that labor should not organize to hamper or oppress any class of toilers." "This is significant," announced the Augusta *Herald*, "when it is considered that the union is composed of skilled workmen—and all white." [31]

Equally significant in 1898 was the action of white workers in Galveston, Texas, during the strike of some 2,300 Negro longshore members of the A. F. of L. against the Malloy lines for an increase of wages from 30 to 40 cents an hour to 40 and 50 cents. The company offered the strikers' jobs to white workers, "but they," the A. F. of L. organizer in Galveston informed Gompers on August 9, 1898, "refused it even at any price. They appreciate the fact that the thorough organization of the Negro, means the ultimate success of organized labor in Galveston. So we are silently staying with the Negro in their demands and have high

* Shown Davidson's letter, Duncan sneered that "his communication is beautiful sentimentality bordering upon the ideal and covers a state of affairs which we all think ought to exist and hope may exist, but at the present time . . . is wholly unwarranted." (James Duncan to Gompers, June 16, 1896, *AFL Corr.*) Under the agreement drawn up by Duncan and the firm of Venable Bros. in Atlanta, Negro workers in the plant who were members of the A.F. of L.'s Quarrymen's Union were replaced with white workers. The Atlanta Federation of Trades went on record as opposing the agreement, and fought for the right of the Negro workers to remain in the plant as recognized members of the A.F. of L. union. (E. A. Davidson to Gompers, May 30, 1896, *AFL Corr.*)

† "The Southern Confederacy of Labor" was launched by the Atlanta *Tocsin* which circulated notices to all *"white labor organizations* in the Southern States" calling upon them to send delegates to a founding convention. There is no evidence that the convention was ever held. (*See* Atlanta *Times,* Jan. 22, 1898.)

hopes of their success." [32] These "high hopes" were not realized; despite
the tremendous militancy of the Negro strikers and the support they
received from the white workers in Galveston, the strike, which lasted
four weeks, was broken after the killing and arrest of some of the
Negroes and the use of the state militia.[33] Nevertheless, the unity of
Negroes and whites that featured the strike was further proof that there
were many white workers in the South who refused to allow the employers' inspired anti-Negro propaganda to blunt their understanding that
Negro and white workers must stand shoulder to shoulder in a common
struggle.

WHITE CHAUVINISM OF LEADERS

It was not, however, on these and other illustrations of Negro-white
unity that the A. F. of L. leaders based their policies, but rather on the
conception that the vast majority of white workers in the South, and
many in the North, would under no circumstances tolerate unity with
Negroes. They urged the Negroes to be patient, and held out the hope
that, in due time, the A. F. of L.'s program of education and "moral
suasion" would break down the barriers separating Negro and white in
the labor movement.[34]

Unfortunately for this theory, the key men who were supposed to do
the educating were themselves guilty of the most chauvinistic attitudes
and practices. For one thing, many A. F. of L. organizers, who in addition to organizing were supposed to educate the workers, publicly and
privately expressed contempt for Negroes, and defended Jim Crow practices in society as a whole as well as in the labor movement. They defended the exclusion of Negroes from machine jobs with the slanderous
argument that they were "clumsy and would be lulled to sleep by the
whirring of the wheels," accused Negroes of being "natural strikebreakers" and thus utterly unsuited to belong to a trade union, and warned
the A. F. of L. national officers that they could not be expected even to
attempt to unite Negro and whites in the same locals.[35]

In explaining his failure to conduct a successful organizing campaign
in the South in 1899,* F. J. McGruder, A. F. of L. southern organizer,

* Early in 1899, the Executive Council voted to launch a "Southern organizing
campaign." It appointed two organizers for one month, and another, Will H. Winn,
for three months. None of the organizers were Negroes, and all three expressed
contempt for the Negro workers. As was to be expected, nothing materialized from
the "organizing campaign" so far as organization of Negro workers was concerned. Gompers was not disappointed by these results, for as he wrote to the
Federation's New Orleans organizer: "while it is desirable to organize them [the
Negroes] . . . yet the organization of white workmen is of paramount importance,
and should not be hazarded." (Gompers to James Leonard, June 28, 1900, GLB.)

who prided himself on being "a full blooded Irishman," wrote to Gompers that he was "up against a hard proposition" in trying to organize "Jews and n - - - - s." "The Nigras there is the most ignorant people in the world," he added. Another A. F. of L. organizer, who was similarly unsuccessful, wrote from Savannah, Georgia: "I try to do the Best I can for all unions. But when you have to Deal with those ignorant negros then you have something else on your hands." That contempt for the Negro was not confined to Southern organizers is revealed in the following comment from an A. F. of L. organizer in Cairo, Illinois: "The only way I will be able to get any body into a union in this place will be to chloroform them and initiate them while under the influence of the drug. There is a reason for all these conditions, and that reason is, that of a population of 12,000, over one-half are Negroes. This place is full of 'n - - - - s.' " [36]

There is no evidence to indicate that Gompers or any of the other top leaders of the A. F. of L. dismissed or even rebuked organizers for such vicious chauvinism. Indeed, the contrary is true.[37] In January, 1898, Gompers published an article in the *American Federationist* by Will Winn, the A. F. of L. organizer in Georgia, and one of the three organizers assigned to the A. F. of L.'s Southern "organizing campaign." Winn wrote that even if the Federation threw all of its forces into a campaign to organize Southern Negro workers, the efforts would end in failure, because the Negroes did not possess "those peculiarities of temperament such as patriotism, sympathy, sacrifice, etc. and which alone make an organization of the character and complicity of the modern trade union possible." Instead of the A. F. of L. wasting its time and money attempting to organize Negro workers who could not be organized, Winn proposed that it support as the best solution of the problem, the colonization of Negroes in Liberia or Cuba.

And this article entitled, "The Negro: His Relation to Southern Industry," was hailed by Gompers who hastened to congratulate the author for having given the labor movement a fair presentation of the subject.[38]

The praise of Winn's slanderous article is not surprising. Most of the top A. F. of L. leaders were themselves masters of racial slander. Gompers who had already used the most vicious epithets in fanning race hatred against Chinese and other Oriental workers in the early years of the A. F. of L., employed racial epithets which revealed contempt for the Negro people. He took delight in telling stories in his public addresses which helped to perpetuate the stereotype of the Negroes, whom he referred to as "darkies," as superstitious, dull, ignorant, happy-go-lucky, improvident, lazy, and immoral.[39] On such vital issues as disfranchisement, lynchings, exclusion of Negroes from jury service, segregation in schools, colleges, railroads and other public places, Gompers was utterly and completely silent. In 1895, the A. F. of L. convention protested against curtailment of the franchise, "especially in Southern cities," called upon "the unions of labor and all other fair minded citizens to take such action as shall thwart all attempts to strike a blow at manhood suffrage," and directed the Executive Council "to lend every aid, and if necessary, take the initiative to carry out the purpose of these resolutions." But Gompers did nothing to carry out these instructions.[40]

Bitterly disappointed, Negro spokesmen, who had hailed the action of the 1895 convention, warned Gompers that the policy he was pursuing was dangerous for the white workers as well as Negroes. Unless the labor movement fought for the political freedom of the Negro people and "unless the white labor unions were willing to fraternize with the black people working in the same trades they must all sink in a condition of hopeless slavery." Rev. Reverdy C. Ramson, Negro clergyman of Chicago, wrote: "White men the country over will one day discover a menace to their own industrial independence and prosperity, as well as to their political liberty, through the degradation by industrial and political serfdom, of the millions of black toilers of the land." [41]

But such warnings made no impression on the A. F. of L. President. On Labor Day, 1902, Gompers participated in the celebration sponsored by the New Orleans trade unions. It was a segregated affair, and Gompers spoke first to the white and then to the Negro unionists. In both speeches, he dealt, for the first time, with the question of Negro disfranchisement. But he assured the Southern white ruling class that it had nothing to fear from his discussion, for he made it clear at the outset that "I do not want to discuss the wisdom of the movement, nor any of its political phases." Instead, in his address to the white unionists he argued that the real menace of illiteracy laws aimed at disfranchising Negroes was that they would disfranchise more whites and thus lay the basis for the decline of the white race and the ascendancy of the Negroes. All this would come to pass because while the Negro child was "being educated by his old black mamy or his aunt or in the schools of your building," the white child was working in the factories and growing up illiterate.

To the Negro unionists Gompers had only one solution for the disfranchisement problem—patience! He admitted that in the South "the black man has been treated in a partial way because of his color. He has been disfranchised. . . . Well, you must hold on and hope for a time. . . . That is politics in the South." [42]

And these were the men who were supposed to lead the fight against the racism fanned among workers by employers! These were the men who told the Negro workers to be patient; that "we cannot overcome prejudice in a day," and assured them that through its program of education and "moral suasion," the A. F. of L. gradually would break down the barriers between Negro and white in the labor movement—barriers which these leaders of the A. F. of L. had themselves helped to erect. Is it any wonder that the Negro people viewed these assurances with scorn! [43]

A. F. OF L. AND FOREIGN-BORN WORKERS

The attitude of the A. F. of L. leadership and that of most of the affiliated craft unions towards foreign-born workers in the middle and late 1890's bore a striking resemblance to their approach to Negro workers. It was an attitude of racism, of contempt and outright hostility, plus a reactionary policy of placing barriers to the entrance of the foreign-born to the country and to the trade unions.

Even if the A. F. of L. leaders had shown any inclination to organize the foreign-born workers, its predominantly craft union structure would have made this almost impossible, for the vast majority were unskilled and semi-skilled.* But the A. F. of L. leaders were anything but interested in organizing the newly-arrived immigrants who were pouring into American industry. On the contrary, they advanced the thesis that these workers were unorganizable, unable to fit into the pattern of American trade unionism as exemplified by the A. F. of L.

This pattern was one of "racial purity." Foreigners, said Gompers and other A. F. of L. leaders, themselves mainly foreign-born, were at best difficult to organize. But the immigrants who entered the country in the decade 1880-1890, when the immigration from southern and eastern Europe first outran "the old immigration" from northern and western Europe, were not only foreigners, but a different kind of foreigners. The A. F. of L. leaders characterized the "old" immigrants as "the sturdy, intelligent and liberty-loving races of Northern and Western Europe," and the "new" immigrants as "the servile and degraded hordes of Southern and Eastern Europe, with their crime and disease-breeding adjuncts of poverty, filth, and slavish willingness to work for almost nothing and to live on less." The "new" immigrants (Italians, Bohemians, Hungarians, Poles, Lithuanians, Rumanians, Russians, etc.), the A. F. of L. leaders charged, could not be organized; unlike the "old" immigrants

---

* Of the 7,048,953 immigrants admitted during the 12 years from 1899 to 1910 and reporting an occupation, 35.9 per cent were laborers and 23.4 per cent were farm laborers. In the year ending June, 1903, nearly one half or 46.5 per cent of all immigrants to this country were either urban laborers or farm laborers, and only 14.5 per cent were skilled workers. (Reports of the Immigration Commissioner, "Statistical Review of Immigration, 1820-1910," *Senate Doc. No. 756*, 61st Cong., 3rd Sess., p. 96.)

(the British, Germans, Dutch, French, and Scandinavians), they were "a heterogeneous stew of divergent and discordant customs, languages, institutions; and they were impossible to assimilate or unionize." They cut wages because they were satisfied with conditions that neither the native American workers nor the "older" immigrants would tolerate. They came not to settle permanently, to take root in America, but to earn a few dollars, primarily through strikebreaking, and return home. They were the "beaten men of beaten races," and their experience and background had deprived them of the unity of purpose and tenacity necessary to successfully build a stable labor movement. They had been oppressed by poverty for so many centuries and had become so degraded that they were unable to lift themselves up to the high level of American workers of the "older" immigrants from northern Europe.[44] *

Even when organized and allowed to become members of the trade unions, the A. F. of L. leaders charged, the "new" immigrants were no asset to the labor movement. The "older" immigrants were amenable to trade unionism; they were patriotic, and democracy was in the very marrow of their bones. Not so with the "new" immigrants. They fell prey to the propaganda of the "anarchists," "socialists," and "radicals of all sorts." They started strikes without cause, and, in general, became "trouble-makers." They were, as Homer D. Call, Secretary of the A. F. of L.'s Amalgamated Meat Cutters and Butcher Workmen, wrote in 1899, "natural kickers," always demanding that "they should be allowed to manage the organization and dictate to the national executive board in all things." The A. F. of L. could do without such workers.[45] As Dr. David J. Sappos put it: "The inclination of the immigrant towards radical doctrines made leaders of the existing unions chary of accepting them as members."[46]

A. F. OF L. AND IMMIGRATION

The racist attitude toward the "new" immigrants was reflected in the campaign waged by the A. F. of L. leaders to restrict or cut off entirely immigration from southern and eastern Europe. In supporting a literacy test for immigrants, Gompers declared that it "will exclude hardly any natives of Great Britain, Ireland, Germany, France or Scandinavia. It will shut out a considerable number of South Italians, and of Slavs and other equally or more undesirable and injurious."[47]

* The arguments of the A.F. of L. leaders was brilliantly and effectively demolished by Dr. Isaac Hourwich in his *Immigration and Labor*, published in 1912. Dr. Hourwich demonstrated that the immigration from southern and eastern Europe had actually encouraged the organization of labor in the United States, and he cited ample evidence in support of this contention.

At the 1896 A. F. of L. convention, Gompers called upon the delegates to endorse the Lodge-Corliss bill in Congress which required that all who sought entrance to America should know how to read or write their own language. The proposal met with bitter opposition. It was "not a labor measure, but came from capitalists," cried one delegate. Another insisted that "the men of wealth were more of a detriment [to organized labor] than the immigrant." "Immigration was not the true cause of the industrial difficulty," said John McBride of the United Mine Workers who pointed to the heroic role played by the "new" immigrants in building his union.

In the face of the determination of the majority of delegates to uphold the A. F. of L.'s widely-proclaimed policy of unity of workers of all races, creeds and nationalities, Gompers' was forced to beat a temporary retreat. The proposal was voted down.[48] However, the A. F. of L. leaders demanded and obtained permission to hold a referendum among the affiliated unions on the question of immigration restriction to guide the 1897 convention.

During the months that the issue was being debated in the affiliated unions prior to their vote, the A. F. of L. leadership joined with the "Immigration Restriction League," an employer-sponsored organization, to distribute the League's literature to members of the Federation—literature which emphasized that "the new immigrants" "are not needed;" "do not increase the wealth of the country;" "lower the standard of living (a) by cheap labor, (b) by willingness to live in a depraved condition;" "are a menace to our national institutions; (a) by foreign speech and customs; (b) by groupings in isolated bodies; (c) because they do not appreciate our institutions and are not interested in preserving them."[49]

Even though President Cleveland vetoed the Lodge-Corliss bill as being against the best traditions of American democracy, the A. F. of L. leaders, together with the "Immigration Restriction League," still pressed for its endorsement by the 1897 convention.* Despite the fact that only a few of of the affiliated unions finally voted in the referendum, the A. F. of L. leaders demanded action in favor of immigration restriction and a literacy test for immigrants by the delegates on the ground that these demands reflected the will of organized labor. A furious debate broke out with delegate after delegate charging that the proposals violated the A. F. of L.'s own declarations in favor of "the brotherhood of man," and ignored the fact that "the best trade unionists were the foreigners." But this time the A. F. of L. leadership had prepared for the contest. With the pro-

* President Cleveland vetoed the bill on March 2, 1897, three days before his term ended. His action was denounced by the A.F. of L. leaders as "a direct blow at the interests of labor." (New York *Journal*, March 3-4, 1897.) The House passed the bill over the veto, but the Senate did not act in time.

administration delegates well organized, the demands for immigration restriction and the passage of a literacy test by Congress won out.[50]

From 1897 on, the A. F. of L. called for more and more stringent legislation to restrict immigration. At the 1901 convention, Edward F. McSweeney, Assistant Commissioner of Immigration, was given full time to launch a vicious attack on the "new" immigrants from southern and eastern Europe in the course of which he appealed to the A. F. of L. to intensify its efforts to keep out this "pauper labor" that was a "menace" to American institutions. Following his address, McSweeney was accorded a vote of thanks.[51]

RESTRICTIONS ON FOREIGN-BORN WORKERS

Although the A. F. of L. leaders, in cooperation with employer-sponsored organizations, southern demagogues, nativist racists, and other political agents of big business, helped to restrict the flow of immigration, they could not stop the demand of the fast expanding industries for labor power. But they could and did make it exceedingly difficult, if not impossible, for these immigrants to become members of the A. F. of L. Special requirements were imposed upon immigrant applicants for membership in many A. F. of L. unions: (1) naturalization, or declaration of intention to become a citizen (some unions even required full-fledged citizenship); (2) payment of high initiation fees, higher fees than were demanded of other applicants (some unions fixed fees as high as $500); (3) approval or consent of the officers of the national union; (4) presentation of the card of a foreign union; (5) special evidence of competency. "It was difficult for an immigrant to get into a building-trades' union," a foreign-born worker recalled years later. "The smallest initiation fee was $25.00; in some cases it was as high as $100.00. Second, even when an immigrant could pay this sum, he was not sure that he could pass the required examination." Referring to another A. F. of L. union, a contemporary labor figure recalled later: "The initiation fee had been placed at $100. If the person seeking membership was favorably regarded the entrance fee could be paid in installments, and if he were [an immigrant and] not so regarded it had to be paid in a lump sum." [52]

A. F. OF L. AND WOMEN WORKERS

In July, 1900, several hundred women workers in Cincinnati, employed in a large variety of trades and callings, sent a petition to the A. F. of L. national office in which they complained: "We have some time ago, made application to join the Trades Unions, but could never get the members to meet us, having always the same excuse. We feel satisfied that they are trying to keep us out of the unions." [53]

The experience of the women in Cincinnati was duplicated by women workers in all parts of the country. Only a small number of the unions affiliated with the A. F. of L. in this period actually forbade the admission of women,* but, as in the case of Negro and foreign-born workers, most of the craft unions achieved the same effect without specific constitutional clauses barring women, through the system of long apprenticeship requirements, the high fees charged for admission, and special examinations which women were required to pass. Some unions admitted women employed in certain branches, but not those employed in others. Usually, in such cases, the women were excluded from the best-paid branches of the trade. Describing an engraving plant he had visited in Bridgeton, New Jersey, an A. F. of L. organizer reported in March, 1900, that of the 1,100 workers employed, about 600 were women who were permitted by the union to work only in the lowest-paid positions in which they received "about $2.50 a week." In the engraving department, he explained, "there are about 50 girls employed but they are not allowed to do the better class of work. The engravers' union . . . will not take them in their organization." [54]

Not only did many A. F. of L. unions keep out women either by constitutional bars, by openly declared policy, or by simply refusing to organize them, but they refused to sanction the granting of a special charter for a women's local to be affiliated directly to the national A. F. of L. Even though these women were excluded from the unions that refused to permit the organization of women's locals, the national leaders of the A. F. of L. refused the charter request.

In 1900, a group of women workers in the shoe industry in Illinois appealed to the A. F. of L.'s Boot and Shoe Workers' Union for permission to become members. Informed what the dues were, they protested that they could not pay such a high sum on the meager wages they earned. They appealed to the A. F. of L. national office to urge the Boot and Shoe Workers' Union to reduce the dues. The request was forwarded, and Horace M. Eaton, Secretary-Treasurer of the Union, bluntly informed Frank Morrison, A. F. of L. Secretary-Treasurer, that the union was not interested in recruiting members "on the bargain counter plan." Morrison informed the women that there was nothing the A. F. of L. could do to force the Union to alter its stand.

Learning this, the women organized a local union and asked the A. F. of L. national office to grant it a charter. They explained again that they were willing to join the Boot and Shoe Workers' Union, and that the

* Among them were the Barbers, the Engravers, the Switchmen, and the Molders. These unions prescribed that only men were eligible for membership, and the Molders even imposed a penalty of a fine or of expulsion on any member who dared to give instructions to female workers in any branch of the trade. (F. E. Wolfe, *Admission to American Trade Unions*, Baltimore, 1912, p. 85.)

only reason they voted not to was that "the dues were to[o] high." The Boot and Shoe Workers' Union vigorously protested against granting a charter to the newly-formed women's local, and the A. F. of L. national office turned down the request.[55]

Meanwhile, the A. F. of L. was passing resolutions urging the organization of women workers, and even urging "those international and national organizations that do not admit women workers to membership . . . to give early consideration for such admission." But nothing was done to give these resolutions meaning. On the contrary, the A. F. of L. leaders spent more time justifying the neglect of women workers by the affiliated unions than they did persuading them to abandon their policy. Women, they argued, did not stay in industry permanently. They obtained jobs just for "spending money." Soon they married and dropped out of the industry. Why, then, should the trade unions tax themselves and expend undue energy attempting to organize women?[56]

Meanwhile, women were entering industry in larger and larger numbers,* and surveys disclosed that the majority depended on their wages for a livelihood, that most of them had dependents, and that the trend for women, married as well as unmarried, was towards entering factories. In its investigation, the Industrial Commission found widespread evidence in 1900 that "the wives—mothers of the family go into the factory and work for a living."[57]

But evidence presented in government and private surveys did not dispel the nonsensical theories advanced by the A. F. of L. officials to justify the refusal of the craft unions to organize women workers. The result, of course, was that women's wages were considerably lower than those of male workers even when they did the same work. In 1897 Commissioner Caroll D. Wright cited 781 instances of men and women engaged in the same occupations and performing their duties with equal efficiency. In only 57 of these cases did the women receive equal pay with men, while in 595 cases their pay was appreciably less. A report drawn up in 1899 showed that in 23 industries where men and women did the same work, men's wages ranged from 150 percent to 300 percent higher than women's wages. The (San Francisco) *Voice of Labor* cited these statistics in demanding the launching of an intensive drive to organize women workers into the A. F. of L., and a "return to the principle of unionism that demands equal wages for the same work, be it performed by male or female." Otherwise, it warned, the wages of the male workers would sink to the level of women workers.[58]

Endorsing this appeal, a male trade unionist declared: "It is useless . . .

* The 1900 Census showed more than five million women employed, and of 303 occupations listed, women were in 296. (*Twelfth Census of the U.S.,* 1900, Special Reports, Occupations, pp. 7-9.)

to attempt to stem the tide of female workers. It now rests with us to bring them into our organizations. . . . To see that they are affiliated with us . . . and that we extend to them the protection which thorough organization affords . . . is a duty which we cannot shirk without grave dangers to ourselves." [59]

Unfortunately, these appeals and warnings fell on deaf ears. The situation in most of the craft unions affiliated with the A. F. of L. was epitomized in 1900 during an exchange between a member of the U.S. Industrial Commission and G. W. Perkins, President of the Cigar Makers' International Union:

"Q. Have you many female members?

"A. Very few, comparatively speaking, to the large number of females employed in the trade." [60]

It was this situation, declared Leonora O'Reilly, militant leader of the Working Women's Society of New York, that was responsible for the fact "that there are 40,000 women in New York City whose wages are so low that they must eke out an existence by charity or starve or worse . . . [and] that girls in San Francisco laundries work sixteen hours a day for 30 cents." [61]

If white women suffered from low wages and other evils as a result, to no small extent, of the practices of the A. F. of L. and its affiliated unions, the lot of Negro women workers was, of course, far worse. They had a double burden to bear: discrimination as women and as Negroes. They were excluded from employment and from unions by both sex and color. [62]

Meager as were the wages of women workers in general, those of Negro women were far worse. Surveys revealed that there was a wide difference in the wages of Negro and white women workers who were doing identical work. Just as women workers in general received from one-half to one-quarter less pay than men for equal work,* so Negro women averaged one-third to one-half less pay than white women for equal work. This differential between white and Negro women workers prevailed in every occupation. Indeed, in many occupations, Negro women never knew what they would receive for their work. In the words of one Negro woman: "You never know what you are going to get; you just take what they give you and go." [63]

"The A. F. of L. affirms as one of the cardinal principles of the trade union movement that the working people must organize, unite and

---

* Professor Brissenden estimates that the earnings of men and women in all manufacturing industries in 1899 were: Men—$587; Women—$314. (Paul F. Brissenden, *Earnings of Factory Workers, 1899 to 1927*, United States Bureau of the Census, Monograph X, Washington, 1929, pp. 29-30.)

federate, irrespective of creed, color, sex, nationality or politics." [64] At convention after convention, these fine and noble sentiments were proclaimed. But they had no relation whatever to reality. Engaged almost entirely in the unskilled and semi-skilled occupations, the Negro, foreign-born and women workers received scant attention from the craft unions who made up the major organizations of the A. F. of L. In addition, they were barred from membership in many of these unions by a complex system of rules, regulations, and practices deliberately designed to achieve their exclusion.

In the years following 1895, the main outlines of the American Federation of Labor were forged and were to be retained down until the 1930's. During these years, the establishment of a "labor aristocracy" became the major objective of the Federation. Despite its frequent proclamation of principles of labor solidarity, the A. F. of L. sought to organize primarily the skilled workers, and refused to make any real effort to organize the unskilled worker. Instead of seeking to organize and unite the working people irrespective of sex, color, or nationality, as it affirmed, the keystone of the A. F. of L. policy was to prevent the organization of the vast majority of the working class.

What accounts for the rapid transformation in the policy of the A. F. of L. leadership towards the organization of workers irrespective of sex, color, or nationality? For certainly the policy pursued on this issue differed sharply from that followed in the early, formative years of the A. F. of L.

Undoubtedly one reason is the rapid decline and disappearance of the K. of L. The A. F. of L. leaders no longer felt the need to compete with the Order for the allegiance of workers brought up in the tradition of labor solidarity. These workers had nowhere else to go but into the Federation so Gompers and his associates in the leadership had no need to convince them that the Federation preserved and continued the finest features of the K. of L. [65]

In a larger sense, however, the policy of the A. F. of L. leadership was part and parcel of a program of class collaboration with monopoly capitalism under which they bought security for the skilled workers at the expense of the unskilled and unorganized workers. As we shall now see, these leaders were prepared to come to terms with the trusts—and, indeed, to become prominent champions of the trusts—provided that their craft unions of skilled workers were allowed to exist in certain limited areas of the giant monopolies. In return, they agreed to do nothing to organize the vast majority of the workers employed by the trusts—the foreign-born, Negro and women workers. [66]

CHAPTER 24

Labor and the Trusts

Despite the Sherman Anti-Trust Act, monopoly in American industry grew at an amazing pace. The Act outlawed the old trust form, but this was speedily replaced by the huge corporations, interlocking directorates, and holding companies.

The severe depression of the mid-nineties accelerated the trend toward monopoly as stagnation in business made it easier for the bigger concerns to acquire properties whose owners were in financial distress, on the verge of bankruptcy, or actually bankrupt. When the economy pulled out of the depression, trustification was in full swing. During 1898, gigantic mergers took place in copper refining, lead, sugar, salt, tobacco, cans, whiskey, baking, street railways, cigarmaking, steel and other lines. In 1900 a Congressional Industrial Commission reported that "industrial combinations have become fixtures in our industrial life."

As huge industrial monopolies were developing, a great financial oligarchy was also emerging in the United States. A few leaders of finance such as J. P. Morgan & Co., the Rockefellers, Kuhn-Loeb, and others came to control large capital resources through the banks and investment companies. By the turn of the century, the big industrialists and bankers were fused into an oligarchy of finance capital (the merger of industrial capital with bank capital). The investment bankers increasingly obtained control of the industrial system through mergers, holding companies, interlocking directorates, voting trusts, etc.

In 1901, the House of Morgan organized and controlled the U.S. Steel Corporation, the trust which produced upward of 60 percent of the nation's iron and steel output. The Rockefeller interests controlled a minority of the directorships in U.S. Steel.

In 1897 the combined capitalization of 82 of the biggest industrial corporations was a billion dollars. In 1901, a single corporation, U.S. Steel, had assets of over one billion dollars. The first billion-dollar corporation, it dominated the basic industry of the country. Through their control of U.S. Steel and other industrial combinations, and of banks, railroads, life insurance and trust companies, the Morgan-Rockefeller interests, combining industrial and banking capital, symbolized the emergence of a power that dominated the entire nation. The real government of America resided in Wall Street, for the trusts controlled the political government, and exercised dominating influence over the press, schools, and all other means of communication. Such a power surely threatened the existence of the entire labor movement.[1]

In 1888, Richard T. Ely, the noted economist, discussing how labor was affected by the rise of the trusts, warned: "Evidence is not wanting to show that these huge monopolies propose to turn their immense power against all combinations of workingmen and crush them just as they have the independent producers." Professor Ely urged labor to join the nationwide campaigns against monopoly, led by small business men and farmers, which sought to achieve legislation outlawing the trusts.[2]

With rare exceptions, however, labor in the 'eighties took little part in the agitation for anti-trust legislation.[3] To no small extent, this was due to fear in labor circles that anti-trust legislation would be used against the trade unions; in fact, many of the anti-trust champions called for control of unions as well as monopolies. When the Sherman Anti-Trust Act was adopted in 1890, labor's fears were all too quickly justified. The anti-trust act became an anti-labor law as a result of judicial interpretation. From 1892 to 1896 the government brought five cases under the act against labor and won four, and five against the trusts and won only one.[4]

It was impossible, however, for labor to remain indifferent to the trust question.

A LABOR PROGRAM TO MEET THE CHALLENGE

"How can the trade union meet the Standard Oil Company, the Sugar Trust, or the other swindling syndicates by which prices and wages are fixed?" John Swinton asked the delegates to the 1895 A. F. of L. convention. Pointing out that profound changes were occurring in the structure of American industry, he inquired whether the trade unions were equipped to meet these changes. He was convinced that the new situation arising from the emergence of the trusts could never be met "under the old methods of the trade unions," and predicted that unless new policies and new tactics were quickly adopted, the dawn of the twentieth century might witness "the doom of labor."[5]

A few months later, George E. McNeill developed the same theme at length in an article, entitled "The Trade Unions and the Monopolies."

The veteran labor leader began by asking: "How can the trade unions successfully combat the giant monstrosities of the nineteenth century?" He conceded that when timid labor leaders considered the forces represented by the trusts, syndicates, monopolies, and their allies—"newspaper managers, rich priests and clergymen, gamblers, dudes, corporation attorneys, sychophants to power and position, and some college professors"—and when they realized that "the power of aggregated wealth is with the monopolists," they concluded "that monopoly was sure of the victory and that the trade unions were powerless." McNeill denied the validity of this conclusion, but he agreed that unless extraordinary measures were taken immediately, the outcome would be a triumph for monopoly and a defeat for the labor movement from which it would take decades to recover.

McNeill urged the A. F. of L. to call a conference of all trade unionists at which a program would be worked out to meet the challenge of monopoly. This program should include: (1) a reevaluation of the problem of trade union structure in order to arrive at the one best suited to organize the mass-production, monopolized industries in which the un-skilled and semi-skilled workers were becoming the majority of the labor force; (2) the launching of a campaign to organize the unorganized regardless of skill, race, creed, color, sex, and nationality, and for which purpose there should be a pooling of the financial resources of the trade unions to establish "a system of revenue . . . commensurate with the seriousness of the work at hand;" (3) cooperation and unity of the craft unions in the trustified industries to match the powerful combinations of the employers instead of leaving it to each craft union individually to tackle a giant, mass-production industry—in short, "guerilla warfare must be replaced with a system of scientific warfare;" (4) provisions for feeding and otherwise assisting the workers who would fight the battles against the trusts and "if need be [they should be] pensioned when hopelessly disabled by lockouts or blacklisting;" (5) alliances should be worked out wtih all organizations and groups, particularly of farmers and small business men, ready to join in opposition "to the power of trusts, syndicates and monopolies," with the trade unions retaining jurisdiction over all matters of wages, shop rules, strikes, etc.; (6) educational clubs should be established, under the leadership and control of the labor movement, to rally the entire population against the monopolies.

"The war for the emancipation of labor is now on," McNeill concluded. "We connot win [against monopoly] by making faces at each other, or at the enemy, or by platform denunciations. We have written platforms, amended constitutions and adopted resolutions. We have cried out, 'agitate, educate and organize,' and all this has been well, but now we must learn as well as teach. We must sacrifice our time, money, and, harder still, our peculiar fads, and join hands with all who will help in the struggle for industrial liberty."

This remarkable outlook and program was widely reprinted in the labor press and aroused widespread discussion in labor circles.[6] A number of trade unionists, particularly in industries which were rapidly becoming trustified, endorsed McNeill's detailed plan of action, and urged the A. F. of L. leadership to call a conference for the purpose of carrying it into effect. Special emphasis was placed upon McNeill's call for instantly initiating a concerted, united drive to organize the unorganized regardless of skill, race, creed, color, sex, and nationality. Henry Weissman, treasurer of the Bakers' and Confectionary Workers' Union, which faced the emerging Cracker Trust, endorsed McNeill's proposal, and warned:

"If the workers fail to organize more successfully and particularly so in the leading industries before the process of concentration is complete and the Trusts are almighty, then indeed, will they be unable to offer organized resistance through either the Boycott, Label or strike. Competition will then be a thing of the past, the strike and boycott will very naturally become obsolete ... and if entire trades are controlled by Trusts before the men have built up their organizations the possibility of organization and subsequently of successful strikes will be remote indeed."[7]

INDIFFERENCE OF A. F. OF L.

This timely warning had no effect on the A. F. of L. leadership. McNeill's call for action and his detailed program to meet the threat of rapidly developing monopoly were ignored. There was no need for concern, the A. F. of L. leaders insisted. The Federation and its affiliated unions had demonstrated the ability of craft unionism to survive the gravest economic crisis in American history up to this time. Time would prove that this type of unionism could effectively meet the needs of the workers even in an era of trustification. The members of the A. F. of L. could rest assured that they belonged to an organization that possessed the power to deal effectively with the problems emerging from the trustification of industry as it had with the problems connected with the severe economic crisis.[8] In fact, those who were spreading alarm in labor circles over the rise of the trusts did not seem to realize that there was nothing especially new in this development requiring radical changes in the A. F. of L.'s policies.

"They do not understand," Gompers wrote optimistically in December, 1896, "that the trust is simply an evolution from the old-time individual establishment merged into partnerships, into corporations, and finally into the company of corporations, the trust. Experience will demonstrate that there is a power growing ... which will prove more potent to deal with the trusts, or if the trusts possess any virtue at all that they shall be directed into channels for the public good. . . . And that power is the much despised labor movement. . . . Wait and see." [9]

The workers waited but what they saw hardly bore out Gompers' optimistic prediction. They saw giant trusts emerging in every phase of American economic life; they saw the majority of the A. F. of L. unions attempting vainly to develop organization along craft lines in industries which had obliterated craft distinctions, and they saw by the turn of the century that the men who had called for a new program and a new form of unionism to meet the challenge of the trusts, had spoken the truth when they warned that the failure to follow this path would be disastrous. By the turn of the century, unionism had hardly scratched the surface of the trustified industries. In the main, small, fragmentary unions existed on the outer fringes of these industries, recognized by a few independent, minor concerns.* If they retained any foothold in these industries, they were only able to gain recognition for a small section of the workers employed by the trusts in return for agreeing not to organize the vast majority of the workers.[10]

CRAFT UNIONISM AND THE TRUSTS

There are hundreds of letters from affiliated unions informing the A. F. of L. leadership of their failure to make any real dent in the trusti-

* Leaders of these unions were unalterably opposed to any suggestions that they launch campaigns to organize the trusts, arguing that to do so was to run the risk of losing the independents who tolerated the union only because possession of the union label gave them a certain advantage, enabling them still to compete in certain parts of the country with the trust. "Should our Organization change its policy, and attempt to organize the American and Continental Companies [the two great non-union trusts in the tobacco industry which, through interlocking directorates were one and the same institution]," wrote E. Lewis Evans, secretary-treasurer of the National Tobacco Workers' Union, A.F. of L., "we should at once lose the confidence of the independent firms . . . They would then drop what support and influence they are now giving us; the Label would be useless to them, as a factor in competition with Trust goods, and they would drop it; . . . and our Organization would lose 90% of its membership. . . ." (E. Lewis Evans to Gompers, Sept. 12, Nov. 14, '99, *AFL Corr.*)

This policy, however, did not save the union; on the contrary, it hastened its decline. The tobacco trust, as it had done since its formation, swallowed up one after another of the independent firms which still recognized the union. In 1903, Secretary Evans acknowledged that for all practical purposes, the union was dead, killed by "a fatal disease that has developed in the trade, called the Tobacco Trust. . . ." (E. Lewis Evans to Frank Morrison, Sept. 23, 1903, *AFL Corr.*; *American Federationist*, September, 1903, p. 68; Herbert R. Northrup, "The Tobacco Workers International Union," *Quarterly Journal of Economics*, Vol. LVI, August, 1942, pp. 606-25.)

fied industries. "I presume you are aware," Gompers was informed early in 1899, "that the Western Union Telegraph Company is opposed to organized labor and that any employee affiliating with such as soon as known is discharged and blacklisted. . . ." The secretary-treasurer of the International Brotherhood of Oil and Gas Well Workers, explaining the reasons for the union's lack of progress, informed Gompers that its main hope had been the workers employed by "the Standard Oil Company and they are the people who are afraid to go into an organization for fear of losing their jobs." [11]

Many of Gompers' correspondents who reported this tragic situation also urged the A. F. of L. leadership to adopt a form of organization suited to meet the problems emerging from the rise of trustified, mass-production industries. "Our present form of industrial organization does not meet the requirements of the hour," W. D. Mahon wrote to Gompers. There is no organization of labor able to meet and defeat the combination of capital that is arrayed against it. . . . Instead of bringing victory and strengthening our cause it [the present form of organization] discourages, weakens and fills the country with discontented workmen. . . . Let us make the Federation something more than it has ever been." [12]

It was a futile appeal. The leaders of the A. F. of L. frowned upon any policy, any program that threatened craft unionism. Industries might be trustified and revolutionized by mechanization and division of labor; the industrial area that lent itself to craft union organization might narrow down and, in many cases, disappear, but nothing must jeopardize the "principle" of craft unionism. Only craft unionism was legitimate unionism; industrial unionism, which would eliminate or diminish craft jurisdictions that gave basic strength and stability to the labor movement, would doom the A. F. of L. as surely as it had doomed the K. of L. and the American Railway Union. [13]

Oblivious to the fact that mechanization had reduced the number and importance of the skilled workers in the iron and steel industry, the leaders of the Amalgamated Association of Iron and Steel Workers clung to the craft union form of union structure that was utterly inappropriate in this mass-production industry. [14] Shattered as an effective organization in the Homestead Strike of 1892, the Amalgamated Association was reduced to a nonentity soon after the formation of the U. S. Steel Corporation. Following a strike in 1901, unionism in the steel trust was crushed. [15] The Amalgamated, in the settlement, agreed not to endeavor to organize non-union mills and workers in return for recognition in the few union mills where it had previously been recognized, except where these had become non-union during the strike. [16]

Thus the steel industry, America's basic and most monopolized industry, operated as an open shop. The A. F. of L.'s craft union in the industry just barely managed to maintain its existence by holding to a handful of skilled workers, employed largely in the small, independent plants.

The basic cause for the lack of unionism in the iron and steel industry was pointed to by a U. S. Senate Committee when it declared after investigating conditions of employment in the steel trust: "The general policy of the Amalgamated Association [of Iron and Steel Workers] . . . had from the beginning been very exclusive, so that the union embraced only the more highly skilled men in a comparatively limited part of the rapidly developing steel industry and the organizations of lodges in the steel mills was in large part merely incidental to the development and strengthening of the organization in what may be called the iron branch of the industry. At no time in the history of the Amalgamated Association was any attempt made to work out a logical scheme for dealing with the highly complex situation in the steel mills." [17]

Despite the evidence that the trust was bent on destroying the unicn, the leadership of the Amalgamated Meat Cutters did nothing to place the organization in a position to effectively defend itself. On the contrary, it continued to divide the workers in scores of craft unions, many of which had contracts containing clauses which forbade the crafts from giving support to other crafts in the event of a battle wtih the powerful stockyard trusts.[18] The weakness of this whole form of organization in a trustified, mass production industry like packing was pointed out in March, 1900, in a letter to Frank Morrison from Chicago, the heart of the industry:

"Our experience proves a separation in this craft is not only detrimental to the interests of the workers but also creates that discord and dissatisfaction which injures rather than advances their cause and the cause of all workers employed in this industry. When a union or rather a divided organization attempts to secure better conditions, in most instances [it has] failed and the workers have lost hope in the union and their reorganization is a most difficult obstacle to overcome. By the separation of the workers under as many heads as there are departments, the solidarity which should be fostered is destroyed." [19]

A report adopted by the 1901 Scranton convention boasted that "the magnificent growth of the A. F. of L. is conceded by all students of economic thought to be the result of organization along trade lines." [20] In the light of the status of its affiliated unions in the trustified industries, the statement was labelled by many students of economic thought as ridiculous. But the A. F. of L. leaders made it clear that what they meant was that nothing had occurred in the process of trustification that had weakened the bargaining power of the skilled workers in the trustified industries, and that there were even aspects of this process which had actually increased their bargaining strength.* As for the unskilled and the semi-skilled, the fact that they were unorganized in nearly all of the trustified industries was not due to any inadequacies in craft unionism, but to the fact that these workers were unorganizable. Composed mainly of Negroes, immigrants from southern and eastern Europe, and women, of different racial, linguistic, and cultural backgrounds, and lacking a tradition of unionism, these workers were unable to fit into any type of union. When they became a homogeneous group instead of a diversified, fragmented mass of separate customs, languages, and institutions, then, argued the A. F. of L. leaders, they might be organized and become part of the American labor movement.[21]

In essence, of course, this racist interpretation of the cause for the unorganized status of the mass of the workers in the trustified industries —an interpretation accepted by too many labor historians [22]—was an excuse for the past failures of the A. F. of L. and furnished its leaders with an alibi for not making any attempts to organize the trusts' workers. These leaders feared the consequences flowing from the organization of the masses of industrial workers, realizing that the large industrial unions containing unskilled workers would form the core of the opposition to class collaboration in the A. F. of L. The rapid organization of these workers would alter the character of the Federation and thus jeopardize the position of those who had a vested interest in maintaining the traditional composition of the organization under which small unions of skilled workers could be easily controlled by a bureaucratic leadership.[23]

A. F. OF L. LEADERS DEFEND THE TRUSTS

"Trusts Seek Labor For Ally," read a newspaper headline in the spring of 1899. The article went on to point out that with the indignant voice of almost the entire nation insisting that monopolies be smashed or carefully regulated, the trusts were relying upon certain leaders of organizations "which are in the American Federation of Labor to help create a friendly feeling [towards the trusts]," and to extol the advantages to labor of concentration in industry.[24]

The proof of this startling statement was not long in coming. On September 13, 1899, Gompers and Henry White, general secretary of the

---

* In 1901, in an interview with Henry George, Jr., Gompers declared that there were special aspects of the nature of production in the trustified industries "which cause me not to fear the threatening attitude of the trusts." He cited the steel trust as proof that labor tended to specialize under the trust, and "the withdrawal of these specialists would reduce the trust to a mass of silent and inert machinery. . . ." (*American Federationist*, Vol. VIII, July, 1901, p. 245.) Just at the precise time this was published, the A.F. of L.'s craft union in the steel trust was being reduced to a powerless nonentity.

United Garment Workers, addressed the widely-publicized Interstate Trust Conference held under the auspices of the Chicago Civic Federation.* Both of these A. F. of L. spokesmen upheld the position that organized labor had nothing to fear from the rise of the trusts. Their argument was that businessmen would pay high wages only if assured of high profits, and this could be done only if the number of firms was limited and cut-throat competition eliminated. The trusts and other industrial combinations were inevitable economic developments, against which legal action would be futile and unwise; but their power could be harnessed by another inevitable economic development, the organized labor movement. No governmental interference was necessary to deal with the new industrial and financial giants. Industrial monopoly could be met by the trade unions. In the closed shop lay the answer to the problems of the trusts. "When labor organizations reached their full development they would take charge of the trusts and control them." [25]

Organized labor, said Gompers, viewed apprehensively the "many panaceas and remedies" offered by theorists to curb the growth and development or destroy the combinations in industry. "We have seen those who know little of statecraft and less of economics urge the adoption of laws to 'regulate' interstate commerce, 'prevent' combinations and trusts, and we have also seen that these measures, when enacted, have been the very instruments employed to deprive labor of the benefit of organized effort. . . . The State is not capable of preventing the legitimate development of a natural concentration of industry."

As Gompers saw it, the real and only evil of the trusts was "their corrupting influence on the politics of the country," but this would have to be endured until the toilers were organized and educated to understand that "the State is by rights theirs. . . ." Meanwhile, labor would continue "to organize and keep pace with the industrial development" symbolized by the rise of the trusts.[26]

Henry White declared bluntly that trusts had more efficient means of production than did small businesses and could give labor better terms. "Workingmen are only too familiar with the disheartening reply when asking for an increase of wages, 'Can't afford it on account of competition.' The trust method, at least, changes that situation as far as ability to concede better conditions are concerned." Moreover, the trusts, by lowering prices, paying higher wages and making employment more

---

* The conference was projected in April, 1899, by Ralph M. Easley, secretary of the Civic Federation of Chicago, who was shortly to become secretary of the National Civic Federation. Easley was extremely anxious to have Gompers attend and address the conference. In that way, the conference would be sure that the labor point of view would be "eminently sane," and would contain "no threats nor forebodings, nor pessimism nor despair." (Ralph M. Easley to Gompers, June 1, July 18, 19, Aug. 5, 8, 22, 1899, *AFL Corr.*)

certain, rendered panics less likely to occur. In short, the workers had no quarrel with the trusts; they simply demanded "a share in the profits." The trusts were evidently willing to concede the workers these benefits because they were recognizing their unions and signing collective agreements with them. To be sure, workers were wondering if they would continue to do so, but he, for one, had no doubt that they would. It would be the height of folly for the trusts to attempt to destroy the unions, for they would then be faced with "wild and revolutionary uprisings." [27]

The speeches of the A. F. of L. spokesmen at the Trust Conference were widely and gleefully reported in the press. White was invited to repeat his address to organizations of businessmen throughout the country, and he readily complied.[28] Gompers was praised for his "calm confidence" in stating that "unions are able to take care of their own interests in connection with these industrial combinations." The Chicago *Record* commented: "Mr. Gompers knows the sentiments of the trade unionists of the country and undoubtedly he represents their views correctly when he expresses opposition to repressive legislation against trusts." [29]

WORKERS PROTEST DEFENSE OF TRUSTS

The editorial writer for the Chicago *Record* was evidently unaware of the fact that reports were pouring into A. F. of L. headquarters at Washington, D. C., contradicting his conclusion. The speeches of the A. F. of L. spokesmen at the Trust Conference aroused widespread indignation in labor circles. Officials of A. F. of L. affiliates who were engaged in a life-and-death struggle with the trusts in the mass production industries reported that their members were furious and were denouncing Gompers and White for "whitewashing" the combines that were destroying their unions.* A. F. of L. organizers informed Gompers that everywhere they went, the workers were "indignant, claiming that you said trusts were a good thing," and that he and White were being labelled "parasites and

---

* Gompers was also attacked for carrying advertisements of anti-union trusts in the *American Federationist,* and a number of journals of A.F. of L. affiliates, replying to requests that they cancel advertisements of open-shop trusts, declared that they saw no reason to do so "while the *American Federationist,* Mr. Gompers' own paper is carrying the advertisements." Complaining to Gompers over the publication of advertisements of the anti-union brewery trust in the *American Federationist,* Charles F. Bechtold, national secretary of the United Brewery Workmen, wrote in October, 1899: "I am sorry that these people received a direct endorsement by the A.F. of L." (E. Lewis Evans to Gompers, June 13, 1899, enclosing clipping from Denver *Industrial Advocate;* August Hertfelder to Gompers, Sept. 27, 1899; Herman Robinson to Gompers, Sept. 22, 1899; J. F. Lawrence to Gompers, Sept. 21, 1899; Chas. F. Bechtold to Gompers, Oct. 9, 1899, *AFL Corr.*)

traitors of the labor movement." The A. F. of L. organizer in Idaho and Montana wrote to Gompers, "You have been attacked upon all sides & called every thing even a McKinl[e]y hireling . . . a tool of the Trust. . . . I was shown a newspaper clipping where you was quoted as supporting the Trusts saying that they was a benefit to the Laborer & should not be restricted." [30]

The reaction of the workers in the Rocky Mountain states to Gompers' defense of the trusts can be clearly understood when it is realized that they were better aware perhaps than any other group of workers of the power of the trusts over the federal and state governments and the use they made of this power to undermine labor's rights. In the spring of 1899, a bitter strike erupted in Coeur d'Alene to raise wages at the Bunker Hill and Sullivan Mining Company, the property of the Standard Oil Trust, and bring the rates in these mines in conformity with the rest of the district.[31] Federal troops, under Brigadier General H. C. Merriam, were called into Idaho. Martial law was declared as soon as the troops arrived, and at least some 600 men were arrested without warrant, hundreds of whom were held for months in a hastily constructed and filthy "bull-pen." The writ of habeas corpus was suspended. Governor Frank Steunenberg, correctly described by labor organizations as "a compliant tool" of the Standard Oil Trust, ordered even employers who recognized the union to cease employing members of the Western Federation of Miners.[32] "Through Governor Steuenberg's order no union man is allowed to work in any mine in the country," James Maher, W.F.M. secretary-treasurer, wrote to Gompers. "It is a well known fact that he is paid for this by the Standard Oil Company and the rich mining companies of the State. These are only a few of the iniquities imposed upon the union men of the Coeur D'Alenes by the minions of the corporations." [33]

Gompers was fully aware of all of the "iniquities imposed upon the union men of the Coeur D'Alenes" by the Standard Oil Trust, for he had received an extremely moving appeal from the men involved in the struggle which went in part:

"Owing to the deplorable conditions of affairs existing in the Coeur d'Alenes, we deem it our duty as members of organized labor to take every opportunity to acquaint the public with the true state of affairs under [the] military rule of the Standard Oil Trust. . . .

"The entire machinery of government backed by federal bayonets are ignoring every form of law and human rights in their endeavor to destroy our organizations and lower our standard of living.

"Our regularly elected and duly qualified officers of the law in the county have been arbitrarily and without cause removed.

"The writ of habeas corpus has been destroyed. We no longer have freedom of speech. We are daily being imprisoned for as much as passing the time of day to a non union man.

"Our brothers are thrown into a vile filthy prison on every pretext and without pretext.

"Our men, women and children are subject to all sorts of insults and indignities at the hands of our oppressors.

"We have mentioned only our most grievous wrongs.

"We do most earnestly ask of you that you continue to use your best efforts that a republican form of government be restored to us that we may again resume our efforts to better the conditions of ourselves and our fellow workmen everywhere.

"We do not sign our names as the privacy of the U.S. mail is not reflected in Idaho under the rule of the Standard Oil Trust [and] a disclosing of our names would mean our imprisonment.

                    "COMMITTEE." [34]

Is it surprising that the men who sent this poignant document to Gompers should have been filled with indignation when they read in the newspapers that the A. F. of L. president had said that organized labor had nothing to fear at the hands of the trusts? Is it surprising that the western workers should have accused Gompers of "emulating Chief Arthur of the Engineers," and of being "a tool of the Trust?" [35] *

SOCIALISTS AND THE TRUSTS

Although many Socialists emphasized the danger of the growing power of trusts in American life, the general tendency in Socialist circles was to oppose all movements which sought to "smash the trust" or to "control the trust." The only real solution was a Socialist society, and all who sought to avoid this solution by seeking to return to the by-gone days of small-scale production were doomed to failure.

Some Socialists carried this position to such an extreme that they hailed

* The western workers were also indignant because Gompers refused to heed an appeal from the W.F.M. to call a national union labor convention in Chicago "to protest against the usurpation of power by Military authorities in Idaho." Gompers even warned all Federation affiliates that he opposed the plan, and advised them not to yield to the W.F.M.'s appeal. The western workers were convinced that the A.F. of L. leaders were actually not averse to seeing the W.F.M. local in Coeur d'Alene destroyed.

The experience in the strike convinced the W.F.M. to remain outside the A.F. of L. and to proceed with its plans to build a separate labor federation in the West. This organization was the Western Labor Union.

(See Ed Boyce, President of the W.F.M. to Gompers, June 28, 1899; Gompers to Ed Boyce, June 30, 1899; Gompers to all A.F. of L. affiliates, June 30, 1899; Jas. O'Connell to Gompers, July 31, 1899; Michael Raphael to Gompers, Butte, Montana, July 17, 1899, *AFL Corr.*)

the position adopted by Gompers and other A. F. of L. leaders on the trust question. At the 1900 A. F. of L. Convention, Max Hayes of the Cleveland typographers, leader of the Socialist delegates, complimented Gompers for taking a sound stand on the trusts. He added that the non-Socialist delegates should not become suspicious if he as a Socialist congratulated Gompers, and went on to point out that on the trust question, Gompers and the Socialists inside the A. F. of L. saw eye-to-eye.[36]

Gompers was correct, these Socialists held, in insisting that monopoly was an inevitable stage in economic evolution and in emphasizing that the rise of the trusts did not menace the labor movement. Indeed, this position revealed that Gompers had a keen grasp of Marxism, and that it only required time for him to draw the logical conclusion already reached by the Socialists, namely, that the trusts should be owned by and operated for the benefit of all by nationalizing them.

These Socialists naively contended that the existing trusts should be preserved and the growth of new trusts should be encouraged. The greater the number of trusts, the easier it would be to establish socialism, for it would be infinitely easier for the government to take over a few large trusts than hundreds of thousands of small business enterprises. In line with this approach, some Socialist journals even published each week a list of newly-formed trusts, and hailed these reports as "a herald of the coming triumph of socialism." [37]

These Socialists, of course, failed to understand that while Marxism agrees that it is impossible to return to the days of small-scale production and that it would be economically backward to attempt to do so, it does not mechanically accept the growth of the trusts as basically a progressive development. Indeed, by cutting themselves off from the struggle inside the A. F. of L. against the stand of the leadership on the crucial question of the trusts, these Socialists were taking an anti-Marxist position. They completely failed to answer the question: just what were the workers who were thrown out of employment by the trusts,* and those, whose unions were being crushed by the trusts and whose conditions in the

---

* Newspapers carried frequent reports of workers who were discharged by the trusts because of the monopolists' program of restricting output and raising prices and profits. A.F. of L. organizers constantly reported that trusts in various parts of the country closed down plants and discharged the workers. A typical report, sent to Gompers by Frank M. Truse, A.F. of L. organizer in Massachusetts on January 14, 1900, read: "The Trust having absorbed the plant of the Salem Wire & Nail Mills has thrown 350 people out of work here and the trusts are tearing out the machinery and shipping it elsewhere." (*AFL Corr.*) For other evidence of such practices by the trusts, *see* John Swinton, "How the Trusts Squeeze Working People," New York *World*, June 13, 1900; *Mark Hanna's "Moral Cranks" and—Others: A Study of To-Day*, by William H. Muldoon, Brooklyn, 1900, pp. 330-31; New York *Tribune*, April 18, 1900.

trustified industries were growing worse, supposed to do until the "coming triumph of socialism?"

Few of the critics of the A. F. of L. spokesmen for the trusts differed with their contention that it would be fruitless to attempt to return to the small, competitive enterprises that characterized American industry before the growth of monopoly. They felt strongly, however, that, as John Swinton put it, "Monopolies or trusts should not have those powers which enable them to play tricks with the price of commodities and to play the deuce with the wages and rights of labor." [38] They felt, therefore, that instead of publicly defending the trusts, the A. F. of L. leaders would do better to join the rising mass movement which sought to curb the power of monopoly. Nor were they impressed too strongly by the argument that to do so would run the risk that unions themselves would be prosecuted as combinations in restraint of trade. By playing an active role in the rising anti-trust movement, labor could exert influence to prevent legislation aimed at curbing the trusts from being used to curb the trade unions. Moreover, if labor did nothing, there would be few unions in the trustified industries to be curbed by any type of legislation. [39]

A. F. OF L. AND ANTI-TRUST MOVEMENT

But to all suggestions that they join the rising anti-trust movement, the A. F. of L. leaders turned a deaf ear. [40] They had responded eagerly when they had been invited by Ralph M. Easley to address the Chicago Civic Federation's Trust Conference in September, 1899. But they were entirely lacking in enthusiasm when they were invited a few months later to address the National Anti-Trust Conference to be held in Chicago in February, 1900.

The second conference actually grew out of the first; a number of the men who attended the conference sponsored by the Civic Federation became convinced during the proceedings "that friends of the 'trust system' were in fact endeavoring to use the conference as a means to strengthen the foundations and further the development of Trusts." Upon the adjournment of the conference, these delegates decided to inaugurate a National Anti-Trust movement, and to launch the venture at a conference on the birthday of Abraham Lincoln, February 12, 1900. [41]

When Gompers ignored two invitations to attend the National Anti-Trust Conference or to send some other delegate to represent the A. F. of L., the chairman of the Committee on Programme and Speakers appealed directly to him to explain how it was possible for the leading labor organization in the country to remain indifferent "to the most vital question now confronting the people of this country."

"Surely the criminal conspiracies, known as Trusts, are a menace to every Trades Union in the United States. The truth of this has been recognized by the great labor organizations of the world. . . .

"The responses to our call from every part of the country indicate that the people are ready to rise in their majestic strength to crush the monopolistic power of the trusts. Is it possible that the Trades Unions are not to unite with the other patriots in this supreme non-partisan effort for liberty and justice?"

Referring to the fear expressed by A. F. of L. spokesmen that unions themselves might be prosecuted as combinations in restraint of trade under legislation proposed by anti-trust movements, the spokesman for the National Anti-Trust Conference wrote:

"You will observe, it is not the principle of association or combination which is attacked in the call.

"The principle of association of men or of capital is one thing, a combination organized to filch from the people their hard earnings through the establishment of monopolies is another and wholly different thing. And it is the latter, not the former, which is the subject of our attack. Is there any reason why the Trades Unions should not join us in this contest?

"The Federation of Labor is based upon the right of the working people to combine for the protection of labor. The exercise of this right is in conformity with the principles of justice and meets with our cordial approval; but the Trades Unions enjoy no special privileges. They are not organized to create monopolies. Should not private monopolies be abolished? Remove the special privileges which directly or indirectly are granted the trusts, and by which they secure undue advantage, and it is believed that the evil in them could not live. At least the trusts could then only survive, like labor organizations, on their merit. . . .

"In view of the great importance of this matter to the country at large, including your organization, we again invite you, provided your organization is in sympathy with us, to send us the name or names of one or more who will represent the Federation of Labor in this great Conference. . . .

"I beg to add that an invitation is hereby further extended to any representative of your organization whom it may select to deliver a brief address." [42]

Silence was the only answer to this moving appeal!

More than a thousand delegates, representing 31 states, two territories and the District of Columbia, met together on Lincoln's Birthday in Chicago to discuss the trust problem. Among them were men like John Peter Altgeld, James B. Weaver, Mayor Samuel J. Jones of Toledo, Mayor Tom L. Johnson of Cleveland, and John W. Hayes, general secretary-treasurer of the K. of L. The delegates voted to set up the American

Anti-Trust League whose members would "give practical effect to their antagonism to trusts by giving preference in their patronage to non-trust products as far as possible." [43]

Not a single delegate from the A. F. of L. was present. Gompers not only would have nothing to do with the gathering, but when he learned that several Federal Labor Unions, affiliated to the Federation, were planning to send delegates, he warned them that they risked expulsion if they did not remove all references to the A. F. of L. in the printed material or releases they issue. The organizations acquiesced and the name of the A. F. of L. did not appear at the National Anti-Trust Conference. [44]

THE NATIONAL CIVIC FEDERATION

Meanwhile, the A. F. of L. leaders were allying themselves with a movement which grew out of the trust conference held under the auspices of the Chicago Civic Federation. On September 25, 1899, the New York *Mail* featured the following report:

"A NATIONAL CIVIC FEDERATION

"Encouraged by the results of the trust conference, recently held under its auspices, the Civic Federation of Chicago has decided upon a larger scope of operations. The president of that organization, Mr. Franklin H. Head, one of the great business leaders of the West, has been authorized to appoint a committee of twenty-five whose duty it shall be to form a National federation."

The committee of 25, with Ralph M. Easley as Secretary, nominated an Advisory Council of 500 to assist in the formation of the National Civic Federation. This Council, Easley boasted to Gompers in April, 1900, was composed of "only representative, conservative, practical men of affairs," and "no federal or state office-holders, professional politicians, cranks, hobbyists or revolutionists have been knowingly included." The proposed Advisory Council was made up of ten divisions: manufacturing, agriculture, college, labor, church, finance, commerce, law, transportation, and general organizations—in short, representatives of employers, wage-earners, and the public, that myth of a supposedly neutral force in the class struggle perpetrated by the powers that be. As Easley pointed out to Gompers, the National Civic Federation would seek to eliminate the class struggle by reconciling labor and capital on the basis of "reason and understanding." [45]

The representatives of big business on the Advisory Council made it clear to the American workers just what they meant by "reason and understanding." Heading the representatives of manufacturers was J. Ogden Armour of Armour & Co., whose workers in the trustified meat packing plants were described by an A. F. of L. investigating committee as "white slaves," and whose products were being boycotted by many trade unions because of the trust's anti-union policies. Another representative of manufacturers was Louis F. Swift, of Swift & Co., which was one of the four packing house firms which had just agreed among themselves never to sign a written agreement with the union. Another was Elbert H. Gary, president of the Federal Steel Company, who had played a leading role in wiping out unionism in this trust. Still another was Cyrus H. McCormick, president of the McCormick Harvesting Machine Company, who had broken the union in this giant industry as far back as 1886 and had blacklisted all workers who had anything to do with labor organizations. Other representatives of manufacturers had also gained notoriety for their anti-union policies. The men who represented the Transportation Division were of the same make-up; most of them had been active in breaking the Pullman strike in 1894, had blacklisted every Pullman striker, and had fought every attempt to organize the mass of the railroad workers. The only unions they tolerated were the conservative brotherhood crafts which represented a small minority of the workers in the industry.[46]

Although neither Morgan nor Rockefeller were proposed for membership on the Advisory Council, the influence of these finance capitalists was nevertheless dominant in the body. By the time the National Civic Federation was organized, the House of Morgan, and, to a lesser degree, the Rockefeller-Standard Oil group, controlled many of the industrial enterprises, railroads, banks, life insurance and trust companies whose officials were proposed for the Advisory Council. Although these men headed their respective corporations, control was definitely maintained by the finance capitalists. Hence they were actually Morgan and Rockefeller representatives on the Advisory Council.[47]

There were 34 representatives proposed for the labor division: four leaders of the railroad brotherhoods, headed by the reactionary Grand Master of the Brotherhood of Locomotive Engineers, P. M. Arthur; one from the K. of L., John N. Parsons, President of the dying Order, and the rest from the A. F. of L. including Gompers, P. J. McGuire, John B. Lennon, John Mitchell, and James O'Connell.[48]

Although the leaders of the railroad brotherhoods were associated with the launching of the National Civic Federation, it was to the A. F. of L. leaders that Easley looked for major support. As Gompers himself pointed out later in his autobiography: "Of course, the N.C.F. was useless without the support of the A. F. of L." [49]

There is no indication that the A. F. of L. leaders nominated for the Advisory Council were concerned by the nomination of so many representatives of the anti-union, trustified, finance capital-dominated corporations for membership. But they were aware that the rank-and-file

Federation members would regard with great suspicion the presence of the A. F. of L. leaders in an organization side by side with many of the most notorious foes of organized labor. Before he replied to Easley's request that he join the Advisory Council, John Mitchell wrote to Gompers and inquired: "I wish you would give me your views as to whether it will be advantageous to the labor movement to accept appointment on this committee." [50]

Gompers replied that he did "not see that there can be any harm at all in accepting a position as a member of the Advisory Council." Reassured, Mitchell joined with Gompers in becoming charter members of the National Civic Federation. Both were also leading officers of the organization, Gompers being the first vice-president and Mitchell one of the top members of arbitration committee. [51]

Early in October, 1900, Easley urged Gompers to spend an evening with him to discuss "the future developments of the Nat[ional] Civ[ic] Fed[eration] and its work. I want you to know about its genesis & aspirations and just what it is & can be, where it can be of great value to the interests you represent and where it can help you personally." Easley cited as an example a conversation he had just had with the general counsel of a large corporation which "does not recognize the union." The man told Easley that if he could be convinced that the union would not make trouble for the corporation, and that it would agree "to 'keep politics out' [he] would favor his firm organizing." "I am sure," Easley added, "if I brought you & him together for instance you could convince him." [52]

In the above letter, the founder of the National Civic Federation laid down the basic purpose of the organization. It was to channelize the labor movement into conservative avenues and to rob it of every semblance of radicalism and militancy. The craft unions would win recognition from the leaders of the trustified industries for a small minority of the workers on condition that they would "not make trouble" for the corporations by organizing the mass of the workers in their plants and factories; that they would not challenge the control exercised by the finance capitalists over the American economy; and that they would not engage in politics, particularly in independent political action. The industrialists, in return for this agreement, would grant the skilled workers certain concessions, and they would be secure in the knowledge that no serious effort would be made to organize the majority of the working class.

It was this concept that was adopted by the leaders of the A. F. of L. when they participated in the founding of the National Civic Federation and began in the fall of 1900 to play leading and active roles in the organization, together with the leading representatives of the trustified, finance capital-dominated industries. As John Mitchell expressed it: "There is no necessary hostility between capital and labor. Neither can do without the other; each has evolved from the other. . . . There is not even a necessary fundamental antagonism between the laborers and the capitalist . . . broadly considered, the interest of one is the interest of the other, and the prosperity of the one is the prosperity of the other." [53]

In a letter to Mark Hanna who, during his brief tenure as first president of the National Civic Federation, was considered as J. P. Morgan's representative on the organization, Mitchell stressed the same theme, emphasizing that as the concept became more widely understood, "strikes and lockouts may become unnecessary." [54]

The whole philosophy and purpose of the National Civic Federation was summed up by the *Catholic World* in an editorial on the occasion of the organization's second annual industrial conference in 1901: "For the first time in this country's industrial life did the accredited leaders of hundreds of thousands of toiling masses look into the sympathetic eye and grasp the friendly hands of men who control much of the invested wealth of the country." The editorial was aptly entitled "Marriage of Capital and Labor." * [55]

* The editorial in the *Catholic World* marked the beginning of a campaign by the Catholic Church to permeate the A.F. of L. with social principles based fundamentally on the ideology of conservative, "pure and simple" trade unionism. This campaign, however, did not really get under way until a few years later and thus belongs outside the scope of the present discussion. For an interesting summary of this campaign and its influence, *see* Marc Karson, "The Catholic Church and the Political Development of American Trade Unions, 1900-1918," *Industrial and Labor Relations Review*, Vol. IV, July, 1951, pp. 528ff.

CHAPTER 25

Labor and Socialism, 1897-1901

In June, 1897, Eugene V. Debs wound up the affairs of the American Railway Union and merged it with the Social Democracy, then being formed at a convention in Chicago.[1] Leading the list of the Social Democracy's demands was the colonization plan which proposed to establish a socialist America by organizing a mass migration to a western state, where cooperative colonies would be formed, from which the movement would spread throughout the nation, and in due time create a socialist United States.

A political platform was also adopted calling for public ownership of all industries controlled by monopolies, trusts and combines; the public ownership of all means of transportation and communication, of all public utilities, all mines and all oil and gas wells; a shorter work day; a system of public works for the employment of the unemployed; the adoption of the initiative and referendum and proportional representation, and the establishment of Postal Savings Banks.

The ruling body of the Social Democracy was to be the National Board. Debs, the dominant figure at the convention, was named chairman; the four other officers had all been prominent leaders of the A.R.U., and all had been in Woodstock jail with Debs. *The Railway Times,* organ of the A.R.U., was transformed into *The Social Democrat,* the new party's official organ.[2]

SOCIAL DEMOCRACY GAINS ADHERENTS

Two months after its founding the Social Democracy gained a most valuable addition to its membership—the Jewish Socialists of the East. Many of these socialists had long been chafing under the domination of Daniel De Leon and the philosophy of the S.L.P. under his leadership. They had followed with intense interest the western developments which

388

culminated in the formation of the Social Democracy. They had a great admiration for Debs, stemming from the time of the Pullman strike, and they regarded the Social Democracy as a genuine American movement led by a native American working class leader of militant convictions and high integrity. On January 7, 1897, the "oppositionists" among the Jewish Socialist members of the New York branches of the S.L.P., led by Dr. Isaac A. Hourwich, Meyer London, Joseph Barondess, Abraham Cahan, Louis E. Miller, and Morris Winchevsky, broke away from the organization. With the founding of the Social Democracy of America, they promptly established Local No. 1 of the new party.[3]

From July 31 to August 2, 1897, the convention of the New York Jewish Socialists met in Chicago. There were present 58 delegates representing 1,200 members of the Socialist Labor Party and about 10,000 trade unionists. Hourwich and London, in behalf of Local No. 1 of the Social Democracy, persuaded the convention, by a vote of 40 to 10, to pass a resolution condemning sectarianism and favoring affiliation with Debs' movement. The resolution stated that the Social Democracy steadily strove to attain the ideal of Socialism.[4]

This welcome addition increased the strength of the party. Another gain of importance was the support given by the Milwaukee Socialists, led by Victor L. Berger. On July 9, 1897, the Milwaukee "Independents," as they were called in Socialist circles, formed a branch of the Social Democracy. This brought to the new party the strong movement that had been built up in the important Wisconsin city. Almost immediately, the Federated Trades Council, the local central body of the A. F. of L., comprising most of the unions in the city, passed a resolution endorsing the Social Democracy by a unanimous vote.[5]

On January 5, 1898, the Milwaukee Federated Trades Council elected five delegates to the first city convention of the Social Democracy, which met to draw up a platform and nominate candidates for the municipal election. The independent trade unions sent special delegates, among them the brewers, the brewery teamsters, the wagon makers, the coopers, the blacksmiths, the joiners, and the hod-carriers. *The Social Democrat,* official organ of the national party, placed great stress on the trade union representation at the Milwaukee convention, declaring on February 3, 1898: "The significance of this will be seen when it is remembered that the S.L.P. in its guerilla warfare on organized labor has made the name of Socialism odious to a good many workingmen. Nevertheless, when labor finds Socialism put forward by a strong, respectful and thoroughly determined American party, it hastens to endorse the movement."

The reference in *The Social Democrat* was, of course, to the formation of the Socialist Trade and Labor Alliance by Daniel De Leon and his followers in the S.L.P. In the opinion of the official organ of the Social

Democracy no more unfortunate step could have been taken, from the standpoint of American socialism, than the formation of De Leon's dual union. It pointed out that the Socialists were being branded as wilful destroyers of the unity of labor; that it drove hitherto socialist-minded trade unionists into the camp of the conservative trade union leaders, and that it had alienated many sympathizers in the labor movement.

A. F. OF L. AND THE SOCIAL DEMOCRACY

There were high hopes entertained in Socialist circles that with Debs as its leader, the Social Democracy would overcome the pernicious effects of De Leon's dual union and that the new party might even obtain official endorsement from the A. F. of L. and its leaders. Debs' activities appeared to justify these hopes, for he did important work during lecture tours in assisting A. F. of L. organizers. On July 1, 1896, Will H. Winn, general organizer for the A. F. of L., wrote to Gompers from Columbus, Georgia: "Mr. Debs was here recently & delivered two addresses to the public, which were well received & will do good. . . . Debs' brief stay here has done us more good on this line (of organizing and educating the workers) than we have done in years."[6]

Winn's enthusiastic appreciation of Debs' contributions was not shared by the top A. F. of L. leadership. Indeed, Gompers, McGuire, and other Federation leaders were alarmed by the reports from organizers telling of the interest among A. F. of L. rank-and-filers in the formation of the Social Democracy, and the feeling on the part of many members "who stand very close to Debs" that "some good might be done by such an organization if it were so managed as to not conflict or interfere with the trade union movement."[7] In an effort to squelch such feelings, Gompers published a sharp criticism of Debs for advocating the colonization scheme, charging that the program was a threat to the trade unions since it sought to draw workers away from the struggles in the industrial areas being led by the unions.[8] Even some of Debs' staunchest supporters in the A. F. of L. agreed with Gompers, but urged him to hold off final judgment until it was clear which way Debs would move. "If he will hold fast to the trade union as well," wrote Robert Askew, secretary-treasurer of the Mine Workers' Union in Michigan, "he will make a success but to abandon the trade union and to enter entirely on [the] cooperative system will only mean failure for his grand idea."[9]

But the A. F. of L. leaders dismissed the suggestion that they postpone judgment on Debs and the Social Democracy. After learning that President M. D. Ratchford of the United Mine Workers had summoned Debs to help the union in the great bituminous strike which began July 4,

1897, in West Virginia,* P. J. McGuire wrote heatedly to Gompers: "The Miners would be better off without men like Debs, as they arouse the ire of the coal operators by their denunciations of capitalists, etc." [10] The A. F. of L. leaders were moving rapidly in the direction of active collaboration with the monopoly capitalists, and were busily engaged in trying to eradicate from the Federation's record the many radical and progressive "policies and methods" that had been characteristic of the organization in its formative years. They were out to prove to the capitalists that the A. F. of L. stood for "policies and methods" that did not challenge the capitalist system—even if to achieve this meant undemocratically overruling the will of the rank-and-file membership.† Nothing was further from their thoughts than to cooperate with a movement led by Debs which stood for a struggle against the capitalists and their entire system.

Nonetheless, Gompers and other A. F. of L. leaders were basically correct in their criticism of the colonization program. Propaganda for achieving socialism through migration of workers to sparsely populated western states, if influential in working class circles, would certainly interfere with the organization of labor into trade unions. Indeed, the colonizers not only had no interest in building the trade unions; they sneered at labor's demands for higher wages, shorter hours and better

* For about a month Debs toured the strike areas, rallying the miners. He was forced to abandon the work after he suffered a severe sunstroke, but the Mine Workers' official journal paid tribute to his assistance in helping the union achieve a victory and to gain the first major contract ever signed by the coal operators which included a pay increase for the miners. (*United Mine Workers' Journal*, Aug. 19, 1897, Jan. 13, 1898.)

† At the 1895 A.F. of L. convention, a motion was adopted which instructed the Federation's secretary "to prepare a code of resolutions passed by former conventions up to the close of this convention." Following the convention, P. J. McGuire, who was elected secretary, proceeded to prepare a code of resolutions. "I have kept within the lines of the instructions given by the convention to not in any respect alter the fundamental law," he wrote to Gompers early in 1896. But Gompers had other plans. On May 7, 1896, he wrote to McGuire: "You know, too, that in the early history of the Federation, some queer looking resolutions were adopted and which now would scarcely look good in print. I write you this with the view of suggesting that the matter might be dropped or deferred until some more opportune time, when trade union opponents will not be so ready to take advantage of every little inconsistency or impracticable resolution. I suppose no one will really call for it so the matter might easily be dropped, providing you give your consent to it."

McGuire readily consented, agreeing with Gompers that many of the resolutions adopted during the early years of the A.F. of L., especially "questions of a political nature," would be embarrassing to the Federation if they appeared in print. The code of resolutions was never published. (*Proceedings*, A.F. of L. Convention, 1895, p. 56; P. J. McGuire to Gompers, Jan. 16, May 31, 1896; P. J. McGuire to August McCraith, May 31, 1896, *AFL Corr.;* Gompers to P. J. McGuire, May 7, 1896, *GLB*.)

working conditions. They called on the workers to give up strikes for these causes and concentrate solely on building colonies in the Western states.[11] Small wonder that even Debs' admirers in the A. F. of L. agreed with Gompers that the Social Democracy, as long as it was dominated by the colonizers, had little more to recommend it to organized labor than the S.L.P.

THE SOCIAL DEMOCRATIC PARTY

The battle over colonization, already in the making from the inception of the Social Democracy, came out in the open at its second convention in June, 1898. Isaac Hourwich, Victor Berger, G. A. Hoehn, and other ex-members of the S.L.P., led the opposition to the colonizers. The party, they argued, should reject the colonization scheme as utopian and ineffective, and should devote itself exclusively to a program of political action and socialist propaganda.

When the issue came to a vote, the colonizationists won by a clear majority—52 to 37.[12] Rather than remain in a convention which had adopted so utopian a platform, the political action group decided to bolt. Led by Berger and Keliher, the bolters proceeded at once to a neighboring hall where they voted to found the Social Democratic Party to be composed only of Socialists who believed in the "principles and program of International Socialism." The new party, basing itself firmly on political methods, would be "a class-conscious, revolutionary, social organization." [13]

The platform adopted by the new party showed clearly the advance the Socialist movement made in casting off the utopian influences of the colonizationists. Although the Social Democracy had, under the leadership of Debs, taken some interest in the trade union movement, the 1897 platform, because of the dominance of the colonizationists, contained no specific provisions about the relationship of the party to the trade unions. The platform of the new party did not neglect this vital question. It distinctly favored cooperation with organized labor, and this issue was regarded as important as the party's program of political action. The organization of labor into national and international unions was encouraged; strikes and boycotts were declared useful and necessary working-class weapons, and the party went on record in support of organized labor no matter what the political affiliation of the trade union was. All Socialists were required to join existing unions and support the union's economic activities. But they must not, under any circumstances, attempt to involve the union in political action. Whatever political action could be organized in working class circles must be channelled into the Social Democratic Party. The duty of the Socialists in the unions was to work for the unity of the workers on the economic front, and to educate union members on the need to join and vote for the S.D.P.[14]

The executive board, elected to direct the destinies of the Social Democratic Party, included Eugene V. Debs, his brother Theodore, Victor Berger, Frederic Heath, Seymour Stedman, and Jesse Cox.[15]

Having rid itself of the colonization incubus, the Social Democratic Party began an earnest campaign immediately after it was founded to gain trade union support. Special efforts were made to win the A. F. of L.'s leadership's approval of the new party. On June 20, 1898, William Mailly of New York, a leader of the S.D.P., reminded Gompers that he had in the past stated that the A. F. of L. leadership did not oppose the Socialists as such but only the anti-trade union principles and activities of De Leon and his followers. He then called Gompers' attention to the resolutions on the trade unions adopted by the S.D.P., and predicted that an era of close relationship between the Socialists and the A. F. of L. was about to open which would "accrue to the best interest of the workers." A similar position was set forth by Joseph Barondess, a member of the committee that drew up the trade union resolution, who assured Gompers that the S.D.P. would do everything that was possible to eliminate the obstacles to friendly relations between the trade unions and the Socialists created by De Leon and his followers.[16]

While it undoubtedly pleased Gompers' vanity to find the Socialists pleading for his approval, he refused to acknowledge that a different situation existed as a result of the friendly attitude adopted by the S.D.P. towards the established trade unions. At one time, he informed Barondess, it had been possible for the trade unionists and the Socialists "to at least agree upon some essentials. Since De Leon's advent no such thing is possible." It was too late to undo the damage inflicted by De Leon and his followers.[17]

The measure of Gompers' hypocrisy is clearly revealed by the fact that less than three weeks before he had written to an S.L.P. leader expressing the hope "that the time may not be far distant when you will see the fundamental truths which the Trades Union teaches, that you will earnestly, thoughtfully and faithfully cooperate . . . for better conditions of labor today and the final emancipation in the time to come."[18] Yet when the S.D.P. leaders offered such cooperation, Gompers said it was too late! It was typical of Gompers' demagogy to offer cooperation to those Socialists whom he knew in advance would reject his overture and to refuse to cooperate with those Socialists who were fully prepared to do so on the very terms he himself had outlined.*

* Apologists for Gompers among labor historians place much of the blame for his bitter denunciation of and opposition to the Socialists in the Federation upon De Leon's dual union policies. (See Selig Perlman, *A History of Trade Unionism*

The S.D.P. leaders still had hopes of converting Gompers. On December 3, 1898, Jesse Cox, chairman of the National Executive Committee, wrote to Gompers and pleaded with him to work for an endorsement of socialism and the S.D.P. at the forthcoming A. F. of L. convention. He conceded that there was "great opposition among the trade unions to the Socialist Labor Party, because of its having organized the socialist trade and labor alliance, which many trade unionists regard as in opposition to the regular trade unions." But he assured Gompers that the S.D.P. not only had no sympathy for the S.L.P.'s dual unionist trade union policies, but had emphasized that its members were obligated to work unceasingly to build the trade unions of which they were members. "I may add, that the platform of the Social Democratic Party regards the Trade Union movement as the foundation of the Socialist movement and that the real Socialist movement must grow out of the trade unions." [19]

On the following day, December 4, the S.D.P.'s Board followed up this appeal by instructing Berger and Stedman to attend the A. F. of L. convention at Kansas City in the role of observers, and to supervise the campaign to secure the desired endorsements. [20]

When Berger and Stedman arrived in Kansas City on December 13, they discovered that the Socialist delegates to the A. F. of L. convention, composed of Social Democrats and the anti-De Leon Social Laborites, had already worked out a strategy which called for the defeat of Gompers and all other "pure and simple" union leaders, for the endorsement of the S.D.P., and for the adoption of a resolution calling for "class conscious propaganda for the abolition of the wage system." [21]

Berger and Stedman immediately expressed disapproval of the plan mapped out by the Socialist delegates. They argued strenuously that the main task of the Socialists at the convention was to obtain the Federation's endorsement of socialism, and insisted that any involvement in internal union controversies would only destroy the possibility of securing such action. Having persuaded the Socialist delegates to abandon their opposition to Gompers, Berger and Stedman paid a visit to the A. F. of L. president and sought to convince him to throw his support behind a Socialist resolution. They were convinced that Gompers' opposition to such a resolution was "unintentional," and Berger felt confident that he could prove to him that he would be serving the best interests of the A. F. of L. by endorsing the proposal.

Gompers was unmoved by Berger's logic. He simply informed the

in the United States, New York, 1922, p. 211.) Actually, Gompers made use of De Leon's mistaken policies to achieve support for his battle against Socialists inside the A.F. of L. De Leon's dual union policies gave Gompers a powerful weapon in this battle, for many workers came to regard all Socialists as destroyers of the unity of labor.

emissaries from the S.D.P.'s national office that the rank-and-file A. F. of L. members were not yet ready to endorse socialism, and that it would be incorrect for the leaders to move ahead of them on such issues.[22]

The failure to win over the A. F. of L. president doomed the Socialist resolution. Despite vigorous convention debate, Gompers' machine remained firm. But the final vote—1,791 against and 493 for the resolution [23] —gave the S.D.P. leaders cause for glee. The fact that more than one-fifth of the vote had been cast for the resolution, despite Gompers' opposition, appeared to them to signify that the A. F. of L. was moving in the right direction. They were convinced that within two years the Federation would take the same "advanced ground for Socialism" as had their brothers in the British Trade Union Congress who had endorsed nationalization of the means of production and distribution. Even Gompers would probably come along, for Berger reported that after the convention had adjourned, the A. F. of L. president had told him: "I have read Karl Marx; I am as much a Socialist as you and I will vote the Social Democratic ticket and advise trade unionists to do so." [24]

While Gompers, as we have repeatedly seen, was quite capable of demagogically expressing diametrically opposite opinions at exactly the same time to different groups there is little evidence to support Berger's optimistic account. In a press interview in the fall of 1896, Gompers had publicly denounced the Socialists as demented men and "enemies of the labor movement." [25] While he referred primarily to De Leon and his followers, he said nothing thereafter to indicate that he thought differently of others in the Socialist movement. On the contrary, it was at the 1898 convention that Gompers expressed his implacable hostility towards the Socialists and their principles, and made it clear that he included all types of Socialists—De Leonites and anti-De Leonites—in his denunciation of them for seeking "to allure our movement into such a vortex of complications and capture our movement as a tail to their political kite." [26]

Events at the A. F. of L. 1899 convention convinced the S.D.P. leaders that they were making enormous progress in converting the Federation to socialism. For the convention adopted a resolution calling upon the "trade unionists of the United States, and workingmen generally, to study the development of trusts and monopolies with a view to nationalizing the same." [27] But this resolution was quickly forgotten in the atmosphere created by the National Civic Federation. At the 1900 convention, a resolution expressing the same policy, introduced by Max Hayes of the Cleveland Typographical Union, was disapproved by the committee to which it was referred. For the original resolution a substitute was offered by the committee to the effect that the best way to combat the trusts "is for the wage earners to organize into respective unions of their trade or craft . . . and we also renew the recommendation that the workingmen study the development of trusts and monopolies." The demand for the nationalization of the trusts had been dropped. Even then, Max Hayes predicted that it was "only a question of a year or two before the Federation went on record for socialism." [28]

THE S.D.P. AND THE INDEPENDENT LABOR PARTY

While the effort to advance the cause of socialism by converting the top leaders of the trade union movement was proceeding at A. F. of L. conventions, the S.D.P. was actively engaged on the the lower levels where, at least, attempts were made to lead the workers in day-by-day struggle. The tremendous victories scored in Haverhill, Massachusetts, where in 1898 and 1899 a Socialist mayor, and Socialist councilmen and assemblymen were elected, flowed from the leadership given by the S.D.P. in a series of strikes of shoe workers and railway workers.[29]

In New York City, too, the S.D.P. reaped the fruits of leadership in the day-to-day struggles of the workers, and had not the party's leaders interfered, the Socialists would have established an important relationship with organized labor on the political front. The Brooklyn trolley strike of 1899, in which the Socialists were active, had convinced many trade unionists "that they must elect their own leaders to public office if they were to win economic justice." Early in the fall of 1899, the leading trade unionists of the city, including many A. F. of L. officials, issued a call for a political convention designed to form an Independent Labor Party. The Socialists were invited to attend; many trade unionists praised them for their role in the trolley strike and agreed that "they were the men" to have in the political movement. The West Side Social Democratic Party and the Social Democratic Association of the Fourth, Fifth, Eighth and Twenty-fourth Assembly Districts accepted the invitation and sent delegates who participated in the formation of the Independent Labor Party and in the nomination of a ticket for the November election.

The alarmed reaction in the A. F. of L. national headquarters to this significant development was proof that a real opportunity existed for the Socialists to achieve on the local level what they had failed to obtain by pleading with the top leaders of the Federation. Gompers sharply criticized Sam Prince, president of the New York Central Federated Union, for having joined hands with the Socialists—"people who have forfeited the confidence of every wage worker"—in the Independent Labor Party. "You are now president of the Central Federated Union," he wrote angrily, "carrying grave responsibilities. You can not now act as you formerly were inclined to when you were plain Samuel Prince, a member of your trade union without any cares or responsibilities other than membership." [30]

But Gompers was not the only person alarmed by the events in New York. The S.D.P. National Executive Board bluntly reminded the New York branches that their participation in the formation of the labor party was a betrayal of basic party principle which forbade all alliance with any other political party.* The New York branches defended themselves by contending that the I.L.P. was a trade union party and that all Socialists were dutybound to support the unions. The S.D.P. Board summarily dismissed the plea; support of the trade unions by Socialists must be confined to the economic front; on the political front, "the trade unions must be supplanted . . . by the Social Democratic movement." Alliances with political movements like the Independent Labor Party would only strengthen the capitalist maneuvers to confuse the workers so as to prevent them from supporting the only party organized to emancipate the working class from wage slavery. Hence the New York branches must instantly recall their delegates from the I.L.P. convention, sever all connections with that party, or stand suspended.[31]

To Gompers' great delight, the New York branches abandoned the I.L.P. The danger of an alliance between the A. F. of L. trade unionists and the Socialists had passed.[32]

DEBS' CONTRIBUTIONS

The fact that the Social Democratic Party was gaining wide support blinded the leadership to the seriousness of the error it was committing in forcing the branches to sever all relations with organized labor on the political front. Although the party was seriously strapped for funds— there was barely two dollars in the treasury when the national office was opened on October 1, 1898—it was growing. Debs made a valuable contribution to this growth by continually touring the country, delivering fiery lectures about the "March of Socialism," selling subscriptions to the *Social Democratic Herald,* the party's official organ, and as an A. F. of L. organizer in New England put it in a letter to Gompers, "making Socialists by the hundreds." [33]

In November, 1899, when Debs visited Los Angeles, the A. F. of L.'s Council of Labor urged affiliated unions to attend his lectures "as important to the cause of organized labor." Large and enthusiastic labor

---

* This policy was formally adopted by the National Executive Board at the March 26, 1899 meeting. All applicants for membership in the S.D.P. were compelled to pledge themselves to sever all connections with other political organizations, never to consent to their fusion or alliance of the S.D.P. with any other political party, and, if nominated for public office, to refuse to accept the endorsement of any other political party. ("Report of the Secretary of the National Executive Board of the Social Democratic Party, June, 1898-January, 1900," typescript, John Crerar Library, Chicago.)

audiences turned out for two meetings, and the Council of Labor expressed gratitude to H. Gaylor Wilshire, a wealthy socialist who financed the trip west, "for making Debs' visit possible." [34]

As in the past, Debs helped A. F. of L. organizers recruit workers into unions wherever he spoke. On May 17, 1900, Chas. Laws, A. F. of L. organizer in Charleston, South Carolina wrote to Gompers:

"We had five unions in the Labor Parade on Debs Day. Painters, about 50—Iron Moulders—Broom Makers—and Carpenters about the same each and Federal Labor (Union) about 200 with mounted marshals, Band, and open carriages for Debs—the Reception Committee and the clergy. Mr. Debs did us all oceans of good. He spoke to 1000 people. The Christian Church with annexes was tendered us freely, as the Opera House holds only about 500. We are now feeling the good effect of his 2 hr. & two minute talk *every day now.* . . . We now have in prospect (1) another Federal Labor Union here, (2) International Typographical Union, (3) Hotel & Restaurant Employes Alliance & Bar Keepers' League, (4) Retail Clerks, (5) Bricklayers, Masons & Plasterers, (6) Federated Industrial Trades & Labor Assembly (central for our unions) and (7) Women Workers Union. Prospects are *very promising* for all as a result of Debs' visit." [35]

By the spring of 1900, the Social Democratic Party boasted a dues-paying membership of 4,636 in 226 branches, organized in 32 states. It also claimed the support of about 25 Socialist newspapers in the United States. In addition to the *Social Democratic Herald* (whose circulation grew from 3,000 in 1898 to 8,000 by the end of 1899), the most important of these papers were Victor Berger's Milwaukee *Vorwaerts,* the *Jewish Daily Forward* of New York City, and Julius A. Wayland's *Appeal to Reason.*[36]

While the Social Democratic Party was growing rapidly and "spreading the light," a major break was occurring in the Socialist Labor Party as members everywhere rose up in revolt against De Leon's dictatorial methods and his sectarian policies. The major bone of contention which was blowing the party apart was the Socialist Trade and Labor Alliance.

DISRUPTIVE ROLE OF THE S.T. AND L.A.

William Z. Foster in his *Bankruptcy of the American Labor Movement* has correctly noted that "The Socialist Trade and Labor Alliance was still-born." [37] In its still-birth, however, the S.T. and L.A. helped to wreck a number of existing unions. In 1892, there were more than 40 unions affiliated with the United Hebrew Trades in New York City, and other organizations of the U.H.T. had been established in other cities too. But by 1897, there were only five or six New York unions left in the United Hebrew Trades! While other factors such as the economic crisis of 1893 played their part, "the decisive factor in the disintegration of the United Hebrew Trades lay in its pursuit of the sectarian policy of Daniel De Leon. . . ." The participation of the U.H.T. in the S.T. & L.A. caused such disruption in its ranks that scores of locals soon went to pieces The same tragedy befell the United Hebrew Trades of Philadelphia after it joined the S.T. & L.A.[38]

There were other tragic results of De Leon's sectarian policies, the most notable being the developments among the textile workers. When the Alliance was initiated, the Socialists were already in the leadership of the National Union of Textile Workers, affiliated with the A. F. of L.* As soon as the Alliance was launched, the Socialist leaders of the union abandoned all attempts at organizing the unorganized textile workers, and concentrated solely on taking the union out of the A. F. of L. and into the S.T. & L.A. In November, 1896, H. Littlewood, the Socialist general secretary of the N.U.T.W., visited Columbus, Georgia, and other Southern textile centers. He spent no time discussing organizational problems with the textile workers, confining himself to bitter denunciations of the A. F. of L. and to appeals for support of the newly-organized Alliance. *The People* endorsed Littlewood's mission, and called upon all Socialists in the textile union to leave the Federation of the "Pure and Simple Labor Fakirs" and organize "strictly upon the lines of the Socialist Trade and Labor Alliance." [39]

At the May, 1897, convention of the textile union, a proposal by the Socialist leadership "that our organization affiliate with the Socialist Trade and Labor Alliance . . . an organization that wage[s] war both on the economic and political field against capitalism" was defeated. Moreover, disgusted by the leadership's concentration on the war against the A. F. of L., the delegates unseated the Socialists and elected a new slate of officers sympathetic to the Federation.[40]

In January, 1898, the National Union of Textile Workers called a strike in New Bedford against a ten percent cut in wages, the vicious fining system, and other abuses. Several thousand workers were involved in the struggle which spread to other New England textile centers and attracted nationwide attention. In the midst of the struggle, the S.T. and L.A. entered the picture. Denouncing the A. F. of L. union for "betraying the srtikers," the Alliance's leadership launched an independent strike, called upon the workers to abandon the existing struggle, leave the N.U.T.W., and join the movement led by the S.T. & L.A. De Leon himself went to New Bedford to further the Alliance's cause. In an address delivered in the City Hall on February 11, 1898, he launched a bitter attack on the

---

* The Union was organized in 1891 and received its charter from the A.F. of L. in the same year. Socialist control took place in 1894 and 1895.

A. F. of L. and the N.U.T.W., accusing the union of betraying the textile workers by leading them in a struggle for higher wages and shorter hours. These "sops" and "concessions" were of no value to the workers. The slogan of the strikers should be "Socialism as the only means of abolishing wage slavery," their weapon should be "the ballot box," and they should tell the textile manufacturers that their days were numbered, for "with the falchion of the Socialist Labor Party ballot, we shall have laid you low for all time." [41]

The disruptive role of the Alliance during the New Bedford strike was denounced by anti-De Leon Socialists and the A. F. of L. leadership alike. Writing to Gompers on March 13, 1898, T. F. Tracy, leader of the N.U.T.W.'s strike committee, pointed out:

"Debs was there [at New Bedford] Thursday night and had a big meeting. Think of it. Every officer of a union in town sat on the platform. He addressed two meetings Friday and formed a branch of the Social Democracy. I had a talk with him Thursday night on his attitude toward trade unions and he favors them. . . . I asked Debs if he endorsed the policy of the S.L.P. and the S.T. & L.A. and their agents in trying to disrupt the unions. He went after them in good shape and advised them to join their unions and it was like throwing a bomb into them. The S.L.P. will not last long in New Bedford as Debs has made an impression on all here and even men with a red button are denouncing De Leon for his attack on the National Union of Textile Workers." [42]

Although Gompers conveniently overlooked the constructive role Debs and the Social Democracy played in the strike, he left no stone unturned in acquainting the entire labor movement of the "treacherous conduct" of De Leon and the S.T. & L.A. [43]

The dual union raids of the Alliance, its interference in strikes called by the A. F. of L., its open strikebreaking role in these struggles, and its unwillingness to fight for immediate demands—climaxed by the events at New Bedford—not only drove many workers into the camp of the conservative labor leaders but even disgusted many of the unions which had affiliated with the Alliance. By the end of 1898, more than half of them had resigned. Following the 1898 S.T. and L.A. convention, the powerful New York Central Labor Federation characterized the Alliance's dual union policies as futile and withdrew in disgust. Between the spring of 1896 and the summer of 1898, the Alliance had issued 228 charters and increased its membership to 20,000. Most of these locals and members withdrew during and after the 1898 S.T. & L.A. convention. The union that was rapidly to revolutionize the American labor movement was left in 1899 with a few thousand members, "for the most part Socialist 'leaders'—a sectarian and impotent letter-head organization." [44]

At its 1900 convention, De Leon completed the process of total self-isolation by cutting out "the tapeworm of immediate demands" from the party's platform, leaving it with but one proposal, for the revolution. The S.L.P. convention also adopted a resolution prohibiting its members, on pain of expulsion, from accepting "office in a pure and simple trade or labor organization. . . . If any officer of a pure and simple trade or labor organization applies for membership in the Socialist Labor Party, he shall be rejected." The resolution passed the convention by a vote of 61 to 2, and it was ratified later by a referendum vote of the S.L.P. membership, the tiny sect of De Leon's followers.[45]

THE SOCIALIST PARTY

At a convention at Rochester, New York, on January 29, 1900, 59 S.L.P. members led by Morris Hillquit, Job Harriman, and Max Hayes, repudiated De Leonism and the Socialist Trade and Labor Alliance, and adopted a position in favor of all trade unions regardless of their political affiliation. With but a single dissenting vote, the convention voted in favor of unification with the Social Democratic Party so that all socialist elements in the country could make a more effective fight against capitalism. A committee was appointed to work out the details of unification and the Social Democrats were invited to appoint a similar committee.[46]

It would be pointless to examine in detail the steps that led finally to a union between the anti-De Leon S.L.P.'ers and the Social Democrats. Suffice it to say merely that in July, 1901, after many conferences, featured by bitter recriminations on both sides, delegates, representing all Socialist groups in the country, except the followers of De Leon, met at Indianapolis to found a united Socialist Party.

Although the De Leonites were not present at the Indianapolis convention their theories found expression during the discussion of the platform. One of the most serious debates took place on the fundamental question of immediate demands. The majority report favored the inclusion of immediate demands in the platform. The minority viewpoint, presented by Delegate A. M. Simons, asked that immediate demands be stricken from the platform. A furious debate followed. The "impossibilists," as they were called, insisted that the party must have a revolutionary platform aiming at the overthrow of capitalism. The inclusion of immediate demands would mean the side-tracking of the essential program of socialism; the party would then sink to the level of any reform movement under capitalism. In short, away with immediate demands and concentrate on socialism.

Those who favored the majority report emphasized that immediate demands were of inestimable value in the struggle for socialism. They bridged the gap between capitalism and the ultimate establishment of socialism; they enabled the Socialists to reach the ears of workers who were not yet ready for the replacement of capitalism by socialism and they educated these workers in the battle for a new social system; they lightened the burdens of the working class under capitalism. In short, they served to attract the workers to the banner of the Socialists and to lead them in achieving socialism.

Morris Hillquit tried to conciliate the opposing views by stating that both the immediate demands and the socialist program were necessary elements in the party's work. Finally, after much controversy, the vote was 82 to 30 in favor of the inclusion of immediate demands calling for present reforms, pending the ultimate establishment of the cooperative commonwealth.

The foes of immediate demands, however, won a victory on the question of the party's position toward the farmers. The debate here centered around the statement that the "interests of the farmers of this country are identical with those of the wage workers of the cities." The opponents of immediate demands insisted that farmers could not be considered members of the working class, and with the delegates supporting this view, it was decided to drop all demands of the farmers.[47]

A third issue which aroused controversy was the Negro question. At the third session a resolution was introduced expressing sympathy for the Negro people and inviting them to join the Socialists. Hillquit objected, declaring that there was "no more reason for singling out the Negro race especially and their attitude than for singling out the Jews or Germans or any other nationality, race, or creed, here present." The spokesmen for the resolution pointed out that there was a *difference* in the status of Negroes and white workers. The Negro faced not only exploitation on the job, miserable wages and long hours, but he was especially discriminated against, was deprived of his citizenship rights in many parts of the country, and faced the constant danger of lynching.

It was not until the eleventh or final session that the matter was settled. A resolution was then passed affirming kinship with "our Negro fellow-workers" who suffered from exploitation and oppression. A warm invitation was given to Negro workers to join the new party in a common effort to bring about economic and political emancipation and a new and better social system.[48]

On other questions there was little disagreement. A resolution was passed unanimously condemning injunctions and the judges who used them to weaken and destroy organized labor. The resolution on trade unions favored complete cooperation with all bodies representing organized labor. It asserted that the Socialists considered "the trade union movement and the Socialist movement as inseparable parts of the general labor movement, produced by the same goal," and that they deemed it "the duty of each of the two movements to extend its hearty co-operation and support to the other in its special sphere of activity." It was acknowledged, however, that each of the two movements had "its own special mission to perform in the struggle for the emancipation of labor," that it devolved upon the trade unions "to conduct the economic struggles of the working class, and that the interests of labor will be best conserved by allowing each of the movements to manage the affairs within its own sphere of activity without active interference by the other." Then followed the heart of the entire resolution:

"The Socialist Party will continue to give its aid and assistance to the economic struggles of organized labor regardless of the affiliation of the trade unions in that struggle, and will take no sides in any dissensions or strifes within the trade union movement. The party will also continue to solicit the sympathy and support of all trades organizations of labor without allowing itself to be made the ally of any one division of the trade union movement as against another." [49]

Having agreed on a platform, the convention easily drew up a constitution, formed an executive committee with Leon Greenbaum as national secretary and established national headquarters in St. Louis. The convention then voted to call the new organization "The Socialist Party of America." * Each state was granted autonomy in matters of organization.

Amid songs and cheers for the new-born Socialist Party, the historic convention adjourned.

Noninterference in union activity, outlined in the resolutions on trade unions adopted at Indianapolis, was basically correct in 1901 when the unions were still smarting from the effects of De Leon's dual union tactics and would have regarded any other position as an endorsement of De Leonism. But, under the Right-Wing leadership of the Socialist Party, it soon came to mean refusal to condemn class collaboration policies of the A. F. of L. craft unions, refusal to condemn and struggle against neglect by these unions of the organization of the semi-skilled and unskilled, refusal to support industrial unionism, and opposition to the Socialist forces who fought Gompersism in the A. F. of L. Neutrality on these basic issues in the trade unions meant betrayal of the working class.

---

* In states where a different name had or might become a legal requirement it was permitted for the Socialists to function under a different name. Wisconsin Socialists kept the name Social Democratic Party.

CHAPTER 26

Labor and the Spanish-American War

Finance capital was dominant in the United States by the closing years of the nineteenth century. And as Victor Perlo points out: "The conquest of the United States economy by finance capital led to the accumulation of a superabundance of capital in a few hands. The law of capitalism is continuous acquisition. The monopolies had to find new fields for investment of their surplus capital. Failing this, their profits would decline in the resulting economic crisis." [1] *

The depression which began in 1893 sharply pointed up the monopolies' need for new outlets for surplus goods and for excess capital outside the continental boundaries of the United States. Increased productivity of the workers had seriously widened the gap between what they produced and what they could purchase with their wages. The surplus goods piled up for lack of foreign markets, bursting the warehouses. With monopoly profits building up record-shattering reserves of capital, the super-returns on investments in colonial areas could not be ignored by the Morgans, the Rockefellers, and their fellow-monopolists.

Spelling out Wall Street's urgent need for empire, the Senate Committee on Foreign Relations reported on March 16, 1898: "The unoccupied territory has been taken up, and while much remains to be done, the creative energy of the American people can no longer be confined within the borders of the Union. Production has so outrun consumption in both agricultural and manufactured products that foreign markets must be

* At the convention of the New York State Bankers' Association in 1896, James H. Tripp, President of the First National Bank of Marathon, emphasized the fact that surplus capital was accumulating at a rapid pace: "Millions of dollars are today lying idle, not yielding one cent of profit to the owner; millions more are being loaned at 1 and 2 per cent, and prime mercantile paper, with occasional exceptions, has for a long time been taken in our great financial centers at 3 and 4 per cent." (*Third Annual Convention of New York State Bankers Association, 1896*, p. 81; see also *American Banker*, Vol. LXIV, 1898, p. 9.)

secured or stagnation will ensue." "Free Cuba," Henry Cabot Lodge, spokesman for American imperialism, declared in 1896, "would mean an excellent opportunity for American capital invited there by signal exemptions. But we have a boader political interest in Cuba. . . ." That "broader interest" was Spain's colonial possessions—Puerto Rico, Guam, the Virgin Islands, and the Philippine Islands.[2]

The problem for American imperialists was to convert the sympathy with the revolutionary struggle of the Cuban people for freedom from Spanish despotism and misrule into support of a war against Spain. In this conspiracy the imperialists had the full support of the jingo press, headed by William R. Hearst's New York *Journal* and Joseph Pulitzer's New York *World*, which unscrupulously played upon the American people's sympathy for the cause of Cuban independence to raise circulation figures, and did all they could to drive the United States into war.[3]

LABOR'S OPPOSITION TO WAR

Still the imperialists did not have an easy time winning popular support, particularly among the organized workers, for their plot to provoke a war against Spain. In 1895, soon after the Cuban people, under the leadership of José Martí, took up arms to secure their independence from Spain, the labor press in the United States reported that meetings were being held "in all parts of the country to discuss the Cuban revolution." and that "in most cases labor organizations are taking the initiative, passing resolutions of sympathy for the insurgents."[4] Such resolutions were passed by the A. F. of L., the K. of L., and labor groups all over the country, and most of them recommended that the President of the United States recognize Cuban belligerency.[5]

The fact that the trade unions correctly sympathized with the struggle of the Cuban people for their liberation did not mean that they called either for war or for imperialism and militarism. On the contrary, the organizations and journals most outspoken in their support of the Cuban revolutionists were also most vigorous in their condemnation of imperialist expansion and the militarism that accompanied it. This does not mean that the labor organizations understood and opposed every aspect of imperialism. In the main, they were silent on such questions as the efforts of U.S. capital to penetrate into Latin America behind the cloak of the Monroe Doctrine, nor did they as a rule see the organic connection between the growth of the trusts and imperialist expansion. For the most part, they spoke out against the actual annexation of foreign territory, fearing that this would lead inevitably to aggressive wars.[6]

Labor's firm opposition to war was voiced time and again throughout the 1890's.[7] Addressing a meeting of the New York Central Labor Union, called to voice labor's opposition to war against Great Britain over the Venezuela Boundary Dispute,* Gompers lashed out at the warmongers:† "Labor is never for war. It is always for peace. It is on the side of liberty, justice and humanity. These three are always for peace. . . . Who would be compelled to bear the burden of a war? The working people. They would pay the taxes, and their blood would flow like water. The interests of the working people of England and the United States are common. They are fighting the same enemy. They are battling to emancipate themselves from conditions common to both countries. The working people know no country. They are citizens of the world, and their religion is to do what is right, what is just, what is grand and glorious and valorous and chivalrous. The battle for the cause of labor, from times of remotest antiquity, has been for peace and for good-will among men." [8]

War was regarded in labor circles as a time-honored method of despots to drown the complaints of their subjects. The publication of reports in the press quoting U.S. Senators as welcoming the war with Great Britain over the Venezuela boundary dispute on the ground that "it would thin the ranks of the unemployed and idle men in the country" aroused the widest indignation among the workers. "Just as we get rid of an infuriated dog by 'sicking him' at something else," cried the *American Federationist*, so did the agents of the capitalists hope to stave off the rising wrath of an aroused working class.[9]

Labor's opposition to war was voiced early in 1897 during the debate in the U.S. Senate over the ratification of the General Arbitration Treaty between the United States and Great Britain. In support of the Arbitration Treaty, Gompers wrote an article in the *American Federationist*, entitled "Let Us Have Peace," which aroused widespread comment, particularly his prediction that the time was soon coming when "the workers of all countries will fraternize and thus once and for all settle these resorts to force of which they become the victims." The Citizens' Committee in favor of ratification of the Arbitration Treaty paid for the mailing of copies of Gompers' article to every U.S. Senator. The Chicago

---

* The *Century Magazine* attributed the peaceful solution of the Venezuela dispute in large measure to "the action of trades' unions on both sides of the Atlantic," and declared that organized labor "gives the present peace movement its substantial basis." (Aug., 1896, pp. 634-35.)

† Neither Gompers nor the A.F. of L. as a whole, however, opposed President Cleveland's effort to use the Monroe Doctrine to assist the penetration of U.S. capital into Latin America. On such an issue, a student points out, "one is greeted by the A.F. of L. with official silence." (Delber Lee McKee, "The American Federation of Labor and Foreign Policy, 1886-1912," unpublished Ph.D. thesis, Stanford University, 1952, p. 39.)

Trades and Labor Congress, the Boston Central Labor Union, many individual trade unions and officials of the leading labor organizations supported the Treaty, pointing out in a memorial to the Senate:

"No section of the population is more vitally interested in the preservation of peace than are wage-workers. It is they who have to bear the brunt of fighting in time of war, and they, also, who feel the effects of war debts more than any other. More than this, as wars and rumors of wars interfere with industrial conditions and economic stability, the laborer is again harmed. Bringing about a situation which minimizes the dangers of war is of the greatest interest and importance to the wage-earning population in this country." [10]

On July 16, 1897, President William McKinley submitted a treaty to the U.S. Senate for the annexation of Hawaii. The response in labor circles was immediate. Opposition to the proposed annexation was voiced by scores of city central labor bodies who informed their Senators at once of the stand they were taking. The *American Federationist*, the *Journal of the Knights of Labor*, and the official organs of many individual unions not only called for defeat of the treaty but demanded that "a halt should be called to this new spirit of jingoism which is subtly being injected into the life of our nation." Workers could gain nothing from "the vain glory of territorial extension," for, declared the *American Federationist*, "behind this cry of glory there exists real danger to the liberties of our citizens, perhaps the decadence of our republic and the degeneration of our people." [11]

The labor movement denounced the proposed annexation of Hawaii as "a scheme of the millionaires," a capitalist conspiracy to reintroduce into the United States the contract labor system outlawed by Congress in 1885. The fact that the Senate had voted down an amendment to the treaty of annexation that would have repealed the contract labor laws in Hawaii convinced many trade unionists that once Hawaii was annexed, the contract labor system would spread to the United States. This feeling was strengthened by statements in the Senate which boasted that if contract labor was good enough for Hawaii, it was good enough for the United States. [12] *

* This feeling was further reinforced by the Arago decision of the Supreme Court, January 25, 1897, in which case (*Robertson v. Baldwin*), the majority ruled that courts could compel seamen to fulfill their contracts, and pointed out that "the contract of a sailor has always been treated as an exceptional one, and involving to a certain extent the surrender of his personal liberty during the life of the contract." However, Justice John M. Harlan protested that there was nothing to prevent succeeding courts from including other occupations in the "exceptional category." Eventually all workers would be compelled to work under the contract labor system. (*U.S. Reports*, Vol. CLXV, New York, 1897, pp. 282-83.)

1897 A. F. OF L. CONVENTION

At the 1897 A. F. of L. convention, the issues of expansion, jingoism, and war were brought clearly to a head. The convention took a clear and decisive stand against territorial expansion by declaring its strong opposition to the annexation of Hawaii and asking the Senate to reject the treaty. On the questions of jingoism and war, however, considerable division arose. The reason is not difficult to discover. On the one hand, labor's passionate hatred of oppression and an equally passionate desire for freedom led delegates to support a resolution which urged that Congress should "waste no more time in useless debates and diplomatic chicanery, but should take such immediate action as [might] tend to put an end to the indiscriminate murder of the common people of Cuba by the Spanish soldiery." Some delegates admitted that the policy advocated in the resolution might lead to a war with Spain, but they insisted that even this might be necessary to remove the "disgrace to our civilization."

The majority of the delegates expressed their sympathy for the Cuban struggle for freedom, but argued effectively that by adopting the proposed resolution, the labor movement would only be adding fuel to the fire of jingoism which "would result in involving the United States in war with the great European powers." One delegate was amazed that "jingoism should find defenders on the floor of the American Federation of Labor"; another said that in a war with Spain, the workingmen would be the sufferers and the trade unions would be disrupted; another asserted that war would play into the hands of the enemies of the trade unions; still another pointed out that "if the Cubans had the independence the American speculator wanted him to have the Cuban would not be independent, because it would simply be a change from the Spanish speculator to the American."

In short, the majority of the delegates saw clearly the dangers involved in permitting their sympathy for Cuban freedom to be used by the imperialists and militarists. They voted to defeat the strong pro-Cuban resolution. The expression of sympathy for the Cuban people, adopted at the 1896 convention, was reaffirmed.[13] "The sympathy of our movement with Cuba is genuine, earnest and sincere," Gompers wrote in a private letter to Frank Morrison, summing up the A. F. of L. position, "but this does not for a moment imply that we are committed to certain adventurers who are apparently suffering from Hysteria but who simply assume the role to attract attention to their unworthy selves." The A. F. of L. would not permit these jingoistic elements to convert sympathy for Cuba into support of a war against Spain.[14]

The opponents of the annexation of Hawaii, spearheaded by labor's effective campaign against ratification of the treaty, forced abandonment of the imperialist drive to acquire the Islands.[15] But it was only a temporary abandonment. The imperialists had already laid plans to revive the annexation move once the United States became involved in the war with Spain.

"REMEMBER THE *MAINE*"

In January, 1898, the jingo press stepped up its campaign for a war with Spain over Cuba. On February 15, 1898, the *Maine* blew up in the harbor at Havana, and the death of 260 American enlisted men and officers fanned the flames of war. A naval court of inquiry investigated the cause of the explosion. In its report, it was scrupulously careful not to imply that Spain was responsible for the disaster, but the jingo press and the imperialist spokesmen in Congress ignored this fact, denounced Spain, and called for war.*

As the clamor for war against Spain increased, as the headlines in the press whooping it up for war became shriller extra by extra, leading trade unions made a valiant effort to stem the tide. The International Association of Machinists mourned for the loss of life on the *Maine,* but the loss of workers' lives in industry was even more horrible and costly. When the *Maine* sank, "men raved and women wept," and the press called for vengeance. Yet the shooting down of workers in strikes, such as the unprovoked killing of 19 miners and the wounding of 35 others by the sheriff and his deputies in the "Lattimer Massacre,"† and the "carnival

---

* To this day it is not known who blew up the battleship *Maine.* (*See* Donald A. Holman, "The Destruction of the *Maine,* Feb. 15, 1898," *Michigan Alumnus,* Winter, 1954.)

† The "Lattimer Massacre," one of the most cold-blooded crimes against the working class in American labor history, occurred on September 10, 1897 during the great coal strike. Sheriff Martin of Luzerne County, Pennsylvania, had issued a proclamation forbidding marching on the highways in an effort to prevent striking miners from visiting the mines and persuading the workers to join the strike. On September 10, the sheriff and about 100 armed thugs, honored by the designation of "deputy sheriffs," ordered a group of miners to halt on the public highway where they were marching to the Lattimer Mine to get the men there to come out. The marchers were made up of Austrians, Hungarians, Italians, and Germans who had originally been imported into the mines by the operators to cut wages, but had begun to organize and to demand higher wages and better conditions. Suddenly, without warning, the deputies opened fire on the unarmed workers, killing 19 miners and wounding 35 others. "The deputies kept shooting at the miners after they were scattered and were running away," the *Review of Reviews* reported with horror on October 1, 1897. "Most of them were shot in the back." (*See also* Hazleton (Pa.) *Times,* Sept. 13, 25, 1897; Hyman Kurtz, "Pennsylvania State Government and Labor Controls From 1865 to 1922," unpublished Ph.D. thesis, Columbia University, History Department, 1953, pp. 123-25.)

of carnage that takes place every day, month and year in the realm of industry, the thousands of useful lives that are annually sacrificed to the Moloch of greed, the blood tribute paid by labor to capitalism, brings forth no shout for vengeance and reparation, no tear, except from the family and friends of the victims.

"Trainmen and switchmen are murdered every day because of the non-equipment of cars with a device that will reduce danger to life and limb to a minimum. . . . Machinists and engineers, firemen and conductors, and all other branches of the railroad service sacrifice their percentage of life and limb to the same insatiable Gorgon. . . . Death comes in thousands of instances in mill and mine, claims his victims and no popular uproar is heard." [16]

The Craftsman, official organ of the Connecticut A. F. of L., also refused to join in the hysteria being whipped up over the *Maine* explosion. It charged that the tragic incident was being deliberately used by the monopolists and their agents to drive the nation into a war against Spain whose outcome would be the end of liberty at home. It warned:

"The concentrated wealth . . . who control the government of the United States . . . are moving with alarming rapidity either to a military despotism, or to such a curtailment of the ballot that the common people will have practically nothing to say in the legislation of the nation. See how this *Maine* disaster has been used. . . . A gigantic . . . and cunningly-devised scheme is being worked ostensibly to place the United States in the front rank as a naval and military power. The real reason is that the capitalists will have the whole thing and, when any workingmen dare to ask for the living wage . . . they will be shot down like dogs in the streets." [17]

Labor had enough evils to fight at home, the *Coast Seamen's Journal* insisted. War was an "expensive proceeding that the working-class pays for and gains least from." While a war lasted "and for a long time afterward, the interest of the working-class are neglected and frequently

---

A coroner's jury condemned Sheriff Martin for the "wanton" killings, and the sheriff and his deputies were placed on trial. But the outcome was a foregone conclusion. The trial was held in the midst of a terrific propaganda barrage against the foreign-born miners. Members of the jury admitted their prejudice against the "foreigners," but were allowed to remain on the jury. As had been predicted, Sheriff Martin and his deputies were acquitted. "Another blot on the history of our country," wrote United Mine Workers' President M. D. Ratchford when the verdict was announced. (Letter to Gompers, Feb. 24, 1898, *AFL Corr.*)

In 1902, the Lattimer Monument Committee, headed by John Mitchel, U.M.W. President, appealed to organized labor and its friends to contribute to a fund "to perpetuate the memory of the Lattimer Martyrs" by erecting a suitable monument. The monument was dedicated on September 10, 1902, the fifth anniversary of the "Lattimer Massacre." (Circular letter, March 25, 1902, *AFL Corr.*)

ruined past redemption." If only labor would announce in no uncertain terms that it would not fight, there would be no war.[18]

The Railroad Brotherhoods echoed these sentiments. The *Railroad Trainmen's Journal* charged that the demand for war came from "certain moneyed gentlemen, familiarly known as the bulls and bears of Wall Street." The workers, organized and unorganized, had nothing to gain from war, and the government should keep clearly in mind the all-important fact that "they are *not* for war." [19]

A few unions did succumb to the pro-war fever, the most important being the United Mine Workers; at the union's ninth annual convention, the delegates adopted a resolution which announced, in reference to the *Maine* explosion, that "we hold ourselves in readiness to demand that justice be done to all concerned, or we will defend the honor of our country by force." But the predominant sentiment in labor circles was definitely anti-war. The *Journal* of the Boilermakers' Union voiced labor sentiments accurately when it declared early in April, 1898: "There is no cause for war; and to plunge this country into war, unless war is declared against us, would be ignoring the history of this republic, and *imitating* the grabbing examples of the monarchies of Europe." [20]

Throughout March and the opening weeks of April, 1898, several leading trade unionists kept hammering away at the theme that war would mean reaction at home, and would put a halt to labor's efforts to secure social and economic gains. "Calm thought and discussion on economic questions will, I regret to say, be forced to the background," Gompers wrote to Henry Demarest Lloyd on March 25, 1898. Three days later, he warned P. J. McGuire that, in the event of a war with Spain, "legislation in the interest of labor will be forced to the rear and defer[r]ed for a very indefinite period." Only a few days before McKinley sent his war message to Congress, Gompers declared publicly that "All the socialism and humanizing influences that have been at work for twenty-five years will have been in vain if war is declared." [21]

"A war will put all social improvements among us back ten years," wrote Bolton Hall, Treasurer of the American Longshoremen's Union in a widely circulated document entitled, "A Peace Appeal to Labor." * "If there is a war, you will furnish the corpses and the taxes, and others will get the glory. Speculators will make money out of it—that is, out of you. Men will get high prices for inferior supplies, leaky boats, for shoddy clothes and pasteboard shoes,† and you will have to pay the bill,

---

* The Appeal was endorsed by Bishop Potter, William Dean Howells, Charles Frederick Adams, Ernest Crosby, and John S. Crosby.

† It is doubtful that even Bolton Hall could have foreseen the extent of corruption in the furnishing of supplies for the American army during the Spanish-American War in which "leaky boats, shoddy clothes, and pasteboard shoes" were supplemented by canned beef which poisoned whole regiments.

and the only satisfaction you will get is the privilege of hating your Spanish fellow-workmen, who are really your brothers and who have had as little to do with the wrongs of Cuba as you have." [22]

SOCIALISTS OPPOSE WAR WITH SPAIN

With one solitary exception, namely the *Jewish Daily Forward,* the Socialist press offered consistent opposition to the mounting war fever. *The People,* De Leon's organ, charged that the issue of Cuban freedom was "but a pretext." "The real object was *War.*" The ruling class needed war, first, because the "promise of prosperity" could not be realized by American capitalism without a war, and secondly, because war would "distract the attention of the workers from their real interests." [23] The organs of the Social Democracy of America saw eye-to-eye with De Leon on the war question. The drive for war, said the *Appeal to Reason,* was simply "a favorite method of rulers for keeping the people from redressing domestic wrongs." *The Coming Nation* characterized the entire pro-war campaign as a plot of the big capitalists. "It has given them an excuse for increasing the army and navy; for issuing more bonds; it has taken our attention from destitution and hard times, and it has developed the sham patriotism of flagism upon which the Republicans depend so much." [24]

In exposing the character of the war and opposing it, the Socialists stressed the identity of interests of the American, Spanish, and Cuban working classes. "It is a terrible thing," wrote a west coast Socialist in the San Francisco *Voice of Labor,* "to think that the poor workers of this country should be sent to kill and wound the poor workers of Spain, merely because a few leaders may incite them to do so." "If war comes," declared the Minneapolis Sections of the S.L.P. on April 10, 1898, a day before President McKinley sent his war message to Congress, "its burden will fall upon the workers in this country and in Spain. Its fruits will be enjoyed by the capitalists in both countries. Our Comrades, the Socialists of Spain, have denounced war. Let us join hands with them."

The statements of labor leaders, the resolutions of trade unions, and the editorials in the labor and Socialist press opposing war carried little weight with an administration prepared to carry into effect the plans of American monopolists to redivide the world. The *Wall Street Journal* reported on March 19, 1898, that "a great many people in Wall Street" were demanding action against Spain at once. Congress, meanwhile, was being deluged with petitions from powerful business groups urging it to support a policy of expansion, and chambers of commerce and boards of trade were pressuring the State Department to safeguard American interests in the far east. [25]

TRADE UNIONS SUCCUMB TO WAR FEVER

On April 9, 1898, Spain completely capitulated to each and every demand by the United States government to achieve a peaceful settlement of the Cuban question. But the political agents of the Wall Street imperialists were not interested in a peaceful solution of the Cuban crisis. President McKinley had already prepared a war bill, and the Assistant Secretary of the Navy, Theodore Roosevelt, with the assistance of Senator Lodge, had already sent a telegram to Commodore George Dewey, ordering him to hold his squadron ready for "offensive operations in the Philippine Islands."

On April 11, two days after he had received Spain's complete capitulation, President McKinley sent his war message to Congress. He devoted nine closely printed pages to arguments based on the assumption that Spain had not given in, and two short paragraphs to the fact that it had. In short, the President deliberately concealed the news that Spain had already conceded every one of the United States demands.[26] War was declared on April 25.

After war was declared, the majority of the trade unions succumbed to the war fever. Most of the unions either came out in support of the war or remained silent.

Many of the American workers were misled by the demagogy of imperialism, and supported the war in the sincere but mistaken belief that it was a just war, a progressive and democratic one. In an article entitled, "Labor and the War," Joseph R. Buchanan, one of the keenest minds in the contemporary labor movement, discussed the question "How does labor feel about the war?" He noted that there were two tendencies at work in determining labor's attitude. On the one hand, the workers were traditionally more patriotic than "the business, professional or leisure classes" and more eager "to resent an insult to the flag [than] the employers." On the other hand, many workers, in deciding what position to adopt towards the war with Spain, had asked themselves: "Isn't this flag they are waving now and calling upon me to defend the same flag that the butchers of Homestead, Pullman, Brooklyn and Lattimer carried? * Are not the militiamen with whom and under whom I am asked to serve those self same butchers? Have I any interest in common with the fellows who make wars, conduct them and generally get richer out of them?"

Ordinarily, Buchanan continued, the workers would have decided that the answer to these questions was not to support the war. But overweigh-

---

* The reference to Brooklyn is to the Brooklyn Trolley Strike of 1895 which was brutally smashed by the militia. (*See* p. 168.)

ing these factors was labor's traditional hatred of monarchical despotism and support for the revolutionary struggles of oppressed people. Thus, while for the bankers and industrialists, the war with Spain was solely a matter of "the bond and the dollar," for the workers it was a question of liberty for an oppressed people and an end to "the cruel domination of Spain over Cuba." [27]

In short, many workers did not at first see through the fog of propaganda that surrounded the war. They had been fooled by the American imperialists and the jingo press into believing that the war was a war for the freedom of Cuba from Spanish tyranny, and that it was their patriotic duty to assist an oppressed people. "Cuba Libre," "Remember the *Maine*" —these slogans enabled the imperialists to put on the false face of anti-imperialism, and with it they misled many workers into supporting and fighting in a reactionary, aggressive, imperialist war.*

But many labor leaders who now joined the war camp knew clearly that they were supporting an imperialist war. Most of them, in fact, had so characterized the war drive before the actual outbreak of hostilities. Thus, Andrew Furuseth, editor of the *Coast Seamen's Journal,* up to April 25 a leading anti-war paper, pledged labor's allegiance to the United States in its war effort. "The working class and particularly the organized section of it," he wrote editorially, "will concur in this view [that the war might have been avoided]. . . . But having got into the war, no matter how or why, we want to win out as speedily as possible and with as little damage as possible. 'How to win' is the only question worth considering now. The answer is, 'by hard fighting.' " The *Railroad Trainmen's Journal,* which had correctly pointed out before the war that the "bulls and bears of Wall Street" were behind the war drive, now came out for war, stating that "there are conditions worse than war, and the greatest of these is national disgrace." Samuel Gompers, who had labeled the onrush of war as a national tragedy, now extolled the war as "a glorious and righteous one as far as the United States is concerned." Gompers was primarily concerned now that organized labor should receive its full credit for its contribution to the war effort. He pointed with pride to the 250,000 trade unionists who, he claimed, had volunteered for military service, and cited this as overwhelming proof of organized labor's loyalty.[28]

Many of the labor leaders who now supported the war rationalized their position with the argument that by proving the loyalty of the trade unions to the flag, they could forestall the attempts of the imperialists to

---

* After the war was over, the *Monthly Journal of the International Association of Machinists* conceded that many members of the union had been taken in by the humanitarian aspects of the pro-war propaganda and had not clearly understood that the "capitalistic system" had been responsible for the war. (Oct., 1898.)

attack the unions as "Un-American," and thus utilize the war hysteria to destroy labor organizations already weakened by the prolonged economic crisis.* Gompers observed in June, 1898, that "because there were some who hoped that this rightful and humane purpose [Cuban freedom] should be secured without the necessity of our country entering upon war, with all that war entails, men have been unjustly and unfairly criticized, their motives impugned, their Americanism questioned. . . ." [29] Out of fear of having their "Americanism questioned," Gompers and other labor leaders who understood the unjust character of the war, climbed aboard the war-makers' wagon and threw overboard their anti-war sentiments. P. J. McGuire put it succinctly in a letter to Gompers a week after the war started, emphasizing that the leaders of the labor movement should quickly abandon their former opposition to the war lest their demands be treated coldly by the government, and that precautions should be taken to make certain that all spokesman for labor who sought favorable legislation in Congress "should be men who favor loyal and unstinted support to our Government against Spain in the present War." [30]

Economic gains resulting from the war were also responsible for silencing labor leaders who had voiced opposition to the war drive right down to the declaration of war. The railroad brotherhoods, leading opponents of the war drive, hailed the effect of the war in increasing work for railroad men as a result of the shipment of military goods. The leaders of the pottery and glass workers, the bricklayers and woodworkers, all of whom had been outspoken in opposing the war drive, pointed joyfully to the economic benefits their membership secured during the war. The leadership of the United Mine Workers felt that the economic results of the war justified the union's stand in supporting a war against Spain even before the outbreak of hostilities. "The coal and iron trades have not been so healthy for some years past as at present," cried a U.M.W. leader. "The larger business and higher coal prices have been the favorable results of the war." "The war with Spain has had a good effect already on the business of the country," the *National Labor Tribune* exulted. "Not alone in the iron and steel industry is the boom felt, but in all other branches." Citing the sums of money spent for food, clothes, and transportation for the army, it concluded: "All this money being placed in circulation cannot fail to have some beneficial effect, and as a result trade in all branches

---

* Three years later, Andrew Furuseth admitted that he had supported the war in the belief that by proving its "patriotism," labor could prevent set-backs during the conflict and even make advances. This was a false concept of patriotism, he conceded, and he should have opposed the war, even after it had started "because, under all the circumstances of the case, war would result in injury and possibly an irretrievable set-back to the cause of the working-class advancement in the United States." (*Coast Seamen's Journal*, May 1, 1901.)

is improving rapidly." "Even if the war should end in sixty days," joy-fully declared a Pacific Coast labor paper, "the impetus given to business will be so great that the 'boom' will keep up." [31]

Actually, the conditions of the majority of the workers grew worse during the war. Not only was there a startling increase in the cost of living, but, in the absence of an income tax, the poor found themselves paying almost entirely for the staggering costs of the war through in-creased levies on sugar, molasses, tobacco, and other taxes on the workers' "breakfast tables." While Gompers was publicly extolling the war, he acknowledged in his private correspondence that the conflict had caused a serious decline in labor's living standards, and that "the increased cost of living" resulting from the war "has been tantamount to a reduction of wages of fully twenty per cent, i.e., in the decreased purchasing power of their wages." [32]

LABOR AND SOCIALIST FORCES OPPOSING WAR

While many of their leaders had betrayed them, the American workers were not without an anti-war and anti-imperialist voice to express their true interests. Even in the early months when the imperialist nature of the war was still not clear to many workers, some opposition to the war appeared in trade union circles. The *Bakers' Journal* voiced its doubts about labor's support in the following editorial comment on June 15, 1898: "How much more cause have the workingmen to enlist in the army of organized labor and to do their duty in the campaigns and battles against the cohorts of capital than those men who have taken the field against Spain. The latter will never enjoy the fruits of their victories." The war, declared the International Association of Machinists in May, 1898, was simply a device of capitalism to distract the workers from the miseries brought about by the present economic system and to thereby "prevent a thorough union of labor's forces. The day will come, however, when laborers will realize that they must fight not each other, but the power by which it is oppressed and then, with the overthrow of that system, war will be no more." [33]

So vigorous was the opposition to the war on the part of the Socialist Labor Party, and all its organs, that the authorities in New York City banned the May Day anti-war parade called by the S.L.P. [34] *

The Social Democrats, Eugene V. Debs was proud to announce, had

* The pro-war May Day parade called by the *Jewish Daily Forward* was blessed by the authorities. That same evening the *Forward* sponsored a patriotic rally at which the speakers were Abraham Cahan, Louis Miller, Michael Zametkin, Meyer London, Morris Winchevsky, and others. Here these so-called Socialist leaders urged the Jewish workers to support the war. (*Jewish Daily Forward*, May 1-3, 1898.)

not been swept off their feet by the war craze. "So far as I know," he told the press in mid-June, 1898: "not one of the 10,000 members of the Social Democracy has enlisted." The only war the Social Democrats would be ready to fight in was a war "to wipe out capitalism, the common enemy of the oppressed and downtrodden of all nations." [35]

The anti-imperialist voice of American labor did not reach too large an audience at the outset of the war. Most trade union leaders either supported the war or were silent. The voice of the Socialist press and leadership was limited in its appeal both by sectarian policies and by its small membership.

As the summer waned, and the course of American imperialism became clearer, the ranks of the anti-imperialists in the American labor movement grew rapidly. Widespread disillusionment began to appear in the trade unions with the annexation of Hawaii in July, a month before the war against Spain ended. To be sure, several trade unions, especially the railroad brotherhoods, supported Hawaiian annexation on the ground that increased trade with the islands would bring more business to American industry and thus provide more jobs and higher wages to American workers.[36] But the editorials in the majority of the labor papers and the resolutions adopted by numerous trade unions reveal clearly that the general sentiment of the labor movement was one of outspoken opposition to annexation. The Pueblo *Courier,* official organ of the Western Labor Union,* observed that Hawaiian annexation proved that "the war which started as one of relief for the starving Cubans has suddenly changed to one of conquest." The Chicago *Labor World* declared: "This has been a poor man's war—paid for by the poor man. The rich have profited by it, as they always do, and now they demand that we shall grab everything in sight, in order that they may profit all the more." Condemning the passage of the Hawaiian annexation treaty in the Senate, the *Journal of the Knights of Labor* asked: "Is this step the beginning of imperialism with which we have been so long threatened?" [37]

Events rapidly demonstrated that these fears were amply justified.

* The Western Labor Union was founded at a convention held at Salt Lake City on May 10, 1898. The delegates, representing the Western Federation of Miners and various trades around the mining camps and towns, emphasized their dissatisfaction with the failure of the A.F. of L. to meet the needs of the western workers, particularly the unskilled, and pointed to the importance of bringing together all workers "irrespective of occupation, nationality, creed or color." The Western Labor Union would "set an example for our fellow-workers in the East that will prove a blessing and sound the death knell of every corporation and trust that has robbed the American laborer of the fruits of his toil, and has so changed the complexion of this government that there is little difference between a republic and a monarchy." (Pueblo *Courier,* May 25, June 3, 1898; San Francisco *Voice of Labor,* May 28, 1898.)

CHAPTER 27

Labor and Imperialism

On December 10, 1898, the Treaty of Peace against defeated Spain was executed. Cuba, it was understood, was to be held by the United States with the immediate prospect of autonomy. Puerto Rico and the Philippine Islands were ceded to the United States. Eleven days later President McKinley proclaimed to the Philippines a policy of "benevolent assimilation," and, at the same time, urged General Harrison Gray Otis, the military commander of the islands, to gain control of important towns and cities as soon as possible.

But the administration had no easy time putting over this betrayal of the Filipino people who had fought two-score rebellions against Spain, who had captured Manila for the U. S. forces, and who were fighting for independence. The *United States Investor* could say blithely: "It is demonstrable that by far the greater proportion of the people of this country either openly favor the acquisition of outside territory at this time, or are so indifferent to the matter as not to care to interpose any obstacle to such a movement." [1] But vast numbers of the American people, shocked by the peace terms, had awakened to the true implications of the war—that in place of Spanish oppression, U. S. imperialism was proposed. And the anti-imperialist sentiment of these Americans was being expressed in resolutions of trade unions, farmers' organizations, Negro people's associations, and of various clubs and leagues. In a leading place in the developing battle against a war of conquest and an imperialist peace treaty stood the American labor movement.

It is true that there were unions which remained aloof from the struggle over imperialism, devoting their entire attention to immediate job problems. It is also true that a section of the labor movement supported imperialism, and became apologists for the policies of the McKinley administration. Unions whose members were beginning to obtain benefits from the robbery of the colonial masses openly proclaimed their endorsement of expansion. The Typographical Union hailed the annexation of Hawaii and the proposal to annex Puerto Rico, Guam, and the Philippines, and freely admitted that it did so because with English being used as the language in the schools of these territories, printing would "flourish more than heretofore." Of Cuba it said in the same selfish terms: "If the occupation of the island by the United States has done no good to anything else, it certainly has immediately benefitted the printing business." With new territories owned by Spain thrown open to American trade, said the *Commoner and Glassworker,* organ of the pottery makers and glass workers, "American glassware in many lines can find new fields of consumption if intelligent effort is made." The journals of the railroad brotherhoods reported joyfully every shipment of American manufactured goods to Cuba, Hawaii, Puerto Rico, and the Philippines, and pointed out that this increased trade meant more jobs and more money for the railroad workers. There were even unions which, voicing the ideology of the ruling class, advanced the thesis that expansion would end the danger of another depression in the United States, since the newly-acquired territories would provide a market for the surplus manufactured goods.[2]

LABOR OPPOSES IMPERIALISM

But the supporters of imperialism in the labor movement were definitely in the minority. "Most of the discussion in labor circles took an anti-imperialist line," concludes Dr. John S. Appel in his study of labor's attitude towards imperialism.[3]

Only a small section of the working class enjoyed the fruits of the post-war expansion, and the majority of the trade unions rejected the contention that imperialism would offer a market for American goods and therefore benefit the American workers. Labor answered that capital would do better by satisfying the demands of the market at home. There was enough demand for food and clothing in America, but the masses of the American people were too poor to consume the products of the mills, factories, mines, and farms. "The workers would gladly consume more," declared the *Leather Workers' Journal,* "but their wages do not permit them to do so; therefore the only outlet for this surplus is foreign markets." Instead of searching for new markets abroad and destroying the liberties of the American and colonial people in the process, "let us have economic expansion and the development of home markets here on our own soil through giving labor a greater share of its own created wealth through higher wages and better living standards." [4]

The argument that the mass of workers would benefit from imperialism was met head on by the trade unions. Imperialism, they said, led to wars which were fought by the workers but from which only the capitalists profited. "Looking at it from a class viewpoint," declared *The Railroad Telegrapher,* "the wonder of it all is that the working people are willing to lose blood and treasure in fighting another man's battle." "How much better off are the workingmen of England through all its colonial possessions?" pointedly asked the Carpenters' journal. On the contrary, it was the trusts and monopolies which benefitted while the workers paid all the expenses.* The Cigar Makers predicted that the expenses of imperialism "will have to be borne by the people while a favored few—trusts and monopolies—will receive all the profits." The *National Labor Tribune,* organ of the Iron, Steel and Tin Workers, agreed that the Philippines "possess wonderfully rich resources. . . . The same can be said of this country, but if anybody were to ask you if you owned a coal mine, a sugar plantation, or railroad you would have to say no . . . all these things are in the hands of the trusts controlled by a few." [5] Imperialism, moreover, would only strengthen the control of the trusts. As George E. McNeill put it:

"The present war against the Filipinos, if endorsed and continued by the people, will certainly strengthen the trusts in the work of debauching public sentiment, and will react against universal suffrage and all free institutions. 'Choose ye this day whom ye will serve God or mammon'— the trade unions or the trusts, the principles of the Declaration of Independence, or an imperial government." [6]

1898 A. F. OF L. CONVENTION

The American labor movement's vigorous and stirring opposition to imperialism was set forth clearly and decisively at the A. F. of L. convention in December, 1898. By that time President McKinley had already toured the country in his campaign to sell imperialism to the people. The President had ended every speech with the question: "Shall we haul down the flag?" At the A. F. of L. convention, Gompers gave the answer

* The experiences of the British working class in England's imperialist war against the Boers reinforced this argument. "In Great Britain," remarked *The Railroad Telegrapher* in November, 1899, in the midst of the Boer War, "the wage earners pay all the cost of the warfare, the same as in other countries. As labor is the sole source of wealth there is no other source from which war supplies can be drawn." (P. 82.) The *Beerdrivers and Stablemen Journal* agreed: "The working people will pay all the cost of the Boer War, but they will get none of the honor or boodle if any result." (March 24, 1900, attached to letter of Frank Thompson to Frank Morrison, April 9, 1900, *AFL Corr.*)

American labor bitterly denounced the British for the Imperialist war against the Boers, and a number of trade unions passed resolutions demanding "that Great Britain make peace immediately with the Boers." (See H. N. Walmsley to Gompers, May 12, 1900, *ibid.*)

of the trade unions: "The flag of the country should never be used as the cloak to hide tyranny." Challenging those who charged that labor should not concern itself with such issues as imperialism, Gompers declared that if labor had supplied the foot-soldiers for the war, "who then but the representatives of labor have the better right to consider the very grave questions which have resulted from our war with Spain?" [7]

Overwhelmingly, the delegates agreed with Gompers. Seven leading delegates signed a statement declaring: "As citizens we protest against forcing our system of government upon an unwilling people; against the maintenance of a large standing army, that has no place in a republic such as ours; we protest against the manifold dangers attendant upon European and Asiatic entanglements, and as workingmen emphatically protest against the unfair competition of the wretched people who would become, without voice or vote, our fellow citizens. We therefore urge upon workingmen to awake to a full realization of the dangers that confront them, and call upon their representatives with no uncertain voice to save them from the dangers of imperialism." [8]

This manifesto against imperialism was endorsed by the convention, as was a resolution condemning the peace treaty, and instructing the officers of the A. F. of L. "to use every honorable means to secure its defeat." Delegate after delegate arose to speak against imperialism, and only one, Samuel Donnelly of the Typographical Union, spoke against the manifesto. Delegate Lloyd of Boston warned that any politician voting for the peace treaty would be "putting himself in deadly enmity to organized labor." The final decision was reached by almost unanimous voice vote, only three votes being cast against the anti-imperialist resolution which read:

"Whereas, As a result of the war with Spain a new and far-reaching policy, commonly known as 'imperialism' or 'expansion' is now receiving the attention of the National Government, and if ratified by the United States Senate will seriously burden the wage-workers of our country, thrust upon us a large standing army and an aristocratic navy, and seriously threaten the perpetuity of our Republic, therefore be it

"Resolved, That this convention offers its protest against any such innovation in our system of government, and instructs our officers to use every honorable means to secure its defeat." [9]

The proceedings of the A. F. of L. convention were widely reported in the press, and even the pro-imperialist papers agreed that the convention had clearly demonstrated that "Labor opposes Imperialism." [10] The anti-imperialist journals joyfully hailed the stand taken by the delegates. "At no time has there been any doubt as to the sentiments of the American Federation of Labor regarding the expansion policy of President McKinley," editorialized the Kansas City (Mo.) *Times*. "But an official expression of the position of the organization was needed and that is now given. Labor is fixed in its purpose to resist the adoption of the American colonial empire of the corporations." [11]

From scores of unions, including the Brewery Workers, the Cigar Makers, the Coast Seamen, the Carpenters, the Hatters, the Journeymen Plumbers, the Meat Cutters and Butcher Workmen, the Machinists, the Patternmakers, the Woodworkers, and the Western Federation of Miners, came letters and telegrams to the A. F. of L. headquarters congratulating the organization for having spoken "in no uncertain voice" against imperialism.[12] A significant letter came also from Erving Winslow, Secretary of the American Anti-Imperialist League. "I want to congratulate you," he wrote to Gompers, ". . . for the admirable and ringing resolutions adopted by the Federation. We should be glad to act upon any suggestions from you for promoting the work among the unions." [13]

The Anti-Imperialist League was born on June 15, 1898, at a meeting in Boston's Faneuil Hall, site of numerous historical meetings in the American Revolution and in the anti-slavery fight. The assembled audience adopted protest resolutions against the war of conquest, and declared that it would be time enough to think of governing others "when we have shown that we can protect the rights of men within our own borders like the colored race of the South and the Indians of the West, and that we can govern great cities like New York, Philadelphia, and Chicago."

The meeting selected an anti-imperialist committee of correspondence to contact "persons and organizations throughout the country." Special attention was to be given to winning labor's support for the cause; the Anti-Imperialist Committee of Correspondence made an appropriation "for the distribution of an anti-imperialist speech recently made by President Samuel Gompers of the American Federation of Labor," and appointed a special sub-committee to "prepare and circulate an appeal to the workingmen of the country to oppose imperialism by resolutions and otherwise." [14]

In its campaign, the League received the cooperation of a number of labor leaders. George E. McNeill was one of the speakers at the Faneuil Hall meeting on June 15, 1898, and served actively with the Committee of Correspondence, helping to draw up and send circular letters to trade unions calling for anti-imperialist protests, In November, 1898, Gompers was elected a vice-president of the League, and thereafter he participated actively in its work, speaking for the organization, assisting in the distribution of the League's circular letters to the unions, and furnishing it with the names and addresses of the secretaries of the principal labor unions in the country.[15]

In the months following the A. F. of L. convention, the leaders of the Federation and the Anti-Imperialist League worked closely together to bring labor's influence to bear on Congress against the Peace Treaty. The joint effort was especially directed towards obtaining resolutions and appeals from local unions to their respective members of Congress. "There is no doubt they can exert a tremendous influence against expansion," Erving Winslow wrote to Gompers.[16] David G. Haskins, Jr., secretary of the League's Committee of Correspondence was convinced that the labor movement was the key to the success of the drive to defeat ratification of the treaty. "Everybody says that the labor unions are the political forces of which the politicians are most in awe," he wrote to Gompers on December 7, 1898, "and I think it extremely important that their influence should be exerted at once before Senators are too strongly committed." [17]

LABOR FIGHTS IMPERIALIST TREATY

Fully aware of its responsibilities, the labor movement acted to bring pressure for the defeat of the treaty. Both the Central Labor Union of New York and the Boston Central Labor Union adopted resolutions calling for the treaty's rejection. The New York body, in addition, joined with other organizations to sponsor the great mass meeting held at the Academy of Music in New York on January 22, 1899. The meeting, addressed by representatives of many of the leading organizations of the country and other prominent citizens, came out vigorously for the defeat of the treaty, expressing itself as being "absolutely opposed to the annexation of the Philippine Islands as a permanent portion of the national domain." [18]

The press agreed that the meeting was the "most striking demonstration" against imperialism "that has been held so far in the country," and clearly revealed the "unanimity and enthusiasm" in the labor movement against the peace treaty. This fact alone, noted the New Orleans *Times-Democrat,* "is certain to have an effect that will be felt, and that will have a tangible result, far beyond the limits of the Empire State . . . and will make many a Senator and many a Representative pause before they commit themselves to the proposed reversal of all our American policies and all our American traditions." [19]

During the session of Congress at which the Spanish peace treaty was considered—December, 1898, through March, 1899—31 petitions were entered in the *Congressional Record* from trade unions opposing the acquisition of the Philippines. These petitions came from such organizations as the Cigar Makers' International Union, the Superior (Wisconsin) Trades and Labor Assembly, the Mine Workers' Union of Michigan, and the San Francisco Labor Council. In addition, thousands of individual trade unionists signed and sent petitions to the President and

Congress which were drawn up jointly by the Anti-Imperialist League and the A. F. or L.* Finally, Gompers was one of 24 signers, along with Carl Schurz, Grover Cleveland, Charles W. Eliot, President of Harvard University, Andrew Carnegie and others, of a Memorial to the Senate which petitioned that body to amend the peace treaty to exclude the annexation of the Philippines and Puerto Rico.[20]

All through the fall of 1898 and the early winter of 1899 the treaty debate went on. The anti-imperialist movement was denounced; opponents of the peace treaty were branded as "unworthy of the name of American citizens"; anti-imperialist writings were barred from the mails, and threats of violence against anti-imperialists, who were denounced in the jingo press as "traitors," were common.[21] Gompers was specifically accused of "treason" for calling upon the organized workers to rise up in protest against imperialism.†

"So far as Gompers' loose talk means anything," angrily declared the pro-imperialist Philadelphia *Telegraph,* "it means treasonable hostility to the Government of this nation. It is not often worth while to take notice of the foolish vaporings of notoriety-seeking spouters, but when a man occupying a representative position goes to the length of uttering treasonable threats against the Government he should be at least repudiated and rebuked by his constituents." [22]

But the anti-imperialists refused to be intimidated or terrorized either by slanders accusing them of being "Un-American" or by threats of violence. The opposition to the peace treaty grew. Thousands of petitions poured into Washington as the Senators prepared to cast their votes. Senator George F. Hoar of Massachusetts, one of the few Republican leaders to oppose imperialism, himself filed 14,500 names, many of them trade unionists in the Bay State, from December 12, 1898, to February 4, 1899, against the treaty. Small wonder that Henry Cabot Lodge, the leader of the imperialists in the Senate, wrote to his jingo colleague, Theodore Roosevelt: "We are going to have trouble over the treaty." [23]

---

* The petitions protested ". . . against any extension of the sovereignty of the United States over the Philippine Islands, in any event; or other foreign territory, without the free consent of the people thereof."

† The hysterical cry in the pro-imperialist press that Gompers was guilty of "treason" mounted in intensity after his speech at a mass meeting in Boston's Tremont Temple, sponsored by that city's trade unions. During the course of his speech, Gompers not only expressed labor's hatred of imperialism but its profound interest in preserving world peace. "If international peace cannot be secured by the intelligence of those in authority," he declared, "then I look forward to the time when the workers will settle this question by refusing to handle materials that are to be used to destroy their fellow men, and the seamen of the world, united in one organization, while willing to risk their lives in conducting the commerce of nations, absolutely refuse to strike down their fellow men, even though they may be employed by a foreign power." (Boston *Globe,* March 20, 1899.)

ROLE OF BRYAN

At this critical juncture, William Jennings Bryan, the supposed anti-imperialist standard-bearer of the Democratic Party, came to Washington, and told shocked Democratic Senators that they should vote for the treaty. His spurious argument was that: (1) it would end the war; (2) after the war was ended, Congress would grant the Philippines independence; (3) if they failed to do this the blame would be on the Republican Party. Actually, Bryan was motivated by selfish political reasons. The Democrats, he was convinced, needed another issue besides free silver for the 1900 presidential campaign. Imperialism would make a good issue, and ratification of the treaty would keep it alive.[24]

Bryan's intervention hastened the formation of a coalition of Republicans and Democrats in favor of the treaty. The Southern Democrats were in the forefront of the coalition, for they saw in American overseas expansion, with the assumption of stewardship over a large overseas colored population in Cuba, Hawaii, Puerto Rico, and the Philippines, an effective weapon to be used against the Negro people in the South. The ideology of the imperialists emphasized precisely the same arguments used by the Southern ruling class to justify exploitation of the Negro people in the South—the essentially innate inferiority of non-whites to whites, their "ineptitude in politics and in the exercise of political responsibility," and their low social and economic status as proof of fundamental defects in Negro character and ability.* When the Southern Democrats lined up with the Republicans in support of the imperialist treaty, they were thinking more about the Negro people in the South than they were of the Puerto Ricans, the Cubans, and the Filipinos.

The treaty was passed by only one vote. Thirty-three Senators stood firm in opposition. Lodge, breathing a sigh of relief, described the struggle for ratification as "the closest, hardest fight I have ever known."[25]

While the treaty transferred the Philippines, Puerto Rico, and Cuba to the United States, it did not determine their future status. The Teller Amendment, adopted at the time the United States declared war against Spain, had committed this country to Cuban independence, and President McKinley had stated publicly that the retention of the Philippines was a transitional stage on the way to Philippine independence. Would the United States carry out these pledges? And how soon?

* For excellent discussions of the relation of racism and imperialism, *see* Herbert Aptheker, "American Imperialism and White Chauvinism," mimeographed pamphlet, New York, 1951; Richard Hofstadter, *Social Darwinism in American Thought,* Philadelphia, 1945, pp. 146-73; Merle Curti, *Social Ideas of American Educators,* New York, 1935, p. 225ff.

The answer would depend on the strength of the anti-imperialist movement. "Robbers never give up their gains voluntarily, no matter under what guise obtained," wrote a labor leader in calling upon the workers to mobilize into action so as to guarantee "that the expansion or imperialistic policy . . . will not be carried into effect." [26]

LABOR AND THE ANTI-IMPERIALIST LEAGUE

No sooner was the Treaty with Spain ratified than the Anti-Imperialist League announced its intention to continue the circulation of literature, to assist in the formation of local and state leagues, and by public meetings and other means to oppose imperialism and a permanently large standing army. In a circular signed, among others, by Gompers, the League urged "all lovers of freedom" to cooperate with it to achieve a suspension of hostilities in the Philippines, the guarantee by Congress that the United States "will recognize the independence of the Philippines and its equality among nations, and gradually withdraw all military and naval forces."

The response to this appeal was widespread. Anti-imperialist leagues sprang up all over the country. In October, 1899, at a mammoth convention in Chicago, the local leagues created a central association, the American Anti-Imperialist League. The national league, with headquarters in Chicago, supplemented rather than supplanted the local groups. [27]

The League grew into a national organization of one-half million members. The national and local leagues held conferences and public meetings, published thousands of manifestos, pamphlets, poems, speeches, and magazine articles. (The national organization alone circulated 1,164,188 items of printed matter, and sent out 169,700 chain cards.) The anti-imperialists won the support of America's outstanding writers—Mark Twain, William Dean Howells, Henry James, Edwin Arlington Robinson, Edgar Lee Masters, Dr. W. E. B. DuBois, Finley Peter Dunne, and others—who contributed poems, essays and short stories to the literature of the anti-imperialist movement. A significant number of the older men who were leading critics of imperialism had worked for the abolition of slavery, notably Carl Schurz and Thomas Wentworth Higginson.

Although the American Anti-Imperialist League and its numerous branches were organized and managed largely by liberal, intellectual reformers, the movement attracted thousands of men and women, Negro and white, of every class and of almost every shade of public opinion. The *National Labor Standard,* official organ of the New Jersey State Federation of Labor, recommended that all trade unionists "who believe in the *Republic* against *Empire* should join the Anti-Imperialist League." [28]*

* The paper sponsored its own league, called the Anti-Imperialist Labor League of New Jersey. (*National Labor Standard,* Sept. 13, 1900.)

Just how many answered this call is not known, for it is impossible to estimate the trade union composition of the national league or any of its branches. A number of labor leaders, however, were active in the movement.

Samuel Gompers became a vice president of the Washington, D. C., Anti-Imperialist League, and when the American Anti-Imperialist League was organized, he became a vice president of the national organization. On July 13, 1899, he wrote to Erving Winslow, secretary of the national league, assuring him that "I certainly prize the privilege of membership in the League . . . and assuring you of my earnest desire to be helpful in every way within my power to attack and defeat this vicious and un-American policy of imperialism." [29]

Gompers participated actively in the League's work. He spoke for the organization, assisted in the distribution of speeches and circulars against imperialism to all A. F. of L. unions, gave his personal and official support to the work in the capital, and donated his office for the meetings of the organization. "It is constant work speaking at public meetings, private meetings," Gompers wrote on June 16, 1899, in the midst of a tour to spread the word among the unions against imperialism. A month later he wrote to Erving Winslow:

"For ten weeks I have been out in the inter-mountain country of the far West, and have addressed more than fifty public meetings; and no opportunity was lost for presenting this question in as fair light as was within my power.

"I know you will be gratified to learn, that every attack made upon the Imperialist policy was received with great acclaim." [30]

John W. Hayes, Grand Master Workman of the K. of L., Patrick A. Collins, and Patrick Ford were some of the other trade unionists who were active in the American Anti-Imperialist League. Although the labor spokesmen played an important role in advancing the League's campaign, their influence in the organization was overshadowed by the business and industrial elements in the leadership. Andrew Carnegie, Richard T. Crane, the Chicago manufacturer, John J. Valentine, President of the Wells-Fargo Express Company, and George Foster Peabody, New York banker, were among the top leaders of the League and enjoyed an influence out of proportion to their numbers—chiefly because they helped to finance the movement. [31]

"We want to keep step with labor," Erving Winslow wrote to Gompers in July, 1899. [32] But the character of the leadership of the national and local leagues made this goal difficult to achieve. Lenin, who called the leaders of the Anti-Imperialist League, "the last of the Mohicans of bourgeois democracy," pointed to their refusal to recognize "the indissoluble bond between imperialism and the very foundation of capitalism. . . ." [33] The League's leaders—businessmen, industrialists, and retired capitalists—

refused to point out the connection between the trusts and imperialism, a fact which was hardly surprising since many of them were themselves benefitting from the monopolistic corporations. They saw imperialism only in terms of annexing territory, while they had no objection to economic penetration and control of colonial or semi-colonial countries by U. S. monopoly capital, without actual annexation.[34]

The literature issued by the League reflected these weaknesses, concentrating almost completely on the religious, constitutional, and humanitarian aspects of the anti-imperialist argument in which references to the working class and to the economic basis of imperialism were few and far between.[35] Thus in the address by George S. Boutwell, President of the American Anti-Imperialist League, entitled "The President's Policy: War and Conquest Abroad, Degradation of Labor at Home," which was probably the most direct appeal to labor issued by the League, the only mention of the relationship between imperialism and the rights of labor in the United States was the oft-repeated and shop-worn argument that a colonial empire would be "followed by the degradation of the laboring population through competition with the laborers of the east and the products of the cheap labor of the east." [36]

It is not difficult, in view of their approach to the issue of imperialism, to understand why the leaders of the Anti-Imperialist League and Gompers were on such good terms. Like them, Gompers refused to acknowledge the connection between the trusts and imperialism; like them he saw imperialism primarily as a question of annexing territory, and like them he blamed the competition of cheap labor upon the inhabitants of the new possessions, rather than upon the capitalists who sought to drive down wages and to employ the cheapest labor possible. Like many leaders of the Anti-Imperialist League, Gompers was repeatedly making chauvinistic references to the colonial peoples. He argued that expansion would "threaten an inundation of Mongolians to overwhelm the free laborers of our country," and described the Philippine people as "perhaps nearer the condition of savages and barbarians than any island possessed by any other civilized nation on earth." [37]

The spreading of such misconceptions about the inhabitants of the new possessions seriously weakened the struggle against imperialism, for it practically conceded the chief argument of the imperialists, namely, that the colonial peoples were not civilized enough to be entrusted with self-government.[38] Yet to Gompers as to many leaders of the Anti-Imperialist League, the issues of competition from labor in the colonial possessions and the so-called danger of mass immigration from these territories were the major considerations.*

* "Gompers, as a cigarmaker, was afraid of the competition from Cuban and Philippine cigarmakers; and as a vigorous advocate of immigration restrictions, he

In many ways, therefore, both Gompers and the leaders of the Anti-Imperialist League were far behind a large part of the rank-and-file trade unionists in the anti-imperialist struggle. While Gompers had no criticism of the approach of the Anti-Imperialist League, many workers correctly felt that the League's leaders had no real understanding of their problems. When the League and Gompers tried to get the trade unions to make Labor Day, 1899, "the occasion for a great demonstration against the imperialist policy," they met with a lukewarm response from the unions who objected to the suggestion that the workers "should march through the streets with banners declaring that American Labor should not compete with 3 cents a day Philippine labor." The issue, the League and Gompers were informed, was insignificant compared with the more basic impacts of imperialism on the labor movement.[39]

The failure of the Anti-Imperialist League to emphasize the direct connection between the expansion overseas and the attacks upon the labor movement at home is not surprising. Workers who remembered the slaughter of men, women and children in the Homestead and Pullman strikes and the destruction of the civil rights of the strikers and their leaders were not overly impressed by the anti-imperialist expressions of men like Andrew Carnegie and Grover Cleveland. Gompers felt puffed-up to be associated with such important personages in the same movement,* but the workers could not forget the smashing of the unions at Homestead and Pullman.[40]

THE COMMON OPPRESSORS

It is true that much of the literature of the labor movement dealing with imperialism at the turn of the century reflected the same vagueness as that issued by the League, with imperialism being loosely associated with expansionism, colonialism, militarism, tyranny, etc. and with all too few references to "the indissoluble bond between imperialism and the very foundation of captialism." Nevertheless, it is in the labor press, in

feared the influx of workers from and via the new possessions. These points were probably the main reasons for the stand he took [against imperialism] and the intensity with which he advocated it." (Delber Lee McKee, "The American Federation of Labor and Foreign Policy, 1886-1912," unpublished Ph.D. thesis, Stanford University, 1952, p. 78.) Gompers, of course, did point out other reasons for opposing imperialism such as "large armaments and frequent wars." (*See* his speech at the conference on Foreign Policy at Saratoga Springs, N. Y., August 1898, *American Federationist*, September, 1898, pp. 139-40.)

* "In the Anti-Imperialist League he [Gompers] was connected with such names as Grover Cleveland, Thomas B. Reed, David Starr Jordan, and Andrew Carnegie. A higher degree of prestige and respectability accrued to the interest of the A.F. of L. leader than had been the case before, even though he was on the unpopular side." (McKee, *op. cit.*, p. 76.)

the proceedings of the trade unions, and in the correspondence of the trade unionists, not in the publications of the Anti-Imperialist League, that one finds set forth the fundamental thesis that the oppressors of the colonial people were also the oppressors of the working class in the United States and that imperialism would lead only to further repression of the American labor movement. A machinist from Chicago, writing of the Filipino people, put it sharply: "Because men such as [Theodore] Roosevelt of New York declare them savages and [say] that they ought to be repressed . . . does not make it so, for if such men as he had it in their power they would repress you and me from becoming members of the International Association of Machinists." [41]

On February 7, 1899, U.S. troops fired on a group of Filipino soldiers and killed 3,000. The war for the conquest of the Philippines was on.

Less than three months later, Federal troops were called into the Coeur d'Alene district of Idaho to crush a strike of the miners against the Bunker Hill and Sullivan Mining Company, the property of the Standard Oil Trust. Since the Idaho militia was on duty in the Philippines, Federal troops had been called in. The action, coupled with the suspension of the writ of habeas corpus and the imprisonment of the striking miners in bull pens, effectively destroyed the union in that area.* It also brought home in dramatic fashion the dangers of imperialism to the working class. Imperialism abroad meant reaction at home; it meant the growth of militarism to put down strikes and curb the progress of trade unionism. It meant, said the Metal Polishers' Journal, "a large standing army in largely populated centers to shoot down the people if the pangs of hunger cause them to revolt." [42]

The unions were quick to draw the lessons of Coeur d'Alene. "Could Imperialism go farther than this," wrote Andrew Furuseth, Secretary of the Sailors' Union of the Pacific. "Militarism in Philippines and Cuba and militarism to suppress the right of organization and take away the right of Habeas Corpus at home. We are certainly moving with striking directness towards the death of the Republic. Whether the people will realize the danger and put in their protest is now an all important question."†

If labor did not protest against the outrages in Idaho, the Hatters' Union warned, the time would soon come when there would be "a squad

* See pp. 230-34.
† In one of his keen comments on the imperialist drive of American capitalism, Furuseth wrote prophetically to Gompers: "About China, why we are going to have a slice of China if the present powers are unsuccessful, of that there is not the slightest doubt in my mind unless China in the meantime learns to fight, then we shall get out with the rest." (A. Furuseth to Gompers, San Francisco, Sept. 25, 1900, AFL Corr.) Furuseth was referring to the sending of American troops to help suppress the Chinese people's "Boxer" rebellion in the summer of 1900.

of soldiers at every factory door." [43] Although Coeur d'Alene, Idaho, was more than 7,000 miles from Manila, the chains of a common oppression had welded them much closer: the struggle of one had become the struggle of the other. "When the Cuban, the Porto Rican, and the Philippinos [*sic*] are deprived of the right of self-government by our ruling class, it is our political rights which are in jeopardy," said a committee report at the 1899 A. F. of L. convention. [44]

This understanding of the interrelationship of the class interests of the American and colonial working class is clearly illustrated in the reactions of the trade unions to labor events in Cuba, Puerto Rico, and the Philippines. When in September, 1899, Brigadier-General William S. Ludlow, military governor of Havana, broke up a strike of Cuban workers by the simple device of throwing the leaders in jail, he reported that the greatest protest came from "a labor organization in Chicago, showing how close was the connection between the two localities." * Gompers agreed that such a "connection" existed, for he pointed out in his Presidential report to the 1899 A. F. of L. convention that "it is but a step from military rule applied to Cuba to the territory constituting the present United States of America. We have seen . . . the attempt made in the Coeur d'Alene district of Idaho and elsewhere." The following editorial from the St. Louis *Post-Dispatch* was reprinted with approving comment in labor papers all over the country:

"How labor will fare under militarism is strikingly shown by the record of the Havana strike. It matters not whether the demands of the strikers were reasonable or not, they had a right to strike, to choose leaders, and to obtain what they wanted by all lawful methods. But the military authorities have broken the backbone of the strike by the simple plan of throwing the leaders into jail, although no violence on the strikers' part has been reported. And that the strikers are thoroughly intimidated is shown by the fact that they are obliged to obtain the authority of the military governor before they can even hold a meeting to call the strike off. The Spaniards did not treat Cuban labor in a more arbitrary manner. This is one of the incidents of military rule." [45]

The trade unions in the United States also protested sharply against the arrest and imprisonment of strikers in Puerto Rico by American military authorities. The New York Central Federated Union voted to "send a contribution to the Porto Rican strikers," and urged all trade unionists to protest to the President and Congress "so that these down-trodden people [of Puerto Rico] may not be mere chattels of trusts and corpora-

* Brigadier-General Ludlow actually accused "certain professional agitators" sent to Cuba by trade unions in the United States of having precipitated the strike. (*Annual Report* of Brigadier-General, William S. Ludlow, U.S. Army, Military Governor of Havana, "Strikes," Oct. 4, 1899, pp. 186-87.)

tions." The *Typographical Union* also urged the "organized workmen of this country . . . to appeal to the administration at Washington to obtain the release of Porto Rican labor officials and relief from further persecution." The official journal of the Indianapolis Central Labor Union declared: "If you want an emphatic evidence of military tyranny, if not downright imperialism, all you have to do is to direct your attention toward Porto Rico. A military edict has just been issued for the suppression of all species of trade unionism on the island, and the presidents, secretaries and other officers have been thrown into prison. . . . It is a cause for serious reflection in the ranks of organized labor." [46]

The strike bans imposed by the military authorities in Cuba, Puerto Rico, Hawaii,* and the Philippines increased anti-imperialist sentiment in organized labor circles in the United States. They proved to American workers that their fears of imperialism were well founded; they demonstrated the use to which the monopolies would employ the military in the United States. The precedent in the colonial possessions had already passed over to the United States, and this, as one labor journal succinctly stated it, was logical: "Expansion leads to imperialism which tends to militarism which leads to despotism, and all four lead to oppression and misery for the toiling masses as sure as the sun rises in the east and sets in the west." If the imperialists were triumphant the future for American workers was replete with danger: "A big standing army and a fort and garrison near every city will be the natural outcome of the policy of the imperialists. Industrial disturbances will be summarily dealt with and rifles and bayonets will be the answer of the trusts to the complaints of the toilers." [47]

ANTI-IMPERIALIST POLITICAL ACTION

Resolutions adopted at union conventions, editorials in labor papers, and utterances of union leaders—all this was to the good, but more was needed if labor's campaign against imperialism was to bear fruit. Calling for independent political action to "stay this sacrifice upon the bloody altar of imperialism," the National Union of United Brewery Workmen declared that "a Protest by paper Resolution is . . . not the kind of protest we want. Let us protest at the Ballot Box. This is the proper place." [48]

Few indeed were the trade unions and labor spokesmen who responded to this call. The very unionists who were most active in the struggle against imperialist annexation were opposed to any suggestion for mobi-

---

* Writing from Honolulu in April 1, 1900, a trade union organizer pointed out: "We have to be very careful as they will throw you in jail for the least thing. . . . You have to get a Permit to hold a meeting of any kind." (J. T. Gomo to Frank Morrison, April 1, 1900, *AFL Corr.*)

lizing labor's voting power to defeat the expansionists, and the Socialists who were the most active in stressing the need for independent working class political action were largely indifferent to the issue of imperialism, regarding it as one which did "not concern the working class." [49] This double weakness rendered ineffective much of labor's activity against imperialism.

Week after week Gompers inveighed against expansion. But when he was asked to help mobilize the A. F. of L. membership into political action to defeat pro-imperialist candidates, he invariably replied that "by a constitutional provision, the A. F. of L. is prohibited from meddling in party politics." When a number of A. F. of L. officials in Minnesota and Arkansas, alarmed "by the adoption of an imperial policy by the McKinley administration and by the appalling development of trusts," organized a sponsoring committee to mobilize political action around the issues of "Anti-Trusts and Anti-Imperialism," Gompers did not even bother to answer their appeal for endorsement and support.[50] When several A. F. of L. unions in Ohio took steps to form an independent political party around the issue of anti-imperialism, Gompers opposed the plan and was responsible for its abandonment. "The establishment of a political party among the workingmen is the division of their forces," he informed the Ohio trade unionists at the same time praising them for opposing imperialism so vigorously.[51]

The Socialist *Cleveland Citizen* was incorrect in characterizing the trade union battle against imperialism as a "waste of time," but it stood on solid ground when it sharply criticized Gompers for opposing the Ohio trade unions in their attempt to form an independent political movement around this issue. Of what value, it asked, were Gompers' lofty statements in defense of freedom for subject peoples in Puerto Rico and the Philippines, if he refused to supplement them with organized political power to defeat the imperialists? Of what use was it for Gompers to call upon the unions affiliated to the A. F. of L. to speak out against the administration's imperialist policies when he sabotaged the chief method of making these protests effective? "The governmental bosses [do not] care a snap for labor's opinion knowing that labor represents no crystallized political power." [52]

AN ANTI-IMPERIALIST THIRD PARTY

While labor remained aloof, an anti-imperialist political movement began to take shape under the leadership of the Anti-Imperialist League. In December, 1899, Erving Winslow, secretary of the New England Anti-Imperialist League, appealed for an all-out unity effort—"Republican, Democrat, Socialist, Populist, Gold-Man, Silver-Man, and Mugwump for

the momentous, vital, paramount issue, Anti-Imperialism and the prese
vation of the Republic." On January 6, 1900, a small group gathered at
the Plaza Hotel in New York in response to a call by the New England
Anti-Imperialist League for the purpose of organizing an Anti-Imperialist
political party. Carl Schurz, Ex-Senator Henderson, Brisbane Walker,
Gamaliel Bradford, Edward Burrit Smith, Professor Franklin Giddings,
Andrew Carnegie and some ten others attended. Labor was conspicuous
by its absence; Gompers and other top A. F. of L. officials had been invited, but they had failed to respond.[53]

Agreement was reached at the meeting to organize a third party and
plans were formulated. Funds were quickly forthcoming with Carnegie's
donation of $15,000 on the spot and a pledge to match dollar for dollar
as much money as the rest could raise. The gathering ended, and the
participants, though regretful that labor had failed to attend, left in jubilant spirits to spread the good word that a real people's party was in the
making.

But trouble soon developed. Carnegie betrayed his pledge. Not only
did he refuse to fulfill his financial promise, but he severed all contacts
with the third party group. Senator Richard F. Pettigrew of South Dakota discovered the reason. The monopolists were planning to form the
world's first billion dollar steel trust, the U.S. Steel Corporation. Of the
400 million dollars of bonds the Pittsburgh steel master was to pocket
160 millions. When the magnates heard of Carnegie's activities in support
of an anti-imperialist third party, "he was waited on by a committee, with
the ultimatum that they would go no further with the organization of
the steel trust unless he abandoned his third party activities and stopped
his contribution toward the movement."[54] Carnegie complied.

This took the heart out of the third-party movement, which had relied
so heavily on Carnegie's financial backing. The lesson Pettigrew drew
was that they failed because they had not gone to the people, and especially to the organized workers, even if it had meant going over the heads
of their leaders, to develop that type of unity urged by Erving Winslow.
Pettigrew correctly concluded: "Undoubtedly we made a mistake to pin
so much faith on the actions of one man—particularly in view of his
business connections."[55]

Yet the leaders of the trade unions were also responsible. If the trade
unions had mobilized labor's full strength behind the movement for an
anti-imperialist third party, the result would have been far different.

Sentiment for an anti-imperialist third party did not entirely die after
the failure of the movement sponsored by the Anti-Imperialist League.
The Republicans had nominated McKinley on a purely imperialist platform, but the Democrats, in nominating Bryan and denouncing imperialism, had adopted a platform which advocated a protectorate for the

Philippines. To the anti-imperialists this platform was literally an endorsement of imperialism. Insisting that the difference between the programs of the two major parties was so slight as to be meaningless, the *National Labor Standard* urged the trade unions to assume the leadership of the movement for a truly anti-imperialist party. It was convinced that if its call was heeded, imperialism could be defeated in the election of 1900. "In spite of the trusts and their ill-gotten millions," observed the official organ of the New Jersey State Federation of Labor, "the year 1900 may witness the end of Imperialism and the dawning of a new and better era of mankind."[56]

Unfortunately, the call went unheeded. The A. F. of L. Executive Council met in Denver in July, 1900, and issued an address to the working people of the country. Not a word was said about the approaching presidential campaign or the need to mobilize the working class into an anti-imperialist political movement. A month later, Gompers declared that it was "the sacred duty" of the workers "to oppose imperialism root and branch," but when asked if this included anti-imperialist political action, he replied that he had no intention of discussing politics.[57] *

ELECTION OF 1900

With no real basis existing for an anti-imperialist third party, the Indianapolis Convention of the Anti-Imperialist League on August 16, 1900, chose the "lesser evil," and voted to support Bryan, the Democratic nominee, as the anti-imperialist candidate. But many would not go along with the decision, and those that did were half-hearted about it.

The number of independent parties running candidates in the 1900 election reached an all-time high of ten, but none of them offered any real basis for winning anti-imperialist votes. Neither of the two Socialist parties which ran candidates, the Socialist Labor Party and the Social Democratic Party, emphasized the issue of imperialism, stressing that "the real issue of the campaign was not imperialism, it was socialism versus capitalism." At the Paris Congress of the Second International, September, 1900, the Socialists unanimously adopted a resolution calling upon the proletariat to fight in every way against imperialist expansion. But the American Socialists ignored these instructions, insisting throughout the

* Gompers' stand was directly in keeping with that adopted by the A.F. of L. leadership at the 1898 convention where a resolution was passed calling upon all Federation members to use all "honorable means" in opposing imperialism. When John C. Dernell of the Cigar Makers' Union introduced a motion directing the A.F. of L. to mobilize its membership for political action to carry the resolution into effect, it was reported to the Committee on the President's Report where it was buried. (*Proceedings*, A.F. of L. Convention, 1898, p. 96.)

presidential campaign that "from the point of view of the working class expansion is . . . something not worth talking about." [58] *

Entirely absent in the 1900 presidential campaign was the labor activity that had characterized the political scene four years previously. "I have been watching the Political campaign with great interest," wrote John B. Lennon, A. F. of L. vice-president, to Gompers, "and I believe if a half dozen prominent Labor men would take hold politically that Bryan could surely win. I feel recreant to my duty as a citizen to keep mum." [59]

But, with rare exceptions, the labor leaders did "keep mum." With no real alternative for the anti-imperialists between Bryan and McKinley, confusion and apathy spread. Bryan did not even stress the anti-imperialist aspect of the campaign. Indeed, addressing a Labor Day mass meeting in Chicago on September 4, 1900, Bryan made the following passing remark on imperialism: "The resolutions adopted by various labor organizations in condemnation of militarism and imperialism justify me in making brief reference to these questions." [60] Then he proceeded to emphasize free silver and the tariff as the major issues of the campaign.

The result was soon evident. Anti-expansionists who were fearful of Bryan's free silver views, turned towards McKinley. Even workers who were fed up with the entire currency panacea were choosing to cast their lot with McKinley.[61]

Denied a real choice, the voters elected President McKinley by a vote of 7,218,491. Bryan recorded an impressive 6,402,926, thus raising the visibility that had his record on imperialism been such as to convince the people he was really an anti-imperialist, he might have been elected.[62] Debs' vote of nearly 100,000, almost three times that of the candidate of the S.L.P. who polled about 34,000 votes, was impressive, but undoubtedly even this vote would have been much larger if the Socialist candidate had taken a forceful stand against imperialism.

The re-election of McKinley was a severe set-back to the anti-imperialists, and it is not surprising that many of them were discouraged. The *Railroad Trainmen's Journal,* a leading labor spokesman for imperialism, urged the trade unions to abandon their opposition to the administration's policies. Since these policies had been upheld at the polls, "the opposition might as well fold up its protests and become witnesses to what is done." [63]

The anti-imperialists differed sharply with this viewpoint and kept up their agitation—demanding investigation of atrocities by American armed

---

* Job Harriman, vice-presidential candidate of the Social Democratic Party in 1900, was a delegate to the Paris Congress. Yet in his report of the Congress, he hardly even mentioned the resolution against imperialist expansion. (See Job Harriman, "Some Questions at the Paris Congress," *International Socialist Review,* Vol. I, 1900, p. 30.)

forces in the Philippines; deluging Congress with petitions insisting that these islands should be independent. The labor press, too, continued to make its contribution to the anti-imperialist struggle, emphasizing as in the past the relationship between events in the colonial possessions and the problems confronting the working class in the United States.

"Our own future is bound up with that of our dependencies," went a typical editorial in the labor press, "and whoever consents to the suppression of organized labor there, is our enemy. Whoever seeks to train an army there in order to use that army eventually against ourselves, is our enemy. . . . If we do not curb the predatory classes by our ballots, they will curb our power and curtail our rights by the bullets of mercenary soldiers." [64]

Enlistment for service in the Philippines was denounced in the labor press as an open betrayal of the working class. "No honorable American will volunteer for service in the Philippine Islands," cried the *National Labor Standard*. "Honorable men won't engage in robbery and man killing." [65]

For several years after the election of 1900, the anti-imperialists fought strenuously to keep the cause alive, but gradually the movement died. By 1905 the original New England organization was the only active survivor of the Anti-Imperialist Leagues. In 1913, Moorfield Storey, president of the Anti-Imperialist League, wrote to Erving Winslow, its secretary: "the truth is that if we come down to facts, you and I are substantially the Anti-Imperialist League." [66]

A. F. OF L. CAPITULATES TO IMPERIALISTS

Within the labor movement, too, anti-imperialist activity gradually receded. While the number of trade unions that endorsed imperialism was never large, there were many who came to accept the fact that Puerto Rico and the Philippines should remain part of the United States. After 1901, the A. F. of L. ceased to condemn the acquisition of Hawaii, Puerto Rico, and the Philippines.[67]

In the spring of 1904, the question of organizing the cigar makers in the Philippine Islands was discussed by the A. F. of L. leadership. Although it was agreed that the Filipino cigar makers were "willing to better organize," it was finally decided that it would not be wise for the A. F. of L. to assist them. The reason: "agitation of Philippine independence, very strong among the better class of workers, and kept up by lawyers and doctors mainly for pecuniary reasons, has to be taken into consideration when organizing these people." Rather than risk the danger of aiding the cause of Philippine independence and thus antagonizing the Wall Street interests, the A. F. of L. leaders agreed not to undertake the organizing campaign.[68]

These betrayals of the earlier anti-imperialist traditions of the A. F. of L. should come as no surprise. It was already foreshadowed in the late 1890's. Even within the struggle against imperialism, the leadership of the A. F. of L. rejected any plan for an attack on the forces behind imperialism—the monopoly capitalists—and for an independent political role for labor against the twin evils of monopoly and imperialist expansion. Old-time labor leaders like George E. McNeill repeatedly reminded the A. F. of L. leadership that it was impossible to wage an effective struggle against imperialist conquests unless it was clearly understood that they were the "tools of capitalism. War is made to serve the investors." [69] But Gompers, for all his oratorical declamations against the evils of expansion, refused to accept McNeill's interpretation. To have done so would have meant changing the entire direction in which he was moving—collaboration with the very forces McNeill blamed for imperialist aggressions.

It was possible to oppose *imperialist annexation* on humanitarian and democratic ground without pointing out the connection between the growth of monopoly and of imperialism. But it was impossible to fight against the rapidly emerging and more characteristic feature of American imperialism—economic and political control of colonial countries without outright annexation—unless one also waged a consistent battle against the monopolists, the imperialists themselves. Hence it is not surprising that when imperialist annexation was no longer the major aspect of American imperialism, the A. F. of L. leaders should quickly abandon their earlier participation in the anti-imperialist movement.

"Imperialism," writes Lenin in his classic study, "tends to create privileged ranks among the workers and to separate them from the broad mass of the proletariat." [70] Just as British imperialists were able to blunt the anti-imperialist sentiments of organized labor in England by corrupting the skilled workers, giving them a share in the spoils of imperialism, so American imperialists succeeded in achieving this in the United States. Out of the surplus profits derived from imperialism, monopoly capitalism in the United States could afford to pay the highly-skilled workers a bit more above the average wage in order to reconcile them to imperialism, to develop among this strata of the working class a subtle sense of superiority, and destroy their solidarity with their fellow-workers and their consciousness of class.

These concessions accelerated the development of theories and practices of class collaboration in the ranks of labor's leadership, accelerated the corruption of the labor aristocracy, and weakened the earlier militancy and revolutionary spirit of the labor movement. As American imperialism expanded and completely outstripped its imperialist rivals, this process proceeded apace.

The essence of this unionism was class-collaboration on behalf of the bourgeoisie. On the economic front it stressed the necessity for immediate gains for a small strata of the working class, the skilled craftsmen, and struggled to achieve for this "aristocracy of labor," "job monopoly," better wages and shorter hours, and very little else, and this, too, at the expense of the mass of the workers who were unorganized. On the political front, it made the organized workers the tail-kite to the political parties of the capitalist class. On both fronts, it meant "policies and methods" which prevented any real expression of the militancy of the working class, which avoided clashes with the trusts and the government, and which bought a limited security and higher wages for the skilled workers at the expense of the rest of the working class. Between the A. F. of L. craft unions and the industrialists a broad area of implicit agreement was reached after 1900. "The unions," one authority points out, "would make no effort to organize the unskilled and Negro workers; the corporations would make certain concessions to the trade unions." [71]

Yet the earlier militant traditions of the American working class were never completely destroyed by the imperialist monopolists and their class-collaboration allies in the labor movement. The struggle against these class-collaboration policies continued. It was, to be sure, made more difficult by the mistaken tactics of many of the most militant elements in the labor movement who isolated themselves from the masses of workers organized in the craft unions. But the important fact remains that the struggle did continue—the irreconcilable class struggle against the capitalists, for the organization of the entire working class in this struggle regardless of skill, race, creed, color, sex or national origin, and for the unity of the workers on the economic and political fronts. The monopolists and their allies in the A. F. of L. bureaucracy won many battles in this struggle. But in spite of all the might on their side and in spite of merciless repression of the militant workers, they were not able to achieve a prolonged victory over the working class. As we shall see in the next volume, they never succeeded in eradicating the irreconcilable class struggle between labor and capital; they never succeeded permanently in forcing the workers to compromise with the capitalists at the expense of the entire working class, and they never succeeded in forcing the militant vanguard to subordinate itself to the agents of the monopolists in the labor movement.

CHAPTER I

1. John Swinton, *Striking for Life*, New York, 1894, preface.
2. *Fourth Annual Report*, Bureau of Labor Statistics, New York, 1887, p. 8; Norman J. Ware, *The Labor Movement in the United States, 1860-1895*, New York, 1929, p. 302; Frederick Engels, *Condition of the Working Class in England in 1844*, London, 1887, preface; George E. McNeill, editor, *The Labor Movement, The Problem of To-Day, Comprising a History of Capital and Labor, and Its Present Status*, New York, 1887, pp. 170-71.
3. Josiah Strong, *Our Country*, New York, 1885, p. 162.
4. *Second Biennial Report*, Wisconsin Bureau of Labor and Industrial Statistics, 1885-1886, Introduction.
5. Eliot Jones, *The Trust Problem in the United States*, New York, 1921, pp. 20-22.
6. *Public Opinion*, vol. VIII, Feb. 22, 1890, p. 478.
7. Lewis Corey, *The House of Morgan*, New York, 1930, pp. 131-80, 245-62.
8. 53d. Congress, 2d. Session, House of Representatives, *Miscellaneous Document* 210, part 8.
9. *The First Annual Report of Labor, March, 1886. Industrial Depressions*, Washington, 1886, p. 80; *Twelfth Annual Report*, New York State Bureau of Labor Statistics, 1894, p. 237.
10. *Report of the (Education and Labor) Committee of the Senate upon the Relations between Labor and Capital, and Testimony Taken by the Committee*, 4 vols., Washington, 1885, vol. I, pp. 757-59. (Hereafter cited as Rep. of the Sen. Comm. on Labor.)
11. *Rep. of the Sen. Comm. on Labor*, vol. I, p. 288.
12. *A Lecture on the Declaration of Principles of the Knights of Labor: Delivered by Ralph Beaumont*, 1887, p. 13; *Rep. of the Sen. Comm. on Labor*, vol. I, p. 631.
13. Hartford *Courant*, reprinted in *John Swinton's Paper*, Dec. 30, 1883; Herbert Morais, "Marx and Engels on America," *Science & Society*, Winter, 1948, pp. 3-21.
14. *Rep. of the Sen. Comm. on Labor*, vol. I, pp. 291-92, vol. II, p. 552; Charles B. Spahr, *An Essay on the Present Distribution of Wealth in the United States*, New York, 1896, p. 114; *Fourth Biennial Report*, Illinois Bureau of Labor Statistics, 1886, p. 83.
15. McNeill, *op. cit.*, p. 581; *John Swinton's Paper*, Dec. 7, 1884, April 8, 1885.
16. *Report of the United States Industrial Commission*, Washington, 1902, vol. XIX, pp. 957, 961.
17. Joanne Erickson, "The Recruitment of European Immigrant Labor for American Industry from 1860 to 1885," Unpublished Ph.D. thesis, Cornell University, Feb. 1952, pp. 434-39.
18. U.S. Bureau of Labor, *Bulletin No. 9*, March, 1897, p. 114; *Rep. of the Sen. Comm. on Labor*, vol. I, pp. 810-11; *John Swinton's Paper*, Dec. 23, 1883, Jan. 6, 20, May 18, Aug. 3, 10, 31, Oct. 5, 1884, Feb. 1, 1885.
19. Wasyl Halich, "Ukranians in Western Pennsylvania," *Western Pennsylvania History Magazine*, vol. XVIII, March, 1935, p. 141; Andrew A. Marchbin, "Hungarian Activities in Western Pennsylvania," *ibid.*, vol. XXIII, March, 1940, p. 165.
20. Erickson, *op. cit.*, pp. 562-63.
21. Philadelphia *Times*, July 6, 1882.
22. Philadelphia *Times*, June 24, 25, 1882; New York *Tribune*, June 25, 29, July 15, 1882; New York *Sun*, July 14, 1882; Erickson, *op. cit.*, p. 523.
23. *Third Annual Report*, New York Bureau of Labor Statistics, 1885, p. 484; 16, 1884; New York *Tribune*, June 5, *Irish World*, Nov. 24, 1883, Aug. 9, 1891, June 23, 1892.
24. Morrell Head, "Business Attitudes Towards European Immigration, 1880-1900," *Journal of Economic History*, vol. XIII, Summer, 1953, pp. 296, 301-02.

25. *Seventh Annual Report,* New Jersey Bureau of Industry and Labor, 1884, p. 295; Erickson, *op. cit.,* p. 521.

26. Erickson, *op. cit.,* pp. 524-25; William M. Leiserson, *Adjusting Immigrant and Industry,* New York, 1925, p. 174.

27. Strong, *op. cit.,* p. 147; *Fifteenth Annual Report,* Massachusetts Bureau of Statistics, p. 464; *Rep. of the Sen. Comm. on Labor,* vol. I, p. 625.

28. Testimony of Thomas O'Donough, *Rep. of the Sen. Comm. on Labor,* vol. III, p. 452; Henry David, *The History of the Haymarket Affair,* New York, 1936, p. 14.

29. *Rep. of the Sen. Comm. on Labor,* vol. III, pp. 452-53.

30. *John Swinton's Paper,* Nov. 18, 1883, April 6, 1884.

31. *Rep. of the Sen. Comm. on Labor,* vol. I, pp. 220, 552-53, 757, 838-39, vol. III, pp. 4, 28, 74, 125; *John Swinton's Paper,* Nov. 18, Dec. 30, 1883, Jan. 13, April 6, 1884; Michigan, *Bureau of Labor Reports,* 1885, p. 34.

32. Printed circular, Augusta, Georgia, Aug. 28, 1886, Terence V. Powderly Papers, Catholic University of America; *John Swinton's Paper,* Nov. 18, 1883, April 6, 1884; *Journal of United Labor,* May, 1883, pp. 460-61; *Pennsylvania Bureau of Industrial Statistics,* vol. XII, 1884, pp. 69-70.

33. Edward and Eleanor Aveling, *The Working-Class Movement in America,* London, 1891, p. 98.

34. "Report on the Condition of Women and Child Wage Earners in the United States," *United States Bureau of Labor,* 1910, vol. I, pp. 334-36; John Peter Altgeld, *Live Questions: Including Our Penal Machinery and Its Victims,* Chicago, 1890, pp. 80-89; New York *Tribune,* May 7, 1890.

35. *Annual Report of the Pennsylvania Secretary of Internal Affairs,* 1880, vol. VII, pp. 244, 354; *First Annual Report of the United States Commissioner of Labor,* 1886, p. 244; *Pennsylvania Bureau of Industrial Statistics,* VII, 1878-1879, pp. 367, 370, 374, 377; Alexander Trachtenberg, *The History of Legislation for the Protection of the Coal Miners in Pennsylvania, 1824-1915,* New York, 1942, p. 84.

36. *Journal of United Labor,* July 2, Aug. 13, Sept. 17, 1887; *Report of the United States Industrial Commission,* vol. VII, Digest, p. 34; *John Swinton's Paper,*

Nov. 28, 1886; P. W. Green to Organized Labor, Phoenix, Alabama, undated circular, American Federation of Labor Correspondence, A.F. of L. Building, Washington, D. C. (Hereafter cited as *AFL Corr.*)

37. Washington *National Republican,* April 17, 1888; Philip S. Foner, *The Life and Writings of Frederick Douglass,* New York, 1955, vol. IV, pp. 109-11.

38. Aveling, *op. cit.,* pp. 42-44, 65-66, 75, 77, 87, 90, 228-31.

39. *Rep. of the Sen. Comm. on Labor,* vol. III, p. 410; *Ninth Annual Report,* Ohio Labor Statistics Bureau, p. 10.

40. *Report of the United States Industrial Commission,* 1902, vol. XIX, pp. 789-90.

41. Hyman Kurtz, "Pennsylvania State Government and Labor Controls From 1865 to 1922," unpublished Ph.D. thesis, Columbia University, History Department, 1953, p. 192; *Legislative Record,* Pennsylvania, vol. II, June 7, 1897, p. 2385; *Journal of United Labor,* May, 1883, pp. 460-61; *John Swinton's Paper,* May 18, 1884.

42. *Report of the Committee on Tenement Houses of the Citizens' Association of Chicago, September, 1884,* Chicago, 1884, p. 3.

43. J. E. Pople, *The Clothing Industry in New York,* University of Missouri Studies, Columbus, Missouri, 1905, pp. 151-55; *Report of the Sanitary Aid Society for the Tenth Ward of the City of New York,* New York, 1885.

44. Louis Levine, *The Woman's Garment Workers,* New York, 1924, pp. 19-20.

45. Aaron Kramer, editor and translator, *Poems of Morris Rosenfeld,* New York, 1955, p. 34.

46. *Report of the New York State Bureau of Labor Statistics for 1885,* p. 289.

47. "Final Report of the Commission on Industrial Relations," *Senate Executive Documents No. 465,* 64th Congress, 2nd Session, pp. 38-55.

48. For detailed discussions of the labor legislation of the period, *see* David, *op. cit.,* pp. 30-53.

49. David, *op. cit.,* pp. 30, 36; John R. Commons and Associates, *History of Labor in the United States,* 4 vols. (New York, 1918-1935), vol. III, pp. 541-43; Aveling, *op. cit.,* pp. 55-56.

50. Rupert Sargent Holland, "The Right of an Employee Against Employers' Black-

lists," *The American Law Register*, vol. XLII, Dec., 1903, pp. 803-09.

51. See especially Pennsylvania Bureau of Industrial Statistics, vol. IX, 1880-81, p. 380; vol. X, 1881-82, pp. 172-73, 189, vol. XII, 1884, pp. 73-74, 77; Proceedings, General Assembly, Knights of Labor, 1881, p. 283.

52. Clarence E. Bonnett, "The Origins of the Labor Injunction," *Southern California Law Review*, vol. V, Oct., 1931, p. 123.

53. Charles Fairman, "Justice Samuel F. Miller," *Political Science Quarterly*, vol. L, March, 1953, pp. 42-43.

54. J. Lochner v. New York, 198, U.S., 445 (1905); Adair v. U.S., 208, U.S., 161 (1908).

55. In re Jacobs, 98, N.Y. 98 (1885); *John Swinton's Paper*, Jan. 25, 1885.

56. Morris Raphael Cohen, *Law and the Social Order*, New York, 1933, p. 76.

57. McNeill, *op. cit.*, p. 455.

58. Richard Hofstadter, *Social Darwinism in American Thought, 1860-1915*, Philadelphia, 1944.

59. William R. Thayer, *Life and Letters of John Hay*, New York, 1916, vol. I, p. 7.

60. Lester Frank Ward, *Glimpses of the Cosmos*, New York and London, 1913, vol. III, pp. 303-04; *Rep. of the Sen. Comm. on Labor*, vol. II, p. 959.

61. Thomas Bailey Aldrich, *The Stillwater Tragedy*, 1880, p. 138.

62. Francis A. Walker, *Political Economy*, New York, 1883, p. 259; A. L. Perry, *Elements of Political Economy*, New York, 1866, p. 122.

63. New York *World* reprinted fifteen years later in *Appeal to Reason*, Nov. 18, 1899.

64. McNeill, *op cit.*, p. 461; Aveling, *op. cit.*, p. 81; Philip S. Foner, *History of the Labor Movement in the United States: From Colonial Times to the the founding of the American Federation of Labor*, New York, 1947, pp. 520-21.

65. Richard J. Hinton, "American Labor Organizations," *North American Review*, Jan. 1885, pp. 33-38.

66. *John Swinton's Paper*, June 1, 1884.

67. *Ibid.*, Feb. 3, 29, Nov. 9, 1884, March 22, 1885, May 9, 1886; Sender Garlin, "The Challenge of John Swinton," *Masses & Mainstream*, Dec., 1951, p. 47.

68. Printed circular and letter of J. P. McDonnell to Terence V. Powderly,

Jan. 23, 1880, both in Terence V. Powderly Papers. (Hereafter cited as *PP*.)

69. *Irish World and American Industrial Liberator*, July 5, 1884.

CHAPTER II

1. *John Swinton's Paper*, Nov. 2, 1884; J. Ehmann to Philip Van Patten, April 8, 1880, Socialist Labor Party Papers, Wisconsin State Historical Society (hereafter cited as *WSHS*); Foner, *History of the Labor Movement in the U.S.*, p. 499; Philip S. Foner, *The Fur and Leather Workers Union*, Newark, New Jersey, 1950, p. 18; Charles McArthur Destler, *American Radicalism, 1865-1901*, New London, Connecticut, 1946, pp. 83-84.

2. Foner, *History of the Labor Movement in the U.S.*, p. 498.

3. *Constitution and By-Laws of the Central Labor Union of New York and Vicinity*, New York, 1887; *Rep. of the Sen. Comm. on Labor*, vol. I, pp. 502-03, 808-13; *John Swinton's Paper*, Oct. 14, 21, 1883; Peter A. Speek, *The Singletax and the Labor Movement*, Madison, Wisconsin, 1917, pp. 25, 317-18.

4. *John Swinton's Paper*, April 8, 1884; *New Yorker Volkszeitung*, July 12, 1886; New York *Sun*, July 19, 1886.

5. Morris Hillquit, *History of Socialism in the United States*, New York, 1903, pp. 286-87.

6. E. Burgin, *The History of the Jewish Labor Movement*, Yiddish, New York, 1915, pp. 68-85; Martin A. Cohen, "Jewish Immigrants and American Trade Unions," unpublished Ph.D., thesis, University of Chicago, Aug., 1941, pp. 35-37.

7. *John Swinton's Paper*, June 7, 1885; Burgin, *op. cit.*, pp. 100-03; Cohen, *op. cit.*, pp. 41-43.

8. *Jewish Life*, April, 1952, p. 12; Burgin, *op. cit.*, pp. 103-12.

9. Morris U. Schappes, unpublished paper on the United Hebrew Trades, presented at 1948 Annual Meeting of the American Jewish Historical Society.

10. B. Weinstein, "The First Years," Yiddish, in Harry Lang and Morris Feinstone, editors, *United Hebrew Trades 50th Jubilee Book*, New York, 1938, p. 32; Cohen, *op. cit.*, pp. 68-69.

11. Eunice Minette Schuster, *Native American Anarchism: A Study of Left-Wing American Individualism*, Northampton, Massachusetts, 1931-32, pp. 162-64.
12. Alan Calmar, *Labor Agitator: The Story of Albert R. Parsons*, New York, 1937, pp. 52-62.
13. E. L. Bogart and C. M. Thompson, *The Industrial State, 1870-1893*, The Centennial History of Illinois, vol. IV, Springfield, Illinois, 1920, pp. 167-68.
14. David, *op. cit.*, pp. 64-69.
15. Richard T. Ely, *The Labor Movement in America*, New York, 1886, pp. 358-63.
16. Samuel Yellen, *American Labor Struggles*, New York, 1936, p. 48.
17. Hillquit, *op cit.*, pp. 217-18.
18. *Socialism and Anarchism, Antagonistic Opposites*, Socialistic Library, No. 6, June 1, 1886, New York, pp. 7-8.
19. Marx and Engels, *Letters to Americans*, pp. 7, 142, 160-87.
20. *John Swinton's Paper*, Oct. 18, 1885; *Workmen's Advocate*, Jan. 8, 1888.
21. *John Swinton's Paper*, Feb. 21, 1886.
22. Karl Marx and Frederick Engels, *Letters to Americans, 1848-1895*, New York, 1953, pp. 289-90.
23. *Arbeiter Zeitung*, Dec. 5, 1890.
24. Aveling, *op. cit.*, pp. 43-44.
25. *Ibid.*, p. 45.
26. Hillquit, *op. cit.*, pp. 319-21.
27. *New Nation*, Jan. 31, 1891; *The Nationalist*, May, 1889.
28. *The Nationalist*, Dec., 1889; *New Nation*, Jan. 31, 1891.
29. Justus Ebert, *American Industrial Evolution*, New York, 1907, p. 66.

CHAPTER III

1. *Cf.* Selig Perlman, *A Theory of the Labor Movement*, New York, 1928, p. 192; Louis Adamic, *Dynamite—The Story of Class Violence in America*, New York, 1931, p. 52; Paul F. Brissenden, *The I.W.W.—A Study of American Syndicalism*, New York, 1920, p. 33; Mary Beard, *A Short History of the American Labor Movement*, New York, 1927, p. 116; Norman J. Ware, *The Labor Movement in the United States, 1860-1895*, New York, 1929, p. xvii.
2. *Proceedings*, General Assembly, K. of L., Philadelphia, 1884, p. 583.

3. Robert Coleman Francis, "A History of Labor on the San Francisco Waterfront," unpublished Ph.D. thesis, University of California, Department of Economics, 1934, p. 43.
4. *John Swinton's Paper*, Aug. 23, 1885.
5. Circular issued by L.A. 1384, K. of L., John Samuels Papers, *WSHS*.
6. *John Swinton's Paper*, Dec. 27, 1885.
7. The three types of boycotts are illustrated in: Charles Crain to Powderly, Dec. 3, 1885; printed circular attached to letter of T. Woodruff to Powderly, Nov. 21, 1885; F. W. Gessner to Powderly, Nov. 24, 1885, *PP*.
8. Hiram Dissyen to Powderly, Feb. 11, 1886, *PP*.
9. *John Swinton's Paper*, Jan. 25, 1885.
10. *Ibid.*, Aug. 17, 1885.
11. George A. Stevens, *New York Typographical Union No. 6*, Albany, New York, 1913, pp. 387-96; Printed Circular of D.A. 99, K. of L., Feb. 25, 1886, *PP*.
12. *Irish World*, Feb. 23, 1884.
13. *The Boycotter*, April 4, 1885.
14. *Irish World*, May 14, 1885.
15. See *John Swinton's Paper*, Jan. 25, 1885.
16. A. Carpes to Powderly, November 29, 1885, *PP*.
17. *The Selected Correspondence of Karl Marx and Frederick Engels, 1846-1895*, New York, 1942, p. 385.
18. S. W. Foss in *Tid-Bits*, undated clipping, New York Public Library, Scrapbooks on Labor.
19. Printed circular, dated Dec. 28, 1882, signed by John Campbell and Thomas H. Hughes; John Campbell to Powderly, May 26, June 21, 24, 1883, *PP*.
20. U.S. Congress, House of Representatives, 49th Con., 2nd Sess., 1887, Report No. 4147, *Investigation of Labor Troubles in Missouri, Kansas, Texas and Illinois*, Part I, p. i.
21. Joseph R. Buchanan, *The Story of a Labor Agitator*, New York, 1903, pp. 70-78, 141-42; Edith Walker and Dorothy Liebengood, "Labor Organization in Kansas in the Early 'Eighties," *Kansas Historical Quarterly*, vol. IV, 1935, p. 284.
22. Harry Frumerman, "The Railroad Strikes of 1885-86," *Marxist Quarterly*, Oct.-Dec., 1937, pp. 395-96.
23. *New York Times*, March 11, 1885; U.S. House of Representatives, Report No. 4147, *op. cit.*, pp. iii-iv, 6-7.

24. F. W. Taussig, "The Southwestern Strike of 1886," *Quarterly Journal of Economics*, vol. I, Jan., 1887, p. 187.

25. *John Swinton's Paper*, Aug. 24, 1885.

26. Commons and Associates, *op. cit.*, vol. II, p. 369.

27. R. W. Drew to Powderly and Turner, telegram, Sept. 4, 1885; Powderly to Jay Gould, Aug. 29, 1885; Jay Gould to Powderly, telegram, Aug. 31, 1885, *PP; John Swinton's Paper*, Aug. 30, Sept. 13, 1885.

28. Reprinted in *John Swinton's Paper*, Sept. 30, 1885.

29. Commons and Associates, *op. cit.*, vol. II, p. 370.

30. For the Hocking Valley strike, *see Labor Enquirer*, July 19, 1884; *John Swinton's Paper*, Aug. 17, 24, 1884, March 1, 1885; *Irish World*, May 17, 1884; Erickson, *op. cit.*, pp. 501-06. For the Saginaw Valley strike, *see* Detroit *Labor Leaf*, July 15, Oct. 14, 1885; *John Swinton's Paper*, July 9, 1885; George B. Engberg, "Labor in the Lake States Lumber Industry, 1830-1930," unpublished Ph.D. thesis, University of Minnesota, 1949, pp. 380-85. For a view contending that the Gould strike had no great effect on the Order, *see* Donald L. Kemmerer and Edward D. Wickersham, "Reasons for the Growth of the Knights of Labor in 1885-1886," *Industrial and Labor Relations Review*, vol. III, Jan., 1950, pp. 219-20.

31. George B. Engberg, "The Knights of Labor in Minnesota," *Minnesota History*, vol. XXII, 1941, p. 369; *Journal of United Labor*, April 10, 1886, p. 2041; D. F. Powell to Powderly, Dec. 23, 1885, *PP*.

32. *Journal of United Labor*, Jan. 25, 1886, p. 1182, March 10, 1886, p. 2019, May 10, 1886, p. 979.

33. Powderly to A. A. Carlton, March 25, 1886, Terence V. Powderly Letter-Books, Catholic University of America (hereafter cited as *PLB); Journal of United Labor*, March 25, 1886, p. 2034, April 10, 1886, p. 2041.

34. *Journal of United Labor*, Sept. 25, 1885, p. 1087, April 25, 1886, p. 2052; Terence V. Powderly, *Thirty Years of Labor, 1859 to 1889*, Columbus, Ohio, 1889, pp. 344-45.

35. The account of the Order in Canada is based on Douglas R. Kennedy, "The Knights of Labor in Canada," unpub-lished M.A. thesis, University of Western Ontario, 1945, pp. 40-47ff.

36. *Constitution of Local Assemblies*, 1878; *Constitution for Local Assemblies*, 1884.

37. Frederick Engels, *Conditions of the British Working Class in 1844*, London, 1887, preface.

CHAPTER IV

1. Martin Irons, "My Experience in the Labor Movement," *Lippincott's Monthly Magazine*, vol. XXXVII, June, 1886, pp. 626-27.

2. William C. Birdsall, "The Problem of Structure in the Knights of Labor," *Industrial and Labor Relations Review*, vol. VI, July, 1953, pp. 540-41.

3. Article 12, Section I, cited in *Proceedings*, General Assembly, K. of L., 1884, p. 776.

4. *Labor Standard*, June 17, 1885; *John Swinton's Paper*, July 19, 1885; *Proceedings*, General Assembly, K. of L., 1883, p. 437 and 500.

5. Augusta E. Galster, *The Labor Movement in the Shoe Industry*, New York, 1924, p. 53.

6. These names are derived from the letter-heads of the assemblies in their correspondence to Powderly, *PP*.

7. James H. Bridge, *A Romance of Millions, The Inside Story of the Carnegie Steel Company*, Aldine, 1903, p. 81.

8. F. J. Weber to Samuel Gompers, no date, *AFL Corr.*

9. Ware, *op cit.*, pp. 41, 72, 93; L. M. Barry to Powderly, March 9, 1888, *PP; Proceedings*, General Assembly, K. of L., 1883, pp. 438, 442.

10. *Proceedings, General Assembly*, K. of L., 1883, p. 459, 1884, pp. 575-76; *Journal of United Labor*, Jan. 15, 1881, p. 82; Pittsburgh *Dispatch*, April 28, 1888; Sidney Glazer, "Labor and Agrarian Movements in Michigan, 1876-1896, "unpublished Ph.D. thesis, University of Michigan, 1932, p. 43.

11. *John Swinton's Paper*, April 4, July 4, 1886, Feb. 6, 1887; *Proceedings*, General Assembly, K. of L., 1890, p. 2.

12. Nicholas A. Somma, "The Knights of Labor and Chinese Immigration," unpublished M.A. thesis, Catholic University of America, June, 1952, p. 37; Powderly to J. W. Adams, Feb. 7, 1883, *PLB*.

13. Calvin Ewing to Powderly, Sept. 2, 1885; Charles F. Adams, Jr. to Powderly, October 28, 1885, *PP;* Somma, *op. cit.,* pp. 46-48; clippings in Burnette Haskell Papers, 1885, Bancroft Library, University of California. (Hereafter cited as *BL*.)

14. John Musekt, Jno L. Lewis to Powderly, Oct. 12, 1885; Powderly to Charles F. Adams, Jr., Oct. 26, 1885; Powderly to T. L. Carlton, Feb. 6, 1886, *PP*.

15. Powderly to Thomas Neasham, Oct. 31, 1885, *PLB*.

16. *Union Printer,* May 31, 1887.

17. *John Swinton's Paper,* July 10, 1887.

18. *John Swinton's Paper,* June 7, 1885.

19. John B. Andrews and W. D. P. Bliss, "History of Women in Trade Unions," *Senate Document No. 645,* 61st Congress, 2nd Session, vol. X, p. 115; Ware, *op. cit.,* p. 348.

20. U.S. Congress, House of Representatives, Report No. 4147, *op. cit.,* p. 85; Andrews and Bliss, *op. cit.,* pp. 123-32.

21. *Irish World,* July 29, 1882.

22. Andrews and Bliss, *op. cit.,* p. 121.

23. Louis Levine, *The Women Garment Workers,* pp. 37-38.

24. *John Swinton's Paper,* May 18, 1884; Yonkers *Statesman,* Feb. 27, 1885.

25. Yonkers *Statesman,* Feb. 27, March 6, 1885.

26. *Ibid.,* May 15, 22, 1885.

27. *John Swinton's Paper,* June 7, 1885.

28. Yonkers *Statesman,* Aug. 22, 29, 1885.

29. Joseph R. Buchanan, *op. cit.,* pp. 198-200. *See also* "Minutes of the Women's Labor League, Knights of Labor, L.A. #5855, San Francisco," March 19, Dec. 15, 1886, *BL*.

30. *John Swinton's Paper,* April 26, 1885; *Journal of United Labor,* July, 1883, p. 517, December, 1883, p. 605.

31. *Journal of United Labor,* July 23, 1887.

32. Andrews and Bliss, *op. cit.,* p. 116.

33. *Report of the International Council of Women Assembled by the National Woman Suffrage Association, Washington, D. C., U.S. of America, March 25 to April 1, 1888,* Washington, 1888, pp. 153-56; *Woman's Journal,* April 7, 1888.

34. Dan (Daniel O'Donoghue) to Powderly, April 29, 1888; Leonora M. Barry to Powderly, Feb. 27, Sept. 4, Oct. 4, 1888, *PP*.

35. Leonora M. Barry to Powderly, March 1, 1888; Powderly to Julia A. Coyle,

Feb. 27, 1888; Powderly to Leonora M. Barry, Feb. 27, March 23, 29, 1888, *PP;* Leonora M. Barry to Rev. Father McEnroe, Mar. 12, 1888, copy in *PP*.

36. *Proceedings,* General Assembly, K. of L., 1890, p. 162.

37. Quoted in Aveling, *op. cit.,* p. 85.

38. Quoted in Andrews and Bliss, *op. cit.,* p. 126.

39. Reprinted in *John Swinton's Paper,* Oct. 4, 1885.

40. *The Boycotter,* Dec. 5, 1885; Sidney H. Kessler, "The Negro in the Knights of Labor," unpublished M.A. thesis, Columbia University, 1950, pp. 48-54.

41. Joe B. Kewley to Powderly, May 14, 1883; Gil (Gilbert Rockwood) to Powderly, May 17, 1883, *PP*.

42. Powderly to Gil (Gilbert Rockwood), May 15, 1883; Powderly to M. W. Pattill, May 15, 1883, *PLB*.

43. Powderly to M. W. Pattill, May 15, 1883, *PLB*.

44. *Proceedings,* General Assembly, K. of L., 1886, pp. 103-04.

45. Thomas Curley, Rec. Sec. L.A. 2387, to Powderly, Jan. 11, 1886, *PP*.; Powderly to Thomas Curley, Jan. 14, 1886, *PLB*.

46. *Proceedings,* General Assembly, 1887, p. 1316.

47. Powderly to M. W. Pattill, May 15, 1883, *PLB*.

48. Powderly to J. M. Bannan, July 8, 1887, *PLB*.

49. Joe B. Kewley to Powderly, May 14, 1883, *PP. See also* New York *Freeman,* March 6,, Nov. 15, 1886; Cleveland *Gazette,* Feb. 20, 1886.

50. New York *Freeman,* May 1, 1886; New York *Evening Post,* May 1, 1886.

51. J. B. Sawyer to Powderly, Denton, Texas, Dec. 14, 1885, *PP*.

52. *John Swinton's Paper,* Oct. 17, 1886, March 20, 1887; Cleveland *Gazette,* Sept. 11, 1886; Sidney H. Kessler, "The Organization of Negroes in the Knights of Labor," *Journal of Negro History,* vol. XXXVII, July, 1952, pp. 257-62.

53. Jeffrey H. Brackett, "Notes on the Progress of the Colored People of Maryland Since the War," *Johns Hopkins Studies in History and Political Science,* 8th Series, VII-VIII-IX, 1890, p. 377; *Second Biennial Report of the Bureau of Industrial Statistics and Information of Maryland, 1886-1887,* Annapolis, 1888, p. 70.

54. *John Swinton's Paper*, May 16, 1886; *Journal of United Labor*, Aug. 6, 1887.
55. Cleveland *Gazette*, May 8, 1886; July 23, 1887; New York *Freeman*, May 8, 1886; *John Swinton's Paper*, July 3, 1887; Huntsville *Gazette*, July 23, 1887.
56. *John Swinton's Paper*, Sept. 19, 1886; New York *Freeman*, Sept. 11, 1886; New Orleans *Weekly Pelican*, July 30, 1887.
57. New York *Freeman*, April 17, Dec. 18, 1886, Jan. 15, Sept. 10, 1887; *Autobiography of Dr. William Henry Johnson*, Albany, New York, 1900, p. 27; *Journal of United Labor*, June 25, 1884.
58. *Journal of United Labor*, Sept. 25, 1886; George Talmadge Starnes and John Edwin Hamm, *Some Phases of Labor Relations in the South*, New York, 1934, p. 74.
59. Richmond *Whig*, Oct. 2, 1886; Starnes and Hamm, *op. cit.*, p. 74.
60. New York *Tribune*, Oct. 11, 1886; Philadelphia *Press*, Oct. 6, 1886.
61. Powderly, *Thirty Years of Labor*, p. 652.
62. *Ibid.*, p. 653; *Proceedings*, General Assembly, K. of L., 1886, pp. 7-8.
63. *Proceedings*, General Assembly, K. of L., 1886, p. 254.
64. Richmond *Whig*, Oct. 7, 1886; *Proceedings*, General Assembly, K. of L., 1886, pp. 175, 194.
65. New York *Tribune*, Oct. 12, 1886; Richmond *Whig*, Oct. 12, 1886.
66. *Cf.* "Knights of Labor and the Color Line," *Public Opinion*, vol. II, Oct. 16, 1886, pp. 1-3.
67. Telegram signed by E. C. Morris and others, Committee of National Negro Press Association, to Powderly, Oct. 19, 1886, *PP.*; Cleveland *Gazette*, Oct. 23, 1886.
68. New York *Tribune*, Oct. 10, 1886; Louisville *Labor Record* reprinted in *Knights of Labor*, Dec. 23, 1886.
69. Philip S. Foner, *The Life and Writings of Frederick Douglass*, vol. IV, p. 382.

CHAPTER V

1. Leaflet attached to letter of James B. Davison to Powderly, Nov. 11, 1887, *PP.*
2. George B. Engberg, "The Rise of Organized Labor in Minnesota," *Minnesota History*, vol. XXI, Dec., 1940, p. 390.
3. *Onward*, Detroit, Dec. 1, 1888; Glazer, "Labor and Agrarian Movements in Michigan," *op. cit.*, p. 246.
4. *John Swinton's Paper*, Dec. 23, 1883; *Proceedings*, General Assembly, K. of L., 1899, pp. 24-50; *The People's Institute of Civics*, pamphlet signed by John W. Hayes, n.p., Nov., 1899.
5. Joseph A. Labadie to Powderly, June 12, 1882, *PP;* Powderly to Joseph A. Labadie, July 5, 1882, *PLB.*
6. Powderly to J. Mulhane, Sept. 28, 1882, *PLB.*
7. Powderly, *Thirty Years of Labor*, p. 464; J. J. Sullivan to Powderly, July 30, 1882, *PP.*
8. J. D. Leydard to Powderly, Dec. 12, 1885, *PP.*
9. Bert Stewart to Henry D. Lloyd, Dec. 22, 1886, Henry Demarest Lloyd Papers, *WSHS.*
10. Douglas R. Kennedy, "The Knights of Labor in Canada," pp. 49-50; St. Paul *Daily Globe*, Sept. 6, 1885; Albert Shaw, "Cooperation in the Northwest," *Johns Hopkins University Study*, Baltimore, 1888, pp. 206-07.
11. Ware, *op. cit.*, pp. 110-11.
12. St. Paul *Daily Globe*, Sept. 8, 1885; W. H. Foster to Gompers, Feb. 8, 1886, *AFL Corr.;* Fred (Turner) to Powderly, May 29, 1885, *PP.*
13. Charles (Lichtman) to Powderly, June 16, 1886; Joseph R. Mason to Powderly, Dec. 7, 1885, *PP; Proceedings*, General Assembly, K. of L., 1884, p. 717.
14. *Proceedings*, General Assembly, K. of L., 1880, p. 169.
15. *Journal of United Labor*, Nov. 15, 1880; p. 66; *Proceedings*, General Assembly, K. of L., 1884, p. 780.
16. Powderly, *Thirty Years of Labor*, p. 283; Powderly, *The Path I Trod*, p. 386; Powderly to B. H. Webster, July 30, 1886, *PLB.*
17. Wesley A. Stuart to Powderly, Nov. 28, 1885.
18. *Unionist*, Detroit, April 17, 1882; Detroit *Labor Leaf*, July 15, Aug. 12, Oct. 14, 1885.
19. *John Swinton's Paper*, Oct. 25, 1885, Jan. 31, 1886; John Taylor Chappel, "How Labor Triumphed in Richmond," *The Comrade*, vol. 1, Oct., 1901, p. 11.
20. Powderly to Wesley A. Stuart, Dec. 2, 1885; Powderly to B. H. Webster, July 30, 1886; Powderly to M. L. Wheat, Aug. 11, 1886, *PLB.*

21. *Journal of United Labor*, Nov. 15, 1880; *Proceedings*, General Assembly, K. of L., 1882, p. 278, 1883, p. 408.

22. *Proceedings*, General Assembly, K. of L., 1880, p. 10; *John Swinton's Paper*, Dec. 9, 1883.

23. See Circular of L.A. 2922, to K. of L., no date, but marked "Received June 1, 1884," *PP*; McNeil, *op. cit.*, pp. 424ff.

24. *Journal of United Labor*, June, 1882; Robert D. Layton to Powderly, March 30, 1883, *PP*.

25. *John Swinton's Paper*, Oct. 3, 1886.

26. Missouri Bureau of Labor Statistics and Inspection, *The Official History of the Great Strike on the Southwestern Railway System*, 1887, pp. 89-95; Harry Frumerman, "The Strikes of 1885-86," *The Marxist Quarterly*, Oct.-Dec., 1937, pp. 398-99.

27. U.S. House of Representatives, 49th Congress, 2nd Session, 1887, Report No. 4147. "Investigation of Labor Troubles in Missouri . . .," Part I, pp. xi-xii.

28. *Ibid.*, Part I, pp. xi-xii, Part II, pp. 438, 44.

29. Ruth A. Allen, *The Great Southwest Strike*, Austin, Texas, 1942, pp. 55, 129-30; *Strike Investigation*, p. 354.

30. See J. L. Pingrey, "Public Opinion and the Gould Strike of 1885-86," Unpublished M.A. thesis, Columbia University, Department of History; Frumerman, *op. cit.*, p. 400.

31. *Strike Investigation*, p. xix.

32. *New York Times*, March 26-28, 1886.

33. *Ibid.*, March 29, 1886.

34. *Strike Investigation*, p. 66.

35. Frumerman, *op. cit.*, p. 403.

36. *Strike Investigation*, p. 82.

37. Allen, *op. cit.*, p. 68-69, 81-83; *New York Times*, April 10, 1886.

38. *Correspondence Between Jay Gould, Terence V. Powderly, et al*, n.d., n.p., pp. 1-3; Allen, *op. cit.*, p. 69.

39. Frumerman, *op. cit.*, p. 404; *Strike Investigation*, Part II, pp. xxiii-xxv.

40. Powderly to Annie A. Wright, May 3, 1886, *PLB*.

41. *John Swinton's Paper*, May 16, 1886.

42. Buchanan, *op. cit.*, pp. 319-21.

43. Letter of G. W. Botford, etc. to Powderly, Nov. 1886, *PP*.

44. "Resolutions passed at private meeting of late strikers of stock yards, November 15, 1886," attached to letter of Michel Cahill to Powderly, Nov. 15, 1886, *PP*.

45. Buchanan, *op. cit.*, pp. 320-21; *Labor Enquirer*, Jan. 5, 1887.

46. Douglas R. Kennedy, *op. cit.*, p. 102; Henry J. Browne, *The Catholic Church and the Knights of Labor*, Washington, D. C., 1949, p. 89.

47. Browne, *op. cit.*, pp. 101-04, 108, 130.

48. Powderly to Tom, Oct. 25, 1886, *PLB*.

49. Powderly to Archbishop Ryan, Oct. 24, 1884, *PLB*.

50. Uriah S. Stephens to James S. Sullivan, n.p., August 19, 1879, Uriah Stephens Letter-Books, Catholic University of America.

51. Phillip Van Patten to Powderly, Sept. 12, 1881, May 20, August 13, 1883, *PP*; Powderly to Phillip Van Patten, Oct. 13, 1881, *PLB*.

52. Powderly to J. Mulhane, Sept. 28, 1882, *PLB*.

53. See newspaper clipping, "Is Powderly a Socialist?" attached to A. M. Dewey to Powderly, Sept. 9, 1887, *PP*.

54. Browne, *op. cit.*, pp. 90-92, 109, 112, 138-39, 140-41, 156-57, 169-70, 300-02.

55. See Harry J. Carman, "Terence V. Powderly," *Journal of Economic History*, vol. I, May, 1941.

56. John P. Bulman to Powderly, April 18, 1883, *PP*.

57. Powderly to Executive Board, Jan. 5, 1883; John S. McClelland to Powderly, Jan. 23, 1883; Gilbert Rockwood to Powderly, Jan. 26, 1883, *PP*.

58. Joseph A. Labadie to Powderly, July 26, 1882, *PP*.

59. Ware, *op. cit.*, p. 103; Powderly to John Hayes, Feb. 22, 1888, *PLB*.

60. Joseph A. Labadie to Powderly, Jan. 7, '83, *PP*.

61. Ira Kipnis, *The American Socialist Movement, 1897-1912*, New York, 1952, p. 12.

62. Marx and Engels, *Letters to Americans*, pp. 162-67.

63. Cf. Theo. F. Cuno to Powderly, June 28, July 3, 8, 15, 1882; Geo. Storm to Powderly, Dec. 14, 1885, *PP*.

CHAPTER VI

1. *Proceedings*, Federation of Organized Trades, 1882 Convention, p. 9.

2. *Proceedings*, Federation of Organized Trades, 1883 Convention, pp. 17-18.

3. *Proceedings*, Federation of Organized

Trades, 1882 Convention, pp. 9-11; 1883 Convention, pp. 7-8.

4. *Ibid.*, 1882 Convention, pp. 9-11; 1883 Convention, p. 8; Senator Wilkinson Call to G. Edmonston, Dec. 4, 1884, *AFL Corr.*

5. *Proceedings*, Federation of Organized Trades, 1882 Convention, pp. 9-11.

6. *Ibid.*, 1883 Convention, p. 8.

7. *Ibid.*, 1884 Convention, pp. 9, 11-12.

8. *New Yorker Volkszeitung*, May 19-20, 1882.

9. New York *World*, New York *Herald*, New York *Sun*, Sept. 6, 1882.

10. New York *Herald*, New York *Sun*, New York *World*, Sept. 6, 1883.

11. *Journal of United Labor*, June 25, 1884, p. 725; *John Swinton's Paper*, Aug. 31, 1884.

12. New York *Herald*, Sept. 2, 1884; *John Swinton's Paper*, July 6, Aug. 31, 1884.

13. *Proceedings*, Federation of Organized Trades, 1884 Convention, p. 23.

14. Leaflet in Albert R. Parsons Scrapbook, *WSHS*.

15. St. Paul *Globe Democrat*, July 19, Aug. 16, 1885.

16. St. Paul *Daily Globe*, Sept. 13, 1885.

17. *American Federationist*, vol. I, Aug., 1894, pp. 128-29.

18. *Proceedings*, Federation of Organized Trades, 1884 Convention, pp. 24-25.

19. *New York Times*, Feb. 4, 1884.

20. *Proceedings*, Federation of Organized Trades, 1882 Convention, p. 19; *John Swinton's Paper*, April 4, 1886.

21. *Proceedings*, Federation of Organized Trades, 1884 Convention, pp. 8, 10-14.

22. *John Swinton's Paper*, Oct. 26, 1884.

23. *Proceedings*, Federation of Organized Trades, 1884 Convention, p. 14.

24. Ella Rose Tambussi, "The Knights of Labor," unpublished M.A. thesis, Department of Economics and Sociology, Mount Holyoke College, p. 95.

25. Commons and Associates, *op. cit.*, vol. II, pp. 377-79.

26. G. Edmondston to Fred Turner, July 26, 1885, copy in Samuel Gompers Letter-Books, American Federation of Labor Building (hereafter cited as *GLB*); *Proceedings*, General Assembly, K. of L., 1885, p. 15.

27. Powderly, *Thirty Years of Labor*, p. 253; Union 56, Brotherhood of Carpenters and Joiners to Powderly, Nov. 21, 1885, *PP*.

28. Powderly, *The Path I Trod*, p. 169.

29. *Proceedings*, Federation of Organized Trades, 1885 Convention, pp. 11-15; "Minutes of the Legislative Committee of the Federation of Organized Trades and Labor Unions of the United States and Canada, November 19, 1881 to December 17, 1887," report of meeting of Dec. 11, 1885, in A.F. of L. Archives; Printed "Appeal to all Trade and Labor Unions," February 1, 1886, signed by W. H. Foster, copy in *AFL Corr.*

30. Cahill, *op. cit.*, pp. 154-55.

31. David, *op. cit.*, p. 164.

32. Powderly, *Thirty Years of Labor*, p. 496.

33. Chicago *Tribune*, April 11, 1886; *John Swinton's Paper*, April 11, 1886.

34. *John Swinton's Paper*, March 2, 1884, June 7, 1885, May 2, 1886.

35. Calmar, *op. cit.*, p. 78.

36. *Ibid.*; David, *op. cit.*, pp. 182-83.

37. *John Swinton's Paper*, Jan. 10, April 18, 1886; David, *op. cit.*, p. 177.

38. See George Gunton, *Wealth and Progress*, New York, 1887, p. 243; *John Swinton's Paper*, March 2, 1884.

39. *John Swinton's Paper*, May 16, 1886.

40. *Bradstreets'*, May 8, 15, 1886.

41. Glazer, *op. cit.*, pp. 71-72.

42. New York *Sun*, May 2, 1886.

43. *Bradstreets'*, May 8, 15, 1886; Cahill, *op. cit.*, p. 159; *John Swinton's Paper*, May 2, 1886; *Proceedings*, A.F. of L. Convention, 1886, p. 6.

44. *Report of the Industrial Commission on the Relations of Capital and Labor Employed in Manufactures and General Business*, Washington, 1901, vol. VII, p. 623.

45. *Proceedings*, A.F. of L. Convention, 1889, p. 42.

CHAPTER VII

1. Yellen, *op. cit.*, pp. 50-51.

2. "Story of McCormick Massacre, 1886," *Daily Worker*, April 29, 1936.

3. David, *op. cit.*, Chapter IX.

4. See especially Chicago *Tribune* and Chicago *Herald*, May 6-10, 1886.

5. *Journal of the Illinois Historical Society*, Dec., 1938, p. 204. See also *John Swinton's Paper*, May 16, 1886.

6. Chicago *Daily News*, May 10, 1889.

7. David, *op. cit.*, pp. 226-27.

8. J. P. Altgeld, *Reasons for Pardoning Fielden, Neebe, and Schwab*, Springfield, Illinois, 1896, p. 8.

9. David, *op. cit.*, pp. 229-31.
10. Calmer, *op. cit.*, pp. 98-100.
11. *The Century Magazine*, April, 1893. My emphasis, *P.S.F.*
12. Altgeld, *op. cit.*, pp. 12-14.
13. See A. R. Parson, *Anarchism: Its Philosophy and Scientific Basis*, Chicago, 1887, p. 53.
14. Manuscript notebook of Albert R. Parsons, containing notes taken during the trial, *WSHS*.
15. *Famous Speeches of the Eight Chicago Anarchists in Court*, Chicago, 1910, pp. 20-24.
16. *Ibid.*, pp. 40-43.
17. *To-Day*, Nov., 1887.
18. *The Century Magazine*, April, 1893.
19. Quoted in David, *op. cit.*, p. 376.
20. *Ibid.*, Chapter XVII.
21. *Ibid.*, pp. 410-11.
22. *Proceedings*, A.F. of L. Convention, 1886, p. 46.
23. Gompers to James W. Smith, Oct. 13, 1887, *GLB*.
24. Samuel Gompers, *Seventy Years of Life and Labor*, New York, 1924, vol. I, p. 187.
25. David, *op. cit.*, p. 410; Powderly, *Thirty Years of Labor*, pp. 544-45.
26. *New York Tribune*, Nov. 6, 1887; David, *op. cit.*, pp. 388, 397-98.
27. David, *op. cit.*, p. 426; *To-Day*, Nov., 1887.
28. *The Commonweal*, Oct. 22, 1887, p. 340.
29. *Ibid.*
30. August Spies, *Autobiography. His Speech in Court, Notes, Letters, etc.*, Chicago, 1887, p. 75.
31. *Freedom*, Nov., 1887, p. 56, Dec., 1887, p. 59.
32. David, *op. cit.*, pp. 426-33.
33. Altgeld, *op. cit.*, pp. 8-10.
34. David, *op. cit.*, pp. 499-500; Glazer, *op. cit.*, pp. 61-62; Clippings in Labadie Collection classified under the head of "Haymarket," University of Michigan. (Hereafter cited as *LC*.)

CHAPTER VIII

1. *Harper's Weekly*, Nov. 3, 1886, p. 726.
2. *Ibid.*, Oct. 25, 1885, Jan. 1, 10, 1886; *The Boycotter*, Jan. 9, 1886.
3. F. Henry Marsh to Powderly, Jan. 18, 1886, *PP*.
4. *John Swinton's Paper*, June 13, Sept.

5, 1886; *New York Times*, June 8, 1886.
5. *John Swinton's Paper*, June 13, 1886; *New York Sun*, May 2, June 6, 1886.
6. *New York Sun*, Sept. 20, 1886.
7. *John Swinton's Paper*, June 13, 1886.
8. *John Swinton's Paper*, June 27, July 11, 1886; *The Boycotter*, May 15, 1886; Gompers, *op. cit.*, p. 311; *Fourth Annual Report of the Bureau of Labor Statistics*, New York, 1886, pp. 666-75, 748-82.
9. *Der Sozialist* quoted in Ely, *The Labor Movement in America*, p. 299.
10. *John Swinton's Paper*, June 13, 1886.
11. *The Boycotter*, July 10, 1886.
12. *Ibid.*, July 16, 1886.
13. *Ibid.*, July 17, 1886; *John Swinton's Paper*, July 18, 1886.
14. *John Swinton's Paper*, July 25, 1886; Louis F. Post and Fred C. Leubuscher, *An Account of the George-Hewitt Campaign in the New York Municipal Election*, New York, 1887, pp. 5-6.
15. *New York Times*, Aug. 20, 1886.
16. Henry George, Jr., *The Life of Henry George*, New York, 1900, pp. 338, 345-41, 449; *New York Times*, April 30, 1884; *Rep. of the Sen. Comm. on Labor*, vol. II, p. 76; Howard Lawrence Hurwitz, *Theodore Roosevelt and Labor in New York State, 1880-1900*, New York, 1943, pp. 114-15.
17. Frederick Engels, *Conditions of the English Working Class in 1844*, 1887 edition, Preface.
18. Hillquit, *op. cit.*, pp. 253-54; *New York Sun*, Oct. 17, 1886.
19. *The Leader*, Oct. 21, 28, 1886.
20. *John Swinton's Paper*, Sept. 5, 12, 19, 26, 1886.
21. *New York Herald*, Sept. 24, 1886; *New York Sun*, Sept. 29, 1886; *The Star*, Sept. 25, 1886.
22. *John Swinton's Paper*, Oct. 3, 1886.
23. Quoted in Nathan Fine, *Labor and Farmer Parties in the United States*. New York, 1928, pp. 44-45.
24. *New York World*, Oct. 6, 1886.
25. *John Swinton's Paper*, Oct. 31, 1886; *New York World*, Oct. 11, 1886.
26. Quoted in Gompers, *op. cit.*, vol. I, p. 312.
27. *Ibid.*, p. 316; *The Star*, Oct. 6, 1886.
28. Wm. Q. McDowell to Powderly, Oct. 7, 1886, *PP*.
29. *New York World*, Oct. 30, Nov. 2, 1886; *New York Evening Telegram*, Nov. 3, 1886.

30. *The Star*, Oct. 25, 1886.
31. *Irish World*, Oct. 16, 23, 30, 1886; *The Morning Journal*, Oct. 25, 1886.
32. New York *Freeman*, Dec. 6, 1886; *The Boycotter*, Oct. 16, 1886; Alex J. Niselson, "The Henry George Campaign in New York City Mayorality Election, 1886," unpublished M.A. thesis, Columbia University, Feb., 1950, pp. 435-37.
33. *Die New Yorker Yiddishe Volkszeitung*, Oct. 1, 8, 15, 1886.
34. *John Swinton's Paper*, Aug. 15, Oct. 17, 1886.
35. *John Swinton's Paper*, Oct. 10, 1886.
36. New York *World*, Oct. 10, 1886.
37. New York *World*, Oct. 4, 1886; *The Morning Journal*, Oct. 11, 17, 1886; *John Swinton's Paper*, Jan. 2, 1887. For copies of *The Reflector* for Oct. 2 and 9, *see* Henry George Scrapbooks, vol. XVII, New York Public Library, *Ms*. Division. (Hereafter cited as *NYPL*.)
38. *The Boycotter*, Oct. 2, 1886; *John Swinton's Paper*, Oct. 24, 31, 1886.
39. Henry George to Gutschow, Oct. 8, 1886; Henry George to E. R. Taylor, Oct. 11, 1886, Henry George Papers, *NYPL*.
40. Gustavus Myers, *The History of Tammany Hall*, New York, 1901, p. 322.
41. *The Star*, Oct. 17, 1886; New York *World*, Oct. 30, 1886.
42. *The Daily Illustrated Graphic*, Oct. 5, 1886; *The Star*, Oct. 21, 1886; New York *World*, Oct. 28, 1886.
43. New York *Post*, Oct. 14, 1886; New York *World*, Oct. 15, 25, 1886.
44. *John Swinton's Paper*, Oct. 31, 1886.
45. New York *Sun*, Oct. 27, 1886.
46. *Irish World*, Nov. 6, 1886; New York *World*, Oct. 27, 30, 1886; Stephen Bell, *Rebel, Priest and Prophet*, New York, 1937, p. 34.
47. *Die New Yorker Yiddishe Volkszeitung*, Oct. 8, 1886.
48. New York *World*, Oct. 31, 1886.
49. New York *Herald*, Nov. 4, 1886; *Post* and Luebuscher, *op. cit.*, p. 169; Henry George to Gutschow, December 31, 1886, Henry George Papers, *NYPL*.
50. *Irish World*, Nov. 6, 1886.
51. *The Nation*, Nov. 4, 1886; New York *World*, Nov. 3; 4, 1886.
52. Karl Marx and Frederick Engels, *Letters to Americans*, pp. 162-63.
53. New York *Herald*, Sept. 24, 1886.
54. *John Swinton's Paper*, Nov. 7, 1886;

James G. Brown to Powderly, Oct. 23, 1886, *PP*.
55. Eugene Staley, *History of the Illinois State Federation of Labor*, Chicago, 1930, pp. 72-73; Edward B. Mittleman, "Chicago Labor in Politics, 1877-1896," *Journal of Political Economy*, vol. XXVIII, May, 1920, pp. 418-19.
56. *Knights of Labor*, Oct. 2, 1886.
57. Fine, *op. cit.*, p. 54.
58. *Knights of Labor*, Nov. 6, 1886.
59. *Knights of Labor*, Nov. 6, 1886; Martin J. Russell, editor Chicago *Herald*, to Powderly, Nov. 9, 1886, *PP*.
60. August Spies, *Autobiography, His Speech in Court, Notes, Letters, etc.*, Chicago, 1887, pp. 120-21.
61. *Proceedings*, Federation of Organized Trades, 1885 Convention, pp. 10, 17-18; *Proceedings*, A.F. of L. Convention, 1886, p. 16.

CHAPTER IX

1. H. O. Cole to Powderly, March 9, April 28, 1883, *PP*.
2. Gompers, *op. cit.*, vol. I, p. 255; W. H. Foster to Powderly, Dec. 24, 1885; W. H. Foster to Gompers, Feb. 8, 1886, *AFL Corr.*; James J. Hawlett to Powderly, Dec. 14, 1885; James J. Haggerty to Powderly, Dec. 16, 1885; James Cristie and Tony Heywang to Powderly, Dec. 9, 1885, *PP*.
3. Printed circular signed by Charles O'Brien, M.W., Peter McCarroll, R.S., L.A. 2985, etc. in *PP*, undated, but marked "Received, Nov. 19, 1885."
4. Ware, *op. cit.*, p. 164; Printed circular, signed by Charles O'Brien, etc., in *PP*, and Printed circular, New York, May 8, 1886, signed by M. Dampf and R. E. Pinner, *PP*; *Proceedings*, General Assembly, K. of L., 1884, pp. 690, 691, 716, 727.
5. Printed circular, New York, May 8, 1886, signed by M. Dampf and R. E. Pinner, *PP*.
6. *John Swinton's Paper*, Jan. 27, June 22, 1884; Gompers, *op. cit.*, vol. I, p. 203.
7. Jas. M. Brady, D.M.W., Mauk Chamberlain, Henry Gerlach, Comm., D.A. 47 to Powderly, April 11, '84; Powderly to Fred and Fred to Powderly, on back of above letter, *PP*.
8. *John Swinton's Paper*, Jan. 27, 1884.

9. Circular Appeal, Cigar Makers' International Union, Feb. 25, 1886, *PP*.
10. *Ibid.*; G. W. Perkins, first vice-president, Cigar Makers' International Union of America, to Gompers, Jan. 28, 1886, *AFL Corr.*; *Fourth Annual Report of the New York Bureau of Statistics of Labor*, pp. 524*ff*.
11. *Irish World*, March 27, 1886.
12. "The Order and the Cigar Makers," Circular, July 2, 1886, *WSHS* and *PP*.
13. *Irish World*, March 27, 1886.
14. *John Swinton's Paper*, May 9, 1886; Gompers, *op. cit.*, vol. I, pp. 256-57.
15. *Cigar Makers' Official Journal*, June, 1886.
16. Powderly to Henry Dettman, Aug. 11, 1886, *PLB*.
17. *John Swinton's Paper*, Dec. 5, 1886.
18. Geo. Blair to Powderly, May 21, 1886, *PP*.
19. Powderly to Adolph Strasser, May 11, 1886; Powderly to Peter J. McGuire, May 11, 1886; Powderly to G. W. Andrews, May 3, 1886, *PLB*.
20. Powderly to Henry Dettman, Aug. 11, 1886, *PLB*.
21. Powderly to Joseph R. Buchanan, Aug. 13, 1886, *PLB*.
22. Buchanan, *op. cit.*, p. 301; *John Swinton's Paper*, May 9, 1886; *Proceedings*, General Assembly, K. of L., Cleveland, 1886, p. 73.
23. *Proceedings*, General Assembly, K. of L., Cleveland, 1886, p. 73.
24. Editorials reprinted in *Cigar Makers' Official Journal*, June, 1886; George A. Tracy, *History of the Typographical Union*, p. 370.
25. *Proceedings*, General Assembly, K. of L., Richmond, 1886, p. 200.
26. Buchanan, *op. cit.*, pp. 313-16.
27. Circular issued by District Assembly 89 in K. of L. Papers, *WSHS*; Detroit *Advance and Labor Leaf*, Feb. 19, 1887; Clippings in Labadie Collection under the head of "Cigar Makers."
28. Lewis L. Lorwin, *The American Federation of Labor*, Washington, 1933, p. 21.
29. *Proceedings of the 1886 Convention of the Federation of Organized Trades and Labor Unions of the United States and Canada*, pp. 10-11.
30. Quoted in Philip S. Foner, *History of the Labor Movement in U.S.*, vol. I, p. 521.
31. *Proceedings of the American Federation of Labor Convention, 1886; John Swin-*ton's Paper, Dec. 19, 1886; New York *Herald*, Dec. 15, 1886; *Labor Standard*, Jan. 9, 1887.
32. *John Swinton's Paper*, Dec. 19, 1886.
33. "Report of the Conference with the Committee of the Knights of Labor," in *Proceedings*, A.F. of L. Convention, 1886, pp. 17-18.
34. *Ibid.*, p. 19.

CHAPTER X

1. *John Swinton's Paper*, Jan. 9, April 24, 1887; *The Union Printer*, April 2, June 4, 18, 1887; *Irish World*, Sept. 24, 1887.
2. *John Swinton's Paper*, April 24, 1887.
3. *Ibid.*, May 15, 1887; Cleveland *Gazette*, April 16, 1887.
4. New York *World*, Nov. 7, 1886; New York *Sun*, Nov. 7, 1886.
5. *The Leader*, Oct. 30, 1887.
6. Peter Alexander Speek, *The Singletax and the Labor Movement*, p. 320.
7. *The Standard*, May 7, 1887.
8. *The Standard*, Dec. 11, 1887; Bell, *op. cit.*, pp. 88-205.
9. *Workmen's Advocate*, Jan. 22, May 28, 1887; Marx and Engels, *Letters to Americans*, p. 167.
10. *The Leader*, July 25, 1887; Speek, *op. cit.*, p. 116; *Cigar Makers' Official Journal*, April, May, 1887.
11. *Workmen's Advocate*, April 2, 1887; *John Swinton's Paper*, May 29, 1887.
12. *The Standard*, May 7, 1887.
13. *Workmen's Advocate*, May 28, 1887; *John Swinton's Paper*, May 15, 22, 1887.
14. *John Swinton's Paper*, May 15, 1887.
15. *The Standard*, Aug. 14, 1887.
16. *Ibid; The Union Printer*, Aug. 6, 1887.
17. Speek, *op. cit.*, pp. 107, 112-20; *Workmen's Advocate*, Aug. 13, 1887.
18. Chicago *Labor Enquirer*, Aug. 20, 1887.
19. *The Standard*, Aug. 6, Sept. 10, 1887.
20. *Ibid.*; Die New Yorker *Yiddishe Volkszeitung*, Aug. 5, 1887; *Workmen's Advocate*, Aug. 20, 1887.
21. *Irish World*, Aug. 27, 1887; *Workmen's Advocate*, Aug. 20, 1887.
22. *Irish World*, Aug. 27, 1887.
23. *The Standard*, Aug. 27, 1887; *Irish World*, Aug. 27, 1887.
24. New York *World*, Aug. 19, 1887.
25. *The Standard*, Aug. 27, 1887.
26. *The Standard*, Aug. 27, 1887; *Irish World*, Aug. 27, 1887.

27. *Freedom* (London), Oct., 1887.
28. *The Leader,* Aug. 23, 1887; *Workmen's Advocate,* Aug. 27, Sept. 10, 17, 1887.
29. *Workmen's Advocate,* Oct. 1, 1887.
30. Chicago *Labor Leader,* Aug. 27, 1887.
31. *Ibid.,* Sept. 24, 1887; New York *Tribune,* Oct. 14, 1887.
32. New York *Sun,* Sept. 19, 1887.
33. New York *Sun,* Nov. 18, 1887.
34. Chicago *Labor Enquirer,* Feb. 23, March 2, 1887.
35. *Knights of Labor,* March 26, 1887.
36. Chicago *Labor Enquirer,* March 26, 1887.
37. Boston *Labor Leader,* Oct. 18, 1887.
38. Staley, *op. cit.,* p. 74.
39. *Knights of Labor,* April 9, 1887.
40. Staley, *op. cit.,* p. 74.
41. Chicago *Labor Enquirer,* Sept. 3, 1887, March 10, 1888.
42. *Ibid.,* March 24, 1888; Staley, *op. cit.,* p. 74.
43. Fine, *op. cit.,* pp. 58-60.
44. *The Standard,* Jan. 8, 1887; *John Swinton's Paper,* Dec. 5, 1886, March 20, 1887; Boston *Labor Leader,* Jan. 15, 1887.
45. Chicago *Labor Enquirer,* Aug. 6, Nov. 26, Dec. 24, 31, 1887; *Workmen's Advocate,* Oct. 1, 1887, April 21, 1888.
46. *Appleton's Annual Cyclopedia,* 1888, pp. 778-79.

CHAPTER XI

1. Leo Wolman, *The Growth of American Trade Unions,* p. 32.
2. New York *Tribune,* Aug. 12, 1889.
3. *Cf.* Commons and Associates, *op. cit.,* vol. II, pp. 414-23; *Report of the Industrial Commission on Relations of Capital and Labor,* Washington, 1901, vol. VII, pp. 9, 420, 423-24, 801.
4. R. T. Crane, "The Knights of Labor in Baltimore," *Johns Hopkins Circulars,* April, 1903, p. 39; S. J. Hickock to Powderly, Jan. 25, 1886, *PP.*
5. Detroit *Advance and Labor Leaf,* Nov. 11, 1885; Frank C. Noyes to Powderly, Dec. 12, 1885; *PP;* O'Sullivan to Gompers, Boston, June 5, '93, *AFL Corr.*
6. For the Massachusetts' shoe strike, *see* Boston *Globe,* May 4, June 22, 23, 1887; *Shoe and Leather Worker,* Sept. 1, 1887; *John Swinton's Paper,* Feb. 13, June 21, 1887; J. O'Keefe to Powderly, May 30, 1887, *PP;* Powderly to Charles Prouty, June 15, 1887,

PLB; for the strike on the Reading Railroad, *see* Powderly to John W. Hayes, Feb. 7, 11, 1888, *PHC;* Powderly to Bob (Layton), April 30, 1888, *PLB;* "Scrapbooks of newspaper clippings relating to strikes, lockouts, etc., in the United States, 1887-1888," *NYPL;* for the steel workers' strike, *see* Pittsburgh *Dispatch,* April 30-May 7, 1888.
7. "Scrapbooks of newspaper clippings . . ., 1887-1888," *NYPL.*
8. Clipping, *LC;* J. O. Keefe to Powderly, May 30, 1887, *PP;* "Scrapbooks . . ., 1887-1888," *NYPL.*
9. *John Swinton's Paper,* March 6, 1887.
10. Crane, *op. cit.,* p. 39; *Arbeiter Zeitung,* Jan. 10, 1888; *Knights of Labor,* Nov. 20, 1886.
11. Official Circular, No. 14, *LC.*
12. "Scrapbooks . . ., 1887-1888," *NYPL.*
13. New York *Herald,* Sept. 12, 1887.
14. Detroit *Advance and Labor Leaf,* July 23, 1887.
15. New Orleans *Times-Democrat,* Nov. 23-24, 1887; *Irish World,* Dec. 3, 1887; *Weekly Pelican,* Nov. 26, 1887.
16. Detroit *Advance and Labor Leaf,* July 23, 1887; W. R. Ramsey to Powderly, Dec. 11, 1887, *PP.*
17. Powderly to McGoughen, Aug. 15, 1887, *PLB;* Powderly to John W. Hayes, July 25, 30, 1887, *PHC.*
18. Scrapbook of clippings on the Minneapolis Convention, Knights of Labor, compiled by Agnes Inglis, *LC; Proceedings,* General Assembly, K. of L., Minneapolis, 1887, pp. 1511, 1525.
19. *Proceedings,* General Assembly, K. of L., Minneapolis, 1887, pp. 1499-1505.
20. *Proceedings,* General Assembly, K. of L., Minneapolis, 1887, pp. 1520-25.
21. Chicago *Labor Enquirer,* Oct. 29, 1887; David, *op. cit.,* p. 418; Browne, *op. cit.,* pp. 301-02; E. E. Cleveland to Powderly, Oct. 7, 1887, *PP.*
22. *Proceedings,* General Assembly, K. of L., Minneapolis, 1887, pp. 1528, 1822; Printed Circular issued by D.A. 86, undated, *PP.*
23. Scrapbooks of clippings on the Minneapolis Convention, Knights of Labor; *The Commonweal,* Oct. 29, 1887.
24. *Mississippi Valley Lumberman,* vol. XII, Oct. 14, 1887, p. 2, quoted in George B. Engberg, "Labor in the Lake States Lumber Industry, 1830-1930," unpublished Ph.D. thesis, University of Minnesota, 1949, p. 393.
25. Saginaw *Evening News,* Nov. 19, 1887.

26. *See* Charles (Lichtman) to Powderly, Feb. 17, 24, April 24, June 27, 1888; *PP;* Powderly to Charlie (Lichtman), Feb. 22, 25, Nov. 25, 1888, *PLB.*
27. Philadelphia *Call,* July 6, 1888.
28. Circulars in *LC* classified under the head of "Brotherhood of United Labor."
29. Newspaper clippings in *LC* classified under the head of "Brotherhood of United Labor."
30. Andrew Roy, *A History of the Coal Miners of the United States,* Columbus, Ohio, 1901, p. 350; New York *Tribune,* Aug. 13, 1889; printed circular issued by Shoemakers' General Label Committee, June 2, 1892, *PP.*
31. William C. Birdsall, *op. cit.,* p. 63.
32. Robert Y. Ogg to Gompers, Nov. 10, 1890, *AFL Corr.*
33. Powderly to John W. Hayes, Feb. 9, May 28, 1889, *PHC.*
34. R. D. Layton to Powderly, Jan. 27, 1888, *PP;* Powderly to James P. Archibold, April 21, 1888, *PLB; Proceedings,* Michigan State Assembly, K. of L., 1887, p. 20.
35. *Proceedings,* General Assembly, K. of L., Atlanta, 1889, pp. 4, 8, 33, 43.
36. *The Standard,* Nov. 23, 1889.
37. New York *Tribune,* Aug. 13, 1889; Powderly to John W. Hayes, Dec. 22, 1889, *PHC.*
38. Kennedy, *op. cit.,* pp. 112-14.
39. *The Industrial Tribune,* Aug. 8, 1891.
40. Powderly to Leonora M. Barry, July 25, 1888, *PLB; Proceedings,* General Assembly, K. of L., 1893, pp. 59-61.
41. Philadelphia *Times,* May 7, 1894.
42. *Proceedings,* General Assembly, K. of L., Philadelphia, 1893, p. 4; Philadelphia *Press,* June 3, 1894.
43. John M. Callaghan to Gompers, July 9, 1892; Henry Abrams to Gompers, Feb. 24, 1893, *AFL Corr.;* Boston *Herald,* Feb. 10, 1893.
44. Brooklyn *Daily Eagle,* Jan. 27, 28, Feb. 16-17, 1895.
45. Circular issued by office of General Assembly, Order of Knights of Labor, Washington, Oct. 13, '97, copy in *AFL Corr.;* Boston *Globe,* Nov. 21, 1899.
46. *Report of the Industrial Commission on the Relations and Conditions of Capital and Labor,* Washington, 1901, vol. VII, p. 9. *See also* John W. Hayes to J. Lortan, November 19, 1908; I. W. Chamberlain to Wm. J. Lortan, March 4, November 3, 1908, Knights of Labor

Papers, Mullen Library of the Catholic University of America.
47. New York *World-Telegram,* Oct. 18, 1949.
48. Boston *Globe,* June 23, 1887.
49. Powderly to Martin Irons, Sept. 27, 1892, *PLB.*
50. Buchanan, *op. cit.,* pp. 361-62.

CHAPTER XII

1. Leo Wolman, *The Growth of American Trade Unions,* pp. 30-35.
2. Robert Schilling to Terence V. Powderly, June 25, 1891, *PP.*
3. Lewis Lorwin, *The American Federation of Labor,* p. 27.
4. Samuel Gompers to J. P. McDonnell, March 21, 1887, J. P. McDonnell Papers, *WSHS;* Detroit *Free Press,* Oct. 18, 1896.
5. *John Swinton's Paper,* May 29, 1887; Gompers to G. Edmonston, April 22, 1887, *GLB.*
6. *Cf.* Letters to Gompers from Theo. Fuehrer, Dec. 1, 1890; C. Evans, Dec. 18, 1890; B. Andrus, Feb. 28, 1891; J. C. Roberts, Nov. 20, 1891; E. H. Cherry, Mar. 17, 1892; W. Eberhardt, June 30, 1892; J. W. Callaghan, June 28, Oct. 23, 1892, *AFL Corr.*
7. Eugene V. Debs, *His Life, Writings and Speeches,* New York, 1910, p. 132.
8. Gompers to F. D. Hamlin, May 6, 1890, *GLB.*
9. "Minutes of the Legislative Committee of the Federation of Organized Trades and Labor Unions of the United States and Canada—From Nov. 1881 to Dec. 17, 1887," meeting of Feb. 3, 1887, AFL Archives.
10. New York *Sun,* Sept. 19, 1893.
11. Letters of Gompers to J. Parker Camp, Feb. 10, 1892; Carroll D. Wright, March 4, 1896; G. Freihoff, Jan. 4, 1893, *GLB; Proceedings,* A.F. of L. Convention, 1889, p. 15; *The Railroad Trainmen's Journal,* vol. VII, No. 9, Sept., 1890, p. 534.
12. Gompers to J. M. Williams, June 29, 1887, *GLB.*
13. Gompers to S. R. Holmes, Oct. 8, 1890, *GLB.*
14. Letters of Gompers to Wm. J. Baxter, Jan. 31, 1893; Geo. Iden, June 17, 1891; Wm. P. Effinger, April 29, 1892; S. R. Holmes, Oct. 18, 1890, *GLB;*

speech of Gompers at International Cigar Makers' Union Convention, Sept. 25, 1893, *AFL Corr.*

15. Gompers to Antoni Rozanaki, June 25, 1889; Gompers to Anonymous, Feb. 1890, *GLB.*

16. Gompers to Henry F. Chamberlain, Sept. 28, 1892, *GLB.*

17. Quoted in Rowland Hill Harvey, *Samuel Gompers*, Stanford University Press, 1935, p. 56.

18. Letters of Gompers to P. J. McGuire, Feb. 26, 1887; G. Andrus, April 24, 1891; Geo. Iden, July 15, 1892; Albert S. Stevens, Nov. 1, 1899, *GLB.*

19. New York *World*, April 11, 1890.

20. New York *Leader*, July 25, 1887; Harvey, *op. cit.*, pp. 59-60; Gompers to C. W. Armstrong, Dec. 21, 1892, *GLB.*

21. New York *Leader*, July 25, 1887; Gompers to H. M. Ives, April 3, 1893, *GLB.*

22. Gompers to Victor Delahaye, August 21, 1891, May 31, 1893, *GLB.*

23. Printed Circular issued by A.F. of L. Executive Council, New York, Jan. 19, 1889, *AFL Corr.*

24. Gompers to H. J. Skeffington, Jan. 3, 1889; Gompers to John O'Brien, Feb. 7, 1889, *GLB.*

25. Printed Circular issued by A.F. of L. Executive Council, *AFL Corr.*

26. "A Ringing Eight-Hour Call, Practical Suggestions by President Gompers," *AFL Corr.;* Gompers to the officers and delegates of the General Assembly of the K. of L., Nov. 9, 1889, *GLB.*

27. George Gunton, *The Economic and Social Importance of the Eight-Hour Movement*, 1889.

28. Gompers to Victor Delahaye, May 31, 1893; *GLB; American Federationist*, vol. I, May, 1894, p. 52.

29. Gompers to James H. Perry, Jan. 22, 1889; Gompers to John O'Brien, Feb. 7, 1889, *GLB.*

30. Gompers to P. J. McGuire, March 20, 1890; Gompers letter dated May 8, 1890; Gompers to the Toilers of America, April 28, 1890, *GLB.*

31. *See* Karl Oberman, "Local No. 1, The Pioneer of the Bakers Union Movement of the United States of America," *100 Years of Progress, Anniversary Journal, Local 1, April, 1950*, p. 20.

32. Preface to the 4th German edition of *The Communist Manifesto*, dated May 1, 1890, in *The Communist Manifesto*

of *K. Marx and F. Engels*, New York, 1930, p. 268.

33. Gompers to August Keufer, May 9, 1890, *GLB.*

34. Chicago *Tribune*, May 2, 1890.

35. New York *Tribune*, New York *World*, New York *Sun*, May 2, 1890.

36. Gompers to the editor of *Labor Tribune*, July 26, 1890, *GLB;* Sidney Fine, "The Eight Hour Day Movement in the United States, 1888-1891," *Mississippi Valley Historical Review*, vol. XL, Dec., 1953, p. 455.

37. Gompers to Emil Applehagen, Sept. 18, 1890; Gompers to August Keufer, May 9, 1890, *GLB.*

38. E. H. Cherry to Gompers, Owosso, Michigan, June 14, 1890, *AFL Corr.*

39. Eleanor Marx Aveling and W. Thorne to Gompers, Jan. 25, 1891, *AFL Corr.;* Gompers to Eleanor Marx Aveling and W. Thorne, Feb. 19, 1891, *GLB.*

40. Gompers to the delegates to the International Labor Congress, August 4, 1891, *GLB.*

41. Gompers to F. D. Hornlin, May 6, 1890, *GLB;* A. B. Schofield to Gompers (1891), *AFL Corr.*

42. Letters of Gompers to W. H. Davis, Feb. 19, 1887; to Albert C. Stevens, Nov. 1, 1889; to F. D. Hornlin, May 6, 1890; to A. D. Bare, Aug. 22, 1890; to Geo. Iden, July 15, 1892; to Albert C. Stevens, Nov. 1, 1889; to Frank M. Nolton, Nov. 10, 1893, *GLB.*

43. Gompers, *Seventy Years of Life and Labor*, vol. I, pp. 317-22; New York *Leader*, July 25, 1887.

44. *Cf.* Letters to Gompers from V. E. St. Cloud, General Organizer, Savannah, Georgia, Nov. 1, 1890; C. J. Duke, General Organizer, Fort Deposit, Maryland, May 9, 1891; F. J. Weber, General Organizer, Milwaukee, Wisconsin, Dec. 23, 1892, *AFL Corr.*

45. McNeill, *op. cit.*, pp. 585-95; Gompers to George W. Perkins, Feb. 8, 1908, *GLB.*

46. *Proceedings*, A.F. of L. Convention, 1888, pp. 8-15.

47. P. J. McGuire to Bro. McAleer, June 18, 1894; H. M. Ives to Gompers, Topeka, Kansas, March 19, 1893; W. W. Exam to August McCraith, San Antonio, Texas, May 21, 1895, *AFL Corr.*

48. John C. Knight to Gompers, Mar. 24, 1893, *AFL Corr.*

CHAPTER XIII

1. Bulletin of U.S. Census, April 30, 1895, reprinted in *American Federationist*, vol. II, July, 1895, pp. 89-90.
2. Eva McDonald Valesh, "Woman and Labor," *ibid.*, vol. II, Feb., 1896, p. 222.
3. *Proceedings*, A.F. of L. Convention, 1888, p. 12; Gompers to Jos. H. Leininger, Jan. 19, 1891, *GLB*.
4. Gladys Boone, *The Women's Trade Union League in Great Britain and the United States of America*, New York 1942, p. 58; Mary Meenin to Chris Evans, June 20, 1892, *AFL Corr.*
5. Lena Ardner to Chris Evans, March 23, 1892, *AFL Corr.*
6. Mrs. Thomas J. Morgan to Gompers, Aug. 20, 1891, *AFL Corr.*
7. *Ibid.*; Chicago *Tribune*, Feb. 21, March 9, 1892.
8. Mrs. Thomas J. Morgan to Gompers, Feb., Mar. 9, 10, 1892, *AFL Corr.*
9. Chicago *Tribune*, Chicago *Herald*, Feb. 21, 25, 1892; Printed Circular issued by the Illinois Woman's Alliance, Mar. 1893, copy in *AFL Corr.*
10. Mrs. T. J. Morgan to Gompers, Sunday 6, 1891, Nov. 27, 1891, April 7, 1892, *AFL Corr.*
11. Mrs. T. J. Morgan to Gompers, April 7, 1892, *AFL Corr.*
12. *The Northern Budget* (Troy), Jan. 11, Feb. 1, 1891.
13. *The Northern Budget*, Feb. 1, 1891; Troy *Daily Times*, Jan. 7, 15, 29, 1891.
14. *The Northern Budget*, Jan. 11, Feb. 1, 1891.
15. Letters to Gompers from H. J. Ogden, Feb. 1, 1891; Mary S. Evaline, Feb. 5, 1891; James P. Hooley, Oct. 4, 1891; Dora Sullivan, Oct. 19, 1891, *AFL Corr.*
16. Joan J. May to Gompers, Dec. 22, 1892, *AFL Corr.*
17. Ida Van Etten to Gompers, Feb. 2, June 18, 1891, Feb. 2, 1892; Eva McDonald-Valesh to Gompers, Dec. 1, 1891, Sept. 11, 1893, *AFL Corr.*
18. Mary E. Kenney to Gompers, May 18, June 31, July 6, Sept. 10, 15, 1892, *AFL Corr.*
19. Samuel Gompers to A.F. of L. Executive Council, Sept. 30, 1892; John B. Lennon to Gompers, Oct. 1, 1892; P. J. McGuire to Gompers, Oct. 3, 1892, *AFL Corr.*

20. John F. O'Sullivan to Gompers, Boston, Dec. 26, 1893, *AFL Corr.*; Gompers to E. F. Pitt, Dec. 29, 1893, *GLB*.
21. "Minutes of the Meeting of the A.F. of L. Executive Council, N.Y.C., Jan. 13, 1894," *AFL Corr.*; *Proceedings*, A.F. of L. Convention, 1898, p. 77.
22. Gompers to Miss Lena Ardener, Nov. 14, 1892, *GLB*.
23. *Proceedings*, A.F. of L. Convention, 1890, pp. 31, 54-56.
24. *Proceedings*, A.F. of L. Convention, 1891, p. 12; Gompers to T. N. Talbot, April 15, 1890; Harry E. Easton, Nat'nl Assoc. of Machinists, to Gompers, April 26, 1891, *AFL Corr.*; Gompers to delegates at convention of Int'l Machinists' Union, May 7, 1892; Gompers to Martin Fox, May 11, 1892, *GLB*.
25. Lee Johns to John McBride, Sept. 27, 1895, *AFL Corr.*
26. *Cf.* Letters to Gompers from Josiah B. Dyer, Nov. 17, 1890; A. S. Leitch, July 15, 1891; Charles Overgard, March 23, 1892; E. M. McGruder, March 20, 1893; R. L. Culdley, March 5, 1893, *AFL Corr.*
27. Letters by Gompers to Frank L. Rist, April 30, 1890; R. T. Coles, April 28, 1891; A. D. Bauer, June 13, 1892; E. M. McGruder, April 3, 1893; Louis F. Klinger, July 18, 1891, Ed. J. Donegan, Dec. 9, 1892, *GLB*.
28. Gompers to James H. White, Sept. 14, 1889; Gompers to H. M. Ives, Nov. 10, 1892, *GLB*.
29. Gompers to Charles E. Archer, June 1, 1894, *GLB*.
30. Charles Overgard, Sec'y Union No. 5618, Temple, Texas, to Gompers, April 7, May 4, 1892; C. C. Tabor to Gompers, Temple, Texas, April 24, 1892, *AFL Corr.*
31. A. S. Leitch to Gompers, June 18, 30, 1891; Geo. L. Norton to Gompers, July 10, 1891; Geo. L. Norton to Chris Evans, Oct. 23, 1891; Geo. L. Norton to Gompers, April 28, 1892, *AFL Corr.*
32. A. S. Leitch to Gompers, June 18, 30, 1891, *AFL Corr.*
33. St. Louis *Globe-Democrat*, April 1, 1892; Cleveland *Gazette*, April 9, 1892.
34. St. Louis *Globe-Democrat*, April 1-2, 5, 1892.
35. Geo. L. Norton to Gompers, April 28, June 19, 1892, *AFL Corr.*; St. Louis *Globe-Democrat*, April 5-8, 1892.

36. Gompers to Geo. L. Norton, April 13, 1892, *GLB;* Charles Overgard to Gompers, Temple, Texas, April 7, 1892, *AFL Corr.*
37. Gompers to Geo. L. Norton, May 3, 1892, *GLB.*
38. Gompers to Geo. L. Norton, June 3, 1892, *GLB.*
39. John M. Callahan to Gompers, May 15, June 12, 1892, *AFL Corr.*
40. John M. Callahan to Gompers, Aug. 3, 1892, *AFL Corr.*
41. Roger W. Shugg, "The New Orleans General Strike of 1892," *Louisiana Historical Quarterly,* vol. XXI, April, 1938, pp. 547, 553.
42. New Orleans *Times-Democrat,* Oct. 23-24, 1892.
43. *Ibid.,* Oct. 28, 1892.
44. New Orleans *Times-Democrat,* Oct. 28, 29, Nov. 1, 1892.
45. *Ibid.,* Nov. 1-4, 1892.
46. New Orleans *Times-Democrat,* Nov. 4, 1892.
47. New Orleans *Daily Picayune,* Nov. 10, 12, 1892.
48. New Orleans *Times-Democrat,* Nov. 5, 8-10, 1892; Shugg, *op cit.,* p. 556; John M. Callahan to Gompers, Nov. 7, 1892, *AFL Corr.*
49. New Orleans *Times-Democrat,* Nov. 11, 1892; B. Sherer to Gompers, Nov. 8, 1892, *AFL Corr.*
50. New Orleans *Times-Democrat,* Nov. 4-11, 14, 1892; B. Sherer to Gompers, Nov. 13, 1892, *AFL Corr.*
51. New Orleans *Times-Democrat,* Nov. 11, 1892; Gompers to J. W. Hammond, Nov. 30, 1892; Gompers to V. Sher, Nov. 21, 1892, *GLB.*
52. R. P. Fleming to Gompers, Nov. 16, 1892, *AFL Corr.;* Gompers to John M. Callahan, Nov. 21, 1892, *GLB.*
53. *See* printed circular issued by the A.F. of L. national office, Dec. 12, 1892, *AFL Corr.*
54. Gompers to R. T. Coles, April 28, 1891, *GLB.*
55. Arthur Mann, "Gompers and the Irony of Racism," *The Antioch Review,* Summer, 1953, pp. 207-09.
56. Gompers to A.F. of L. Executive Council, March 26, 1894; Gompers to Adlai E. Stevenson, April 4, 1894, *GLB.*
57. Letters to Gompers from J. Morgan, Aug. 5, 1891; E. J. Denney, July 29, 1891; Thos. O'Dea, Jan. 4, 1892; John McBride, March 17, 1893; John F. O'Sullivan, July 29, 1893, *AFL Corr.*

58. Tacoma (Washington) *News,* June 23, 1893.
59. *Cf.* Thos. O'Dea to Gompers, Jan. 4, 1892; John F. O'Sullivan to Gompers, July 29, 1893; P. J. McGuire to Chris Evans, April 4, 1891, *AFL Corr.*
60. Marx and Engels, *Letters to Americans, 1848-1895,* p. 242.

CHAPTER XIV

1. Jesse S. Robinson, *The Amalgamated Association of Iron, Steel and Tin Workers,* Baltimore, 1920, pp. 17-21; John A. Fitch, *The Steel Workers,* New York, 1911 p. 89.
2. J. Bernard Hogg, "The Homestead Strike of 1892," unpublished Ph.D. thesis, University of Chicago, Department of History, 1943, pp. 32-34.
3. James H. Bridge, *The Inside Story of the Carnegie Steel Company: A Romance of Millions,* New York, 1903, pp. 203-04; George Harvey, *Henry Clay Frick—The Man,* New York, 1928, pp. 164-65.
4. *Proceedings of the Annual Convention of the National Lodge, Amalgamated Association of Iron and Steel Workers,* 1893, vol. XIII, pp. 4250-54.
5. *National Labor Tribune,* June 11, 1892.
6. U.S. Congress, House of Representatives. Committee on the Judiciary. *Employment of Pinkerton Detectives.* House Report 2447, 52d Congress, 2d Session, Washington, 1893, pp. 32-35, 88-89.
7. New York *Herald,* July 3-4, 1892.
8. Pittsburgh *Commercial Gazette,* July 6, 1892.
9. Wm. A. Carney to Gompers, June 29, 1892, telegram; William Weihe to Gompers, July 16, 1892, *AFL Corr.;* Pittsburgh *Commercial Gazette,* July 18, 23, 1892.
10. U.S. Congress, Senate, *Select Committee for Investigation in Relation to the Employment for Private Purposes of Armed Bodies of Men, or Detectives, in Connection with Differences between Workmen and Employers.* Senate Document 1820, 52d Con., 1st Sess., Washington, 1893, pp. 161-62.
11. *Senate Report 1280,* pp. 141-43.
12. Hogg, *op. cit.,* p. 90.
13. *See* New York *Tribune,* July 8, 1892.
14. Letters to Gompers from John M. Callaghan, July 9, 1892; N. Morse, July 9, 1892, *AFL Corr.*

15. Gompers to Executive Council, A.F. of L., July 7, 1892; Gompers to P. J. McGuire, July 8, 1892, *GLB;* James J. Daly, chairman of the Central Labor Union, New York City, to Gompers, July 11, 1892; newspaper clipping attached to L. S. Mathews to Gompers, July 21, 1892; Moses Oppenheimer to Gompers, July 8, 1892, *AFL Corr.*

16. William Weihe to Gompers, July 7, 21, 1892, telegrams, *AFL Corr.*

17. Yellen, *op. cit.,* p. 88.

18. Hugh O'Donnell to Gompers, July 18, 1892, telegram, *AFL Corr.*

19. Harvey, *op. cit.,* pp. 133-34.

20. William Weihe to Gompers, July 14, 1892, *AFL Corr.;* Pittsburgh *Press,* July 10, 11, 1892.

21. Report of Major General Snowden, *Pennsylvania Official Documents,* vol. V, 1892, pp. 75-76.

22. New York *Herald,* July 18, 1892; Wm. Weihe to Gompers, July 24, 1892, *AFL Corr.*

23. Columbus (Ohio) *State Journal,* July 24, 1892.

24. Hogg, *op. cit.,* p. 120.

25. Stephen Madden to Chris Evans, Aug. 26, Sept. 2, 1892, *AFL Corr.*

26. *National Labor Tribune,* Sept. 10, 24, 1892.

27. Hogg, *op. cit.,* p. 126.

28. *Senate Report 1280,* pp. xv-xix.

29. Wm. Weihe to Gompers, Oct. 5, 1892, *AFL Corr.*

30. Pittsburgh *Dispatch,* Oct. 11, 1892.

31. Thos. J. Crawford to Gompers, Oct. 13, 1892, *AFL Corr.*

32. M. M. Garland and J. C. Kilgallon to Gompers, Nov. 5, 1892, *AFL Corr.*

33. Edward Bemis, "The Homestead Strike," *Journal of Political Economy,* 1893-94, pp. 383-85; Hogg, *op. cit.,* pp. 149-50.

34. Gompers to M. M. Garland, Nov. 8, 1892, *GLB;* M. M. Garland to Gompers, Nov. 12, 1892, *AFL Corr.*

35. Printed Circular, headed "Homestead Day," New York, November 19, 1892, *AFL Corr.*

36. There are hundreds of such letters in *AFL Corr.*

37. Hogg, *op. cit.,* p. 134.

38. *Ibid.,* pp. 134-35.

39. *National Labor Tribune,* Aug. 17, 1893.

40. J. C. Kilgallon to Chris Evans, Oct. 26, 1893, Jan. 31, 1894; J. C. Kilgallon to August McCraith, Feb. 2, 1895, Jan. 28, 1896, *AFL Corr.*

41. Harvey, *op. cit.,* p. 176.

42. Robinson, *op. cit.,* pp. 25ff.

CHAPTER XV

1. I am indebted to Mr. Peter Seeger for furnishing me with the text of the song.

2. Blake McKelvey, "The Prison Labor Problem: 1875-1900," *Journal of the American Institute of Criminal Law and Criminology,* vol. XXV, 1937, pp. 254-70.

3. Walter Wilson, "Historic Coal Creek Rebellion Brought an End to Convict Miners in Tennessee," *United Mine Workers Journal,* November 1, 1938, p. 10; *New York Times,* July 22, 1891.

4. James Dombrowski, "The Story of the Coal Creek Rebellion," unpublished paper, 1943, copy in possession of Mr. Peter Seeger, Beacon, New York.

5. Memphis *Ledger,* July 6-7, 1891.

6. Memphis *Ledger,* July 6-7, 1891.

7. Chattanooga *Times,* July 8, 1891; Memphis *Ledger,* July 7-8, 1891.

8. Memphis *Ledger,* July 11, 1891.

9. Wilson, *op. cit.,* p. 11.

10. Knoxville *Ledger,* July 11-12, 1891; Wilson, *op. cit.,* p. 11.

11. Knoxville *Ledger,* July 11-12, 1891.

12. Dombrowski, *op. cit.,* p. 100.

13. *Ibid.,* pp. 100-02; Louisville *Times,* July 13, 1891; Nashville *Banner,* July 13, 1891.

14. Memphis *Ledger,* July 21-22, July 26, 1891; Chattanooga *Times,* July 26, 1891.

15. Chattanooga *Times,* Sept. 23, Oct. 14, 1891.

16. Nashville *Banner,* Oct. 17, 19, 1891.

17. Chattanooga *Times,* Oct. 29, 1891.

18. Memphis *Ledger,* Nov. 1-2, 1891; Chattanooga *Times,* Nov. 1-2, 1891.

19. Chattanooga *Times,* Nov. 3, 1891; Nashville *Banner,* Nov. 3, 1891.

20. Dombrowski, *op. cit.,* pp. 121-22.

21. *Ibid.,* pp. 120, 121-23.

22. Chattanooga *Times,* July 16, 1892; *United Mine Workers' Journal,* August, 1892, p. 89.

23. Dombrowski, *op. cit.,* pp. 123-24.

24. *Ibid.,* pp. 124-25; Chattanooga *Times,* Aug. 12-13, 1892.

25. Nashville *Banner,* Aug. 14-15, 1892.

26. Nashville *American,* Aug. 16, 1892.

27. Chattanooga *Times,* Aug. 15, 1892.

28. *Ibid.*, Aug. 17-18, 1892; Nashville *Banner*, Aug. 17-18, 1892.
29. Chattanooga *Times*, Aug. 20-21, 1892; Wilson, *op. cit.*, pp. 12-13.
30. Nashville *Banner*, Aug. 20-21, 1892; Chattanooga *Times*, Aug. 21-22, 1892; Dombrowski, *op. cit.*, pp. 138-39.
31. Nashville *Banner*, Aug. 23-30, 1892; Chattanooga *Times*, Aug. 23-30, 1892; *United Mine Workers' Journal*, Sept., 1892, p. 64.
32. Nashville *Banner*, Aug. 21, 1892.
33. Wilson, *op. cit.*, p. 13.
34. Dombrowski, *op. cit.*, pp. 142-43.
35. Chattanooga *Times*, April 20-22, 1893.
36. Blake McKelvey, "The Prison Labor Problem, 1875-1900," *Journal of the American Institute of Criminal Law and Criminology*, vol. XV, 1934, p. 265.
37. William D. Haywood, *Bill Haywood's Book—The Autobiography of William D. Haywood*, New York, 1929, p. 83. See also Albert Williams, "The Miner and his Perils," *Chattauquan*, vol. XVIII, 1893, pp. 429-32.
38. Frank Aley, "Only a Man in Overalls," *Miners' Magazine*, July, 1900; Peter Paulson, "The Western Federation of Miners, 1890-1910," unpublished M.A. thesis, Columbia University, 1951, p. 41.
39. Vernon H. Jensen, *Heritage of Conflict: Labor Relations in the Nonferrous Metals Industry up to 1930*, Ithaca, New York, 1950, pp. 10-24.
40. Robert Wayne Smith, "The Idaho Antecedants of the Western Federation of Miners: Labor organization and industrial conflict in the Couer D'Alene Mining District of Colorado," unpublished Ph.D. thesis, University of California, 1937, pp. 31-43.
41. Jensen, *op. cit.*, p. 27; Smith, *op. cit.*, pp. 53-54.
42. *Appleton's Annual Cyclopedia*, 1892, p. 338.
43. T. A. Rickard, *A History of American Mining*, New York, 1932, pp. 327-28.
44. Smith, *op. cit.*, pp. 72-75.
45. *Appleton's Annual Cyclopedia*, 1892, pp. 338-39.
46. Job Harriman, *The Class War in Idaho*, New York, 1900, p. 6.
47. Smith, *op. cit.*, pp. 110-12, 128-29.
48. *Appleton's Annual Cyclopedia*, 1892, pp. 338-39.
49. Smith, *op. cit.*, pp. 139.
50. *Ibid.*, pp. 156-78.

51. John O'Brien to Gompers, Aug. 31, 1892, *AFL Corr.*
52. Smith, *op. cit.*, pp. 190-96; Gompers to P. J. McArthur, Feb. 15, 1893; Gompers to Mary Fitch, Feb. 23, 1893, *GLB;* P. J. McArthur to Gompers, Feb. 19, 1893, *AFL Corr.*
53. Harriman, *op. cit.*, pp. 9-10.
54. P. J. McArthur to Gompers, Feb. 19, 1893, *AFL Corr.*
55. Peter Breen to Gompers, March 23, 1893, *AFL Corr.*
56. *Miners' Magazine*, June, 1901, p. 21.
57. *Miners' Magazine*, June, 1901, pp. 21-22; Smith, *op. cit.*, pp. 233-34.
58. Western Federation of Miners, *Convention Proceedings*, 1893, pp. 4-6, 20.

CHAPTER XVI

1. F. S. Philbrick, *The Mercantile Conditions of the Crisis of 1893*, Lincoln, Nebraska, 1894-1902, University Studies of the University of Nebraska, vol. II, p. 106.
2. Albert C. Stevens, editor of *Bradstreets'*, to Gompers, Dec. 20, 1893, *AFL Corr.; Proceedings*, A.F. of L. Convention, 1893, p. 19.
3. J. J. McCook, "A Tramp Census and Its Revelations," *Forum*, vol. XV, Aug., 1893, pp. 735-66.
4. Albert Shaw, "Relief for the Unemployed in American Cities," *Review of Reviews*, vol. IX, January, 1894, pp. 29-33; Donald L. McMurry, *Coxey's Army: A Study of the Industrial Army Movement of 1894*, Boston, 1929, p. 10; Leah Hannah Feder, *Unemployment Relief in Periods of Depression: A Study of Measures Adopted in Certain American Cities, 1857 through 1922*, New York, 1936, pp. 46-47.
5. Feder, *op. cit.*, pp. 152-53.
6. New York *World*, Aug. 13, 1893; "Printed Circular," signed, "Organized Labor Conference for the Relief of the Unemployed," *AFL Corr.*
7. New York *World*, Aug. 20, 1893.
8. *Ibid.*, Aug. 22, 1893.
9. Samuel Lesem to Gompers, Aug. 24, 1893, telegram, *AFL Corr.*
10. George E. McNeill to Gompers, Oct. 18, 1893, *AFL Corr.*
11. See S. J. Kent to Gompers, March 5, 1894, Lincoln, Nebraska, *AFL Corr.*
12. George E. McNeill to Gompers, Oct. 18, 1893, *AFL Corr.*

13. *Journal of the Knights of Labor*, Aug. 24, 1893; Feder, *op. cit.*, p. 95.
14. *American Federation of Labor; History, Encyclopedia, Reference Book*, Washington, 1919, p. 27; Shaw, *op. cit.*, pp. 29-33; Feder, *op. cit.*, pp. 46-47, 94.
15. *Emergency Relief in Cincinnati, 1893-1894*, Cincinnati, 1894, p. 13.
16. *American Federationist*, vol. I, March, 1894, p. 13.
17. P. J. Maas, "The Situation To-Day," *ibid.*, vol. II, May, 1895, pp. 42-43.
18. New York *World*, Feb. 1, 1894.
19. *Proceedings*, A.F. of L. Convention, 1893, pp. 11, 37.
20. *Arena*, vol. IX, May, 1894, pp. 822-26.
21. McMurry, *op. cit.*, pp. 20-33, 128-29.
22. *American Federationist*, vol. I, May, 1894, p. 53; Carl Browne to Gompers, March 14, 1894; Lewis C. Fry to Gompers, March 16, 1894, *AFL Corr*; Grace Heilman Stimson, *Rise of the Labor Movement in Los Angeles*, Berkeley, Calif., 1955, pp. 155-57.
23. Maurice S. Paprin, "American Labor and the Reform Movement," unpublished M.A. thesis, University of Wisconsin, 1941, p. 167; J. T. Joyce, general organizer, A.F. of L., Richmond, Indiana, to Gompers, May 15, 1894, attaching printed copy of song, *AFL Corr.*
24. Boston *Post*, April 8, 1894.
25. Boston *Post*, April 8, 1894; McMurry, *op. cit.*, pp. 110-16, 167.
26. *Ibid.*, p. 117.
27. Philadelphia *Times*, May 7, 1894; *American Federationist*, vol. I, June, 1894, p. 76.
28. *American Federationist*, vol. I, pp. 3, 52, 119, 204, 263-64; vol. II, pp. 61, 124.
29. Printed Circular, Tonawanda Lumber Shovers' Union, Tonawanda, N. Y., June 20, 1893; W. J. Smith to Gompers, Sept. 17, 1894, *AFL Corr.*
30. Wm. Hunter, etc. to General Council, A.F. of L.; Gompers to Executive Council, A.F. of L., Oct. 27, 1893; Gompers to Wm. J. Smith, Sept. 28, 1894, *AFL Corr.*
31. Benjamin McKie Rastall, "The Labor History of the Cripple Creek District," *Bulletin of the University of Wisconsin, No. 198*, Madison, 1908, pp. 15-58; Jensen, *op. cit.*, pp. 38-53.
32. *Journal of the Senate of the Thirty-Ninth General Assembly of the State of Illinois*, Springfield, Illinois, 1896, pp. 28-29.
33. John McBride to Chris Evans, April 16, 1894; John McBride to Gompers, April 21, 1894, telegram, *AFL Corr.*
34. "Report of President McBride of the United Mine Workers," *American Federationist*, vol. II, 1895, pp. 8-10; ibid., vol. I, pp. 53, 59, 77, 83, 101, 105, 108, 109, 115, 231, 259; vol. II, pp. 69, 107.
35. Joseph R. Buchanan to Gompers, April 6, 18, 23, 24, 1894; G. W. Perkins to Gompers, April 5, 1894; "Call for a Labor Conference," New York, March 31, 1894, *AFL Corr.*
36. *Official Report of Conference of Labor Representatives Held at Philadelphia, April 28-29, 1894*, pp. 2-3.
37. *Official Report . . .*, pp. 2-7; Joe (Buchanan) to Gompers, June 23, 1894, *AFL Corr.*
38. *Railway Times*, Jan. 1, 1894.

CHAPTER XVII

1. William W. Bennett, "The Railroad Enginemen Brotherhoods and Collective Bargaining," unpublished Ph.D. thesis, Princeton University, 1932, p. A-52; *Railway Times*, Jan. 1, 15, 1894; *Chicago Herald, Chicago Tribune*, Feb. 7, 1895; Fred H. Anthony to Gompers, Feb. 25, 1895, *AFL Corr.*
2. *Fifth Annual Report of the Commissioner of Labor*, 1899, Railroad Labor, 51st Cong., 1st Sess., H. R. Exec. Doc. No. 336, Washington, 1890, pp. 131, 145.
3. *Locomotive Firemen's Magazine*, Jan. 1894, p. 52.
4. Ray Ginger, *The Bending Cross: A Biography of Eugene V. Debs*, New Brunswick, N. J., 1949, pp. 46-47; Donald L. McMurry, "Federation of Railroad Brotherhoods, 1889-1894," *Industrial and Labor Relations Review*, vol. VII, October, 1953, pp. 75-76.
5. *Locomotive Firemen's Magazine*, Dec., 1886, p. 712; Feb., 1887, pp. 71-72; McMurry, *op. cit.*, pp. 74-75.
6. Ginger, *op. cit.*, p. 47, 56; *John Swinton's Paper*, Jan. 10, 1886.
7. Ginger, *op. cit.*, pp. 56-58; *Firemen's Magazine*, April, 1888, pp. 246-48.
8. Thos. Neasham to Powderly, Feb. 28, 1888, *PP.*
9. McMurry, *op. cit.*, p. 77.
10. *Ibid.*, pp. 77, 79.

11. The Constitution of the Supreme Council is in the *Proceedings of the First and Second Annual Sessions and Intervening Special Sessions of the Supreme Council of the United Orders of Railway Employees: First Annual Session, Chicago, Illinois, June 3, 4, 5, and 6, 1889. Galensburg, Ill.,* 1890, pp. 1-12. A copy of this bound volume, probably the only one in existence, is in the Meyer London Library, Rand School of Social Science, New York City.

12. *Ibid.,* "Proceedings, Second Session of the Supreme Council . . .," June 16 and 17, 1890," p. 37.

13. *Ibid.,* pp. 14-32, 47.

14. McMurry, *op. cit.,* p. 81.

15. "Proceedings of the Supreme Council . . . Held at Houston, Texas, October 9, 1890," in *op. cit.*

16. "Proceedings of the Fourth Annual Session of the Supreme Council United Orders of Railway Employees, Chicago, Ill., June 20, 1892," in *op. cit.*

17. Buffalo *Express,* Aug. 13, 15-19, 1892.

18. *Ibid.,* Aug. 24, 1892.

19. *Ibid.,* Aug. 25, 1892.

20. *Locomotive Firemen's Magazine,* Dec., 1892; *Railway Trainmen's Journal,* vol. IX, Sept., 1892, p. 725; McMurry, *op. cit.,* pp. 87-88.

21. Buffalo, *Express,* Aug. 25, 1892.

22. G. W. Howard to Gompers, Jan. 21, Sept. 5, 1892, *AFL Corr.*

23. *Proceedings,* Brotherhood of Locomotive Firemen Convention, 1892, pp. 370-73.

24. Chicago *Times,* June 13, 1894.

25. Ginger, *op. cit.,* pp. 92-93; United States Strike Commission Report, *Senate Executive Document No. 7,* 53rd Congress, 3rd Session, Washington, 1895, p. xxiv.

26. Chicago *Times,* June 13, 1894; American Railway Union, *Proceedings of the First Quadrennial Convention . . .,* Chicago, 1894, p. 4.

27. *Machinists' Journal,* vol. V, June, 1893, p. 187.

28. Chicago *Intelligencer,* Jan. 7, 1894.

29. Chicago *Intelligencer,* Jan. 7, 1894. *See also* Eugene V. Debs to T. V. Powderly, Jan. 4, 1894, *PP.*

30. Chicago *Intelligencer,* Jan. 7, 1894; *Railway Times,* Jan. 1, 15, 1894.

31. *Railway Times,* May 1, 15, June 1, 1894; Ginger, *op. cit.,* pp. 102-07; Almont Lindsey, *The Pullman Strike,* Chicago, 1942, p. 113.

32. Salt Lake *Tribune,* reprinted in *Railway Times,* June 1, 1894.

33. *Railway Times,* Jan. 1, 15, 1894; United States Strike Commission, *Report on the Chicago Strike of June-July, 1894,* p. 209.

34. Columbus *Dispatch* reprinted in *Railway Times,* Jan. 1, 1894.

35. Chicago *Times,* June 13, 1894.

36. *Railway Times,* Jan. 1, 15, 1894.

37. T. Odell, "On the Necessity for Similar Associations to the Chicago General Managers' Association," *Record of Proceedings of Gen'l Managers' Association of Chicago, 1892-1893,* bound volume (vol. II) of typed manuscript, John Crerar Library, Chicago, No. 12, August 17, 1893, pp. 9-13. Marked "Confidential." (Hereafter cited as *JCL*.)

38. *Rec. of Proc. Gen. Man. Assoc., 1892-1893,* No. 12, p. 4, *JCL.*

39. *Rec. of Proc. Gen. Man. Asssoc., 1892-1893,* No. 8, pp. 12, 13, No. 13, pp. 4, 5, *JCL;* U.S. Strike Commission, *Report on the Chicago Strike . . .,* pp. xxix-xxx, 223.

40. *Rec. of Proc. Gen. Man. Assoc., 1892-1893,* No. 14, pp. 3-12, *JCL.*

41. U.S. Strike Commission, *Report on the Chicago Strike . . .,* pp. xxix-xxx, 223; Chicago *Herald,* Feb. 6, 1895; U.S. Industrial Commission, *Report,* Washington, 1900, IV, pp. 509-10.

CHAPTER XVIII

1. Almont Lindsey, *The Pullman Strike,* pp. 38*ff.*

2. Foster Rhea Dulles, *Labor in America,* New York, 1949, p. 172.

3. Lindsey, *op. cit.,* p. 103.

4. *Ibid.,* pp. 103-05, 122-23.

5. *Ibid.,* pp. 128-31.

6. U.S. Strike Commission, *Report on the Chicago Strike of June-July, 1894,* Washington, 1895, pp. xxxix, xliv; U.S. v. Debs et al. *Federal Reporter,* vol. LXIV, p. 763.

7. New York *Tribune,* July 3, 1894.

8. Debs to O. L. Vincent of Clinton, Iowa, July 4, 1894, printed in *U.S. vs Debs,* Proceedings in Information for Attachment for Contempt, U.S. Circuit Court, Northern District of Illinois, n.p., n.d., p. 91. (Copy in Baker Library, Harvard University); Chicago *Tribune,* Jan. 31, 1895.

9. Stuart Daggett, *Chapters on the History of the Southern Pacific*, New York, 1922, pp. 144-46; Grace H. Stimson, *Rise of the Labor Movement in Los Angeles*, pp. 166-67.

10. Wm. Boas to Gompers, July 4, 1894, *AFL Corr.*

11. *New York Times*, July 9, 1894.

12. *Ibid; Railway Times*, July 15, 1894.

13. Allan Nevins, *Grover Cleveland*, New York, 1931, p. 616.

14. Lindsey, *op cit.*, p. 154; Clarence Darrow, *The Story of My Life*, New York, 1932, p. 61; *Proceedings of the General Managers' Association of Chicago*, June 25, 1894 to July 14, 1894, bound volume in *JCL*, p. 113.

15. Edward Berman, *Labor and the Sherman Act*, New York, 1930, p. 23.

16. Felix Frankfurter and Nathan Greene, *The Labor Injunction*, New York, 1930, pp. 20-24.

17. New York *World*, July 2, 1894.

18. Ginger, *op. cit.*, p. 132.

19. United States Strike Commission, *Report . . .*, p. xx.

20. Harry Barnard, *Eagle Forgotten: The Life of John Peter Altgeld*, New York, 1938, pp. 276, 295-305.

21. Lindsey, *op. cit.*, pp. 191-93.

22. Lindsey, *op. cit.*, pp. 310-11; New York *Tribune*, July 3, 7, 9, 1894; New York *Herald*, July 8, 9, 1894; Chicago *Evening Post*, July 7, 10, 1894; Boston *Commercial Bulletin*, July 7, 1894.

23. Joseph Dorfman, *Thorstein Veblen and His America*, New York, 1934, pp. 108-12; *Christian Intelligencer*, July 12, 1894.

24. Yellen, *op cit.*, p. 122.

25. Chicago *Tribune*, Jan. 31, 1895.

26. Lindsey, *op. cit.*, pp. 278-79.

27. U.S. Strike Commission, *Report . . .*, pp. 143-44, 161.

28. Lindsey, *op. cit.*, p. 222-24.

29. *Ibid.*, p. 225.

30. Gompers to P. J. McGuire, July 9, 1894; Gompers to P. M. Arthur, July 9, 1894, *GLB*; Gompers to John B. Lennon, July 10, 1894, *AFL Corr.*

31. Gompers to John B. Lennon, July 10, 1894; P. J. McGuire to Chris Evans, July 10, 1894, telegram, *AFL Corr.*

32. Philadelphia *Record*, March 28, 1900. P. J. McGuire to Gompers, April 3, 1900, *AFL Corr.*

33. "Proceedings of Briggs Conference," *American Federationist*, vol. I, August, 1894, pp. 131-33.

34. *Cf.* Detroit *Free Press*, Oct. 18, 1896; W. W. McArthur to Gompers, July 30, 1894, *AFL Corr.*

35. Gompers, *op. cit.*, vol. I, pp. 404-06.

36. P. J. McGuire to Friend Sam (Gompers), June 14, 1894, *AFL Corr.*

37. F. W. Arnold to Chris Evans, July 28, 1894; F. P. Sargent and F. W. Arnold to Chris Evans, Aug. 8, 1894, *AFL Corr.*

38. Lindsey, *op. cit.*, pp. 231-33, 282.

39. *In re Debs*, 15 Sup. Ct., 900, 912.

40. U.S. Strike Commission, *Report . . .*, pp. 150-51.

41. *Ibid.*, vol. IV, pp. 503-25; Chicago *Tribune*, June 27, Oct. 25, 1899.

42. "The Strike and its Lessons," *American Federationist*, vol. I, August, 1894, p. 124.

43. *Railway Times*, Aug. 1, 1895. *See also* Debs to Gompers, Aug. 30, 1894, *AFL Corr.*

44. *Proceedings, First Annual Convention Industrial Workers of the World*, Chicago, 1905, p. 162.

45. *New York Times*, July 13, 1894.

CHAPTER XIX

1. Herbert Miller, "Socialism in the United States," *American Federationist*, vol. II, August, 1895, p. 97.

2. The best account of De Leon's life before he became the S.L.P. leader is James B. Stolvey, "Daniel De Leon, A Study of Marxian Orthodoxy in the United States," unpublished Ph.D. thesis, University of Illinois, 1946, 19-34.

3. Stolvey, *op. cit.*, pp. 132-38; Daniel De Leon, *The Burning Question of Trade Unionism*, New York, 1947, p. 20.

4. Tom Mann and Ben Tillett, *The 'New Trades Unionism,' A Reply to Mr. George Shipton*, London, 1890, p. 4.

5. Lucien Sanial, *The Socialist Almanac and Treasury of Facts*, New York, 1898, p. 225.

6. Ernest Bohm to Gompers, July 13, 1890; Central Labor Federation of N. Y. to Gompers, Aug. 11, 1890, *AFL Corr.*

7. Gompers to August Keufer, May 9, 1890, *GLB;* Ernest Bohm to Gompers, Nov. 1, 1890, *AFL Corr.;* Gompers to Ernest Bohm, Nov. 7, 1890, *GLB.*

8. *The People*, May 10, 1891; Gompers to Ernest Bohm, Nov. 7, 1891, *GLB.*

9. *Proceedings*, A.F. of L. Convention, 1890, pp. 12-21.
10. *Ibid.; American Federationist*, vol. I, April, 1894, p. 30.
11. *Proceedings*, A.F. of L. Convention, 1890, pp. 12-21.
12. Gompers to Ernest Bohm, Dec. 27, 1890; Gompers to William Martin, Dec. 23, 1890; Gompers to Geo. A. Schilling, Jan. 6, 1891, *GLB*.
13. Robert Y. Ogg to Gompers, Detroit, Dec. 29, 1890; Ida M. Van Etten to Gompers (Dec., 1890), *AFL Corr.*
14. Gompers to Victor Delahaye, August 21, 1891, *GLB*.
15. Gompers to Fred Engels, Jan. 9, 1891, *GLB*.
16. *Science and Society*, vol. VII, p. 369.
17. Engels to Schluter, January 29, 1891, Marx and Engels, *Letters to Americans, 1848-1895*, pp. 233-34.
18. August Delabar to Gompers, May 11, 1891, *AFL Corr.;* Gompers to August Delabar, May 19, 1891, *GLB*.
19. *See* printed leaflets, "Central Labor Federation of New York to Organized Labor Throughout the Country," *AFL Corr.; The Union Record*, St. Louis, Dec. 26, 1891.
20. *The People*, May 10, Aug. 2, 1891, and *The People* quoted in letter of Frank K. Foster to Gompers, Jan. 26, 1893, *AFL Corr.*
21. *The People*, Dec. 24, 1893.
22. Hugo Miller to Gompers, New York, April 16, 1892, *AFL Corr.*
23. Morris C. Feinstone, "A Brief History of the United Hebrew Trades," in *Geverkshaften*, 1938, p. 18.
24. Phillip Van Patten to George A. Schilling, Hot Springs, Arkansas, July 2, 1893, *LC;* Gompers to W. C. Owen, July 10, 1893, *GLB*.
25. *Proceedings*, A.F. of L. Convention, 1893, pp. 31, 37-38.
26. New York *Herald*, Jan. 7, 1894.
27. *Ibid.;* (Wm. C.) Hollister to Gompers, Jan. 18, 1894, marked "Confidential," *AFL Corr.; The Tailor*, March, 1894.
28. New York *Herald*, Jan. 7, 1894.
29. W. MacArthur to Gompers, Dec. 28, 1893, *AFL Corr.;* Gompers to W. McArthur, Jan. 3, 1894, *GLB*.
30. Handwritten article by Tom Mann addressed to American Socialists, *AFL Corr.*
31. Edward Murry and others to Gompers, Sept. 6, 1894, *AFL Corr.*
32. Boston *Labor Leader*, Jan. 27, 1894; Cleveland *Citizen*, Dec. 30, 1893. *See also AFL Corr.*
33. P. J. McGuire to Chris Evans, Nov. 3, 1894, *AFL Corr.*
34. P. J. McGuire to Gompers, Nov. 3, 1894, *AFL Corr.*
35. P. J. McGuire to Gompers, Nov. 23, Dec. 4, 1894; Frank K. Foster to Gompers, Nov., Dec., 1894, *AFL Corr.*
36. *See Cigar Makers' Journal*, Feb., 1895, Sept., 1896.
37. *Proceedings*, A.F. of L. Convention, 1894, pp. 14-15, 31, 36-37, 38-43.
38. "Report of R. Pohle, Delegate to the National Convention of the American Federation of Labor from the International Machinists' Union," Thomas J. Morgan, *Mss.*, University of Chicago.
39. *Proceedings*, A.F. of L. Convention, 1894, pp. 41-42; P. J. McGuire to August McCraith, June 17, 1895; (Thomas J.) Morgan to James Duncan, Mar. 21, 1895, *AFL Corr.; Proceedings*, A.F. of L. Convention, 1895, pp. 41-42, 80-82.
40. *The People*, Dec. 23, 1894; (Thomas J.) Morgan to James Duncan, March 21, 1895, *AFL Corr.*
41. John McBride to Thomas J. Morgan, May 10, 1895, *AFL Corr.*
42. Thomas J. Morgan to John McBride, May 18, 1895, *AFL Corr.*
43. *American Federationist*, vol. II, March 1895, p. 17; Charles Rawbone to John McBride, March 5, 1895, *AFL Corr.*
44. P. J. McGuire to August McCraith, Oct. 31, 1895, *AFL Corr.; Proceedings*, A.F. of L. Convention, 1895, p. 96.
45. Joseph Brickell to Gompers, May 10, 1895, *AFL Corr.;* Kipnis, *op. cit.*, p. 14.
46. *Proceedings*, General Assembly, K. of L., 1893, pp. 39-40, 55-56.
47. Syracuse *Evening Herald*, June 9, 1894.
48. *Journal of the Knights of Labor*, Nov. 16, 1893; *The People*, Dec. 2, 1894.
49. James R. Sovereign to De Leon, Jan. 7, 1895; De Leon to James R. Sovereign, Daniel De Leon Correspondence, *WSHS; The People*, Sept. 29, 1895.
50. Stolvey, *op. cit.*, pp. 74-75.
51. Kipnis, *op. cit.*, pp. 15-17; *The People*, Dec. 1, 1895.
52. *The People*, April 12, 1896; *Proceedings of the Ninth Annual Convention of the Socialist Labor Party*, July 4, 1896, pp. 28-31.
53. N. I. Stone, *The Attitude of the S.L.P. Toward the Trade Unions*, New York, 1900, p. 8.

54. P. J. McGuire to August McCraith, Feb. 18, 1896; E. Kurzenknabe to Gompers, March 12, 1896; Chas. F. Bechtold to Gompers, May 23, 28, 1896, *AFL Corr.*
55. Chas. F. Bechtold to August McCraith, Feb. 18, 1896; P. J. McGuire to August McCraith, Feb. 18, 1896; Gompers to Walter McArthur, May 5, 1896, *AFL Corr.*
56. *Proceedings of the Ninth Annual Convention of the Socialist Labor Party, July 4, 1896,* pp. 25-32.
57. Kipnis, *op. cit.*, p. 86.
58. Kipnis, *op. cit.*, pp. 26-27.
59. Fred E. Martin to S.L.P. National Executive Committee, Feb. 2, 1895, Daniel De Leon Papers, *WSHS.*

CHAPTER XX

1. *Nebraska Folklore Pamphlets, No. 18,* Federal Writers Project, Lincoln, Nebraska, 1938, p. 1.
2. John D. Hicks, *The Populist Revolt, A History of the Farmers' Alliance and the People's Party,* Minneapolis, 1931, p. 115; *Proceedings,* General Assembly, K. of L., 1889, pp. 46, 53; *National Economist,* Nov. 7, 1889.
3. Hicks, *op. cit.*, pp. 156, Appendix.
4. F. L. McVey, *The Populist Movement,* New York, 1896, p. 139; *Boston Labor Leader,* May 9, 1891; *Cleveland Citizen,* June 12, 1891.
5. *National Economist,* March 5, 1892.
6. Chas. F. Bechtold to Gompers, Nov. 14, 1890, *AFL Corr.; Cleveland Citizen,* July 25, Aug. 15, Sept. 5, 26, Nov. 14, 1891; Frank Drew, "The Present Farmers' Movement," *Political Science Quarterly,* vol. VI, June, 1891, p. 301.
7. Detroit *Free Press,* June 16, 17, 1892.
8. Thomas E. Watson to Powderly, Jan. 30, March 7, April 13, May 24, 1892, *PP.*
9. *Bakers' Journal,* Oct. 3, 1891, Jan. 31, 1892; Boston *Labor Leader,* Aug. 8, 1891; Eva McDonald-Valesh, "The Strength and Weakness of the People's Movement," *Arena,* vol. V, April, 1892, p. 728; Eva McDonald-Valesh to Gompers, Aug. 2, Oct. 23, 1891, Mar. 19, 1892, *AFL Corr.*
10. Cleveland *Citizen,* July 2, Aug. 6, Sept. 3, Oct. 8, Nov. 5, 1892.
11. *Ibid.,* Jan. 9, April 23, June 18, July 9, Aug. 13, Sept. 3, Nov. 5, 1892; F. L.

McVey, *op. cit.*, p. 143; Hicks, *op. cit.*, pp. 230, 427-44; Destler, *American Radicalism,* pp. 16, 17-18, 28-30; Maude A. Gernes, "The Influence of the Labor Element in the Populist Party," unpublished thesis, University of Minnesota, June 9, 1924, copy in Minnesota Historical Society, pp. 10-13.
12. New York *Herald,* Aug. 26, 1892.
13. *The People,* April 30, May 17, 31, June 7, 21, 1891, Sept. 4, 25, 1892; George H. Knoles, "Populism and Socialism with Special Reference to the Election of 1892," *Pacific Historical Review,* vol. XII, 1943, pp. 299-300.
14. Engels to F. A. Sorge, Jan. 6, 1892, Marx and Engels, *Letters to Americans, 1848-1892,* p. 239; *The People,* June 7, 14, 21, Aug. 24, Sept. 6, 1891; F. A. Cornell to Daniel De Leon, Feb. 1, 1895; G. W. Hopping to De Leon, March 4, 1895; H. W. Young to De Leon, March 15, 1895, Daniel De Leon Correspondence, *WSHS.*
15. *The People,* Sept. 6, 1891; Stolvey, *op. cit.*, pp. 51, 53.
16. *Proceedings,* 1889 Convention, A.F. of L., pp. 14-15; *Report of T. J. Morgan to Chicago Trades and Labor Congress,* p. 9; Alonzo Crouse, E. S. Browne, D. D. Glasgow, Exec. Comm., "Farm Hands Labor Union," Bellaire, Ohio, Aug. 27, 1892, *AFL Corr.*
17. Gompers to V. P. Smith, Feb. 10, 1892; Gompers to John McBride, Feb. 6, 1893, *GLB* and *AFL Corr.*
18. H. M. Ives to Gompers, Topeka, Kansas, Feb. 18, 1892, *AFL Corr.*
19. Gompers to H. M. Ives, Feb. 23, 1892, *GLB.*
20. *North American Review,* vol. CLV, August, 1892, pp. 93-95.
21. New Orleans *Times-Democrat,* Oct. 3, 1892.
22. E. J. Moffitt to Gompers, Nov. 8, 1892; E. H. Cherry to Gompers, Sept. 25, 1892; W. R. Kolley to Gompers, Aug 8, 1892; *AFL Corr.*
23. Gompers to Chris Evans, Sept. 15, 1892; Gompers to Alonzo Crouse, Sept. 23, 1892, *AFL Corr.*
24. H. D. Lloyd to Gompers, July 20, 1892. See also H. G. Wilshire to Gompers, July 17, 1892, *AFL Corr.*
25. Hicks, *op. cit.*, p. 267.
26. Gernes, *op. cit.*, pp. 14-18.
27. Cleveland *Citizen,* Nov. 17, Dec. 17, 1892; Destler, *op. cit.*, p. 168; Knoles, *op. cit.*, p. 302; George Harmon Knoles,

"The Presidential Campaign and Election of 1892," unpublished Ph.D. thesis, Stanford University, 1939, pp. 288-96.
28. Gompers to L. D. Lewelling, Jan. 3, 1893, *GLB*.
29. *Report of Speech by John Swinton to the 1892 Convention of the American Federation of Labor*, pp. 4-5.
30. *Proceedings*, A.F. of L. Convention, 1892, p. 43.
31. Ben Terrell to Gompers, Dec. 21, 26, 1892, *AFL Corr.*
32. Gompers to H. M. Ives, Feb. 10, 1893, *GLB*.

CHAPTER XXI

1. *New York Herald*, Jan. 7, 1894.
2. Cleveland *Citizen*, Sept. 30, Oct. 14, 1893; *The Tailor*, Sept., 1893; *Western Laborer*, reprinted in Boston *Labor Leader*, Sept. 16, 1893.
3. James E. Murray to Gompers, Aug. 19, 1894, *AFL Corr.*
4. Oneida (N.Y.) *Herald*, June 27, 1894; Tacoma (Washington) *News*, June 23, 1893; Los Angeles *Herald*, July 27, 1894.
5. McMurry, *op. cit.*, pp. 110-11, 229-30, 271-74; *New York Times*, April 22, 24, 1894; Cleveland *Citizen*, April 21, May 5, 1894.
6. Vernon H. Jensen, *Heritage of Conflict*, pp. 49-51; *Bill Haywood's Book*, pp. 63-64.
7. Boston *Labor Leader*, July 17, 21, 1894; James G. Clark to Gompers, July 27, 1894, *AFL Corr.*
8. Alonzo Crouse to Gompers, Sept. 24, 1894, *AFL Corr.*
9. Edward B. Mittleman, "Chicago Labor in Politics, 1877-96," *Journal of Political Economy*, vol. XVIII, May, 1920, p. 423.
10. Ginger, *op. cit.*, p. 131.
11. Cleveland *Citizen*, Aug. 19, 26, 1893.
12. *The Arena*, vol. XIV, Nov., 1895, pp. 369-84; Hicks, *op. cit.*, p. 333.
13. Boston *Labor Leader*, Sept. 23, 1893; Cleveland *Citizen*, Aug. 19, Sept. 23, 1893.
14. Cleveland *Citizen*, Nov. 25, 1893.
15. Cleveland *Citizen*, July 3, Aug. 1, 1891; Nov. 25, 1893.
16. There are literally hundreds of letters and telegrams in the A.F. of L. Correspondence from organizers, unions, city centrals and state federations of labor all over the country supporting free coinage of silver.
17. Chicago *Tribune*, Aug. 2-4, 1893; Printed circular, copy in *AFL Corr.*
18. Chicago *Daily Tribune*, Sept. 7, 1893; *Western Laborer*, Oct. 28, 1893; Thomas Hines to Gompers, Oct. 5, 1894, *AFL Corr.*; *Labor Advocate*, Dec. 14, 1894.
19. R. C. Martin, *The People's Party in Texas*, Dallas, Texas, 1933, pp. 67-68.
20. Willis J. Abbott, "The Chicago Populist Campaign," *Arena*, vol. XI, Feb., 1895, p. 330.
21. For a detailed biography of Henry D. Lloyd, *see* Caro Lloyd, *Henry Demarest Lloyd, 1847-1903*, 2 volumes, New York, 1912. For a brief biography, *see* Charles McArthur Destler, *American Radicalism, 1865-1901*, pp. 136-38.
22. Henry Demarest Lloyd to Gompers, Jan. 31, Feb. 5, 1894, *AFL Corr.*
23. Henry Demarest Lloyd to Gompers, Jan. 31, Feb. 5, 1894, *AFL Corr.*
24. Destler, *op. cit.*, pp. 168-69; *Railway Times*, May 1, 8, 15, 22, 29, 1894.
25. Thomas J. Morgan to Gompers, March 6, 1894, *AFL Corr.*; Thomas J. Morgan to Henry D. Lloyd, February 21, 1895, Lloyd Papers, *WSHS*.
26. Destler, *op. cit.*, pp. 169-70.
27. *Ibid.*, p. 170.
28. *Eight-Hour Herald* (Chicago), May 10, 1894; M. H. Madden to Henry D. Lloyd, June 27, 1894, Lloyd Papers, *WSHS*.
29. Max L. Shipley, "The People's Party in Illinois," unpublished M.A. thesis, University of Illinois, 1927, pp. 57-58; Destler, *op. cit.*, pp. 171-73.
30. *Railway Times*, July 19, 1894; Destler, *op. cit.*, p. 180.
31. Chicago *Times*, Aug. 6, 1894; *Railway Times*, Sept. 1, Oct. 15, 1894; Destler, *op. cit.*, pp. 186-87.
32. D. M. Feins, "Labor's Role in the Populist Movement, 1890-1896," unpublished M.A. thesis, Columbia University, 1939, pp. 53-54; Destler, *op. cit.*, p. 188.
33. Cleveland *Citizen*, Feb. 24, March 10, April 28, June 2, 23, 30, July 28, Aug. 4, 18, 25, Sept. 8, 1894; Boston *Labor Leader*, Aug. 4, Sept. 29, 1894; *American Federationist*, vol. I, March, 1894, pp. 9-10, 14; *Coast Seamen's Journal*, Oct. 24, 1894; Feins, *op. cit.*, pp. 62-70; Donald Edgar Walters, "Populism in California, 1889-1900," unpublished Ph.D. thesis, University of California, 1952, pp. 242-57; Henry Nichols to

Gompers, March 1, 1894; F. B. Wakeman to Gompers, March 15, 1894, *AFL Corr.*

34. Albert Shaw, "William V. Allen, Populist," *Review of Reviews*, vol. X, July, 1894, p. 130.
35. Cleveland *Citizen*, Aug. 25, Dec. 1, 1894.
36. Henry Demarest Lloyd to Gompers, July 30, Aug., 1894, Lloyd *Mss., WSHS.*
37. Laurence Grolund to Gompers, Aug. 9, 1894, *AFL Corr.*
38. J. M. Guelle to Gompers, June 18, 1894, *AFL Corr.*
39. *Railway Times*, Aug. 15, 1894.
40. Samuel Gompers to Joseph A. Labadie, Sept. 13, 1894, *GLB* and *LC.*
41. Mimeographed circular letter, Sept. 24, 1894, *AFL Corr.*
42. Letters to Gompers from Art C. Herrick, Oct. 1, 1894; F. J. Weber, Milwaukee, Sept. 5, 13, 1894; M. C. Whelan, Wyandotte Co., Kansas. Oct. 2, 1894; D. W. O'Fallon, Piqua, Ohio, Sept. 30, 1894; Harry Clark, San Diego, California, Oct. 3, 1894; H. Godegast, Sacramento, California, Oct. 2, 1894; Henry F. Frederick, Oct. 28, 1894, *AFL Corr.*
43. *See* letter of District Council, Cook County, Illinois, United Brotherhood of Carpenters and Joiners, Oct. 13, 1894; John Calderwood to Gompers, Victor, Colorado, Oct. 1, 1894; J. W. Deane to Gompers, Chicago, Oct. 6, 1894; M. C. Duffy to Gompers, Grand Rapids, Michigan (1894), *AFL Corr.*
44. Printed circular, Nov. 3, 1894, collection of handbills and leaflets in Lloyd Papers, October, 1894, *WSHS.*
45. Willis J. Abbott, *op. cit.*, p. 334.
46. *Cf.* Gompers' editorial, "A Word in Season," *American Federationist*, vol. I, Oct., 1894, pp. 172-73; Henry George to William L. Garrison, Oct. 5, 1894, Henry George *Mss.*, N.Y.P.L.
47. Destler, *op. cit.*, p. 200.
48. Chicago *Daily Tribune*, Oct. 7, 1894. Lloyd's address is reprinted in full in Destler, *op. cit.*, pp. 213-21.
49. Chicago *Times*, Nov. 1, 1894.
50. *American Federationist*, vol. I, Dec., 1894, p. 246; Wm. N. Martin to Gompers, Nov. 8, 1894; James Brettell to Gompers, Nov. 8, 1894, *AFL Corr.*
51. *Cf.* Art C. Herrick to Gompers, Lincoln, Nebraska, Oct. 1, 1894, *AFL Corr.*

52. Destler, *op. cit.*, pp. 189, 208; Staley, *op. cit.*, pp. 100-04.
53. Chicago *Daily Tribune*, Oct. 15, 1894; New York *Tribune*, Oct. 17, 1894.
54. Abbott, *op. cit.*, p. 336; Destler, *op. cit.*, pp. 208, 210-11.
55. Donald L. McMurry, *Coxey's Army*, p. 286; Chicago *Daily Tribune*, Nov. 10, 1894; Boston *Labor Leader*, Nov. 17, 24, 1894; *Coast Seamen's Journal*, Nov. 14, 1894; Gernes, *op. cit.*, pp. 88-90.
56. Hicks, *op. cit.*, p. 338.
57. Unpublished M.A. thesis, University of Wisconsin, 1941, p. 180.
58. Henry Demarest Lloyd to Dr. Benjamin Andrews, Feb. 19, 1895, Lloyd *Mss., WSHS.*

CHAPTER XXII

1. Thos. E. Watson to Powderly, May 24, 31, 1892, *PP.*
2. Hicks, *op. cit.*, p. 344.
3. L. W. Fuller, "History of the People's Party in Colorado," unpublished Ph.D. thesis, University of Wisconsin, 1933, pp. 174-75; T. Vandervoort to Henry D. Lloyd, Jan. 1, 1895; Phoebe W. Couzins to Henry D. Lloyd, Dec. 30, 1894, Lloyd Papers, *WSHS.*
4. Henry D. Lloyd to Clarence Darrow, Nov. 23, 1894, Lloyd Papers, *WSHS;* W. J. Abbott, *op. cit.*, p. 336.
5. Destler, *American Radicalism*, pp. 200-03; *The People*, Nov. 18, 1894; W. E. Kearns to Gompers, Topeka, Kansas, Dec. 31, 1895, *AFL Corr.*
6. *The People*, Dec. 9, 1894; H. E. Taubeneck to Henry D. Lloyd, December 10, 1895, Lloyd Papers, *WSHS.*
7. Cleveland *Citizen*, Dec. 22, 1894; Destler, *op. cit.*, p. 229.
8. St. Louis *Labor*, Jan. 5, 1895.
9. *American Federationist*, vol. I, Dec., 1894, pp. 242-45.
10. *Proceedings*, A.F. of L. Convention, 1894, p. 15.
11. *Railway Times*, March 15, 1895; *Coast Seamen's Journal*, July 3, 1895; Henry D. Lloyd to John Burns, Feb. 6, 1895, Lloyd *Mss., WSHS.*
12. *The Coming Nation*, Jan. 26, 1895; *St. Louis Labor*, Jan. 5, 1895.
13. *National Watchman*, Feb. 22, 1895.
14. *The Coming Nation*, Feb. 23, 1895.
15. Destler, *op. cit.*, pp. 241-42; Cleveland *Citizen*, Feb. 23, 1895; Henry D. Lloyd,

"The American Labour Movement," (London) *Labour Leader*, May 11, 1895 (Copy in British Museum, London).

16. Destler, *op. cit.*, pp. 250-51; Boston *Labor Leader*, April 6, 1895.
17. *National Watchman*, April 12, 1895.
18. Cleveland *Citizen*, April 20, 1895.
19. Cleveland *Citizen*, Nov. 17, 24, 1895; Boston *Labor Leader*, Nov. 17, 24, 1895.
20. *Appleton's Annual Cyclopedia*, 1895, pp. 10, 314, 424.
21. Helen McKay Blackburn, "The Populist Party in the South, 1890-1898," unpublished M.A. thesis, Harvard University, 1941, pp. 89-94.
22. *Union Workman*, Dec. 28, 1895; *Eight-Hour Herald*, Dec. 1, 4, 1895.
23. *Coast Seamen's Journal*, April 25, 1895; *Proceedings*, New Jersey Federation of Trades Convention, 1895, p. 5.
24. *Proceedings*, A.F. of L. Convention, 1895, pp. 17-18, 82, 85-86.
25. *Proceedings*, A.F. of L. Convention, 1895, p. 82.
26. *Union Workman*, Jan. 25, 1896; Cleveland *Citizen*, Jan. 11, 18, 1896.
27. Leaflet entitled, "To the Laboring Men of America," June 12, 1895, *AFL Corr.*; Cleveland *Citizen*, Feb. 1, April 18, June 13, 1896.
28. *Review of Reviews*, vol. XIV, Aug., 1896, p. 140.
29. J. Martin Klotsche, "The United Front Populists," *Wisconsin Magazine of History*, vol. XX, June, 1937, p. 387.
30. Jack Abramowitz, "The Negro in the Populist Movement," *Journal of Negro History*, vol. XXXVIII, July, 1953, pp. 287-88.
31. Klotsche, *op. cit.*, p. 387.
32. Henry Demarest Lloyd, "The Populists at St. Louis," *Review of Reviews*, vol. XIV, Sept., 1896, pp. 299-300.
33. *People's Party Paper*, Nov. 13, 1896.
34. Henry Demarest Lloyd to J. H. Ferris, Aug. 6, 1896, Lloyd *Ms.*, *WSHS*.
35. *Proceedings of the Ninth Annual Convention of the Socialist Labor Party*, p. 10.
36. *Ibid.*; *The People*, Sept. 6, 1896; *The Coming Nation*, Aug. 1, 15, 29, 1896.
37. *The People*, Nov. 12, 1896.
38. Printed circular, Gompers and McCraith to affiliated unions, March 16, 1896; M. R. Grady to August McCraith, April 20, 1896; George A. Schilling to Gompers, May 28, 1896, *AFL Corr.*
39. *Cf.* A. Todtenhausen to Gompers, Knox-ville, Tenn., Sept. 23, 1896; Edward Boyce to Gompers, Aug. 8, 1896, *AFL Corr.*
40. *Railway Times*, Jan. 1, 1897.
41. *New York Journal*, Oct. 30, 1896; pamphlet, *Labor for Bryan, AFL Corr.*
42. Mimeographed copy of report in *AFL Corr.*
43. *Journal of the Knights of Labor*, Sept. 17, 1896.
44. John B. Lennon to Gompers, July 9, 1893; M. M. Garland to Gompers, July 12, 1896, Feb. 20, 1897, *AFL Corr.*
45. J. H. McWilliams to Gompers, Los Angeles, July 22, 1896, *AFL Corr.*
46. *Railway Times*, Aug. 1, 1896.
47. J. D. Vaughan to Gompers, July 18, 1896; John M. Farquahr to Gompers, July 17, 1896, *AFL Corr.*; Denver *Republican*, July 13, 1896.
48. *Coast Seamen's Journal*, Aug., 1896.
49. *New York Daily News*, Aug. 8, 1896; Denver *Daily News*, Sept. 18, 1896; *Denver Evening Post*, Aug. 17, 1896.
50. John B. Lennon to Gompers, July 20, Oct. 29, 1896, *AFL Corr.*
51. W. H. Milburn to Gompers, Aug. 16, Sept. 16, 1896, *AFL Corr.*
52. P. J. McGuire to Gompers, Sept. 9, 1896; Gompers to P. J. McGuire, Sept. 11, 1896, *AFL Corr.*
53. Springfield *Republican*, Aug. 19, Sept. 26, 1896; Letters to Gompers from John P. Brunn, Oct. 5, 1896; P. E. Kenney, Oct. 5, 1896; J. T. McKenchie, Sept. 14, 1896; Martin J. Gallery, Oct. 21, 1896; Henry White, Oct. 22, 1896, *AFL Corr.*
54. Matthew Josephson, *The Politicos*, New York, 1939, p. 699.
55. Henry F. Pringle, *Theodore Roosevelt*, New York, 1938, p. 124.
56. Theo. Nelson to Gompers, Sept. 13-96, *AFL Corr.*
57. Cleveland *Citizen*, Aug. 22, Oct. 24, 1896; San Francisco *Examiner*, Aug. 27, 1896; *Chautauqua*, vol. XXIV, Aug., 1896, p. 357; *The Coming Nation*, Sept. 5, Oct. 17, 1896; H. F. Taggart, "Party Realignment of 1896," *Pacific Historical Review*, vol. VIII, 1948, p. 445; Cleveland *Citizen*, Aug. 22, Oct. 24, Dec. 1, 1896.
58. San Francisco *Examiner*, Sept. 27, 1896.
59. *Typographical Journal*, Oct. 15, 1896.
60. Harry White to Gompers, Oct. 22, 1896, *AFL Corr.*
61. *New York Journal*, Oct. 29, 1896.

62. John W. Stewart to Justin S. Morrill, Nov. 11, 1896, Justin S. Morrill Papers, Library of Congress. (Hereafter cited as *L. of C.*)

63. William Diamond, "Urban and Rural Voting in 1896," *American Historical Review*, vol. XLVI, Jan., 1941, pp. 281-305.

64. Henry White to Gompers, Nov. 4, 1896, *AFL Corr.*

65. Thomas Stanton to William Jennings Bryan, Nov. 10, 1896; James R. Sovereign to William Jennings Bryan, Nov. 10, 1896; Henry White to William Jennings Bryan, Nov. 9, 1896, William Jennings Bryan Papers, *L of C;* Henry White to Gompers, Nov. 4, 1896, *AFL Corr.*

66. Gompers to E. Kurzenknabe, Dec. 5, 1896, *AFL Corr.*

67. A. Furuseth to Gompers, Nov. 10, 1896, *AFL Corr.*

68. Jesse Cox to Henry Demarest Lloyd, Nov. 24, 1896, Lloyd Papers, *WSHS.*

69. *Eight-Hour Herald*, Nov. 17, Dec. 8, 22, 1896, Jan. 5, Feb. 2, 1897; *American Federationist*, vol. III, Nov., 1896, p. 188; *Proceedings*, A.F. of L. Convention, 1896, p. 15.

70. Henry D. Lloyd, "The American Labour Movement," (London) *Labour Leader*, May 11, 1895.

71. F. B. Tracy, "Menacing Socialism in the Western States," *Forum*, vol. XV, May, 1893, pp. 332-43.

72. *Cf.* Michigan, Federation of Labor, *Year Book*, 1896, p. 5.

CHAPTER XXIII

1. *American Federationist*, vol. IV, Oct., 1897, p. 188.

2. M. D. Ratchford to Gompers, Feb. 5, 1898, *AFL Corr.*

3. John B. Lennon to Gompers, Oct. 14, 1897, *AFL Corr.*

4. Leo Wolman, *The Growth of American Trade Unions, 1880-1923*, New York, 1924, pp. 32, 110-21; Gompers to Henry Demarest Lloyd, March 15, 1898, *GLB.*

5. Gompers to Joseph Brichell, March 11, 1896; Gompers to John F. O'Sullivan, March 7, 1896; Gompers to J. Kent, March 25, 1898; Gompers to R. S. Novick, April 13, 1899, *GLB;* Adolph Strasser to August McCraith, July 30, 1896; P. J. McGuire to Gompers, April 28, 1898; Jas. O'Connell to Gompers, Aug. 22, 1901; F. J. Brown to Gompers, St. Louis, Mo., Feb. 8, 1896; W. H. Stokes to Gompers, Muncie, Indiana, Aug. 26, 1896, *AFL Corr.*

6. Jas. O'Connell to John McBride, March 25, 1895, *AFL Corr.; F. E. Wolfe, Admission to American Trade Unions,* Baltimore, 1912, p. 120; Jas. O'Connell to Gompers, Feb. 26, 1896; Jas. O'Connell to Frank Morrison, March 20, 1903, *AFL Corr.*

7. Gompers in *Locomotive Firemen's Magazine*, July, 1896, p. 65; Gompers to F. P. Sargent, Aug. 17, 1896; Gompers to George W. Perkins, Oct. 27, 1896; Gompers to W. D. Lewis, April 9, 1897, *GLB;* W. S. Carter to Frank Morrison, May 12, 1897, *AFL Corr.*

8. Fred Johnson, Grand President, Brotherhood of Boiler Makers and Iron Ship Builders, to Gompers, March 9, 1896, *AFL Corr.*

9. John T. Wilson to Gompers, Aug. 19, 1903, *AFL Corr.;* Samuel Gompers, "Unity Drawing Nearer," *American Federationist*, vol. VII, Feb., 1900, pp. 34-35.

10. W. E. B. DuBois, editor, *The Negro Artisan*, Atlanta, Ga., 1902, p. 157.

11. John S. Durham, "The Labor Unions and the Negro," *Atlantic Monthly*, vol. LXXI, February, 1898, pp. 22-31.

12. DuBois, *op. cit.*, pp. 158-60.

13. *Ibid.*

14. F. L. McGruder to Gompers, Mar. 17, 1899, Mar. 24, 1899, Atlanta, Ga., Mar. 25, 1899, Lithuania, Ga., April 22, 1899, Mobile, Ala., April 27, 1899, Meridian Mississippi; Prince W. Greene to Gompers, Sept. 18, 1899, Columbus, Ga., Nov. 19, 1899, Phenix, Ala.; Samuel Mitchell to Gompers, Oct. 18, 1900, Charleston, S. Car., *AFL Corr.*

15. William W. Davis to Gompers, Norfolk, Va., Jan. 1, 1901; T. J. Naughton to Frank Morrison, Savannah, Ga., Oct. 11, 1900; M. S. Belk to Gompers, Newport News, Va., Feb. 6, 1901; Henry M. Walker to Gompers, Nov. 22, 1899, *AFL Corr.;* Gompers to Henry M. Walker, Nov. 8, 1899, *GLB.*

16. J. E. Porter to Gompers, New Orleans, Mar. 4, 13, April 20, May 19, June 15, 1900; James Leonard to Gompers, March 12, June 7, 23, 1900, *AFL Corr.;* Gompers to J. E. Porter, March 9, April 25, May 23, 1900, *GLB.*

17. *Proceedings,* A.F. of L. Convention, 1900, pp. 22-23, 112-29, 263; Gompers to M. C. Wallace, June 6, 1900, *AFL Corr.*

18. New York *Tribune,* Dec. 13, 1901.

19. Gompers to the press, April 19, 1901, *AFL Corr.;* Washington *Star,* April 20, 1901; Rayford W. Logan, *The Negro in American Life and Thought, The Nadir, 1877-1901,* New York, 1954, pp. 149-50.

20. Sterling D. Spero and Abram L. Harris, *The Black Worker,* pp. 220-21.

21. *Proceedings,* A.F. of L. Convention, 1898, p. 94.

22. George Sinclair Mitchell, "The Negro in Southern Trade Unionism," *Southern Economic Journal,* vol. II, January, 1936, pp. 27-28.

23. *Ibid.;* Herbert R. Northrup, *Organized Labor and the Negro,* New York and London, 1944, pp. 2-5.

24. Andrew F. Hilyin, Chairman Committee Hampton Conference, to Gompers, April 21, 1899, *AFL Corr.*

25. Northrup, *op. cit.,* pp. 103, 110.

26. *Ibid.*

27. P. J. McCarthy to A. Kennedy, Jan. 20, 1896, attached to E. A. Davidson to Gompers, May 30, 1896, *AFL Corr.*

28. E. A. Davidson to Gompers, May 30, 1896, *AFL Corr.*

29. *Ibid.*

30. E. A. Davidson to Gompers, May 30, 1896; James Duncan to Gompers, June 16, 1896, *AFL Corr.*

31. Augusta (Ga.) *Banner,* Feb. 3, 1898.

32. T. W. Dee to Frank Morrison, Galveston, Texas, Sept. 9, 1898, *AFL Corr.*

33. Galveston *Daily News,* Sept. 16, 25, 29, 1898.

34. Gompers to Henry M. Walker, Nov. 8, 1899, *GLB.*

35. *Cf.* J. F. Grimes to Gompers, Houston, Texas, Oct. 4, 1898; F. L. McGruder to Gompers, Augusta, Ga., Oct. 4, 1899, April 20, 1899, Mobile, Ala.; R. S. Brady to Frank Morrison, Savannah, Ga., Nov. 25, 1899, *AFL Corr.*

36. F. L. McGruder to Gompers, May 26, Oct. 4, 1899; T. J. Naughton to Gompers, Feb. 18, 1901; R. E. McLean to Frank Morrison, July 5, 1901, July 8, 1901, *AFL Corr.*

37. Gompers to F. J. McGruder, May 27, 1899, *GLB.*

38. Will Winn, "The Negro: His Relation to Southern Industry," *American Federationist,* vol. IV, February, 1898, pp.

269-71; Gompers to Will Winn, Jan. 19, 1898, March 9, 1899, *GLB.*

39. Indianapolis *Star,* Sept. 8, 1903.

40. *Proceedings,* A.F. of L. Convention, 1895, pp. 41, 45.

41. San Francisco *Voice of Labor,* April 16, 1898; *The Public,* Dec. 3, 1898.

42. *American Federationist,* vol. X, October, 1902, pp. 706-07, 709.

43. Arthur Mann, "Gompers and the Irony of Racism," *The Antioch Review.* Summer, 1953, p. 214; Andrew F. Hilyin to Gompers, April 21, 1899, *AFL Corr.*

44. Joseph H. Taylor, "The Restriction of European Immigration and the Concept of Race," *South Atlantic Quarterly,* vol. L, January, 1951, pp. 27-28.

45. Homer D. Call to Frank Morrison, Jan. 21, 1899; Aaron Roth to Gompers, Oct. 28, 1897; Henry Weissman to Gompers, July 1, 1897, *AFL Corr.*

46. David J. Saposs, *Left Wing Unionism,* New York, 1926, p. 114.

47. Joseph H. Taylor, *op. cit.,* pp. 27-28.

48. *Proceedings,* A.F. of L. Convention, 1896, pp. 18, 99-100.

49. Prescott F. Hall, Secretary, Immigration Restriction League, to Gompers, June 16, 1897, *AFL Corr.*

50. *Proceedings,* A.F. of L. Convention, 1897, pp. 95-98.

51. Gompers to President William McKinley, June 23, 1899, *GLB; Proceedings,* A.F. of L. Convention, 1901, pp. 76-83.

52. Wolfe, *op. cit.,* pp. 25-27, 61-65, 99-102, 103-04; Hourwich, *op. cit.,* p. 31; Max Naft, "Jewish Workers in the Building Trades," *United Hebrew Trades 50th Jubilee Book,* pp. 195-98.

53. Petition, dated Cincinnati, Ohio, July 20, 1900, attached to Frank L. Rist, to Frank Morrison, July 23, 1900, *AFL Corr.*

54. Wolfe, *op. cit.,* pp. 85-86.

55. Frank Morrison to O. Mattie Hill, June 6, 1900; O. Mattie Hill to Frank Morrison, Pontiac, Ill., June 12, 1900; H. M. Eaton to Frank Morrison, Boston, Mass., June 20, 1900, *AFL Corr.*

56. Gladys Boone, *The Women's Trade Union League,* New York, 1942, p. 169.

57. *Report of the Industrial Commission,* vol. VII, p. 541.

58. Paul F. Brissenden, *Earnings of Factory Workers, 1899 to 1927,* United States Bureau of the Census, Monograph X, Washington, 1929, pp. 29-30; (San

Francisco) *Voice of Labor*, Sept. 22, 1897.
59. Wolfe, *op. cit.*, p. 88.
60. *Report of the Industrial Commission*, vol. VII, p. 168.
61. Leonora O'Reilly, "Message to Women Workers," Labor Day, 1898, in Leonora O'Reilly Papers, Radcliffe College Library.
62. John O'Sullivan to August McCraith, July 6, 1895, *AFL Corr.*
63. "Negro Women in Industry," *Bulletin of the Women's Bureau*, No. 20, p. 5.
64. Samuel Gompers, *The American Labor Movement*, pp. 33-35.
65. Gompers to Andrew Furuseth, Sept. 18, 1900, *GLB*.
66. Lyle W. Cooper, "Organized Labor and the Trust," Journal of Political Economy, vol. XXXVI, 1928, p. 737.

CHAPTER XXIV

1. Lewis Corey, *The House of Morgan*, New York, 1930, pp. 147, 199-213, 245-62; Anna Rochester, *Rulers of America*, New York, 1936, pp. 72-87; Victor Perlo, *American Imperialism*, New York, 1951, pp. 9-10.
2. Lyle W. Cooper, *op. cit.*, p. 737.
3. Sanford Daniel Gordon, "Public Opinion as a Factor in the Emergence of a National Anti-Trust Program," unpublished Ph.D. thesis, New York University, 1953, p. 282.
4. Thurman W. Arnold, *Anti-Trust Law Enforcement, Past and Present*, Washington, 1940, pp. 218, 225.
5. *American Federationist*, vol. II, Feb., 1896, pp. 218-19.
6. *Southern Economist and Trade Unionist*, May 1, 1897.
7. Henry Weissman to Gompers, Nov. 25, 1896, *AFL Corr.*
8. Adolph Strasser to August McCraith, July 30, 1896, *AFL Corr.*
9. *American Federationist*, vol. IV, Dec., 1896, p. 217.
10. *Ibid.*, vol. II, Feb., 1896, p. 229; *Report of the Industrial Commission*, 1901, vol. VII, pp. 384-405.
11. E. G. Wells to Gompers, Feb. 6, 1899; Frank M. Trusse to Frank Morrison, March 7, May 8, 1899; Jay H. Mullen to Gompers (Jan., 1901); John Schudel to Gompers, Feb. 14, 1898, *AFL Corr.*
12. W. D. Mahon to Gompers, Nov. 26, 1898, *AFL Corr.*

13. P. J. McGuire to Bro. Gompers, April 28, 1898, *AFL Corr.*
14. *Report of the Industrial Commission*, 1901, vol. XII, pp. 384, 385, 388-89.
15. John Fitch, *The Steel Workers*, p. 89; Corey, *op. cit.*, p. 278.
16. W. O. Weyforth, *The Organizability of Labor*, Baltimore, 1912, pp. 207-08; New York *Tribune*, July 20, Aug. 3, 1901.
17. *Report on Conditions of Employment in the Iron and Steel Industry in the United States*, Washington, 1910, vol. II, pp. 113-14.
18. John R. Commons, "Labor Conditions in Meat Packing and the Recent Strike," *Quarterly Journal of Economics*, vol. XXXIX, Nov., 1904, pp. 1-4.
19. Chas. A. Baustian to Frank Morrison, Chicago, March 31, 1900, *AFL Corr.*
20. *Proceedings*, A.F. of L. Convention, 1901, pp. 11, 239-41.
21. Carroll D. Wright, "Influence of Unions on Immigrants," *Bulletin*, U.S. Bureau of Labor, No. 56, January, 1905, pp. 1-7; Washington *Star*, Feb. 7, 1905.
22. *Cf.* A. L. Gitlow, "The Communist Threat to Labor," *Southern Economic Journal*, Vol. XVI, April, 1950, pp. 858-59. For an effective refutation of this entire concept, *see* Isaac Hourwich, *Immigration and Labor*, New York, 1912.
23. Gompers to Andrew Furuseth, Sept. 18, 1900, *GLB*.
24. Toledo *Daily News*, March 18, 1899.
25. W. H. Roche to Gompers, Oct. 25, 1899, *AFL Corr.*
26. *Chicago Conference on Trusts, Held September 13-16, 1899*, Chicago, 1900, pp. 323-29; *American Federationist*, vol. VI, October, 1899, p. 195.
27. Chicago Conference on Trusts, *op. cit.*, pp. 323-29.
28. Buffalo *Express*, Nov. 17, 1899.
29. Chicago *Record*, Nov. 2, 1899; Henry W. Blair to Gompers, April 12, 1900, *AFL Corr.*
30. Letters to Gompers from E. Lewis Evans, Dec. 2, 1899; W. D. Mahon, Nov. 3, 1899; Jas. O'Connell, June 10, 1900; Harvey Schlamel, Oct. 14, 16, 1899, *AFL Corr.*
31. Idaho *Tribune*, May 3, 1899, reprinted in "Couer d'Alene Mining Troubles," 56th Congress, 1st Sess., *Sen. Doc. No. 24*, vol. IV, p. 30.
32. *Ibid.*, pp. 16-18; Denver *Daily News*, June 26, 1899.

33. James Maher to Gompers, Butte, Montana, Sept. 27, 1899, *AFL Corr.*
34. Handwritten letter, Gem, Idaho, June 22, 1899, *AFL Corr.*
35. Harvey Schlamel to Gompers, Oct. 14, 16, 1899; Michael Raphael to Gompers, Sept. 2, 1899, *AFL Corr.*
36. *Proceedings,* A.F. of L. Convention, 1900, pp. 149-50.
37. *Social Democratic Herald,* July 9, 1898, June 10, 24, 1899.
38. John Swinton, "How the Trusts Squeeze Working People," New York *World,* June 13, 1900.
39. Cooper, *op. cit.,* pp. 722-24.
40. Gompers to E. Lewis Evans, Dec. 4, 1899, *GLB;* Henry White to Gompers, Nov. 24, 1899, *AFL Corr.*
41. M. L. Lockwood to Gompers, Oct. 2, 1899, *AFL Corr.*
42. M. L. Lockwood to Gompers, Jan. 8, 24, 1900, *AFL Corr.*
43. *Official Report of the National Anti-Trust Conference, Chicago, Feb. 14, 1900,* Chicago, 1900, pp. ii, 119-45.
44. Gompers to Henry B. Bischoff, Dec. 4, 1899, *GLB;* Henry B. Bischoff to Gompers, Dec. 7, 1899, *AFL Corr.*
45. Ralph M. Easley to Gompers, April 6, 1900; "Proposed Advisory Council of the National Civic Federation," printed list marked "Confidential," attached to Ralph M. Easley to Gompers, April 6, 1900, *AFL Corr.*
46. "Proposed Advisory Council of the National Civic Federation," *op. cit.;* Jas. O'Connell to Gompers, June 10, 1897; N. D. Call to Gompers (July, 1899); M. Donnelly to Frank Morrison, April 3, 1900, *AFL Corr.*
47. Corey, *op. cit.,* p. 276.
48. "Proposed Advisory Council . . ."
49. Samuel Gompers, *op. cit.,* vol. II, p. 106.
50. John Mitchell to Gompers, April 7, 1900, *AFL Corr.*
51. Gompers to John Mitchell, April 9, 1900, *GLB;* John Mitchell to Gompers, April 12, 1900; Ralph M. Easley to Gompers, June 21, 1900, *AFL Corr.;* Gompers to R. M. Easley, April 14, 1900, *GLB.*
52. Ralph M. Easley to Gompers, Oct. 10, 1900; Ralph M. Easley to Gompers, Oct. 2, 16, 1900, Oct. 14, 1900, *AFL Corr.*
53. Gompers to R. M. Easley, Oct. 10, Nov. 30, 1900, *GLB;* John Mitchell, *Organized Labor,* Philadelphia, 1903, p. ix.
54. Ralph M. Easley, "Senator Hanna and the Labor Problem," *The Independent,* vol. LVI, March 3, 1904, p. 484; John Mitchell to Mark Hanna, March 20, 1901, John Mitchell Papers, Mullen Library of the Catholic University of America.
55. *Catholic World,* vol. LXXIV, Jan., 1902, pp. 531-32.

CHAPTER XXV

1. *Railway Times,* Jan. 1, 1897.
2. *Ibid.,* June 15, 1897; *The Social Democrat,* July 1, Nov. 4, 1897.
3. Harry Rogoff, *An East Side Epic: The Life and Work of Meyer London,* New York, 1930, pp. 10-13.
4. *The Social Democrat,* Aug. 12, 1897.
5. Marvin Wachman, *History of the Social-Democratic Party of Milwaukee, 1897-1910,* Urbana, Illinois, 1945, pp. 9-24.
6. Will H. Winn to Gompers, July 1, 1896, *AFL Corr.*
7. W. D. Mahon to Gompers, May 26, 1897; Gompers to P. J. McGuire, May 1, 1897, *AFL Corr.*
8. Gompers to W. D. Mahon, May 24, 1897; Gompers to Wm. Mudge, July 20, 1897, *GLB;* Wm. Mudge to Gompers, July 26, 1897, *AFL Corr.*
9. R. Askew to Frank Morrison, Ispeming, Michigan, June 23, 1897, *AFL Corr.*
10. P. J. McGuire to Gompers, July 20, 1897, *AFL Corr.*
11. *The Social Democrat,* Feb. 17, June 16, 1898.
12. *Ibid.,* July 16, 1898.
13. *The Social Democratic Herald,* July 9, 1898.
14. *Ibid;* Kipnis, *op. cit.,* pp. 65-66.
15. Ginger, *op. cit.,* p. 199.
16. William Mailly to Gompers, June 20, 1898; Joseph Barondess to Gompers, Aug. 20, 1898, *AFL Corr.*
17. Gompers to Joseph Barondess, Aug. 24, 1898, *GLB.*
18. Gompers to R. McKeown, Aug. 9, 1898, *GLB.*
19. Jesse Cox to Gompers, Dec. 3, 1898, *AFL Corr.*
20. "Report of the Secretary of National Executive Board of the Social Democratic Party, June, 1898-January, 1900," typescript, *JCL.*
21. Isaac Cowen and M. S. Hayes to Gom-

pers, Dec. 3, 1898; Thos. F. Croal to Gompers, Dec. 5, 1898, *AFL Corr.*

22. "Report of the Secretary of the National Executive Board of the Social Democratic Party, June, 1898-January, 1900," typescript, *JCL.*
23. *Ibid.*
24. *Ibid.*
25. Detroit *Free Press,* Oct. 18, 1896.
26. *Proceedings,* A.F. of L. Convention, 1898, pp. 121-22; Gompers to Henry Demarest Lloyd, Nov. 20, 1897, *GLB.*
27. Kipnis, *op. cit.,* pp. 63-64.
28. *Proceedings,* A.F. of L. Convention, 1900, pp. 131-32; Max S. Hayes, "American Federation of Labor Convention," *International Socialist Review,* vol. I, January, 1901, pp. 419-21; "Socialism at the A.F. of L. Convention," *Brauer-Zeitung,* Dec. 29, 1900.
29. *Boston Globe,* Nov. 8, 1899.
30. Kipnis, *op. cit.,* p. 78; *New York Times,* Sept. 1, 1899; Samuel Prince to Gompers, Aug. 26, Sept. 1, 7, 8, 1899, *AFL Corr.;* Gompers to Prince, July 17, 20, Aug. 24, 29, 1899, *GLB.*
31. "Report of the Secretary of the National Executive Board of the Social Democratic Party, June, 1898-January, 1900," typescript, *JCL.*
32. Gompers to Samuel Prince, Oct. 14, 1899, *GLB.*
33. *Social Democratic Herald,* Nov. 12, 1898; Samuel Ress to Gompers, New Bedford, Jan. 25, 1898, *AFL Corr.*
34. Grace H. Stimson, *Rise of the Labor Movement in Los Angeles,* p. 223.
35. *Social Democratic Herald,* March 17, 1900; Ginger, *op. cit.,* pp. 200-01.
36. *Social Democratic Herald,* Dec. 10, 1898.
37. New York, 1922, p. 28.
38. I. Gerson to Daniel De Leon, Jan. 29, 1896, De Leon Correspondence, *WSHS.*
39. Will H. Winn to Gompers, Columbus, Ga., Nov. 5, 12, 1896, *AFL Corr.*
40. Printed Circular, James Reid, Gen'l Sec'y, N.U.T.W., to all affiliated unions, March 5, 1897; P. J. McGuire to Gompers, May 10, 1897, *AFL Corr.*
41. Circular, N.U.T.W., to all organized labor, copy attached to H. S. Mills to Frank Morrison, Mar. 3, 1898; H. S. Mills to the General Council of N.U.T.W., Feb. 8, 1898, *AFL Corr.;* Lowell (Mass.) *Sun,* Jan. 1, 1898; *The Evening Standard* (New Bedford), Feb. 12-14, March 10, April 4, 1898;

What Means This Strike? Address delivered by Daniel De Leon in the City Hall of New Bedford, February 11, 1898, pamphlet.
42. T. F. Tracy to Gompers, North Adams, Mass., March 13, 1898, *AFL Corr.*
43. Gompers to Joseph Barondess, Aug. 24, 1898, *GLB.*
44. De Leon, *What Means This Strike? . . .,* p. 30; *The People,* July 3, 1898.
45. *Proceedings of the Tenth National Convention of the Socialist Labor Party, 1900,* New York, 1901, p. 211.
46. *The Social Democratic Herald,* Dec. 10, 1898, Feb. 18, 1899, March 17, 1900.
47. *Proceedings of the National Convention of the Socialist Party, 1901,* fourth session, pp. 9-11; sixth session, p. 30; seventh session, p. 12.
48. *Ibid.,* third session, p. 22; eleventh session, p. 3.
50. *The Social Democratic Herald,* Aug. 17, 1901.

CHAPTER XXVI

1. Victor Perlo, *American Imperialism,* New York, 1951, pp. 9-10.
2. 55th Congress, 2nd Session, House of Representatives *Report No. 1355,* p. 62.
3. Marcus M. Wilkerson, *Public Opinion and the Spanish-American War: A Study in War Propaganda,* Baton Rouge, La., 1932 and Joseph E. Wisan, *The Cuban Crisis as Reflected in the New York Press,* New York, 1934.
4. *Journal of the Knights of Labor,* Oct. 31, 1895; *American Federationist,* vol. II, Nov., 1895, p. 168; *Painters' Journal,* Oct., 1895, p. 9; George Stevens, *New York Typographical Union No. 6,* New York, 1913, p. 605; United Brotherhood of Carpenters and Joiners, *Convention Proceedings,* 1896, p. 245.
5. *Journal of the Knights of Labor,* July 11, 18, Nov. 28, 1895; *Proceedings,* G.A., K. of L., 1895, pp. 73-74; *Proceedings,* A.F. of L. Convention, 1895, pp. 63, 102; 1896, pp. 53-54; John S. Appel, "The Relation of American Labor to United States Imperialism, 1895-1905," unpublished Ph.D. thesis, University of Wisconsin, 1950, p. 31.
6. Delber Lee McKee, "The American Federation of Labor and Foreign Policy, 1886-1912," unpublished Ph.D. thesis, Stanford University, 1952, pp. 38-40.

7. *Proceedings*, A.F. of L. Convention, 1896, pp. 53-54.
8. Alfred J. Boulton to Gompers, Dec. 30, 1895, *AFL Corr.*; Ernest Howard Crosby, "Work and War," *American Federationist*, vol. II, Dec., 1895, p. 221.
9. George A. Powles to Gompers, Dec. 30, 1895, *AFL Corr.*; *The People*, Dec. 22, 29, 1895; *American Federationist*, vol. III, Feb., 1896, p. 22.
10. E. R. Gould to Gompers, Jan. 23, Feb. 11, 1897; R. U. Johnson to Gompers, Jan. 25, 1897, *AFL Corr.*; *American Federationist*, Feb., 1897, pp. 259-60.
11. Andrew Furuseth to Gompers, June 23, 1897, *AFL Corr.*; *Iron Molders' Journal*, June 18, 1897; *American Federationist*, Nov., 1897, pp. 215-17; *Journal of the Knights of Labor*, July 1, 1897.
12. Harry C. Walker to Gompers, Oct. 28, 1897, *AFL Corr.*; *Congressional Record*, 55th Congress, 2nd Session, Part 7, pp. 6341, 6533.
13. *Proceedings*, A.F. of L. Convention, 1897, pp. 56, 89-91; San Francisco *Voice of Labor*, Jan. 1, 1898.
14. Gompers to Frank Morrison, June 2, 1897; Frank Morrison to Gompers, May 28, Aug. 11, 1897, *AFL Corr.*
15. *Cf.* Sylvester K. Stevens, *American Expansion in Hawaii, 1842-1898*, Harrisburg, Pa., 1945, Chapter XI.
16. *Monthly Journal of the International Association of Machinists*, April, 1898, pp. 191-92.
17. *The Craftsman*, April, 1898, p. 87.
18. *Coast Seamen's Journal*, Feb. 23, March 2, April 6, 1898; G. H. Bates to Gompers, April 5, 1898, *AFL Corr.*
19. *Railroad Trainmen's Journal*, Jan., 1898.
20. *United Mine Workers' Journal*, March 17, 1898; *Journal of the Brotherhood of Boilermakers and Iron Shipbuilders*, April, 1898.
21. Gompers to Henry Demarest Lloyd, March 25, 1898; Gompers to P. J. McGuire, March 28, 1898, *GLB.*
22. Copy in *AFL Corr.*
23. *The People*, April 17, May 1, 1898; *The Coming Nation*, March 12, 1898; *Appeal to Reason*, March 26, April 16, 1898; *Jewish Daily Forward*, Feb. 23, March 1, 1898.
24. San Francisco *Voice of Labor*, April 16, May 21, 1898; *The People*, April 10, 24, 1898.
25. Julius W. Pratt, *America's Colonial Experiment*, New York, 1950, p. 61.

26. *The Nation*, April 21, 1898.
27. San Francisco *Voice of Labor*, June 11, 1898.
28. *Coast Seamen's Journal*, April 27, 1898; *Railroad Trainmen's Journal*, May, 1898; New York *Tribune*, Aug. 1, 1898; *Proceedings*, A.F. of L. Convention, 1898, pp. 19-20.
29. *American Federationist*, July, 1898, p. 92.
30. P. J. McGuire to Gompers, April 28, 1898, *AFL Corr.*
31. *Railroad Trainmen's Journal*, June, 1898, pp. 516-17; *The Wood Worker*, May, 1898; Appel, *op. cit.*, pp. 137-40; *United Mine Workers' Journal*, July 14, 1898.
32. *The Public*, May 21, 1898; Gompers to Chas. J. Peeve, July 18, 1898, *GLB*; Boston *Post*, Aug. 3, 1898.
33. *The Bakers' Journal*, June 15, 1898, p. 358; *Monthly Journal of the International Journal of Machinists*, May, 1898, pp. 255-56.
34. *The Weekly People*, May 8, 1898; Morris U. Schappes, "Jewish Labor in the Nineties," *Jewish Life*, June, 1950, p. 16.
35. Minnesota *Union Advocate*, June 17, 1898; Ginger, *op. cit.*, p. 203.
36. *Railroad Trainmen's Journal*, July, 1898, clipping in A.F. of L. Corr.; Appel, *op. cit.*, p. 113; Troy *Advocate* reprinted in New York *Evening Journal*, July 14, 1898.
37. Pueblo *Courier*, June 24, 1898; Chicago *Labor World*, July, 1898; *Journal of the Knights of Labor*, July, 1898; A. Furuseth to Gompers, Aug. 23, 1898; John B. Lennon to Gompers, Aug. 26, 1898, *AFL Corr.*; Gompers to John B. Lennon, Aug. 16, 24, 1898, *GLB.*

CHAPTER XXVII

1. *United States Investor*, Boston, vol. X, pp. 60-61.
2. *Typographical Union*, May 1, 1899, p. 383; *The Commoner and Glassworker*, *Railroad Trainmen's Journal*, September, 1898, pp. 763-64.
3. Appel, *op. cit.*, p. 155.
4. *Leather Workers' Journal*, vol. III, Nov., 1900, p. 65; *The Carpenter*, Nov., 1898, p. 3; *Cigar Makers' Journal*, Dec., 1898, p. 8; Gompers to F. B. Thurber, Nov. 25, 1898, *AFL Corr.*; *American Federationist*, Dec., 1898, pp. 205-07.

5. Undated clipping from *Railroad Trainmen's Journal* in A.F. of L. Corr.; *The Carpenter*, Aug., 1898; *Cigar Makers' Journal*, Feb. 1899, p. 8; Pueblo *Courier*, May 19, 1899.

6. Quoted in *American Pressman*, Oct., 1899, p. 269.

7. *Proceedings*, A.F. of L. Convention, 1898, pp. 18-20, 90.

8. *Ibid.*, p. 92.

9. New York *World*, Dec. 16, 1898; *Proceedings*, A.F. of L. Convention, 1898, pp. 92-96; *Coast Seamen's Journal*, Dec. 27, 1898.

10. New York *Journal*, Dec. 14, 1898.

11. Kansas City (Mo.) *Times*, Dec. 17, 1898; *see also* Los Angeles *Herald*, Dec. 14, 1898; Helena (Montana) *Independent*, Dec. 13, 1898; Muncie (Indiana) *Herald*, Dec. 23, 1898.

12. *National Labor Tribune*, Nov. 24, 1898; *Amalgamated Meat Cutters and Butcher Workman Journal*, Aug., 1900, pp. 12-13; *International Woodworker*, Feb., 1899, p. 14; Pueblo *Courier*, March 26, 1899; *Patternmakers' Journal*, May, 1899, p. 9.

13. Erving Winslow to Gompers, Dec. 21, 1898, *AFL Corr.*

14. Maria C. Lanzar, "The Anti-Imperialist League," *Philippine Social Science Review*, vol. III, Aug., 1930, pp. 7-13.

15. David G. Haskins, Jr. to Gompers, Nov. 2, Dec. 7, 1898; Erving Winslow to Gompers, Nov. 22, 1898, *AFL Corr.;* Gompers to David G. Haskins, Jr., Oct. 29, Nov. 4, 1898, *GLB.*

16. Erving Winslow to Gompers, Dec. 21, 1898, *AFL Corr.;* Gompers to Erving Winslow, Dec. 23, 1898, *GLB.*

17. David G. Haskins, Jr. to Gompers, Dec. 7, 21, 1898, *AFL Corr.*

18. New York *Evening Journal*, Dec. 28, 1898; Boston *Globe*, March 20, 1899; John Devoy to Gompers, Jan. 4, 1899, *AFL Corr.*

19. Pittsburgh *Post*, Jan. 24, 1899; Syracuse *Telegram*, Jan. 27, 1899; Worcester (Mass.) *Post*, Jan. 24, 1899; Chicago *Tribune*, Jan. 23, 1899; Rochester *Union-Advertiser*, Jan. 23, 1899; New Orleans *Times-Democrat*, Jan. 24, 1899.

20. *Congressional Record*, 55th Cong., 3rd Sess., pp. 398, 781, 882, 1443, 1639, 2427; G. W. Perkins, Intn'l President to the officers and members of local unions, Cigar Makers' International Union of America, Dec. 23, 1898; G. W. Perkins to Gompers, January 17, 1899; H. White to Gompers, March 2, 1899; *Official Proceedings*, San Francisco Labor Council, Jan. 20, 1899; David G. Haskins, Jr. to Gompers, Dec. 7, 1898; Erving Winslow to Gompers, Jan. 31, 1899; J. W. Ines to Gompers, Jan. 3, 1899, *AFL Corr.*

21. Fred H. Harrington, "The Anti-Imperialist Movement in the United States," *Mississippi Valley Historical Review*, vol. XXII, Sept., 1935, p. 225.

22. Philadelphia *Telegraph*, Jan. 23, 1899.

23. Walter Millis, *The Martial Spirit*, New York, 1931, p. 392.

24. *Ibid.*, pp. 392, 402-03; Richard F. Pettigrew, *The Course of Empire*, New York, 1920, p. 271.

25. John A. Garraty, *Henry Cabot Lodge: A Biography*, New York, 1953, p. 121.

26. D. J. O'Donoghue to Frank Morrison, March 22, 1899, *AFL Corr.*

27. Erving Winslow to Gompers, Feb. 28, 1899, *AFL Corr.*

28. *National Labor Standard*, Sept. 27, 1900.

29. W. A. Croffut to Gompers, Sept. 17, 1899; W. L. Mize to Gompers, Oct. 27, 1899, *AFL Corr.;* Gompers to Erving Winslow, July 13, 1899, *GLB.*

30. Letters to Gompers from Edwin Burritt Smith, June 24, Aug. 22, 1899; Edward Atkinson, June 30, July 3, Aug. 23, 1899; Erving Winslow, Aug. 22, Sept. 23, 1899; Bolton Hall, Sept. 14, 1899; Gompers to Frank Morrison, June 16, 1899, *AFL Corr.;* Gompers to Erving Winslow, July 13, 1899, *GLB.*

31. Appel, *op. cit.*, pp. 178-79n.

32. Erving Winslow to Gompers, July 11, 1899, *AFL Corr.*

33. V. I. Lenin, *Imperialism, the Highest Stage of Capitalism*, New York, 1939, p. 88.

34. Harrington, *op. cit.*, p. 235.

35. Brooklyn *Citizen*, Dec. 31, 1898.

36. Pamphlet, Chicago, American Anti-Imperialist League, Jan., 1900; *see also* Erving Winslow to Gompers, Dec. 27, 1899, Jan. 12, 20, 24, 1900, *AFL Corr.*

37. McKee, *op. cit.*, pp. 68-70; *American Federationist*, vol. V, 1898, p. 92.

38. Clarence Darrow to Thomas I. Kidd, Dec. 14, 1898, *AFL Corr.*

39. James L. Slayden to Erving Winslow, attached to Winslow to Gompers, July 20, 1899, and Winslow to Gompers, Aug. 15, 1899, *AFL Corr.*

40. Erving Winslow to Gompers, Aug. 15, 1899, *AFL Corr.*

41. Machinists *Monthly Journal*, March, 1900, p. 104; Boilermakers and Iron Shipbuilders *Journal*, January 1, 1899, p. 24.
42. *Metal Polishers' Journal*, Jan., 1899, pp. 587-88.
43. A. Furuseth to Frank Morrison, May 22, June 9, 1900, *AFL Corr.*; International Association of Machinists, *Monthly Journal*, Dec., 1899, p. 789; Pueblo *Courier*, May 26, 1899, p. 3; *Miners' Magazine*, Feb., 1901, p. 5.
44. *Proceedings*, A.F. of L. Convention, 1899, pp. 148-49.
45. *Annual Report* of Brigadier-General William S. Ludlow, U.S. Army, Military Governor of Havana, "Strikes," Oct. 4, 1899, pp. 186-87; *New York Times*, Sept. 23-30, 1899; J. E. Bloom to Gompers, Havana, April 14, 1900, *AFL Corr.*; St. Louis *Post-Dispatch* reprinted in *The Reveille* (Butte, Montana), Oct. 16, 1899.
46. Printed Circular, "To Organized Labor," New York, Feb. 25, 1900, in *AFL Corr.*; *National Labor Standard*, Oct. 11, 1900; *Typographical Journal*, Nov. 15, 1900, p. 417.
47. *Cigar Makers' Journal*, March, 1900, p. 9; *The Carpenter*, Oct., 1899, p. 4; *Coast Seamen's Journal*, Dec. 27, 1899, p. 7.
48. *Journal of the Knights of Labor*, Oct., 1898; Appel, *op. cit.*, p. 225; Pueblo *Courier*, May 19, 1899, p. 1; Julius Zorn to Gompers, July 3, 1899; *AFL Corr.*
49. *International Socialist Review*, vol. I, Sept., 1900, pp. 132-33.
50. Gompers to A. F. Jenson, May 9, 1899, *GLB.*
51. Chas. Shenkin to Gompers, Little Rock, Ark., April 22, 1900, enclosing newspaper clipping, *AFL Corr.*; Gompers to Patrick Dolan, President, District 5, U.M.W., June 28, 1898; Gompers to N. D. Cochran, May 23, 1899; Gompers to J. A. Cannon, July 12, 1899, *GLB.*
52. Cleveland *Citizen*, Dec. 10, 1898.
53. *First Annual Report of the New England Anti-Imperialist League*, Dec., 1899; Erving Winslow to Gompers, Dec. 27, 1899, *AFL Corr.*
54. Pettigrew, *op. cit.*, pp. 324-25.
55. *Ibid.*, p. 125.
56. Thomas A. Bailey, "Was the Presidential Election of 1900 a Mandate On Imperialism?" *Mississippi Valley Historical Review*, vol. XXIV, June, 1937, p. 44; *National Labor Standard*, Aug. 16, 1900.
57. Minutes of A.F. of L. Executive Council, July, 1900, *AFL Corr.*
58. *International Socialist Review*, vol. I, 1900, p. 303; McKee, *op. cit.*, p. 305.
59. John B. Lennon to Gompers (1900), *AFL Corr.*
60. W. J. *Bryan to United Labor, Speech at Chicago Labor Day 1900*, pamphlet; Indianapolis *Journal*, Sept. 4, 1900.
61. Bailey, *op. cit.*, pp. 47-48; Appel, *op. cit.*, p. 187.
62. Bailey, *op. cit.*, pp. 48-51.
63. *Railroad Trainmen's Journal*, Jan., 1901, p. 68.
64. *National Labor Standard*, May 2, 23. 1901; *Coast Seamen's Journal*, May, 1901, p. 6; *Shoe Workers' Journal*, Oct., 1902, p. 21.
65. *National Labor Standard*, Nov. 29, 1900. See also ibid., July 18, Aug. 8, 1901; *Railroad Trainmen's Journal*, Nov., 1902, pp. 861-64.
66. Lanzar, *op. cit.*, pp. 226-27.
67. McKee, *op. cit.*, p. 134; *Proceedings*, A.F. of L. Convention, 1903, pp. 204-06; *American Federationist*, Oct., 1903, p. 760.
68. G. W. Perkins, Pres., Cigar Makers' International Union, to Gompers, April 26, 1904; Gompers to Ed Rosenberg, May 5, 1904; Gompers to G. H. Patterson in Manila, May 12, 1904; Ed Rosenberg to Gompers, May 22, 1904; Gompers to G. W. Perkins, June 4, 1904, *AFL Corr.*
69. *American Federationist*, vol. VI, 1899, p. 149.
70. Lenin, *Imperialism*, p. 110.
71. Ray Ginger, *The Bending Cross*, p. 217. See also McKee, *op. cit.*, p. 132, and David R. Weimer, "Myth in the American Federation of Labor, 1881-1914," unpublished Ph.D. thesis, University of Minnesota, 1954, pp. 70-74.

INDEX

INDEX